A TIME TO TEAR DOWN
and
A TIME TO BUILD UP

A TIME TO TEAR DOWN
and
A TIME TO BUILD UP

A Rereading of Ecclesiastes

Michael V. Fox

WILLIAM B. EERDMANS PUBLISHING COMPANY
GRAND RAPIDS, MICHIGAN / CAMBRIDGE, U.K.

© 1999 Wm. B. Eerdmans Publishing Co.
255 Jefferson Ave. S.E., Grand Rapids, Michigan 49503 /
P.O. Box 163, Cambridge CB3 9PU U.K.

Printed in the United States of America

04 03 02 01 00 99   7 6 5 4 3 2 1

Library of Congress Cataloging-in-Publication Data

A time to tear down and a time to build up: a rereading of Ecclesiastes /
Michael V. Fox.
p.   cm.
Includes bibliographical references.
ISBN 0-8028-4292-5 (pbk.: alk. paper)
1. Bible. O.T. Ecclesiastes — Criticism, interpretation, etc.
2. Bible. O.T. Ecclesiastes — Psychology.
3. Bible. O.T. Ecclesiastes — Language, style.   I. Title.
BS1475.9.F695   1999
223′.806 — dc21   98-53602
CIP

Contents

v

CONTENTS

Preface: On Rereading Qohelet

This book began as a revision of my 1987 study *Qohelet and His Contradictions* (JSOT Supplement 71). But as I worked once again through the difficulties and conundrums that Qohelet thrusts upon us, the revision went deeper and deeper. At some point, I realized that this was no longer the "same" book.[1]

Reading Qohelet is not a once-for-all effort. For me, at least, the meanings and tones of the book have shifted and modulated over the years. The book is like a mountain that reveals new shape and colors as you approach it from different angles. In part, however, I have improved upon my earlier interpretations.

I have sought to clarify, strengthen, and synthesize my ideas and arguments. In some cases I take issue with "Fox 1987" and leave the alternative proposals to the reader's judgment. I have modified and expanded the exegesis in numerous details and have attempted to refine the definitions of Qohelet's key words, a task which is crucial to exegesis and cannot be left to listing glosses.

I have not, however, changed my basic theses about Qohelet's message, even though my understanding of it has evolved and deepened in numerous ways. In particular, I now give greater attention to the constructive phase of Qohelet's thought, the "building up." I also examine more carefully the un-

1. I am indebted to the Wisconsin Society for Jewish Learning for financial support in this research. I thank my student Rick Painter for his assistance in the preparation of the manuscript and the indexes.

ix

derlying, unspoken premises that express themselves in Qohelet's conclusions, even the strangest and most contradictory of them. It is on this deep level of premises that Qohelet's true consistency is to be found, not on the bumpy surface that scholars have tried so hard to smooth out.

I also draw upon and respond to some more recent scholarly literature. Some valuable and thought-provoking works have appeared (or come to my attention) since the earlier book was completed. I have found the following especially interesting, though I have not been able to make full use of the more recent ones in the present work.

Norbert Lohfink, *Kohelet* (Neue Echter Bibel), 1980.

Man is an ephemeral being in an unchanging world, with whose oppressive fullness he cannot cope (1:4-11; Lohfink labels this unit cosmology). Happiness is powerful, but in the face of death all human abilities and achievements are a "vapor." Happiness itself is allotted by God, not securely produced by man, who must enjoy what he is given in the fear of God (1:12–3:15; anthropology). Social criticism is the theme of 3:16–4:16. In the center of the book, Qohelet also offers critical evaluation of piety (4:17–5:6; religious criticism). Observations of social injustice and fragmentation reinforce the anthropology of "vapor" and "fear of God" (5:7–6:10; social criticism). The basic dogmas of wisdom, in particular the principle of just recompense, are undermined (6:11–9:6; ideological criticism). The "fear of God" alone can guide man. Man cannot comprehend God's work and consequently may think it arbitrary and amoral. Man must manage the best he can, accept what the moment brings, and enjoy God's gifts (9:7–12:7; ethics). The book ends with two orthodox appendices (12:8-11, 12-14). In a series of subsequent studies (see bibliography), Lohfink has modified and refined his views.

Lohfink's portrayal of Qohelet's structure seems forced. His subject headings could fit equally well elsewhere. I would also disagree that Qohelet's arguments are directed against wisdom. Also, Lohfink finds many quotations and paraphrases of repudiated ideas where signs are lacking; see the introduction to 8:1b-9 in the commentary below.

James L. Crenshaw, *Ecclesiastes* (OTL), 1987.

Qohelet directs a radical, unrelentingly negative attack on the traditional beliefs of the sages. He repudiates wisdom's claim to secure one's existence and denies the reality of a moral order. Chance determines everything, including the time of death, and the future — indeed all of reality — remains utterly hidden. All that is left is to enjoy life's little pleasures in order to soothe the troubled spirit. This, at least, has God's approval.

This profile, in my view, is too grim. Qohelet also seeks ways to adjust to life. Nor is "chance" the issue. On the contrary, Qohelet has no concept of chance at all, in the sense of randomness in events. God is the determinant, but even he does not determine everything. Also, Qohelet is not attacking wisdom's doctrines, or at least does not see himself as doing so. Nor does he simply deny the moral order, though he is distressed to see it violated.

Roland E. Murphy, *Ecclesiastes* (WBC 23A), 1992.

A variety of attitudes are heard in Qohelet. These are sometimes contradictory and sometimes in dialogue. Qohelet affirms the values of life, wealth, toil, and wisdom, but they prove inadequate when seen under the shadow of death. Qohelet is often in conflict with traditional wisdom teaching, especially its claim to provide security, yet he affirms wisdom and remains within its traditions, employing its methods and literary genres. It is because Qohelet loves life and wisdom that he is grieved by death and by life's vanity.

I am largely in agreement with Murphy's reading of Qohelet, which was reached by a different angle of approach from my own.[2] Two main differences are that Murphy does not recognize the decisive role of contradiction in Qohelet's construction of the universe and does not identify the collapse of *meaning* as the central crisis that Qohelet confronts. See further my critique of "relativization" in the introduction to 8:1b-9 in the commentary.

T. A. Perry, *Dialogues with Kohelet*, 1993.

The book of Qohelet is a dialogue between a pious sage-narrator, the "Presenter" (P), who transmits and debates the wisdom of the skeptical persona, Kohelet (K). K is the man of experience. He is deterministic and skeptical and rejects wisdom and faith except insofar as they emerge from his own experience. He teaches that we should embrace pleasure because it is within our power to do so and should fear God because of human ignorance. P, the man of faith, uses K's words to provoke thought and provide a basis for argument. P affirms the value of labor, pleasure, and wisdom. God is to be feared because he is unpredictable, and his justice and freedom are not bound by human conceptions of justice. At the end, P modifies his own position by recognizing that life is vanity but we are to fear the God as the ground of our transience.

Perry's is the boldest application of the ancient theory that the book is a

---

2. This also shows that A. Wright's intricate structural analysis (1968, discussed below at §10.2), which Murphy basically accepts, does not determine a particular reading and is not the "key" to what he calls the "Riddle of the Sphinx."

dialogue, and like it, his produces a pious and optimistic author, though this author is not Qohelet. Perry accepts my idea that there is a frame-narrator who purports to transmit and quote and buffer the words of the fictional Qohelet (see Excursus II). Perry, however, believes that he can identify the voice of this narrator throughout the book, even to the point of prying apart single sentences and assigning one segment to Qohelet, another to the "presenter." I criticize this approach in §1.54.

Daniel C. Fredericks, *Coping with Transience*, 1993.
Qohelet confines his observations to the transient, human realm, avoiding the realm of the eternal. He offers ways of coping with transience, finding value in wisdom, in the joy of work, and above all in simple pleasures, which are man's major consolation. Man's duty is to resign himself to God's will and accept circumstances beyond human control.

Fredericks's reading is a traditional one. My objection is that this approach — much like the overly negative reading — must find ways to override one major aspect of Qohelet's teaching in favor of another, though Qohelet himself provides no guidance in making the choice.

Choon-Leong Seow, *Ecclesiastes* (Anchor Bible), 1997.
Seow's comprehensive commentary appeared too late to be used in the present study. I will only quote his summary of Qohelet's message:

> In sum, Qohelet always begins his reflection with humanity and the human condition. He concludes at every turn that mortals are not in control of the things that happen in the world. They are not in control of their destiny. That is why Qohelet says that everything is *hebel*. He does not mean that everything is meaningless or insignificant, but that everything is beyond human apprehension and comprehension. But in thinking about humanity, Qohelet also speaks of God. People are caught in this situation where everything is *hebel* — in every sense of the word. God is transcendent and wholly other, but humanity is "on earth." Yet God is related to humanity, and God has given humanity the possibilities of each moment. Hence people must accept what happens, whether good or bad. They must respond spontaneously to life, even in the midst of uncertainties, and accept both the possibilities and limitations of their being human. (pp. 59f.)

Tremper Longman III, *The Book of Ecclesiastes* (NICOT), 1998.
Longman translates *hebel* as "meaningless" and describes Qohelet's message as skeptical and pessimistic. The message of the *Book of Ecclesiastes,* how-

ever, is determined by the authorial voice in 12:9-14. The book's final message is that life is meaningless *without God.* Verses 13f., moreover, introduce an eschatological perspective. I agree with the important distinction between Qohelet and the book of Ecclesiastes, but I see less of a contrast between the messages of the two (see Excursus III). Longman draws upon his work on the autobiographical form in ancient Near Eastern literature, on which see §10.21, below.

Also of value are the linguistic and stylistic studies of D. Michel, gathered in his *Untersuchungen zur Eigenart des Buches Qohelet* (1989), and the meticulous linguistic analysis of A. Schoors, *The Preacher Sought to Find Pleasing Words* (1992), of which the first volume has appeared, and the careful probing of Qohelet's thought in its Hellenistic context by L. Schwienhorst-Schönberger, *"Nicht im Menschen gründet das Glück"* (1996). (I have been able to address the latter work in only a few footnotes.)

In conjunction with the present work, I am writing a commentary on Qohelet for the Jewish Publication Society, which is intended for use in the synagogue and lay study. That book may be consulted for a deeper engagement with traditional Jewish exegesis, as well as for some thoughts on the significance of the book to the modern Jewish reader.

M. V. F.
Department of Hebrew and Semitic Studies
University of Wisconsin, Madison

Abbreviations

AEL	*Ancient Egyptian Literature,* Lichtheim, 1973ff.
Aq	Aquila
AV	Authorized Version (King James translation)
AW	*Altägyptische Weisheit,* Brunner, 1988a.
B	Papyri Boulaq
BDB	Brown, Driver, and Briggs, *Hebrew and English Lexicon of the Old Testament*
BH	Biblical Hebrew (incl. Ben Sira)
BHK	R. Kittel, *Biblia Hebraica*
BHS	*Biblia Hebraica Stuttgartensia*
BTM	*Before the Muses,* B. Foster, 1993
DJD	Discoveries in the Judaean Desert
esp.	especially
ET	English translation
FS	Festschrift
GBH	*Grammar of Biblical Hebrew,* by Joüon and Muraoka, 1991
GKC	Gesenius' Hebrew Grammar (ed. Kautzsch-Cowley)
HALAT	*Hebräisches und aramäisches Lexikon zum AT,* ed. Baumgartner et al.
HB	Hebrew Bible
HSS	Harvard Semitic Studies
IBHS	*An Introduction to Biblical Hebrew Syntax,* by Waltke and O'Connor, 1990
JPSV	The Jewish Publication Society version of the Bible, 1962ff.

K-R	Kennicott-Rossi
LEWL	*Late Egyptian Wisdom Literature,* by Lichtheim, 1983
lit.	literally
LSF	*Die Lese- und Schreibfehler im AT,* by Delitzsch, 1920
mg.	margin (glosses and corrections in Ben Sira)
MT	Masoretic Text
Rab.	Rabbah: a compilation of Midrash
RH	Rabbinic (Mishnaic) Hebrew
RSV	Revised Standard Version
sim.	similarly
S^c	Sinaiticus corrector
SPOA	*Les Sagesses du Proche-Orient Ancien,* Paris, 1963
SyH	Syrohexapla
Sym	Symmachus
Syr	Syriac (Peshiṭṭa)
TAOT	*An Aid to the Textual Amendment of the Old Testament,* by J. Kennedy, 1928
TDOT	*Theological Dictionary of the OT,* ed. by G. J. Botterweck and H. Ringgren, 1977ff.
Tg	Targum
Theod	Theodotion
TSSI	*Textbook of Syrian Semitic Inscriptions,* vols. I-III, by J. Gibson, 1971ff.
UT	*Ugaritic Textbook,* by C. H. Gordon
Vul	Vulgate
ZAW	*Zeitschrift für die alttestamentliche Wissenschaft*

Other ancient works are abbreviated in accordance with the Society for Biblical Literature style sheet. Commentaries are referenced by author's name only, other works by author and date. Publication and translation information on ancient texts (Ptahhotep, Merikare, etc.) is integrated in the bibliography by name of putative author.

Transliteration and Sigla

I use a broad transliteration, with diacritics for vowel-length added only when necessary, such as when introducing a new word, discussing morphology, or proposing emendations. The purpose of this transliteration is to call to mind the word rather than represent the MT precisely, which is, after all, always available.

- Compound shewas: $ě$ $ŏ$ $ă;$ vocal shewa = ^{e}
- y indicates the *mater lectionis yod* after *ṣere*
- h = *heh* as consonant and *mater lectionis*
- *-hh* = *heh-mappiq*
- Word-initial gemination not represented.
- Roots are represented by uppercase letters.

{ }	later addition
< >	emendation (except for revocalizations or changes required for the Hebrew that do not affect the translation)
*	in bibliography: indicates commentaries referenced by name of author only.

CHAPTER 1

On Reading Contradictions

§1.1. Qohelet's Contradictions

One of the first reported discussions of Qohelet centers on the book's contradictions. Some of the early rabbis, the Tannaim, report that the book was almost consigned to oblivion for that reason:

> R. Judah b. Samuel b. Shilath said in Rav's name: The sages sought to withdraw [*lignoz*] the book of Qohelet because its words are mutually contradictory [*sotrin zeh 'et zeh*]. Why then did they not withdraw it? Because it begins with words of Torah and it ends with words of Torah. (b. Shab. 30b)

According to this tradition, the sages considered the presence of contradictions serious enough to raise doubts about the suitability of the book for general reading. Similar queries arose with regard to Ezekiel, with its dangerous visions,[1] and Proverbs, where the problem was the (trivial) contradiction in 26:4-5 (ibid.). The discussion of "withdrawal" *(genizah)* of Biblical books has nothing to do with their status as inspired or canonical literature, which was not in doubt. It is precisely sacred books and objects that are put in *genizah*. The question was whether these books were suitable and "safe" for general use.[2]

---

1. When discussing Ezekiel, they told an admonitory tale of a child being burnt to death by electrum while studying Ezek 1 [b. Hag. 13a].
2. See M. Haran 1996:301f. and chap. 5.

Another problem was the danger that the words of Qohelet might "cause an inclination to heresy" (Qoh. Rab. on 1:3[3]). The verses quoted as examples of this danger, Qoh 11:9aβ and 1:3, are not the ones modern commentators consider most radical. The rabbis in question apparently feared that 11:9aβ ("... and follow your heart, and the sight of your eyes") might be conducive to licentiousness (see the comment ad loc.), and that the "toil" decried in 1:3 ("What profit does man have in all his toil at which he labors under the sun?") might be thought to include the study of Torah. In both cases, the danger envisioned lies not in an attack upon doctrine but in the susceptibility of these verses to misinterpretations that might have practical consequences.

Both problems were solved by adducing the book's orthodox frame, supplied by Qoh 1:3 (understood to praise exertions in the study of Torah[4]) and 12:13 (which concludes by insisting that what is ultimately important is the fear of God and obedience to his commandments). This frame provided a sufficient buffer for the book's internal inconsistencies and other doctrinal difficulties.[5] This is a surprisingly liberal hermeneutic. Qohelet-Solomon — writing in the Holy Spirit, and not just in his own wisdom[6] — was allowed to explore dangerous territory, provided that he began and ended in professions of faith and obedience. Later rabbis (quoted in b. Shab. 30b, in the continuation of the above passage) did try to resolve some contradictions, but this was a scholastic exercise. The book's canonicity was not in doubt. (These and similar stylized discussions are homiletic devices raising difficulties to be resolved by exegetical dexterity. They are not disputes about canonicity, which was resolved much earlier.)

3. *Maṣĕ'u bo dĕbarim Maṭṭim lĕṣad miynut.* The variant in Lev. Rab. 28.1 reads *noṭin* "incline" (intrans.). *Maṭṭim* (Qoh. Rab. 1.3) is the better reading. The sentences the rabbis discussed are never suspected of being in themselves heretical, but of being liable to lead others astray.

4. The school of R. Yannai interpreted Qoh 1:3 as asserting the futility of activities "under the sun" (i.e., mundane activities) while affirming the value of matters "before the sun" (namely, the study of Torah, for the Torah was created before the sun) (b. Shab. 30b).

5. According to Avot de R. Natan A 1:4, "Originally they used to say, Proverbs, the Song of Songs, and Qohelet had been withdrawn, because they speak proverbs [*mᵉšalot*] and do not belong to Scripture [*kᵉtubim*]. So they withdrew them, until Hezekiah's men [thus read] came and interpreted them." The problem in Qohelet was the recommendation of pleasure in 11:9, which was susceptible to a hedonistic interpretation.

6. Another view was put forth by R. Shimon ben Menasia in b. Meg. 7a, "Qohelet does not make the hands impure, because it is (merely) Solomon's own wisdom" and not written in the Holy Spirit. This opinion is ascribed to anonymous Tannaim in T. Yad. 2:14. In Avot de Rabbi Nathan (quoted in n. 5), Abba Shaul says that the Solomonic books were for a time thought to be "mere proverbs." But these are minority opinions or fictions and not serious options for the Tannaim.

2

I too take Qohelet's contradictions as the starting point of interpretation. My primary thesis is a simple one: The contradictions in the book of Qohelet are real and intended. We must interpret them, not eliminate them.

To be precise, Qohelet is not so much contradicting himself as *observing* contradictions in the world. To him they seem to be *antinomies,* two equally valid but contradictory principles. He does not resolve these antinomies, but only describes them, bemoans them, and suggests how to live in such a refractory world. The contradictions do not make the book incoherent. On the contrary, Qohelet's persistent observation of contradictions is a powerful cohesive force, and an awareness of it brings into focus the book's central concern: the problem of meaning in life. The book of Qohelet is about *meaning:* its loss and its (partial) recovery.

I use "contradiction" in a broad sense. Contradictions are not only violations of the canons of logic, assertions of *A and not-A.* Qohelet's views on wisdom, for example, can be resolved into a logically tolerable statement, but wisdom is still mired in keen and painful contradictions, *as he sees it.* Some of the contradictions Qohelet observes do violate logic, but others consist of unresolved tensions between incongruous and incompatible observations, and the sticking-point is sometimes more a matter of feeling that something *should not* happen than the conviction that the occurrence of the conflicting events is impossible; in other words, it is a violation of sensibilities rather than of logic. Ultimately, interpretation must explain the antinomies on some level or it can have nothing coherent to say, but that level must encompass both sides of the polarity without overriding either.

Qohelet's contradictions are the starting point but not the message of the book. He marshals them to *tear down* meaning, but he does not stop there. He is not a nihilist. He also *builds up* meaning, discovering ways of creating clarity and gratification in a confusing and indifferent world. Nor does Qohelet employ paradox, Zen-like, as a means to enlightenment. He discovers paradoxical truths, but the paradoxes give no flashes of insight into some greater, ineffable meaning.

To interpret Qohelet's contradictions we must clarify their terms and context and determine as precisely as possible what conclusions he draws from them. This task requires us to describe systematically and abstractly ideas that Qohelet expresses unsystematically and concretely. Such a redescription is not identical with the thought it describes; in fact, it inevitably entails some distortion. No systematic discussion can (or should) replicate Qohelet's thought, with its episodic, discontinuous, staccato character. Qohelet "goes about" the world observing and reacting to events, actions, qualities, and values as he encounters them. His response to something in

3

one place need not be the same as his response elsewhere. And even a single response may be compounded of various attitudes or remain resolutely unstable (as in 8:10-14). Again, these complexities and instabilities must be set forth and elucidated, not eliminated or paved over.

While I seek to understand Qohelet's thought by probing the meaning of the contradictions, I do not presume that Qohelet is written in a code that only a scholarly key can decipher. The book of Qohelet is not mysterious or esoteric. After all, Qohelet is said to have taught *the people* wisdom. Nor does the book fail to communicate broadly, for its fundamental teachings and many of its secondary ones have been understood in essentially the same way by most commentators. With the help of C. D. Ginsburg's lengthy survey of the history of interpretation in his commentary of 1861, along with some more recent surveys, in particular S. Blank's 1970 prolegomenon to Ginsburg's commentary, this consensus can be encapsulated in three points.[7] It is similar to what one often hears from laymen who have read Qohelet in translation.

> (1) Everything in this life is, in some way, inadequate — worthless, vain, futile, transient, or senseless, and injustices abound. (2) There is no point in striving too hard for anything, whether wealth or wisdom. (3) It is best simply to enjoy what you have when you have it and to fear God. To this the traditional interpreters add: and study Torah.

This is the surface message, but the surface no less than the depth belongs to a text's meaning. I consider my own interpretation essentially a refinement of this widespread understanding. But within these three points, there is still much room for variation, and the way the propositions are expressed is far from obvious. I differ from previous interpreters mainly in regard to point 1, the nature of the inadequacy. I also regard the contradictory observations, rather than the pessimistic statements and complaints by themselves, as the means by which Qohelet defines and demonstrates life's failings.

§1.2. Words and Ideas

The following essays cluster around four themes: (1) The absurd (chapter 2); (2) justice and its violation (chapter 3); (3) knowledge and ignorance (chap-

---

7. I have an extensive survey of the history of Qohelet exegesis forthcoming in the *Dictionary of Biblical Interpretation* (Abingdon Press).

ters 4–5); (4) efforts and results (chapters 6–8), and (5) the premises of Qohelet's thought (chapter 9). It is followed by a commentary (chapters 10–11) and three excursuses, which provide the exegetical basis for the earlier chapters. The themes cannot be approached directly, but require careful attention to his peculiar lexicon. While Qohelet does not give words unparalleled meanings, he gives them a twist in application. His lexicon not only expresses his ideas; to some extent it constrains their formulation.

These studies converge on the following main thesis: Qohelet is primarily concerned with the meaning of life, rather than with the value of possessions, the duration of existence, or the benefits of human striving. Qohelet denies life's meaningfulness by calling everything *hebel,* "absurd" and *re'ut ruaḥ,* "senseless." But even when meaning collapses, meaningfulness remains an irreducible value, and local meanings can be reconstructed.

"Meaning" in language is a predictable connection between signifier and signified. That which is signified must be something other than the signifier itself, whether in external reality, in thought, or in language. Transferring the idea of meaning to nonlinguistic realities, we say that an action or quality is meaningful when it accomplishes something external to or commensurate with the action. To say that a person's *life* has meaning implies that the sum total of his deeds and experiences achieve or prove something beyond themselves. In other words, they *do* something.

§1.3. Context

To understand the source and significance of Qohelet's ideas we must set them within the context of his intellectual background. For this we look primarily (but not exclusively) to didactic Wisdom Literature, because the book of Qohelet is closest to this genre in form, subject matter, and, to a large extent, ideology. The comparisons with Wisdom Literature will show that it is not the propositional content of Qohelet's individual observations that is radical so much as his reaction to what he sees.

"Wisdom"[8] should not be identified with a putative Wisdom School, for which there is no evidence in Israel (*or* in Egypt; see Fox 1996). In BH, *ḥakam* refers to a wise man, an individual possessing wisdom, and only

8. The word will be capitalized when referring to the genre of Wisdom Literature, in lower case when referring to the faculty or knowledge. At the start of sentences it will be disambiguated where necessary.

rarely to a member of the class of teachers or scholars, such as the authors of Wisdom writings.[9]

There is no reason to assume that different literary genres in ancient Israel were produced by different "schools," or that each intellectual tradition was attached exclusively to tradents ignorant of or hostile to other traditions. The same people can participate in more than one intellectual tradition and literary genre. After all, the scholars (called *ḥăkamim*) whose proverbial wisdom is collected in *Avot* participated as well in the creation of midrash and halakhah. There weren't separate "schools" for wisdom, homiletics, and jurisprudence.

The intellectual framework in which Wisdom Literature was molded and transmitted may be called the Wisdom *tradition,* a term implying that certain types of text or oral teaching were cultivated and transmitted in a way that preserved their special formal and ideological features, and that these expressed a fairly coherent group of attitudes, assumptions, methods, and beliefs.

§1.4. Parallels

§1.41. Greek[10]

To read a book in its intellectual context does not require ferreting out parallels, influences, and external sources. Nevertheless, these may throw light on the text and help define the issues. One area often explored is Qohelet's rela-

---

9. I concur for the most part with Whybray (1974:15-54) on the non-professional status of the *ḥăkamim.* I do not, however, agree that *ḥakam* is *always* a personal attribute rather than a group identification. See the commentary on 12:9f.

10. The book of Qohelet is dated by most modern scholars to the Hellenistic period, which is to say, the third century B.C.E. (Ben Sira alludes to Qohelet and partially quotes him in the early second century B.C.E.). Qohelet undertakes a sort of philosophical analysis without parallel in the ancient Near East prior to Hellenism. There seems to be a background awareness of Greek thought, sketched in the following paragraphs, though not necessarily direct knowledge of Greek philosophy.

Qohelet's Hebrew is transitional between Biblical and Mishnaic Hebrew. This view was cogently argued as early as 1875 by Franz Delitzsch (pp. 189-202) and supported by several studies of R. Gordis (1946/47, 1949/50, 1952, 1960) and by A. Schoors' painstaking analysis of the book's morphology and syntax (1992) and underscored by the survey by Bianchi (1993). Seow (1996) also argues that the language is definitely post-exilic but is *no later* than the fourth century B.C.E. Solid arguments for this *terminus ad quem* have not yet been presented. The absence of Greek borrowings is hardly definitive, since Sira too lacks Graecisms. See also the Commentary on 2:19.

tion to Hellenistic philosophy.[11] It is worth noting that Qohelet's affirmation of individual experience, in particular the experience of pleasure, seems to bear a significant similarity to Hellenistic popular philosophy, whose central purpose was to find a way to individual happiness by the use of human reason alone. The Epicureans sought happiness through pleasure and freedom from fear, the Stoics through the shedding of desire and passions.[12] Both schools agreed that the inner realm of human experience is the locus of freedom and happiness, as does Qohelet.[13] Others looked to virtue and duty, without, however, setting social change as the goal. Qohelet did not choose these precise paths, but in his fundamental goals and methods, he bears significant similarities to Hellenistic philosophy. Qohelet's question about the profitability of human action is likewise the problematic of philosophical anthropology in Greek thought (Braun 1973:168).

A number of scholars, notably A. Palm (1885), H. Ranston (1925), R. Braun (1973), M. Hengel (1974:1.115-28),[14] C. Whitley (1979:165-75), J. G. Gammie (1985), and L. Schwienhorst-Schönberger (1996:251-332), have weighed the possibility of various sorts of Hellenistic-Greek influences on

11. R. Braun 1973 has extensive surveys and bibliography on this issue. Loretz (1964:45-57) argues against Greek influence by showing differences of detail. But influence is not replication, and such distinctions as he notes are not decisive.

12. J. G. Gammie (1985) argues for the Stoic connection and concludes "that the Stoics, along with other Hellenistic philosophies, had an impact on the ancient Israelite sage, not only in specific teachings of divine causation, the cyclical nature of events, the relative value of education/wisdom, etc., but also in form of argumentation and, because of its advanced philosophy of language, possibly also in making Qoheleth more sensitive to the range of connotations in his use of terms such as *hebel*" (p. 185). In other ways, Gammie says, Qohelet was closer to the Epicureans, Skeptics, and Cynics and was arguing against the Stoics (p. 180).

13. Schwienhorst-Schönberger (1996:294f.) sees a deep difference, insofar as Qohelet does not believe in the absolute autonomy of the inner realm. Man cannot create happiness *(Glück)* but can only receive it from God. "For this reason, in Qohelet — in contrast to the Hellenistic philosophy — the inner attitude *(Einstellung)* plays no role" (p. 295). Throughout this book (see esp. §§5.4; 8.42; 9.5) I will argue the opposite, that Qohelet locates freedom and happiness precisely in the inner realm. God controls the means of pleasure, but man alone chooses to experience the enjoyment, and this choice can bring happiness. Likewise, the exercise of rational thought, with all of its severe limitations, is within man's control.

14. Hengel sums up the traces of Hellenism in Qohelet in six points: the individuality of personality; radical criticism of the doctrine of retribution; the loss of a personal relationship between God and man; the insinuation of terms for destiny between God and man; the counsel of resignation and a *via media;* and the "bourgeois ethic" (p. 126). I do not agree with the accuracy of all these characterizations, but Hengel does succeed in locating Qohelet in the Hellenistic thought-world.

Qohelet and, in the overall, made the case for situating Qohelet in the thought-world of Hellenistic philosophy. Schwienhorst-Schönberger (1996) offers a balanced assessment of Qohelet's thought in the context of Hellenistic thought, in a chapter on "The Book of Qohelet Between Jewish Wisdom and Hellenistic Philosophy," pp. 232-332). The pivotal question of both Hellenistic philosophy and Qohelet is the nature of human happiness and the limitations of its possibilities, especially with respect to the individual life (p. 275). This concern is present in earlier Wisdom, of course, and a Jewish author of the third century could be stimulated by both external and traditional thought on this subject. Moreover, the devaluation of that which cannot be controlled (e.g., possessions, health, progeny, death) belongs to the common program of Hellenistic philosophy (p. 293) but not, it might be added, to earlier Wisdom Literature.

The most significant parallels may well be the least provable: affinities in attitude, epistemology, fields of inquiry, questions addressed, and the types of answers offered (though not necessarily the specific answers themselves). Qohelet's particular attitudes need not have had an immediate "source" in Greek philosophy in order to have shared some of the diffuse concerns and attitudes of various philosophies current in the Hellenistic age, that sought to achieve individual happiness in an indifferent universe. Among the notable parallels are Qohelet's affinities with Epicureanism, which regarded sensory experience as the ultimate source and arbiter of knowledge, and which affirmed pleasure (intellectual as well as physical) as the only good for man. Most significant is the conviction Qohelet shared with the Stoics that happiness can be achieved only in shaping one's inner attitude toward the world, not in changing externals.

§1.42. *Qohelet and Camus*

Parallels need not be close in time and place to be valuable. Throughout my study of Qohelet I have been impressed by the affinities between his thought and that of Albert Camus, especially in his *Myth of Sisyphus*. The epigraphs to the following essays and additional quotations from Camus are suggestive of some of these affinities. My point is not to prove the similarities but to use them — to call upon Camus's words for help in expressing key points of Qohelet's thought.[15]

15. Two recent studies that use Camus as a path to understanding and describing Qohelet are Wm. Brown 1996:131-39 and E. Christianson 1997:36 and forthcoming.

Brown emphasizes the key difference: the smile of Camus's Sisyphus expresses "a

My purpose is not to draw comparisons between Qohelet and existentialism, a concept I would not attempt to define, and which Camus refused to apply to himself.[16] Nevertheless I note Lohfink's observation that "Im modernen Denken ist ihr die Existenzphilosophie erstaunlich verwandt" ("In modern thought, existentialist philosophy is surprisingly akin to [Qohelet's thought]") (p. 14), the reasons for which may be found in similar social changes in Judea in the Hellenistic period and in Europe of the first part of the twentieth century. For a brief sketch of some lines of resemblance see K. James 1984. Worth noting is his understanding of the significance of joy for Qohelet: "If the security of 'conceptual knowledge' is taken away from us, we still have a center that feels strongly about life, and it is to this emotional center that Qoheleth turns as a possible source of meaning in life" (James 1984:89). This insight, which James does not develop further, is close to my understanding of the function of pleasure in Qohelet's value system; see §8.42.

On the other hand, two keystones of modern existentialism do not seem to apply to Qohelet. The assertion of the radical freedom of individual choice and the belief in individual choice as the ultimate determinant of value are of dubious relevance to Qohelet. Qohelet believes, though not consistently, that God's control extends to the human heart (2:26; 3:11, 14).

Qohelet was certainly not a "religious existentialist," a stance identified above all with Kierkegaard and, in Judaism, with Martin Buber and Franz Rosenzweig. The values that Qohelet does construct are not an "absurd" leap to faith and trust in God.

The affinity between Qohelet and Camus resides above all in their sensitivity to the absurd.[17] Qohelet's key-word *hebel*, I argue in chapter 2,

---

clever joy that is motivated by scorn and defiance of the gods who have condemned him to such labor," while "futile labor for Qoheleth is infused with an overwhelming sense of acceptance of one's lot in life that allows a person to cherish the few brief moments of rest when the boulder is delicately balanced and the cool breeze is savored before the chase begins again" (p. 139).

16. Christianson (1996, 1997, and forthcoming) undertakes to read Qohelet in the light of existentialism. The key themes of existentialism that Christianson identifies and uses as axes of comparison are the role of extreme circumstances, the confrontation with absurdity, and (particularly in relation to the existential legacy of the Holocaust) the individual struggle with or against death and fate (1996:215 and forthcoming). Christianson too senses a deep affinity between the worldviews of Qohelet and certain existentialists, in particular Camus and Viktor Frankl.

17. In a review of a biography of Camus, John Weightman comments: "Not that the concept of the Absurd is an original invention. On the contrary, it has occurred at intervals throughout history, whenever a thinker or a literary artist has become acutely aware of the

means "absurd" in nearly the same sense it has for Camus. The two thinkers are aligned also in their unflinching determination to strip away illusions and to face life's harsh irrationality. They are aligned also in their sense of the world's opaqueness, in their exaltation of the value of lucidity, and in the *zest* with which they invoke the power of unaided reason to undermine its own foundations — true instances of deconstruction long before the notion was invented.[18]

The example of Camus is especially valuable because it shows that to see life as absurd does not mean becoming a nihilist. Recognizing the absurd is not the end of the road. A thinker can find, or create, meanings and values in an absurd world. Even *The Myth of Sisyphus,* written at the nadir of the War (1942) and considered the darkest of Camus's works, "sums itself up for me," he says, "as a lucid invitation to live and to create, in the very midst of the desert."[19] Camus sees a sort of redemption (though not escape) in man's lucid awareness of his fate. Camus dedicated *The Rebel* (written in 1951) to repudiating the moral sloth and indifference of nihilism and to finding an answer beyond the absurd even while not denying its reality. *The Plague* (written in 1946) shows how a man can *create* meaning — for himself, in his own little sphere — by choosing and living his mission in a world epitomized by a plague, recalling Qohelet's perception of "an evil sickness" pervading events (5:15; 6:2).

Qohelet, like Camus, judges the world absurd and unfair by measuring it against a strict standard of values and rationality. This incongruity, more severe than any of the inconsistencies the commentators have focused on, dominates Qohelet's thought. This too should not be smoothed over in art or in life (as Camus accuses various philosophers of trying to do), because it is faithful to a disparity perceived in reality.

Like Qohelet, Camus seeks to build up as well as tear down. Though they repudiate the claim of explanatory systems to control the refractory and inconsistent phenomena we face, they both insist on the value of knowledge, understanding, experience, and courage in a world whose irrationality seems to confound all values. Both demonstrate the resiliency of

---

gap between the human power of understanding and the unintelligibility of the universe. Its basic principle is that man has no access to the so-called 'transcendent,' and must work out how best to live with the knowledge that all religious mythologies are unconformable projections of the human imagination, sometimes with good, but often with very bad consequences" (*New York Review of Books* 45.1 [1998]: 26).

18. M. Sneed (1997) describes Qohelet as a deconstructionist who undermines the traditional dichotomies of wisdom/folly and profit/debit.

19. Preface to the *Myth,* English edition, 1955, p. v.

the human spirit by living with this contradiction and in affirming values despite it, and this resiliency makes them both far less negativistic than is commonly thought. Both, in fact, are *moralists.* They deconstruct life's logic by exposing its absurdities, then affirm life's value by recovering meanings and morals.

That is not to say that Camus's ideas (which themselves varied over the course of time) can be transferred whole to the book of Qohelet. The most profound difference is that Qohelet does not believe the world is masterless, though his universe with an incomprehensible master has little more to say to man than the void Camus sees. Nor does Qohelet advocate "rebellion," Camus's (not quite appropriate) catchword for man's unflinching willingness to confront his fate and push against the restraints it places on him. For Qohelet, to recognize and embrace life's limited possibilities accords with God's will. For Camus, the gods are gone, and only their indifference remains, yet man's possibilities are not all closed. But for all their divergences, the kinship between Qohelet and Camus runs deep.

Interestingly, Camus mentions Qohelet, but he sets him at a certain distance, because he assumes that Qohelet is calling everything "vanity," and he reads Qohelet as a pessimist in the extreme. In describing Don Juan, whose illusionless choice of the quantitative ethic makes him a hero of the absurd, Camus says that it is a great mistake to see in this character "a man brought up on Ecclesiastes. For nothing is vanity to him except the hope of another life" (*Myth,* p. 52). Camus implies that to see everything as vanity is a more profound negation of life's value than to regard everything as absurd, and he does not demand such nihilism of "l'homme absurd." For within the realm of the absurd it is possible to restore values and truths. Not everything is "vanity," meaning worthless or trivial. Qohelet asserts the irrationality of life and the impenetrability of God's will, but he also seeks to recover meanings, values, and truths, to discern a Way of Life through the murky wasteland. So does Camus.

§1.43. The Absurd in Ancient Near Eastern Literature

Qohelet was not the first author to observe life's absurdities and injustices, nor was he the most pessimistic of the ancients with regard to life's value and meaning.

In the Egyptian "Dispute Between a Man and his Ba" (*AEL* 1.163-69), a man addresses his Ba (the separable soul) and bitterly laments the cruelty and alienation he sees about him; for example:

11

To whom shall I speak today?
The criminal is one's intimate,
The brother with whom one dealt is a foe. (*AEL* 1.167)

To whom shall I speak today?
Wrong roams the earth
And ends not. (*AEL* 1.168)

He longs for death, and his Ba finally agrees to stay with him at death. The Ba's concession may imply his agreement to suicide. The book is nihilistic toward this world, but it may (though this is uncertain) hold out hope for the afterlife.

An often-noted parallel is the "Harper Song" supposedly from the tomb of King Antef (it appears in a later papyrus, Harris 500).[20] The skepticism of this poet is directed at a belief of supreme importance to the Egyptians, the efficacy of the mortuary cult: Can it really ensure immortality, when tombs crumble or are violated? Perhaps it was the Atenist tomb depredations that provoked this lament:

A generation passes,
Another stays,
since the time of the ancestors.
. . .
Yet those who built tombs,
their places are gone,
What has become of them? (*AEL* 1.196)

The poet's solution is a carpe diem: enjoy the pleasures of life in *this* life. Let *them* give you a taste of immortal paradise, since we cannot know what follows:

Follow your heart as long as you live!
Put myrrh on your head,
Dress in fine linen,
Anoint yourself with oils fit for a god.
Heap up your joys,
Let your heart not sink!

---

20. Translation in *AEL* 1.196-97. For a philological and literary analysis, see "A Study of Antef," Fox 1977b. The actual dating of the text is probably the Amarna period (1365-49) or shortly thereafter. See ibid., 402f.

Follow your heart and your happiness.
Do your things on earth as your heart commands!
When there comes to you that day of mourning,
The Weary-hearted [Osiris] hears not their mourning,
Wailing saves no man from the pit!

Refrain: Make holiday,
Do not weary of it!
Lo, none is allowed to take his goods with him,
Lo, none who departs comes back again! (*AEL* 1.196f.)

This poem initiated a series of tomb poems repudiating "Antef's" skepticism and insisting that we can indeed prepare for a blessed eternity.[21]

"The Babylonian Theodicy" (*BTM* 2.806-23) is a dialogue between a sufferer, who sees injustice pervading society and blames the gods for it, and a friend who defends the justice of the gods. The conclusion is unclear, but in the friend's last speech he is apparently moved by the sufferer's pessimism and he too blames the gods for creating man evil and heaping upon him miseries and death (2.813).

A Wisdom text from Emar, known also in a variant version from Ugarit, dwells on the finality of death: "Where are [ancient heroes]? . . . Where are the Great Kings who lived from days of old until now? In fact, they have never been conceived; they have never been born."[22] The response is to choose joy: "A gloomy life, what advantage does it have over death? . . . Cast off all griefs, ignore troubles!"[23]

The closest parallel to Qohelet's "absurdism" — though not his affirmation of values and meanings — is the Babylonian "Dialogue of Pessimism" (BTM 2.815-17), which also focuses on contradiction to dismantle life's meaningfulness. A man proposes an undertaking, such as driving to the palace and founding a household. His servant replies by encouraging him to do so and supplies reasons. When the master changes his mind, the servant immediately agrees and gives reasons for refraining:

"Servant, listen to me." "Yes, master, yes." "Quickly bring me water (to wash) my hands, give it to me so I can sacrifice to my god." "Sacrifice,

---

21. See Fox 1977b:421f.

22. Emar VI.4:767, 17f. Translation by A. Gianto 1998: 475f., who observes significant parallels between Qohelet and another Emar text.

23. Ibid., lines 19, 21.

13

master, sacrifice. The man who sacrifices to his god makes a satisfying transaction, he makes loan upon loan." "No, servant, I will certainly not sacrifice to my god." "Do not sacrifice, master, do not sacrifice. You will train your god to follow you around like a dog. He will require of you rites or a magic figurine or what have you."

After several such exchanges, the master asks, "What, then, is good?" The servant answers:

"To break my neck and your neck and throw (us) in the river is good. Who is so tall as to reach to heaven? Who is so broad as to encompass the netherworld?" "No, servant, I will kill you and let you go first." "Then my master will certainly not outlive me even three days!" (2.817)

There is indeed humor in this dialogue, as some interpreters say, but it is a grim humor with a sharp barb: If everything and its opposite are "good," no action is better than its opposite, and all actions are stripped of meaning. Qohelet, in spite of 9:1-4, is not nearly so nihilistic. He too asks what is "good for a man to do under the heavens during the few days of his life" (2:3). He has several answers. A couple of times these seem to include death, but those are passing outbursts, and death is really the reason to grasp life's pleasure, not a solution to life's frustrations.

§1.5. Making the Rough Places Plain

There can be no question of masking the evidence, of suppressing the absurd by denying one of the terms of its equation.

Camus, *Myth*, p. 37

One of the few things that Qohelet's commentators agree on is that the book is full of contradictions. To be sure, most insist that the contradictions are only apparent and can be eliminated, but if so, then at least the *appearance* of contradiction is a datum that requires explanation. Interpreters who feel that the contradictions are illusory should attempt to explain the cause or function of so many illusions, but this has not been done. Commentators who remove the roadblocks never explain why the author put them there in the first place.

There are a number of hermeneutical techniques for resolving the in-

14

consistencies, apparent or real. Since I am proposing that Qohelet intends the contradictions to be understood as such, I must first show that these techniques do not work. But, in a sense, the best argument may be that they work *too* well, that they are too elastic and allow the exegete with a minimum of scholarly ingenuity to arrive at the expected conclusions.

§1.51. *Harmonizing Discords*

The traditional approach is harmonization, the reconciling of apparently contradictory statements by showing that they use the same words differently or deal with different matters. In the discussion in b. Shab. 30b, the Amoraim apply this technique in explaining how their predecessors proved Qohelet acceptable for general access. For example, "I praised *śimḥah*" (8:15) is said to pertain to the joy that comes from fulfilling commandments, whereas "and *śimḥah* — what does this accomplish?" (2:2) dismisses specifically pleasure that does not proceed from the commandments. The problem with such harmonizations is that nothing in the text indicates the supposed distinction, and if the author wanted the readers to recognize essential distinctions, he could have given them some guidance. In actuality, the context within which these interpreters are reading these verses is not the immediate literary unit or even the book of Qohelet as a whole, but rather their own system of religious axioms. They know in advance what Qohelet-Solomon's meaning *must* be. The grand system washes over Qohelet and effaces much of his individuality.

The most skilled harmonizer was Abraham Ibn Ezra. Believing that "even the least of the wise would not write a book and contradict his own words in his book" (in his comment on 7:3), he provides the means for eliminating all the apparent contradictions in Qohelet by assigning each potential contradiction to one of four conditions, as summarized by M. Zer-Kavod (1973:26): (1) Two sentences are in themselves correct, each in different circumstances. (2) Sentence A is conditional, sentence B is absolute. (3) Sentence A is the exception, sentence B is the rule. (This is actually a formulation of a contradiction, not its resolution.) (4) Sentence A is someone else's opinion, sentence B is Qohelet's. An example of #1: "Irritation rests in the breast of fools" (7:9) means that irritability remains with fools at all times, whereas the wise man's irritation or anger, commended in 7:3, is timely and brief. An example of #2: "It is good . . . to eat and drink, etc." (5:17), applies only to the fool, who strains to grow rich and never pauses to enjoy his earnings, whereas "Better to go to a house of mourning than to go to a house of feasting" (7:2) is valid without restriction to person or situation. M. Zer-

Kavod (p. 27) adds two categories of his own: (5) A contradiction is produced by one sentence being taken out of context. (6) A contradiction is produced by a certain (extraneous) supposition. Zer-Kavod can then defend Qohelet against suspicions of inconsistency by wielding whichever rule seems to work best in any particular verse.

H.-W. Hertzberg's principle of the "Zwar-Aber Tatsache" (or "Aussage") has been widely used in Qohelet exegesis. (Literally this means "the 'to be sure'-'however' fact" or "statement"; in other words: a concessive assertion.) This was intended to resolve contradictory propositions by assigning them to different objects or different points of view. In a "Zwar-Aber Tatsache," one statement expresses the commonly held idea, and a second declares the first to be true only in relation to a limited perspective.[24] For example, in 2:13-16, Qohelet is saying: Granted that wisdom has (as they say) a practical advantage over folly, nevertheless the wise man and fool both die, so wisdom has no real advantage (my paraphrase, based on Hertzberg, pp. 91f.). Or in 8:11-14: Granted that as a rule the righteous live long and the wicked die young, nevertheless there are cases where the opposite happens (my paraphrase, based on Hertzberg, pp. 174f.).[25]

The "Zwar-Aber Tatsache" implies a philosophical adjudication between rival ideas that affirms the second — the "Aber" — and pushes the first, the "Zwar," to the periphery. Qohelet is paraphrasing a notion held by others, which he accepts as partly valid ("zwar"), but then declares its inadequacy by presenting his own opinion (cf. Hertzberg, pp. 30f., 175). (Again, this is actually a contradiction, not a resolution.)

The problem with this hermeneutic is that it allows us to assign one of the contrary propositions to someone other than Qohelet with no indicator besides a presupposition about what kind of thing Qohelet would say. Hertzberg rightly observes that in certain passages (but not in all those he lists), two viewpoints confront without invalidating each other. For Qohelet, however, the result is not a comfortable compromise, but only a declaration of dissatisfaction in which he declares the situation to be a *hebel*. Sometimes he reinforces this assessment by calling it "a senseless thought" *(rĕ'ut ruaḥ),* "a great evil," or "an evil sickness." These expres-

---

24. This accords with Ibn Ezra's resolution of the tension between 5:17 and 7:2; see above.

25. Hertzberg (p. 30) regards the following as examples of the "Zwar [Z]-Aber [A] Tatsache": 1:16 = Z and 17f. = A; 2:3-10 = Z and 11 = A; 2:13-14a = Z and 14b ff. = A; 3:11a = Z and 11b = A; 3:17 = Z and 18ff. = A; 4:13-16a = Z and 16b = A; 7:11f. = Z and 7 = A [note transposition]; 8:12b-13 = Z and 14-15 = A; 9:4b = Z and 5 = A; 9:16a = Z and 16b = A; 9:17-18a = Z and 18b, 10:1 = A; 10:2-3 = Z and 5-7 = A.

sions of frustration and protest would make no sense if Qohelet felt he had found a satisfactory resolution.

Qohelet does not merely restrict the "Zwar" in favor of the "Aber." The "Zwar" is as much Qohelet's belief as the "Aber" is, and Qohelet does not propose the latter happily. The "Aber" — the recognition of anomalies — *imposes* itself on Qohelet, who would prefer to retain the rule, the "Zwar," uncontested. He observes the superiority of wisdom, then bewails the treatment it receives. He protests the certainty of divine judgment, then complains of injustice. The relation between the two propositions is "this is true *and* — alas — that is true," and it is this conjunction that makes the world so absurd.[26]

J. Loader (1979) pursues a harmonization of a subtler sort. He points to numerous sets of apparent contradictions and distinguishes in each a "pole" and a "contra-pole." These, Loader says, are held in "tension." This is an important insight, but Loader abandons it for a harmonistic exegesis that ascribes one side of each of the contradictions to another party, namely the advocates of conventional Wisdom, which Loader calls the "general *ḥokmah*." Like the appeal to the "Zwar-Aber Tatsache" and the theory that Qohelet is a disputation or diatribe (below, §1.55 and n. 33), Loader's method has Qohelet raising "chokhmatic" ideas in order to override them, and all real tension in the polarity is discharged. Loader's procedure allows him to conclude that "[e]xcepting the epilogue, not a single palpable contradiction can be found in the book" (p. 133). On Loader's interpretive method see further chapter 5, n. 5. Moreover, as G. Wilson observes in a review of Loader (1987), several of the oppositions Loader isolates are not truly polar, and that Loader's positive-negative schema often produces forced interpretations.

Some measure of harmonization is a necessary part of the reading process, for one must always interpret one passage in light of others in order to gain a coherent picture of an author's thought. A reader must work toward consistency on some level. At several points, I too will explain apparent contradictions by fine-tuning the definitions of terms. But this need for holistic reading does not justify applying harmonization to the extent required for the elimination of Qohelet's major contradictions and incongruities.

Appeal to extraneous factors (such as divine commandments in the discussion of *śimḥah*) and to ad hoc definitions (such as the two types of *śimḥah*

---

26. Ellermeier 1967:125-29 argues that the Zwar-Aber Tatsache has been used as a "magic wand." In the cases he studies, 3:17aβγ and 8:12b-13, the relationship is not one of relativization but "ein glatter Widerspruch" — "a plain contradiction" (p. 127). Ellermeier prefers to regard these as glosses.

that Ibn Ezra descries) makes for forced and unpersuasive harmonization. Harmonistic interpretations become objectionable when they call upon makeshift, contrived devices, such as Zer-Kavod's grab-bag of six princi- ples, to achieve consistency. This is a form of scholasticism that textual scholars, ancient and modern, are comfortable with but that could not be ex- pected of most readers — and Qohelet taught "the people" (12:9).

§1.52. Subtracting Later Additions

When harmonization begins to collapse of its own weight, some commenta- tors ease the tension by assigning some of the opposed propositions to a later hand. This approach was popular in the nineteenth and early twentieth centu- ries and is represented in the commentaries of Siegfried, Barton, McNeile, and Podechard. Currently it is followed (more cautiously) by Crenshaw in his commentary. The hypothesis of additions is a reasonable one, because in the ancient world, texts unquestionably underwent glossing, supplemen- tation, and correction in the course of transmission.

Yet this hypothesis creates a dilemma of its own: where do we locate Qohelet's thought? The passages most often considered secondary are not mere explanatory glosses or theological embellishments, but statements of ideas that both bear directly on the central issues of the book and rebut the ideas that are supposed to be authentic. The text with these passages is a very different book from the text without them.

The attempt to bring consistency into Qohelet by excisions of suppos- edly later material runs into several difficulties:

(a) The sentences commonly eliminated are often intertwined syntacti- cally with material that is certainly original, as evidenced primarily by their unorthodox thought and secondarily by style. (Style, however, can be imi- tated, whereas ideas would not be imitated by the very people who were try- ing to defuse them.)

For example, the praise of wisdom in 2:13-14a (assigned by Siegfried to an annotator) is introduced by a phrase of perception typical of Qohelet, *wěra'iti 'ăni še-*. Moreover, 2:12a looks forward to a statement about wis- dom, which is lacking if vv. 13-14a are excised. The bitter remark about the universality of death in v. 15 — certainly original to Qohelet — could not follow directly upon v. 12, because without v. 14a there is no antecedent for *kullam*, "them both" (or "all") in v. 14b. And if even a single strong commen- dation of wisdom is allowed the original author (as Podechard and Barton concede must be done here), there is no reason to attribute (as they do) other such statements to a "Chakam." In the same way, the affirmation of divine judgment in 3:17aβ (an addition by a "Chasid," according to Siegfried, McNeile, Barton, Podechard, and Crenshaw) begins in v. 17aα in a locution typical of Qohelet ("I said in my heart"), and it is followed by a motivation characteristic of Qohelet's thought and cast in his distinctive vocabulary (v. 17b). The orthodox sentiments of 8:12bβ *(yihyeh . . .)* to 8:13 are linked to the complaint of 8:11-12a by the phrase *ki gam yodea' 'ăni 'ăšer.* Also, by this hypothesis the putative annotator left the severe complaint of 8:14 untouched, though he could have softened it too by placing his addition *after* it.

(b) As a rule, a corrective gloss can be expected to follow the statement it is supposed to correct; otherwise the glossator's views are themselves neutralized. In the passages at the center of this discussion — 2:12-16; 3:17; 8:5-7; and 8:10-14 — it is the "skeptic" who is allowed the last word.

(c) The proposed glosses do not fulfill the purposes ascribed to the glossators. A scribe reading 8:11-12a + 14 alone would face a sharp repudiation of God's absolute justice. If he wished to make the text assert God's justice unequivocally but was unable to eliminate the offending words, he might have added (after v. 14) an assertion that the day of reckoning will eventually come. As it is, however, the hypothetical scribe, in spite of pious motivations, has let Qohelet's painful doubts have the last word and has merely created an uneasy tension between observations of injustice and assertions of justice. Though a tension might serve the purposes of a bold thinker who wishes to portray the world's absurdities, it offers no comfort to a pious believer in God's unwavering justice.

(d) Even with all the additions that Podechard, McNeile, and Barton claim to have discovered, the skeptical and pessimistic character of the book remains blatant. If the book was considered so offensive as to require extensive glossing, why (as Gordis asks [p. 71]) didn't the glossators take the simpler and more effective step of suppressing it altogether? That is to say, why did they choose to copy it? The addition hypothesis requires us to assume that a scribe (or several scribes) who fundamentally disagreed with Qohelet undertook to copy the work, then inserted additions that were supposed to counterbalance Qohelet's skepticism and yet manifestly fail to do so.

Nor does this method succeed in achieving consistency. For example, McNeile, Barton, and Podechard (among others) attribute 3:17; 8:5-7; 8:11-13; and 11:9b to a *hasid*-glossator. Galling assigns 3:17aβγ; 8:5; 8:12b-13; and 11:9b to a later redactor. Crenshaw does the same for 2:26a; 3:17a; 8:12f.; 11:9; perhaps 5:18 and 7:26b.[27] Nevertheless these four commenta-

---

27. P. 48, but in the commentary proper, he is uncertain on some of these verses.

19

tors leave 5:5b and 7:17 to Qohelet, though both verses affirm retribution no less clearly than the verses they deny him. If we leave the book with any significant inconsistencies in central issues such as wisdom and justice, we are undercutting the criteria whereby the supposed additions were identified to start with.

§1.53. Discovering Quotations

Currently the favored means for resolving contradictory propositions is to assign one of them to another speaker, whose opinion Qohelet is said to be citing for the sake of rebuttal. In my view, there very likely are quotations in the book, but identifying them is not crucial. If the author considered it important that we recognize that another person is speaking this or that sentence, he could have let us know. But he does not.

The quotation hypothesis was advocated by L. Levy and, most vigorously, by R. Gordis. According to the latter, Qohelet (and other Biblical writers) frequently quotes other sources for various purposes, of which Gordis identifies four types, with various sub-types. Quite often these lack a *verbum dicendi*. In many cases Qohelet quotes traditional Wisdom in order to refute it. More recently, R. Whybray (1981) has sought to develop a typology of quotations in Qohelet in order to determine which come from traditional Wisdom. D. Michel (1988, 1989) finds numerous quotations from various sources, including conservative sages, pessimistic contemporaries, and Qohelet himself.

None of these scholars has succeeded in finding non-arbitrary and replicable criteria for identifying quotations. There are plenty of ways to mark quotations in Hebrew. Qohelet could just once say, "The sages say . . . , but I say . . ." But the closest he comes to a quotation is in 8:17, $w^e gam$ 'im yo'mar $he\d{h}akam$ $lada$'at . . . , lit., "And even if the wise man says to know . . ." This, however, is not exactly a quotation, but an ascription of attitude. Even so, Qohelet has no problem in identifying the "speaker" of this attitude. When he quotes himself (for example, in 1:16; 2:1, 2, and 15), he does not lack the means for marking the quotation as such. Yet he does not do so in the thorniest, most refractory passages.

An example of a subtle application of the quotation hypothesis is the way D. Michel sorts out 8:2-9 (1989:262; 91-100). He identifies vv. 2-5 as a quotation from a "wisdom text" which declares that the man who knows the teaching of "time and order" has nothing to fear even from the powerful king. This is followed by Qohelet's commentary (vv. 6-9), in which he asserts that man cannot guarantee the desired result by knowing the right moment. There does seem to be a jumble of opinions in this passage, but there is no indicator which belong to Qohelet, which (if any) to another sage. Nothing in the passage asserts that man *can* guarantee a particular result. Not even conservative wisdom would say so.

In 5:10-11 (discussed by Michel 1989:246; 187-90), Qohelet is said to quote two *mᵉšalim* that criticize wealth by pointing out its disadvantages. Then he sets forth his own opinion in 12-16, namely that "wealth in itself is no guarantee for happiness" (p. 189). According to Michel, the derivative origin of the meshalim is supposedly shown by the lack of forms of argumentation and observation characteristic of Qohelet. But nothing is gained by designating vv. 10-11 as quotations, because: (1) Qohelet himself is hardly unaware of the disadvantages of wealth. (2) There are many passages lacking characteristic formulas. That means that the *absence* of such formulas is compatible with Qohelet's style. (3) 5:10-11 and 5:12-16 reinforce each other in observing the disadvantages of wealth. Why assign one and not the other to Qohelet? It does not matter much whether Qohelet has composed vv. 10-11 or is quoting them, for they are now *his* own.

R. Whybray (1981) proceeds with formal criteria rather than starting from the difficulties and using the hypothesis of quotations to solve them. According to Whybray, a saying (specifically, a distich) may be considered a quotation if it is (1) self-contained; (2) closely similar in form to sayings in Proverbs 10–29; (3) thematically consistent with Proverbs while standing in some sort of tension with Qohelet's earmark ideas; and (4) free of late linguistic features (p. 438). On these grounds, Whybray identifies eight "clear examples": 2:14a; 4:5; 4:6 (omitting "and a striving after wind"); 7:5; 7:6a (omitting "This too is *hebel*"); 9:17; 10:2; 10:12.

So far, Whybray may well be right. Sayings such as "The wise man has his eyes in his head, while the fool goes about in darkness" (2:14a) and "The fool locks his hands together and eats his flesh" (4:5) do have the ring of traditional coinages. But Qohelet himself, according to the epilogue, composed proverbs (12:9), and these may be among them. Their language is not archaic or even archaizing. More important, even if Qohelet did not write these proverbs, he used them as his own words. That's what proverbs are for. Unless the quoter distances himself from the idea, it becomes his own. The sages in Pirqey Avot use unmarked quotations to express their own ideas; for example, in 4:19:

> Samuel the younger used to say: When your enemy falls, rejoice not, and when he stumbles, let your heart not rejoice. Lest the Lord see and be wroth, and turn his anger away from him.

21

Samuel's favorite saying is Prov 24:17, but nothing identifies its source. Ben Sira too used unmarked quotations extensively,[28] as did Egyptian Wisdom.[29]

Whybray recognizes that Qohelet "quotes" sayings not to reject them but to make them serve his own ideas (pp. 445-50). That too is generally how proverbs are used. This means that even certain knowledge of the sources of these proverbs (as we have for Avot 4:19) would not resolve the question of their role in Qohelet's thought.

Quotations that express the speaker's viewpoint need not be marked, for their source is not decisive for interpretation. It is quite likely that Qohelet quotes other authors and popular adages to make his point. One indicator of this kind of quotation is that part of it diverges from the topic, for example at 10:18. In such cases — which I too will try to identify — it does not matter much whether Qohelet is quoting or inventing the proverb. Once he uses it for himself, it may as well be his own creation.

On the other hand, we can expect quotations expressing an opinion contrary to the author's to be marked in some way so as to allow the reader to separate them from the author's present view. The more important for interpretation it is for the reader to dissociate certain words from the primary speaker, the more clearly the writer must mark them as belonging to someone else.

Marking may be explicit, using a verb of speaking or thinking, or it may be virtual. Three forms of virtual marking are (1) the mention of another person besides the primary speaker in the immediate context, to allow the reader to easily associate the words with another voice; (2) a virtual *verbum dicendi* (e.g., a reference to "mouth" or "words" or something else that implies speech); and (3) a shift in grammatical number and person. I discuss the marking of quotations more fully in my article, "The Identification of Quotations" (1980).

There is no marking, explicit or virtual, in Qoh 8:12b-13, or in the other verses that Gordis identifies as quotations of views not Qohelet's (2:13-14a; 4:5, 8bα;[30] 9:16aαβ, 18a). Nevertheless, Gordis supplies a transition phrase in translating 8:12: "though I know the answer that" (in 2:13 he substitutes "I have heard it said" for the Hebrew "I saw," which is certainly misleading). Although Gordis probably did not intend these phrases as literal translations,

28. Duesberg-Fransen 1966:698-711.

29. See the numerous examples in Brunner 1979.

30. Gordis supplies, *"He never asks himself."* In other words, this is supposedly a quotation of something the toiler never said, in fact, never even *thought* of saying. (Can we call this a "quotation"?) With such flexibility, there are few difficulties a commentator cannot easily eliminate, or at least conceal.

they are not even implicit in the Hebrew. *Yodea' 'ăni 'ăšer* means "I know that," not (even as paraphrase) "I know the answer that." There is no clearer way to say that you know something than "I know that."[31]

In the absence of quotation markers, we could just as well attribute 8:11-12a + 14 (the "skeptical" remark) to someone else — to a pupil, for example — and say that Qohelet rejects this idea. That is almost what Podechard does, by extracting all of 8:11-13 as a later addition of a "Chasid," who is supposedly echoing Qohelet's sentiments in vv. 11f. and expressing his own in v. 13. Levy regards all of 8:11 + 12aβ-13 as a quotation of the pious explanation for the delay of retribution.

If Qohelet could pronounce teachings like 4:17–5:6; 7:1-12; and 10:8-20, as well as scattered maxims of a traditional cast, there is no reason to deny him other conventional statements.

The traditional commentators often used a similar tactic. The Targum, for example, makes the *skeptical* remark of 2:16 into a quotation: "And as people say, the end of the righteous is like the end of the guilty." Ibn Ezra says that 9:4b, "a living dog is better off than a dead lion," is "the thought of people," but not Qohelet's. Similarly, he ascribes 9:10, the denial of activity in Sheol, to people whose hearts are full of madness (mentioned in 9:3b), while the affirmation of divine judgment in 3:17a he considers Qohelet's own thought, "the truth." The uses to which quotation-identifying can be put are limitless.

§1.54. Hearing Dialogue

Similar to the quotation theory is the approach that construes the book as a dialogue. Some early commentators ascribed the skeptical opinions to someone less wise than Qohelet, such as an "inquirer" or "student."[32]

A. Miller (1934) describes the book as a condensed literary rendering of a school-disputation in which the master raises and dismisses the opinions

---

31. Qohelet's use of the perfect of *yada'* to introduce his own ideas in other passages does not (contrary to Hertzberg) indicate that the participle in this one marks the knowledge as someone else's. On the contrary, the participle emphasizes the presentness of this knowledge more than the perfect would, for the perfect might be understood as introducing an idea held in the past.

32. For commentators that take this approach see C. D. Ginsburg's summaries of Heinemann (p. 84), du Hamel (p. 165), Herder (p. 184), Eichhorn (p. 185), and Nachtigal (p. 192). The understanding of "Qohelet" as referring to an "assembly" (*qᵉhillah*) of individuals with different views is mentioned (and rejected) by Ibn Ezra (on 7:3).

of "friends and students" who include representatives of the "Weisheits-ideal" ("wisdom ideal") and "Lebensfreude und hohen Lebensführung" ("joy in life and high living," p. 109).[33]

T. A. Perry (1993) gives precise boundaries to the voices in the dialogue. Surrounding Qohelet's voice is that of a pious man (the Presenter, "P"), who transmits and debates the wisdom of the skeptical Kohelet ("K"). For example, K speaks 6:1-2, and the discussion continues:

> P: (3) "If a man begets a hundred children and lives a long life: despite the length of his days, if he does not take satisfaction in these good things. . . ."

> K: ". . . and have a proper burial, I would say that the stillborn child is better off than he."

> P: (4) "Yet, as you would argue, in vanity he comes and in darkness he goes forth. . . ."

The same problem dogs this approach as the hypothesis of quotations: that there is no marking of change of speaker. Whatever Perry considers more pious and cautious, he ascribes to "P," thereby *creating* that voice. Even with this liberty, Perry finds it necessary to reverse the import of numerous sentences by tendentious translations or by treating them as rhetorical questions, or even by embedding quotations of "K" in "P's" questions.

§1.55. Detecting Dialectic

R. E. Murphy takes a more subtle approach to the description of "dialectic" in Qohelet. He recognizes that Qohelet belongs to the stream of traditional Wisdom (that is to say, the Wisdom instructions) and does not assume that Qohelet is quoting someone else's words. Rather, he posits that Qohelet is stating the ideas of earlier, more conventional sages, and responding to them in a variety of ways, usually by modifying their validity (and thus coming close to the "Zwar-Aber Tatsache"). In a number of passages, Murphy depicts Qohelet as pronouncing traditional ideas and appending his own remarks, or commenting on them by using one traditional idea against another, usually in order to "relativize" the traditional doctrines' validity. I discuss

---

33. Allgeier and Lohfink (p. 10) classify Qohelet as a diatribe and use this assumption in similar ways.

this type of analysis in the commentary to 8:1-9, which contains some indisputably traditional wisdom.[34]

The basic problem is, again, that no one can provide *a priori* criteria for recognizing "traditional" ideas, and even when such ideas can be identified, and even when they are virtually quotations of extant proverbs (as in 8:1-5), we are still no closer to knowing Qohelet's attitude toward their truth-value, since he may be incorporating them into his own thought as well as limiting or rejecting them. It is evident that Qohelet gives no guidance in making this determination, since the commentators agree so little on where the traditional materials lie or what their function is.

Qohelet undoubtedly was in dialectic with his predecessors, but this is true of all Wisdom Literature, which is to say that Wisdom books always incorporated earlier wisdom, reshaped it, and went beyond it. Amenemope, for example, took a new direction when he gave prominence to the ethic of personal piety and resignation to one's fate. In effect, he redefined the nature of wise behavior so as to give centrality to the virtue of humble receptivity to divine will, whereas earlier (and contemporaneous) Wisdom laid greater emphasis on ways to shape one's future and influence events. Various Egyptian sages debated a theory of education, sometimes quoting and vehemently rebutting each other, sometimes entering into an actual dialogue of two parties (in Anii); this is discussed in Fox 1997b. In Proverbs, the authors of the personification poems in chapters 1–9 (1:20-33; 8:1-36; 9:1-18) elevated the old wisdom of practical and moral counsels to the status of an eternal and transcendent power and personified it as a woman. Ben Sira, whose attitude toward past sages was one of deep reverence, made a major innovation when he transformed wisdom by making Torah its highest realization. The Wisdom of Solomon turned wisdom into the governing force in history. All these books were in dialectic, sometimes antithetical, with the wisdom of the past. Qohelet is doing the same, but it is a dialectic of his book with the past, not of parts of his book with other parts.

Different sages had different ideas, and dialectic was unending, because Wisdom was a living, growing literature for some 2500 years, in an area stretching from Egypt to the Persian Gulf. For that reason it is caricature to depict "traditional" wisdom as a monolithic body of orthodox doctrines against which a radical Qohelet is bravely rebelling. Qohelet certainly does not see himself that way. He sees himself as learning the wisdom of the past

---

34. N. Lohfink (in his commentary, *passim*) and D. Michel (1989, esp. chap. 10, *passim*) take a similar approach, but they more often try to identify actual quotations and tend to sharpen the opposition from modulation into polemic.

and continuing in its path (1:16), and the epilogist agrees with this assessment, even while aware that Qohelet's wisdom has its thorny parts (12:9f.). Nor does Qohelet ever say or imply that the sages claim one thing but *he* says another. He never sets himself against traditional wisdom, but simply folds traditional (which is to say, earlier) wisdom into his own teachings and moves in a direction of his own. That is what all the sages of Wisdom Literature did.

§1.56. A Fragmented Psyche?

K. Galling (1932:281 and passim) diagnoses Qohelet's contradictions and tensions as symptoms of a disturbed soul. Qohelet (or the author) may well have been disturbed, but a psychologistic explanation is not an interpretation. A disturbed soul could be brutally consistent in expressing its disquiet.

Qohelet may not have organized his book schematically, but he still retains his composure. Though troubled by what he sees, he does not lose his equilibrium. He is not merely caught up in inconsistencies (though this does happen occasionally). Rather, he ferrets out the contradictions and even sharpens them as evidence for his claim that "everything is absurd." He is not merely flailing about.

All of these exegetical techniques have their place, but when overused they become a magic wand for making difficulties vanish, and intriguing complexities and subtle disruptions may disappear with them. Excessive exegetical ingenuity may succeed in making an author consistent at the price of making him incoherent — or insipid.

And it is not necessary. On a lower level, within the foundational assumptions that produce the surface contradictions, Qohelet (Qohelet-the-observer) *is* consistent (these are discussed in §9.4). And so too, on a higher level, in what he says *about* the contradictions he observed, is Qohelet (Qohelet-the-reporter[35]). We should listen to the uneasy dissonances that ring in his attitudes and worldview. The contradictions may reside in the world itself. Qohelet just describes things the way he sees them.

---

35. This is the voice of Qohelet as he looks back and reports his earlier experiments and experiences, which included observation of contraries. See Excursus III.

26

CHAPTER 2

Hebel *and* R^eut Ruaḥ

. . . [W]hat is absurd is the confrontation of the irrational with the
wild longing for clarity whose call echoes in the human heart.

Camus, Myth, p. 16

§2.1. *Hebel* in the Hebrew Bible[1]

Qohelet begins and ends his teaching with the declaration that all is *hebel*, and
throughout the book he calls things he sees *hebel*. What exactly does he mean
by this? And what does he mean when he applies this word to *everything?* This
chapter examines how Qohelet uses a common word in a new way.[2] It will also
consider the meeting of *r^eut/ra'yon ruaḥ*, which is appended to a *hebel*-judg-
ment ("This is *hebel*" or "X is *hebel*") in most of its occurrences.

The basic meaning of *hebel*, the literal sense from which the others
are derived,[3] is *vapor*. This sense is evident in Isa 57:13; Prov 13:11;

---

1. *Hebel* occurs sixty-four times in the Bible and two in the extant Hebrew of Sira.
Of these, thirty occurrences are in Qohelet.

2. For a survey of the etymology and the distribution of the term in the Bible, see
Loretz 1964:218-25, as well as the commentaries and Seybold, *hebhel, TDOT,* III, 313-20.

3. This is a conceptual derivation. We cannot trace the historical development
within BH, but given the evidence for the base-meaning "vapor" in cognate languages, as
well as the probability of development from literal to metaphorical uses, it is safe to say
that "vapor" was the original meaning as well.

21:6; and Ps 144:4, as well as in RH, Jewish Aramaic, and Syriac. It is usually used in ways easily derived by metaphoric transfer from the qualities of vapor.

(a) Ephemerality

Some verses show how the literal sense of vapor can easily connote ephemerality, such as Job 7:16 ("I am disgusted. I won't live forever. Let me alone, for my days are *hebel*"); Ps 39:6, 12; Prov 21:6; and Ps 144:4 ("Man is like *hebel;* his days are like a passing shadow"). D. Fredericks (1993:11-32) believes that this is the dominant sense in Qohelet too.

(b) Vanity

The traditional gloss "vanity" means something worthless or trivial. An effort that achieves nothing, or nothing worthwhile, is in vain. Elsewhere in the Bible, *hebel* has this sense several times. Examples: Isa 49:4 ("And I said, 'In vain [*riq*] I have toiled, for emptiness [*tohu*] and vanity [*hebel*] I wasted my strength'"); Isa 30:7 ("Egypt will help only in vain [*hebel*] and emptily [*riq*]"); Job 9:29; Lam 4:17. Human plans are vapor — trivial, ineffectual (Ps 94:11).

The interpretation of *hebel* in Qohelet as vanity goes back to the Septuagint's ματιότης and is maintained as "vanity" or "vain" (and foreign equivalents) in most translations. What was meant by "all is vanity," in the older translations at least, is that the things of this world — "under the sun" — are of little consequence, as opposed to the life of the spirit — "over the sun" — namely piety, Torah, and eternal life. But Qohelet's negation is not a pious renunciation of worldly goods. No one in the Bible advocates enjoying them as warmly as he.

(c) Nothingness

Loretz (1964:223) and Ginsberg (p. 13) gloss *hebel* as "nothing." Since the world is not actually nothing, this interpretation substitutes one metaphor (zero) for another (vapor). Ginsberg also says that *hebel* is "air" in the sense of empty space, not the gas that fills the space. Even if this were so, "empty space" would be the vehicle of a metaphor no less flexible than "vapor," and itself requiring explication. But in fact, *hebel* never actually means "nothing."

(d) Incomprehensibility, Mystery

Hebel does imply incomprehensibility, but that is not all. Because of the proximity of this concept to the absurd, it will be given special attention below, in §2.4.

The following concepts have not been proposed as the meaning of *hebel* in Qohelet, but they do pertain elsewhere in the Bible and their connotations are relevant to Qohelet's usage:

(e) Deceit

Hebel is often a synonym of words for lies and deceits, such as *kazab, šeqer, 'awen,* and *maʿal.* Examples are Zech 10:2; Ps 62:10; Prov 31:30; Job 21:34 *(//maʿal);* etc.

The connotations of inefficacy and deceit make *hebel* a fitting epithet for false gods. In Jer 16:19b, the foreigners say, "Truly our fathers inherited deceit *(šeqer)* — *hebel* in which there is no efficacy *(moʿil)*"; sim. Deut 32:21; 2 Kgs 17:15; Jer 2:5; 8:19 *(//pʿsileyhem);* 14:22; Jon 2:9; Zech 10:2.

(f) Senselessness, Nonsense

This use combines the connotations of (b) and (e). Words and statements that fail to communicate, or that communicate an illusion, are senseless or nonsensical. Examples include Jer 10:3 ("For the ordinances of the peoples are *hebel,* for they cut a tree from the forest [to make an idol]"); 10:8 *(musar hăbalim* = "a senseless teaching"); Ps 39:7.

The move from "deceit" to "nonsense" is a slight one. Job says, "You have all seen (this). Why do you emit vapor *(hebel tehbalu)?*" (27:12). Here Job is accusing the friends of deliberately, hence deceitfully, speaking nonsense. But when Elihu says that Job "opens his mouth vaporously *(hebel),* ignorantly *(bibli daʿat)* heaping up words" (35:16), he is accusing him of speaking foolish, senseless words rather than of lying.

In these verses, *hebel* could easily be translated "senseless" or even "absurd," which is the meaning I believe it has in Qohelet. There is thus a background for Qohelet's usage, but no precise parallel to the way that Qohelet predicates *hebel* of facts and scenarios that violate logic. Qohelet has new things to say and must push the limits of the available vocabulary.

§2.2. *Hebel* in Qohelet

We cannot move directly from the literal sense of *hebel* to its meaning in Qohelet, because vapor in itself is a multipurpose metaphor. While some qualities of vapor, especially ephemerality, might be thought applicable in some verses (e.g., 3:19 and 11:10), no quality of actual vapors can be directly transferred to the facts and scenarios that he judges to be *hebel* (e.g., 2:23). Qohelet has taken the term some distance from its literal sense. The meaning of *hebel* must be derived from context.

We may test a few of the common glosses on 8:14:

> There is a *hebel* that happens on the earth: there are righteous people who receive what is appropriate to the deeds of the wicked and there are wicked people who receive what is appropriate to the deeds of the righteous. I said that this too is *hebel*.

Here the two *hebel*-judgments frame a fact.[4] The only antecedent available for the pronoun in the last sentence is the entire preceding statement, namely the fact that *there are* such occurrences.

To call this fact "vaporous" gives no information about it; none of the qualities usually associated with vapors apply. It is not "transitory" or "fleeting" — if it were, that would be all to the good. Nor is it insubstantial, a "nothing," an absence. It is quite substantive, very much a reality. Nor is it "vain," inconsequential. Far from it! Nor is it futile. It is true that the deeds of the righteous may prove futile insofar as they aim at a reward, but the passage also describes the fate of the wicked, and their receiving what the righteous deserve does not imply any futility in *their* actions. Nor does "incomprehensible" adequately capture the disturbing quality in the events that disturbs Qohelet.

§2.3. The Absurd

Hebel in Qohelet means "absurd," understood in the sense described at length in Albert Camus's classic description of the absurd, *The Myth of Sisyphus.*[5]

---

4. Compare the framing with *ra'* "evil," "misfortune," in 6:1-2.

5. English "absurd" means the same as French "absurde" because the contemporary sense of the term in English has been shaped largely under Camus's influence. Although a

The absurd is a disjunction between two phenomena that are thought to be linked by a bond of harmony or causality, or that *should* be so linked. Such bonds are the sine qua non of rationality, and all deduction and explanation presupposes them. Thus the absurd is irrational, an affront to reason — the human faculty that seeks and discovers order in the world about us.

The quality of absurdity is not inherent in a phenomenon but is a relational concept, residing in the tension between a certain reality and a framework of expectations:

> There are absurd marriages, challenges, rancors, silences, wars, and even peace treaties. For each of them the absurdity springs from a comparison. I am thus justified in saying that the feeling of absurdity does not spring from the mere scrutiny of a fact or an impression but that it bursts from the comparison between a bare fact and a certain reality, between an action and the world that transcends it. The absurd is essentially a divorce. It lies in neither of the elements compared; it is born of their confrontation. (Camus, *Myth,* pp. 22f.)

Hence "the absurd depends as much on man as on the world" (p. 24).

Absurdity arises from a contradiction between two undeniable realities: "'It's absurd' means 'It's impossible,' but also: 'It's contradictory'" (*Myth,* p. 22).

Life is saturated with absurdity: it is humanity's condition of existence. Connotations very similar to the absurd as Camus described adhere to Qohelet's use of *hebel:* alienation from the observed world; a distancing of the observer from the event;[6] alienation of the observer from the self ("Forever I shall be a stranger to myself" [*Myth,* p. 15]); a frustrated longing for coherence; a stale taste of repeated and meaningless events, even

---

noun, *hebel* usually has a descriptive function and may be translated as either a noun or adjective.

Since "absurd" in common usage has connotations of the ludicrous, in a translation for popular use another gloss, such as "senseless," might be more appropriate. In this book I prefer "absurd" because of its associations with a philosophical tradition that I consider akin to Qohelet's thought.

6. H. Gese has well described this sense of alienation in Qohelet: ". . . the wisdom of Koheleth shows a mutation of structure in comparison with the earlier Israelite wisdom. This may be described as the distancing of the person — of the 'I' — from the event with which he appears to be associated, as the detachment and self-removal of the observing subject. According to Koheleth, the essence of the person is determined not only in that one perceives oneself as an individual but also in that one sets oneself against world affairs as a stranger to the world" (ET L. Grabbe, 142f. [orig. Gese 1963:141]).

31

resentment at the "gods," the powers believed to reign above man, whatever they may be.

W. P. Brown (1996:129-34) has developed the idea of absurdity as a relational term, an indicator of *"how the self is positioned in relation to the world in its totality"* (p. 131; italics in original). Brown draws upon Thomas Nagel's exposition of the notion of absurdity (1971) and observes that

> Absurdity acknowledges both the incomprehensible nature of the world and the individual's relationship to it, which can only be recognized by the individual's capacity to "step back" and view both the world and the self as a meaningless whole. Thus, the absurd is integrally a matter of character. Qoheleth's notion of the absurd is forged not only from a collision between his expectations and the world, but also from a collision within himself. (pp. 131f.)

Humans have a "special capacity to step back and survey themselves, and the lives to which they are committed, with that detached amazement which comes from watching an ant struggle up a heap of sand" (Nagel 1971:720). This is a feature of Qohelet's "empirical" epistemology, to be discussed in chap. 4.

The sense of the absurd is much older than Camus. As one scholar of Camus observes, "Whatever the special character of Camus's conclusions, the absurd itself remains a contemporary manifestation of a skepticism as old at least as the Book of Ecclesiastes" (Cruickshank 1959:44).

The sense of the absurd is even older than that, for there are ancient Near Eastern writings that can fairly be called absurdist (§1.43). And even apart from such pessimistic works, absurdities are recognized and exploited for various ends. The Egyptian "Prophetic Lament" genre dwells on them. For example:

> The weak-armed is strong-armed,
> One salutes him who saluted.
> I show you the undermost uppermost,
> What was turned on the back turns the belly. (Neferti; *AEL* 1.143)

> Order is cast out,
> Chaos is in the council hall;
> The ways of the gods are violated,
> Their provisions neglected. . . .
> He who gave orders takes orders,
> And the hearts of both submit. (Khakheperre-Sonb; *AEL* 1.147-48)

Lo, citizens are put to the grindstones,
Wearers of fine linen are beaten with [sticks].
Those who never saw daylight go out unhindered,
Those who were on their husband's beds,
"Let them lie on boards," [one repeats]. (Ipuwer, *AEL* 1.153)[7]

Neferti is prophesying *(ex eventu)* the restoration of order by a future king. The other two texts do not have clear constructive goals, but they too may be praising the present order by contrasting the anarchy supposedly rife in the recent past with the present order. Even if they are "literary" exercises (*AEL* 1.146), they are all heartfelt complaints about troubles that the authors believe they see or that once pertained.

Absurdity is thus by no means a modern concept, a notion that might be set aside as *a priori* impossible in an ancient composition. I am not aware, however, of any single word in Hebrew, Egyptian, or Akkadian that expresses this notion as well as *hebel* does in Qohelet's usage.

§2.4. The Incomprehensible

There are other words in the semantic field of the counter-rational that have been suggested as equivalents of *hebel*. E. Good (1965:176-83) gives *hebel* the sense of "incongruous," a notion close to "ironic," and indeed most of the phenomena that are called *hebel* do involve incongruities and ironies. But as a definition, this is too soft. One can stand aloof from incongruities. Incongruities and ironies may be merely puzzling or amusing, and they may even be concomitants of justice, as when a man is caught in the trap he himself set. Justice, on the other hand, is never absurd. *Hebel* for Qohelet, like "absurd" for Camus, is not merely incongruous or ironic. It is oppressive, even tragic.

Hebel is sometimes thought to mean *incomprehensible* or the like. The implication of such renderings is that Qohelet is asserting the limitations of human reason.

Rashbam, who understands *hebel* to mean "futile" in most contexts, says that in 8:10 and 14 it means that which people wonder at *(tohim)* and are amazed at *(mištom^{e}mim)*. In his comment on 8:10-13 Rashbam explains "this too is *hebel*" as "a matter which is hidden from men and which they are unable to perceive clearly and do not understand. . . . [Qohelet] calls this *'hebel,'* for people wonder and are amazed at it."

7. Compare Qohelet's laments in 10:5-7.

Staples (1943) believes that in many of its uses outside Qohelet, *hebel* has a "distinctly cultic flavor" and originally referred to Canaanite rites. He finds justification for this conclusion in the fact that the word is sometimes applied to foreign gods and idols. "The word *hebhel,* therefore, originally carried some such idea as cult mystery, and so something unfathomable, something unknown or unknowable to man" (pp. 65f.). Staples's reasoning is manifestly a string of false analogies based on mistaken premises.

Pennacchini (1977:508) glosses *hebel* as "absurd," but he interprets the concept as an assertion of incomprehensibility relative to a cultural climate (p. 496). But the phenomena that Qohelet calls *hebel* are absurd not only relative to a particular setting, as if he were complaining that his society's perspectives were limited while implying that his own was broader. Nor is he just complaining about the inadequacy of the human mind to penetrate the murk. The murk is all there is.

Ogden (1987:17-21) says that Qohelet applies the word *hebel* to "scenarios"[8] or "situations to which even the sage, the philosopher theologian, has no answer" (p. 21). The word "conveys the notion that life is enigmatic, and mysterious; that there are many unanswered and unanswerable questions. The person of faith recognizes this fact but moves forward positively to claim and enjoy the life and the work which God apportions" (p. 22). But Qohelet is not a "person of faith," and he is not holding silence before life's mysteries.

Hebel designates not the mysterious but the *irrational and meaningless.* To call something *hebel* is a phenomenological observation. Whether or not there is meaning beneath or beyond the visible surface of events, that surface, which is the world as it presents itself to humans, *is* warped. That surface *is* our reality.

It is true that *hebel* includes the notion of incomprehensibility. In 8:17a, "man cannot grasp [*yimṣaʾ*] anything that God makes happen" is equivalent to "everything is absurd and senseless [*wᵉhinneh hakkol hebel urᵉʿut ruaḥ*]" in 1:14b (see the alignment in §6.23). But that is not the entirety of its meaning. "Incomprehensible" indicates that the meaning of a phenomenon is opaque to human intellect but allows for, and may even suggest, that it is actually meaningful and significant. To call something "absurd," on the other hand, is to claim some knowledge about its quality: the fact that it *is* contrary to reason — perhaps only to human reason, but that is the only reason we have access to, unless one appeals to revelation.

---

8. This means the recurrent complexes of circumstances and events which Qohelet observes and judges (Ogden, p. 17).

Qohelet is not bowing his head in pious humility before life's mysteries or modestly confessing an inability to unravel puzzles too great for him. He has discovered that some things are inequitable and senseless. This *knowledge,* and not the ignorance, is what makes him unhappy, for "whosoever increases knowledge increases pain" (1:18).

In addition to calling phenomena *hebel,* he also calls some things "an evil" (6:1), "a sick misfortune" (5:12, 15; 6:2), "a great evil" (2:21), or (lit.) "evil upon me" (2:17) — judgments not properly applicable to a simple mystery.

Moreover, some of the things Qohelet calls *hebel* are not mysterious. Pleasure is not mysterious. The fact that the toiler's wealth is passed on to someone who did not work for it is not "unknowable" or "mysterious." Growing wise produces no permanent distinction between the wise and the foolish. The reason for this, though not its rationale, is quite knowable.

Qohelet does not exclude the possibility that beyond the sphere of events "under the sun" or within the divine intellect there might be a resolution of absurdities, but he (unlike the author of Job) does not affirm or even suggest that there is one. Such a resolution is simply of no use to Qohelet, any more than the unknowable possibility of an afterlife is the solution to the problem of mortality for the living. Absurdity is defined in terms of human reason, and any resolution inaccessible to this power is irrelevant. A philosophical mouse caught in a trap would consider his fate absurd, and he would be right, however explicable and justified his misery might be in the "broader picture."

§2.5. How Qohelet Uses *Hebel*

Qohelet applies the term *hebel* to various types of phenomena: beings, life or a part thereof, acts, facts, and recurring, typical events or scenarios. In almost all cases, it means "absurd."[9]

A word can, of course, be used in various ways in a single book, but Qohelet's thematic declaration that everything is *hebel* and the formulaic character of the *hebel*-judgments show that for Qohelet there is a single dominant quality in the world and that this quality inheres in the particular *hăbalim* that he identifies.

The approach taken by JPSV, which uses eight different glosses to ren-

9. A. Barucq (1968:55) says that life appears to Qohelet "absurd" "in certain aspects."

der *hebel,* gives us no hint that 1:2 and 12:8 generalize the conclusions reached in the course of Qohelet's investigation. If Qohelet were saying, "X is transitory; Y is futile; Z is trivial," then the summary, "All is *hebel*" would be meaningless. Indeed, it would be specious reasoning or a rhetorical device — arguing from disparate categories that share only a multivalent label. To do Qohelet justice, we must look for a concept that applies to all occurrences, or, failing that, to the great majority of them. Then the summary statement "all is *hebel*" can use the word in the sense established in the particulars.

The attempt to determine the meaning of *hebel* in Qohelet often runs up against a grammatical stumbling block: it is frequently difficult, sometimes impossible, to identify what "this" refers to in "this too is *hebel*." But even when this ambiguity cannot be resolved, it is often possible to follow Qohelet's underlying reasoning, to discover what it is in the scenario that troubles him and provokes his complaint.

Rather than examining the thirty-eight occurrences of the word in Qohelet, I will probe some passages where the meaning of *hebel* is most clear and others where there is ambiguity. The others will be treated in the commentary.

(a) Toil and Wealth

In 2:18-26, Qohelet complains that the wealth he earned will go to someone else after his death, someone who did not work for it. Qohelet broods on this event, formulating it in various ways and calling it *hebel* four times (2:19, 21, 23, 26), as well as *ra'ah rabbah* and a *rᵉ'ut ruaḥ*. What exactly is being judged in this passage?

It is not the wealth itself that Qohelet is calling *hebel.* If wealth itself were "a great evil" (v. 21) or even merely worthless, Qohelet would not be so resentful at the thought of its going to the unworthy. Nor is brevity of possession the thorn in Qohelet's flesh. He does not mention it. Also, it sometimes endures as long as life.

Nor is Qohelet here speaking of the futility of wisdom or efforts to achieve one's goal, for wise labor does achieve its immediate goal, at least. The problem is what happens next. Throughout the passage Qohelet describes a single scenario: one man toils and another enjoys the benefits. This is unreasonable, senseless, absurd.

Even worse absurdities are entangled in this scenario. First of all, the recipient *may* be a fool. This throws the correlation of deed and outcome even further out of joint. Then there is the infuriating fact that the lucky, possibly foolish, recipient manifestly enjoys God's favor. Indeed, God even gives him "wisdom," meaning either the fruits of the toiler's business acumen or the good sense not to work too hard. The toiler, it would seem, must be offensive to God, while the beneficiary (as the benefits prove) must somehow be pleasing. But neither God's favor nor the fortunate man's "wisdom" makes the situation reasonable or just, for the favor is unearned and the wisdom is not the instrument of the acquisition but just another windfall.

It is not the thought of losing wealth that pains Qohelet so much as the affront to his sense of propriety and justice. The crisscrossing of effort and result is unfair and absurd, and it is God's doing.

In 6:1-2, Qohelet complains about the evil of God giving a man wealth and preventing him from consuming it, but giving it instead to a stranger to enjoy. This is essentially the situation called *hebel* in 2:19, 21, and 26. There is no labor mentioned that might be reckoned futile or ephemeral. The wealth itself is not what Qohelet calls "evil" and "an evil sickness"; if it were, its loss (or transience) would be no misfortune. "This" refers to the entire scenario.

Qoh 4:7-8, describing the solitary man, views the wasted-toil scenario from another angle: the transfer of wealth to a stranger. A loner labors and scrimps and saves with no one else to benefit. One might think that it is the toiling that is judged *hebel,* in which case the word might mean "futile" (though the statement would be rather tautological). But the formulation of v. 8 ("there is") shows that what is *hebel* is the scenario described in v. 8a: not the work of the loner but *the fact that* there is a man (namely, Qohelet) who does this. This is an *'inyan ra',* and *'inyan* in 5:13 and 8:16 (and probably elsewhere, but less clearly) refers to an event, not an action. Qohelet describes cases or scenarios that not so much limit the principle[10] as confound it.

In 4:4 ("And I saw that all toil and all skilled work are [merely] one man's envy of another. This too is *hebel* and *r^{e}ut ruaḥ*"), the *hebel* is either skilled work or the fact that skilled work is motivated by envy. No further reason is given for the statement, but one may be implicit in the association of work with envy, a self-destructive passion (Prov 14:30).

In 5:9, the subject of the *hebel*-judgment is a fact: the person who loves wealth is always dissatisfied with what he has. Again, this is well described as "senseless" or "absurd."

---

10. As Hertzberg's description of the "Zwar-Aber Aussage" would explain them; see §1.51.

(b) Pleasure

In 2:1, Qohelet previews the results of his experiment with pleasure, described in 2:3-11, and declares pleasure inane and fruitless. Qohelet is not assessing only frivolous amusements. To call them *hebel* would be a banality by any definition of *hebel*. He is complaining that all pleasures, even legitimate and reasonable ones such as described in 2:4-9, fail to prove meaningful and are thus "inane" *(m^{e}holal)* and irrational. They are still the best thing around, and in substance they are no different from the ones recommended in 9:7-10.

According to Qoh 6:9, "the sight of the eyes" — the immediate experience of pleasure (even without real satisfaction) is better than the "wandering of the appetite" (a yearning that goes entirely unmet). Yet the former too is *hebel*. Both items of the comparison are psychological experiences and not in themselves occupations or pursuits that could properly be judged "futile."

Qoh 7:6 is ambiguous. It is unclear whether *hebel* is predicated of the merry noise of fools (in which case the observation is rather trite) or of the rebuke of the wise, judged absurd because their wisdom is vulnerable to lust for gain (v. 7).

(c) Justice

Several passages (including 2:15, 26; 6:1-2; 8:10b-14; and 9:1-2) describe inequities. Earlier (§2.2) I tested some common glosses of *hebel* on 8:14. The entire passage, 8:10b-14, ponders a single injustice: lifespans sometimes (perhaps often) fail to be proportionate to moral deserts and may even be the opposite. Not only do the wicked and righteous alike die (in itself senseless), but the righteous sometimes die younger than the wicked. This is the epitome of absurdity.

"This too is *hebel*" in 8:10b is best taken as an introduction to 8:11-14 and refers to the same inequity as described in 8:11-14 (see the commentary). If, however, this phrase concludes the preceding observation (8:10a), the antecedent of "this" is still an inequitable scenario: the wicked receiving a fine burial while the corpses of the righteous lie unattended.

(d) Wisdom

Far from being futile or trivial, wisdom has great advantages (2:13-14a; 7:11-12, 19). It is no more fleeting than man himself, and in any case that is not the failing in view here. What is absurd is either Qohelet's becoming very wise or (more likely) the paradoxical situation described: what *happens* to wisdom, namely that the wise man and the fool end up the same (2:14b-15).

This is unjust, incongruous, and contrary to reason, for the lives of antithetical types of people to have the same outcomes. It is important to observe that (as in the case of righteousness, work, and pleasure) it is not an intrinsic quality of the behavior that is being judged *hebel,* but its outcome, or, more precisely, the violation of reason implicated in its outcome. Elsewhere the absurdity infecting wisdom is observed in 2:15; 4:16; and 7:6 [uncertain].

In spite of the difficulties in 4:13-16, it appears that the anecdote exemplifies how the very wisdom that can gain one power is quickly and inevitably undone.

(e) Speech

In 6:11a, "For (if) there are many words, they only increase absurdity, and what is the advantage for man?", the root-sense "vapor" is a live metaphor, since a speaker emits breath, but this statement is, of course, meant figuratively, not as a physiological truism. What is it that "many words" increase? Not transience or futility. Though the words themselves are transient and may accomplish nothing, they do not *increase* these defects. What swells with such talk is the quantity of blather in the world. The context of 6:11 concerns disputes with God. In such a dispute, words are only meaningless, even ludicrous, sounds — in other words, absurdity.

Qoh 5:6, where the plural *hăbalim* is used, is obscure, but since the verse warns against excessive speech (again in the context of speaking to God, cf. 5:1), *hăbalim* is probably used similarly to *hebel* in 6:11.

(f) Living Beings

The *hebel* of living beings is at issue in 3:19; 6:12; 7:15; and 9:9; 11:10. It could well mean "ephemeral" in such cases, though this is not necessarily so.

If *hakkol* in 3:19 *(ki hakkol habel)* means "both," referring to man and beast, then "ephemeral," rather than "absurd," would be the best rendering of *hebel* here, for the death of animals is not absurd. It is, however, possible that *hakkol* in 3:19 means "all" or "everything" (as in 1:2; 1:14; 2:17; 3:11; 11:5; and 12:8). Then man has no advantage over beast because both inhabit an irrational world that blots out meaningful distinctions.

In 11:10 ("for youth and juvenescence are *hebel*"), the time of youth is called *hebel.* While youth may be absurd in various ways, that quality is not the point of this statement, for 12:1 shows that it is the brevity of youth that increases the urgency of seizing the opportunities it offers. *Hebel* therefore means "ephemeral" in this verse. Nevertheless, the connotations of absurdity

39

the word bears elsewhere are not absent from this statement either. The conjunction of deceitfulness and *hebel* in regard to beauty shows how the two qualities interpenetrate. Prov 31:30a says that "Grace is a lie [*šeqer*] and beauty is *hebel.*" Physical beauty is deceitful precisely because it is ephemeral. If a man loves a woman for that quality alone, he invests too much in too little, and finds what he cared about most to be illusory. Like toil, youth's significance is quickly undone. Like pleasure and wisdom, it is at once good *and* absurd.

In 6:12 ("the few days of his life of *hebel*"), 7:15 ("in the days of my *hebel*"), and 9:9 ("all the days of your life of *hebel*"), *hebel* designates human life, and it is impossible to determine which of life's qualities Qohelet has in mind. "Ephemeral" or "absurd" (or a number of other adjectives) could apply equally well.

(g) Death (11:8)

In 11:8, *kol šebba',* "all that comes" is all that follows death. None of the meanings commonly ascribed to *hebel* is appropriate here. Death (not the process of dying, but the eternity spent in death) is not futile, for only an effort with a goal can be futile. It is not vain or trivial, for it is of ultimate existential significance and overwhelmingly powerful. It certainly is not transient. And *hebel* never means literal nothingness. Qohelet is warning us not to expect greater meaning or rationality after death than we face before it. In 3:19-20 he implies that if beings of different status had different fates at death, death might be other than absurd. But this possibility is beyond knowledge, so death retains its absurdity.

(h) "All"

Hăbel hăbalim, 'amar qohelet,
hăbel hăbalim, hakkol habel. (1:2; sim. 12:8)

First of all, what is "all"? It need not encompass absolutely *everything*. "All" is the sum of events, but this does not encompass everything whatsoever that happens or is done.

"All" is restricted to the sphere of human life.[11] The natural processes

---

11. Lohfink (1989) maintains that *hakkol* is "anthropological" rather than "universal." That is, it refers to the human sphere, not to all that exists. Lohfink's main argument is that *hakkol* does not have a universal sense elsewhere in the Hebrew Bible. Qohelet's vocabulary, however, cannot be confined to the usual Biblical usages, especially in his key concepts.

are described by way of analogy; perhaps they too are absurd, but Qohelet is not interested in nature in its own right. *Hakkol* in 1:2 and 12:8 means the same as *hakkol* in 1:14, where it rephrases *kol hammaʿăśim šennaʿăśu taḥat haššameš,* "all the events that occur under the sun." The same statement appears in 2:17, where the conclusion is *hakkol hebel ur$^{e^c}$ut ruaḥ,* which is equivalent to *hakkol habel.* The same use of *hakkol* appears in 3:11, "He made everything appropriate in its time" *('et hakkol ʿaśah yapeh b$^{e^c}$itto),* where *hakkol* refers to actions and events like the examples in vv. 1-8.

Even within this sphere, "all" is not absolute. The fear of God, for example, or justice (when it works), or wisdom (when it is not violated) is not absurd. There are also realities that are meaningful. It is not, after all, absurd (or, if one prefers, "vain" or "futile" or "nothing," etc.) that wisdom proves more beneficial than an inheritance (7:11) or that one's property may be damaged if one fails to pay one's vows (5:5). It is not absurd (or "futile" or "vain" or "nothing," etc.) that wisdom saved a city (9:13-15) — only the subsequent treatment of the wise man was absurd. It is not absurd that "God will judge the righteous and the wicked" (3:17); the absurdity lies in the delay in the execution of the sentence. The fact that "all" is absurd does not exclude the possibility of local, limited significance.

Hakkol includes not every event but events as a collectivity, what happens in life taken as a bundle. If a number of bad things happen in one day, we can say it was a "rotten day," even if some, or most things, were satisfactory. Similarly, within the totality of events many things are not absurd — some values stand, some basic principles are valid, some things are pleasant — but the absurdities taint all.[12]

Hebel in 1:2 and 12:8 must be used in the sense predominant in the book, for those verses summarize Qohelet's thought and encapsulate his

---

12. Schwienhorst-Schönberger argues that the main function of the *hebel*-statements is "the relativizing of traditional values" (1996:282-93, at 292), whose purpose is to determine the true good. It is true that Qohelet uses the *via negationis* to pare away false hopes and pointless efforts, but the cuts go deeper than a mere "relativizing" of values. Qohelet applies the *hebel*-judgment not just to traditional values (which are human preferences and assumptions), but to the way the world works, to the operation of deed and consequence (which is divine governance itself).

Schwienhorst-Schönberger rightly argues that "all is *hebel*" is not "universal" in scope (p. 283). It applies only to the human sphere and not even to absolutely everything within that. But contrary to Schwienhorst-Schönberger (p. 293), within that sphere, the judgment is not narrowly "anthropological," in the sense of evaluating (mistaken) human values. It is also "ontological," for *hebel* is predicated of the nature of being, the way things are at core, and not only of accidentals: what is done or thought or the durability of beings.

hebel-judgments.[13] The statement "all is absurd," unlike the ones produced by the other renderings, is true of much more of what Qohelet describes, even in passages where he does not use the formulaic *hebel*-judgment. He describes many situations that, though not specifically called *hebel,* may well be judged absurd, such as the fool being given elevated status (10:5-7 — an "evil") or a man being forgotten by the city he saved (9:13-15). Understanding *hebel* in the sense of "absurd" brings out the book's unity in a way that a less generally applicable translation (such as "vain," "insignificant," or "fleeting") does not.

"All" is called *hebel* in two other verses. If we emend *hkl* to *hbl* in 9:2aα (see the commentary), then 9:1bβ-2aα says *hakkol lipneyhem habel* "All before them" (= everything people see) is *hebel.* "All before them" reformulates *maʿăśeh haʾĕlohim* (8:17aα) and *hammaʿăśeh ʾăšer naʿăśah taḥat haššemeš* (17aβ). This "all" is the events of life, all that God brings to pass. Everything man sees is absurd, thus incomprehensible.

In 6:4, *hebel* is an epithet of life (a substitution metaphor): "For he comes into *hebel* and goes into darkness." *Hebel* does not refer to the individual lifetime, but to the sphere of human existence into which the newborn enters. *Hebel* does not mean "ephemerality" here, because life's brevity would not support Qohelet's assertion that one who has lived is worse off than the stillbirth, whose existence was, after all, less than brief. *Hebel* is a quality worse than nothingness, worse, even, than pointlessness, for the existence of the man who loses his wealth is no more pointless than the stillbirth's. But his existence is more *absurd,* for he has seen and borne life's irrationality.

§2.6. *Rᵉʿut/Raʿyon Ruaḥ*[14]

Along with *hebel,* Qohelet calls a number of phenomena and situations *rᵉʿut ruaḥ*[15] and *raʿyon ruaḥ.*[16] Though *rᵉʿut* and *raʿyon* have distinct meanings

13. Schwienhorst-Schönberger (pp. 291f.) restricts the application of 1:2 to the issue of profit (1:3) and 12:8 to the course of human life: youth, illness, old age, and death — but not to joy. Nevertheless, he also maintains that these verses, as a motto and frame, echo the entire range of senses the word has throughout the book (p. 291). This seems contradictory, for if "all is *hebel*" is indeed the frame and motto, the range of "all" cannot be restricted to the immediate context and applied to two very different things. The range of application of "all" is, rather, defined by the entirety of phenomena called *hebel* in the body of the book.

14. The closely related *raʿyon libbo* occurs in 2:22.

15. 1:14; 2:11, 17, 26; 4:4, 6; 6:9.

16. 1:17; 4:16.

elsewhere, there is no discernible difference in the way Qohelet uses them. They appear in the same constructions and contexts and are handled the same in the versions, so a single meaning has to be found for both.

§2.61. Etymology

Formally *r^eut* and *ra'yon* derive from the consonantal root RʻH (RʻY[17]), but there are several homophonic roots based on Rʻʻ and RʻH, and these generate words that mean "pursue," "shepherd," "desire," "thought," "friendship," "breaking," and "badness." Some of these words may be expansions of a single biconsonantal root but now have distinct meanings. It is often impossible to assign a word to one of the categories to the exclusion of others.

Several roots with the consonants RʻH or Rʻʻ have been suggested as the source of Qohelet's usage:[18]

(a) Desire, Will (from Aramaic RʻY)[19]

This is the meaning of *r^eut* in Aramaic. LXX's προαίρεσις πνεύματος, "choosing (or purpose) of wind," used consistently for this phrase in Qohelet, reflects this understanding, and many modern scholars accept it as well; e.g., Delitzsch, McNeile, Barton, et al., and translate "desire of wind" or the like.

(b) Thought (from Aramaic RʻY)

This is the meaning of *ra'yon* in Aramaic and RH. It is generally considered a variant meaning of (a) RʻY "desire."

(c) Shepherding, Pursuit (from RʻH)

This is the usual understanding, supported by the parallel between *ro'eh ruaḥ* and *rodep qadim* "shepherds the east wind" in Hos 12:2, as well as the equivalence of *y^ebaqqeš* "seek" and *yir'eh* in Prov 15:14. However, as I will note in the following remarks, most of the phenomena and experiences called *r^eut/ra'yon ruaḥ* are *not* pursuits. Moreover, "shepherding" or "pursuing"

17. I follow the convention of using "H" for "final-weak" roots in Hebrew, "Y" for Aramaic.
18. A homophonic *r^eut* in BH has the sense of "neighbor," "fellow," the feminine of *rea'* (e.g., Exod 11:2; Jer 9:19; Esth 1:19). But this is not applicable to Qohelet.
19. *R^eut* = "desire," "will" in Ezr 5:17 and 7:18.

the wind conveys the notion of a futile effort, one that either cannot attain its goal or whose goal is worthless. But in Qohelet, the activities that are called *re'ut ruah* do attain their immediate goals.

Judging from the puns and plays on these words (especially in the Song of Songs), Hebrew speakers felt the words for "desire," "companionship," "shepherding" (or "feeding") and "pursuing" to belong to the same semantic cluster. The following words are outside this cluster.

(d) Breaking (R")

The Peshitta *(turapa' druha')* and the Targum *(t^ebirut ruha')* parse *re'ut* from R" "break," an Aramaic root used in Hebrew too. "Breaking of spirit" does suit Qohelet thematically, but the root R" in this sense does not have R'Y as a byform.

(e) Badness (R")

The Vulgate sometimes renders *re'ut ruah* as *afflictio spiritus,* associating the word with R" "break" or, perhaps, with *ra'ah* "bad" (etymologically from R").[20] Jerome attributes this interpretation to a "Jewish man" who helped him read the Scriptures. He says that the sense of 1:14 is: "I considered all that is done in the world and I observed nothing but vanity and evils, i.e., miseries of the spirit by which the soul is afflicted by various thoughts" (*Corpus Christianorum,* 72:259f.; the entire passage is quoted by Murphy, pp. 12f.). In this way, Jerome combines the notions of affliction and thought, which may be an intended ambiguity in the use of *re'ut/ra'yon ruah.*

A "bad spirit" is an unhappy or conflicted one. In 1 Sam 16:15, 16 etc., a *ruah 'ĕlohim ra'ah,* a "bad divine spirit" afflicts Saul and provokes disturbances we would label paranoia and depression. In Judg 9:23, a "bad spirit" between Abimelech and the citizens of Shechem means suspicion and hostility.

Apart from actual etymology, *re'ut ruah* as a play on words can suggest both "breaking of the spirit" and "badness of the spirit," and both these connotations are relevant to Qohelet. It is significant that the Aramaic-speaking translators of the Peshitta and Targum associated *ra'yon/re'ut* with the pro-

---

20. Thus in 1:14, 17; 2:17; 4:16. The phrase is rendered by other words for worry elsewhere: *adflictionem animi* in 2:11, *cassa sollicitudo mentis* in 2:26, *cura superflua* in 4:4. Qoh 6:9 is different: *praesumptio spiritus* = "imagination of the spirit." In 2:2, *adflictione spiritus* is used.

ductive Aramaic root R" "break." The author of Qohelet was, after all, almost certainly an Aramaic speaker. A Hebrew speaker too could easily feel an affinity between these words, as well as between *r^eut* and *ra'ah* "bad."

§2.62. *The Meaning of* R^eut/Ra'yon Ruah

It is difficult to distinguish the contextual meaning of *r^eut ruah* from that of *hebel,* since in all but two of the nine times that the former occurs it is appended to a *hebel*-judgment and has precisely the same contexts and referents. On the face of it, *r^eut ruah* could be either a synonym added for emphasis or a different concept that adds a further undesirable nuance to the assertion of absurdity. A certain difference is suggested by the fact that *r^eut ruah* is not precisely parallel to *hebel.* Close synonymy would probably be expressed by *hebel w^eruah.* But in context there is no sharp and consistent difference.

Neither *r^eut* nor *ra'yon,* in my view, is a neologism. Both essentially retain their well-known Aramaic meanings, "desire" and "thought" respectively. These concepts, however, cannot be sharply distinguished in either language or reality, and Qohelet uses them as one. In Aramaic, especially in Syriac, R'Y produces verbs for both thinking and wishing. Both *r^eut ruah* and *ra'yon ruah* mean "senseless thoughts." Some of them (not necessarily the ones called *r^eut*) are desires, others (not necessarily the ones called *ra'yon*) are thoughts, but Qohelet is not making a distinction. Both forms of the phrase refer to a jumble of thoughts, imaginations, and desires that fill the mind.

§2.63. *The Uses of* R^eut/Ra'yon Ruah

(a) *R^eut/Ra'yon Ruah* Alone

The contexts of most of the occurrences of this phrase have been discussed above, since it is usually conjoined to *hebel.* In two verses it is used alone (1:17 and 4:6), and in one (2:22), the related phrase *ra'yon leb* occurs.

Qoh 2:22 uses a phrase, *ra'yon leb,* whose meaning is clear elsewhere in the HB: "For what does a man get out of his toil and the *ra'yon* of his heart at which he toils under the sun?" *Ra'yon leb* in Aramaic (and RH) means "thought of the heart." The phrase occurs in Dan 2:30: *ra'yoney libbak tinda'* "that you may understand the thoughts of your heart." *Ra'yon* in Daniel is always a confused, disturbing thought, either in a dream (2:29, 30) or in reaction to a dream (4:16; 5:6, 10; 7:28). In a recurrent phrase, these thoughts are said to "disturb" *(bahel)* the one who has them (Dan 4:16; 5:6, 10; 7:28). Daniel also calls them *ḥezwey re'ši* "the visions of my head" (7:15). Such thoughts are involuntary and disjointed, the sort of notions and anxieties that buzz around in one's head at night (Dan 2:29, 30; 7:28; cf. Dan 7:1, 15). They are not productive ideas or coherent plans, and they are certainly not the thoughts of wisdom.

The syntax in Qoh 2:22 is difficult, with *ra'yon* a second direct object of *'amel,* but it is clear that "his heart's thoughts" is a concomitant of toil. Qohelet goes on to describe the thoughts that accompany toil in 2:23: (a) *ki kol yamayw mak'obim waka'as 'inyano,* (b) *gam ballaylah lo' šakab libbo* "(a) for all his days his business is but pain and irritation, (b) and not even at night does his heart find repose [lit., lie down]." Daytime toil leaves the drudge's head ("heart") agitated and bubbling with all sorts of thoughts — worries, wishes, regrets, plans, yearnings — that rob him of rest even at night (and compare 5:11). Also dreams (which Daniel calls *ra'yonot* in 2:29f.[21]) can be excited by daytime activities, according to Qohelet 5:2. Senseless thoughts such as these are what Qohelet designates *re'ut/ra'yon ruaḥ.*

When Qohelet calls his seeking of wisdom a *ra'yon ruaḥ* in 1:17,[22] this is usually understood to mean that the effort is a "pursuit of wind" insofar as the goal is beyond human reach. But in this very unit Qohelet emphasizes that he *did* attain wisdom, and it troubled him. He concludes that wisdom is, paradoxically, *ra'yon ruaḥ,* senseless mental activity, because "in much wisdom there is much irritation [*ka'as*], and whosoever increases knowledge increases pain [*mak'ob*]" (1:18). *Ka'as and mak'ob* accompany *ra'yonot* in 2:22-23 as well.

One portion of calm *(naḥat),* that is to say, of wealth earned calmly and without strain, is better than twice as much *'amal ur^e'ut ruaḥ* — toil when accompanied by *r^e'ut ruaḥ* (4:6). Here *r^e'ut ruaḥ* is not an abstraction, "senselessness," but rather refers to certain *thoughts:* the pointless wishes and worries that accompany labor and ambition. The opposition between *naḥat* and *r^e'ut ruaḥ* shows that the latter denotes an undesirable condition of the mind. It does not really make sense to translate *r^e'ut ruaḥ* as "useless pursuit" here, because the labor *has* attained its goal.

---

21. I use the Hebrew plural form throughout to include Aramaic references.
22. The phrase "inanity and folly" is probably secondary; see the commentary.

(b) "All"

The same phenomena, scenarios, situations, and facts that are called *hebel* are called *r^eʿut/raʿyon ruaḥ*. In fact, *everything* is so designated, though not in the thematic declaration in 1:2 and 12:8. "All" means the events of life viewed globally; see above, §2.5(h).

Qohelet calls "what happens under the sun" *(hamma ʿăśeh šennaʿăśah taḥat haššameš) hebel ur^eʿut ruaḥ* in 2:17. This is not an activity or a pursuit, but the totality of events. The event that sparks Qohelet's anger is first of all the fact described in 2:16, that "the wise man dies just like the fool" and is quickly forgotten. From this particular *maʿăśeh*, "event," Qohelet deduces the absurdity and senselessness of the entirety of events. He expresses a similar global judgment in 1:14. This statement previews the results of his investigation and pertains to all he observes.

(c) Other Uses

The "sight of the eyes" — the experience of pleasure (6:9) — is absurd and, paradoxically, *r^eʿut ruaḥ*. It would not make sense to call the "sight of the eyes" a "useless desire" — understanding *r^eʿut* in the narrow sense, since it is not a desire but the satisfaction (at least partial) of desire. Nor is this a "pursuit." It is an experience that, though good, is senseless.

In commenting on the scenario in 2:26 — one man toils, another (possibly a fool) benefits — Qohelet uses both *hebel* and *r^eʿut ruaḥ*. Understanding *r^eʿut ruaḥ* as "pursuit of the wind" = "futile pursuit" in 2:26 would require taking the antecedent of "this" to be the toil of the disfavored man, and it would be banal to call such toil merely a pointless pursuit. Nor can we isolate "desire" as the issue in question, for none has been mentioned. Rather, what Qohelet sees is a senseless scenario, one that cannot be rationalized or fit into a meaningful pattern.

In 4:16, *hebel* and *raʿyon ruaḥ* are not predicated of a pursuit or an effort or even a desire — none is mentioned. Rather, Qohelet is evaluating the scenario: the success of wisdom being buried in public fickleness. This is senseless, not so much from the standpoint of the protagonist (who is dead and forgotten) but from the perspective of the observer, Qohelet. *Raʿyon ruaḥ* is a "senseless thought."

§2.64. *What Is* Ruaḥ?

If *rᵉᶜut* and *ra'yon* mean "thoughts" (including but not restricted to desires), what is the function of *ruaḥ?*

Staples (1943:96) raises the possibility that *ruaḥ* is the human spirit or mind, equivalent to "heart" in *ra'yon libbo* (2:22). He translates *rᵉᶜut ruaḥ* as "the striving of mind." But *libbo* has a possessive suffix and is not a precise syntactic analogy. Also, the term *rᵉᶜut/ra'yon ruaḥ* is clearly a negative evaluator. Compare how what is essentially the same scenario is called both *hebel urᵉᶜut ruaḥ* (2:26) and *hebel woḥŏli ra'*, "an absurdity and an evil sickness" (6:2), whereas to call something "the striving of mind" would not in itself condemn it. (In 2:22, the undesirable quality is implicit in "his heart's thoughts" with no further qualification, because the thoughts belong to an unhappy toiler.)

The genitive in *rᵉᶜut/ra'yon ruaḥ* is best understood as a genitive of material, "thought(s) of wind" = "windy thought(s)." This implies chaotic, aimless thoughts. (Compare how the physical *ruaḥ* moves incessantly [1:6] and unpredictably [11:4].) *Rᵉᶜut/ra'yon ruaḥ* is equivalent to *da'at ruaḥ* in Job 15:2, which is Eliphaz's opinion of Job's words: nonsensical and ineffectual; sim. 6:26. Similarly, plans, *maḥšabot,* that are *hebel* (Ps 94:11) — a nearsynonym of *ruaḥ* — are ineffectual and unstable. *Ruaḥ watohu* means lacking in substance, meaningless, and is the equivalent of *'epes* "nothing" (Isa 41:29).

Ruaḥ in *rᵉᶜut/ra'yon ruaḥ* is thus senselessness, from either an internal perspective (a person's senseless, irritating thoughts and desires) or an external one (a phenomenon that strikes the observer as senseless).

§2.7. How Everything Is Absurd

Qohelet calls "all" *hebel,* because he is probing not only the value of human actions but the logic of the system of worldly events. Sometimes he adds the term *rᵉᶜut/ra'yon ruaḥ* to reinforce his judgment.

An action or type of behavior may be called absurd with respect to its performance or its outcome. When the intention is to condemn the performance, the performer is blamed, for he could have simply desisted from the action. This is the way in which one might call idolatry or drunkenness absurd. When, however, we believe that an action is in principle good, or at least constructive, and yet observe that it does not yield the right results, then it is not essentially the action that is absurd but rather the event itself, which

48

reveals the *fact* of the disparity between reasonable expectations and actual consequences. When Qohelet calls laboring for wealth and growing wise absurd he is bemoaning the violation of the just causal nexus of cause and effect, behavior and deserts. This violation renders the human condition absurd, and not only specific actions within it.

Underlying Qohelet's *hebel*-judgments is the assumption that the system that relates deed to outcome *should* be rational. For Qohelet, this means that actions should reliably produce appropriate consequences. Qohelet stubbornly expects this to happen; see 3:17; 5:5; 7:17; 8:12b-13. He believes in the rule of divine justice. That is why he does not resign himself to injustice, but is continually shocked by it. It clashes with his belief that the world *must* work equitably. Injustices are offensive to reason. And the individual absurdities are not mere anomalies. Their absurdity infects the entire system, making *everything* absurd.

"All is absurd" is ultimately a protest against God. This emerges most clearly in 7:13, *r^eʾeh ʾet maʿăśeh haʾĕlohim, ki mi yukal l^etaqqen ʾet ʾăšer ʾiww^eto*, "Observe what God has brought to pass! Who can straighten out what (God) has warped." That "twisting" or distortion deprives human deeds of significance. The vision of the absurd is, quite literally, de-moralizing; it fills the heart with "evil" and "inanity" (9:3).

The causal order fails, leaving only disconnected occurrences, which are meaningless from the human perspective — and no other perspective does us any good. We live out our lives "under the sun," and our reason must stand or fall in that arena alone.

When the belief in a grand causal order collapses, human reason and self-confidence fail with it. This failure is what God intends, for after it comes fear, and fear is what God desires (3:14). And that is not the end of the matter, for God allows us to build small meanings from the shards of reason.

CHAPTER 3

Justice

§3.1. The Contradiction

Qohelet believes that God is just but the world is full of injustices. Qohelet is painfully aware of this contradiction. He is describing a paradox he sees about him: God is a just judge who allows inexplicable inequities. This is truly an absurdity, and it is one faced by many others who believe in a just God.

§3.2. *Mišpaṭ* and *Ṣedeq*

The terminology in the semantic field of justice is very difficult in English as well as in Hebrew, and an attempt to formulate proper definitions would end up as a discourse in ethical philosophy. I will suggest working definitions without attempting to determine what justice *is*. Understanding Qohelet's ideas about justice does not depend on the exact definitions of the Hebrew terms for judgment and justice, nor can his contradictions be resolved by lexical fine-tuning. But words from two roots, ṢDQ and ŠPṬ, are used frequently in this context and require examination.[1]

Ṣedeq[2] is the right and just state of affairs as well as the abstract quality or ideal of justice, and the behavior that promotes that condition.

---

1. A helpful comprehensive treatment of *mišpaṭ/šapaṭ* is Liedke 1971. For *ṣedeq* see esp. Fahlgren 1932 and Ho 1991.
2. Only *ṣedeq* is used in Qohelet. Elsewhere, *ṣᵉdaqah* is a close synonym.

Mišpaṭ has a broad range of uses: justice, judgment,[3] trial and adjudication, right measure, law, and customary behavior. The verb *šapaṭ* is used of making judicial decisions, administering a social or political unit justly, carrying out justice, executing the just judgment, and giving someone his due.[4] This last kind of *mišpaṭ* (e.g., Ps 10:18; 1 Sam 24:16; Ezek 7:3) goes beyond forensic justice to include norms not embodied in law; see Weinfeld 1995:40-43. "Making (or keeping) things right" comes close to the basic meaning of *šapaṭ,* and the essence of *mišpaṭ* may be defined as "das, was einem zukommt" ("what is due one"; Liedke 1971:100). Administrators, military leaders, judges, and judges in particular should exercise *mišpaṭ* to bring about the right state of affairs, which is also called *mišpaṭ.*

Mišpaṭ in Qohelet is usually the act and execution of judgment. In 3:16, 17; 11:9b; and 12:14, *šapaṭ/mišpaṭ* is a forensic concept, a rendering of a decision at a particular time, not an ongoing state or goal. *Mišpaṭ-ṣedeq,* the hendiadys implied in the distributed word-pair in 3:16, means "righteous judgment," which is what the courts should provide. In 11:9b and 12:14, God's *mišpaṭ* is a future event that should occur within an individual's lifetime. It is a judicial act, a moment when God *brings* people and their actions into judgment and allocates the appropriate rewards and punishments. According to 3:17, God will "judge" the righteous and wicked. This can happen any time and includes not only the decision but also the execution of the sentence, for the decision alone would be static and provide no solution to the problem of injustice. In Qoh 7:15, *ṣedeq* is the condition of the righteous man. *Ṣedeq* and *mišpaṭ* are joined in hendiadys (*mišpaṭ waṣedeq;* 5:7) and in a distributed word-pair (*hammišpaṭ//haṣṣedeq;* 3:16), both combinations being equivalent to a bound pair, *mišpaṭ ṣedeq,* "righteous judgment."

Mišpaṭ can also be equivalent to "rights." *Gezel mišpaṭ waṣedeq* in 5:7 is the robbery of others' *just due* within the government bureaucracy. (Compare Deut 10:18: the orphan and widow possess a *mišpaṭ* ["the *mišpaṭ* of the orphan and widow"] which God "does" or carries out.) The phrase *'et umišpaṭ* in 8:5f. may mean "the appropriate, proper time," for *mišpaṭ* may mean "appropriate," "customary" situation or behavior. Alternatively, it can mean "a time of (divine) judgment," in this instance referring to the moment when the despot will be called to account for his deeds.

---

3. *Judgment* is an instrumental act consisting of a decision about guilt or innocence. "Judgment" may also include the execution of that decision.

4. To "judge" the widow and orphan does not mean to render a decision in a case to which they are a party, but to give them their *mišpaṭ,* what is rightly theirs (Deut 10:18), and to save them from oppressors (e.g., Isa 1:17; Ps 82:3-4).

§3.3. The Affirmation of Justice

The word "justice" designates (1) a correlation between behavior and its consequences and (2) a principle that causes and preserves that state. Justice is ideally distributive: the ledger of every individual life must balance, with happiness or misfortune poised precisely against the goodness or evil each person has done. A state of pure justice is rarely achieved. A human court offers judgment, and when it works well we may say that justice is done. But the judge must come as close as possible to true justice, or *equity,* with a precise balance of behavior and consequence. Only God can achieve this. Does he?

Justice operates in two different ways: natural causation and divine intervention.

§3.31. Natural Justice

A few times, Qohelet asserts or assumes the natural working of justice, picturing the just consequences of actions ensuing as effect from cause. Fools harm themselves; wise men do better (10:12f., 15). Laziness spoils one's property. The wicked and foolish die before their time (7:17). Deeds have appropriate, if unexpected, effects.

Qohelet does not, however, give much attention to the "deed-consequence nexus." When he employs the "pit-topos" and variants in 10:8f., he puts it to a new use. Elsewhere "He who digs a pit will fall into it" is a paradigm that is supposed to be applied to situations where the causal link is less transparent and conveys the principle of peripety: "[The schemer's] iniquity rebounds on his own head, and upon his own pate his lawlessness falls," as the psalmist glosses the saying (Ps 7:16).

Qohelet uses this topos more ambiguously, as a paradigm not only of wicked deeds, but of ordinary, innocent actions as well. The four variants of the pit-topos declare that deeds may have unexpected consequences. As 10:14b asks, "Man does not know what will happen, for who can tell him what will happen afterwards?" These deeds are not necessarily wicked. They are ordinary tasks in farming: digging pits or cisterns, breaking down walls, moving stones, and splitting wood. Surprises are not necessarily just.

Natural causation can operate on the background of God's will. To say that God made everything fitting *(yapeh)* in its time (3:11) is an affirmation of the fundamental rightness of the divine order. Once God has made things in this way, man will bear the natural and fitting consequences

53

of his conformity to this order. In other words, if a man plants at the right time, his work is more likely to bear fruit, and no continuous divine intervention is necessary.

On the plane of natural causality, the relation between deed and result can be described in terms of a "Tat-Ergehen Zusammenhang," "deed-consequence nexus," as developed by K. Koch in his influential article, "Gibt es ein Vergeltungsdogma im Alten Testament?" (1972; ET 1983). Koch claims that the Hebrew Bible lacks a concept of retribution ("Vergeltung") in the strict sense. He defines "retribution" narrowly:

> . . . an essential part of the concept of *retribution* is that a *judicial process* must take place. In this process, the personal freedom and economic circumstances of the person, which up to that point have not been affected by his actions, are now indeed affected by some "alternation" in the person's circumstances relative to possessions, freedom, or maybe even life, as that person receives either a "reward" or "punishment." *In such a case, punishment and reward are not part of the person's nature, nor part of the essence of the action."* (trans. T. H. Trapp, p. 59; p. 133 in original)

I do not agree that the "Tat-Ergehen Zusammenhang" is the exclusive, or even the dominant, principle of justice in the Bible. Koch argues for his thesis by a rather forced exegesis. Certainly many verses Koch discusses, such as "Wait for the Lord and he will save you" (Prov 20:22b), show God doing more than just facilitating a natural causal process. Even Prov 24:12b, "Surely he who weighs hearts understands [sc., the truth], and he who guards your soul knows [it], and he will requite [$w^e he \check{s}ib$] a man according to his actions," makes the requital depend upon God's knowing what happened. Koch's protean exegesis seems able to make every case of reward and punishment fit the formula.[5] The "deed-consequence connection" — or, better,

---

5. H. Gese (1958:45-50) showed that the "Tat-Ergehen Zusammenhang" is not the only one in Proverbs, but he assumed — without adequate evidence — that there was a historical development from the assumption of a world order with built-in recompense, to the belief in God's free intervention in human affairs, which is supposedly a "Sondergut," a special possession, of Yahwism.

P. D. Miller, Jr. (1982:121-39) shows that there is greater complexity and variation in the formulation and presuppositions of the passages supposed to exhibit the "Tat-Ergehen Zusammenhang." He demonstrates that Koch's analysis is highly oversimplified and often erroneous. Miller's conclusions include a recognition that many passages Koch musters do not suggest an internal relation between deed and consequence, and that many of them emphasize the *correspondence* between sin and punishment rather than conthe "character-consequence connection"[6] — is, however, a good description of one *type* of retribution, which I here call "natural" retribution. Since God is omnipotent, any deserved consequence can be regarded as divine judgment (thus in Pss 7:11-14; and 9:16f.; see above). In other words, God's judgment subsumes natural causality.

Natural retribution is a matter of probabilities, not an invariant process. The causal analogies in 10:8-10 do not represent a certainty or a constant formula. Not everyone who digs a pit falls in it, and one who chops wood is only *endangered* by it (10:9b). Qohelet is describing probabilities or typical cases, not invariant causal linkages.

§3.32. Divine Justice

When Qohelet speaks of justice directly wrought by God he sounds more definite and absolute. God, after all, does not have to play the odds. Qohelet sometimes declares that God judges, rewards, and punishes (mostly the latter).

When Qohelet warns against slackness in paying vows — "lest God grow angry at your voice and destroy the work of your hands" — (5:5b), he is assuming that God punishes those who anger him. The punishment fits the crime: God damages the earnings of the man who deprives God of the possessions due *him*. The punishment is not an inevitable aftereffect of the deed (a Tat-Ergehen Zusammenhang), but rather a consequence of God's displeasure (5:3bα). God's "getting angry" — an independent divine decision — precedes the punishment.

God's archetypal, and decisive, judgment is realized in lifespans: the righteous live long and the wicked die young (8:12b-13). Like the other Bib-

---

sequentiality. Furthermore, there is often a clear sense of judgment as retribution, in which Yahweh's decision precedes the punishment.

L. Boström (1990:97-133) examines Proverbs in detail and shows that while the consequences of behavior are often formulated impersonally, in many sayings God is explicitly active in retribution, but, given the nature of the genre, the sentences do not indicate just how the consequences will be realized. It is enough to know that God will not let the righteous go hungry (10:3), for he can fulfill this promise in numerous ways.

6. L. Boström (1990:90) observes that Proverbs does not usually speak of consequences of deeds but of one's behavior and character as a whole. He prefers to speak of "character-consequence relationship." This modification is important, because Proverbs is not so mechanical as to imagine a precise correlation between every action and its consequence. The fool will behave in such a way that, on the overall, his life will be an unhappy one, but the unhappy circumstance may not be the immediate result of the one condemned in a particular proverb.

lical authors, Qohelet distinguishes normal death from premature death. "Death" as a punishment means premature death, just as "life" as a reward means a lengthening of one's lifetime. When Proverbs says, for example, "righteousness saves one from death" (11:4b), it does not mean that the righteous are immortal, but that they will be spared the sudden and untimely death that befalls the wicked in a "day of wrath" (11:4a).

This distinction presupposes that everyone has "his time" (*'et*), meaning an expected, proper time of death. This is Qohelet's assumption in 8:12b-13 and, most clearly, 7:17, "Do not be very wicked or act the fool, lest you die before your time [*bĕlo' 'itteka*]." This is not a rigidly predestined moment, an ineluctable fate. It is more a matter of ripeness, just as an apple has its "time," when it will fall from the tree, unless it is plucked sooner. For humans, this time is, optimistically, about seventy or eighty years (Ps 90:10).[7]

Dying sooner is a punishment. In 8:12b-13, in the midst of remarking on the unjust fate that some people suffer (see below on 8:11-12a, 14), Qohelet insists that lifespans match merits, with fear of God as the decisive factor:

> (12b) . . . I also know that it will go well with the God-fearing, because they are afraid of him, (13) and that it will not go well with the wicked man, and, like a shadow, he will not live long, because he does not fear God.

"Going well" and "not going well" here allude primarily to life and death (as 12a and 13a show), and it is God who determines the length of life (12a).

These sentences sound so orthodox that commentators often seek to ascribe them, or the opinion expressed in them, to someone else. Gordis reads them as quotations of conventional wisdom, which Qohelet repudiates (see §1.53). But Qohelet states these principles as something *he* knows, as a fact rather than an opinion of which he is aware. Qohelet gives no sign that he rejects this piece of knowledge any more than he signals rejection of the injustices he points out in 8:11-12a + 14. Hertzberg reads the passage as a "Zwar-Aber Tatsache" (see §1.51) in which 8:12b-13 is the commonly accepted principle whose general validity Qohelet concedes but restricts in 8:11-12a, 14. Hertzberg is right about the logical relation between the two components, but the logical relationship is the problem not the solution. The "Zwar" is not someone else's idea whose validity Qohelet coolly critiques and restricts.

---

7. "Time" is used also of the actual time of death (9:12), which may occur before one's "time" in the sense of right time; see the introduction to 3:1-15 in the commentary.

Qohelet holds intensely to the "Zwar"; that is why the "Aber" weighs on him so heavily.[8]

Qohelet speaks of a special *time of judgment* for everyone. This is not an apocalyptic day of judgment for the world, a concept foreign to Wisdom Literature, but the time in each individual's life when God will intervene to right the remaining wrongs. After observing wickedness in the place where justice should reign, namely the courts, Qohelet reassures himself that "God will judge the righteous and the wicked, for there is a time for every matter . . ." (3:17). Judgment *must* come, because it too has a time, a right time, set by God himself, and when the circumstances are right, the judgment will be realized.

In 8:5-6a, a difficult passage, Qohelet again speaks of the future judgment:

> (5) He who keeps a command will experience nothing bad. And the wise man's heart knows time and procedure, (6a) for every matter has a time. . . .[9]

The command is the king's order, mentioned in v. 4, not God's. The wise man can patiently bear up under the ruler's wrath, because he remembers that everything, including the behavior of the powerful and seemingly immune, will at some time face judgment.

Qoh 11:9b too declares the inevitability of divine judgment: ". . . And know that for all these things [the pleasures of youth] God will bring you to judgment." Qohelet does not say how or when this will occur, but the assertion is clear and confident.

The book concludes with another resounding profession of divine judgment (Qoh 12:14): "For God will bring every deed into judgment, (even) every secret deed, whether good or evil." This tenet, whether written by an editor or by the author, is not without parallel in the body of the book (compare 3:17 and 11:9b), although it is more emphatic and dogmatic in tone than most of Qohelet's pronouncements on justice. The epilogue, however, does not raise the problem of the delay of justice.

In sum, Qohelet sometimes depicts a tidy world in which retribution works both naturally and through God's judgment. But Qohelet also sees blotches in this picture.

---

8. Among the passages dealing with justice, Hertzberg includes 3:17-20 as well as 8:5-6 + 8b among the instances of the "Zwar-Aber Tatsache."

9. But, as 6b goes on to say, man suffers because he does not know this time.

§3.4. The Recognition of Injustice

Judgment too has its time, but it sometimes comes too late to do any good.

Qohelet asserts confidently the equitable allocation of fates and fortunes (8:12b-13, see above), but then he immediately restates the disturbing observation of v. 12a in 14:

> (14) There is an absurdity that happens on the earth: there are righteous people who receive what is appropriate to the deeds of the wicked, and there are wicked people who receive what is appropriate to the deeds of the righteous. I said that this too is absurd.

Qohelet "knows" that such things happen, although he *also* knows that the God-fearing will have good fortune and the wicked die before their time (8:12b-13). He believes that the evildoer's sentence will eventually be carried out (8:11a), yet he is troubled that it may be delayed. The rule stands: righteousness produces (long) life, wickedness produces (early) death (cf. 7:17b). But it is also true that the rule is violated.

The formulation using "there is" *(yeš)* in 8:14[10] shows that Qohelet is pointing out anomalies, though not necessarily rare ones. Ibn Ezra (commenting on 7:3) says that 8:13a states the usual case, while 7:15bβ tells what happens on rare occasions *(lipraqim mě'aṭim)*.[11] But this observation does not neutralize the fundamental tension between justice and injustice, for the exceptions *are* the problem. The rule is not stated as a statistical generality of mortality patterns, but as a fact of God's rule. Thus every exception, especially every premature death, breaches God's justice.[12]

Delays in justice, even if they are exceptional, vitiate the admonitory value of retribution as *musar* (discipline, chastisement): "Truly man's misfortune weighs heavy upon him, for he does not know *what* will happen, for who can tell him *when* it will happen" (8:6b-7). Consequently, "people's hearts are intent on doing evil" (8:11b). Even if it is true, say, that career

---

10. Absurdities and evils are introduced by *yeš* in Qoh 2:21; 4:8; 5:12; 6:1; 7:15; 8:14; and 10:5.

11. Barton too, though attributing 8:11-13 to a wisdom glossator, understands 8:13a in this way.

12. Zer-Kavod, who seeks to make Qohelet conventional as well as consistent, believes that Qohelet is humbly admitting his incomprehension of the exceptional cases while declaring (in 3:17) his faith that judgment will eventually come to pass (p. 36). But again, the "exceptions" are the injustice, and they do not disappear just because we do not understand them.

criminals have a higher mortality than most law-abiding citizens, when people see even a few crooks growing old and rich, they may conclude that there is no justice. And what does it matter if offenders eventually do meet the death due them? It is no deterrent to crime when an eighty-year-old mob boss is gunned down (or, worse, expires of illness) after a life of prosperity. It may be fitting for him to die by the violence by which he lived, but "judgment" of this sort is feeble retribution. And the inequity is sometimes pushed even further: Not only may the righteous and the wicked fail to receive their respective rewards and punishments, they may get the *opposite* of what they deserve. This is unfair and absurd.

And it gets worse. Beyond the local delays or reversals of justice, which befall the lives of *some* people, stands the universal unfairness of death. Regardless of when death comes, its excessive egalitarianism afflicts all and ignores all distinctions of virtue, talent, and status. Wise and fool die and are forgotten (2:14-16). Even if God does judge the righteous and the wicked (3:17), death in and of itself, whatever its circumstances, finally wipes the slate clean and levels man and beast (3:18-20). Then, unless God's judgment can reach beyond the grave, what good can it do? "And who knows whether the spirit of man goes upward while the spirit of the beast goes down to the ground?" (3:21). The rhetorical question tacitly concedes that an afterlife would distinguish man from beast and make true rectification possible. But an unknown possibility cannot account for a known injustice.

§3.5. Justice and Injustice According to the Sages

What Qohelet sees and says is not entirely out of line with the observations and teachings of the other sages of Wisdom and other genres of Biblical literature. Wisdom Literature does, of course, believe emphatically in retribution: a good person will — sooner or later — receive the proper measure of good fortune, while a bad person will — sooner or later — suffer the deserved misfortune. The sages usually speak of retribution as a natural, automatic result of behavior, as if in the normal course of events a person's deeds are adequately punished or rewarded by their effects upon him. God has created an orderly world in which good deeds have good effects, bad deeds bad ones. But they were well aware that between behavior and consequence there is an opening for injustice, and they sought ways to plug it up.

Throughout the Bible, injustice provokes complaints much like Qohelet's.[13] Jeremiah's can be quite caustic: "Why are the wicked successful, and the treacherous at ease? You planted them and they have taken root; they give ever more fruit" (Jer 12:1b-2a).[14]

Many Wisdom texts too struggle with the problem of injustice. This is obviously true of Job, but even more orthodox texts, in which God's justice is unquestionably affirmed, are aware of the same facts as Qohelet. The psalmist of Psalm 73, a Wisdom psalm,[15] comes to believe that God will destroy the wicked (vv. 18-19), though he remains aware that the wicked may prosper (vv. 2-5) and even be "ever at ease" (*šalwey 'olam;* v. 12). The revelation he receives strengthens and comforts him, but it does not rebut the facts that trouble him. The author of Psalm 49 knows that the wise may die (sc., young) and leave their wealth to others (v. 11). Both psalms assert the belief that the injustice will eventually be set right. Ps 37 makes this point at length.

Even didactic Wisdom Literature, with its dogmatic-sounding teachings of reward and punishment, is aware of exceptions to the neat rule of recompense. The pedagogical rhetoric of didactic Wisdom naturally tends to categorical formulations of reward and punishment. Such dicta as "Righteousness delivers one from death" (Prov 10:2b) and "The hand of the diligent makes (him) rich" (Prov 10:4b), with their grand generalizations, are more impressive and memorable than more cautious formulations would be, for example, "Righteousness usually saves one from early death" or "The hand of the diligent will, barring unforeseen circumstances, bring a degree of prosperity." Most proverbs make unhedged threats and promises, such as "The fear of the Lord increases one's lifetime, while the years of the wicked are cut short" (Prov 10:27), and "No

13. Crenshaw (1970) discusses "popular questioning of justice" in ancient Israel. He includes in this two very different categories: outcries against injustices from people who believe in God's justice, as in Jeremiah, Psalms, Job, and Qohelet; and putative quotation of remarks that express a cynical attitude about God's justice (e.g., Mal 1:7; 2:17; 3:14-15; cf. Ezek 8:12; Ps 10:11; Job 22:13-14).

14. No one finds it necessary to attribute Jer 12:1a to an orthodox glossator or to a quoted voice, though Jeremiah contradicts himself in Jer 12:1-4 no less than Qohelet does in Qoh 8:11-14. The prophet too insists that God is just while complaining that he allows injustices. Jeremiah points to a contradiction: Since you, God, are just, how can you tolerate injustices? The answer he gets is a command to be patient, with a hint that rectification will yet come (cf. Hab 1:13 and 2:3). Jeremiah is willing to wait for this. Qohelet makes his judgments on the basis of what he sees *now*.

15. Apart from the didactic psalms (1; 19:8-15; 34; 37; 111–112; and 119, there are psalms that show affiliations with speculative wisdom, especially Pss 49 and 73. They reflect on the problem of justice rather than simply lamenting wrongs.

evil will befall the righteous, while the wicked are full of misfortune" (Prov 12:21), and so on throughout most of the book of Proverbs. Such unqualified generalization gives an impression, not entirely unjustified, of self-assured dogmatism.

In fact, as J. G. Williams (1981:18f.) observes, Proverbs speaks of typical cases. Wisdom's ideology (as opposed to its rhetoric) does not insist that "all X leads to Y" and "Y is always the result of X" (ibid.). This is true of proverbial sayings throughout the world. We cannot read dogma directly from proverbs. Wisdom Literature describes or epitomizes principles and patterns, not absolute and invariable facts. Since it seeks to imbue the pupil with expectations and attitudes, it is naturally formulaic and condensed, but its rules should not be construed as philosophical absolutes. R. Van Leeuwen (1992) has shown that Proverbs, far from being the repository of naive dogmatism (which many Qohelet exegetes think is the target of his polemic), is very much aware of anomalies and injustices and sometimes presents them in contradiction to the principle of retribution.

> *In general,* the sages clearly believed that wise and righteous behavior did make life better and richer, though virtue did not *guarantee* those consequences. Conversely, injustice, sloth, and the like generally have bad consequences. . . . We must first learn the basic rules; the exceptions can come later. (R. Van Leeuwen 1992:32)

While emphasizing the positive, didactic wisdom is quite aware of exceptions to their rules.[16] A good or industrious man may suffer poverty, or illness, or mockery; a wicked or lazy one may be prosperous or respected. This is the insight of Prov 11:24: "There is[17] one who scatters (his money) about and yet gets more, and one who saves out of honesty yet ends up needy."[18]

16. See the discussion by G. von Rad (1970:166-70). Gladson (1978) examines proverbs in Prov 10–29 that show recognition of injustices by the sages. He is too quick, however, to explain "retributive paradoxes" as dissent from the dominant Wisdom doctrine of retribution and to take them as evidence for diversity of thought within Wisdom. The most orthodox believer could not deny that injustices occur, and a single sage can affirm a rule in one proverb and concede exceptions in another. There can hardly be a doctrine of retribution without recognition that there exist wrongs to be righted.

17. Using *yeš;* see n. 10.

18. Even if Prov 11:24a is to be construed as a commendation of almsgiving (thus JPSV), v. 24b is clearly paradoxical. *M^{e}pazzer,* "scatters," does refer to almsgiving in Ps 112:9, but there the poor are the explicit recipients. Elsewhere *pizzer* means scattering about, with no necessary implication of charity. This interpretation is supported by Sir 11:11f., a reworking of this proverb.

Furthermore, if the authors of Proverbs believed in a strict causal connection between one's merits and wealth, they would not so earnestly urge mercy toward the poor.[19]

The sages knew that vicissitudes of fortune do not invariably correspond to personal merits. One is obliged, in fact, to be aware of such slippages, lest one become contemptuous of others' poverty and sufferings or arrogant about one's own good fortune. As one widespread teaching puts it: "Do not boast of the morrow, for you do not know what the next day will bring" (Prov 27:1). Earlier, the Egyptian sage Anii expounded this truth (MS B 21.3-6). Because you cannot ensure your wealth, he teaches, be generous to others as a hedge against future fluctuations of fortune. Wealth is, Qohelet would say, subject to "time and accident" or (what amounts to the same thing) to God's not entirely predictable will.[20]

While undeserved poverty is not necessarily a calamity (after all, "better a little with righteousness than great harvests without justice," according to Prov 16:8), the premature death of the innocent most certainly is. The highwaymen's plan to "lie in wait for the innocent" (Prov 1:11) may be expected to backfire, and they themselves will die — but sometimes, at least, this will happen after they have murdered their victim. In fact, the sages concede the existence of injustices every time they condemn the wicked for perpetrating them. Prov 13:23 says, "The tillage [nîr] of the poor[21] [produces] much food, but there are some people who are swept away unjustly."[22] "Those who are taken to death," whom we are charged to rescue (Prov

19. As they do in 14:21, 31; 17:5; 19:17; etc.; see Gese 1958:38. By excluding the *ungodly* poor as objects of charity (12:4-5), Ben Sira implies that some poor people are worthy.

20. Contrary to Gese (1958:45-50), the idea that God determines the outcome of deeds independently of human action is not a Yahwistic invention. The sayings that Gese regards as declaring God's control of the "world order" do indeed make such an assertion, but nothing in any Wisdom book denies free and active divine control. The world order assumed by Wisdom is not a rigid set of causal formulas (nor does "Ma'at" have that meaning in Egyptian Wisdom). The world order is the orderly working of justice in natural processes guaranteed by the supervision and intervention of divinity; see Fox 1995.

21. LXX's δίκαιοι does not witness to Hebrew *yěšarim* (contrary to *BHS*), because the Greek rendering of this verse is too paraphrastic to allow secure retroversion. The LXX turns the verse into theodicy, as do various modern commentators.

22. The first stich is a pun, for *nir* can mean offspring (1 Kgs 11:36; 2 Kgs 8:19), and the stich can be translated, "The offspring of the poor possess much food," in other words, the house of the poor man will eventually come into prosperity. In this way v. 23a reiterates the preceding verse: "The good man will pass on an inheritance to his son's sons, while the wealth of the offender is stored up for the righteous." Justice *will* be done, even if it must wait until the next generation.

24:11f.), are not criminals sentenced to capital punishment, but innocent people wrongfully condemned.

Occasionally we hear a note of indignation as the sages observe violations of the proper order — indignation directed not, as usual, at the violators, but at the very occurrence of the violation. In such cases, the author is not simply saying that people should not do this or that, but that such things *should not happen.* A proverb exclaims: "A muddied spring and a polluted well: a righteous man crumbling before a wicked man! (Prov 25:26). In other words, dirty things happen in life. Note that the analogy is to events (a spring becoming muddied, a well becoming polluted), not to a person (a righteous man).

Throughout Biblical literature, even in didactic Wisdom, we find clear recognition that injustices, even severe ones, do occur. Qohelet is not facing a sudden crisis brought on by social dislocations or historical disasters. He is not an innovator or a radical in recognizing the existence of injustices. But the others were better able to explain them away.

§3.6. How Injustices Were Explained

Only the most resolute naivety or dogmatism could blind a person to the reality of injustices and delays in judgment, and this does not happen in Wisdom Literature.[23] The sages developed several types of theodicy to account for injustices while maintaining faith in God's unbroken justice. The essence of theodicy is to see things differently. Seen in a different perspective, incidents of injustice become insignificant or subordinated to a greater, more meaningful whole.

In a perspective extended to psychology, some exterior injustices may be outweighed by an interior good. For example, "Better a dry morsel with repose than a house full of contentious sacrifices" (Prov 17:1). Zophar says that the sinner gets sick to his stomach, probably from agitation and worry (Job 20:14-16). Ben Sira says that all mankind suffers anxiety, but the wicked are afflicted by it sevenfold (40:1-11).[24] The Wisdom of Solo-

---

23. The author of Ps 37 comes close to this, proclaiming "I was young and now have grown old, but I have not seen a righteous man abandoned or his descendants begging bread" (v. 25), but he seems to have in mind their *eventual* salvation rather than their present state, for he promises that "the humble will inherit the earth" (v. 11a and *passim*).

24. See Crenshaw (1975:57) for this interpretation of Sir 40:8. In Sira, Crenshaw says, "the marginal situations of life, particularly sleep, fantasy, and death, become occasions of divine vengeance" (p. 60).

mon strongly endorses the psychological solution (17:2-6, 14-16)[25] and also rationalizes the premature death of the righteous first by claiming that old age is measured by its wisdom not its years and by supposing that God may wish to extricate a righteous person from a potentially corrupting environment (4:7-15).

Another approach to theodicy tries to situate the injustice within the perspective of a greater order which cannot be directly observed but whose existence can be deduced from the wonders of observable creation. Thus even when the wise man is ignorant of the rationale for the apparent injustice, his wisdom consists in knowing that there *is* one. Ben Sira appeals to human limitations in this way: "No one can say, 'This — why is this?,' for everything was created[26] for its need" (Sir 39:21). The book of Job teaches a theodicy of this sort. The prologue shields the principle of justice by first suggesting that more goes on than meets the eye. Then God's reply argues that God created and guarantees a greater order, one that is beyond man's comprehension but whose existence man can deduce from the providential order he *can* see.

Another perspective that can justify God is human triviality. When we look at mortals through the wrong end of a moral telescope, so to speak, they are shown to be so inconsequential and base that injustices done to them do not matter much, or are even justified *a priori* by native corruption. (Eliphaz takes this tack in Job 4:17-21 and 15:16.)

The most important perspective of theodicy is an extended time line. Justice will surely come, and the faithful will wait for it. The promised rectification may be either individual or collective. In Wisdom Literature, including Qohelet, it is always individual. This is the solution proposed by Ps 37: when you see the prosperity of the wicked man, remember that "his day" (v. 13), the day of his death, awaits him. This is not a fixed moment of death but the "right" time (*'et*) for his death, the day when he *should* die. On the concept of right time, see the commentary on 3:2. The righteous may have their ups and downs, the psalmist grants, but the wicked will be extirpated. Ps 34:20 offers similar assurance: "Many are the afflictions of the righteous, but God will deliver him from them all." Ps 92 likewise employs the "long run" principle, insisting that only the fool does not see its validity (vv. 7f.). The psalmist of Ps 73 too finds a solution in the belief that the wicked will die suddenly (vv. 17ff.).

25. Ibid., p. 63.
26. Thus the Greek. The Hebrew has *nibhar*, "chosen," but rabbinic evidence (b. Shab. 77b; y. Ber. 9:2) supports the Greek; see Segal, *Ben Sira*, p. 263.

To promise eventual justice is to admit that there is injustice in the meantime. How, then, does one rationalize the present injustice? Ben Sira responds to this problem by insisting on eventual rectification: the bottom line of the account is what matters: "It will go well at the end with him who fears the Lord. On his final day he will be blessed" (1:13; cf. 9:11; 18:22, 24). At that time, forgetfulness will blur the significance of earlier wrongs (11:25-28).

When rectification comes, the just state, unlike the unjust, will be permanent: "The righteous man may fall seven times and rise, but the wicked will founder in evil" (Prov 24:16; cf. Ps 37:24). After seven falls, the righteous rises and stays up. Once the evildoer falls, he stays down. Ben Sira recognizes that the wicked can get rich, but, he insists, only the wealth of the godly endures (11:17). Furthermore, although the pious may be poor, God can suddenly make a man rich (11:21).

Another approach was to regard suffering as a test of piety, and to see trust in God and patience as the answer. A near-contemporary of Qohelet, the Egyptian (Demotic) book of Phebhor (Pap. Insinger), explores the paradoxes of justice and retribution at length. In each of twenty-five "instructions," Phebhor warns against a vice, such as gluttony or not educating one's son, and extols the corresponding virtue. At the end of each instruction, however, he reminds us that reward and punishment lie with the unpredictable will of God. For example, the fifteenth instruction warns: "Do not be greedy lest your name stink," and he goes on to admonish about greed and generosity. At the end, however, he says,

> He is not greedy and stingy who has a reserve in the storehouse.
> It is the god who gives wealth and poverty according to that
>   which he has decreed.
> The fame and the fortune that come, it is the god who
>   determines them. (*AEL* 3.198)

Lichtheim says that these paradoxes were "designed to qualify the teaching of the chapter by pointing out that through the agency of fate and fortune the god may bring about conditions which are contrary to the expectation embodied in the moral teaching" (*AEL* 3.185). Phebhor thus observes the same sort of paradoxes as Qohelet does but draws the lesson — one reminiscent of the Stoa and probably inspired by it — of resignation and piety. The wise man endures suffering with patience and devotion, for "It is the god who gives patience to the wise man in misfortune" (*AEL* 3.200).[27] Though

27. Lichtheim describes the intellectual context of Phebhor and Onchsheshonqy in *Late Egyptian Wisdom Literature* (1983); see esp. pp. 138-50, 184-91.

Qohelet sees much the same paradoxes, this is not his teaching, except in 3:14:

> I know that whatever God makes happen is always what will be. It is impossible to add to it, and impossible to take away from it. And God has done (this) so that people will fear him.

§3.7. How the Explanations Fail

Theodicy does not work for Qohelet. He takes generalities as absolutes, and he will not subordinate the anomalies he observes to the beliefs he accepts. Injustices are intractable distortions (1:15; 7:13) that warp the larger pattern rather than fading into it.

(1) Qohelet has no hope that human action can correct or even alleviate wrongs. He takes a deterministic, passive attitude toward injustice. It is not that specific injustices are fated, but that injustice itself is built into the world and nothing can be done to remedy it.

When Qohelet recognizes a social wrong, he bemoans it in weary resignation. He does not even urge us to comfort the afflicted (which is something that *could* be done, even in a world that offers little scope to human effectiveness). He merely laments the wrongs he sees — or, more precisely, the fact that he must see them, and envies the unborn for being spared the unpleasant sight. (He assumes that the reader is outside the company of the oppressed.) When faced with governmental corruption and abuses, all he has to offer is lame advice not to be surprised at the sight, because that's just the way things are (5:7). All we can change is the way we feel about them. Again it is the realm of internal responses, intellectual and emotional, that draws Qohelet's attention rather than actions and remedies.

Such resignation is foreign not only to prophecy but also to Wisdom Literature, which demands the pursuit of righteous actions and charity and assumes that the individual can further social justice; see, for example, Prov 14:31; 19:17; 22:9, 22; 24:11-12; 29:14; 31:9.

When Qohelet speaks of despots (8:1b-9), he just assures the reader that the day of reckoning will come, but he does not demand that the despots change their ways or even suggest how the reader can ease their victims' distress. The reader is only taught how to minimize harm to *himself,* to avoid arousing the ruler's wrath (8:1b-2, 5b; 10:4).

When Qohelet describes violations of justice in the courts (3:16), he does not demand righteous judgment or even bother to condemn the unjust judges. He merely reminds himself that God will eventually judge the innocent and the guilty (3:17). But having deferred all hope of justice to the indefinite future, he realizes that this will not set things right (3:18-22). Pervasive injustice is a fact of life, and "nothing warped can be straightened out" (1:15).

(2) Qohelet sees death as the utter end. Other thinkers cared about the quality of the death and the things that survived the individual. They distinguished a "good death," the lot of one who dies at a ripe age, at peace, leaving behind heirs, from a bad one, a premature demise without heirs (Bailey 1979:48-51). Qohelet does refer to such distinctions, but he is only interested in the negative, viewing it from the standpoint of the man who suffers the misfortune (5:12-16), not the one who benefits. All qualitative distinctions are lost in the eternal void (2:13-16; 3:19). Other sages promised that the memory of the righteous will live on beyond life, while the wicked are forgotten or remembered only as a curse (Prov 10:7; Job 18:17; Sir 41:11). Qohelet does not believe that *anyone* is remembered (Qoh 2:16; 9:5). Death traps everyone, suddenly and unpredictably (9:12). Nothing blunts death's assault.

(3) Without seeing a different reality than the other sages, Qohelet has a different focus — injustice rather than justice. This focus determines his worldview. Consider how the effect of 8:10b-14 would differ if Qohelet had made the same observations in a different order, if he had said:

> (8:10b) This too is an absurdity: (11) the sentence for a wicked deed is not carried out quickly — that is why people's hearts are intent on doing evil. (12a) For an offender may do evil for years but live long. (14) There is an absurdity that happens on the earth: there are righteous people who receive what is appropriate to the deeds of the wicked, and there are wicked people who receive what is appropriate to the deeds of the righteous. I said that this too is absurd. (12b) And I also know that it will go well with the God-fearing, because they are afraid of him, (13) and that it will not go well with the wicked man; like a shadow, he will not live long, because he does not fear God.

In the rearranged version, stubborn faith overrides uncertainty. A similar effect can be produced by putting 3:17 after 3:21 or 8:5-6a after 8:7. This is, in effect, how pious readers like Ibn Ezra and Zer-Kavod resolve the problem[28] — but not Qohelet. Qohelet's statement concedes that there will be judgment

---

28. See §1.51, with reference to Zer-Kavod's principle 2.

but makes the anomalies decisive, and this makes the world absurd. Qohelet does not affirm divine justice *in spite* of life's injustices. He is not a hero of faith, defying logic on behalf of a deeper loyalty. He does not acknowledge that divine plans are hidden then bravely hold fast to faith in God's justice. He does cling to the assumption of divine justice, yet this assumption cannot dislodge the exceptions from the center of his consciousness.

When Qohelet looks at life he sees it colored by the exceptions rather than the rule. It is a matter of weighting premises. One person might infer from the fact that most babies are born healthy that God is beneficent and life is orderly and meaningful. This is the religious temperament of most Wisdom authors, the author of Job included. Another might consider that some babies are born autistic and conclude that life is arbitrary and unjust. This is the temperament of Job in his anger and of Qohelet throughout. For Qohelet, God's absolute control makes each individual case an ethical microcosm, so that the local injustices — which are in fact all over the place — are irreducible and undermine the coherence of the entire system.

§3.8. No Resting Place

J. Loader (1979:123) makes "tensions" the key to Qohelet's thought. He recognizes that unlike other "crisis literature" (such as Job), the book of Qohelet does not "discharge" the tension in its discussion of retribution. But, contrary to Loader, the tension is not between "dogmatized wisdom" and "protesting wisdom," nor does Qohelet "combat" the doctrine of retribution and repudiate it (ibid.). (That would resolve the tension.) Qohelet sees the tension as a clash between two truths, neither of which he dismisses or ascribes to another form of wisdom. Nor does he reconcile the tension by abandoning belief in divine justice or by embracing a theodicy such as described earlier. Qohelet does not choose any such way out.

Qohelet is in distress. He is not polemical, directing a "sustained argument against the doctrine of retributive justice" (contrary to J. G. Williams 1981:20). He is not even *skeptical* about this doctrine, in the sense of doubting its validity. To differ is not to attack. Nor is he disputing theodicy. He treats the inequities he observes as an intractable problem, not as evidence for or against a particular solution.[29] He accepts one principle of

---

29. In an influential article, "Vorsehungsglaube und Theodizee im AT" (1934), W. Eichrodt defined theodicy as an attempt to balance the present state of the world with the all-inclusive government of a just and beneficent God. This concern he believes was

theodicy, future judgment, but this does not solve the problem or ease his malaise.

Qohelet does not repudiate or cast doubt on any of Wisdom's doctrines of justice. He sets himself among the wise and shows no awareness that his observations clash with the beliefs of other sages. If Wisdom Literature had dogmatically denied the existence of injustices, then for Qohelet to expose them might be an implicit attack on Wisdom, or at least a symptom of a crisis brought on by a sudden awareness that the old rules have exceptions. But Wisdom Literature makes no such denial. The sages were not that smug or thickheaded. Qohelet's peculiarity does not lie in his being a more acute or realistic observer than the other sages, or even in being more skeptical about doctrines. It lies in his refusal to let the "broader view" diminish the significance of individual suffering in the here and now.

If Qohelet is inconsistent, he is not erratic, now declaring for divine justice, now denying it. He maintains a single, but conflicted, view: God is just, but there are injustices. This, as Qohelet is well aware, is contradictory. The contradictions are not only in Qohelet's mind; they are in the world, as Qohelet sees it. Qohelet is complaining not only about injustices but also, more fundamentally, about the irrationality of the world which holds such contradictions. It is absurd.

---

an invention of "Spätjudentum" ("late Judaism") — which for Eichrodt seems to start with the return from the Babylonian exile. The only texts Eichrodt mentions as exhibiting this balance-scale theodicy are Chronicles, a few verses in Nehemiah, and Pss 17; 26; and 59. Job's friends are also said to exemplify this *(spätedomitische?)* theology. But then, he says, came "a breakthrough from the God of rational abstraction to the living God of revelation" (p. 64), a movement he finds in texts "which throw off all the crutches of theodicy" (ibid.), namely Pss 22, 73, Job — and Qohelet.

Eichrodt's history of theodicy is artificial. First of all, theodicy is present in the pre-exilic prophets too, because prophetic eschatology *is* a form of theodicy. And the "eschatological solution" was hardly abandoned in "Spätjudentum." Conversely, the "striving toward a true theodicy" (ibid.), however the concept is defined, emerges well before Ezekiel. Both Proverbs (and its Egyptian predecessors) and the Deuteronomic writings teach a distributive justice of the sort that Eichrodt identifies with "late-Jewish" theodicy. Eichrodt, like so many theologians who characterize post-exilic Judaism as "verhängnisvolle Verengung des Gesichtskreises" ("a fateful narrowing of perspective"; p. 63), ignores evidence for the phenomenon in question in pre-exilic texts while highlighting similar features in documents considered post-exilic. Contrary ideas that are in undeniably "late" texts are attributed to a struggle against the prevailing "late-Jewish" attitude. (His dating of texts is circular, based on where they fit in the hypothesized scheme of development.)

Theodicy does not work for Qohelet, but he is not attacking it. And he hardly finds a solution in "the living God of revelation."

It is frustrating to stop here. We want to know what Qohelet *really* believes. But Qohelet goes no further. He is at a dead end. *He* is frustrated, and his readers should be too. Life *is* frustrating, and Qohelet refuses to make it any easier for us. His only response — not solution — is to urge us to embrace the good things that come to hand. We must tend our garden, though it will wither.

CHAPTER 4

What Is Wisdom?

The mind's first step is to distinguish what is true from what is false.

Camus, *Myth*, p. 12

§4.1. Qohelet's Epistemology

The deepest innovation in Qohelet's teaching is not his complaint against life's injustices and absurdities. This has parallels in various Psalms, in Job, and in several skeptical and pessimistic works from elsewhere in the ancient Near East (§1.43). Qohelet is most innovative in his concept of human wisdom, not so much in recognizing its limits as in redefining its scope.

Qohelet's evaluations of wisdom are disparate and contrary; the next chapter will define them. But first we must ascertain the nature of this wisdom, whose means Qohelet employs, whose applications he teaches, and whose powers he assesses.

Epistemology asks, What can we know and how do we know it? Everyone who claims to know something has at least implicit epistemological assumptions answering these inseparable questions. Qohelet has an explicit epistemology. The problem of epistemology is one of the main concerns of his book — in a sense, the central one.

Qohelet's epistemology is inchoate and unsystematic, and it lacks the refinements in vocabulary necessary to make some distinctions important for

71

clarity in this matter.[1] Yet it is not chaotic. Qohelet deliberates on the ways and possibilities of gaining knowledge and on the scope of the knowledge to be gained. His thoughts on these matters form a coherent whole, even though they contain tensions and contrary observations and sometimes seem to pull in all directions at once.

§4.2. Words for Wisdom

Ḥokmah, traditionally translated "wisdom," is different from its English counterpart. "Wisdom" in English denotes sagacity, the ability to take the long view, to judge things by moral as well as practical criteria, and to discern the best ends as well as the best means. Wisdom also entails the will to pursue those ends, for we would not call one wise who knew the right course but did not take it. Qohelet never uses *ḥokmah* or *da'at* specifically of this sort of wisdom.

In Biblical usage, *ḥokmah* (and *ḥakam*) includes sagacity but embraces other realms of skill and knowledge as well, such as the craftsman's skill (e.g., Exod 35:31; 36:4; Isa 40:20, and often), the statesman's and ruler's savvy (2 Sam 2:22; Isa 10:13; 29:14; Jer 49:7; and often), the merchant's know-how (Ezek 28:5), the sly man's wiles (2 Sam 13:3), as well as learning and erudition, such as in booklearning (e.g., Dan 1:4 and Sir 38:24) and the mantic and magical arts (Gen 41:8 and Isa 44:25). In short, *ḥokmah* is expertise of all sorts. It would be unwieldy to avoid the term "wisdom" in discussing Biblical *ḥokmah* and Wisdom Literature, but it is important to remember that when translating *ḥokmah*, English "wisdom" means something different from the ordinary and philosophical sense of the word in English usage. When Qohelet describes the failures of wisdom he is not necessarily talking about the kind of sagacity that directs one in leading a moral and prudent life, but about a more neutral faculty.

Ḥokmah (like English "intelligence" or "intellect" but unlike English "wisdom") is ethically neutral. Wicked men and nations may have *ḥokmah* (e.g., 2 Sam 13:3; Isa 29:14; 47:10; Ezek 28:5), and this *ḥokmah* is genuine, even when abused.[2] Proverbs is unique in insisting that *ḥokmah* is *ipso facto* a moral virtue.

---

1. For example, Qohelet uses *ḥokmah* both of the faculty of reason and of the knowledge to which reason can lead. *Ra'ah* is applied both to the perception of data and to the inference of conclusions on the basis of that data. *Yada'* is used both of the awareness and the understanding of facts.

2. God destroys and confounds the wisdom of his enemies (e.g., Isa 29:14; 44:25), which would be unnecessary if this were not actual, effective wisdom.

Wisdom — *ḥokmah* — has two aspects: faculty and knowledge. As a faculty, wisdom is an intellectual power similar to intelligence in the uses to which it can be put. It encompasses common sense and practical skills. It includes the faculty of reason, that is, the capacity for orderly thinking whereby one derives valid conclusions from premises. *Ḥokmah* also exists as knowledge: that which is known, the communicable content of knowledge. Knowledge gained and transmitted by study of books and lore is "learning" or, if extensive and deep, "erudition" (e.g., Qoh 1:16; Jer 8:8; 9:22; Dan 1:4).

The sages treat this compound of faculties and knowledge as a unity, though their language was able to distinguish different components of wisdom.[3] It is assumed that the successful imparting of the teacher's *ḥokmah* (knowledge) to the pupil also imbues him with the *ḥokmah* (faculty) needed to make the right decisions and act correctly in new situations.

Qohelet does not tap into the rich vocabulary for wisdom that Proverbs employs, rarely using any terms besides *ḥokmah* and *da'at*. The latter is used as a pendant to *ḥokmah* in a way that prevents us from drawing distinctions between the two (they are virtually indistinguishable in Proverbs as well).[4] Qohelet calls all the knowledge he acquired, including the sort that caused him discomfort, both *ḥokmah* and *da'at* (1:16, 18; 2:21; 7:25). He occasionally also uses *kišron* ("skill"; 2:21; 4:4; 5:10) and *ḥešbon* ("calculation"; 7:25, 27; 9:10), terms absent from Proverbs, which cover a more restricted range in the same semantic field.

Wisdom in Qohelet's usage manifests itself in three ways: ingenuity, good sense, and rational intellect. The type so important in Proverbs, the sagacity of ethical-pious living, is a subset of the second, but Qohelet never treats it by itself. Qohelet calls these three forms of wisdom *ḥokmah*. He does not define these categories or analyze wisdom into different types of intelligence. I do so for purposes of description.

(1) Ingenuity

Ḥokmah includes ingenuity, expertise in solving problems and attaining one's goals. A person with this kind of wisdom is said to be ingenious or smart. Examples elsewhere are 2 Sam 14:2; 20:16; Jer 18:18; Job 5:13. One area of ingenuity is skill in the crafts (e.g., Exod 35:31; 36:4; Isa 40:20).

3. Several words in the semantic field of wisdom are hyponyms of *ḥokmah*, covering part of its semantic field but not all, e.g., *tušiyyah, 'eṣah, mᵉzimmah, tᵉbunah;* see Fox 1993b.

4. To the extent a distinction is discernible, *ḥokmah* is expertise, unusual or special knowledge and skill in a certain domain, while *da'at* is knowledge itself — *any* knowledge.

Ingenuity is power. With it, one can devise clever stratagems that can deliver a city from siege (9:13-15). Hence it is more powerful than a warrior's might (9:16) and weapons of war (9:18). It can even enable a poor youth to rise from prison to kingship (4:13-14). Ingenuity brings wealth. Qohelet believes that one who toils "in *hokmah*" will grow rich, as he himself did (2:9, 19, 21).

Through wisdom as ingenuity, one should be able to unravel obscurities. "Who is <so> wise, and who knows the meaning of anything?" (8:1a; see the commentary) is a wry exclamation of exasperation at the possibility of ever understanding women (7:27-29). Though understanding is beyond wisdom's reach in this thorny matter, the exclamation in 8:1a shows that it is usually employed in seeking the explanation *(pešer)* to puzzling matters. Moreover, the exclamation indicates that *hokmah,* even in Qohelet's view, is expected to succeed in this task; otherwise it would not be remarkable that no one is wise enough to penetrate the mystery.

(2) Good Sense

Hokmah includes good sense, the practical intelligence that promotes success in personal behavior and human relations. Examples elsewhere include 1 Kgs 5:9; Job 39:17; Sir 11:1. Good sense includes prudence, the ability to recognize and pursue the behavior that will advance one's interests in the long run and in the broad view. Good sense is a practical intelligence insofar as its goal is effective action rather than knowledge as such. Good sense requires no unusual insight beneath the surface of reality, no special learning, not even an unusual cleverness in maneuvering through life. (Good sense that is especially penetrating and can scan a wide horizon of factors and values is called *sagacity.*) Examples in Qohelet are 2:3; 7:10; and 8:1. In some cases, *hokmah* can be either ingenuity or good sense (7:11, 12; 9:16, 18).

(3) Rational Intellect

Hokmah includes the rational intellect, the faculty used in the investigation and derivation of new truths. This faculty aims at increasing knowledge, apart from its practical or prudential value, though decisions about behavior may and should be based on the knowledge it produces. This faculty naturally overlaps with ingenuity, but there is a difference. Whereas ingenuity aims at problem-solving and reaches its resolution when the solution is found, rational intellect engages in an open-ended search for new knowledge and deeper understanding. Examples: Qoh 1:13, 18; 7:23; 8:16; 9:10 (?).

Strangely, no other Biblical author associates this faculty with *ḥokmah,* or, for that matter, even describes its operation, though the author of Job 28 is aware of it. *Ḥokmah* occasionally means theoretical or speculative knowledge, as in Prov 30:3,[5] and perhaps a few times in Job, and *da'at* refers to an understanding of the mysteries of God's ways in Ps 139:6.

Outside Qohelet, wisdom (designated by *ḥokmah* or a synonym) is never an instrument in open-ended exploration. Proverbs teaches us to seek wisdom, not to seek something else *by* wisdom. The truths that Wisdom Literature would have us learn are already given, and one need only imbibe them to make them one's own wisdom. If you call to wisdom and go forth to meet it, you will find it (2:4-5; 8:17, 35). Once you have found wisdom, you need only embrace it, hold to it. Wisdom is and always has been out there, waiting for your embrace. (There will always be *more* knowledge than mankind can know, but whatever is learned, somehow existed prior to the learning.) The uninitiated must invest effort in learning and applying the truths of wisdom, but at no stage were they unknown to all.

A wisdom-word with a narrower scope is *ḥešbon* (7:25, 27, 29; 9:10), which seems to be close in meaning to English "calculation." A calculation is not inevitably wise or successful. In 7:27 the *ḥešbon* is the result of a (metaphorically) arithmetical reckoning. In 9:10, it refers to the activity of calculation in the abstract. In Sir 42:3, *ḥešbon* is a business calculation. In 9:15 Ben Sira may have business dealings in mind, though the context allows for a broader application. In 2 Chr 26:15, *ḥiššᵉbonot* refers to the products of devisings, namely military devices.

§4.3. Qohelet's New Path

In preparation for the task he took upon himself, Qohelet amassed wisdom surpassing that of his predecessors (1:16). This wisdom (called *ḥokmah* and *da'at*) must be knowledge (learning), not a faculty (reason), because it is something learned and extended. It was a body of traditional teachings, since Qohelet says that he carried it beyond his predecessors, meaning that they too possessed it.

Qohelet does not say exactly what the content of this learning was. We

5. Agur, as I understand this difficult passage, is contrasting *ḥokmah* (= *binah*), which he did not learn, with *da'at 'ĕlohim,* which he *does* possess. The former is *studied* or *learned,* which must be something like "theology" — a knowledge of doctrines and theories derived from human investigation and speculation. The latter comes from God's word (v. 5) and is knowledge of God's will and ways (Hos 4:1; 6:6).

75

should not assume that it was coterminous with the genre we call Wisdom Literature just because it is called *ḥokmah*. But the wisdom that Qohelet learned and surpassed certainly included this genre, since his lexicon, style, and presuppositions are deeply rooted in that tradition. Didactic Wisdom Literature, above all the book of Proverbs, assumes and asserts the power of the unaided human intellect to gain, grasp, and use the truths necessary for attaining a good life. Wisdom Literature teaches the profitability of wisdom, promises wealth and happiness, and professes the certainty of justice (see §3.5). This complex of doctrines and convictions is the foundation and starting-point of Qohelet's thought.

Qohelet does not distinguish his wisdom from that of the other sages except in degree. He calls what he is doing simply "wisdom" and considers it an extension of the wisdom he studied. In 8:17 he calls the man "wise" who does exactly what Qohelet himself did ("intends to understand . . . the events that happen under the sun"). The way that Qohelet generalizes that effort suggests that some of the author's contemporaries were embarked on similar explorations.

Once the investigation is under way, the wisdom that is used is not the wisdom that was learned. Qohelet never openly deploys his vaunted learning in his inquiry, but relies only on his own powers of observation, analysis, and reason. He never invokes (though he may quote) the teachings of other sages to support his conclusions. The wisdom that serves as his sole instrument of investigation is his independent rational intellect.

Though he does not seem aware of the fact, the author is introducing a radical innovation into the notion of wisdom: the notion that one may use his independent intellect to discover new knowledge and interpret the data of individual experience.

This approach may be termed (somewhat loosely) "empirical," inasmuch as it assumes that the foundation of knowledge is experience.[6] That does not mean that it is empirical *in practice*. In actuality, much of what Qohelet says gives the impression of stemming from traditional learning, impulse, or vague deduction. Many of his ideas are formulated *a priori* (e.g., 3:17; 8:12b) or derived from assumptions that lack experiential grounding (e.g., 7:11-12). Yet the "empirical" label is justified, first by Qohelet's conception of his investigative methodology, which looks to experience as the

6. If we translate Qohelet's thoughts on knowledge into the concepts of Western philosophical empiricism, we can say that he holds a primitive form of the "weak" type of empiricism, which maintains that all knowledge comes from experience because every proposition is either a direct report on experience or a report whose truth is inferred from experience. See the *Encyclopedia of Philosophy* II, p. 499.

source of knowledge (§4.4), second, by his method of argumentation, which appeals to his own experience as evidence and testimony (§4.5), and third, by his ontology of knowledge, which views knowledge as created by thought and dependent on perception (§4.6).

§4.4. Methodology

Qohelet's investigation is based, in principle, on experience. He seeks experience, observes it, judges it, then reports his perceptions and reactions.

Qohelet first describes the investigation he undertook in 1:12-18, mentions it again in 7:23, 25, 27; and 8:16, and maintains its continuity by periodically reporting how he "turned" *(panah, šub,* or *sabab)* from one thing to another, or urged his heart to experience something new. All his teachings and observations lie within the framework of this report, and thus, it is implied, were discovered during the investigation introduced in 1:12-18, which started from wisdom (1:16), aimed at wisdom (1:17; 7:23b), and proceeded by wisdom (1:13).

Qohelet seeks out experience as a source of knowledge. After a preliminary meditation, he introduces himself and reports his decision "to investigate and explore with wisdom all that occurs under the heavens" (1:13; see the commentary). He then proceeds to relate how he investigated various activities, facts, and situations. In 2:11 he chose his object of study, namely pleasure, then directed his heart to experience it and to observe its effects. He tried out pleasures not in order to enjoy them, but as a means of answering a practical philosophical query: "What is good for a man to do?" (2:3). So Qohelet did not merely go through life commenting on what he noticed. He chose a heuristic procedure deliberately and pursued it with determination, if not with consistency. This, I believe, is unparalleled: a sage choosing to seek out sensory experience as a path to insight.

Before experience can become knowledge, it must be sifted and interpreted by reason. Qohelet uses *ḥokmah* in the sense of reason, as an instrument of guiding, organizing, and interpreting experiences (1:13). He says that he "spoke to" (or "with" or "in") his heart (1:16; 2:14, 15; etc.), "set" *(natan)* his heart (1:13; 1:17; 8:9, 16), "set" something "upon" *('el)* his heart (8:9; 9:1), "explored" in his heart (2:3), "turned with" his heart (7:25), "said to [his] heart" that he will make it experience pleasure (2:1). He reports that he did not withhold pleasure from his heart (2:10) and that he rid his heart of illusions (2:20). His heart, for its part, "sees" wisdom (1:16), conducts itself in wisdom (2:3), and receives pleasure (2:10).

Qohelet does not consistently distinguish his heart from his self — the "I" or ego that speaks to the heart. Yet the prominent role he gives his heart in the passages where he discusses his investigation (1:12–2:26) suggests that he does ascribe distinctive functions to it. Qohelet mentions his heart twelve times in 1:12–2:26,[7] a frequency 13.8 times greater than elsewhere in the body of the book. (He mentions his heart elsewhere only in 7:25; 8:9, 16; and 9:1 [twice, emending to *wlby r'h*].[8]) This uneven distribution indicates that Qohelet's interest in his heart is not merely a reflex of style. He speaks of it so frequently in 1:12–2:26 because he is reflecting on the process of perception and discovery, and the heart has a central role in this process. He is not only exploring but also observing himself explore. He is his own field of investigation.

We may schematize the heart's role thus: (1) The person (Qohelet, the "I") desires knowledge and (2) directs his heart to attaining it (1:13; 2:1a; 8:9). It seems that Qohelet must persuade his heart to take part in the investigation (we might say: he must persuade himself). (3) The person does something so that his heart may "see" or "observe" (usually R'H) the sensation it causes (2:1a, 10bα). (4) Since the heart is the seat of wisdom/reason (1:13, 16, 17; 2:3), it can assimilate and evaluate the sensations it perceives, in order to produce knowledge and report this knowledge to the person. Thereupon the person realizes *(yada')* a fact. We see the heart's experience ("e") enabling the person to attain knowledge ("k") in several places: 1:16 (e) — 1:17 (k); 2:1a (e) — 2:1b (k); 2:3abα (e) — 2:3bβ (k); 7:25 (e) — 7:26 (k); and 8:16 (e) — 8:17 (k).[9]

---

7. He also twice refers to the heart of the toiler in this unit (2:22, 23), where he is generalizing from his own situation.

8. Qohelet refers to a "man's" heart (in the third person) in 2:22-23, where he sees himself as an example of such a man.

9. A similar conception of the heart's function is expounded in the Egyptian "Memphite Theology": "Sight, hearing, breathing — they report to the heart, and it makes every understanding come forth. As to the tongue, it repeats what the heart has devised" (*AEL* 1.54). In other words, the senses (Qohelet, less specifically, says "I") transmit sensations to the heart, which organizes them into knowledge. The heart then passes this knowledge to the tongue (again, Qohelet says "I"), which speaks what it is told. Since Qohelet is more concerned with understanding, whose agent is the heart, than with the senses and speech, he subsumes the eyes, ears, and tongue to the "I," while frequently distinguishing the heart from the person.

§4.5. Argumentation

Qohelet's argumentation, though uneven, is likewise experiential, for he appeals to what he has "seen" as evidence for his conclusions. One form of empirical argumentation is *testimony,* in which one claims to have observed the fact that is being asserted or the data from which the conclusion is drawn. Qohelet uses testimony most prominently in 2:1-10, where he attests to the value of pleasure on the basis of his own experience with it.[10] Another form of empirical argumentation uses experience as *validation,* appealing to publicly observable facts for premises and validation. In 2:21-23, for example, Qohelet bases his assertion of the absurdity of toil on the undisputable fact that at death (if not before) a toiler must leave his wealth to someone else (see also 2:3-9 and 5:7-8).

Qohelet's new epistemology engenders a new rhetoric: the introspective autobiography. Qohelet's report of his explorations, though eschewing the usual claim of traditional authority, strengthens his rhetorical ethos. Qohelet bares his soul, not only his ideas, because he seeks to persuade by empathy. He bares his soul in all its twistings and turnings, ups and downs, taking his readers with him on an exhausting journey to knowledge. If the readers can replicate the flow of perception and recognition as it developed for Qohelet, they will be more open to accepting the author's conclusions as their own.

As part of this introspective reporting, Qohelet often evaluates situations and activities not by an independent external standard but by their effect on himself. "Of amusement I said, 'Inane!' and of pleasure, 'What does this accomplish?'" (2:2). Thinking about the unfairness of death made him "disgusted" with life (2:17). He "found" woman to be more bitter than death (7:26). An event he "saw" (a wise man saving a city) he considered significant (as he puts it [lit.] "it was great upon me"; 9:13). The *hebel*-judgment too expresses a psychological datum, for absurdity exists only as presented to the mind.

Qohelet constantly interposes his consciousness between the reality observed and the reader. It seems important to him that the reader not only know what the truth is, but also be aware that he, Qohelet, saw this, felt this, realized this. He is reflexively observing the psychological process of discovery as well as reporting the discoveries themselves.[11]

---

10. See also the appeals to experience in 4:1-2, 15; 5:12-13; 6:1-2; 7:15-16; 8:9 and 10.

11. In his perceptive study of the role of the ego in Wisdom Literature, Höffken (1985:125f.) points out the unusual importance Qohelet gives the ego and explains its role as criterial — Qohelet will evaluate transmitted teachings *(Bildungsgut)* by the measure of his own experiences. In my view, however, Qohelet is only occasionally and incidentally concerned with evaluating or testing ideas of others.

§4.51. *Wisdom and Experience According to the Sages*

Wisdom epistemology is not empirical.[12] Although the teachings certainly derive in part from experience, the other sages do not *present* their experience as the source of new knowledge.

A number of passages that purport to describe immediate observations are often thought to exhibit empirical reasoning, but in fact they do not claim the observation as the source of new knowledge or even as proof of the principle taught. The teacher in Proverbs 7 "saw" a woman enticing a youth to fornication, yet he does not even claim to have observed the consequences. These he already knows quite well. The author of Prov 24:30-34 says that he "saw" what happened to a lazy man's field. A lesson follows upon the observation, but it is presented as a fact called to mind rather than as a truth discovered or inferred. The author does not say that he saw a field gone wild, looked for the cause, and found that its owner was lazy, nor does he claim to have looked at lazy farmers and observed what happens to their fields. Rather he came across a field gone wild, and this inspired reflection on its causes. Experience was simply an occasion for thought. Likewise, when a sage tells the pupil to go to the ant (6:6-8), he is merely using the ant as a teaching device to illustrate diligence. He does not even call on the observable facts of ant behavior to prove his point, but merely to drive it home. And note that the teacher does not himself "go to" the ant. He doesn't have to, since he already knows the principle being taught. He just sends the pupil to see for himself.[13] Similarly Aḥiqar 105a and 112.

Personal experience is more often cited in theodicy, both by the sufferer and by the defenders of divine justice. The sufferer in particular infers truths from what he has undergone (though we cannot presume that all his statements are to be understood as knowledge from the *author's* point of view). The defender too, whether in dialogue or in argumentative monologue, sometimes appeals to experience to support his tenets. For example, the poet of Ps 37 claims that he never saw a righteous man abandoned (v. 25), and that he did see the wicked cut down (vv. 35-36). Eliphaz says he ob-

12. D. Michel describes Wisdom as empirical (1989:27). The example he gives, Job 4:7-8, comes from theodicy, on which see below.

13. G. von Rad (1970:56-58) recognizes the essentially rhetorical function of the "autobiographical style" in Wisdom Literature, a genre he considers a "traditional style-form" (p. 57). He observes that in these passages there is a tension between the form, which implies personal experience, and the content, which is impersonal and general. In this way the teacher shows that such knowledge must be anchored in the life of the individual.

80

served evildoers reaping what they sowed (Job 4:8). Ben Sira uses personal testimony in the same cause: "Many such things my eyes have seen, and mightier things than these my ears have heard" (16:5). The events he recounts in vv. 8-10 are examples of punishment in ancient times, things "heard" rather than "seen." The psalmist and Eliphaz adduce their experiences in order to underscore the obvious. Observation in theodicy testifies to old truths; it does not uncover new ones.

Qohelet's appeal to experience does have certain parallels in theodicy. He differs in the greater importance he gives to the "I" in his argument and, most significantly, in his purposes. While the sufferers and defenders try to understand what they observe, they, unlike Qohelet, do not observe *in order* to gain knowledge.

It seems reasonable to look for external factors that could inspire such a fundamental innovation, one that might accurately be called a paradigm shift, except that it remained peculiar to its initiator. Qohelet's epistemology is, as far as I can tell, foreign to the ancient Near East. It is, however, paralleled in his Hellenistic environment. R. Braun's thorough and partly convincing study of Qohelet's Hellenistic background raises this possibility in passing:

> It may confidently be concluded from the preceding investigations — and it has repeatedly been emphasized by Jewish scholars — that [Qohelet] was influenced in the presuppositions of his rhetoric and motives by Greek popular philosophy and the literary training of early Hellenism, which was also an intrinsic component of popular philosophy. [This is the case] in regard to his empirical methods, his unbiased questions, and his personal individualistic-cosmopolitan self-understanding. (Braun 1973:178)[14]

Qohelet's thought does not belong to a particular Greek philosopher or school, and not even to Greek empiricism generally. We need not suppose that the author had read the Greek philosophy or even heard about it in particulars. He does, however, share the fundamental tenet of Greek philosophy: the autonomy of individual reason. This is the belief that the individual can and should proceed toward truth by means of his own powers of

---

14. "Dass er aber in seiner empirischen Methode, in seinem vorurteilslosen Fragen und seinem persönlichen individualistisch-kosmopolitischen Selbstverständnis, in seinem rhetorischen und motivischen Voraussetzungen von der griechischen Popularphilosophie und der literarischen Bildung des Frühhellenismus, welche auch konstitutiver Bestandteil der Popularphilosophie war, beeinflusst war, ist aufgrund der Ergebnisse der vorliegenden Untersuchungen mit Sicherheit anzunehmen and wird auch von jüdischen Wissenschaftlern immer wieder betont."

perception and reason, and that he can in this way discover truths previously unknown.[15]

§4.6. The Ontology of Knowledge

Qohelet conceives of knowledge as a product of thought and discovery, not as an entity independent of the individual mind. He does not phrase his idea in this way, of course, but such a notion is implied by his description of what happens when he reaches the boundaries of knowledge. Having surpassed his predecessors in wisdom, he sets out on his own "to investigate and explore with wisdom all that occurs under the heavens" (1:13). He pursues knowledge not merely by absorbing existing wisdom and elaborating on it or applying it intelligently, but by attempting to push back the frontiers of wisdom and create knowledge that did not exist before his investigation.

In one verse Qohelet does speak of *hokmah* and *da'at* being given by God to a favored man (2:26). That, however, refers either to the products of (another person's) wisdom or to wisdom in the sense of a disposition to do what is sensible. It is not a statement about the source of knowledge. *Hokmah* and *da'at* in 2:26 do not refer to a deeper understanding of life's workings and values such as Qohelet sought, for that wisdom brings discomfort (1:16-18), which is hardly an expression of divine favor.

It is of course possible for an individual to increase his wisdom by learning from others, as Qohelet himself did (1:16). But Qohelet believes that an individual can also reach truths never before known, and not only absorb transmitted knowledge. Within the investigation that Qohelet reports in his monologue, he does not picture himself as learning truths others already know, but as discovering new ones that would not otherwise be known. Above all, Qohelet's awareness that "all is absurd," which encompasses many of his other conclusions, is a new perception. He never suggests that anything other than his own investigations led to that discovery.

Qohelet's new wisdom he calls *da'at* and *hokmah* (1:17-18), just like the wisdom he believes other people can have (1:16; 2:12-14; etc.). He

15. Gordis (pp. 56f.) recognizes influence of this sort. We may compare the way a contemporary author can introduce Freudian concepts and terminology into his writing (probably with some vagueness and distortion) even without having read Freud. This "Freudianism" does not come from direct "influence" but from the assumptions and knowledge built into one's cultural environment. Schwienhorst-Schönberger (1996:232-332) describes numerous affinities between Qohelet and Hellenistic philosophy and locates Qohelet in the "tension-field of Hellenism and Jewish wisdom."

clearly believes that at least some of his most important findings are fundamentally new knowledge, not merely truths long known that he might have garnered from others' wisdom. He does not bring this perception into confrontation with his statement that "there is nothing whatsoever new under the sun" (1:9), but the two ideas do not necessarily contradict each other. The statement in 1:9 refers to events *(mah šehayah, mah šenna'ăśah),* and it is unlikely that Qohelet would apply it to anything as abstract as thoughts or items of knowledge. If, however, he does intend to assert that ideas cannot be innovative, he is first of all contradicting himself (which, to be sure, he is quite capable of doing) and second, he is simply wrong, as his book itself proves.

Qohelet's epistemology makes the validity of knowledge (at least knowledge of the sort that interested the sages) dependent on the knower's perceiving it. For Qohelet there is no body of truth standing above the individual and demanding assent, no abstract wisdom that could be personified as a woman who was created before mankind and who would exist even if all humans were fools.

Qohelet alone of the sages speaks with "a voice that justifies itself by reference to the good sense of the individual's reflections on his experiences" (J. G. Williams 1981:85). But argumentation based on experiential justification could well turn against the speaker, weakening the rhetorical ethos it is meant to strengthen. It is open to the challenge that one person has no right to look about and within himself and come up with things not known to contemporary wise men, let alone to the wise men of old. In relativizing knowledge, Qohelet sacrifices the right to claim certainty or built-in authority for the wisdom he teaches. This loss may exacerbate his frustration at the impossibility of attaining the kind of certainty he longs for (7:23-24; 8:16-17).

§4.61. *The Ontology of Wisdom According to the Sages*

In the usual Wisdom conception, wisdom is essentially independent of the individual mind. What the individual knows would be known even without him. Knowledge exists "out there," waiting for man to appropriate. It need not be proved, only discovered and applied. This notion is nowhere stated, but it is implicit in the way wisdom is personified and by the way the sages speak about the way it is gained.

Personified wisdom in Proverbs (1:20-33; 8:1-36; 9:1-12) and Ben Sira (14:20–15:8; 24:1-29) represents the same wisdom that is taught and praised elsewhere in the Wisdom texts. If personified wisdom meant something fundamentally different from wisdom elsewhere,[16] the figure of wisdom as a person would communicate nothing about the wisdom the sages were trying to inculcate. The personification represents wisdom as existing, archetypally, in essence if not in specifics, prior to mankind.[17] The preexistence of the essential substance of wisdom — knowledge itself — is expressed most clearly by Ben Sira. He says that wisdom proceeded (at creation) from the mouth of God (24:3), and that those who desire wisdom need only come to her and satisfy themselves from her produce (24:19-22). She was present at the first and available to the first man (24:28). What place can there be in such a conception for the individual to increase the total store of knowledge in the world by observing life and noting his own reactions? A human being, whether as Lady Wisdom's plaything (Prov 8:31) or as a passer-by invited to her noble banquet (Prov 9:1-7), can hardly expect to make significant additions to this awesome force, but can, at most, seek to refine and express it in new ways.[18]

The conception of wisdom as a static entity, independent of the human mind, is manifest also in the sapiential idea of the way wisdom is gained. One gains wisdom by absorbing and applying existing knowledge. The sages prided themselves not on making discoveries or creating knowledge but on having taken knowledge to themselves and applied it. Whereas Qohelet's favorite verb of perception is "seeing," theirs is "hearing."[19] The Egyptian sage Ptahhotep describes the pupil's duty as "hearing" his father's teaching in order to recount it to his own children, thereby "renewing the teaching of his father" (ll. 588-95). The teacher in Proverbs 1–9 (where alone in Proverbs we find much reflection on the process of acquiring and transmitting wisdom) enjoins the pupil to "hear" and "keep" his father's wisdom. Whereas for Qohelet "seeking" and "finding" wisdom refer to exploration and discovery, in Proverbs these concepts imply striving for and succeeding in absorbing existing truths. For the most part, the sages of didactic Wisdom sought not to discover truths but to inculcate them. This attitude is attested in Wisdom Literature throughout its history.

Since knowledge, in the sapiential view, is not created by the individual's perception and reason, its truth and authority need not be established by

16. Such as the world-order or the "self-revelation of Creation," as von Rad understands it (1970:189-228).

17. See Fox 1997a:627-30.

18. Ben Sira says, "If a man of understanding hears a wise saying, he will praise it and add to it" (21:15). This means that the essence of the saying, the idea it teaches, is already there, and the wise man elaborates it.

19. "Seeing" implies immediate experience, not necessarily visual; "hearing" implies mediated, reported knowledge (Job 42:5).

argumentation. Wisdom Literature, as noted earlier, uses argumentation less to prove its propositions than to establish the speaker's ethos and to motivate the pupil. Mainly, Wisdom argues deductively, inferring truths from axioms or extending the application of given concepts.[20] Wisdom Literature shows very little attempt at argumentation from individual experience. In fact, there is little argumentation of any sort. The sage need not prove the truth of his wisdom, because if it *is* wisdom, it is not essentially his. He has partaken of it, not produced it. He does not know everything, of course, and he may be mistaken in what he thinks he knows, but the knowledge he does have, confirmed by its conformity to tradition, is secure.

Job 28 resembles Qohelet in conceiving of wisdom as the product of discovery, but the author of the former presents this concept only in order to insist on the invalidity of such an approach. Westermann (1977:132) correctly calls Job 28 radical and polemical. It is, in a sense, more skeptical than Qohelet, for it insists that whatever man can attain by his skills and efforts is not to be reckoned as wisdom, whereas Qohelet believes that the knowledge the human intellect is able to grasp is truly wisdom, though the confines of this wisdom are tight and oppressive.

Usually, however, the sages conceived of wisdom as existing independently of the human mind and always available for appropriation. In brief, if one could ask a more conventional sage, "How do you know this?" I believe he would answer: "Because I learned it." To this question Qohelet would reply: "Because I saw it." The shift is profound.

§4.7. Qohelet's Skepticism

Qohelet is usually thought to be skeptical about conventional beliefs, to doubt the validity of doctrines held by *others*. But this does not accurately describe Qohelet's skepticism. He does not hold up other people's beliefs and disparage or undermine them. He does not set himself apart from conventional beliefs, in the "they say . . . but I know . . ." mode. His skepticism is of a deeper sort, not directed at other people's knowledge, but at knowledge itself.

---

20. P. Höffken (1985) says that in traditional Wisdom Literature (Proverbs, Ps 37, and the friends' speeches in Job), the primary functions of the teacher's ego are deduction (as in Prov 24:30-34) and affirmation. As I see it, although deduction is the main form of reasoning in Wisdom Literature, virtually the only function of the interposition of the teacher's ego in didactic Wisdom is (in Höffken's terminology) *affirmation,* i.e., the strengthening of traditional teachings by appeal to the "geballte Lebenserfahrung des Ego" — the "concentrated life-experience of the ego" (1985:122).

The assumption that knowledge proceeds from perception is conducive to epistemological skepticism, for the subject is liable to recognize that his own knowledge is inherently fallible and unverifiable. In 6:12 Qohelet seems to do just that. He ironically undermines his own — quite serious — series of statements about what is "good" (7:1-12) by first denying the possibility of knowing "what is good for man" (6:12). This is not a radical epistemological skepticism; Qohelet believes his knowledge is genuine. It is, however, an awareness that no human knowledge can lay claim to certainty.

This reflexive skepticism is more dangerous to Wisdom beliefs than are direct statements about the limitations and frailties of wisdom, for such skepticism undercuts confidence not only in specific items of knowledge but in knowledge itself. Not only is there much that man cannot know (as all would agree), but even what one *does* know is in doubt. Qohelet is led to doubting his own wisdom, saying paradoxically that although he had wisdom (1:16), he could not become wise (7:23). Other sages reveal no such self-doubt. They would, I believe, have found it incomprehensible.

CHAPTER 5

Is Wisdom Foolish?

To begin to think is to begin to be undermined.

Camus, Myth, p. 4

§5.1. What's Wrong with Wisdom

Qohelet extols wisdom, spells out its practical benefits, and judges it to be as superior to folly as light is to darkness. Yet he also teaches that human wisdom has blinders on it and inevitably falls short of its goals. Qohelet's ideas on wisdom pull in all directions, yet they do cohere, uncomfortably and unstably.

§5.11. Wisdom Is Deficient

Qohelet's methods and conclusions *are* wisdom, yet they do not lead to an understanding of the rationale of life's events. That kind of knowledge ever eludes him, because God places barriers to human insight.

As Qohelet sees it, "finding" or "grasping" *(maṣa')*[1] reality — "that

---

1. *Maṣa'* and *yada'* can both mean "understand." More precisely, *maṣa'* signifies attaining the understanding and knowledge designated by *yada'*. The near-synonymity of *maṣa'* and *yada'* is seen in 8:17b: even if the wise man intends to "know" (YD'), he cannot "find" or "grasp" (MṢ') the events of life. *Maṣa'* refers to attaining understanding in, e.g.,

which is" or "that which happens" — is a goal of wisdom (7:24-26; 8:17). This undertaking is doomed to failure, because God has also "placed <toil> [*he'amal*] in their hearts, without man being able to grasp [*yimṣa'*] in any way whatsoever what God has brought to pass" (3:11). God has created the world in such a way as to make it impossible to "grasp anything (that might happen) afterwards" (7:14b), and thus to know the consequences of an action. Qohelet himself strove for wisdom day and night (8:16), but he learned that "man cannot grasp [*limṣo'*] anything that God makes happen, that is to say, the events that occur under the sun, for even if a man seeks arduously, he will not grasp [*yimṣa'*] (them)." And *even if the wise man* intends [*yo'mar*] to understand" — though he is the one best equipped and most worthy to do so — "he is not able to grasp [*limṣo'*] them" (8:17).

Though Qohelet was the wisest of men and possessed the wisdom necessary for examining life, he feels that he failed: "All this I tested with wisdom. I said, 'I shall become wise [*'eḥkamah*],' but it was far from me. Far off indeed is that which happens, and very deep: who can find it [*yimṣa'ennu*]?" (7:23-24). The unattainable wisdom is defined by its object, "that which happens" (7:24). It is a secure understanding of the meaning and rationale of events. Other kinds of wisdom are attainable: learning, ingenuity, good sense. Wisdom as rational intellect too is accessible. But wisdom of the sort Qohelet yearned for is beyond man's reach.

The future too is beyond knowledge. Man "does not know *what* will happen, for who can tell him *when* it will happen?" (8:7). No one "can tell man what will happen afterwards under the sun" (6:12). Indeed, God made good and bad fortune alternate unpredictably "so that man is unable to grasp anything (that might happen) afterwards" (7:14; sim. 3:22b). Hence it is foolish to speak too much (10:14). And, of course, man does not know when he will die (9:12).[2]

Judg 14:18b; Job 11:7; and 37:23. Appropriate renderings of *maṣa'* are "discover," "come to an understanding of," "grasp," as well as "find." These are all extensions of the root-meaning "reach," "overtake," "catch" (see Iwry 1966:35-39). Note esp. Sir 31:26 [34:22], in which *tmṣ' 'mry,* "understand my words," is rephrased as *tśyg 'mry,* "attain/grasp my words," in the doublet.

Etymologically, two protosemitic roots may be conflated in Hebrew MṢ'; see the discussion by Ceresko (1982:552-57). The effect is that in Hebrew, MṢ' means both "find" and "reach." Both these aspects are conducive to an extension of the meaning to a third sense: "understand," "grasp." Ceresko (pp. 557-69) also explores how Qohelet exploits the ambiguities of MṢ'.

2. Qohelet's recognition of the futility of metaphysical speculation is not unique. Agur declares that wisdom is beyond him (Prov 30:3-4). Ben Sira says, "Who has seen [God] and can tell about it? Who can extol him as he is? There is much hidden that is

§5.12. Wisdom Is Vulnerable to Folly and Fickle Fortune

Wisdom is vulnerable to man's folly and life's vicissitudes. Therefore it cannot guarantee the advantages that it *should* produce and that it *deserves* to produce.

Though wisdom is mightier than weapons, stupidity is, in a sense, even more powerful, because one offender (9:18) or one bit of stupidity (10:1) can foul up what much ingenuity has achieved.

Though an intelligent man's wisdom might gain him wealth (2:19b, 21a), he may easily lose it in an unfortunate incident (5:13). Worse, someone who did not work for it may obtain it (2:18-19). Worse yet, the recipient may be lazy or stupid. In that perverse case, the fortunate man must be reckoned as if he had received wisdom from God (2:26). After all, the industrious man had toiled in "wisdom, knowledge, and skill" [*b^eḥokmah ub^eda'at ub^ekišron;* 2:21], and the favored man gets it all. This wisdom may be understood as the material gains of wisdom or as the good sense not to strain for wealth, or both. The really smart man turns out to be the one who sits around and enjoys himself until someone else's hard-earned fortune falls into his lap. Wisdom reveals itself as folly and folly as wisdom. This is truly absurd.

Even when wisdom brings a man wealth, it cannot *guarantee* him sustenance, let alone wealth and public favor (9:11), because all efforts and talents may founder on the shoals of happenstance (v. 12). "The race does not belong to the swift" etc. (9:11f.) does not mean that the swift never win the race or that the mighty never prevail in war or that clever men never earn their bread, for they usually do. Rather, what oppresses Qohelet is the realization that such talents cannot secure their rightful rewards in the face of chance misfortunes.

Though the wise surely merit high esteem, people honor wealth more, even to the point of holding the wisdom of a poor man in contempt (9:16b) and quickly forgetting him, even if he saved their city from capture (9:13-15). Though wisdom (whether in the form of ingenuity or good sense) may carry a man from prison to the throne, he too will soon be supplanted, the fickle public will turn its attentions elsewhere, and he will be lost to memory (4:14-16).

---

greater than these things, for we see but little of His works" (43:31-32; cf. 11:4b; 16:20-22; 18:4-7). In a similar vein Zophar asks: "Can you discover the mystery of God? Can you discover the limit of the Almighty? It is higher than heaven — what can you do? It is deeper than Sheol — what can you know?" (Job 11:7f.). This is also the message of Job 28.

§5.13. Wisdom Is Overwhelmed by Death

Most disheartening is the way God treats the wise in the crucial matter of death: exactly as he treats the foolish. Both die and soon slip into oblivion (2:16). The crude egalitarianism of death makes Qohelet fed up with life itself (2:17).[3] Death disregards the distinctions that seem to make individual differences significant. As R. E. Murphy observes (1979:237), 2:15-16 is not a repudiation of wisdom but a complaint about its failure to deliver. Qohelet's protest against the wrong done *to* wisdom presupposes its intrinsic value. The unfairness does not obliterate the qualitative difference between wisdom and folly. Rather, the difference exacerbates the unfairness.

§5.14. Wisdom Hurts

Ironically, insofar as wisdom succeeds in gaining knowledge, it causes pain. The rational intellect uncovers galling truths.

Qohelet applied his heart "to gaining wisdom and knowledge" (1:17a[4]), and he succeeded, but he soon realized "that this too is senseless, for in much wisdom there is much irritation, and whoever increases knowledge increases pain" (1:17b-18). For wisdom exposes life's absurdity, an absurdity aggravated by the immutability of events. Hence (to paraphrase 7:16) you should not become extremely righteous or perceptive, lest you see things that will shock you, such as the wicked living long and the righteous dying young (7:15). Wisdom is an "unfortunate business" (1:13), because when a wise man (Qohelet has himself in mind) persists in pondering life, he comes face to face with the irredeemable senselessness of the universe.

---

3. Qohelet is reporting an earlier experience of despair. All of 1:13–2:26 is an account of an earlier experience. The conclusions he arrived at remain valid, but the hatred he reports having felt toward life and wealth (*'amal*) is an extreme reaction that did not stay with him, since whatever their flaws, life and wealth remain "good things" in Qohelet's store of values.

4. Delete "inanity and folly"; see the commentary.

§5.2. Qohelet and the Wise

Qohelet's critique of wisdom is often considered a polemic against the wise or the supposed Wisdom School.[5] Zimmerli, for example, says of Qohelet's task (apropos of 8:17):

> All his [sc. Qohelet's] endeavor is basically a great polemic against wisdom, which believes itself able to understand the things of the world in their connections, and thereby also (to understand) God, and to construct thereon its confident knowledge of life. (1962:223)[6]

This is a misreading of 8:17. When Qohelet says, "And even if the wise man intends[7] to understand, he is not able to grasp (the events that occur under the sun)" (8:17b), he is not blaming or deriding the wise man for presumptuous claims. He is intensifying the complaint of 8:17a: No one, *not*

5. For example, J. Fichtner (1933:8) says that Qohelet undertakes "a radical critique of the value of wisdom." According to von Rad, "That Qohelet turns against the dominant teachings cannot be doubted" (1970:301; ET 233), and ". . . indeed, Qohelet turns not only against offshoots of the traditional teaching, but against the entire undertaking" (ibid.). Loader concludes that ". . . Qohelet is constantly polemizing [sic] against general *hokmā* by turning its own topoi against it, by using its own forms and types with antichokmatic function and by categorically opposing the very heart of chokmatic optimism" (1979:117). H. Schmid says that it is generally granted that Qohelet takes a stance critical of wisdom (1966:186). Zimmerli (1962:132-35) too regards the book as a polemic. Kroeber (1963:270) is one of the few who denies that the purpose of the book is polemical. He understands the dialectic with the older worldview to be itself a form of wisdom.

R. E. Murphy (pp. lxi-lxiv) offers a more nuanced assessment of Qohelet's ambivalent attitude toward wisdom. He describes the relation between Qohelet and the older wisdom as dialectical rather than polemical and summarizes Qohelet's relation to traditional wisdom as follows: "First, it is within this tradition that he thought and wrote; his work is intelligible only in this perspective. Second, even while he quarrels with views of traditional wisdom, his goal remains that of an Israelite sage: the discovery of what is good for humans to do (Eccl 2:3b). He does not simply jettison past teaching; he purifies and extends it. His grief against classical wisdom is its claim to security, not its methodology. Third, his argument is not theoretical; it is practical . . ." (lxiv). The characterization is apt, though I would disagree with the last point. Qohelet is trying hard to arrive at a theoretical and abstract (as well as practical) evaluation of all he surveys.

6. "All seine Bemühung ist im Grunde ein grosses Kampfgespräch mit der Weisheit, die meint, die Dinge der Welt in ihren Zusammenhängen, und damit auch Gott, verstehen zu können und die darauf ihre zuversichtliche Lebenskunde baut" (1962:223). See also pp. 132-35.

7. *Yo'mar* = "intends," not "claims"; see the commentary.

even the wise man, who is best able to seek understanding and most deserving of success, can discover the rationale of what happens in life. There is a note of sadness and even indignation here, a feeling that it is unfair to deprive a man of the knowledge he desires, a desire imposed on him by God (3:11).

Qohelet's critique of wisdom is not an attack on its foundations so much as an expression of disappointment and a warning not to expect too much of it. He is indignant that the wise man is denied the full rewards of his wisdom, in the same way that he is rankled by such inequities as a toiler losing the full benefits of his earnings (6:1-6) or the wealthy being made to "sit in lowly places" (10:6). Life's insults to the wise do not make Qohelet repudiate wisdom, any more than death's indifference to righteousness makes him discard moral virtue (7:14; 9:2-3).

Wisdom falls short of the grand goals that Qohelet (sharing the attitudes of the more conventional sages) sets for it. This failure is due not so much to the inherent feebleness of human intellect as to the cussedness of life. An absurd world thwarts understanding. Qohelet's complaints are not an attack on wisdom, but a complaint against life on wisdom's behalf.

In complaining about the limits of wisdom, then, Qohelet's stance is not polemical but protective. He himself is a wise man and a sage, and he shares the sages' esteem of wisdom. He distinguishes his wisdom from theirs only in its amplitude. Therefore he feels chagrin at the world — and thus, indirectly, at God — for denying wisdom its just rewards.[8]

§5.3. How Wisdom Succeeds

Qohelet has a high appreciation of wisdom. He seems to revel in the mind's power to reach far and deep. He believes that wisdom is to stupidity as light is to darkness (2:13), a polar distance. This is not only a ratio; it is also a metaphor for knowledge. Sight is better than blindness (ignorance), regardless of what we see. We should embrace "activity and calculation and knowledge and wisdom" when we can, because there are none of these in Sheol (9:10). The limit death sets to all human powers and endeavors makes them precious whatever their inadequacies.

The type of wisdom that Qohelet praises and recommends is usually

8. C. Reines harmonizes the judgments by assigning the negative ones to "wisdom *alone,* regarded in the usual empirical sense as the observation of the facts of (social) life," while the positive ones refer to the *"moral* worth of (true) wisdom" (1954a:80). But Qohelet does not draw such distinctions, and when he praises wisdom it is for its practical, not moral, worth.

the practical faculties of ingenuity or good sense. He himself possessed such wisdom. It enabled him to keep his wits about him (*w^{e}libbi noheg^9 bahokmah;* 2:3) and to monitor his own experiences even while immersed in distractions.

Such wisdom is unquestionably advantageous. The wise man's speech is pleasant and careful (10:12), his face cheerful (8:1b). He has a feel for the right time and type of behavior, such as when dealing with the authorities: "and the wise man's heart knows time and procedure" (8:5). This makes the sensible man's soft-spoken speech more effective than a ruler's bellowing is among fools (9:17).

Wisdom, as ingenuity and good sense, is effective. It helps one do things well (10:2). Through it one can earn wealth (2:19b, 21a). It is more powerful than a warrior's might (9:16a) and weaponry (9:18a; cf. 13-18).

When things take a turn for the worse, is it not wise (that is to say, discreet) to ask why this is so (7:10)? The prudence to refrain from such questions spares one the frustrations of futile inquiry. (Yet it is precisely "in wisdom" — rational intellect — that one inquires into such matters.)

The mind of the sensible man is his blessing, the fool's his bane (10:1) — so much so that wisdom "keeps its possessor alive" (7:12). If Qohelet would concede that there are any *yitronot* "profits" under the sun, wisdom would surely be one.

Human intellect is feeble but not futile. It *can* reach knowledge. The possession of knowledge in and of itself gives the living, however unhappy, at least one advantage over the dead: "the living know they will die, while the dead know nothing" (9:5). Though death inevitably is oppressive, the living should keep this truth ever in mind (7:2) and let their thoughts ever dwell in the "house of mourning" (7:4). Some truths have slipped through the barriers God placed before human knowledge. The fact of death is one, and it is wise to face facts. This too is wisdom.[10]

§5.4. The Wisdom Imperative

Qohelet both affirms and denies the value of wisdom, but on balance he unquestionably prefers it to ignorance. Nevertheless (and there is always a

9. Or vocalize *nāhōg;* see commentary.
10. Plumptre paraphrases 2:13-14: "A man is conscious of being more truly man when he looks before and after, and knows how to observe." He compares the *Iliad,* xvii 647: "And if our fate be death, give light, and let us die" (similarly Barton).

"nevertheless" with Qohelet), he also cautions us against becoming too wise, lest we become dumbfounded (7:16). The wisdom that might do this can only be the awareness of harsh facts such as the injustice he describes in v. 15. In 4:3 he says that it is better never to have been born than to have seen life's evils. He once even recommends dulling the ache of consciousness: A man allowed to steep himself in pleasure "will not much call to mind the days of his life, since God is keeping <him> occupied with his heart's plea-sure" (5:19).[11] The anodyne did not, however, work for Qohelet (2:1-2, 11), who, by persisting in his search for knowledge, proves that he is driven to strive for enlightenment rather than to eliminate the concomitant pain. Qohelet seeks out and reports maddening absurdities and injustices because he feels that it is imperative that he — and we — know these truths. But he never says why.

The motive of this imperative is not a moral equation between wisdom and righteousness. In sharp contrast to Proverbs (but not to most of the Bi-ble), Qohelet does not assume that *hokmah* is inherently a virtue of piety or ethics. Proverbs' central principle — that it is smart to be righteous and being righteous makes you smart — is not a truism. It is a new doctrine being ex-pounded programmatically by some of the authors and redactors of the pro-verbial and literary materials that grew into the book of Proverbs. It is a doc-trine that Ben Sira absorbed better than Qohelet.

Qohelet does not claim that his moral virtue grew with his wisdom. Likewise, the "wise" youth who displaces the old king (4:13) shows no par-ticular moral virtue, nor does the man who labors in wisdom (2:19, 21), or even the poor man whose wisdom saved his city (9:13-16). Qohelet does pair righteousness and wisdom in 7:16 and 9:1, but he is coupling the categories as positive values, not equating them. Qohelet never says that wisdom ensues from righteousness or fear of God or that it brings these virtues in its wake. It is wise to be virtuous, but wisdom (outside of Proverbs) is not an intrinsically moral virtue.[12]

Yet even without the assumption of wisdom's intrinsic moral excel-lence, and quite apart from its utility, wisdom in Qohelet's view has auton-omous, irreducible value. He is convinced that wisdom is vastly better than

---

11. Reading *ma'ănēhû*. Murphy's comment nicely grasps the pathos of this verse: "humans can be induced to forget their pitiable condition. God tranquilizes them, as it were, by the (erratic) pleasures given to them, holding out nostrums as a distraction from the misery of the short lives of human beings" (1991:579).

12. Proverbs was the first to assert the intellectual foundations and prerequisites of piety and righteousness and to insist on the obligation to seek wisdom apart from any spe-cific virtue. See my forthcoming article, "What the Book of Proverbs Is About."

stupidity. He seems to have carried over from conventional wisdom a feeling for the moral excellence of wisdom without assuming the ethical or religious substance ascribed to it there. He advocates wisdom while fully aware of its irritations and defects, and he is convinced that the wise, however they manifest their wisdom, deserve a better fate than the foolish. He does not explain the reason for wisdom's excellence, which seems independent of its benefits.

There is an affinity between Qohelet's eagerness for wisdom and Albert Camus's embrace of *clairvoyance*, "lucidity." Both thinkers look hard at life, rake up its unfairnesses and absurdities, and spurn easy consolations. They realize that man's knowledge is constricted, his achievements randomly undone, and his merits plowed under by death. As Camus states and Qohelet demonstrates, lucidity allows man to rise above this helplessness, to look at the world with an unflinching gaze, and to assay it by human measuring rods. Lucidity is not pleasant or pragmatically advantageous, but it is quintessentially human. It is the moment of Sisyphus' victory and the domain of his freedom. This too is man's portion. Qohelet is a Sisyphus aware of his fate but unaware of his triumph.

> To a man devoid of blinders, there is no finer sight than that of the intelligence at grips with a reality that transcends it. (Camus, *Myth,* p. 41)

§5.5. Wisdom and Beyond

The book of Qohelet contains two statements about wisdom that do not come from Qohelet. These belong to the epilogist (12:9-12) and the author of the postscript (vv. 13b-14), who are probably different persons.

The epilogue, I argue in Excursus III, is probably the comment of a frame-narrator — who presents and quotes the (fictional) persona Qohelet — rather than being added by a later and extraneous "editor." But whether author or editor, the epilogist has a different idea of wisdom from Qohelet's, one that encompasses and controls Qohelet's view without repudiating it. The epilogist considers Qohelet *wise* and his teachings *knowledge,* yet he knows the danger of Qohelet's kind of wisdom.

The epilogue serves to buffer the words of Qohelet and to assure the reader of their legitimacy. It does so by identifying Qohelet's words with wisdom and praising them as lovely and true, while cautioning against pushing wisdom too far. Then a postscript sets boundaries on wisdom, namely the religious principles of piety and obedience — "Torah," in rabbinic usage:

"Fear God and keep his commandments. For this is (the substance) of every man" (12:13b).

Though the postscript does not speak about wisdom explicitly, it does set a limit to wisdom. It is not redefining wisdom as Torah or even subsuming wisdom to it. (Ben Sira will do that.) Rather, it allows wisdom its realm but makes Torah the final arbiter of what is right and valuable. The realm of wisdom is excellent, but it is bounded by faith and God's law.

The caution in both vv. 10-12 and in vv. 13b-14 is directed not toward Qohelet's words alone, but toward wisdom as such, to which Qohelet's teaching belongs. Wisdom can and should be conducive to piety, but it is not tantamount to it. By giving piety the final word, the postscript blunts the thorns imminent in the roamings of human intellect at the very same time it allows Qohelet — and other intellectuals — freedom of movement for their inquiries. All wisdom may be heard and considered, so long as it is finally subject to the controls of piety in attitude and behavior. Qohelet pushed wisdom to the edge. The last verse in the book marks the boundary. To use God's words to Job (38:11): "This far you may come, but no farther."

CHAPTER 6

Deed and Event

Qohelet pronounces heavy judgments on a range of deeds and events — what people do and what happens to them. Words in the semantic fields of deeds and events intersect in the terms studied here.[1] Their connotations range from unpleasant (ʿML, ʾNH) to neutral (ʿŚH, HYH).

§6.1. ʿAmal "Toil" (Noun and Verb)[2]

§6.11. ʿAmal in Biblical Hebrew

Throughout the Bible, ʿamal carries gloomy connotations. It first of all means toil — arduous, wearisome work. This is its etymological meaning, broadly represented in cognate languages.[3] It can refer to the wealth that

---

1. Actions are a subset of events: an event that has an agent is an action. D. Davidson defines "agency" in accordance with a semantic criterion: "A person is the agent of an event if and only if there is a description of what he did that makes true a sentence that says he did it intentionally" (1980:46, and see chap. 3, *passim*). Making agency a semantic category circumvents the problem of determinism in discussing act and event. While it may be the case that God "gives" a man the task of toiling (2:26), that toil is intentional from the man's standpoint.

2. The writing ʿamal conveniently can indicate both the noun ʿāmāl and the verb ʿāmal. Their meanings are easily commutable.

3. E.g., Arabic ʿamila "to exert oneself"; Syriac ʿamlaʾ "labor"; and Akkadian nēmelu "profit," the result of effort.

these labors produce. It can also be extended to denote difficulties and evils apart from labor.

When signifying activity, *'amal* always means onerous, strained labor, "overdoing" rather than simply "doing." This is the usual meaning of *'amal* in Qohelet. Elsewhere in BH, this meaning is infrequent. This sense is clearly attested for the verb only in Jon 4:10; Ps 127:1; Prov 16:26; and Sir 11:11 and for the noun in Deut 26:7; Isa 53:11; Prov 16:26; Sir 31[34]:3, 4b. Even in these verses, the noun *'amal* may mean "misery" rather than "toil."

The implications of trouble and burden can detach themselves from the notion of work and stand alone, so that *'amal* can mean "(causing) trouble," "misery," or the like. Job describes his sufferings as "nights of *'amal*" (7:3). This phrase shows that *'amal* can refer to an experience that does not involve actual labor. The *'amel* is a "miserable" person in Job 3:20 (*//marey napeš*). Jeremiah (20:18) calls his suffering *'amal weyagon,* "misery and anguish." *Maḥšebet 'amal* in Sir 13:26 refers to unhappy thoughts.[4]

Sometimes *'amal* refers to an activity or behavior that is burdensome not from the standpoint of the agent but from the standpoint of the effect it has on someone else, the "patient" of the action or an observer. The psalmist of Ps 73:16 says that he regarded the prosperity of the wicked as *'amal* — unpleasant and burdensome on *him,* the observer, not on the evildoers or their victims. *'Amal* here refers not to the wickedness as such but to the injustice the speaker observes. Job calls his friends *menaḥămey 'amal,* "burdensome comforters" (16:2), alluding not to the burden *they* bear but to the effect of their comfort on *him.*

Sometimes *'amal* refers to "life's toil" generally, and not only to labor. Joseph uses the word in this way when he says, "God made me forget all my *'ămal*" (Gen 41:51). The *'amal* is not his work as slave or vizier, but rather the hardships he has borne. When Job curses his birth-day because "it did not close the doors of my [mother's] womb and hide *'amal* from my eyes" (3:10), the *'amal* he is alluding to is the tragedy he has recently suffered, not his productive pastoral labors of earlier years. In Job 5:7a ("For man is born to *'amal*), Eliphaz means that misery, and not only labor, is the human condition.

'Amal clearly means "wealth" only in Ps 105:44, but there too it carries the connotation of burdensome toil. The psalmist uses *'amal* to mean wealth in order to remind us that Israel's special blessing was to inherit what *others* toiled for, a motif employed in Deut 6:11 and Josh 24:13 as well.

---

4. "Unhappy thoughts (make) the face full of brooding and anger" (cf. Segal, *Ben Sira*). Di Lella, less plausibly, translates the line "withdrawn and perplexed is the toiling schemer."

The trouble implied by *'amal* may be *evil. 'Amal* is frequently collocated with or parallel to words meaning wickedness, deceit, and disaster; for example: *'awen* (Isa 10:1), *hawwot* (Ps 94:20), *šod* (Prov 24:2), *'awen* and *šeqer* (Ps 7:15), and *ra'* (Hab 1:13).

The semantic shifts of *'amal* from the etymological meaning "toil" to "misery" to "evil" are presumably historical, but in the Biblical texts the differences cannot be arranged chronologically, and the relations must be considered conceptual and synchronic. For the speaker of BH, the notion common to the various uses of *'amal* was, approximately, "trouble." This could then apply in context to burdensome and troublesome work, events, behaviors, persons, situations, and more.

§6.12. *'Amal in Qohelet: "Toil"*

Among the words by which Qohelet designates work, the most important is *'amal.* It stands conspicuously in the leading rhetorical question, "What profit does man have in all his toil at which he labors under the sun?" (1:3). The word occurs frequently — the verb 22 times, the noun 13 (of a total of 23 and 57, respectively, in the Bible + Sira). The word has sombrous connotations that almost by themselves exclude the likelihood of adequate reward for the efforts it designates.

In a number of places, *'amal* clearly means "hard labor"/"to work hard." In 4:4, *'amal* (as well as *kišron hamma'ăśeh*) must refer to toil. *'amal* is occupational labor in 4:8; 5:15; and 6:7. This sense is sometimes interlaced with others. In 2:21 ("For sometimes a man whose toil [*'ămalo*] is [performed] in wisdom, knowledge, and skill ends up giving it as a portion to someone who did not toil for it [*š^elo' 'amal bo*] . . ."), both the verb and the noun clearly refer to the activity of labor, although the suffix of *yitt^enennu,* "giving it," points to the unmentioned but implicit product of the toil.

§6.13. *'Amal in Qohelet: "To Earn," "Property"*

Ginsberg says that in Qohelet the verb *'amal* "almost always" means "acquire" or "possess" *(qnh wrhš)* and the noun means "possessions," "wealth" (p. 14). (Rashbam recognized this usage in 2:18, 19, and 24.)

'Amal (noun and verb) means "property" or "to earn" in 2:18: "And I came to detest my wealth for which I had toiled [*kol 'ămali še'ăni 'amel*] under the sun, since I would be leaving it to a man who will come after me."

The verb *'amel* designates the end-result of the effort, and the noun *'ămali* must be the earnings, because these alone can be left to a later generation. In 2:19, Qohelet says that this successor will "control" all his *'amal,* which can only refer to his wealth. Yet the real target of Qohelet's "detestation" is not his wealth but the work he invested in acquiring it. It might be more precise to say that *'amal* means "toil" when it appears in 18a, but its product when referred to in the suffix of *'ănihennu.*

In several occurrences of *'amal,* it is nearly impossible to determine the intended sense. In 2:10, for example, Qohelet can be saying that he got pleasure from his earnings (itself a metonymy for what he purchased with them) or, equally well, indirectly, from the labor that produced them. In 2:11 he may be calling his toil or his wealth absurd. And there are passages where he seems to vacillate rapidly between the two senses; see the commentary on 2:18-26. We may try to identify the most appropriate sense in any particular occurrence, but the grounds for decision are often extremely slight and perhaps not relevant to Qohelet's thought, for both his earnings and his efforts fail him. I translate "toil" whenever possible, for this can be understood as a metonymy for earnings where appropriate, but in a few cases, "wealth" or "to earn" is required by context.

Even when the word is ambiguous, the meaning of the passage can be clear. When Qohelet affirms the value of *'amal* as a source of benefit,[5] it is clear that what is actually being praised is toil's product, whether *'amal* means "toil" or "wealth." Qohelet nowhere advocates labor for any intrinsic value such as, say, disciplining the spirit or occupying the mind. Toil is a source of pleasure only insofar as it provides the means of pleasure. Thus *lismoah ba'ămalo* (and variants) does not mean exactly "to take pleasure in his toil," for Qohelet does not preach the "joy of labor" (though he does praise activity in 9:10). *Samah be'amal,* lit. to "take pleasure in toil," may mean (1) to enjoy pleasure *during* one's (life of) toil, or (2) to get pleasure (indirectly) *by means* of toil. 8:15 makes sense (1) more likely, because the usual phrase *lismoah ba'ămalo* is expanded into *we'lismoah we'hu' yilwennu ba'ămalo.* It makes more sense to say that eating, drinking, and experiencing enjoyment will accompany a man *during* his toil (that is to say, during his burdensome life) than to say that these things "will accompany him *by means of* his toil," which feels incomplete. Also, in 11:9, *se'mah be'yalduteyka* is parallel to "in the days of your prime," so the *beyt* must mean *during.*

When Qohelet deprecates toil for not yielding a profit (1:3; 3:9) or for being absurd and senseless (2:11), is it the work or the wealth that is so

5. Qoh 2:10; 2:24; 3:13; 5:17; 8:15; 9:9; similarly 3:22 with *ma'ăsim.*

judged? In other words, is the warning directed against materialism or against working too hard? No syntactic features resolve the question.

In two key verses, 1:3 and 3:9, Qohelet clearly speaks of toil, not wealth. Since nothing in the poems preceding 3:9 and following 1:3 deals with remunerative work, the value of wealth is not at issue. The issue is undoubtedly the efficacy of arduous efforts. The similarity of 2:11 to 1:3 and 3:9 (all three deny that there can be any *yitron* in *'amal* "under the sun") suggests that *'amal* means "toil" in 2:11 as well.

The toil/earnings ambiguity faces us in several other verses, and I will attempt to resolve them in the commentary. But the problem may be partly circumvented by identifying the actual target of Qohelet's anger. For whatever the precise meaning of *'amal* in a particular verse, it is not the toiling itself that really troubles him so much as its failure to achieve a profit.

§6.14. 'Amal *"Life's Strains"*

At its broadest reach, *'amal* covers virtually all human endeavors. This is not a separate lexical meaning of the word, but a broader application of the concept of toil.

'Amal refers to much more than occupational labor aiming at remuneration. Even walking to the city is *'amal:* "The fool's toil exhausts him, because he doesn't even know how to get to town" (emended; see the commentary) (10:15). Of course, anyone's *'amal,* by definition, tires him. In the fool's case, the reason for the fatigue is his ignorance: he does not know how to get to the most obvious and well-known site in the region.

For Qohelet, even *thinking* can be *'amal.* The attempt to understand life is *'amal* in 8:17aβ: *'ăšer ya'ămol ha'adam lᵉbaqqeš,* lit. "even if a man toils to seek," that is, seeks arduously. Mental activity is called *'amal* in 2:22: "For what does a man get out of his toil [*'ămalo*] and his heart's thoughts [*ra'yon libbo*] at which he toils [*'amel*] under the sun?" The verb *'amel* here has two direct objects, "his toil" and "his heart's thoughts." (The construction is difficult to convey in translation.) This shows that thinking is an action that one can *'ml* — "perform laboriously." (This observation applies even if we interpret *ra'yon libbo* as "his heart's desire" or "pursuit.")

The scope of *'amal* is so broad in Qohelet that life's experiences in general can be subsumed under this heading. In 4:9, "Better two than one, because *they* have a good reward in their *'amal,*" the *'amal* seems to refer not only to the companions' work but to all that they do in life, and not only their work, because the benefit they get in (or during) their *'amal* is exemplified by

101

incidents such as falling down, lying down in the cold, and being attacked (4:10-12). Nor does '*amal* here mean "wealth," because the context does not speak of the benefits of property.

The conclusion Qohelet draws from observing the fixity of "times" in 3:1-9 is the negative assertion implied by the rhetorical question, *mah yitron ha'ośeh ba'ăšer hu' 'amel,* "What profit does one who does something have in what he toils at?" (or "from the fact that he toils") (v. 9). Most of the events and actions mentioned in vv. 2-8 are not instances of toil or other burdensome activities. They exemplify human deeds in their entirety, but also events that *happen* to people. Therefore the conclusion in v. 9 must apply to far more than occupational labors. Also, Qohelet refers to the agent in v. 9 as *ha'ośeh,* "one who does" (sc., something), which is the broadest term for activity.

Another comprehensive use of '*amal* is 8:15:

> So I praised pleasure, because there is nothing good for man under the sun but to eat, drink, and experience pleasure, and this will accompany him in his toil [*ba'ămalo*] throughout the days of his life, which God has given him under the sun.

These pleasures accompany a man not only during his *labors,* but throughout life, which Qohelet perceives as an ongoing strain. In view of the persistent connotations described above, we could paraphrase *b*^e*kol 'ămalo* (1:3) as "in all his misery." The functional synonymity of '*amal* and "life" is shown by the way that having pleasure in one's '*amal* (3:13) is equivalent to taking pleasure in one's life, *ḥayyayw* (3:12).

In spite of this breadth, not every action would be called '*amal*. Taking advantage of what falls to one's lot would not be included. Nor would behaving righteously or paying vows, for these do not push against the constraints of reality. But all efforts that aim at achievements, even fairly moderate ones, fall in the category of '*amal*. To live is to toil.

§6.2. '*Aśah* "Do," "Happen"; *Ma'ăśeh* "Deeds," "Events"[6]

Qohelet draws other words into the ambit of '*amal*. Words from the broader and connotationally neutral root 'ŚH are used as near equivalents of '*amal*.

6. There is little practical distinction between the plural and singular of *ma'ăśeh*. *Ma'ăśeh* is usually a collective, equivalent to a plurality of actions. *Ma'ăśeh ha'ĕlohim,* always in the singular, is God's work in its totality, his "opus." This can, however, be phrased as *hamma'ăśim šenna'ăśu taḥat haššemeš,* which are individual events.

Judging from 3:9, discussed above, a "doer" may (but need not) "toil." In 9:10, the *ma'ăśeh* that is absent from Sheol is the same as the *'amal* that one performs in life (v. 9). Man can get pleasure in his toil (or his toilsome life) (2:10; 5:18) and in his "works" (3:22; cf. 9:7), and no practical distinction can be drawn.

§6.21. 'Aśah *"Do"*; Ma'ăśeh *"Deed(s)"*

In Qohelet, as in BH generally, the derivatives of 'ŚH can refer to actions and mean "do," "deeds," and the like. Activity as such is *ma'ăśeh* (sg.) (9:10), indicated by the verb in 2:3. God's actions are *ma'ăśim* (3:11b; 8:17; 11:5, etc.), though these might also mean "make happen," see below. Working for wealth and property is *ma'ăśim* (2:4, 5, 6; 4:4; etc.). Eating and drinking are *ma'ăśim* (9:7).

Qohelet does not call mental activities *ma'ăśim*. The terms in 9:10, *ma'ăśeh, ḥešbon, da'at,* and *ḥokmah,* refer to the two types of human activity: *ma'ăśim,* which are external actions (primarily working), and *ḥešbon, da'at,* and *ḥokmah,* which are mental activities.

§6.22. 'Aśah *"Earn"*; Ma'ăśeh *"Property"*

As in the case of *'amal,* the derivatives of 'ŚH can designate the products of work, as observed by Ginsberg (p. 14). This is not a frequent usage outside Qohelet, but *'aśah* clearly means "acquire" in Gen 12:5. *Ma'ăśeh* (*ma'ăśim*) occasionally refers to the products of work, especially in the phrase *ma'ăśeh yad* (Cant 7:2; Deut 4:28; Ps 102:26).

In Qohelet, *'aśah/ma'ăśeh* and *'amal* are sometimes collocated as near equivalents (2:11; 3:9; 4:4 etc.) or used in equivalent contexts (compare 2:10 and 5:18 with 3:22), and the words are subject to the same ambiguity. *'Aśah* clearly means "acquire" in 2:5, 6, and 8. Nowhere does *ma'ăśeh* alone unequivocally mean "property," except in the phrase *ma'ăśeh yadeyka* (5:5). It may have that sense in 2:4, 10f., but this is uncertain.

§6.23. 'Aśah, Na'ăśah *"(Make) Happen"*; Ma'ăśeh *"Event(s)"*

Ginsberg (pp. 15-16) makes the important observation that derivatives of the root 'ŚH often denote "occurrence and happening" (*q^eriyyah* and *wa'ăriyyah*). He notes that *ma'ăśeh* often means "occurrence" in RH. This observation is important to understanding Qohelet's message. He is examining what happens in life — which is to say, life itself — and not only human deeds. *Maʿăśeh haʾĕlohim* in Qohelet is God's ongoing governance of the world, and not the original creation. Of course, God's "making happen" is something he "does," so this is not a distinct meaning of *maʿăśeh*. But in Qohelet, *maʿăśeh haʾĕlohim* is a special category of divine action, namely God's ongoing control of events. Underlying this usage is Qohelet's deterministic worldview, according to which all that happens, including events with human causation, are, in large, "acts of God" and ultimately brought about by him.

Maʿăśeh haʾĕlohim is used not only of a particular occurrence, but at a higher level of abstraction, it designates divine activity as a whole, as a system. P. Machinist observes that *maʿăśeh* sometimes refers to "a planned life pattern of activity characteristic of each individual *and God*" (e.g., 3:11; 7:13; 8:14, 17) (1995:171; emphasis added). The notion of a "life pattern" of God, which can be called his *maʿăśeh,* is intriguing. It is particularly in the fore in 3:11, according to which God's *maʿăśeh* can be thought of as having boundaries, a beginning and an end — not temporal but conceptual. What God does, what happens on earth, is not just a collection of scattered deeds, but constitutes a single *maʿăśeh,* which is, in a sense, the universe: all that God causes to be or happen.

Words from ʿŚH are often ambiguous. I will examine a few sentences that establish this usage, and will leave the others to the commentary.

When God is the semantic subject, *maʿăśeh* means "event" or, as a collective, "events." *ʾAśah* means "cause" or "make happen" in 3:14; 7:14; 8:17; and 11:5. In 3:11 and 7:29, *ʾaśah haʾĕlohim* does mean "God made." (Ginsberg concedes only the latter exception.)

More difficult, but very important to Qohelet's meaning, are cases where the subject is indefinite. In the recurring phrase *hammaʿăśeh ʾăśer naʿăśah taḥat haššemeš* (and variants), the *maʿăśim* are usually thought to be man's activities, in particular his restless exertions to get rich. I understand the phrase to mean "the events that occur under the sun" and to be equivalent to *maʿăśeh haʾĕlohim.* Qohelet is interested in human activities as a subset of these events.

Two passages in particular are important because of their programmatic nature: 1:13f., in which Qohelet says what he intended to do, and 8:16f., in which he looks back to report on what he accomplished. In the following alignment, key components are identified by letter:

(1:13) (a) *wᵉnatatti ʾet libbi*
             lidroš wᵉlatur baḥokmah

(8:16) (aʹ) *kaʾăśer natatti*
              ʾet libbi ladaʿat ḥokmah
              wᵉlirʾot ʾet

(b)   *'al kol 'ăšer na'ăśah*   (b') *ha'inyan 'ăšer na'ăśah*
      taḥat haššamayim   *'al ha'areṣ . . .*

(c)   *hu' 'inyan ra' natan*   (c') *ki gam bayyom uballaylah*
      'ĕlohim libney ha'adam   *šenah bᵉ'eynay<> 'eynenn<y>*
      la'ănot bo   *ro'eh*

(14) (d) *ra'iti 'et*   (17aα) (d') *wᵉra'iti 'et*
      (e) *kol hamma'ăśim šenna'ăśu*   (e') *kol ma'ăśeh ha'ĕlohim*
           taḥat hašameš
      (f) *wᵉhinneh hakkol*   (g') *ki lo yukal ha'adam limṣo'*
      (g) *hebel urᵉ'ut ruaḥ*   (f') *'et hamma'ăśeh 'ăšer*
                                                   na'ăśah taḥat haššemeš . . .

In 1:13f., Qohelet designates the object of his investigation as (b) *kol 'ăšer na'ăśah taḥat haššamayim* and (e) *kol hamma'ăśim šenna'ăśu taḥat haššameš*. These phrases refer to the totality of what happens in this world. The scope of Qohelet's investigation throughout the book (which he defines in these verses) includes much more than human deeds. He mostly examines things that happen to people, such as undeserved gain, social injustices, the unfair allocation of lifespans, the obliteration of distinctions by death, and death's oblivion.

In 8:16f. Qohelet sets up a series of equations, which also echo the components of 1:13f.: (f') *hamma'ăśeh 'ăšer na'ăśah taḥat haššemeš* resumes (e') *kol ma'ăśeh ha'ĕlohim* (not *ma'ăśeh ha'adam!*), which in turn restates (b') *ha'inyan 'ăšer na'ăśah 'al ha'areṣ*. Just as phrase (e') is not restricted to human actions, so neither is (b') or (f'). Phrase (f') in turn cannot be distinguished from (b) and (e). The object of Qohelet's examination (1:13a, 14a; 8:16αβb) and evaluation (1:14b; 8:17) is what *happens*, which is to say, life itself, not only what people do. In other words, "all that happens under the sun" is equivalent to "God's works" or "what God brings to pass," and these are all absurd.

There are additional cases where the two concepts are equated. In 7:13, *ma'ăśeh ha'ĕlohim* is God's making some things irreparably warped. In 1:15, the same proverb is used in reference to *hamma'ăśim šenna'ăśu taḥat hašameš* in the preceding verse. 3:11 says that man cannot grasp *(maṣa')* *hamma'ăśeh 'ăšer ha'ĕlohim*, and 8:17 says that man cannot grasp *hamma'ăśeh 'ăšer na'ăśah taḥat haššemeš*.

The equation of *ma'ăśeh ha'ĕlohim* and *hamma'ăśeh šenna'ăśah taḥat haššemeš* allows us to recognize that the latter phrase consistently refers to events. This is the likely sense in 1:9 (verb, 2x); 1:13 (verb); 1:14 (verb, noun); 2:17 (verb, noun); 3:11b (noun); 3:14 (verb, verb); 4:3 (noun, verb); 7:13 (noun); 8:9 (noun, verb); 8:14aα (verb); 8:16 (verb); 8:17 (noun 2x, verb); 9:3 (verb);[7] 9:6 (verb); 11:5 (verb, noun). Ambiguous cases are 4:1 (verb, niphal) and 7:14 (verb). Some cases are necessarily ambiguous.

When humans are the semantic subject (that is, explicitly or implicitly the agent of the verbal notion of the ʿŚH derivative), *ʿasah* means "do"/ "deed[s]," "activity," or the product thereof.

- *ʿasah:* 2:2, 5, 6, 8, 12; 3:9, 12; 4:17; 7:20, 29; 8:3, 4, 10, 12; 9:10 (2X); 10:19; and 12:12
- *naʿăsah:* 8:11 and 16
- *maʿăśeh:* 3:17; 4:4; 5:5; 8:11, 14 (2X); 9:7, 10; and 12:14.

§6.3. *ʿAnah, ʿInyan* "Be Busy," "Business," "Task"[8]

ʿInyan means "business," "occupation." "Business" with attention to the etymological sense, "busy-ness," is often a good English equivalent. When the activity or business is imposed on someone, "task" is an appropriate rendering, but the notion of imposition or requirement is drawn from the context, not from the word's denotation. *ʿInyan* — busyness — need not have an agent. In that case, it refers to an event (5:13) or the bustle of events that fill life, as in 8:16, see §6.23. The scope of this term continues to expand in RH, where it means, approximately, "matter" or "subject."

The verb *ʿanah* appears in paronomasia with *ʿinyan* and presumably has a corresponding meaning, "to busy oneself with" (qal 1:13; 3:10). In Sir 42:8, *ʿoneh biznut* means "busies himself with fornication." In Qoh 1:13 and 3:10, *laʿănot* may pun on the homonymous root ʿNH "to suffer." The hiphil in 5:19 means "occupy," "keep busy." The root ʿNH "busy" is better attested in Aramaic (in Syriac *ʿnah* = "be busy, engaged [with]") and is probably an Aramaism in Qohelet.

---

7. Here *naʿăsah* is unequivocal. The subject of *naʿăsah* is (the fact) "that all have the same fate." Of course, it can be said that God has "done" this, but that kind of divine deed cannot be distinguished from event.

8. *ʿInyan* is found in BH only in Qohelet. The noun occurs eight times, the verb *ʿanah* (in the relevant sense) three times, as well as once in Sir 42:8.

§6.4. *Hayah* "To Be," "Occur"

The verb *hayah,* usually rendered "to be," is in practice often best translated "to happen" or "occur." This is a well-established sense of *hayah* (BDB 224f.). With respect to events, "being" and "happening" are not distinct concepts, and often a translation can use either. In 1 Sam 4:17a, for example, we can translate *maggepah gᵉdolah hayᵉtah (baʿam)* as "there has been a great slaughter" or "a great slaughter has happened."

Sometimes, however, the context is concerned not with the static fact of existence but with an event, for which a criterial feature is duration in a limited time frame. In Qoh 1:9, *mah šehayah huʾ šeyyihyeh* (usually translated "that which has been is that which shall be") does not mean that a certain entity will once again come into existence; that notion is quite foreign to Qohelet. It means that certain typical events recur *ad infinitum.* The events Qohelet has in mind are illustrated in 3:1-8, the listing of the "times," whose idea is recapitulated in 3:15: "Whatever happens [*hayah*] already has happened, and what is going to happen [*lihyot*] already has happened [*hayah*]. . . ." The rendering of *hayah* as "to be" could lead to misunderstanding, as it has in 3:14, where translations such as "whatever God does endures forever" (NRSV) imply the durability of God's works (thus Crenshaw) or the eternality of the created world (Lauha). Such notions are not relevant to this context or Qohelet generally.

CHAPTER 7

The Best Things in Life

Qohelet calls some things good. Some of them he recommends doing, others he considers impossible to attain. This chapter examines his terminology in the positively evaluated realm of experience and the implications of this lexicon for his system of thought.

§7.1. *Ḥeleq* "Portion"

A man can have a *ḥeleq* in his work (2:10) yet lack a *yitron* (2:11). This fact irritates Qohelet, but this is not exactly where the contradiction lies. Qohelet's statements on portions and profits can be reconciled by a careful examination of his use of these two terms. In brief: one's work or good fortune might get him a *piece* — a *ḥeleq* — of the pie, but Qohelet feels that this is not enough. If it were, it would be a *yitron*. A *ḥeleq could* be enough; the word itself does not imply insufficiency. But Qohelet sees no *ḥeleq* that qualifies as a *yitron*.

How does *ḥeleq* differ from *yitron*? Many scholars contrast the two terms on an axis of duration, with *ḥeleq* taken to mean temporary gain as opposed to permanent gain, which is how *yitron* is understood. This interpretation is found in Rashbam: "*mah yitron:* What reward or gain (*śakar wᵉrewaḥ*) does a man have in all his toil at which he toils under the sun, inasmuch as he will finally pass away and cease to be in the world and will no longer have any pleasure [*ṭob*]?" E. Wölfel distinguishes the terms as follows: "The former [*yitron*] refers to what endures; the latter [*ḥeleq*] remains within (the realm of) the temporal and transitory. It remains moreover in the realm of enjoyment of material pleasures" (1958:75; followed by Hertzberg, p. 89).

Of course, all possession is temporary, since it must end when life does. But the word *ḥeleq* does not in itself imply temporariness. In 9:6 it would be pointless to complain that the dead have no more *temporary* portion among the living. Likewise, in 2:21, we would not translate "but to one who has not toiled for it, [God] will give it as his *temporary* portion," since Qohelet's complaint here is that someone who comes later may, if God-favored, receive unearned benefits, not that these benefits are transitory. On the contrary, the complaint would be diluted if the word *ḥeleq* itself reminded the reader that the fortunate recipient too is receiving merely a fleeting benefit. Furthermore, the portions that man can possess may last as long as life itself (9:9). There is no point in complaining that there is no enduring profit in life when man himself does not endure.

Galling's statement that *ḥeleq* is "plainly a technical term for the space allotted to human existence"[1] does not say what is distinctive about this word, and the suggested meaning is awkward in context. In 2:21 we cannot say that the toiler must turn over his wealth as the "space allotted to human existence" to "a man who has not worked for it." The fortunate successor already possesses the "space allotted to his existence"; he will receive something additional to enjoy within that "space." When Qohelet declares that it is good for a man to "take [NŚʾ] his *ḥeleq*" (5:18), this *ḥeleq* is not an allotted "space," since he fully possesses that independently of any volition on his part. It is something existing within the "space" allotted to a man, who can choose to take his *ḥeleq* or to ignore it.

Ḥeleq does mean "portion," "part," but Qohelet does not use it to contrast a part with the whole, contrary to Zimmerli's definition: "In Qohelet, the word 'portion' (*ḥeleq*) places the accent on limitation: God grants a *portion;* the *whole* he retains in his hand"[2] (1963:135; ET 325). What could "the whole" that God retains *be,* other than the whole world? As for possessing everything realistically accessible to man, the point of the Solomonic fiction is to say that Qohelet did "have it all," and yet he lacked a *yitron.*

A *ḥeleq* is a portion in the sense of possession, something one gets, irrespective of whether it is adequate or satisfying or deserved or durable. This is consistent with the word's use elsewhere. One may receive a *ḥeleq* as booty

---

1. "[G]eradezu *terminus technicus* für den der menschlichen Existenz zugewiesenen Raum" (p. 89).

2. "Das Wort 'Teil' (*ḥeleq*) enthält bei Kohelet den Akzent der Begrenzung. Gott 'teilt' zu — das 'Ganze' behält er in seiner Hand."

(e.g., Gen 14:24; Num 31:36), as an inheritance (e.g., Gen 31:14), or as an allocation (e.g., Josh 15:13). Only in Qohelet does a *ḥeleq* come from earnings (2:10), though perhaps the priestly "portions" may be so regarded (Lev 6:10). A portion may be good (usually) or bad (as in Isa 61:7[3] and Job 20:29).

A *ḥeleq* is usually only a fraction of what is available, but partialness is an incidental feature. In almost all contexts, the significant quality of a *ḥeleq* is its *belonging* to someone rather than its being fractional or partial. (Even the indivisible God himself can be called a "portion," as in Num 18:20 and Ps 16:5.) If one received the whole pie (which, in a sense, "Solomon" did), his *ḥeleq* would still be a "portion."

In Qohelet, a portion is sometimes the material wealth itself (2:21; cf. 11:2). More often a portion is the pleasure derived from wealth (2:10; 3:22; 5:17, 18; 9:9). To be precise, a man's portion is the pleasure *potential* in his wealth. It is possible to be given material assets without being allowed to enjoy them: "Furthermore, if God gives anyone wealth and property and enables him to partake of it *and to take his portion* [*wᵉlaśeʾt ʾet ḥelqo*] and to get pleasure in his toil — that is a gift of God" (5:18). God must both grant (or at least allow) the means of pleasure *and* enable the recipient to experience it (2:24; 3:13; 5:18b).[4] He doesn't always do so. Sometimes God snatches the wealth away (5:12-16; 6:1-6). But if one is permitted to "take" *(naśaʾ)* his portion, he himself must do so (5:18). *There* is where human freedom lies. In other words, God can give you a piece of the pie but *you* must eat it. If you keep it in the cupboard it won't do you any good.

Possessing a portion does not depend on deserving it or having earned it. If something falls into one's possession through divine favor, it belongs to the lucky recipient and is his portion to enjoy. After all, its possession is a sign of God's enigmatic favoritism (2:26).

Pleasure is just one type of portion. Other experiences too are portions: "Even their love, their hatred, and their jealousy have already perished, and they never more have a portion in all that happens under the sun" (9:6). Our portion in life includes the potential to experience the array of feelings, sensations, and cognitions the living can have. This includes emotions such as love, hatred, and jealousy, some of which are not necessarily pleasant or even *good,* but they are our portion. They belong to us, if just for the moment.

---

3. Read *kᵉlimmāh wārôq* "shame and spittle," with *BHS* et al.

4. "Experience" in this situation means the physical sensations attendant on indulging in sensory pleasures rather than pleasurable emotions, which might not come at all.

§7.2. *Yitron* (*Motar*,[5] *Yoter*[6]) "Advantage," "Profit"

Still, one might hope for a *ḥeleq* that is really worthwhile, a real profit — a *yitron*.

Yitron means "advantage" (when two things are being compared) or "profit" (when used absolutely).

> (1) "Advantage" (Comparative) (2:13 [twice]; 3:19; 5:8; 6:8, 11; 7:11, 12; 10:10, 11)

When two things are being compared, the preferable thing has, or is, a *yitron*. The second term of comparison (the *comparatum*) is sometimes vague, especially when Qohelet is denying the existence of an advantage.

In four occurrences of *yitron,* the comparison is explicit, marked by *min* ("more than," "over"): 2:13 (twice; *yitron* is used); 6:8 *(yoter); and* 3:19 *(motar).* In other verses, the comparison is implicit, and the *comparatum* is to be supplied from context: 10:10 (the advantage of the skilled man over others who must use brute force [*ḥăyalim*]); 10:11 (the advantage of a snake charmer over certain others, which is nullified); 7:11, 12 (the advantage of wisdom over wealth); 6:11 (the *lack* of advantage of much speech over silence, which is implicitly advised in vv. 10 and 12); and perhaps 5:8 (obscure, but there seems to be an implicit comparison between the land mentioned in this verse and the unfortunate state mentioned in the preceding one).

> (2) "Profit" (1:3; 2:11; 3:9; 5:15)

Outside of comparisons, *yitron* (as all commentators agree) means "profit," probably in a commercial sense. This meaning is inherent in the comparative usage: the margin of value or benefit of one thing over another.

Qohelet uses the word in the strict sense of surplus return on an investment of labor. If somebody opens a store that provides him with sufficient take-home pay to keep going day to day *and no more,* never producing a surplus and putting the business in the black, Qohelet would call the take-home pay the man's "portion." He would even allow that the food and drink he buys with it is "good." Yet by Qohelet's severe accounting, the business realizes no profit.

---

5. *Motar* means "advantage" in 3:19.

6. *Yoter* is a synonym of *yitron* in 6:8, 11; and 7:11. In 2:15 and 7:16 it is an adverb meaning "very," "exceedingly." In 12:9 and 12, *yoter* is a conjunction meaning "furthermore," lit. "something more (is)."

"What profit does man have in all his toil at which he labors under the sun?" (1:3) is not a nihilistic denial that there are good things in life or that nothing has an advantage over anything else (a *yitron* in the comparative sense). Rather it declares that no human toil and endeavor can achieve a net gain. Life (even for the natural phenomena in 1:4-8) is a treadmill. The fact that the "times" are beyond human control proves, to Qohelet's mind, that man cannot really get ahead of the game (3:9).

For Qohelet, pleasure is a good portion (2:10). But since it is not, in his view, meaningful or truly productive — it "does" nothing, achieves nothing beyond itself (2:1f.) — it is not adequate remuneration for the effort invested in earning it (2:11).

§7.3. *Śimḥah, Śamaḥ* "Pleasure"

Śimḥah in Qohelet means pleasure, not happiness and certainly not joy.

Happiness, pleasure, and joy are not the same thing. *Pleasure* is not an independent emotion or sensation, but an experience or, more precisely, a "feeling-tone" attached to a more comprehensive experience.[7] A *pleasure* may also be something that stimulates that feeling, but the two uses are distinct. One may indulge in "pleasures" — parties, movies, eating rich desserts — yet not get the *feeling* of pleasure from them even momentarily, let alone happiness. *Happiness* is an emotion, a condition that permeates the entirety of consciousness while it is active. Pleasure is at most a contributing factor to happiness. Some people may have pleasure in what they are doing (such as eating) while at the same time feeling unhappy, whereas some people are happy even when denied pleasure. *Joy* refers to an intense and stable type of happiness directed at a worthy object (one's family, accomplishments, etc.).

In BH, *śimḥah/śamaḥ* is applied to the entire range of pleasant experiences. Sometimes *śimḥah* is happiness or joy of the deepest sort (e.g., Isa 30:29; Ps 21:7; 122:1; 126:3). But often, perhaps usually, it means "pleasure," without necessarily connoting happiness, and sometimes without any implication of emotion.

Śimḥah can refer to the externals of pleasure. Gary Anderson has shown that *śimḥah* (which he glosses "joy") has a distinct behavioral aspect (1991, chap. 2). A *yom śimḥah* is a feast day (Num 10:10; cf. *yom mišteh*

---

7. "For the pleasantness of an experience does not indicate a feature of the external object, but a way in which it *affects me,* i.e., a way I 'feel.' In other words: pleasure is a *feeling-tone*" (Duncker 1940:400).

w^e*śimḥah* in Esth 9:18). The verb *śamaḥ* often means "to celebrate," as when Israel is commanded to hold festivities before the Lord (e.g., Lev 23:40; Num 10:10; Deut 12:7, etc.; ibid., p. 19). *Śimḥah* frequently consists of the activities and ingredients of merriment. In 1 Sam 18:6, *śimḥah* refers to the sounds of merrymaking, alongside tambourines and triangles; cf. Gen 31:27. *La'ăśot śimḥah,* lit. "to do pleasure" (Neh 8:12; 12:27; 2 Chr 30:23), means precisely "to make merry." Two rabbinic dicta define the basics of ritual *śimḥah* bluntly: *'eyn śimḥah 'ela' b^ebaśar,* "*śimḥah* comes only by means of meat" (when the Temple was standing) and *'eyn śimḥah 'ela' b^eyayin,* "*śimḥah* comes only by means of wine" (in the present age) (b. Pes. 109a).[8]

The diversions called *śimḥah* may be trivial and even self-destructive amusements, as in Prov 21:17: "He who loves *śimḥah* is an impoverished man. He who loves wine and oil will not grow rich." Pleasures may be joyless, as those that Isaiah describes as "gaiety and pleasure [*śaśon w^eśimḥah*], killing cattle and slaughtering sheep, eating meat and drinking wine" (Isa 22:13a). These are dismal and forlorn amusements, whose participants declare, "Eat and drink, for tomorrow we will die" (13b). *Śimḥah* may take place even when the spirit is bitter and devoid of all agreeable feelings, as in Ps 137:3, "And our tormenters [demanded of us] *śimḥah,*" that is, cheerful song.[9]

Qohelet uses *śimḥah* in two ways: (1) enjoyment, the sensation or feeling-tone of pleasure, and (2) *a* pleasure, a means of pleasure: something that is supposed to (but may not) induce enjoyment, such as wine and music. It is sometimes impossible to know which sense applies in a particular occurrence of *śimḥah*. The word is ambiguous in the repeated commendation of pleasure (3:12; 5:18; 8:15 [twice]; and 11:8), but both senses are clearly attested in the book.

(1) *Śimḥah* = the sensation of pleasure: *Libbi śameaḥ,* "my heart had pleasure," is the outcome of Qohelet's pleasurable activities (2:10b), the consequence of not withholding his heart from any *śimḥah* (10a — which thus belongs in category 2). In 2:26 *śimḥah* is an internal state or event, alongside wisdom and knowledge; likewise in 5:19; 9:7 *(///leb ṭob);* 10:19; and probably 4:16.

8. Anderson (1991:23-25) describes the close connection of "joy" and sacrificial feasting in rabbinic law. These externals of celebration are the minimum constituents of "joy," not the entirety of the experience.
9. Anderson (1991:43f.) explains this "rejoicing" as a cultic act, the singing of declarative praise, which was forbidden during mourning. But the Babylonians would not have been, or thought to have been, sensitive to such nuances.

(2) *Śimḥah* = the means of pleasure, pleasant things and actions, merry-making: In 2:1, 2, and 10b *(mikkol śimḥah),* Qohelet refers to the pleasurable activities Qohelet tested, namely the ones listed in vv. 4-8. *Śimḥah* has this meaning in the phrase *beyt śimḥah* (7:4), which is a synonym of *beyt mišteh* "house of feasting" (7:2). In fact, 4QQoh[a] has *śimḥah* for *mišteh* there. The verb *śamaḥ* means to have fun, to pursue pleasures, in the sentence *śᵉmaḥ baḥur bᵉyalduteyka* (11:9). The young man is told to *do* something, not to *feel* something; thus the parallel "follow your heart."

As the following considerations show, *śimḥah* never means happiness in Qohelet. Indeed, the pleasures called *śimḥah* never even seem to produce happiness in him.

(1) Qohelet lists some of the things that constituted his *śimḥah* — food, wine, gardens, singers, concubines, and so on (2:1-8). These are all pleasurable (v. 10). Nevertheless, as Qohelet makes clear in v. 11, they do not yet constitute happiness. Even living with a woman one loves (9:9), though a more significant (and for many, joyful) type of pleasure, does not seem to constitute happiness in Qohelet's eyes. It is just one recommendation among several, including food, wine, oil, and clean clothes.

(2) Qohelet himself had a great deal of *śimḥah,* as he testifies (2:10), but little happiness, as he shows.

(3) Qohelet could not reasonably call happiness or joy inane, absurd, and unproductive (2:1-2). Happiness and joy are inherently desirable states, whereas pleasure can be hollow.

(4) There is no need to urge people to be happy; everyone wants happiness. On the other hand, urging people to embrace *pleasure* and calling this the best thing available in life is not a truism. To the contrary, this proposition is disputable and can be affirmed only by insisting on the worthlessness of much else that is commonly deemed valuable and conducive to happiness.

(5) It is in any case pointless to *advise* happiness ("Just be happy!"), because happiness is not something people can impose upon themselves. They can choose to indulge in pleasures and to take in the experience, and perhaps they can even choose to have fun, but they cannot make themselves happy at will. On the other hand, the advice to undertake pleasurable activities *can* be carried out. One can indulge in such things even when the heart is heavy. Qohelet is a "preacher of pleasure" — not because he is a hedonist who relishes sensual delights, but because, *faute de mieux,* pleasure remains *ṭob,* "good," whatever its inadequacies.

§7.4. *Ṭob* (Noun, Verb, and Adjective) "Good," "Pleasure"

Ṭob (or *ṭobah*[10]) is the word of positive evaluation Qohelet uses most frequently. It means "beneficial," "efficacious,"[11] "virtuous,"[12] and "good fortune," "fortunate."[13] I will here consider those uses that overlap the semantic
field of pleasure.

Goodness can be of any sort, and it is often difficult to determine just
what kind of "goodness" is meant. Elsewhere in the Bible, it rarely refers to
the feelings experienced during merrymaking and feasting. Only in Qohelet
does "to see good" mean to enjoy oneself, but it is not stretching the meaning
of the word to apply it to the enjoyment of food and wine and other diversions. "Good of heart" is often used in this way. This can imply some degree
of inebriation (explicitly in 1 Sam 25:36; 2 Sam 13:28; probably in Judg
16:25; Esth 1:10; and 5:9 [Haman is *śameaḥ wᵉṭob leb*]). Prov 15:15 reverses
the usual cause and effect: "One who is 'good of heart' (merry) has a perpet-
ual 'feast.'"

(1) Noun *Ṭob/Ṭobah:*
    (a) The experience or feeling of pleasure: 4:8;[14] 7:14 (lit. "be in
        good"). *Ṭob* has this sense in the phrase *ra'ah (bᵉ)ṭob,* lit. "see
        good" = experience enjoyment: 2:1; 3:13; 5:17; 6:6; 2:24
        (her'ah 'et napšo ṭob).
    (b) Pleasurable things, the activities and means of pleasure: 3:12
        (la'ăśot ṭob "do pleasurable things"); 5:10 (*ṭobah* = "goods,
        valuables"); 6:3 (one should get satisfaction "from the *ṭobah*").
(2) Adjective:
    (a) "Pleasing": 2:26 (twice) and 7:26 (pleasing to God); 11:7
        ("pleasing to the eyes").
    (b) "Pleased," "merry": 9:7 ("a merry heart").
(3) Verb:

10. There is no discernible difference in meaning between the masculine and feminine. I will use the masculine for both.
    11. Qoh 2:3, 24; 3:12, 22; 4:6, 9; 5:4, 17a; 6:9, 12; 7:1, 2, 3, 5, 8a, 8b, 11, 18; 8:15;
9:16 (or "virtuous"?), 18a (or "virtuous"?); 11:6. The verbal equivalent of *ṭob* in this sense
is *yiyṭab,* "to benefit (intran.)," "be improved" (cf. 7:3b).
    12. Virtuous person: 9:2 (twice); virtuous (behavior): 7:2; 12:14.
    13. Noun: 7:14; 8:12, 13; 9:18b; adjective: 4:3, 9, 13; 6:3b; 7:10; 9:4.
    14. *Mᵉhasser 'et napši miṭṭobah* is equivalent to *mana'ti 'et libbi mikkol śimḥah*
(2:10). This might be the sense in 6:3 as well. But since *ṭobah* does not elsewhere have the
article when it means pleasure, it probably means "goods" in 6:3, as in 5:10.

"Give pleasure," in *y^eṭib^eka libb^eka* = "let your heart give you pleasure" 11:9.

Qohelet makes no distinction between *ṭob* and *śimḥah* when they designate good feelings and experiences. (*Tob* can also mean moral goodness, where *śimḥah* would not apply [7:20; 9:2, twice]. Also *ṭob* can mean "better" in comparisons, as in 3:22; 4:3, 6, 9; and often.) Elsewhere in the HB *ṭob* often means "pleasurable," "pleasant" (sc., to the senses), e.g., Gen 41:5; Prov 24:13; Cant 1:3; see BDB, p. 373b. In Esth 9:19, *yom ṭob* is synonymous with *śimḥah umišteh* (cf. v. 22). Similarly *ṭub lebab* ("goodness of heart," "cheer"; = *śimḥah* in Deut 28:47); *ṭob leb* in Judg 16:25 (the merriment of feasting and intoxication); 1 Sam 25:36 (the merriment of drunkenness); *ṭob . . . l^ema'ăkal* ("good to eat") (Gen 3:6).

§7.5. *Ś^eḥoq* "Laughter," "Merriment"

Ś^eḥoq basically means "laughter," as in 3:4 and 7:3. In 7:6 *ś^eḥoq* refers to the sound of laughter and is compared to the noise of crackling thorns. It also signifies, *pars pro toto,* the noise of merrymaking, parallel to the "song" of fools (v. 5).

By a further extension, *ś^eḥoq* becomes a metonymy for "amusement," "merriment." "Laughter" is too restricted a translation for the word in 10:19: "For *ś^eḥoq* they prepare food . . . ," because feasting is a requisite of merrymaking, not of laughter. In 2:2, *ś^eḥoq* refers to pleasures such as described in 2:4-8.

Ś^eḥoq is not necessarily trivial gaiety or frivolous diversion. It includes this but much more as well. The *ś^eḥoq* of the returning exiles, for example (Ps 126:2; cf. Job 8:21), is an expression of a joy as deep and worthy as any called *śimḥah*. *Ś^eḥoq* cannot be contrasted with *śimḥah* as trivial gaiety versus deeper happiness.[15]

15. A number of commentators draw this contrast in discussing 2:2. Crenshaw regards *ś^eḥoq* and *śimḥah* as two poles, "frivolity and profound joy," with Qohelet's experiment "running from the one extreme to the other." Ginsberg sees a similar antithesis. Barton believes that "unrestrained merriment is represented by laughter [i.e., *ś^eḥoq*] and pleasure in general by 'joy' [i.e., *śimḥah*]" (p. 79).

Glasser (1970:46) extracts the following out of the word *ś^eḥoq:* "Laughter is to be understood in the pejorative sense it has in 7:3, 6. It is the dissipated, stupefying, and entirely superficial life of the fool, who has never reflected on the enigma of the human condition, or who simply manifests his unawareness of what is serious in life." ("Le rire est à entendre au sens péjoratif qu'il a en 7,3.6; c'est la vie dissipée, étourdissante et toute

In 2:2, $s^e\dot{h}oq$ and $sim\dot{h}ah$ refer to the same types of pleasures and are alike judged senseless. Qohelet has some harsh things to say about certain manifestations of $s^e\dot{h}oq$. The $s^e\dot{h}oq$ — actual laughter — of fools is irritating and meaningless (7:6), but that is because it is the fool's. When the rich prepare food and wine for their amusement (10:19), it is neither their feasting nor their merriment that is contemptible, but only their excess: they start in the morning and drink to drunkenness. Observe that in this verse, $s^e\dot{h}oq$ is what *food* — a necessity — produces, while wine — an inebriant — is said to cause $sim\dot{h}ah$ ($y^e\acute{s}ammah$). This is the opposite of what we would expect if $s^e\dot{h}oq$ was inherently more frivolous or immoderate than $sim\dot{h}ah$.

§7.6. Śaba' (Noun and Verb) "Satisfaction," "Get Satisfaction"

In Qohelet, as elsewhere in the Bible, the verb $\acute{s}aba'$ means both (1) "derive satisfaction from, enjoy," when it governs *min,* "from" and (2) "be satisfied, sated," "get enough of," so that one does not desire any more, when it governs a direct object. The noun has corresponding uses. There are too few occurrences of $\acute{s}aba'$ *min* to determine whether the distinction is systematic.[16] Recognition of this dual meaning is present also in the English word "satisfaction." Deriving satisfaction from something (1) is, in Qohelet's opinion, possible (6:3), while being satisfied (2) is not (4:8; 5:9; cf. 6:7). This distinction corresponds to the one between *heleq,* something one derives from toil, and *yitron,* a true profit.

(1) "Derive satisfaction from": Qohelet says that a toiler has wasted his life if "his appetite does not get satisfaction from [*lo' tiśba' min*] his goods" (6:3), implying that this result is both desirable and possible. It is equivalent to "experiencing pleasure [*ra'ah tobah*]" (6:6).

(2) "Be satisfied, sated": $\acute{s}aba'$ in this sense is synonymous with "be full," as in 6:7, "but the appetite is never filled." This is the meaning in 1:8b, where *tiśba'* governs the infinitive as a direct object: *lo' tiśba' 'ayin lir'ot,*

---

superficielle de l'insensé, lequel n'a jamais réfléchi à l'énigme de la condition humaine ou tout simplement manifeste son inconscience du sérieux de la vie."

16. $\acute{S}aba'$ used absolutely or with a direct object almost always means "be sated, have one's fill (of something)," to the point of not desiring more; e.g., Gen 25:8; Exod 16:12; Isa 1:11; 2 Chr 31:10; Mic 6:14; and often. Possible exceptions are Ps 17:15 and Prov 5:10, where $\acute{s}aba'$ + dir. obj. may mean "derive satisfaction from." $\acute{S}aba'$ *min* means either "derive satisfaction from" (e.g., Isa 66:11) or "be sated," "have one's fill" (e.g., Ps 104:13; Job 19:22; Prov 1:31; 14:14).

"The eye is not sated with seeing" — can never get enough of it. The toiler works endlessly, yet *ʿeyno loʾ tiśbaʿ ʿošer* "his eye is never sated with wealth" (4:8). (Hence he is always driven to struggle for more.) One who loves money — seeking it as an end rather than as a means — *loʾ yiśbaʿ kesep,* "will not be sated with silver" (5:9). The corresponding nominal use is *haśśabaʿ,* a surfeit of property, "wealth" (5:11).

CHAPTER 8

Toil and Pleasure

> One does not discover the absurd without being tempted to write
> a manual of happiness.
>
> Camus, Myth, p. 90

§8.1. The Contradiction

Qohelet toiled and grew rich, and his wealth purchased the means of pleasure. He set out to examine pleasure (2:1a), for this could be "what is good for a man to do under the heavens during the few days of his life" (2:3b). He states in advance what he found:

> But I realized that this too is absurd. Of amusement [$s^e\dot{h}oq$] I said, "Inane!" and of pleasure, "What does this accomplish?" (2:1b-2)

But he is getting ahead of himself. He first tries out various pleasures, and he comes to a happier result:

> (2:10) Whatever my eyes saw I did not withhold from them. I did not restrain my heart from any sort of pleasure, and my heart received pleasure from all my toil, and this was my portion from all my toil.

But quickly he seems to change his mind:

(2:11) But when I turned (to consider) all the things my hands had done and the toil I had laboriously performed, I realized that it was all absurd and senseless and that there is no profit under the sun.

But 2:11 does not cancel v. 10. *Śimḥah* is still good. In fact, "There is nothing better for a man <than> to eat and drink and show himself enjoyment through his toil" (2:24; 3:12). Why then is there no profit in life?

Qohelet seems to be in a tangle here. The tangle cannot be undone, but its strands can be described.

§8.2. Tearing Down

Wealth and pleasure have some intrinsic flaws, but these are not the main target of Qohelet's complaints. He values wealth for supplying the means of pleasure and is grieved at the thought of its loss. Property gained through toil is tainted by the aches and frustrations of the labors, but wealth and the pleasures it can buy are not intrinsically absurd or senseless, not even "worthless" or "vain." If they were, their gain would not be a sign of God's favor or their loss evidence of his displeasure.

The true target of Qohelet's anger when he criticizes pleasure is toil. Pleasure is good but not good *enough* to redeem toil. How does toil fail?

(1) Toil is unpleasant, even oppressive (2:22f.), almost by definition. By choosing a term freighted with dreary overtones to designate human endeavors, Qohelet is prejudging the issue (§6.1f.). Then he associates other words for activity with *'amal* so as to prejudge them all.

To be sure, he does distinguish, though inconsistently, *ma'ăśeh* from *'amal* — work from overwork — and he prefers the former (see §8.41). But this does not resolve the contradiction. Pleasure is man's portion in his *toil*, and pleasure is good. *And yet* man has no profit in his toil, and both his toil and his pleasures are absurd.

(2) Toil does not produce adequate compensation for its unpleasantness. For one thing, man is insatiable (4:8; 5:9; 6:7; cf. 1:8), and his gains will never be adequate to his desires. This is man's failing. But there is also a failing inherent in toil: it cannot achieve a profit, by Qohelet's strict definition, and anything less is not enough.

Qohelet makes this clear from the start, by the analogy of nature. Since the prodigious labors of nature accomplish nothing new (1:4-11), surely no human exertions, however protracted or intense, can do so (v. 3). The Catalogue of Times (3:1-8) makes a similar point. Every type of action has its time, which man does not know. Hence straining in one's work has no advantage; it produces no profit.

(3) Whatever toil does produce it cannot secure. Wealth can be lost or go to another person (2:21, 26; 5:13; 6:1f.). This will happen, inevitably and universally, at death (2:18f.; 5:15).

Qohelet is troubled not that the wealth is ephemeral, because so is he. What galls him is his inability to secure the fruits of his toil. Without an exclusive relation between effort and possession, work is defective. The possibility that the recipient of Qohelet's wealth may be a stranger or a fool exacerbates the unfairness but is not the heart of the problem. 2:19aα is parenthetical, and the possibility of the recipient being a fool is not mentioned again.

(4) Toil's best product, pleasure, isn't all that good. The negative judgment in 2:1-2 is not overridden by 2:10 or the other commendations of pleasure. It is sealed by 2:11 and reinforced by 7:2-4, where Qohelet declares it better to be in a house of mourning than in a house of feasting (*beyt mišteh* [7:2] = *beyt śimḥah* [7:4]).

Qohelet does not explain just why he found pleasure unsatisfying and meaningless, except insofar as he hints at it in the exclamatory question, "what does this accomplish?" (or "do") (2:2). Pleasure may be nice, but it leads nowhere. It sweetens life's bitterness somewhat, but the sweetener is not a profit. (Think of it as saccharin, which tastes sweet but "does nothing.") It is certainly not good enough to redeem human exertions from their absurdity. Pleasure is pleasant, and that is the end of the story. Diversions of all sorts, however legitimate, crackle with emptiness. Pleasurable feelings don't suffice for Qohelet. If he were a hedonist, they would.

§8.3. Some Harmonizations

Before turning to the positive side of work and pleasure, we should consider a common way of reconciling the two judgments, namely the drawing of various distinctions between two types of *śimḥah,* one commended, the other condemned.

(1) Frivolous versus Deep?

A distinction often drawn is between foolish, trivial, or degenerate forms of amusement (supposedly the objects of the investigation and repudiation in 2:1-11) and pleasures of a deeper, quieter sort, which are more conducive to happiness. C. D. Ginsburg expresses a common understanding when he says that Qohelet is denouncing "pleasure and mirth" while allowing "innocent cheerfulness and pleasure" (p. 276). Zimmerli labels the deficient pleasures the "blind self-surrender to joy" ("das blinde Sich-Hingeben an die Freude"; p. 157).

In fact, the pleasures Qohelet disparages in 2:1-2, describes in vv. 4-9, and indirectly judges absurd in v. 11, are his portion (v. 10), and they do not differ from those he lauds elsewhere. He uses the same words for both: *śimḥah, ṭob, ra'ah bᵉṭob,* and *ḥeleq bᵉʿamal* (2:1, 2, 10). Even *śᵉḥoq* (v. 2), while not used in the positive passages, does not in itself designate trivial mirth (§7.5). And the *śimḥah* Qohelet condemns in 2:2 and describes in vv. 4-9 does not differ qualitatively from the *śimḥah* he commends to the reader elsewhere.

The diversions described in 2:4-9 are not indecorous or particularly shallow. They are all reasonable forms of enjoyment, indisputably legitimate for a king who earned his wealth through work and wisdom. The enjoyment of wine too is permissible and recommended. Its anesthetic value is appreciated by Proverbs (31:6f.), and Qohelet himself endorses it (9:7). ("Drinking" [2:24; 3:13; etc.] refers to wine and possibly beer.) The sages, of course, censured excess in eating and drinking, as Qohelet does in 10:17 and 19, but nothing suggests that Qohelet got drunk or advises doing so. To be sure, the MT of 2:3 says that he decided to "take hold of folly" until he could discover what is good for a man to do. But this cannot mean that the *śimḥah* described in vv. 4-8 was a special type of pleasure, namely foolish ones, for if those deeds were foolish, then his conclusion in v. 10 would mean that man's portion and best course was *foolish* pleasure, since the amusements he calls his portion in v. 10 are none other than those described in vv. 4-10.

(2) Passively Received versus Actively Pursued?

Another harmonization (proposed by Hertzberg; similarly Lauha) distinguishes two types of pleasures according to the way they are obtained. Foolish pleasures, "the way of folly" (p. 86), are reflective, that is to say, deliberately pursued, whereas wise pleasures are nonreflective: they are not pursued as a goal but bestowed by God on a passive recipient. This distinction too is unjustified, because some of the passages that recommend pleasure speak of it as coming from toil, although in Hertzberg's terms this pleasure is "reflective" and should be repudiated. Excessive striving can, to be sure, hinder enjoyment of pleasures, but this is because the toiler *neglects* to make enjoyment an immediate goal, not because he aims at it. This is the reverse of what should be the case according to Hertzberg.

Zimmerli and Hertzberg describe the rejected type of pleasure in contrary terms. But neither description is to the point, because Qohelet does not distinguish two types of pleasure. Enjoying what one has is a wise course and deliberate goal. Though some people are lucky enough to have pleasures drop into their lap without pursuing them, the pursuit of pleasures in itself, provided it is not excessive, need not prevent their enjoyment. One must just pause to savor them.

(3) Practical versus Absolute?

Gordis recognizes that it is ordinary physical pleasure that Qohelet describes and recommends in 2:1-10. Gordis, however, believes that Qohelet "denies that pleasure is an adequate goal in life, in the *absolute* or philosophical sense — but it remains the only *practical* program for human existence" (p. 216). Pleasure falls short because it is not an "enduring good" (p. 139). Barton too regards pleasure's brevity as its true failing (p. 47, and see his comments on 2:1-11 and 2:24). But, contrary to this harmonization, Qohelet is not holding out for an "absolute" or permanent good and rejecting whatever is transitory. He is not *that* demanding. He is looking for anything that is good in this life, "under the heavens" (2:3). To say that something is "inane" and "absurd" and "achieves nothing" does not merely mean that it falls short of absolute value.[1] Of course Qohelet commends pleasure as a "practical good," but this label does not reduce the conflict between the two judgments. The pleasures called inane in 2:1-2 are, after all, the product of a practical program, an attempt to find out "what is good for man to do" (2:3b). They are not "absolute" or "philosophical" values.

§8.4. Building Up

Just because man cannot earn enough does not mean that he cannot earn *anything*. Work can, or at least may, provide the means of pleasure — and pleasure, Qohelet concedes, is good.

---

1. Gordis paraphrases Qohelet's negative judgment on pleasure as a flaccid demurral: "He then discovers that pleasure is no more satisfactory than wisdom as an attainable goal" (p. 139). But pleasure surely *is* an attainable goal (2:10), as is wisdom of some sorts (see 1:16).

§8.41. How to Work

Since man must work, he should do so in moderation, within the constraints placed upon him. Qohelet recommends "passive," receptive sorts of behavior, ones that flow with the stream rather than swimming against it. This is the message of his teachings on how to approach work.

This is the positive side of the Catalogue of Times in 3:1-9, whose negative side, the inefficacy of toil, was discussed earlier. Every type of action and occurrence has its time. Success requires performing the action in *its* time, adjusting to the constraints of events. For Qohelet, these constraints deprive toil of profit (3:9; cf. 3:14f.). Yet as a *modus vivendi,* one can try to live within them. (See the introduction to 3:1-15 in the commentary.)

Qohelet has a cluster of pointers on how to get along in one's work in 11:1-6: Try various possibilities, help out various people, because you do not know how the game of chance will play out (11:1-2). What will be, will be (v. 3), so don't waste time speculating about the future (v. 4). You are ignorant of God's plans (v. 5), so do what you must do at a variety of times, which is to say, in a variety of ways. His advice is analogous to recommending diversification of investments on the grounds that it is impossible to outguess the stock market. One of your investments might pay off (v. 6), though you can't know which. In sum, don't try harder, don't attempt to outguess God, just wager on various possibilities, invest your assets and labor (in moderation) in many different ventures, and let the flow of events do what it will with them. But mainly (he goes on to say), take hold of pleasure when you can.

Qohelet's criticism of toil is not a recommendation of inactivity, a withdrawal from the world of business and thought. There are two ways to go wrong in labor: by sitting immobile and destroying oneself (4:5), and by toiling and worrying day and night (4:6). Both are folly. One should go about one's business in inner repose, *naḥat* (4:6), working in a measured way: "All that you are able to do, do <in accordance with> your strength [<k>*ᵉkoḥăka*]" (9:10a), without excessive calculations (11:3-4). But you should not overdo it, that would be *ʿamal*. Qohelet's attitude is similar to that of Prov 10:22: "The Lord's blessing is what makes one rich, and straining [*ʿeṣeb*] adds nothing to it." God does not wish passivity, but one cannot push beyond the blessing he grants. To attempt to do so is hubris.

That is not to say that Qohelet's "solution" is just to take it easy. Taking it easy is not really something one can choose to do. Qohelet feels that some people — he has himself in mind — are driven to incessantly strive for more, whether of wisdom or wealth (6:7). Qohelet is aware that he is laboring for no one's benefit (4:8) yet finds himself unable to stop. Since the activity (*'inyan*) of constant, fruitless striving is "given" to the "offender" by God himself (2:26), there is little hope of escape. Yet perhaps one can moderate the intensity of his efforts.

Qohelet does counsel moderation in work, but that does not solve his problem any more than his commendation of pleasure does. He usually places all efforts in the category of *'amal,* even when he uses the less freighted term *ma'ăśeh* (2:10, 11; 3:22). Worse, Qohelet seems determined to view all life's efforts — indeed, life itself — as *'amal* (§6.12). He is not only warning against overwork, against struggling day and night to get rich. All human effort, life itself, is drudgery. Qohelet uses *'amal* to characterize human efforts so as to tarnish them with the somber overtones of that word.

§8.42. Enjoying Life

Qohelet is by no means a "preacher of joy," as Whybray calls him (1982). That is not what Qohelet means by *śimḥah* and *śeḥoq* (§§7.3; 7.5). He does not speak of *'ośer* or *gil,* terms that unequivocally have that sense. But he does have affirmative things to say about pleasure, the product of toil. It is "good" (2:24; 3:12, 22; 5:17; 8:15). It is man's "portion" (2:10; 5:17; 9:9). It is what God wants man to do (9:7). It is God's gift (2:24, 26; 3:13; 5:18). Indeed, pleasure is the *best* thing in life (3:22). He goes so far as to say (in hyperbole) that it is the *only* good thing:

> So I praised pleasure, because there is nothing good [*'eyn ṭob*] for man under the sun but [*ki 'im*] to eat, drink, and experience pleasure [*liśmoaḥ*]. . . . (8:15a; cf. 3:12)

However long one lives, if he has not experienced pleasure, he is no better off than the stillbirth (6:3). This implies the converse, that the life of one who does experience pleasure is at least a bit better than nonexistence. Therefore Qohelet recommends the enjoyment of pleasures throughout life (11:7), but especially in youth, because the ability to enjoy oneself fades as one grows old (11:9–12:1). Qohelet's endorsement of pleasure is especially expansive in 9:7-9: eat and drink in pleasure, wear white garments, anoint yourself with oil, and enjoy life with a beloved woman, for this is what God wants you to do (v. 7b). After all, he made it possible. But we must still ask why Qohelet considers it *good.*

One benefit of pleasure that Qohelet mentions is distraction: a man who tastes the fruits of his labor "will not much call to mind the days of his life, since God is keeping him occupied [reading *maʿănēhû*] with his heart's pleasure" (5:19). Pleasure anesthetizes the pain of consciousness. This seems to be the unspoken reasoning in 8:15 as well. To be sure, this remedy did not work for Qohelet. But Qohelet can recommend to others an escape that he seems constitutionally denied. He does not return to this line of reasoning except to counter it in 7:2, and it does not play an important role in his thought.

Another reason that pleasure is "good" is that it *feels* good. This is the point of Qohelet's argument by testimonial, in which he declares that he "found" or "realized" *(maṣaʾ)* that pleasure is good (cf. 3:12, 22; 5:17; 8:15). There is a certain circularity in testifying that *śimḥah* is good, since *ṭob* is often used as a synonym (§7.4), to denote agreeable sensory experience (2:1; 3:13; 5:17; etc.). This usage makes the praise of pleasure sound self-evident: experiencing *ṭob* is *ṭob*. This tactic may be Qohelet's way of convincing himself as well as others.

Yet, apart from this word play, it is not self-evident or tautological to say that pleasures (*śimḥah* in the sense of pleasurable things) feel good or are good. Fun is not always really good, really gratifying. A person may be eating and drinking and displaying merriment at a party while suffering melancholy and knowing well that the fun is hollow, even ridiculous: "Even in merriment [*śᵉḥoq*] the heart may ache," as Prov 14:13 observes. But then, the very same melancholy that soured the fun may bring the party-goer to a "positive" conclusion: Since everything in life is so dreary, surface pleasures are, all in all, the best available option. Qohelet's ambivalence is of this sort. Toil, pleasure, and life itself are absurd but not without their good aspects.

The most important reason Qohelet gives for enjoying life's pleasures is that this is man's portion, his *heleq*. Qohelet says this several times, for example in 3:22: "And I saw that there is nothing better than that a man take pleasure in his works, *for that is his portion,* for who can enable him to see what will happen afterwards?" And "Enjoy life with a woman you love during all your absurd days that God gives you under the sun, all your absurd days, for this is your portion in life and in your toil at which you labor under the sun" (9:9; similarly 5:17). Other verses imply that it is beneficial to have a portion (2:10, 21; 5:18).

The fact that an experience is one's portion is, for Qohelet, a reason why it *should* be embraced. To understand the force of this reasoning we should consider what themes lead into the exhortations to enjoy life; these are:

(1) The unfair distribution of rewards. This happens when one man toils and another ends up with his wealth (2:20-23), or a man earns wealth

then suddenly loses it (5:12-16). It occurs also when fates are not commensurate with moral deserts (8:14).

(2) Human ignorance, as seen in man's inability to understand what God brings to pass (3:10-11) and in human ignorance of what follows death (3:21).

(3) Death itself, which eliminates human distinctiveness (3:19-20), erases all trace of the once-living (9:5-10), and extends to eternity (11:7-10).

The common denominator in all these reflections is human helplessness. People do not control their fate, during life or thereafter. They cannot secure wealth by hard work or assure long life by righteousness. They are blind to the future and cannot plan for it. They cannot hold on to existence or even traces of it. Control of wealth, knowledge, and life is not man's portion.

To be a portion by Qohelet's implicit definition, something must be at least temporarily in the owner's possession and *under his control*. Pleasure is a portion but *one must take it*. When Qohelet's frustration at human helplessness peaks, he urges taking one's portion, pleasure. This is almost a counsel of despair. We cannot do much, we control next to nothing, but this at least we *can* do and can *choose* to do. If God allows us the means of pleasure, we can elect to enjoy it. Qohelet counsels a true carpe diem: seize the moment, experience what you have while you have it. Since God allows it, it must be what he wants, and refusing to take the gift would be to deny his will.

Of course, God must make it possible to take the pleasure. The reminder that this is a gift of God is frequently joined to pleasure-advice (2:25; 3:13; 5:18; 9:7). This means that God determines who will have the potential for pleasure, not that he induces the experience of pleasure or instills the psychological predisposition for it.[2] God operates on externals. According to 2:24, eating and drinking and "showing (oneself) enjoyment [*ṭob*] through one's toil" is "from the hand of God." The way God gives these things is explained in v. 26: he turns over a toiler's earnings to a fortunate recipient. The nature of God's gift is defined also in 5:18: "Furthermore, if God gives anyone wealth and property and enables him [*hišliṭo*] to partake of it [*le'ĕkol mimmennu*] and to take his portion [*wᵉlaśe't 'et ḥelqo*] and to get pleasure in his toil — that is a gift of God." God's gift lies in *enabling* a man to experience enjoyment. Qoh 6:2, by describing the opposite of this happy situation,

2. Schwienhorst-Schönberger (1996:277) says that Qohelet, in contrast to traditional wisdom, insists that God is not only the giver of good things but also the one who makes their enjoyment possible. This is true only in the sense that God may or may not take them away from a man, not in the sense of controlling the predisposition or inclination to experience pleasure and happiness or not.

shows that God's "enabling" a man to consume his wealth means simply that God does not take it away from him. God neither imposes nor blocks the experience of pleasure in one's possessions as long as they are held. Divine determination does not penetrate the inner experience.[3] *That* is man's realm. That is where he finds his portion.

Qoh 7:14 encapsulates the rule of inner freedom: *bᵉyom ṭobah hĕyeh bᵉṭob*, "in a day of good fortune, enjoy the good." When you find yourself in good circumstances, enjoy them — literally, "be in good." The covert rhetoric of the paronomasia equates the two phenomena called *ṭob*. But good fortune does not guarantee enjoyment. In a good day we will be "in good" only if we put ourselves there. The first "good" in the sentence is not in our control; the second is.

For similar reasons, Qohelet praises other experiences besides pleasure. In 9:7-10, he recommends pleasure as man's portion, then expands the scope of this recommendation to all activities, including mental ones. He urges the reader to perform, in accordance with his ability, whatever he undertakes, on the grounds that there is no activity in Sheol, neither in deed *(maʿăśeh)* nor in thought *(ḥešbon, daʿat,* and *ḥokmah)*. He recommends these pursuits not because they are necessarily rewarding or pleasing (they are not), but because they are what you have *now*. You *can* work, even if one day you lose what you gain. You *can* think and calculate, even if you cannot find the answers. These potentials, whatever their flaws, are human powers. They define our humanness, and they will soon evaporate.

Pleasure is the best of man's portions, but it is not the only one. Love, hate, and jealousy are also the "portions" of the living (9:6). Love is commendable (4:9-12; 9:9), but the other two emotions are not. Nevertheless, 9:4-6 implies that even *their* cessation at death is regrettable. Even disagreeable experiences such as these, as well as the ponderous consciousness of mortality, in some way constitute an advantage of the living over the dead, "for the living know they will die, while the dead know nothing and no longer have any recompense, for their memory is forgotten." To live is to possess the *potential* for knowing.

Pleasure, like the gesticulations of a lunatic, may be senseless, but for the lunatic it makes sense to gesticulate. These actions have some sort of meaning in his private, circumscribed world, and he seems somehow compelled to make them. They are *his*. In Qohelet's eyes, even normal people are

---

3. Qoh 3:14b does not show otherwise, for it is to be translated, "And God has done (this) so that people will fear him"; see the commentary. Qoh 5:19 (as emended) means that God distracts a man by allowing him the means for distracting himself.

mad (9:3), and their actions are no more meaningful. But these actions are their portion, and it is fitting that they embrace them.

This explanation does not eliminate the contradiction, because if something is beneficial, it does make sense, it does "do" something, and most people would consider this a "profit." But Qohelet demands more.

Qohelet's affirmation of the intrinsic value of willed experience is at odds with his stated preference for oblivion in 4:3 and distraction in 5:19. He is ambivalent about experience just as he is about the value of life itself. Is it better to live and taste life's bitterness or to be dead and at peace in the void? Just as Qohelet chooses life though he is sometimes tempted by death, so he chooses awareness though he is sometimes tempted by oblivion. He ends up affirming awareness as the substance of consciousness and the arena of human freedom.

> . . . it is clear that death and the absurd are here the principles of the only reasonable freedom: that which a human heart can experience and live. (Camus, *Myth,* p. 44)[4]

---

4. Camus is speaking of the condemned man, who, on the morning of his execution, is possessed of "that unbelievable disinterestedness with regard to everything except for the pure flame of life" (p. 44).

CHAPTER 9

The End of the Matter[1]

I want to know whether, accepting a life without appeal, one can also agree to work and create without appeal and what is the way leading to these liberties.

Camus, *Myth,* p. 83

§9.1. Meaning: Loss and Recovery

The book of Qohelet is about meaning. What unites all of Qohelet's complaints is the collapse of meaning. What unites all of his counsels and affirmations is the attempt to reconstruct meanings.

Qohelet is frustrated that life cannot be "read," that the multiplicity of disjointed deeds and events cannot be drawn together into a coherent narrative with its own significance. Qohelet's other complaints are secondary to the failure of meaning. He is not primarily lamenting the brevity of life, the futility of work, the pervasiveness of injustice, or the vanity of worldly goods and pleasures. He does observe these things and complain about them, but he does so mainly to demonstrate and strengthen his main grievance: the irrationality of the world we find ourselves in. From this flow all human limitations — and limitation is humanity's earmark. But even while observing this, Qohelet tries to rebuild — at least in part, at least locally.

1. See the commentary on 12:13a.

133

The Viennese psychiatrist Viktor Frankl developed a philosophy of healing called logotherapy. He was forced to put it to the ultimate test as prisoner #119104 in the Nazi slave-labor camps. Logotherapy teaches that humans have a basic *will to meaning,* and that they can bear up under incredible afflictions if they believe that their life has meaning, which is to say that they have a vocation or mission in life, something that needs doing and that *they* can do. The loss of this sense of meaning leaves a vacuum, the well-known "existential vacuum."[2] And how better to say "existential vacuum" in Biblical Hebrew than *hebel,* "vapor"?

§9.2. Qohelet's Soul

Qohelet is a man of faith, who trusts in God and his justice. He is also a man of doubt, who knows the realities that violate his belief. Yet he insists on "taking hold of the one while not letting go of the other."

The contradictions that Qohelet observes are antinomies, two contradictory but supposedly valid principles. How then can he assert them, which means affirming both sides of the contradiction? Early commentators had trouble believing that he could make statements denying the preeminence of wisdom or the reliability of divine justice. Modern commentators find it harder to credit him with the affirmations of wisdom and avowals of divine justice.

Even without systematically harmonizing the text, the reader tends to push Qohelet to one side or another, because the Western model of rational assent regards consistency as a primary truth test. But Qohelet continues to straddle two views of reality, wavering uncomfortably but honestly between them. If it seems impossible that Qohelet could hold both at once, that he could remain divided against himself, consider that this is the condition of many believers nowadays.

It would be a greater cause for surprise if Qohelet did *not* hold to the affirmative, apparently conventional beliefs that constitute one side of the antinomies. These beliefs are perceptual frames, models of reality belonging to his inherited world-construction; they are the way he sees the world. From social inheritance and from the endless sifting of individual experience, all humans hold mental models that guide perception and thought

2. Frankl has written eloquently on logotherapy and his own experience in *Man's Search for Meaning* (1962), *The Doctor and the Soul* (1963), and *The Will to Meaning* (1969).

(J. Bruner 1986:47). These models allow us to register and organize the massive and incessant flow of details that enter our consciousness without our having to devote full attention to them all, insofar as the input conforms to the models. The models are structures of expectations. Occasionally our expectations are violated so frequently, or so inescapably, that we must modify or even replace our models. One *can* move away from inherited perceptual frames, but it is no surprise when one does not do so. Qohelet does so only in part.

Qohelet's peculiar logic cannot be explained entirely in terms of philosophical choices. There are qualities of temperament that make him look where he looks and see what he sees. (I speak of the temperament of Qohelet, who is a fictional persona, not the author's. For the distinction, see Excursus III. But the author knew whereof he was writing.) These qualities are perfectly captured by William James's classic distinction between two religious temperaments, the "healthy minded" and the "sick soul," in *The Varieties of Religious Experience* (1902:77-162). It must be stressed that James uses these terms non-judgmentally, and it turns out that it is the "sick souls" he really esteems, for it is they who can push forward to a more profound and fervent religious belief, while the healthy minded are content to stay right where they are. James himself placed Qohelet among the sick souls. I will quote at length from James's description of this temperament (the subject of Lectures VI and VII), because it is an incomparable description of Qohelet's mind-set.

"Healthy mindedness" is "the tendency which looks on all things and sees that they are good" (p. 86). The religion of the healthy minded person

> . . . directs him to settle his scores with the more evil aspects of the universe by systematically declining to lay them to heart or make much of them, by ignoring them in his reflective calculations, or even, on occasion, by denying outright that they exist. (p. 125)

On the other side stands

> a radically opposite view, a way of maximizing evil, if you please so to call it, based on the persuasion that the evil aspects of our life are of its very essence, and that the world's meaning most comes home to us when we lay them most to heart. (p. 129)

For the healthy minded, evil (meaning misfortune as well as wickedness) is incidental and accidental, and thus curable in the mortal sphere, while for the sick soul evil is radical and essential. It cannot be cured by any alteration of circumstances or displaced by simple happiness in life. For the sick soul,

> [t]o ascribe religious value to mere happy-go-lucky contentment with one's brief chance at natural good is but the very consecration of forgetfulness and superficiality. Our troubles lie too deep for *that* cure. The fact that we *can* die, that we *can* be ill at all, is what perplexes us; the fact that we now for a moment live and are well is irrelevant to that perplexity. (p. 137)

Whatever solutions or accommodations one may come up with, death trumps them all. James quotes Qohelet himself as the epitome of this attitude:

> Back of everything is the great spectre of universal death, the all-encompassing blackness: —
>
> "What profit hath a man in all his labour which he taketh under the Sun? I looked on all the works that my hands had wrought, and behold, all was vanity and vexation of spirit. For that which befalleth the sons of men befalleth beasts; as the one dieth, so dieth the other; all are of the dust, and all turn to dust again. . . . The dead know not anything, neither have they any more a reward; for the memory of them is forgotten. Also their love and their hatred and their envy is now perished; neither have they any more a portion for ever in anything that is done under the Sun. . . . Truly the light is sweet, and a pleasant thing it is for the eyes to behold the Sun: but if a man live many years and rejoice in them all, yet let him remember the days of darkness; for they shall be many."
>
> In short, life and its negation are beaten up inextricably together. But if the life be good, the negation of it must be bad. Yet the two are equally essential facts of existence; and all natural happiness thus seems infected with a contradiction. The breath of the sepulchre surrounds it. (pp. 136f.)

Qohelet looks at life and sees darkness, but he also glimpses some lights sparkling within it.

§9.3. Qohelet's God

Qohelet's God is a hard ruler. He shows the world a steely countenance. He does not seem to love mankind, nor does Qohelet seem to love *him*. Qohelet

136

fears God, certainly, but without warmth or fellowship. His God is unpredictable. He lays down the rules and judges those who transgress them, but he does so inconsistently and, from the human perspective at least, rather erratically.

God runs the world like a distant monarch ruling a minor province. The ruler must be feared, not cherished. His subjects await his decisions nervously. He may expropriate one subject's property and give it to a favorite. Disobey him and he will harm you. Obey him and you'll be spared harm. Maybe. Renege on what you owe him and he'll punish you in kind. He offers little aid or assistance to his subjects.

God does lay down the laws of the kingdom. These laws constitute a static world order that man cannot alter. God allows no changes in his realm. Man may push and strain against the barriers but cannot budge them, any more than an icon in a video game can rewrite the software that generates its world.

God assigns man tasks. He sets him to the quintessentially human chore of trying to understand the world, yet he deprives him of adequate tools for the job. He imposes on man a life of toil without real profit. If the toil does bear fruit, God may let the worker enjoy it, or he may take it away in a "bad business" and give it to someone else.

One does not turn to such a God for aid or comfort. Qohelet never says we should call upon God, whether to beseech him for help or vindication or to protest about wrongs done us. "I, I the Lord am your comforter," Isaiah's God says (51:12). In Qohelet, the oppressed have no comforter, none at all.

What is one to do in such a realm? Mainly, look inward to find one's own strengths and to savor pleasant feelings. Man is an actor playing a bit-part in a great drama whose script he cannot change. His freedom is interior.

Daniel's world, too, especially in the visions in chapters 7–12, is a drama scripted in advance, but man's role there is clearer, to keep faith while terrifying historical forces rage about him. The visions of Daniel were written against the backdrop of the mammoth empires of the Seleucids and Ptolemies, a time of titanic forces and human impotence. The book of Qohelet has the same feel but abstracted from history and distant from external oppression. There is the same sense of helplessness, the same tone of resignation, but without the faith in impending deliverance and universal justice.

Qohelet's God is hard and mostly indifferent but not hostile. He has created an orderly world and set things running so that everything has its right and appropriate circumstance. We can be confident that God will act at the right time — for himself if not for us.

God has not entirely deprived man of freedom and happiness. A man can choose how to live his life and how to respond to events as they impinge upon him. God's most congenial quality is that he *wants* man to enjoy himself, to drink of life's sweetness. If you are doing this, it is not because you have wrested a moment of respite from a hostile deity. It is what God wishes you to do. Indeed, he must have *already* chosen this for you (9:7). Knowing this may turn pleasure into happiness.

Though we may be thwarted in our search for understanding, it is God who implanted in us this thirst for knowledge. He has set us to the task of seeking it, and he has given us a mind to pursue it with. He has allowed us wisdom, the most divine of human faculties, however lowly the degree in which we possess it. We can *see.* The lucidity that Camus praises as the first act of rebellion is, for Qohelet, not defiance but conformity to God's will. He has laid on us a hard chore, but it is a lofty one. Sisyphus pushes his rock, after all, upwards.

What was Sisyphus' crime? Many answers are given, but most sources agree that Sisyphus was the trickster of the gods who evaded death by a ruse, and the rock was his punishment. Camus's Sisyphus *wrests* his moment of respite and his lucidity from his toil in defiance of his fate. In Qohelet, man gains his respite and his little pleasures and his flashes of lucidity as God's gift. His rock is not a punishment but the condition of all life, all things, under the sun.

This is an uncomfortable theology, and one need not accept it as valid — the other Biblical authors wouldn't have — but this *is* Qohelet's teaching, and it should not be muted. The truths and teachings of the Bible are not all packed into every book, every source, every verse. All truths are partial, all thinkers inadequate. Qohelet's hard and lonely theology is only one vision of the Infinite. His words should be heard as one tone among the multitude of sounds that together make up the Biblical symphony.

§9.4. A Time to Tear Down: The Subversion of Meaning

The source of Qohelet's dilemma lies in his peculiar *construction* of reality, which perceives contradictoriness in all phenomena. This construction does not arise from noticing some reality unknown to or denied by earlier thinkers, but from a central premise. This premise is unspoken but can be deduced from his expectations. These in turn are revealed by what *violates* them and provokes surprise, dismay, and the *hebel*-judgment.

Qohelet's central premise is that meaningfulness requires that an action or quality X produce the appropriate consequence X', and that not-X *not* produce it. To be appropriate, a consequence must be

(1) immediate (8:10f.)
    If the punishment for an evil deed is not executed in a timely fashion, people are demoralized.
(2) individual (2:18, 26; 6:2)
    The person who earned the wealth, and he alone, must get its enjoyment.
(3) recognizable (8:11)
    People must see justice done.
(4) consistent (8:12a, 14; 6:1; 10:5; and often)
    Even a preponderance of right outcomes would not suffice. The fact that *there are* anomalies undercuts the effect of justice.
(5) final (3:21; 4:15-16)
    The differences achieved by effort or status must not be wiped away by the passage of time.

If a consequence violates these stipulations, it is absurd and senseless. It seems that only a consequence that met such strict criteria would qualify as a *yitron*, a "profit," in Qohelet's eyes, and in the absence of a *yitron*, all human virtues are devoid of meaning. This is true of work, wisdom, and righteousness, the three great areas of human endeavor. Qohelet seems determined to see absurdity everywhere. He posits criteria for meaningfulness so rigorous that almost nothing can meet them. Even if something is good, it can still be absurd.

The foundation of this entire concept of meaningfulness is Qohelet's belief in a deity who, in principle, guarantees the working of right causation. An absolute ruler with absolute powers can and *should* ensure invariable justice. Anomalies cannot be pushed to the periphery, because God's power reaches everywhere. *Everything* that happens is *maʿăśeh haʾĕlohim*. Injustices cannot be explained away by promises of future rectification, because they are unjust *now*, and God *could* rectify them immediately. Wisdom need not fail, for God could guarantee its invariable success. Death need not wipe out differences, because it is God who determines lifespans and could even conquer death.

§9.5. A Time to Build Up: The Reconstruction of Meaning

At the same time that Qohelet is tearing down, he is building up, identifying things that are good, offering maxims and counsels on how to live, suggesting how we can make the best of the bad deal that is life. Tearing down and building up are two movements in Qohelet's thought, but they are not two sequential phases. Toward the end of the book, however, the emphasis is increasingly on the constructive.

"Sickness of soul," as James describes it, is a variety of religious experience, not a pathology, and it is not the end of the road. The sick soul must be "twice born" to find happiness. He must find redemption apart from this world of evil and disorder. Qohelet does not do this. His horizon is confined to the world under the sun. But within these confines he discovers some moments of meaning. These belong to his teaching no less than does the absurdity he reveals, and, in the end, they are what make life worth living. The best Qohelet can offer is some ephemeral, local tactics for coping with the vacuum.

Qohelet set out to discover "what is good for a man to do under the heavens during the few days of his life" (2:3b). He does have some answers to this question, often in the form of maxims. These are not solutions but *accommodations*. The answers come down to embracing the very activities that elsewhere he calls senseless: work and pleasure, wisdom and righteousness. These things are allowed value for the moment only. They allow humans to find good things — *little meanings* — within the vast absurd.

Qohelet calls something "good" if it is better than its alternative. Goodness is relative to the alternative. It is not enough to satisfy Qohelet. It does not redeem the world from absurdity or constitute a profit for man's labor, but it is at least *possible*. Qohelet's stipulations for meaningfulness are not applied to the criterion for goodness. Something need not be the immediate and exclusive consequence of right behavior to be good. For example, the lucky recipient of someone else's earnings (2:26) has something good, even if it isn't exactly a "profit." Likewise, a good thing need not be permanent. Hence a name is good (7:1) though quickly forgotten (2:16). A moment of pleasure is good (2:24), though it might quickly slip away (2:25f.). A good thing need not be secure or invulnerable. Wisdom is neither (9:16f.). It need not even be pleasant. Going to a house of mourning and hearing a rebuke are not (7:2f.). To be good, something just has to be in some way advantageous, a very modest requirement.

Life, Viktor Frankl says, can be made meaningful in three ways:

140

first, through *what we give to life* (in terms of our creative works); second, by *what we take* from the world (in terms of our experiencing values); and third, through the stand we take toward a fate we no longer can change (an incurable disease, an inoperable cancer, or the like). (1969:15)

Qohelet does not consider the first. This may be judged an inadequacy in Qohelet, one that leaves many readers looking for a completion else-where. Qohelet seeks meaning in the second and third ways. In the sec-ond path, Qohelet seeks to find out "what is good for man to do," and he has some suggestions in this regard. The third way is Qohelet's too, though he does not speak from the standpoint of individual tragedy. He sees all humanity as subject to an inescapable fate, compounded of falli-bility, ineffectuality, and mortality.

Qohelet deems several activities and experiences to be good. Others, which he does not happen to call "good" but still praises and recommends, belong in the same category, since they too are advantageous.

Many of Qohelet's affirmations of goodness are in the form of compar-isons: X is better than Y. There are two types of comparison: (1) X is neutral or bad and is called *ṭob* "better" only because Y is worse. The purpose of such comparisons is to denigrate Y. An example is 4:3: those who have not lived are "better than" (that is to say, better off than) the living and the dead. Similarly, refraining from vows is better than vowing but not paying (4:5), and being stillborn is better than living a long but pleasureless life (6:6). Sometimes Y is negative but X is still on the positive side of the scale, if peo-ple have a propensity for Y, as in 6:9, "Better the sight of the eyes than the wandering of the appetite." (2) X has some benefit in itself, and Y too is better than neutral. For example, "A name is better than good oil" and "Better to go to a house of mourning than to go to a house of feasting" (7:2). Com-parisons that accentuate the value of X provide the examples for the "good things" that Qohelet recommends. These may be placed in six groups:

(1) Miscellaneous

Qohelet calls a variety of things good[3] or recommends them in various max-ims: repose (4:6); being young and smart (4:12); avoiding excess verbiage, especially in vows (5:5); peaceful sleep (5:11); companionship (4:9); reputa-tion (7:1); going to a house of mourning (7:2, 4); the end of a matter (7:8);

---

3. To be precise, he sometimes calls the *possessors* of these things good, as in 4:9, *ṭobim haššᵉnayim min ha'eḥad,* "Better [that is, "better off"] are two than one. . . ."

avoiding extremes (7:18); obeying the king and not angering him (8:2f., 5; 10:4); and having a temperate ruling class (10:17).

Other recommendations belong to the major areas of contradiction and have been examined in the preceding chapters.

(2) Pleasure

Pleasure, however trivial and evanescent, *feels* good, and it is man's portion. This slight plus is enough to make life, with all its miseries, preferable to death (6:6).

(3) Work

One's efforts *may* provide the means of pleasure. Activity, especially if it is accommodated to the constraints of reality, is good (11:1-6). And work too is the portion of the living, something we have and can do (9:10).

(4) Justice

Though justice is often violated, it is unquestionably the way things *should* be, while corruption and oppression are, of course, bad. Righteousness, which is the foundation of justice, is indisputably good. Strangely, however, Qohelet advocates justice and righteousness less often than other virtues. He implicitly affirms righteousness when he declares that God will judge persons and their deeds (3:17; 11:9b). He admonishes us not to be "very wicked," and not to act the fool, lest we die early (7:17) — a lukewarm moralization, to be sure. (This advice, like the teachings of 11:1-6, advocates accommodation to the pressures of reality.) Qohelet certainly does not repudiate righteousness just because its pay-off is uncertain. Maybe he regards it as a less problematic virtue, or perhaps he is less convinced of the practical utility of righteousness than of wisdom, and since he is mainly concerned with the practical management of life, he gives less attention to inculcating the moral virtues.

(5) Wisdom

Whatever wisdom's frailties, it is the greatest of human powers. Wisdom, which includes know-how, cleverness, and good sense, works pretty well in practical matters, especially in comparison to stupidity, which earns contempt and makes a mess of things. More fundamentally: wisdom is *worthy*.

Wisdom — for Qohelet more than for his predecessors in wisdom — includes the free exercise of intellect. As the book opens, Qohelet has surpassed his predecessors in wisdom. All he subsequently does — his seeking, his discoveries, his counsels — are his alone, the fruit (sometimes sour) of his own mental efforts. Wisdom means *lucidity*, the ability to stare into the darkness and say honestly what one sees. Qohelet chooses this uncomfortable path and pursues it with determination, even zest.

Not only Qohelet, but the epilogist (whether author or editor; the effect is the same) implies the moral validity, if not the efficacy, of intellectual inquiry, by using Qohelet as a model of the wise seeker and including him in the ranks of the sages who taught knowledge framed in elegant words. Qohelet's audacious probing of life belongs to the acts and achievements of wisdom.

(6) Life

Qohelet loves life, even though he is grieved by its injustices and obscurities. Life, or, to be precise, the experience of living, is good:

> (7) Sweet is the light,
> and it is good for the eyes to see the sun.
> (8) Now even if a man live many years,
> he should take pleasure in them all,
> and remember that the days of darkness are many.
> All that comes is *hebel*. (11:7f.)

This goodness is not an ethical virtue or an objective value. The book so far has shown that life as a whole cannot be called "good" in the way it can be called "meaningless." Qohelet is rather describing how people feel about seeing the light, about just being alive. Verse 7 does not give advice, but states a fact of human nature. Verse 8 is distinct. It is an exhortation to take pleasure *(śimḥah)* during one's time on earth. To "see the sun" means simply to be alive (7:11; cf. 12:2). Just to be alive is "good" the way pleasure is "good," in spite of its deep inadequacies, and "a live dog is better off than a dead lion" (9:4).

Most of the good things man can have are interior and individual: knowing what one can know, or at least exercising the mind in the quest for knowledge; tasting pleasure while it lasts; enjoying moments of repose and sleep; adjusting our expectations to the constraints of reality; "seeing the light" and savoring the sweetness of just being alive. These good things are available to everyone, and everyone is free to choose them or not.

Although Qohelet does not preach happiness, does not even have a word for it, the book is, for all its shadows, "quelque manuel du bonheur" — "something of a manual of happiness" — as *The Myth of Sisyphus* describes itself (p. 99), for it gives guidance in moving somewhat closer to happiness, if not quite reaching it. Qohelet teaches how to make the best of a bad situation, where to find "portions" and "good things," how to look inward to feel the pleasures that come to us and to exercise whatever wisdom we are granted. Implicit in his words but not quite stated is the inherent preciousness of human experience. In the eternal void, there will be no activity, knowledge, or sensation, so we should embrace these things now. By realizing our slender and faltering powers we become most fully human and, perhaps, happy.

Hakkol hebel is a generalization, not a precisely calibrated description. It grasps in two words the feel of human reality as a whole and is not meant to apply to every moment, act, experience, and virtue in the world. Even if the aggregate lacks meaning, we possess, and we can create, passing moments of goodness and clarity. These flicker briefly, like sparks in the infinite darkness. But so do we.

§9.6. The End of the Matter

The book ends not with "all is absurd" but with a postscript (12:13f.), which modern commentators virtually ignore when describing the meaning of the book of Qohelet. The postscript is probably by a later scribe, but it now belongs to the book:

> Fear God and keep his commandments. For this (is the substance) of every man. For God will bring every deed into judgment, (even) every secret deed, whether good or evil. (12:13b-14)

This addition is not an irrelevant appendage. It is a conclusion that reasonably builds on Qohelet's words. The author of the postscript, probably a later scribe who was perhaps the book's copyist, did not delete or refuse to copy *hakkol hebel*. (He could have done so, and we would not know the difference, because the version we have descends from the postscript-writer's manuscript.) By leaving that statement and the like intact, he is conceding its validity, to a degree. The book now says: Even if everything is absurd, *nevertheless* we must fear God and keep his commandments.

Man's duty to fear and obey God and God's ultimate judgment on man are, for Qohelet too, bedrock truths that experience can collide with but not dislodge. We may wander around bruised and bewildered. We may see the meaning of life crumble if we stare at it too carefully. But we can still do what we are supposed to do. And we *know* what this is, even if we are ignorant of its consequences. That is no small thing.

One must imagine Sisyphus happy. (Camus, *Myth,* p. 99)

CHAPTER 10

Commentary: Introduction

§10.1. Literary Structure

At first reading, and even after many readings, the book of Qohelet seems rather disorganized. Though one idea often leads into the next, for the most part, the book moves from one topic to another without any evident organizing principle embracing all the parts. The book as a whole seems to lack design and hierarchy of topics. Is this a literary-philosophical flaw, or is it evidence of the book's composite authorship, or is it just the way Qohelet wrote it?

Since the Enlightenment, and perhaps under its sway, commentators have set themselves the task of discerning the "design" of the book.[1] Starting in the 1960s, this activity came to be considered *de rigeur* for "literary criticism," but now scholars began basing the analysis on formal features more than on the philosophical structure of argumentation. On the basis of recurring words and motifs, the scholar traces a literary structure, which is then supposed to provide the key to interpretation. This approach has produced numerous structural proposals in Qohelet, with little agreement among them except with regard to the borders of many literary units. (These proposals are conveniently summarized by A. Wright [1968:315-17] and R. E.

---

1. Judging from C. D. Ginsburg's survey, this activity commenced with Piscator (1612) among the Christians (Ginsburg, p. 123) and David Friedländer (1788) among the Jews (pp. 79f.). Piscator's gross division of the book into two parts, "Doctrinal" and "Admonitory," does characterize the emphasis of each half of the book fairly well.

Murphy [pp. xxxv-xli].) Few proposals have persuaded anyone but their authors, with the exception of Wright's proposal, which he considers the solution to "The Riddle of the Sphinx" (1968). The main outline, marked out by various verbal repetitions and inclusions, is as follows:

> Initial poem (1:2-11)
>   I. Qohelet's investigation of life (1:12–6:9)
> II. Qohelet's conclusions (6:10–11:6)
>   Introduction (6:10-12)
>   A. Man cannot find out what is good for him to do (7:1–8:17)
>   B. Man does not know what will come after him (9:1–11:6)
>   Concluding poem (11:7–12:8)
>   Epilogue (12:9-14)

These units are subdivided, yielding an intricate, well articulated, hierarchical design. Wright's article should be consulted for details and argumentation.

Murphy (1992: pp. xxxix-xli), Mulder (1982), and Schoors (1982b) accept this proposal in large degree. It would seem, however, that partial agreement with Wright's proposal is disagreement, since Wright is proposing more than feasible unit-divisions and patterns of thematic emphasis. His theory is a scaffolding that collapses when posts and cross-beams are moved, because its validity depends on the tight organization of the hierarchical patterns and the determinative significance of every unit marker.

There are flaws in Wright's methodology, and these are common to other proposals of "literary structure" in Qohelet.

(1) The criteria for unit division (particularly in part II) are not well-defined phrases, but word-groups of dubious cohesiveness, such as "not knowing," which is any negative + any form of YD' (in 9:10 *da'at* occurs third in a list of four nouns).

(2) The words and phrases chosen as unit markers are not always the most prominent ones. Other choices, equally justifiable, produce very different designs. The marker in part I is said to be *hebel w^{e}ra'yon/r^e'ut ruah,* but since the presence of *hebel* is optional, the marker is actually only *ra'yon/r^e'ut ruah.* Yet the reader's attention certainly focuses on *hebel,* which 1:2 sets forth as the book's leitmotif, rather than on *ra'yon/r^e'ut ruah.*

(3) The key phrases are frequently not where we would expect them to be according to Wright's schema. For example, the end-marking phrases in 1:15; 1:17; 2:10; 9:5; and 10:12, 14 are followed by one sentence or more before the unit ends, while the beginning-markers in 1:14; 2:3; 2:4; 2:21; 5:1; 9:16f.; and 11:4 are each preceded by a sentence or two.

148

(4) The plan does not match the thought. Wright frequently gathers a variety of topics under an inappropriate or vague rubric. The array of themes labeled "Qohelet's conclusions," for example (p. 325), which supposedly is the subject of 6:10–11:6, are not confined to those verses but are introduced from the start. Qoh 4:17–6:9 supposedly teaches that "one can lose all that one accumulates," but this theme cannot subsume the variety of topics discussed there. Conversely, Wright passes over or subordinates major unit divisions that are clear and significant even though not formally marked; e.g., after 3:22; 5:6; 7:12;[2] 7:22; 10:3; and 10:20. If unit divisions are of any rhetorical significance, the reader should be able to sense their presence even without having them recovered in erudite "rhetorical" criticism.[3]

There is an even deeper problem: the proposed structure has no more effect on interpretation than a ghost in the attic. A literary or rhetorical structure should not merely "be there"; it must *do* something. It should guide readers in recognizing and remembering the author's train of thought, even if there is no unanimity on the precise disposition of the material. The design Wright unearths does not seem to have left an impression, even a vague one, on earlier interpreters. It does not affect the way they grouped verses in their discussion or determine the themes they emphasized. Nor do the numerous more recent interpreters who outline the book's contents show any awareness of *this* design. It doesn't even seem to have much effect on the exegesis of the few interpreters who basically accept it, such as Murphy.[4]

A text can be coherent even without a neat design. Compare how Ludwig Wittgenstein, an intensely systematic thinker, described the structure of his *Philosophical Investigations:*

> The thoughts which I publish in what follows are the precipitate of philosophical investigations which have occupied me for the last sixteen years. They concern many subjects: . . . I have written down all these thoughts as *remarks,* short paragraphs, of which there is sometimes a fairly long chain about the same subject, while I sometimes make a sudden change, jumping from one topic to another. — It was my intention at first to bring all this to-

2. Or 7:19, if that verse is placed after v. 12, as I have done.
3. See further the critiques by Schoors (1982a:97f.) and J. Mulder (1982), whose objections in part overlap the above.
4. In subsequent studies, Wright claims to uncover numerological codes. The self-validating nature of such "decoding" is evident, and in any case I cannot imagine why the author of Qohelet would embed such codes to start with, leaving them there unnoticed for more than two millennia. He had more important things to do.

gether in a book whose form I pictured differently at different times. But the essential thing was that the thoughts should proceed from one subject to another in a natural order and without breaks.

After several unsuccessful attempts to weld my results together into such a whole, I realized that I should never succeed. The best that I could write would never be more than philosophical remarks; my thoughts were soon crippled if I tried to force them on in any single direction against their natural inclination. — And this was, of course, connected with the very nature of the investigation. For this compels us to travel over a wide field of thought criss-cross in every direction. — The philosophical remarks in this book are, as it were, a number of sketches of landscapes which were made in the course of these long and involved journeyings. (1968:ix)

This description could be applied unaltered to Qohelet's "philosophical investigations." His book too is a report of a journey of consciousness over the landscape of experience (1:13). The terrain has few highways or signposts, the journey has scant order and progression. This mode of organization is akin to the form of composition of many ancient Near Eastern Wisdom books. The classical, pre-Demotic Egyptian Instructions are composed of short discourses on different topics, strung together without any overall principle of organization. The Mesopotamian instructions show some topical clustering but no overall design. The same is true of Proverbs and Sira too. In the latter, the central units (chaps. 4–43) are composed of a mixture of proverbs, sometimes clustered thematically, as well as short discourses on various themes (themselves incorporating proverbs), without an overall principle of organization.

If, however, we look beneath the jagged literary surface and consider Qohelet's methodology of discovery and reporting (described in §4.4), we find strong *conceptual* organization. The body of the book, 1:3 to 12:7, argues for a single proposition: "all is absurd." The book opens with this central thesis and proceeds to establish it by reporting on Qohelet's quest for knowledge, which led to and validated this thesis.

In pursuing a single idea from start to finish, the book, for all its bumpiness, is unusually methodical for an ancient Wisdom text. Qohelet's conceptual organization is reinforced by uniformity in tone, ideas, and style. The book's lexical and thematic uniformity is charted by O. Loretz (1964:212-17 and 135-217).

Structure and unit division are important but not always decisive in interpretation. Scholars argue vigorously about how to segment the text and what passages are subordinate to others. They argue, for example, about

150

whether 7:23f. *really is* the start of a unit (Fox 1987), or whether it ends one (as maintained in the present study). Such determinations, however, are scholarly constructs, valuable in parceling out the text and grouping thoughts, but not always representing a decision on the author's part.[5] Put another way, the significance of a unit division is proportionate to its clarity. When the author changes to a completely fresh topic, as at 3:1, we know it, because it *is* a fresh topic. When he maintains continuity from one topic to the next, as in 2:12 and 2:18, it is a matter of exegetical preference whether we designate this as a single unit (2:1-26) or three (2:1-11, 12-17, 18-26). As the reader moves from one "unit" to the next, he does not put out of mind what he has just read, nor does he ignore pauses and changes of direction within a single unit (such as 1:3-11). Qoh 7:23f. is partly attached to both preceding and following material, and it is also partly independent of them. Unit division would be more significant if we knew that the book was stitched together by a later editor from originally independent mini-texts, but there is too much cohesiveness in Qohelet to suppose that was the case.

The book's cohesiveness inheres above all in the constant presence of a single brooding consciousness mediating all the book's observations, counsels, and evaluations. In most Wisdom books, few sentences reveal the particular situation or personality of the author, real or fictional. The typical overshadows the individual.[6] In most books, the person of the sage disappears almost entirely after the introduction, and we rarely hear his "I" again, at least not before the epilogue. In Proverbs, the teacher's "I" is more pronounced in chapters 1–9, though it is in the person of a generic wise man, not a particular person. The individual experience of the teacher is prominent in the body of the instructions only in Amenemhet and Merikare. (In the former, the authorship is certainly fictional, because the speaker is dead, and someone else was remembered as the actual author.[7]) Amenemhet and Merikare are organized largely according to the sequence of events in the lives of the speakers. Their teachings suppos-

---

5. This is mainly a modern scholarly preoccupation. The fact is that most readers do quite well with little attention to structural matters, as can be verified by an examination of early commentaries — or by discussing Qohelet with a lay group. The more significant a structural design is, the more it works on its own.

6. Examples of sentences that do seem to reflect the circumstances of the sage who speaks in the work are Onchsheshonqy 8,9-10; 26,1-8; 28,10 and Aḥiqar sayings 59 (lines 139f.), 76 (169b-170), and 80 (175f.), But the apparent relevance of such sayings to the narrative may be accidental or secondary. In the case of Aḥiqar, Lindenberger (1983:17-18 and *passim*) argues that the frame-narrative was joined to the proverbs secondarily and that these three sayings are editorial additions.

7. In the New Kingdom Pap. Chester Beatty IV (6.13-14), the author of Amenemhet is identified as the scribe Chety.

edly derive from their own experiences but not from a premeditated attempt to sift experience through examination and reflection. The ego of the teacher is more significant in Sira than in most Wisdom books, and he is one of the few who projects a clear image of personality. But he does not constantly state facts as things he saw, nor does he describe their impact on his observations to the same extent Qohelet does.

The book of Qohelet is not just a collection of proverbs. Some of the material is well placed. The book begins with a general principle (1:3), continues with a thematic prelude, introduces the persona and his background, describes his task, previews his results, and then proceeds with his investigation. The last unit, 12:1-7, is climactic and could stand nowhere else. These things are evident to all. But expectations of a structured discourse are mostly frustrated by the rather haphazard arrangement in other parts of the book. This lack of sequential organization is not a "riddle" but a characteristic of style, and it need not be repaired by scholarly ingenuity.

What finally convinces me that the proposed structures are off the mark is that they have no effect on my reading. I have read the book innumerable times and have never sensed that halfway through the book, in 6:10, there is a sudden move to a new theme, even though I do sense a great emphasis on the constructive in the latter part of the book. And even when I read the book with Wright's structure in mind, 7:1–8:17 fails to block itself off as a discrete unit on the theme, "Man cannot find out what is good for him to do." If the issue is a structure that governs reading, then it should do so.

Even a book with little schematic design can have units and subunits, and interpretation is aided by identifying them and reading them as local contexts with their own structure and flow of thought. In the commentary that follows I am less concerned with discovering hierarchical and symmetrical patterns than with tracing the movement of thought, especially within the units. At the beginning of a unit that is not simply aphoristic, I trace, by outline or paraphrase, the structure of argumentation found in it. Sometimes I employ indentation to show levels of logical subordination. The purpose of letters and primes is to draw attention to repetitions of ideas or phraseology.

The boundaries between literary units are not impermeable. Neither author nor reader needs to stop thinking about one topic when he moves to the next, and one passage is inevitably, and properly, read in the light of its surroundings. The most important feature is the relations among the ideas of the argument, since the argument is primary, and the most important formal features are introduced to help communicate it. The unit divisions and subdivisions I propose are not meant to reflect a blueprint the author held in his head but to show how the text is most naturally phrased and parsed.

152

There is, in fact, considerable scholarly agreement about the articulation and rhythm of the book, since one commentator may mark out a longer unit but then subdivide it, while other commentators treat those subdivisions as relatively independent units.

§10.2. Genre

A literary work does not have a single genre. Genres are sets defined by criterial features. A literary work may belong to several genres, which is to say, it may be a member of various sets.

There is no close parallel to Qohelet's genre, but it combines elements known from other works, particularly in Wisdom Literature: autobiography, proverbs, reflections, and counsels. The broad genre of Qohelet is Wisdom Instruction, because it purports to teach the reader the rules of successful living, doing so without appeal to divine revelation or specific traditions, but only by recourse to human reason. Here I will consider two genre classifications, royal autobiography and reflection.

§10.21. *Royal Autobiography*

The body of the book of Qohelet (1:3–12:7) purports to be the words of a king, who recounts his deeds, experiences, and findings.

As is widely recognized, the royal fiction is not active beyond chapter 2, for neither Qohelet nor the epilogist has further need for the guise. But neither is it cancelled, and the book as a whole is formally spoken by "king" Qohelet. The guise serves to reinforce the validity of the conclusions, because it makes Qohelet a Solomon-like figure. He is endowed with the means for indulging in a great array of pleasures, and he possesses the wisdom to evaluate his experiences and to assess wisdom itself. This guise prevents the reader from writing off Qohelet's complaints as ignorance, sour grapes, or personal grievances.

Some features of the book of Qohelet, particularly in 1:1–2:26 (or as others divide the units, 1:1–2:11), resemble royal autobiographies from elsewhere in the ancient Near East.

(1) Within Wisdom Literature, the "royal testament" provides a parallel to Qohelet 1:12–2:26. The genre of 1:12–2:11 is sometimes identified as royal testament (K. Galling 1932:298; G. von Rad 1970:292 [ET 226]). There are two such works in early Egyptian Wisdom Literature, the (posthu-

mous) instruction of Amenemhet and the instruction for Merikare. In the testaments, the teachers both speak of their own experience and give counsel to their successors. Qohelet differs insofar as he never addresses his successor, and, in the passages in which his royalty is relevant, he does not give advice.

(2) Didactic autobiographies in Akkadian, in particular the Cuthean legend of Naram-Sin, the Adad-guppi inscription, and the "Sin of Sargon," show some resemblance to Qohelet's narrative technique. T. Longman (1991:6-129) describes a genre he calls "fictional Akkadian autobiography with a didactic ending." He compares Qohelet to the Cuthean legend of Naram-Sin. Naram-Sin, of the twenty-second century BCE, is for the author a figure in the distant past. In the Late Assyrian version (eighth-seventh century; *BTM* 1.262-69), the text presents itself as a stela, though it is not one. Naram-Sin introduces himself and reminisces about a crisis he faced. In defiance of divine counsel, he entered battle against a foreign enemy and suffered severe consequences. Having learned his lesson, Naram-Sin gives advice to future rulers ("governor, prince, or anyone else") and blesses those who heed his words. There is no resemblance to Qohelet in the protagonist or the details of the narrative, and the Cuthean legend lacks an editorial frame. But there is a similarity in the basic mode of presentation: a king from the past introduces himself, recounts his experience and reflects on it, and gives advice based on that experience. Similar also is the reflexive reporting. Naram-Sin tells the reader what he said to his heart. Three times he says, "Speaking to my heart [*kiam aqbi ana libbîya*], thus I said" (Longman, p. 122). Compare Qohelet's reflexive reporting: "I spoke with my heart, saying" (1:16) and "I said in my heart" (Qoh 2:1, 15; 3:17, 18). Seow too classifies Qohelet as a fictional autobiography and adduces a number of parallels from West Semitic and Akkadian royal inscriptions (1995).

(3) Qohelet's retrospective self-glorification also calls to mind royal celebratory or "historical" inscriptions, though these lack pessimistic conclusions such as Qohelet's. An example is the Phoenician Karatepe inscription (eighth century BCE), which begins:

I am Azitawada, blessed by [or, vizier of] Baal, servant of Baal, whom Awarku, king of the Danunians, made powerful. Baal made me a father and a mother to the Danunians. I revived the Danunians. I extended the land of the plain of Adana from the rising of the sun to its setting. And in my days the Danunians had everything (that was) good, and plenty (of grain), and fine food; and I filled the granaries of Pahar. And I acquired horse upon horse, and shield upon shield, and army upon army, by the grace of Baal and the gods. . . . (trans. *TSSI* 3.48)

Qohelet uses the stereotypical royal boasts ironically, for he does not believe that such accomplishments bring immortality; on the contrary, they matter not at all. "The legendary acts, wealth, and wisdom of Solomon turned out not to have abiding significance after all. The genre of a royal inscription is utilized to make the point about the ephemerality of wisdom and human accomplishments" (Seow 1995:284).

The book of Qohelet is only loosely related to the texts discussed above. Qohelet may be classed in the broad genre of royal autobiography, with the above three groups, and with genres 1 and 2, it can be designated as a fictional royal testament.

One significant similarity between Qohelet and the texts in groups 1 and 2 is their self-critical tone. Amenemhet is dissatisfied with his failure to be on guard against attack. (He apparently was assassinated.) The father of Merikare chastises himself for tomb desecrations perpetrated by his underlings. Naram-Sin reproaches himself for disregarding an oracle. Qohelet is displeased with his failure to achieve a profit of the sort that would satisfy him, though this is more a matter of disappointment with his efforts than reproach for an individual inadequacy.

The book of Qohelet draws upon the settings, tones, and formulas of these genres for its own purposes. It is likely that the ancient reader of Qohelet could easily have classified the book as a royal autobiography and would probably have recognized the attribution to "king" Qohelet as a convention. The reader would have felt that "that's how kings speak."

§10.22. Reflection

Another salient feature of Qohelet's form is his use of reflection. A reflection is a report of an inner contemplation of an issue — "inner" insofar as the ideas were not spoken to another person during their formation, but only post-facto. The reflection is characteristic of Qohelet. Ellermeier (1967:89-92) and Braun (1973:153-59) subdivide this category in ways that "seem subtle and even unnecessary" (Murphy, xxxii). Parallels are few, since most Wisdom Literature is addressed to an audience, real or fictive. The words of Khakheperre-sonb (*AEL* 1.146-49) are meditations, spoken to his heart. Ps 73 is the best parallel, for in it the poet describes his past thoughts and how he came to resolve his quandary. Some of the royal autobiographies mentioned above have elements of reflection. Perhaps the best way to characterize Qohelet would be "reflective autobiography," as opposed to a celebratory autobiography that narrates deeds and accomplishments.

§10.3. The Greek and Syriac Translations

If used carefully, the Septuagint and, to a lesser degree, the Peshiṭta, can provide reliable variants to the Hebrew text of Qohelet, since they are both narrowly mapped translations.

The Greek translation is *mimetic* in approach, remaining close to the Hebrew, particularly in its consistency of word-correspondences. It is Aquilan in quality, though probably not the actual Aquilan translation (thus Hyvärinen 1977:88-99, 112).[8] The mimetic (or formal-mapping) nature of the translation allows us to retrovert from the Greek with some confidence and requires us to account for the resulting variants, unless obviously erroneous, as potentially valid alternative readings.

The Peshiṭta (Syr) to Qohelet likewise remains close to the Hebrew. Kamenetzky's text-critical study of the Syriac translation of Qohelet (1904) is still valuable. In the commentary, "Syr" refers to the base text of the Leyden Peshiṭta, which, in the case of Qohelet, is the Ambrosian codex. In a survey of the manuscripts used for the Leyden Peshiṭta, D. J. Lane (1979) says that the manuscript tradition for Qohelet is homogeneous, showing only minor variations. He also argues that doublets represent different understandings of a single underlying text rather than later assimilation to the Hebrew.

In this context, it might be mentioned that modern exegesis makes frequent use of the rule of *lectio difficilior probabilior,* giving preference to the more difficult text on the grounds that the simpler one may have resulted from simplification in transcription or translation. While such simplification does occur, *lectio difficilior* is, as B. Albrekson has shown (1981), invalid as a working principle. If applied consistently, *lectio difficilior* would produce the worst possible text. If in fact we know that the variant that seems more difficult to us is earlier than a simpler variant, then we can explain the appearance of the former *post facto* by appeal to *lectio difficilior.* But we cannot use the rule to select variants because, as Albrekson says, "There are cases where a *lectio difficilior* may be more difficult simply because it is wrong" (ibid., p. 11). Moreover, the rule is suspect because it is never — ever — used to support a variant *against* the MT. In 8:6, for example, instead of MT's *ra'at*, there is a well-attested variant *da'at,* requiring the translation "for the knowledge of man is great upon him." No one prefers *da'at,* though it is cer-

---

8. Hyvärinen points out significant deviations in LXX-Qoh from Aquilan techniques in lexical and syntactical matters and argues against an Aquilan origin for LXX-Qoh. The latter notion was first suggested by H. Graetz (1871:173-79) and argued by McNeile (1904:115-34).

tainly the more difficult. Nor does anyone emend to *w*ᵉ*lo' bošet,* "and not to be ashamed," in 10:17, with LXX and Vul, on the grounds that it is the *lectio difficilior.* Even commentators who frequently appeal to *lectio difficilior* to support the MT will reject a difficult non-Masoretic variant precisely because it *is* difficult.

§10.4. Translation

A fairly close translation accompanies the comments on each unit. When quoting Qohelet elsewhere I use that translation, except when a slightly different (usually more literal) wording serves to bring out certain features of the passage in question or to highlight other interpretations.

The translation tries to preserve ambiguities present in the Hebrew text, so that the reader will see immediately some of the problems the commentary must address. Removal of ambiguities is usually left for the comments.

CHAPTER 11

Commentary

◆ **1:1-2**

(1) The words of Qohelet, son of David, king in Jerusalem:
(2) Utterly absurd, said Qohelet, utterly absurd. All is absurd.

The authorial voice (also heard in the epilogue, 12:9-12) introduces Qohelet in the third person and summarizes his message. The motto in 1:2 and 12:8 brackets his words.

1:1 The title associates Qohelet with Solomon. Since Qohelet takes on the role of king in 1:12–2:11, there is no reason to restrict the original title to the phrase "words of Qohelet" (thus Galling) and assign the rest of the identification to a later editor. The vast wealth and wisdom of Qohelet reflect traditions about Solomon, probably with direct dependence on 1 Kgs 3:12; 5:9-14; 1 Chr 29:25; 2 Chr 1:12; etc.

But it is also a fact that this verse does *not* call the speaker Solomon. The title does not say that Solomon is the author, as has always been assumed both by those who reject the accuracy of the ascription as well as those who accept it. Instead, the author creates for his persona a fictional king *based on* Solomon. Though he wants us to imagine the persona's wisdom, power, and prosperity as Solomonic in quantity and quality, he is not trying to make us believe that the author truly is Solomon or to give the book full Solomonic authority. Though this fact evades most commentators, it seems to me clear that if the author wanted us to believe that the author was Solomon he would have called him by that name, as did the authors of Solomonic pseudepi-

159

graphic books in the Bible and Jewish Hellenistic writings, namely Proverbs, Psalm 72, the Odes of Solomon, the Psalms of Solomon, the Testament of Solomon, and the Wisdom of Solomon.

Qohelet speaks in this book, but he is not its author. In Excursus III, I point out several reasons to identify the author with the speaker of the epilogue (12:9-11a) and to regard Qohelet as his persona. But even if the author of the epilogue is not the author of the body of the book, we can be sure that Qohelet is a fictional character, hence not the author. Qohelet presents himself as a king called Qohelet, but, to state the obvious, there was no such king. If, as the naive view holds, Solomon wrote the book using an alias, was he trying to hide his identity? If so, why did he provide the other information identifying himself? In any case, a Solomonic dating is impossible. And even if there was an actual person (not Solomon) known as Qohelet, and he wrote the book, the fact that he makes himself a king shows he was *re-creating* himself as a fictional character, and we cannot simply identify the author with his fictional spokesman. The book belongs to the genre of fictional autobiography, like Onchsheshonqy and Aḥiqar and the Hellenistic apocryphal "testaments."

The persona was created not for the proclamation of secure and timeless truths. That could be better achieved by impersonal statement, such as we have in most of Wisdom Literature, even in texts with an identified author. Qohelet states his observations and evaluations as such. His subjectivity is on display. The book is about *meaning,* and that, the author realizes, exists relationally, by means of perception.

Qōhelet: A feminine common noun appearing both with the article (7:27 <*'amar haqqohelet*>; 12:8) and without it (1:1, 2, 12; 12:9, 10). Most commentators explain the word as a title of office, comparing the likewise mysterious *soperet* (Ezr 2:55; Neh 7:57) and *pokeret haṣṣᵉbayim* (Ezr 2:57; Neh 7:59). These seem to be titles that came to be epithets of individuals. Both appear in a list of names of men who, interestingly, are cultic functionaries called "the sons of Solomon's servants." Like *qohelet, soperet* can appear with the article (Ezr 2:55) or without it (Neh 7:57). The use of a feminine office-title to designate the male office holder has a parallel in *mmlkt* "kingdom" (fem.), equivalent to *melek* "king," in Phoenician and Hebrew (*mamlakah* = "king" in 1 Sam 10:18 [in pl., with masc. pple.] and perhaps elsewhere; see *HALAT* 2.595b).

In Aramaic (Syriac), the G-stem verb *qᵉhal* is intransitive and means "to assemble," "come into assembly," that is, a group is assembled or assembles itself. This is the meaning that the G-stem would be expected to have in Hebrew, and it indicates an action that cannot be predicated of a single person. Thus Qohelet cannot be "one who assembles himself" — apart from the problem of gender.

We should not assume that *qōhelet* is the participle of (an unattested) qal of QHL. It is best explained as a noun-from-noun denominative from *qāhāl* "assembly." B. Kedar-Kopfstein has examined nouns in the *qôṭēl* pattern and shown that the qal active participle is only a subclass of them (1977; cf. *IBHS* §52d). A number of them are fixed designations of occupations or social roles, such as *bôqēr* "cowherd" from *bāqār* "cattle," *ḥôbēl* "sailor" from *ḥebel* "rope," *kōrēm* "vintner" from *kerem* "vineyard." In some cases, the *qôṭēl* nouns lack a link to a verbal root in the qal, such as *nôqēd* "sheep-raiser," *kôhēn* "priest," *rôzēn* "prince," and *šôlēm* "man of peace," "ally" (*šolᵉmi* in Ps 7:5). Most nouns in this category are, loosely, doer nouns or occupation-nouns, but their meaning cannot be simply projected from the qal.

A *qohelet* would be someone who does something in the assembly, just as *korem* is one who does something in a vineyard, and *hobel* is one who does something with a rope. There is also a class of nouns supported by verbal roots that appear only in the derived stems (Kedar-Kopfstein, p. 163), e.g., *noqeš* from NQŠ, attested in niphal, piel, and hitpael, and in *soken* "steward" from SKN, which appears in the hiphil. This opens the possibility that *qohelet* is (the office of) *maqhil*, "one who assembles." But, as in the case of "sailor"-"rope," the connection may be tangential or unpredictable, and the morphology allows no further precision.

The Greek rendering ἐκκλησιαστής, meaning "member of the ἐκκλησία, the assembly," may be right. Alternatively, *qohelet* may mean "speaker in assembly" (thus Qoh. Rab. 1:1, §2). Sir 15:5 says that wisdom enables her devotees to speak in *qahal*. The *qahal* is not necessarily a formal assembly. It can be an informal, non-institutional gathering, such as a *qahal* of peoples (Gen 28:3) or of ghosts (Prov 21:16). We might imagine him speaking to any gathering of people. This recalls Lady Wisdom's preachments in the busy parts of the city (Prov 1:20f.; 8:1-3). Lady Wisdom is, after all, a teacher, and so was Qohelet.

The traditional translation, "the Preacher," is reasonable, but "preacher" tends to connote one who inculcates a given religious viewpoint of which he is confident. Thus "public teacher" might be better, and that is exactly what 12:9 says that Qohelet was.

1:2 *Hăbel hăbalim 'amar qohelet hăbel hăbalim hakkol habel:* This is the book's motto, phrased as someone else's summary of Qohelet's central, but not sole, message. It is not "an extremely misleading editorial summary of

Qohelet's statements" ("im allerhöchsten Grade misverständliche Summierung Qoheletscher Aussagen") (Ellermeier 1967:100). Even though this sentence in 1:2 and 12:8 is formulated as another person's quotation of Qohelet, it is an effective encapsulation (or "thematization") of Qohelet's thought. Of course it is an oversimplification, but that's what summaries are. There is no need to ascribe it to an editor who did not read Qohelet's message quite right.

In fact, the motto is best ascribed to the author, who is here paraphrasing Qohelet, who is his creation. Qohelet implies that *everything* is absurd by "going around" the world and attaching that word to the numerous things he observes. The same idea appears in 1:14, where Qohelet says that "all the events that occur under the heavens" are *hebel* — a statement equivalent to "all is *hebel*." 2:17 is a similar generalization.

Ellermeier (1967:98-100), who understands *hebel* to mean "Nichtigkeit" ("nothingness"), claims that the phrase *hăbel hăbalim* cannot convey the notion of "in the highest degree," for there are no degrees to nothingness. Furthermore, he says, if we take *hăbel hăbalim* to mean "*hebel* in the highest degree," then the end of the verse, "all is *hebel*," is a weakening of the opening statement, "(all) is utterly *hebel*." Ellermeier explains *hăbel hăbalim* as iterative: "immer wieder 'hebel'" ("again and again [Qohelet said] '*hebel*'"), but he gives no examples of similar phrases having an iterative sense, and it is doubtful that a superlative (as Ellermeier grants this phrase to be) can have an iterative meaning, unless iteration is part of the semantic content of words themselves.

Understanding *hebel* as meaning "absurd" answers the difficulties Ellermeier raises, for there *are* degrees of absurdity, depending on the intensity of the tensions in the contradictions judged absurd. The motto says that life, taken as a whole, is absurd to the highest degree. It is true that *hakkol habel* is weaker than *(hakkol) hăbel hăbalim,* but this weakening serves a rhetorical purpose. The phrase *hakkol habel* provides the subject of *hăbel hăbalim* and resumes the predicate in a de-emphasized form. In the final occurrence of the predicate *(habel),* some weight is given to the subject ("*all* is absurd"), while in the first two occurrences *(hăbel hăbalim . . . hăbel hăbalim),* emphasis is placed on the predicate. In this way, the motto expresses first the intensity of the *hebel*-judgment and then its universality.

The quoting-phrase, '*amar qohelet,* controls the rhythm of the motto. It provides a slight caesura that makes us pause and absorb the notion of utter absurdity rather than jumbling the words together and gliding over the clause, as we would do if we read *hăbel hăbalim hăbel hăbalim hakkol habel.* It also interposes the frame-narrator (see Excursus III) between Qohelet and the reader. The frame-narrator is an interpreter, who, by abstracting this idea from Qohelet's teachings and bracketing the monologue with it, points out the central idea and determines the way we read the rest of Qohelet's words.

The book's motto is a thesis that the reader can expect to see validated in the following monologue, and this expectation channels the interpretation. After 1:2, 1:4-7 cannot be a celebration of the glorious stability of the natural order. Instead we immediately ask: what is it about these natural processes that is *hebel?* At the same time, we begin to redefine *hebel* in accordance with what we read, and we will continue to do so throughout the book. Likewise, the practical counsels Qohelet offers later will not be understood as guides to achieving a mastery of life and its meaning, since such control is precluded by the pervasiveness of the quality of *hebel.* The five-fold repetition of *hebel* sends reverberations throughout the book, so that all the subsequent *hebel*-judgments are subsumed to the opening declaration and wrapped up by the closing one. This strong interpretive guidance allows the monologue to wander about *(latur!)* without going astray.

◆ **1:3-11**

(3) What profit does man have in all his toil at which he labors under the sun?

(4)   A generation goes and a generation comes,
*   but the world remains forever the same.*
(5)   The sun rises and the sun sets,
*   then goes panting to its place,*
*   whence it rises.*
(6)   Going to the south,
*   and rounding to the north,*
*   round and round goes the wind,*
*   and on its rounds the wind returns.*
(7)   All the rivers flow to the sea,
*   but the sea is never filled.*
*   That place to which the rivers go,*
*   there they go again.*

(8)   Words are all weary;
*   man is unable to speak.*

> *The eye is not sated with seeing,*
> *nor the ear filled by hearing.*
> (9) *That which happens is that which shall happen,*
> *and that which occurs is that which shall occur,*
> *and there is nothing whatsoever new under the sun.*

(10) If there be something of which one could say, "Look, this is new!" — *it has already happened in the aeons that preceded us. (11) There is no remembrance of things past, nor of the things yet to come will there be remembrance among those who come still later.*

A. 1:3. Thesis
B. 1:4-7. Argument by analogy
C. 1:8. Reaction to observations in B
D. 1:9. Conclusion abstracted from B and justifying A
E. 1:10-11. Prose addendum, reinforcing A

If the mighty efforts of nature can achieve nothing new, surely man's toil is futile. Since there is nothing new, man's toil can achieve nothing that would not have occurred anyway.

The generalization in v. 2 leads into the description of eternal repetition just as the same generalization in 12:8 flows out of the description of human mortality. This unit is naturally read as evidence for the principle in v. 2 and the rhetorical question in v. 3. Even if one starts the unit with v. 4 (as many do, including Galling, Lohfink, and Crenshaw) the unhappy implications of vv. 2 and 3 inevitably reverberate into the verses that follow.

The description of nature in vv. 4-7 serves only to demonstrate the thesis about human toil in v. 3. Verse 8 returns to the human realm, and v. 9 points back to v. 3 by echoing the phrase "under the sun." What the patterns of nature model, we now learn, is the fact that nothing new ever happens, and this fact validates the opening statement that toil is never adequately compensated. Vv. 10-11 form a prose addendum to the preceding section, wrapping up the argument of vv. 4-9 in rather scholastic fashion by accounting for impressions one may have to the contrary.[1]

---

1. E. Good (1978) carefully reconstructs and analyzes the dynamic process of reading this unit as it unfolds.

A. 1:3. Thesis

"What profit does man have in all his toil . . . ?": This is a rhetorical question whose negative answer is implicit in the choice of the word *'amal* to designate human activities (see §6.1) as well as in the negativism of the preceding verse. No labors are properly rewarded. This may be learned from the analogy of the elements of nature, which, though mighty and incessant, seem to accomplish nothing in particular.

'Amal here is not only labor that aims at gaining wealth, but all human efforts (§6.12).

Taḥat haššameš "under the sun" (alternatively "heavens"; 1:13; 2:3; 3:1) is used twenty-five times to designate the domain of human life, in short, "the world." It excludes the underworld (see 9:6) and the heavens, God's domain ("for God is in heaven and you are on the earth"; 5:1b). Certainly God is not *hebel*.

There are two ways in which "under the sun" might be intended: restrictively and inclusively. In the first, the purpose of the phrase would be to modestly restrict the application of Qohelet's observations to this world *alone,* excluding other domains that are beyond human ken. In this case, Qohelet would be holding out the possibility of a different situation elsewhere, namely in the heavens. This is the traditional understanding of the phrase. It makes Qohelet out to be pious and modest in his claims and even hints at hopes for a better life above and beyond this one. If the sense of "under the sun" is inclusive, Qohelet's purpose is to underscore the *breadth* of his observations, claiming that such-and-such is true in the *entire* world "under the sun," not just in part of it. The inclusive function is more likely, for if the phrase were restrictive, 1:9 would be saying that only under the sun is there nothing new, thereby conceding the possibility of something new occurring elsewhere than in the human domain, though in other domains "newness" does not seem relevant. Nor is Qohelet likely to concede that toil may have a profit elsewhere than in this life (1:3), as if man's work could pay off in heaven or in the underworld. Furthermore, since most of the facts that Qohelet observes "under the sun" can hardly be imagined to exist in any other domain but human life, there is no need for him to exclude other domains of reality. Rather, he focuses on life "under the sun" and insists on the broad applicability of his observations to that realm.

B. 1:4-7. Argument by Analogy

The staticity of nature. Each of these verses makes the same point: "le plus ça change, le plus c'est le même chose." All this is meant to show that, by analogy and *a fortiori,* man's toil cannot be expected to affect the course of events.

1:4 This verse is commonly understood to contrast the permanence of the earth with the ephemerality of the generations. Yet the permanence of the physical earth has no relevance to the individual life. The key to understanding this verse lies in recognizing that *ha'areṣ* here does not mean the physical earth, but humanity as a whole — "le monde" rather than "la terre." Good examples of this usage are Gen 11:1; 1 Kgs 2:2; and Ps 33:8.

The flow of generations is not intended to call to mind human transience. The other images in 1:4-8 do not show the disappearance of the entities in the cycle. The point of 1:4 is the fact that humanity "remains always the same." *'Amad* here means "remain as is," as in Lev 13:5; Jer 32:14; and Ps 33:11. Qohelet observes that the procession of generations does not alter the face of humanity, just as the rivers' incessant flow downstream does not change the sea. No sooner does one generation depart — note that "going" precedes "coming" — than another moves in to fill the gap. Thus the "world" never changes in spite of appearances to the contrary. The procession of generations is one of the natural phenomena that move in cycles without achieving anything new.

1:5 The sun's great, laborious journey across the sky merely brings it back to its starting point. The strain of the trek is implied by *šo'ep*, "pant." Even if the author intended *šo'ep* to be primarily understood as if from ŠWP, "to walk, proceed" (thus Rashi, Gordis, Ginsberg; similarly Tg, "crawls and goes"), the reader would naturally associate the writing *š'p* with *šo'ep* (Š'P), "pant."

1:6 The wind, which might well be perceived as wandering aimlessly, in Qohelet's vision follows a fixed circuit. *Sobeb sobeb* is adverbial to *holek*.

1:7 The rivers' endless flowing does not fill up the sea conclusively. The sea can always take more water, always absorb the rivers' labor and leave no trace of the water they sent forth.

Vul and Sym seem to imply the presence of *mšm* before *šm* and require the translation "To the place [from] which they flow . . ." (JPSV). By this emendation, the verse mentions the return of the waters to the rivers' sources. Without emendation, the MT describes the endless flow toward the sea without mentioning the return. Ibn Ezra explains the process precisely: the sea waters evaporate and become clouds, whose rain supplies the sweet waters to the springs, which feed the rivers.

C. 1:8. Reaction to Observations in B

The *d^ebarim* that are weary are not the "things" mentioned — the world, sun, wind, and rivers. *Dabar* is nowhere used of physical entities. Rather, it is *words* that are weary, too feeble to communicate. These are Qohelet's words, of course, and he is weary. Repetition and routine wear one down:

> But one day the "why" arises and everything begins in that weariness tinged with amazement. "Begins" — this is important. Weariness comes at the end of the acts of a mechanical life, but at the same time it inaugurates the impulse of consciousness. (Camus, *Myth,* p. 10)

"The eye is not sated with seeing" *(lo' tiśba' 'ayin lir'ot): śaba'* with the direct object means "be satisfied, get enough of" (see §7.6). Sir 42:25 uses this construction in stating the opposite: <umi> yiśba' lir'ot to'ar "and who can be sated with seeing the appearance (of God's works)?" Sir 42:21-25 seems to be directly dependent on Qoh 1:3-9 and to be gently reinterpreting it by turning 1:8 into an exclamation of awe. For Sira, the natural world is so lovely and purposeful that no one can get enough of contemplating it. For Qohelet, the natural world is so dreary and aimless that no one can fully and satisfactorily contemplate it.

A possible, and even expected, reaction to the constancy of these phenomena would be exultation in the stability and reliability of God's creation. How glorious that the sun always rises and generation always follows generation! (Lohfink [1981] reads it this way, and understands the absence of newness as something good.) Qohelet, however, reacts with frustration. The futility of all effort, as he sees it, is inherent in the nature of things. This fact is not *bad,* it's just the way things are. But it *is* absurd, and absurdities escape the powers of sight and speech, which is to say, comprehension and expression. Sights and sounds may inundate the senses but they cannot provide understanding. Isa 6:9-10 also speaks of a kind of hearing and seeing that consists of superficial absorption of sense impressions devoid of understanding (LXX-Isa makes the distinction explicit).

"The eye is not sated with seeing, nor the ear filled by hearing," recalls 5:9a, "He who loves silver will not be sated with silver," and 6:7, "All a man's toil is for his mouth, but the appetite [*hannepeš*] is never filled [*lo' timmale'*]." Just as an appetite for wealth is never sated by amassing possessions, so is Qohelet's appetite for understanding never appeased by amassing hearing and seeing. Someone else might experience this insatiable appetite as a lively intellectual curiosity, but Qohelet feels it as an inadequacy and a source of frustration.

D. 1:9. Conclusion Abstracted from B and Justifying A

As in the natural world, so too in human life there is no true change, only dreary repetition. As Augustine observed, Qohelet is speaking of recurrence of *types* of beings and events:

> Even monstrous and irregular productions, though differing from one another, and though some are reported as solitary instances, yet resemble one another generally, insofar as they are miraculous and monstrous, and, in this sense, have been, and shall be, and are no new and recent things under the sun.[2]

Archetypal events (including deeds viewed as events) — birth, death, war, embracing, and so on — come to realization in specific manifestations: the birth of particular individuals, particular acts of embracing, the outbreak of particular wars, and so on. The concept of archetypes reduces the reality of specific, non-repetitive events. As Mircea Eliade says,

> Hegel affirmed that in nature things repeat themselves for ever and that there is "nothing new under the sun." All that we have so far demonstrated confirms the existence of a similar conception in the man of archaic societies: for him things repeat themselves for ever and nothing new happens under the sun. But this repetition has a meaning . . . it alone confers a reality upon events; events repeat themselves because they imitate an archetype — the exemplary event. Furthermore, through this repetition, time is suspended, or at least its virulence is diminished. (1954:90)

The last sentence does not apply to Qohelet, who felt the repetitiveness as a heavy burden. But the notion that repeated event-types alone are real, or are, we might say, more real than other events, does apply to Qohelet. The assertion that "there is nothing new under the sun" cannot apply to events as specific, unique occurrences. World War II, the book of Qohelet, the death of Lincoln — these had not happened before. But in some sense Qohelet would regard their reality as inhering in their realization of archetypes: war, book, assassination. Only in that way can he deny their newness. An analogy to this notion is a video game. The icons can do different things, but there is no real "newness" in their actions. They are simply instances of visual effects gener-

---

2. *City of God*, XII, 13 (trans. M. Dods). Augustine also considers it possible that 1:9 speaks of predestination.

ated by the software. Novelty is a delusion. And without novelty, what real achievement can there be?

Na'ăśah here probably means "happens." The recapitulation of this idea in 3:15 omits *na'ăśah*, suggesting that *na'ăśah* + *hayah* in 1:9 can be rephrased by *hayah* ("be," "happen") alone. The MT always vocalizes *n'śh* as a qatal *na'ăśāh* rather than the expected participle *na'ăśeh*. A possible reason for this is suggested in the comment on 8:11.

E. 1:10f. Prose Addendum

When people think something is new, that is only due to the defectiveness of the collective memory. This same defect means that not only do events repeat themselves, but the *experience* of events is also always the same. *Ri'šonim* and *'aḥăronim* refer not to earlier and later generations (as Crenshaw says), but to earlier and later events, since the issue in this passage is not whether people are remembered but whether events are.

Verse 11a could be translated as a question ("Is there something . . . ?") and answer ("It has already occurred . . ."). Michel (1989:186) says that *yeš* is used in argumentation to introduce for discussion a case or opinion other than the usual one. He follows Lohfink's translation, "Zwar gibt es bisweilen ein Ding, von dem es heisst: Sieh dir das an, das ist etwas Neues" ("To be sure, sometimes there is a thing of which it may be said: Take note, this is something new"). Crenshaw notes the effective juxtaposition of *yeš* and *'eyn:* the consideration introduced by the latter knocks down the supposition introduced by the former.

This passage has a peculiarly argumentative or forensic quality of a sort unusual in Biblical literature. It is manifest in the attempt to anticipate counter-arguments and forestall them by reference to psychology: The immense and startling assertion in v. 9 might well meet opposition, for people do think that this or that event is unprecedented. But they are mistaken, because the same thing happened in earlier times as well. Why would they think this? They are misled by a faulty collective memory. And it will always be thus. Not only do events repeat themselves, but the *experience* of events is also always the same.

◆ 1:12-18

(12) I am Qohelet. I have been king over Israel in Jerusalem.

(13) I set my heart to investigate and explore with wisdom all that occurs under the heavens. (It is an unfortunate business that God has given people to busy themselves with.) (14) When I observed all the events that occur under the sun, I realized that everything is absurd and senseless.

(15) Nothing warped can be straightened out,
*No deficiency can be ⟨filled out*ᵃ⟩.*

*(16) I spoke with my heart, saying: "See, I have amassed wisdom far beyond anyone who preceded me over Jerusalem." And my heart observed much wisdom and knowledge. (17) But when I applied my heart to gaining wisdom and knowledge,*ᵇ *⟨. . .*ᶜ*⟩ I realized that this too is senseless.*

(18) For in much wisdom there is much irritation,
and whosoever increases knowledge increases pain.

ᵃ*lᵉhimmālôt* (MT *lᵉhimmānôt*)
ᵇ*wāda'at* (MT *wᵉda'at*)
ᶜMT has *hôlēlôt wᵉśiklût* "inanity and folly," a gloss.

1:12-18 is composed of two sections, with the second looking back at the inquiry described in the first, reflecting upon it and reacting to its results.

    A. 1:12-15. Introduction of inquiry
       1. 1:12. Self-presentation
       2. 1:13. The undertaking: using wisdom to gain an
          understanding of the world
       3. 1:14-15. Conclusion: everything is absurd
    B. 1:16-18. Narration and evaluation of inquiry
       1. 1:16-17a. Method and process of inquiry
       2. 1:17b-18. Reflection on the inquiry itself:
          it is a miserable task

    Qohelet introduces himself as king, describes the investigation he undertook, and previews its discomforting conclusion, from which he learns that the success of his wisdom was also its bane. In the next unit, he will describe his wealth, his experience, and his conclusions.

1:12 This verse can be rendered either "I, Qohelet, have been king . . . ," or "I am Qohelet. I have been king. . . ." The latter translation seems the more appropriate, since the speaker has not yet introduced himself and could be expected to do so before identifying his office. (1:1 is the title, not Qohelet's words, and 1:2 is the author's summary of what Qohelet said.) "I am Qohelet" resembles the opening of various royal inscriptions, e.g., "I am Kilamuwa, the son of Hayya" (*TSSI* 3.34); "I am Azitawada, blessed by Baal, servant of Baal, whom Awarku, king of the Danunians, made powerful" (ibid., 48); "I am Yehaumilk, king of Byblos, etc." (ibid., 95). These introductory self-identifications, like Qohelet's, precede autobiographical accounts of the speaker's virtues and exploits. The qatal form, *hayiti melek,* refers to the present rule of the king, just like *mlkty* and *yšbty* in West Semitic royal inscriptions (Seow 1995:280). Nevertheless, Qohelet's words, just like the royal inscriptions, have a past orientation and are appropriately translated by the present perfect.

The phrase "king over Israel" shows that the author is thinking of a king of the United Monarchy. Of them, only David and Solomon ruled "in Jerusalem." We are to think of Qohelet in terms of Solomon; Solomon is his model. But, as I argued above, that does not mean that the speaker (let alone the author) *is* Solomon.

1:13 "Under the heavens": Though emendation to "sun" is not necessary, it does have a good claim to a Hebrew origin, being attested by Syr, Jerome, Tg, and most of the LXX tradition. The interchange between the functional synonyms *šemeš* and *šamayim* may have occurred in the transmission of texts or in the process of translation.

Na'ăśah and *hamma'ăśim* in 1:13f. refer to events. Qohelet determines to investigate what *happens* in life, rather than all of man's activities. See the discussion of these verses in §6.23.

The sentence, "it is an unfortunate business that God has given people to busy themselves with" (v. 13b) is parenthetical. The antecedent of "it" *(hu')* is not *kol 'ăšer na'ăśah taḥat haššamayim* (13aβ), for neither "what happens" nor "what is done" (if *'ăšer na'ăśah* does refer to actions) is "given" to man. The "unfortunate business" mentioned in 1:13 is the effort to understand what happens on earth. This effort is an aspect of wisdom. Qohelet believes that this task was imposed by God (see further 3:10, as emended). It is a fruitless one, for even if pursued day and night (8:16b) by the most competent persons (8:17b), its goal cannot be attained (8:17a). One cannot make sense out of something that is senseless (1:14).

Hertzberg and Ellermeier (1967:177-86) take the object of *lidroš* ("to investigate") and *latur* ("to explore") to be "wisdom" rather than "all that happens under the heavens," arguing that TWR elsewhere governs a direct object or, in the hiphil, the preposition *b-* (Judg 1:23), never *'al*. But the object of exploration is never introduced by a *b-* either, when the verb TWR is in the qal. Also, it is doubtful that *'al* can indicate "dasjenige, in Hinsicht worauf oder vielleicht noch besser: weswegen Qohelet die Weisheit unter die Lupe nehmen wollte" ("that in respect to which or, perhaps better, because of which, Qohelet would scrutinize wisdom") (Ellermeier, p. 179, who gives no examples of a similar usage). In any case, wisdom is only one of the objects of Qohelet's study; his field of investigation, as 1:2 and 12:8 show, is "everything," i.e., "all that happens" under the sun. "Wisdom" is best understood (with most commentators) as the *means* by which Qohelet investigates life. *Tûr* usually governs a direct object, but it is intransitive in Num 15:39 (followed by *'aḥărey*) and Qoh 2:3, where it means "go about," so there is no difficulty in modifying the verb by a prepositional phrase headed by *'al,* as here, indicating the "territory" of the exploration. For *daraš + 'al* meaning "inquire with regard to" see 2 Chr 31:9; also 11QT 56,2.

Verse 15, repeated in 7:13, has the ring of a traditional proverb that can be applied in various ways. Originally, Crenshaw suggests, it may have described an intractable pupil. In the present context, it elaborates on Qohelet's statements in v. 14 about "everything": what is distorted in this world cannot be corrected, what is missing cannot be supplied. These flaws, 7:13 declares, are God's doing.

Ḥesron "lack" echoes its opposite, *yitron* "profit." The *ḥesron* is the *yitron* absent from life (Crenshaw).

The emendation of *lhmnwt* to *lhmlwt* (*l*e*himmālôt*) "be filled," a Mishnaic-type spelling of a III-' verb, makes good sense (see L. Levy, who credits H. Ewald), though it lacks support in the versions.[3] The interchange of *nun/lamed* is an attested scribal error; see Perles, 1895:53 and *TAOT* 89.[4] MT means "that which is lacking cannot be numbered," but this is a pointless truism, not a complaint about the immutability of wrong situations, as the parallel phrase is. MT cannot mean "an untold number of things are lacking" (Barton), which is in any case banal.

In preparation for his investigation, Qohelet sought to amass wisdom and knowledge. He succeeded in this venture, but found that his success brought with it deep malaise.

---

3. The evidence Levy brings does not actually witness to the suggested reading. Sym represents this word not by ἀναπλῆσαι but by ἀναπλῆσαι ἀριθμόν, a contextual translation of *lhmnwt.* Also R. Bar Hehe's remark *h'y lhymnwt lhml'wt myb'y,* "this *lhymnwt* should be *lhml'wt*" (b. Ḥag. 9b), is not (contrary to Levy) evidence for *lhmlwt* but rather for MT. Bar Hehe is remarking on *lhmnwt* as a peculiarity requiring an exceptional interpretation.

4. Good examples are Job 15:35 (LXX reflects *tkyl* for *tkyn*); Neh 3:30; 12:44; 13:7 (*nškh* for *lškh* in these three verses); and 1 Sam 6:18 (*'bl* for *'bn;* cf. v. 14 and LXX).

1:16 Qohelet acquired wisdom beyond all his predecessors. The boast of great wisdom is a standard motif in royal inscriptions. The inscription of Idrimi boasts: "Nobody understood the things I understood" (Seow 1995:281).

As well as acquiring wisdom, Qohelet *observed* it. The phrase *lir'ot hokmah* means to observe wisdom and to consider its consequences, as in 2:12. In 9:13, *ra'iti hokmah* could mean "I saw as [an example of] wisdom." But *hokmah* is probably an addition there.

1:17 The phrase *holelot w^eśiklut,* "inanity and folly," looks like an addition based on 2:12a or 7:25. It could have been inserted by a scribe seeking to provide a more acceptable target for the *hebel*-judgment. A reference to folly in 1:17 is premature. 1:16-18 speaks of the consequences of wisdom alone. The conclusion "this too is senseless [*gam zeh hu' ra'yon ruah*]" has a singular pronoun as its subject, showing that Qohelet is judging one thing, not two, and furthermore v. 18 gives the reason only for an evaluation of wisdom.

The Masoretes linked *w^eda'at* to *holelot* by *merkha'-tipha'* and placed the disjunctive *'atnah* on *w^eśiklut,* thus making *da'at* an infinitive with "inanity and folly" as direct objects. We should vocalize *w^eda'at* as *wādā'at* (an understanding implied by LXX), treating *hokmah wādā'at* as a word-pair, as in v. 16. The pair stands in a distributed parallelism in v. 18. Though not reflected in the above translation, words from YD' are used five times in vv. 16-18. "Knowledge" is clearly the theme of the passage.

The phrases *yada' hokmah* and *yada' da'at* (lit. "know wisdom" and "know knowledge") mean to learn or possess wisdom/knowledge; compare *yada' hokmah* in Prov 1:2 and 24:14, *yada' da'at* in Prov 17:27 and Dan 1:4, and similar phrases with synonymous verbs *(hebin, binah)* in Prov 4:1; 17:24; 19:25; Job 38:4; etc. A clear example of this usage is Balaam's description of himself as *yodea' da'at 'elyon,* "one who *possesses* knowledge of [= from] the High One" (Num 24:16); see also Isa 29:24 and 2 Chr 2:12. Thus, strictly speaking, it is not wisdom as such that Qohelet is calling absurd. "This" in the *hebel*-judgment refers to the knowing — the acquisition and possession — of wisdom. He is not faulting wisdom as such, but only the human experience of it. Similarly, it is the experience of "becoming so very wise" (expressed by the verb, *hakamti*) that he deplores in 2:15 and "becoming excessively wise" that he warns against in 7:16.

1:18 Whatever wisdom's advantages, too large a dose causes discomfort, as Qohelet learned firsthand. Great wisdom is a source of pain and chagrin, for it enables, even forces, its possessor to see life's absurdities.

Verse 18b is, lit., "He increases knowledge — he increases pain." This is probably a virtual conditional, with the simple juxtaposition of two clauses; cf. esp. Prov 18:22. The subject is indefinite and may be translated, "whosoever, etc." For the construction see *GBH* §167a and compare the rabbinic usage, as in Avot 2:7b, *qanah šem ṭob, qanah leʿaṣmo* "if one has obtained (only) a reputation, he has obtained it for himself (alone)"; sim. Avot 1:13a. Alternatively, *yosip* (twice) can be described as a nominalized finite verb (on which see Grossberg 1979:31-33), but many of these nominalizations are actually elliptical constructions.

Kaʿas refers to a range of emotions from anxiety (e.g., 5:16) to anger (e.g., 7:3), and it is frequently uncertain which English word is the best translation. I translate "irritation" throughout for consistency, and because it too can refer both to anger directed at someone and to a diffuse discomfort.

◆ **2:1-26**

Chapter 2 is a single unit composed of three major sections.

    A. 2:1-11. Pleasure and toil
    B. 2:12-17. Wisdom and folly
    C. 2:18-26. Toil and pleasure, wisdom and folly

This unit continues the narration of Qohelet's investigation begun in 1:13 (note the "too" in 2:1b). Because of the length of the unit, the three sections of 2:1-26 will be translated and discussed separately, but the continuity should not be overlooked. The three sections belong to a single train of thought.

A. 2:1-11. Pleasure and Toil

(1) I said in my heart, "Come, let me make you experience pleasure. Enjoy yourself!" But I realized that this too is absurd. (2) Of amusement I said, "Inane!" and of pleasure, "What does this accomplish?"

(3) I went about in my heart, drawing my body with wine and leading[a] my heart by wisdom, and taking hold of folly, until I might see what is good for a man to do under the heavens during the few days of his life.

(4) I did great things: I built myself houses, planted myself vineyards, (5) made myself gardens and orchards and planted in them fruit trees of all kinds. (6) I made myself pools of water from which to irrigate a wood growing with trees. (7) I acquired male and female slaves, and I had home-

born servants as well. I also had many herds of cattle and flocks, more than all who were before me in Jerusalem. (8) I also amassed for myself silver and gold and treasures of kings and provinces. I acquired for myself singers and songstresses and the pleasures of men — a good number of concubines. (9) I grew far greater than anyone before me in Jerusalem, and also my wisdom stood by me. (10) Whatever my eyes saw I did not withhold from them. I did not restrain my heart from any sort of pleasure, and my heart received pleasure from all my toil, and this was my portion from all my toil.

(11) But when I turned (to consider) all the things my hands had done and the toil I had laboriously performed, I realized that it was all absurd and senseless, and there is no profit under the sun.

^a *nāhōg* (MT *nōhēg*)

A. 2:1-11. Pleasure and toil
   a. Qohelet sets out to examine pleasure (2:1a)
   b. Conclusion in advance: pleasure is absurd (2:1b-2)
   c. Account of inquiry (2:3 general; vv. 4-9 specifics)
   d. Summary finding: pleasure was his portion (2:10)
   e. Reflection on this finding: his toil was absurd (2:11)

Paragraphs a and b together form the introduction to the unit, c and d describe the experiment (its procedure and outcome), and e (separated from the foregoing by the phrase "I turned") reflects upon the finding and draws its implications.

Qohelet tells how he undertook to amass wealth and to immerse himself in pleasures of all sorts. He produces some of the resources himself (2:4-6), and others he purchases (vv. 7-8). His purpose is to discover what is good to do. The answer is pleasure, though this too is senseless. The feeling of pleasure is not enough to imbue pleasurable actions with meaning. Therefore the toil that produced the means of pleasure proved to be absurd.

1:12-18 and 2:1-11 are structured similarly. They report the undertaking of an inquiry (of the world; of pleasure), immediately state a finding (all events are absurd; pleasure is absurd), report more expansively on the procedure (amassing wisdom; amassing wealth and pleasures), then ponder the value of the efforts of the undertaking (amassing wisdom is absurd; toiling is absurd).

The very common word *lî* "for me/myself" is surprisingly infrequent in Qohelet, especially considering the work's autobiographical-reflexive cast. It appears once in 12:1, but in the latter it does not refer to Qohelet. Otherwise, it appears only in 2:4-9, eight times in nine verses. It is attached to almost every verb of production and acquisition in 2:4-8 (not exactly reflected in the above translation):[5] "I built myself . . . planted myself . . . made myself . . . made myself . . . there were to me . . . there were to me . . . I also amassed for myself . . . I acquired for myself. . . ." This repetition puts great emphasis on the self-centered drive for acquisition, a sort of intense consumerism. Yet the love of possessions cannot be filled by possessing them — a lesson Qohelet puts into a maxim in 5:9. Qohelet works obsessively to fill a massive craving, but his real desire is not for material goods.

2:1 A cohortative (*'ănass^ekah,* "let me make you experience") and an imperative (*ur^e'eh,* "enjoy yourself," lit. "and see!") are in parallelism. In 11:9 too an imperative is parallel to a wish-form (a jussive). Qohelet is addressing his heart as "you" and giving it a command. Note how his heart is treated as a distinct "person" in 1:16 and 7:25.

Hinneh at the start of a sentence usually indicates participant perspective together with a sense of discovery (Andersen 1974:94f.). This has a focusing effect that tends to subordinate a preceding verb of perception (or intention, or the like) and make it a virtual circumstantial clause. The translation above seeks to reflect this subordination.

There is a gap between the intention, expressed as an invitation to his heart to try pleasure (v. 1a), and the realization that pleasure is absurd, introduced by *hinneh* (v. 1b). The subsequent narrative will fill in the gap with the background experiences. The *hebel*-judgment in v. 1b is not something Qohelet knew at the start. It is a preview of what he discovered by experiment and reflection.

It is difficult to discern a difference between *ra'ah b^etob(ah)* (2:1) and *ra'ah tob* (3:13; 5:17; 6:6; sim. *r^e'eh hayyim,* 9:9). *R^e'eh b-* means "examine, scrutinize" in 11:4, and that might be the nuance here. Podechard (p. 258) says that *b-* with verbs of perception, especially *ra'ah,* indicates taking a special interest in the object; similarly BDB §907b-908a. Though this nuance is appropriate to the present verse, some occurrences of this phrase definitely contradict Podechard's observation; e.g., 1 Sam 6:19 (even a glimpse, let alone a scrutiny, of the ark would prove fatal); Esth 8:6

5. In the translation, "I had" (twice) in v. 7 and "with me" in v. 9 also represent Hebrew *li.*

(it was not only scrutiny of the Jews' destruction that Esther could not bear; *any* perception of it would be too much). Ginsberg (p. 92) explains R'H in this phrase as a variant of RWH, "drink one's fill, be saturated." But this interpretation implies that Qohelet requires nothing less than complete hedonistic satiation. Satiation is an impossibility (6:7), whereas "seeing good" — experiencing pleasure — *is* possible, and it is recommended. "Experience" is well attested as a meaning of *ra'ah* (BDB 907a; with *tob:* Job 9:9, 25).

In the conclusion "this [lit. "it"] too is absurd," the only available antecedent is the experience of pleasure. *Tob* and *śimḥah* both mean pleasure, not happiness; see chapter 7.

Tur-Sinai places the words *bayyayin 'et bᵉśari wᵉlibbi noheg* in v. 3 after *'nskh* in v. 1. The resulting text can be translated: (1a) "Come, let me anoint my body with wine and my heart behave in pleasure and see enjoyment ["goodness"]. . . . (3) I went about in my heart to draw wisdom and to seize folly, until I could see which was good for man to do. . . ." This emendation is interesting but too radical in the absence of external evidence. Also, Qohelet is not investigating wisdom here, as the emended text implies (cf. Gordis). Furthermore, the verb *nasak* elsewhere takes the poured-out liquid as its object and not the thing *on which* it is poured. *Nissah* means both "experience" and "give experience"; see Greenberg 1960:276.

2:3 *Tarti bᵉlibbi:* TWR + inf. here is the equivalent of SBB + inf. (2:20; 7:25), showing the beginning or the next stage in Qohelet's investigation, as he "turns" or "goes about" from one thing to another. ŠWB functions similarly (4:1, 7; 9:11). *Tûr* designates the action of the spies in Num 13, *passim,* where the object of investigation (the land) appears as the direct object. The heart is the area *within which* Qohelet pursues his exploration, not its object. Though he claims to have actually done the deeds listed in 2:4-10, these are preparations for a thought experiment. Qohelet is not examining material pleasures so much as his responses to them. Hence he goes about, meditates, *within* his heart.

The idiom *limšok bayyayin 'et bᵉśari* literally means "to draw my flesh with wine." A number of unparalleled meanings have been assigned to *limšok* here, such as "tempt" (JPSV) or "cheer" (NRSV) or "stimulate" (Barton, Gordis), but these are all guesses. The emendation to *lᵉśammēaḥ* (cf. Ps 104:15), proposed by Joüon (1930:419), is distant graphically.

The near-synonymity of *nhg* and *mšk* suggests that there is an overlooked parallelism in this verse. As vocalized by MT, 2:3abα reads

i	*tartî b*ᵉ*libbî*			
ii	*limšôk bayyayin 'et b*ᵉ*śārî*	a	b	c
iii	*w*ᵉ*libbî nōhēg bahokmāh*	c′	a′	b′
iv	*w*ᵉ*le'ĕhōz b*ᵉ*siklût*		a″	b″

i   I went about in my heart
ii drawing my body with wine,
iii and leading my heart by wisdom,
iv and taking hold of folly.

The submerged image in the first three lines is of a shepherd leading animals, such as sheep, on a cord. One of Qohelet's "sheep" is his flesh, which is drawn by the "cord" of wine. A comparable use of a metaphorical cord to draw something is Jer 31:3, *'al ken m*ᵉ*šaktik hased* "therefore have I drawn you with mercy." Also Hos 11:4, *b*ᵉ*habley 'adam 'emš*ᵉ*kem/ ba'ăbotot 'ahăbah,* "I drew them with human cords, with ropes of love." "Human cords" probably means emotional ties. Since the force of *'emš*ᵉ*kem* extends to the second stich too, Hos 11:4 shows the usage "draw . . . with ropes of love." Metaphorical pulling appears also in Isa 5:18: *hoy moš*ᵉ*key he'awon b*ᵉ*habley haššaw' w*ᵉ*ka'ăbot ha'ăgalah hatta'ah,* "Woe to those who draw iniquity with cords of deceit, and sin as with cart-ropes." Here the drawing is imagined as the pulling of a wagon. An apt Talmudic parallel to the usage in Qoh 2:3 is *'ymšyk btryyhw,* "He let himself be drawn after them (wine and bath)" (*'Ab. Zar.* 27b). "Drawn" means to be attracted. In the present verse, the infinitive *limšok* indicates concomitant action and explicates the verb *tarti* "I went about." (For the usage see *GBH* §124o.)

NHG-qal is apparently intransitive in Sir 3:26 and 40:23. In the Bible *nahag* is always transitive, meaning "lead" or "drive," often with animals as the object (Gen 31:18; Exod 3:1; 1 Sam 30:20, etc.). In the present verse it is parallel to *limšok* and so probably has its Biblical sense of "lead, draw." If *noheg* is transitive, the subject of the participle is easily supplied from the first-person in the preceding context. Examples of an attributive participle qualifying an immediately preceding first-person pronominal suffix are Ps 103:2f.; Hab 1:5; Zech 9:12; and Mal 2:16; cf. *GBH* §121r. While this construction is possible, it is awkward here, since it is coordinated with two infinitives and has the same gerundive (adverbial) function. It is likely that the vocalization *nōhēg* (written *lene*) is a Masoretic misunderstanding, based on the assumption that *noheg* means "behave." We should probably vocalize the word as an inf. abs.: *nāhōg*.

In 2:3 (lines ii-iii in the above), Qohelet says that he led his body by *(b-)*

means of physical influence, namely wine, while leading his heart by *(b-)* means of intellectual influence, namely wisdom.

"Taking hold of folly": Though Qohelet *examines* folly, he nowhere admits to indulging in it. In 2:9 he states "and still my wisdom remained with me." "Folly" refers to material pleasures, which have all been prejudged as foolish (2:2), but not to a particular type of pleasure that is more foolish than others, because no subgroup of pleasures has been singled out. Qohelet will take hold of, and try, something that will *prove to be* foolish. The pleasures he tries are not intrinsically foolish; they are the very same ones he recommends elsewhere. But even these, when measured against the criterion of profitability, are foolish. *BHS* (accepted in Fox 1987) emends *l'ḥz* to *l' 'ḥz* = *lō' 'ōḥēz,* "and not seizing (folly)." Though this does make sense, the emendation is not necessary. Since pleasure has been called inane in v. 2, it can be called *siklut* here.

The question Qohelet puts before himself is what is good for man to do (*'ey zeh* = "what," as often in RH, not "which [of two things]"). To ascertain this, Qohelet tried out various diversions. He toiled to amass silver and gold and spent his wealth on pleasurable things. He describes and judges toil and pleasure together.

Getting rich requires wisdom — or luck. Qohelet refers to the man whose wealth was gained through "wisdom, knowledge, and skill" (2:21), he himself being the prime example (2:20c). And, as Qohelet stresses, his wisdom remained with him throughout his labors and his pleasures. Nevertheless, as we will learn, toil is bitter and profitless, and the one who gains good things *without* toil must be reckoned wiser than the toiler (2:26).

Qohelet seeks to discover "what is good for a man to do under the heavens during the few days of his life." He gives the answer in 2:10: to take pleasure in what one's toil produces. He will repeat this answer, using lang*uage reminiscent of 2:3, in his recurrent recommendation to "see good" and "do good," that is to say, pleasurable things, during our short lives.

2:4-8 Still imitating royal inscriptions, Qohelet boasts of his material accomplishments. He uses the genre ironically, for his point is that these achievements do not matter (Seow 1995:284).

Ma'ăśay in v. 4 may mean either "actions" or "property" (translated above ambiguously as "things" in 2:4 and 11). *'Aśah* in vv. 5, 6, 7, 8 means "make" in the sense of "earn," "acquire" (as in English "make money"), and is synonymous with *qaniti* in v. 7.

179

2:8 "A good number of concubines" *(šiddah wᵉšiddot):* Ibn Ezra glosses *šiddah wᵉšiddot* as "women"; similarly, Gordis and Whitley 1979:21f. *Šiddah wᵉšiddot* is in apposition to *taʿănugot bᵉney haʾadam,* which seems to allude to women. As Ibn Ezra observes, Qohelet is surveying (by example) all the types of worldly desires, and women as objects of sexual pleasure are not mentioned elsewhere in his report. *Šiddah wᵉšiddot* as an expression of multiplicity may be compared to singular-plural iteration in *dor dorim* (Ps 72:5; 102:25). For "concubine," see Whitley 1979:21f. The derivation of *šiddah* is uncertain. Ugaritic *št* (from **šdt?*) "lady" is a possible cognate. (The relevance of the supposed Amarna gloss *šāditum* to the ideogram *salumûn* "concubine" has been disputed by Moran 1975:151). Gordis explains *šiddah* as a feminine form of *šad* "breast," but that form does not exist elsewhere. Ibn Ezra derives the word from *š-d-d* "plunder," hence "women taken as booty." This sort of acquisition too was considered acceptable (Deut 21:10-14). Others derive *šiddah* from RH *šiddah* "strongbox," "chest" (for safekeeping). Gold and silver would go in a strongbox, but not all the "pleasures of men."

2:9 In *wᵉgadalti wᵉhosapti,* the latter verb has adverbial force, since it has no object. For *hosip* = "to exceed," "do more than," see, for example, 1 Kgs 10:7; 16:33. West Semitic and Mesopotamian royal inscriptions often proclaim the king's superior accomplishments (Seow 1995:281f.). Kilamuwa boasts "And I, Kilamuwa son of PN, that which I accomplished their predecessors had not accomplished" (*TSSI* 1.34, I.4-5). "Grew far greater" may specifically refer to amassing wealth.

"My wisdom stood by me" has two implications: Qohelet did not lose his good sense while amassing property, but did so wisely and soberly; and his acumen served him well in earning his wealth.

2:10 *Kol śimḥah: kol* sometimes means "all sorts of"; e.g., Cant 3:6; see GKC §227b.

ʿĀmāl (noun, twice) is ambiguous in both occurrences. It may refer to the immediate source of pleasure, namely Qohelet's wealth, or to the farther source, namely his toil.

Libbi śameaḥ mikkol . . . : The unusual use of *min* with *śamaḥ* may mark the *indirect* source of benefit (thus Delitzsch), in which case *ʿamal* refers to labor. This explanation fits 2 Chr 20:27, where the piel of *ŚMḤ* governs *min.* To be sure, Prov 5:18, the only other place the idiom occurs, does not support this explanation. There is, however, some evidence for the reading *bᵉ(śimḥah)* (Syr, Vul, Mid. Shoḥer Tov *ad loc.,* and some Heb MSS).

2:11   Whether *ma'ăśim* and *'amal* refer to the effort or to its product is uncertain, but the similarity of this verse to 1:3 and 3:9, where wealth is not at issue, favors the former. In any case, what essentially troubles Qohelet throughout 2:1-26, especially in 2:18-26, is not that wealth itself is trivial, but that human *efforts* are robbed of their significance by death and chance. I discuss the reasons for this judgment in §8.2, namely the inanity of pleasure (2:1-2) and the unjust allocation of the toiler's wealth, the second reason reinforcing the first.

The phrase "in toil" is implicit in the statement "there is no profit under the sun," as it is explicit in the similar verses 1:3 and 3:9. For a clear case of implicit restriction of a *yitron*-statement, see 6:11.

B. 2:12-17. Wisdom and Folly

(12) And I turned to observe wisdom and inanity and folly, for what will the man be like who will come after <me, who will rule^a> over what <I earned^b> earlier?

(13) And I saw that wisdom has an advantage over folly as great as the advantage of light over darkness:

(14) The wise man has his eyes in his head,
while the fool goes about in darkness.
But I also realized that the very same fate befalls them both.

(15) So I said in my heart, "What happens to the fool will happen to me too, so to what purpose, then, have I become so very wise?" And I said in my heart that this too is absurd. (16) For the wise man, just like the fool, is never remembered, inasmuch as in the days to come both are soon forgotten. Oh, how the wise man dies just like the fool!

(17) So I came to detest life, for I was distressed by what happens under the sun, for it is all absurd and senseless.

^a *' aḥăray hammōlēk* (MT *'aḥărêy hammelek*)
^b *'ăśîtîw* (MT *'āśûhû*)

B. 2:12-17. Wisdom and folly
  a. The undertaking (v. 12)
  b. The finding: wisdom is superior (vv. 13-14a)
  c. A reflection on this finding: the wise man is not treated fairly (vv. 14b-16)
  d. Reaction to the reflection (v. 17)

Note the similarity of the procedure in this section to that of 1:12-18 and 2:1-11: Qohelet tells how he undertook an investigation, reports the finding, tells how he pondered the finding, and reports his reaction.

Qohelet says that he drew upon two resources in his labors: work and wisdom (2:9, 10, 19). He reflects upon these resources, now turning to the latter. He mentions folly in 2:12a only in passing, in the course of evaluating wisdom.

2:12a Qohelet says he will examine wisdom and folly. The latter is expressed in two words *holelot* and *siklut,* "inanity and folly," which form a hendiadys meaning "inane folly." They are indistinguishable for practical purposes. Qohelet is observing only two things, wisdom and folly.

Galling transposes v. 12a and 12b because the latter seems to intrude between intention (12a) and result (13), and because 12b, though obscure, seems to motivate the judgment in v. 11. But v. 12b can be parenthetical, explaining the thought that led Qohelet to reflect on the consequences of wisdom and folly (v. 11a).

Qoh 2:12b makes no sense as it stands and is certainly corrupt, but some of the damage can be repaired by a revocalization of two words, proposed by Ginsberg, and aided by one consonantal emendation. The result is a partial solution: *kî meh hā'ādām šeyyābô' <'aḥărāy, hammōlēk> 'ēt 'ăšer kᵉbār <'ăśîtîw>,* lit., "for what is [the quality of] the man who will come after me, [the man] who will control what I have already earned?" We can make sense of the complaint implied in 2:12 by comparing its components with their equivalents (indicated by ≈) in 2:18-19:

- *ḥokmah* and *holelot wᵉsiklut* ≈ *ḥakam* and *sakal* in v. 19a.
- *meh ha'adam* ≈ *umi yodea' heḥakam yihyeh,* etc. For *mah* meaning "what is the quality of?" see Num 13:18; but an emendation to *mî* "who" may be warranted.
- *'aḥărāy* (MT *'aḥărey*) ≈ *'aḥăray* in v. 18. The time-modifier *kᵉbar* "already" (or "earlier"), referring to the production of the wealth in v. 12, matches the "after" in both 12b and 18b, which speak of the time *after* the life of the toiler (exemplified by Qohelet) when the lucky man will enjoy the wealth that was *already* earned by another.
- *hammolek 'et* "who rules over," "controls" ≈ in *yišlaṭ b-* "will control" in v. 19. *Malak,* however, should govern *'al,* and this is a weak spot in the emendation. Ginsberg compares the Arabic cognate which means "to possess" and takes an accusative.
- *<'ăśitiw>* ≈ *'ămali* in v. 19. MT's *'aśuhu* could be understood as an imper-

sonal third-plural equivalent to a passive. The LXX reads this as *'āśāhû* "*he* did it." But an emendation to *'śyty* or *'śytyw ('ăśîtîw)* seems justified. In various scripts, there is considerable resemblance between *heh* and *taw,* and *waw* and *yod* are sometimes indistinguishable. In either case, the word refers to earnings and corresponds to *'amalî* in v. 19. *'Ăšer . . . 'ăśitiw* "that which I earned" means the same as *ma'ăśay,* "my works." A mistaken *'śwhw* could have given rise to MT's *hammelek.*

With these correspondences in mind, we can paraphrase 2:12 thus: I next decided to observe the effects of wisdom and folly, for I wondered about the sort of a man who will succeed me and control what I had earlier earned. The answer comes in 2:18f.: He who succeeds me and controls my wealth may as easily be a fool as a wise man.

2:13-14a The wise man has knowledge while the fool lives in ignorance. On the relation between 2:13-14a and 14b see §§5.13, 5.3. Qoh 2:13-14a is a superlative affirmation of the advantage of wisdom over folly. Light and darkness are polar opposites.

Michel (1989:25-30) argues that *ra'ah* in 2:13 (as in 1:14, 16; 2:12) means "(prüfendes) betrachten" (to contemplate carefully and critically) rather than "see." He believes that 1:13 is a citation of an opinion Qohelet examines rather than a conclusion he affirms. Gordis too considers vv. 13-14 a quotation that Qohelet rejects in v. 15. Gordis expresses this relation by supplying "I have heard it said" before v. 13. But *ra'ah* with a "that"-clause always introduces a proposition the speaker believes true. When the direct object is a noun, on the other hand, *ra'ah* means "see," "look at," "consider," and the like; and since the object of observation has no propositional content, the verb does not imply validity. It is special pleading to assign this statement to another viewpoint while leaving other affirmations of wisdom's value (such as 7:11f.) to Qohelet.

Miqreh (Qoh 2:14, 15; 3:19; 9:2f.) (translated above as "what happens to") means "fate" in the sense of what happens to someone, whether by predetermination or chance, as opposed to what he does to himself. In its four occurrences outside Qohelet (including the synonym *qāreh*), *miqreh* refers to an occurrence that is unexpected and unforeseeable to humans. A *miqreh* is a *type* of occurrence, which, from the *human* perspective, may be chance, but that does not exclude divine determination. Qohelet uses *miqreh* only in reference to death, and at a higher level of abstraction. (P. Machinist, 1995:165-70, q.v. for an analysis of Qohelet's concept of *miqreh* and fate.)

The concepts of "folly" *(siklut, sekel, kesel)* and "fool" *(sakal* or *k^esil)* have no moral content in Qohelet, unlike in Proverbs. The old king's folly (4:13) consists of senile witlessness, not moral debasement. The fool in Qohelet is characterized by obtuseness and ignorance (2:13f.; 9:17), verbal ineptitude (5:2; 10:12), and general incompetence (10:2, 15). The *k^esilim* who delay in paying vows are foolish not because the act is sinful but because it is self-destructive (5:5), hence shortsighted and stupid.

2:15 In spite of wisdom's superiority, the foolish and the wise come to the same end. This leveling makes it pointless to grow very wise, but it does not, to Qohelet's mind, eliminate wisdom's superiority.

Ginsberg says that taking *yoter* as adverbial ("why then have I become *greatly* wise") produces a banality, because if the wise man dies like the fool, it is not worthwhile to grow wise *at all.* But here, as in 1:18 and 7:16, Qohelet warns against *much* wisdom, for it opens one's eyes to painful realities. Some wisdom, like some labor, is necessary and valuable, but too much of either inflicts discomfort and dismay. Since Qohelet did grow "very wise," it is natural for him to describe himself in those terms.

The antecedent of "this too is *hebel*" may be the fact that the fool and the wise man (namely, Qohelet) share the same ultimate fate. More likely, it is Qohelet's "becoming very wise," a process called *ra'yon ruaḥ* in 1:17.

2:16 More precisely, "in the days to come both will have already been forgotten": the forgetting precedes the near future. Qohelet would not agree that "the memory of the righteous is for a blessing, while the name of the wicked will rot" (Prov 10:7). For Qohelet, there is neither blessing nor curse: *everyone* is consigned to oblivion. *Hayyamim habba'im* is an adverbial accusative referring to the near future, as shown by the adverb *k^ebar* "already" or (depending on context) "soon," "a long time since." *K^ebar,* used nine times in Qohelet but nowhere else in the Bible, is an Aramaism frequent in RH.

2:17 *Ma'ăśeh šenna'ăśah* here is a collectivity of events, for what Qohelet has just observed is not a deed. It has no agent, which is what distinguishes deed from event.

Qohelet's reflections on the leveling power of death (2:12-16) brought him to a nadir of anger and despair. For a moment he came to detest life. But this is Qohelet looking back. As his account moves forward, he tempers his frustration with discoveries of good things, and his affirmation of life grows stronger.

184

C. 2:18-26. Toil and Pleasure, Wisdom and Folly

(18) And I came to detest my wealth for which I had toiled under the sun, since I would be leaving it to a man who will come after me (19) (and who knows whether he will be wise or foolish?) and who will control all my wealth for which I had toiled in wisdom under the sun. This too is absurd.

(20) So I turned to rid my heart of illusions concerning all the toil at which I had labored under the sun. (21) For sometimes a man whose toil is (performed) in wisdom, knowledge, and skill ends up giving it as a portion to someone who did not toil for it. This too is an absurdity and a great evil. (22) For what does a man get out of his toil and his heart's thoughts at which he toils under the sun? (23) For all his days his business is but pain and irritation, and not even at night does his heart find repose. This too is absurd.

(24) There is nothing better for a man <than^a> to eat and drink and show himself enjoyment through his toil. I saw that this too is from the hand of God, (25) for who will eat, or who will fret, except as <he^b> determines? (26) For to the one God favors he gives wisdom and knowledge and pleasure, while to the one who is offensive he gives the business of gathering and amassing in order to give [the wealth] to the one whom God favors. This too is absurd and senseless.

^a*miššeyōʾkal* (MT *šeyyōʾkal*)
^b*mimmennû* (MT *mimmennî*)

Section C progresses by a series of statements and motivations. Levels of subordination are shown by indentation in the following outline. This section, reversing the procedure of sections A and B, proceeds *from* Qohelet's reaction ("I came to detest") rather than towards it. This reaction is explained by reporting the observations that led to it. Qohelet identifies a single situation — one man toils and another gets his wealth — and broods on it, reiterating it in several ways, as if poking at a sore spot in his own flesh, then judging it absurd and justifying his judgment. He chains his reasons and evaluations in such a way as to give the appearance of developing and reinforcing an extended argument.

This section is composed of a long reflection, in which one thought leads into the next, followed by a practical conclusion, whose value is immediately restricted.

C. 2:18-26. Toil and pleasure, wisdom and folly
  a. Reflection on the absurdity of toil (18-23)
    i. Reaction to the unfairness to the toiler (disgust) (18a)

ii. Reason for i: the injustice to the toiler (18b-19a)

iii. Judgment of ii: it is absurd (19b)

iv. Reaction to iii: disillusionment (20)

v. Reason for iv: the injustice to the toiler (21abα)

vi. Judgment of v: it is absurd and evil (21bβ)

vii. Reason for vi: the misery of the toiler (22-23a)

viii. Judgment of vii: it is absurd (23b)

b. Practical conclusion: nothing is better than enjoyment of pleasures (24)

i. Limitation: God determines who will be allowed this (25-26abα)

ii. Evaluation of the scenario: it is absurd (26bβ)

Toil yields no profit, even if it brings wealth, because there are cases of one man toiling (in wisdom) and another (who may be a fool) coming into his earnings. Qohelet does not say how often this happens, but the fact that it *can* occur is an absurdity.

Enjoyment of what you have while you have it is the only reasonable recourse. This advice is here incidental to the complaint, and Qohelet's praise of pleasure as God's gift easily slides back into this complaint, now formulated theologically: God's inexplicable will (rather than human effort) determines whether one will have the possibility of enjoying life.

Two senses of 'amal are almost inextricably intertwined in this passage: the toilsome labor itself, and earnings, the material fruits of toil.

- In 2:18, the 'amal (noun) that Qohelet hates seems to be his earnings, since the suffix of 'anniḥennu can apply only to property, for that alone is what Qohelet can (and must) turn over to his successor. (The verb 'amel here means "gained through toil.")
- In 2:19, 'ămali means "earnings," for that, and not the toil, is what the successor will receive. The verb thus means "gained through toil."
- In 2:20, he'amal še'amalti is ambiguous. "Toil" seems more appropriate (for both noun and verb) since Qohelet already spoke of his disillusionment with his wealth in v. 18, and v. 20 seems to address a new issue ("so I turned"), namely the failure of toil to secure its goals.
- In 2:21a, the adverbial phrases "in wisdom, in knowledge, and in skill" modify the activity of toiling, yet the suffix of "giving it" refers to earnings. 'Ămalo here binds the two ideas most closely.
- In v. 21b, the verb 'amal means "toil" (as even Ginsberg concedes) not "earned," because it governs *bo,* "for it," not the accusative as in v. 19b.

Also, the point of the sentence is that the fortunate man did not invest effort (*'amal* = "toil") in it.

- In 2:22, *'amal* (twice) means "toil," for it is collocated with *ra'yon libbo*, "his heart's thoughts," which is a mental activity, not a material possession.
- In 2:24, *'ămalo* is ambiguous. It may mean "his toil," indicating the indirect source (or possibly the temporal context) of his pleasure.

2:18 The "man" in *la'adam* is generic (cf. *la'adam* in v. 22). He is whoever happens to receive Qohelet's wealth.

Just as Qohelet can say in v. 17 that he came to detest life (an outburst that will recur [4:3; 6:3] but that does not define his basic attitude), so can he lash out here at his wealth. He holds both in contempt, at least temporarily, because they have failed to live up to his earlier expectations. But at root Qohelet believes that possession of wealth is a blessing and its loss grievous. Wealth makes pleasure possible, and God gives it to the one he favors.

2:19 This verse is parenthetical. The injustice is, of course, more severe if the toiler was wise and the recipient a fool, but even if the recipient of Qohelet's wealth happens to be wise, the basic injustice remains: one person worked and another benefited.

Seow (1996) argues for an Achemenid dating of Qohelet on the grounds that he uses the verb *šlṭ* in the sense of "to have legal right of possession" (2:19; 5:18; 6:2; sim. *šalliṭ* = "proprietor" in 7:19; 8:9 and *šilṭon* = "authority, right" in 8:4, 8. After the fourth century, according to Seow (p. 654f.), this usage was displaced by derivatives of RŠH. But the documentary evidence is inadequate to justify the conclusion that ŠLṬ *ceased* to have the indicated sense in the third century B.C.E. In fact, ŠLṬ means "rule," "control," or "ruler" — supposedly the later usage — in Qoh 8:4, 8, 9; 10:5; and probably 7:19. In 5:18 and 6:2, *hišliṭ* means "allow," not "give the right of proprietorship." "To have legal right of possession" is a feasible interpretation only in 2:19, but there too "rule" or "control" is possible. Qohelet uses ŠLṬ exactly as in RH or Aramaic, where it is used of control of such things as jealousy, sleep, the evil inclination, or of the angel of death's control over mortals. Hence Qohelet's use of ŠLṬ favors a *post*-Achemenid dating.

2:20 In 2:11, Qohelet "turned" to disabuse his heart of any illusions he might have about toil. This verse resumes and develops the "turn" in the development of his thought marked in v. 11, and the entire section C elaborates the reasons for the *hebel*-judgment in that verse.

L^eya'eš means "to disillusion (oneself)," "to give up hope," as in RH. The illusion to which Qohelet was subject, judging from the reasons he gives for surrendering it, was the profitability of toil.

2:21 "For sometimes a man, etc.": lit., "there is a man, etc." The fact that there are such instances is enough, in Qohelet's view, to subvert the profitability of toil. The basic injustice is the irrelevance of toil and wisdom to inheritance (Murphy). Murphy says that Qohelet seems insensitive to considerations of family. But such considerations would be irrelevant if, as seems to be the case (4:8b), Qohelet has no family, for then his wealth will inevitably end up in the possession of a "stranger" (anyone outside his family). And even if a man's wealth goes to his son, that does not solve the problem, for the son may be a fool, and at any rate he will not have labored for the wealth that drops into his lap. Still, it does seem that if one has a son, it is a good thing to have wealth to bequeath him (5:13), and the lack of a son or brother makes toil even more senseless (4:8).

2:22 *Meh howeh la'adam b^ekol 'ămalo,* lit. "For what is there for a man . . ." is equivalent to *mah yitron la'adam b^ekol 'ămalo* in 1:3 (C. D. Ginsburg et al.). D. Michel (1989:33) explains the use of the (Aramaizing) participle *howeh* as emphasizing the quality of duration ("das Dauerende, Bleibenden"). This seems correct (and Jastrow, *Dictionary,* gives "enduring" as one of the connotations of the participle), but that does not distinguish it from *yitron.*

This sentence is a rhetorical question prompting the answer: "nothing." This does not mean absolutely nothing, since even if a man has no "profit" he can still have a "portion" in his work, which means he will possess *something.* The negation here refers to the man who grimly slaves away for wealth (v. 23) and then loses it to another (v. 21). The wealth becomes the other man's portion, not the toiler's. In contrast, one who pauses for moments of respite and pleasure does have something — a portion — in his toil.

2:23 V. 23 reiterates the themes of v. 22, with *'inyano* resuming *kol 'ămalo* and *lo' šakab libbo* resuming *ra'yon libbo.* The workaholic's *'inyan* — "business" or "activity" — is pain and irritation insofar as it produces these feelings. At night, he tosses and turns in worry (cf. 5:11) or in nightmares induced by daytime disquiet (cf. 5:2). Ben Sira too describes this unhappy condition: "When [man] rests on his bed, the sleep of night alters his mind [*t^ešanneh 'et da'to;* perhaps "drives him mad"] (40:5b, cf. 6-8). Ben Sira moralizes this distress, claiming that while it afflicts all people to some degree, for the wicked it is seven times worse (v. 8). Qohelet blames nocturnal malaise and restlessness on obsessive and excessive work rather than on wickedness.

2:24 The minor correction of a haplography, from *b'dm šy'kl* to *b'dm mšy'kl,* with a comparative *mem* as in 3:22, seems hardly in doubt. It has apparent support in Syr, Vul, and Tg, and S^c, but these would have been forced by context to supply an "except" in some form. LXX, however, mechanically imitates the MT.

2:25 *Yaḥuš* means "worry," "fret," a sense clearly attested in Job 20:2; thus Aq, Sym, SyH; Tg *ḥšš'*. See the thoroughgoing study of this verb in Ellermeier, 1963a. It is a byform of RH *ḥašaš* "be uncomfortable, worry." Alternative glosses are "abstain" (Gordis), "enjoy" (Barton), and "rejoice" (Murphy), but these have little philological basis. The man who "frets" is none other than the "offender" of v. 26, while the one who "eats" (that is, "consumes") is the recipient of God's favor.

Mimmennî should be emended to *mimmennû,* a minuscule change (thus LXX, Syr, SyH, some Heb MSS): "except for him" meaning except for God, unless God wills. The MT has Qohelet saying that no one will eat or drink other than himself, which is neither pertinent nor true. Indeed, vv. 21 and 26 indicate that someone else *will* do so. Verse 25 as emended is paralleled by 3:13 and 5:18, which state that whether or not one will "eat and drink" depends on God. Calling to mind God's all-determining will brings Qohelet back to his main complaint, which he formulates theologically in the next verse.

2:26 Qohelet calls the toiler a *ḥoṭe',*[6] which usually means "sinner" but here must mean "one who is offensive, offender." A true sinner toiling for the benefit of a God-favored man would not be *hebel* by any definition. Furthermore, Qohelet has just said that the fortunate recipient may be a fool (2:19) and the unfortunate man may toil in wisdom (v. 21). Certainly the *ḥoṭe'* and the man who is "good before God" are not simply sinner and saint.

As many interpreters recognize, the *ḥoṭe'* here is not a transgressor against the law or moral norms, but rather one who has somehow incurred God's disfavor. Still, the concept of *ḥoṭe'* is not diluted to the point of being

---

6. This verb is consistently pointed with a segol rather than ṣere in Qohelet (2:26; 8:12; 9:2, 18), being treated as a III-*heh* verb; similarly *môṣe'* "find" in 7:26. In RH the III-*aleph* verbs merge with the III-*heh*s, but RH pointing is found in earlier texts as well (e.g., 1 Sam 22:2; examples in *GBH* §78g). This phenomenon has never been well explained. It is probably an intrusion of later morphology into Masoretic vocalization rather than the preservation of the authors' phonological peculiarities in oral tradition.

merely an "unfortunate" man (thus Ginsberg). ḤṬ' always denotes offensive-ness to someone. Since the offense in question is usually of a moral nature (even in Qohelet: 7:20; 8:12; 9:2), the translation "sinner" is usually accurate, but not always so. In Qoh 10:4, the ḥăṭa'im "offenses" that enrage a ruler cannot be presumed to be moral trespasses. They are any actions that irritate him. (Note that the ruler resembles God also in bestowing inexplicable favor on some people: 10:5-6.) Occasionally elsewhere in the Bible ḤṬ' lacks moral implications, but only when it refers to an offense against humans. Bathsheba says that she and her son will be ḥaṭṭa'im if Adonijah succeeds (1 Kgs 1:21), meaning that they will be offensive to him or treated as offenders, not that they will be guilty of moral infractions. See also 1 Kgs 8:31 (the defendant may not have *sinned* — the case has not yet been adjudicated — but he has offended the plaintiff); Gen 40:1 (pharaoh's butler and baker have somehow offended him, but there is no implication of a moral failing on their part); and Prov 20:2 (the person who angers a king in effect commits an offense against *himself*). In Qoh 2:26 and 7:26 the ḥoṭe' is someone who is offensive to God.

One thing that can offend God is a man's toiling endlessly, pushing too hard for gain, an idea shared by Prov 28:20, "A man of faith has many blessings, but he who hurries to grow rich will not be exonerated." God wants man to enjoy life (Qoh 9:7), and "remembering" one's Creator (12:1) is a motive for doing so. Though Qohelet does not frame this in moral terms, the wise would have understood the hurried and strained attempt to grasp wealth as arrogance, the delusion that one can control life by his own exertions, and hence the opposite of "faith" (Prov 28:20). But there is a strange twist in this reasoning: A man displeases *(ḥoṭe')* by toiling, and consequently he is set the task of toiling for the benefit of another. His "offense" is also his punishment. In other words, his obsession breeds itself.

The unit ends with another twist: "For to the one God favors he gives wisdom and knowledge": the fortunate non-toiler has been granted wisdom. The wisdom God bestows here is not the content of knowledge, for that might well increase its possessor's misery, as it did for Qohelet. The "wisdom" and "knowledge" transferred to the fortunate man can be understood in two ways. First, *ḥokmah* can refer to the *products* of wisdom, as in 1 Kgs 10:4 and Ezek 28:7. Alternatively (or perhaps at the same time) the fortunate man's "wisdom" could be the *good sense (da'at, ḥokmah),* the savvy, to do what benefits him, which in context means taking it easy and enjoying what falls to one's lot. This is what Qohelet recommends doing, and he naturally considers this behavior wise, even if he himself lacks this type of wisdom.

The toiler has turned out to be foolish and "offensive," while the fortu-

190

nate, easygoing man has seen wisdom or its fruits fall into his lap, and it was certainly wise of him not to exert himself. But for all that, there has been an asymmetry of effort and result, and this is absurd. It offends Qohelet's sense of fairness. There is, however, a well-known psychological feedback mechanism whereby suffering provokes a sense of guilt, even when this is objectively unfounded. The sufferer feels he must have done *something;* he feels the taint of offensiveness just because of his misery.

Qohelet is pained at the thought that he, as one who labored merely to pass his wealth on to someone else, is displeasing to God, like a person condemned by a "futility curse."[7] He regards himself as a *hoṭe'* — and here the usual connotations of sinfulness are in play — without regard to whether he has actually sinned.

◆ **3:1-15**

> *(1)   For everything there is a season,*
> *a time for every matter under the heavens:*
> *(2)   a time to be born,*
> *and a time to die;*
> *a time to plant,*
> *and a time to uproot what is planted;*
> *(3)   a time to kill,*
> *and a time to heal;*
> *a time to tear down,*
> *and a time to build up;*
> *(4)   a time to weep,*
> *and a time to laugh;*
> *a time of mourning,*
> *and a time of dancing;*
> *(5)   a time to cast stones,*
> *and a time of gathering stones;*
> *a time to embrace,*
> *and a time to shun embrace;*
> *(6)   a time to seek,*
> *and a time to lose;*
> *a time to keep,*
> *and a time to cast away;*

7. "Futility curses" are discussed by D. Hillers 1964:28f. Examples are Job 31:8 ("May I sow and another eat") and Deut 28:30-31; Amos 5:11; Mic 6:15. They are reversed in the blessing in Isa 65:22.

> *(7) a time to rend,*
> *and a time to sew;*
> *a time to keep silent,*
> *and a time to speak;*
> *(8) a time to love,*
> *and a time to hate;*
> *a time of war,*
> *and a time of peace.*

(9) What profit does one who does something have in what he toils at?

(10) I have seen the business that God has given man to occupy himself with: (11) He made everything appropriate in its time, but he also placed <toil^a> in their hearts, without man being able to grasp in any way whatsoever what God has brought to pass.

(12) I realized that there is nothing good for <man^b> but to have pleasure and to get enjoyment in his life. (13) And for any man to eat and drink and experience pleasure in all his toil, this is the gift of God.

(14) I know that whatever God makes happen is always what will be. It is impossible to add to it and impossible to take away from it. And God has done (this) so that people will fear him. (15) Whatever happens already has happened, and what is going to happen already has happened. And God seeks what is pursued.

^a*he'āmāl* (MT *hā'ōlām*)
^b*bā'ādām* (MT *bām*)

Every event and deed has its right time, a set of circumstances in which they should happen or be performed, and God determines when this is. So in whatever one may do, he should wait until the time is ripe rather than straining and pushing against the grain. But there's a catch: God has denied man the knowledge of when these times are.

A. 3:1-9. The Catalogue of Times
   a. The principle: everything has its time (1)
   b. Instances of the principle (2-8)
   c. Conclusion: there is no profit in toiling (9)
B. 3:10-15. The implications of this principle
   a. with respect to the search for wisdom: man cannot understand the events of life (10-11)
   b. with respect to practical conduct: enjoy life (12-13)

c. with respect to power: man does not control the course
of events (14-15)

3:1-15 constitutes a single unit with a continuous train of thought. Vv.
1-8 require a conclusion that applies their theme to human life, and this is
supplied by 3:9. The connection of vv. 10-15 to the preceding verses is evident in v. 11a, *'et hakkol 'aśah yapeh bᵉ'itto,* which is a theological recasting
of 3:1. When Qohelet's train of thought hits up against the blunt fact of human ignorance in v. 11, he parenthetically recommends enjoyment of life in
vv. 12f. In v. 14, he underscores divine control. Finally, v. 15 wraps up the
unit by abstracting a principle from vv. 1-8: for everything (every type of action and event) to have a time (vv. 1ff.) means that there is a limited number
of classes of events.

A. 3:1-9. The Catalogue of Times
There are several intricate designs proposed for this unit (surveyed by
Murphy, pp. 32f.), but none correspond to my experience of reading or seem
to govern other commentators' readings. One structural element that does
make an impression, however, is the pairing of positive and negative actions.[8] "Negative" includes destructive or unpleasant events, "positive" their
opposites. Positive and negative appear in no apparent sequence.

+ being born	- dying
+ planting	- uprooting
- killing	+ healing
- tearing down	+ building up
- weeping	+ laughing
- mourning	+ dancing
- (?) casting stones	+ (?) gathering stones
+ embracing	- shunning embrace
+ seeking	- losing
+ keeping	- casting away
- rending	+ sewing
- (?) silence	+ (?) speaking
+ loving	- hating
- war	+ peace

8. J. Loader [1979:11-13] labels them "desirable" and "undesirable" and finds an
intricate structure of chiasms within chiasms.

The valence of each item is clear in most cases. If gathering stones is for the purpose of building, then casting may be a "negative." Keeping silent can be counted as a negative insofar as it is an absence of activity.

The pairs are not precisely complementary. Qohelet does not say, for example, "to plant and to harvest" or "to sew and to cut." Nor are the pairs merisms, indicating totality by mentioning the extremes, since the antitheses do not all bracket a continuum. A phrase like "south and north" (11:3) can be a merism because it can indicate everywhere in between as well, but war and peace, planting and uprooting, and tearing and sewing, for example, have no relevant continuum between them. The Catalogue does imply totality, not by merism but by illustration, offering a broad range of examples of the "everything" mentioned in v. 1.

The positive-negative pairing teaches that everything in life, even unfortunate and destructive deeds and events, have their right times. God "made everything appropriate in its time" (3:11).

Exegesis follows the excursus.

EXCURSUS I

Time in Qohelet's "Catalogue of Times"

1. Time and Circumstance

In the "Catalogue of Times" (3:1-8), Qohelet declares that "everything has a time" and proceeds to illustrate the principle by fourteen pairs of examples. The following verses, vv. 9-15, draw conclusions from this fact. In spite of the repetition, it is not evident what it means for everything to have a time. It is not even clear what a "time" (*'et*) is. The present study seeks to clarify the notion of "time" in Qohelet and its implications for the meaning of the Catalogue.

An older, supposedly "anthropological," approach to the understanding of time in the Hebrew Bible tried to grasp its peculiar meaning not in terms of the Hebrew lexicon or literary contexts but by reference to "Hebrew mentality." In his influential *Israel* (1926, esp. 487-91), J. Pedersen maintained that in the mentality of ancient Israel, "time is identical with substance" (p. 487) and that "[t]imes of the same substance are therefore identical" (p. 488). Similarly, T. Boman (1960:129-63) maintained that "the Semitic concept of time is closely coincident with that of its content without which time would be quite impossible" (1960:139). In one sense, the same could be said of the Mach-Einstein concept of time, which holds that the spatiotemporal structure of the universe depends on the distribution of all matter in it, and that time is unimaginable apart from the other dimensions. But if Pedersen and Boman intend this idea to be non-trivial (and non-Einsteinian), they are saying that in the Hebrew "mind," every harvest time is the "same" time and every war-time is the same time, for somehow the Hebrews saw time eternally looping back on itself.[9]

The Israelites were, however, quite aware that there were different years and different springs and different wars. It seems to me that Boman's error in this case[10] lies in failing to recognize an ambiguity inherent in words for time in both Hebrew and English. Spring comes at springtime every year, which may be called the "same" time of the year, but we can distinguish one spring from the next, just as we can speak of what happens in "wartime" either as a category of occurrence or as the phase of a specific war.

Despite its flaws, Pedersen's and Boman's viewpoint has value insofar as "time" in Hebrew (*'et* and *z^eman*) is *sometimes* defined by its content, whether this content is an event (or event-type) or a structure of circumstances. In this regard, ancient Israel's concept of time is the same as ours.

'Et means "time" and covers much of the range of the English word.[11] This meaning may be divided into two main categories, depending on whether "time" is defined temporally (as a location on the time-continuum) or substantively (in terms of events or configurations of circumstances). I will concentrate on category 2 and its subdivisions, since they are pertinent to the present passage:

1. Temporally defined: a segment of time of any duration
    1.1. unique
        e.g., 3:05 p.m. on December 15, 1997; or the era of
        Deborah's judgeship

---

9. The methodological issues in analyzing the Biblical concept of time are examined in James Barr's *Biblical Words for Time* (1962). The thrust of this work is critical and methodological, and he does not examine the actual uses of the time-words.

10. His approach to "Hebrew thought" in general was thoroughly dismantled by J. Barr (1961:72-82 and *passim*).

11. Unlike English "time," *'et* does not denote time in the abstract (the non-spatial dimension in which events succeed each other), nor does it designate one of a series of recurring instances ("the second time").

1.2. periodic

e.g., wintertime (defined by dates rather than by the cold);
noon

2. Substantively defined: events and their configurations
(Biblical examples are discussed below.)

2.1. Actual occurrence

2.1.1. unique

any one-time event

2.1.2. periodic

e.g., the time of rains

2.1.3. sporadic

e.g., the times in which there *are* wars, such as 1914-
18 and 1939-45 CE

2.2 Configuration of circumstances

2.2.1. unique

e.g., the situation when it is right for a certain person to
get married

2.2.2. periodic

e.g., the time to wake up in the morning; the time to
plant

2.2.3. sporadic

e.g., the circumstances in which one should invest ("a
time to invest") in wheat futures; the time when it is
right to go to war

The distinction between categories 1 and 2 is subtle but significant. The period when lakes are frozen (December-March, where I am) is defined by the event in that period, whereas winter, defined by a time-slot (winter solstice to vernal equinox), will always be winter regardless of how severe global warming becomes. Put otherwise, a "time" in category 1 (for example, March 1949, or March every year) would be the "same" time regardless of what happened then, whereas in category 2, a "time" (for example, a "good time to ski") exists as such only insofar as it fits the requisite conditions (a good snow cover); if it does not, it is not *that* time. The subordinate distinctions are sometimes hard to determine but they too can be important. Lexically, the "time of mourning" *(ʿet sᵉpod)* might mean when one actually mourns (2.1) or when one *should* mourn (2.2).

2. Fate or Opportunity

The question of Qohelet's meaning cannot be resolved on the lexical level, since both main senses of "time" appear in the book, though not in the passage under consideration. We must ask just what kind of time Qohelet has in mind in the Catalogue and in what sense there is a time "for" everything.

If by *'et* Qohelet means a unique moment on the time-line, he is assuming a strong determinism: every act and event is assigned in advance a moment at which it will occur. Qohelet would be saying that people will (contrary to Jer 50:16) inevitably harvest at harvest time. This represents one line of interpretation of the present passage. In an earlier study (1987:191), I interpreted the Catalogue as a statement of the divine determination of all that occurs. R. E. Murphy, too, reads the passage as a statement of strong determinism:

> We may readily grant ignorance and lack of control of our births and deaths, but the religious person lets this rest in the beneficent Providence of God. Qohelet will have none of this. He seizes upon this poem on time in order to underscore the sad human condition. These are *God's* times, not our times. They happen to us; they are under divine control. (p. 39)

I now interpret this passage as presuming a less rigid sort of determinism. Qohelet does believe in divine control. God controls what will happen on the large scale, creating the world the way it is, and on the small scale he repeatedly and unpredictably intrudes and overrides human efforts. He makes man die at apparently arbitrary times. He radically circumscribes human freedom and effectuality. Nevertheless, Qohelet does not hold to a strict fatalism. God does not predetermine exactly what will happen and when. He has the power to do so but does not always use it. The Catalogue speaks about the *right* times, the circumstances when, in the proper course of events, something should happen or be done. But these are not the times when things will inevitably occur.[12]

---

12. J. Wilch (1969:126f.), arguing against the fatalistic interpretation, observes that if Qohelet had intended to say that God determines all man's actions, he would probably have used *mo'ed* rather than *'et,* since *mo'ed* is used of times that are specifically appointed or fixed.

A *mo'ed* is a time that is appointed, whether by agreement between two parties (e.g., 1 Sam 20:35) or by the decision of one person, usually God (Lev 23:4 and often, with respect to the festivals). A *mo'ed* is not, however, ineluctably predestined: it *should*

In other words, the fact that there is "a time for war" does not mean that God predestined the Congressional declaration of war against Japan on December 8, 1941. Rather, there are conditions right for war, situations when war is called for and can be effectively prosecuted. One such occasion arose immediately after the attack on Pearl Harbor. Earlier, a declaration of war would not have had popular support; later, Japan would have solidified its hold on the Pacific. In like manner, the sin of the Amorite was not "complete" *(šalem)* in Abraham's time (Gen 15:16). When this came to pass in Joshua's time, that could be called a "time for war." Ripeness is all.[13]

"Time" *('et;* pl. *'ittim, 'ittot)* in Qoh 3:1-8 is not a specific time or date (meaning 1, above). It is an *occasion,* a type or configuration of circumstances (2.2), whether on the grand scale of world history (such as war and peace) or on the minute scale of an individual's routines (such as planting and keeping silent). J. Wilch accurately observes that "Koheleth does not have moments of time in mind, but rather *occasions* or *situations* (1969:123). This is not to say that in Qohelet (or in "Hebraic thought") time is identical with its content. It is not the act of sewing that makes a certain moment a "time to sew." The Catalogue of Times would be a tautology if a "time to sew" were merely any moment when someone happens to be sewing. "Time" in Qohelet's sense is more like a hole in a pegboard, defined by its shape rather than its contents. A "round" time, so to speak, calls for a "round" action that will fit it.

3. *'Et* and *Z^eman* in Biblical Hebrew

Here are some examples of *'et* used elsewhere in the Bible in the relevant sense (category 2.2).

---

be kept (Lev 23:4; 2 Sam 24:15) but *can* be transgressed (Jer 46:17). A *mo'ed* is not a unique date. When Ben Sira says, "Speed the end and bring about the appointed time [*p^eqod mo'ed*]" (36[33]:10), he shows that a *mo'ed* can occur earlier or later yet be the same *mo'ed.* (*Mo'ed* does mean a "destined time" in Daniel [11:27, 29, 35; perhaps 8:19], but that is an expression of apocalyptic fatalism rather than a lexical development.)

'Et does not in itself indicate the notion of "appointment," of the designation of a certain moment or period in advance. To convey that notion, Ezra 10:14 and Nehemiah 10:35; 13:31 add an adjective and speak of *'ittim m^ezummanim,* "appointed times." Similarly, 2 Sam 24:15 speaks of *'et mo'ed,* lit. the "time of the appointed-time."

13. In this sense, contrary to Wilch (ibid.), Qohelet is indeed referring to "situations for decision," except in the case of birth and death.

2.2.1. Unique occasion

- Sir 12:16b: If an enemy "finds an opportunity [*mṣ' 't*]," he will drink one's blood insatiably.
- Ezek 16:8: "and behold, your time was the time for love [*wᵉhinneh 'ittek 'et dodim*]." Israel was in a stage of life *suitable* for love. The first *'et* is in category 1.1, the second in 2.2.1.
- Ps 31:16: "My times [*'ittotay*]" — that is, the situations I find myself in — "are in your hand." God can make them good or evil. Each one is unique.

2.2.2. Periodic (natural seasons, as defined by the events appropriate or habitual in them)

- Lev 15:25: "If a woman has an emission of blood for several days when it is not the time of her menstruation . . . [*bᵉlo' 'et niddatahh*]," that is, the time of the month in which she regularly menstruates.
- Jer 5:24: ". . . the Lord our God, who gives the rain and the early rain and the late rain (each) in its time. . . ." God's blessing is to give the rain when it does the most good ("Rain has a time," Qohelet would say). As punishment, God may withhold rain when it is needed. Similarly Lev 26:4 et al.
- Jer 50:16: "I will cut off the sower from Babylon, and the sickle-wielder at the time of harvest." Even if there is no one to work the harvest in Babylon at harvest time, it will still *be* harvest time, the time when the grain *should* be harvested. Here, time (harvesting time) is not exactly *identical* with its contents, namely not-harvesting, but is defined by the configuration of circumstances that makes harvesting the *appropriate* "content."
- Jer 8:7: "Even the stork in the sky knows her seasons [*moʿădeyha*],/And the turtle dove, swift, and crane/Keep the time of their coming [*šamᵉru 'et 'et boʿanah*],/But My people pays no heed [*lo' yadᵉʿu*]/To the law of the Lord [*mišpaṭ YHWH*]" (JPSV). This example is particularly relevant. "Paying heed to" (lit. "knowing") God's law is comparable to "keeping" a time. Both are the right and wise things to do, and anyone with any sense does things that way, but this is not the only possibility. Israel's refusal to heed God's law is, as v. 8 makes clear, a failure of *wisdom*.
- Isa 33:6: The verse is a crux, but the phrase *'ĕmunat 'itteyka* "the reliability of your times" is itself significant. Obviously it does not mean, say, that the first of Iyyar will always fall on the first of Iyyar. It means that what should occur at certain times (such as rain after the planting) will reliably do so, for Yahweh will be their guarantor.

2.2.3 Sporadic

- Isa 13:22b: "Its time is coming nigh, and its days won't be prolonged." "Its time" is the disaster in store for Babylon. It is imagined as something mobile.
- Isa 60:22: God will "hurry it (the increase of the nation) in its time." If this "time" were a specific date in the future, salvation could not be "hurried." "Time" is the right set of circumstances. God will bring salvation as soon as possible, but only when the time is ripe for it, not prematurely.
- Similarly, "time of trouble" (Isa 33:2); "time of evil" (Jer 2:27f.); and often. Contrast "time of favor" (Isa 49:8).

The events and deeds listed in Qohelet's Catalogue are typical, not specific. Every *type* of event and deed has an *'et,* a set of circumstances (whether recurrent or unique) in which it is appropriate. The proposition "for everything there is a season/time" in 3:1 is a restatement of 1:9: "That which happens is that which shall happen, and that which occurs is that which shall occur, and there is nothing whatsoever new under the sun." Qoh 3:1 is in turn rephrased by 3:15a, at the end of this unit: "Whatever happens already has happened, and what is going to happen already has happened." It is clear that 1:9 and 3:15a (and probably 15b) speak of types or categories, not incidents. John F. Kennedy's death or World War II does not recur, but assassination and war as event-types do. We should also observe that the recurrence is not necessarily cyclical. Qohelet does not here speak of time as a cycle in which crying follows laughing, which follows crying, and so on *ad infinitum.* Several "crying times" may follow in succession before it is right to laugh. Rather, he describes a binary pairing of opposed event-types as a structural property of reality, not as a temporal sequence.

'Et sometimes has this meaning elsewhere in Qohelet. *'Et umišpaṭ* in 8:5-6 means the right time and manner, which is something a wise man should know, for everything has a "right time and manner." An "evil time" in 9:12b (but not 12a!) is defined substantively. It is not a temporally defined moment of time but rather the disaster itself, which may come at different moments and can "fall" on man as he moves along the path of life. According to 10:17, sensible rulers feast *ba'et* "at the proper time." This is not merely non-morning; more is expected of prudent rulers than just not feasting before noon. The "time" here is when circumstances are appropriate to feasting.

The synonym *z^eman* is used parallel to *'et* in 3:1. In Biblical Hebrew, *z^eman* (an Aramaism) denotes an appointed time, whether unique (such as the time fixed for Nehemiah's return, Neh 2:6) or periodic (such as 14-15

Adar every year, Esth 9:27, 31; sim. Sir 43:7). Z^eman does not seem to mean a propitious or right time, nor does it ever clearly designate time as a configuration of circumstances. Thus it is not precisely apropos in Qoh 3:1, but it is used to complete the parallelism. The examples listed in vv. 2-8 are all called *'ittim,* and this is the word that conveys the meaning of the passage.

4. Times That Cannot Be Chosen

The timing of most of the actions in the Catalogue is to some degree in man's control. God does not force a person to do his sewing on a specific date. One can choose whether to sew his garment or not, and whether to do it tomorrow or next month. When he actually does the sewing is not necessarily the "time to sew." That would be when the rip is big enough to be worth fixing but small enough to be reparable. If he sews it a month later, it may be too late, and working at it all night (that would be *'amal* "toil") might not undo the damage. The situation that calls for sewing is *sewing's* time, not man's. At best, man can adapt himself to it.

Birth and death epitomize events and deeds that are beyond human control, for God is their sole agent. The timing of conception is irrelevant here, as is murder, since the events in this passage are seen from the standpoint of the subject, the one who is born or dies. (Verse 2 does not speak of a "time to beget" or a "time to kill"; the latter belongs to the next verse.) Suicide too is irrelevant; there is no question of someone choosing the right time to kill himself.

The "being born"–"dying" pair has often been used as the key to the meaning of the entire passage, supposedly showing that the point of the Catalogue is the predetermination of all events rather than the existence of opportune times (thus Fox 1987:192). Yet the concept of *'et* is the same in v. 2 as elsewhere. There is a right and appropriate time for birth and death, even though man has no influence over the timing.

There are two senses in which "time" (in both English and Hebrew) could apply to birth and death: the actual time (moment) and the right time (circumstances).

(1) *The actual time* (category 1.1), a moment in the chronological continuum. (This "moment" can be of any duration.) In this sense, Kennedy's "time to be born" was May 29, 1917, and his "time to die" was November 22, 1963. It is in this sense of *'et* that Kennedy's time "fell upon him suddenly" (9:12).

This is not the meaning of *'et* in the Catalogue. If Qohelet were saying that every death has its date, the verse would be either a tautology (everyone dies on the day of his death) or an expression of rigid fatalism (as if November 22, 1963, had been destined to be Kennedy's death-day from the start, and had he gone to New York rather than Dallas, death would have met him in New York). This notion of time as fate ("kismet") is foreign to Qohelet. If he held it, it would make no sense for him to speak of the possibility of premature death, calling it a demise $b^e lo'$ 'itteka "not in your time" (7:17), for such a thing would be inconceivable. And to say that an individual's birth happens in its fated time would imply that human souls were somehow waiting to be born on a predestined day, which is also foreign to this author. When 'et is used of the particular date of death, as in 9:12a, it can be said to be a person's time — "his time" — only post facto.

(2) *The right time* (category 2.2). There is a time of readiness for birth, and a time that is ripe for death. These are the right and appropriate times even though humans cannot determine when they will be or even *aim* at them. Yet we pretty much know when these times are, and they are the same for all people.

The "time to be born" need mean nothing more abstruse than the moment when the embryo is mature and ready for birth, nine months after conception. This, of course, is no small matter. The fact that most animals are born at their "time to be born," after full gestation, is a wonder and an act of providence. God reminds Job of his ignorance of the birth-time of wild animals: "Do you know the time ['et] when the rock-gazelles give birth [ledet], can you watch over the birth-labors of the deer? Can you count the months they must fulfill, and do you know the time ['et] they give birth?" (Job 39:1f.). Of course not, but God does, and he makes the gazelles deliver just then. Consequently they bear live young and "multiply in the field" (vv. 3-4). Hos 13:13, a difficult text, speaks of the timely emergence from the womb, apparently calling this moment an 'et.[14] Hosea facetiously says that Ephraim is not "wise" enough to appear at *mašber banim,* the cervical opening (or perhaps the moment of cresting). A fetus born before its time is premature and may die, and a belated birth can be devastating to the mother and child.[15]

14. Unless we emend ky 't to kî 'attāh "for now," as the hexaplaric and Lucianic readings (διότι νῦν) suggest. However, 'et by itself can mean the proper time, as in Job 22:16, 'ăšer qumm^etu w^elo' 'et, lit., "who were cut off and not in the (proper) time." In either case, Hosea mentions the right time for birth as a metaphor for timely repentance.

15. Isa 66:7-11 imagines Zion as a woman who gives birth early, *before* the birth pangs. Here is a rare case of something happening outside its time and nevertheless being *good.* But for that very reason it is a metaphor of a miracle, something outside the natural rhythm of the times. In the same way, in the eschaton, the usual lifespan will be expanded to more than a hundred years.

It is, so to speak, "wise" to be born at the right time. This time is periodic and recurrent for the species, though not for the individual.

The "time to die" is the natural and *right* age for departing life. This too is essentially the same for all people. It is when a person is ripe for death, like an apple about to fall from the tree. The psalmist places this at about seventy or eighty years (Ps 90:10). Kennedy's "time" in this sense would have been in approximately 1997, had he not died *b*ᵉ*lo' 'itto*, as Qohelet puts it (see 7:17).

Judging from the bound constructions in 3:4b, 5bβ, and 8, the "time to die" could be phrased as a genitive: *'et mawet*, "the time of dying" or "dying's time." In a sense, this time "belongs" to dying, just as, we might say, planting cereals "belongs" to the time for planting.[16] But the time to die can also be called a *person's* time, as is shown by the fact that it is possible to say that one died before *his* time or (in the second person) *b*ᵉ*lo' 'itteka* "before your time" (7:17). (In this sense, John Kennedy's time had not yet come in 1963.) "Your time" in this sense is not necessarily when you die, but when you *should* die.

Dying before one's time is the expectation for sinners. They are, Eliphaz insists, snatched away *w*ᵉ*lo' 'et* "before their time," lit., "and not at (the) time" (Job 22:16), that is, the natural and expected time. Eliphaz also calls this the evildoer's "day" (15:32).[17] In other words, everyone has a "time" or "day" when, if all is in order, he will die, and this is when his fruit is ripe, in old age. So Eliphaz believes. And if one sins, he warps the moral "space" around him, whereby *his* time (seventy to eighty years) ceases to be *God's* time, the time of death demanded by God's justice.

There is no mention of dying *after* one's time (an event made possible by modern life-support systems). The fortunate condition at death is being "sated with days."

An untimely death can also occur for ethically inexplicable reasons, and this occasions theodicy. An untimely death that is undeserved must be explained, perhaps by reference to hidden factors that make a certain moment the truly right one in the case at hand. The need to explain why God overrode the "right time" in a particular case, when the justification is not ev-

16. The Gezer calendar is a list of agricultural seasons, with each item in the construct, e.g., *yrh qṣr śʿrm* "a month of harvesting barley" (l. 4; *TSSI* 1.2).

17. "Before his day, it withers [reading *yimmal* for *yml'*], and his boughs are not verdant." "It" is apparently *t*ᵉ*murato* (v. 31), which seems to mean "produce." (The likely etymology of *t*ᵉ*murah* is MWR "exchange," hence "what is received in exchange for labor," namely earnings. In 20:18, *t*ᵉ*murato* is parallel to *yaga'* which, like *'amal*, can refer to the product of toil.)

ident, can lead to smug and self-justifying rationalizations, such as the ones Job's friends come up with.

Qohelet is not one to take the easy way out. He knows well that not everyone dies at the right time, but rather: "an offender may do evil for years[18] but live long" (8:12a) and: "there are righteous people who receive what is appropriate to the deeds of the wicked, and there are wicked people who receive what is appropriate to the deeds of the righteous" (8:14aβb). In context this refers to tardy and premature deaths respectively, in other words, deaths synchronized with the times or seasons of a normal life.

God *could* make all things happen in their times (understanding "times" as right times), but he does not necessarily do so. He sets the times man is to aim for, yet, paradoxically, he himself does not always act then. The "times" such as Qohelet lists are not precisely *God's* times. They are not always coordinated with God's prior plans, and he must sometimes override them.

This paradox arises because the times may be viewed from two angles. From the perspective of divine plans and principles, God must be said to do everything in its right time. But from the perspective of human life and natural processes, there may be a gap between the "right" or "ripe" time and the time God chooses. A "time to die" is "dying's time," which is not necessarily God's. God may, as punishment, intervene in the normal flow of events and make things happen at an inopportune time. He might withhold the rain in its time, the season it should fall (a possibility implied by the reverse of what is promised in Deut 11:14; 28:12, etc.), he might bring darkness at noon (Am 8:9), or he might make someone die "before his time" (Qoh 7:17). This is further evidence that the times in the Catalogue are not predestined, since man may overlook them and God can override them.

The "time to be born" and the "time to die" belong in the Catalogue as the cardinal instances of events of which God is the sole agent. This could be the case with many other events, such as rain-time and disaster-time. People cannot choose when they will occur, though behavior and prayers may influence God's decision. Birth and death head the Catalogue as evidence that this is the way the world works: all things, whether their agent is human or divine, have a right and proper configuration of circumstances for their occurrence. But birth and death are not the problem. The problem is with events that do lie within human control, for then we should aim to get their timing right. But can we?

18. Reading *mē'āz*, lit. "from of old," for MT's *me'at* "a hundred of."

204

5. When the Timing *Can* Be Chosen

Man *should* do things in their times, but he does not necessarily do so. He may transgress the times — by laughing at a funeral, for example, or delaying the planting. This is not the sort of determinism that locks man helplessly into his every step,[19] but it does constrict his range of possibilities and powers. There is a right time to mourn, or, we could say, there are right *times* to mourn (again, defined not by date but by circumstances). Man should adjust his own mourning actions to mourning's time. He should weep at the time fixed for weeping — funerals, say — and laugh when it is appropriate to do so.[20]

The practical message of 3:1-9 is reformulated in 11:1-6: things will happen when they will (and *where* they will: 11:3), and man can only cover his bets and do things at a variety of times. The only sensible way to do something is to adapt oneself to the constraints of reality, not to strain — *la'ămol* — against them. Man is ignorant: "Just as you cannot understand what the life-breath does <in the limbs> (of the fetus) in the womb of a pregnant woman, so you cannot understand the work of God, who makes everything happen" (11:5). Therefore: "In the morning sow your seed, and in the evening let not your hand go slack, for you do not know which will prosper, this or that, or whether both will be equally good" (11:6). Planting has a (right) time; that time belongs to planting, not to man. What man can do is to plant at various times, in the hope that one of his efforts will pay off.

This concept of the right time is shared by other sages. Proverbs exclaims, ". . . and a word in its time — how good it is!" (15:23b). Sira believes that God supplies every need *bᵉʿitto* "in its time" (39:16, 33). Sira (in 39:30b) takes reassurance from the doctrine of times because he is confident that God

---

19. Aḥiqar seems to articulate such a concept: "For it is not in man's power to lift up their foot or set it down, apart from (the gods)" (122). But even this can mean that while man ordinarily controls his actions, ultimately they are in the gods' control, for they can always intervene and decide otherwise.

20. There are strong affinities between Hesiod's teaching of the times and Qohelet's. Hesiod teaches that there is a right time for, among other things, plowing, sowing, and reaping (*Works,* 390f.). "When ploughing-time comes, make haste to plough" (448f.). There is a right day for a wise man to be born, as well as for the birth of a girl and boy (792ff.). (Note that these are events outside man's control. Compare Qoh 3:2.) There are propitious and hazardous days. "The man is happy and lucky in them who knows all these things and does his work without offending the deathless gods" (822ff.). Whitley (1979:174f.) goes so far as to argue that Qohelet is dependent on Hesiod, but the concept of a right time is too widespread to show this. In Chinese folk belief, for example, there is a complex and detailed calendar of right times and propitious days for various activities.

will choose to act in ways beneficial to humanity (if not individuals). God can do "everything in its time" because he *made* everything for its time (note that this is *its* time). He knows just when something is ready and really needed. Hence: "Do not say, 'This is worse than that,' *ky hkl b'tw ygbr* for everything dominates in its own time" (39:34).[21] (One possibility "dominates" over other potentialities in the sense of moving from latency to reality.) In other words, do not say that hail or wild beasts are evil. God has a purpose for them too, and in the right circumstances (namely, a time of judgment [v. 29; cf. Ezek 14:21]), he will deploy them to fulfill this purpose. Even the disasters and ills that afflict mankind "were created for their purposes [*lṣwrkm*, lit., "needs"], and they are kept in [God's] storehouse for (that) time [*l't*]" (Sir 39:30b[22]). That time is the day of visitation, "the time of trouble ['*et ṣar*], the day of battle and war [*yom qᵉrab umilḥamah*]" (Job 38:23). Note the near-synonymy of "need" and "time." "Time" in Qohelet's Catalogue is when a certain "need" presents itself.

Different conclusions might be drawn from the fact that everything has a time, such as the rule that we should try hard to act at the right time. Qohelet's conclusion is both more pessimistic — such efforts can only fail — and more moderate — there is no point in straining, since we are ignorant of when the right times are. This counsel of moderation does not, however, solve his problem. Toil (which for him is the stuff and texture of life) *should* produce a sure profit, and its failure to do so demonstrates the frailty of human powers.

In 3:11a, Qohelet sums up the point of the Catalogue by stating that God made everything appropriate in its time, and in 3:14 he restates the idea that God is the cause of all that happens (meaning that he is creator and ruler, not that he is a puppeteer). Qoh 3:17 also explicates v. 1. After observing social injustices in v. 16, Qohelet comforts himself, at least momentarily, with the thought that God "will judge the righteous and the wicked, for there is a time for every matter." The "time" here is not something that man chooses. Like birth and death, it is beyond his reach. The point is that judgment has a right time; therefore when the time is ripe, God will surely execute judgment. But, as Qohelet quickly recognizes, what is the right time for God may be too late for man.

---

21. In MS B at v. 21.

22. Reading Sir 39:30bβ with B mg.: *whmh b'ṣrw l't ypqdw*. The body of the text has *whmh b'wṣr wl't ypqdw* "and they are in his storehouse for the time [= *ulᵉᵉēt*] they will be mustered" or ". . . and at the (right) time [= *wᵉlā'ēt*] will be mustered." The '*oṣar* is God's storehouse of punishments, on which see Sir 39:17, 30; 43:14; cf. Job 38:22; Jer 10:13.

3:1 On *'et* and *z^eman,* see above.

Ḥepeṣ means both "desire," "pleasure" (Qoh 5:3; 12:1, 10 — its etymological meaning), and "deed," "affair" (3:1, 17; 5:7; 8:6), in which case it is synonymous with *ma'ăśeh* (5:7, in reference to an occurrence; elsewhere possibly in Isa 58:13 and Sir 10:26; 11:23).

3:2 Though the qal of YLD always means "beget" or "give birth," the pairing of *lāledet* with *lāmût* "to die" shows that the former has an intransitive sense here, "being born." The infinitive expresses an abstract verbal notion and can be indifferent to voice (*GBH* §124s; e.g., *liṭboaḥ* in Jer 25:34). Modern commentators are virtually unanimous in this interpretation. Wilch, however (1969:120f.), argues for an active sense, "to give birth," on the grounds that the events in 3:2-8 occur in the experience of mankind generally, and "in this sense the giving and losing of life form perfect opposites" (p. 121). But they don't. That would be "to give birth and to kill."

3:3 The last verb in the verse, *la'ăqor,* does not mean to harvest but to uproot and destroy unwanted plants, as when clearing a field for new cultivation. This is an instance of "tearing down," a negative action. The pair does not refer to seasonal chores, but to sporadic beginnings and ends of enterprises. The actions may represent sudden changes in one's life-path, when one clears the table and begins anew. The pair "to tear down" and "to build up" reiterates this idea.

3:4 *'Et s^epod,* "a time of mourning," etc. In vv. 4b and 5aβ, the construction changes, with the infinitive construct appearing as a bare noun, like an infinitive absolute. This is essentially the same construction as *'et* + noun in v. 8b. The different syntax in various verses is reflected in the above translation, but there can be no distinction of meaning between the nominal constructions and the one with *lamed* + inf. used in the other lines. Note how v. 5a sets the bound construction parallel to the infinitive. This equivalence suggests that the *lamed* + inf. too is semantically possessive rather than purposive: "a time *to* be born" = "a time *of* being born" or a "being-born time."

3:5 The acts of casting away and gathering stones have been variously explained. Qoh. Rab. says that the time for the former is when one's wife is ritually clean, and for the latter it is when she is menstrually impure. Many commentators, medieval and modern, follow this interpretation and decode these actions as euphemisms for having and abstaining from sexual relations (L. Levy, pp. 144ff., argues for this at length). But *k^enos* means to *gather in* or assemble, not to hold back or refrain. Possibly a woman could be said to "gather" the "stones," if the latter were really a cipher for semen. Of course, that sort of "gathering" happens at the same moment as the "casting," but the statement is still valid. Still, there is no good reason to regard these actions as ciphers. Stones were cast on fields as a punitive act of war (2 Kgs 3:19, 25, using the same verb), and in peacetime they were gathered and removed from land prior to cultivation (though this is properly called *siqqel,* e.g., Isa 5:2). Also, stones might be collected to build terrace walls, houses, and grave heaps. It is not necessary to identify one of these circumstances for casting and gathering stones as the sole intent of this sentence. The acts of casting and gathering stones have various purposes. In their mundane character, they resemble the other ones listed in vv. 3-8a and may in fact be mentioned for this reason, to emphasize that the principle of opportune times extends to the most ordinary of activities.

"A time to embrace, and a time to shun embrace": This line (rather than the preceding) may allude to sexual intercourse, but it can just as well include all types of friendly embrace.

3:6 "A time to lose" is puzzling. When is there ever a good time for that? Perhaps *le'abbed* is declarative: to give up on something, to declare it lost (Ehrlich; Gordis; *HALAT*). But *'ibbed* is not used in this way elsewhere. One can imagine circumstances when it is best to lose something, but Qohelet may have no particular situation in mind. He begins with his postulate that there is a time for everything and applies this rule not only to clearly useful actions, but even to ones that may seem useless or even deleterious. This idea is reiterated in v. 6b. Qoh. Rab. gives the example of a captain tossing his merchandise overboard to save his ship from sinking. (*Le'abbed* can refer to such a deliberate loss.) Even if one does not intend to lose something, at a certain time that may be for the best. The disappearance of the asses of Saul's father (1 Sam 9:3) is an example of a fortuitous loss.

3:9 *'Amal, 'ŚH (mah yitron ha'ośeh ba'ašer hu' 'amel):* This is the climax and explanation of the Catalogue of Times. Qoh 3:9 does not (contrary to Ginsberg) mean "What is the profit of one who earns (something) in what he gains?", for the preceding verses do not speak of a person's earnings, nor do vv. 10-11 relate to the unprofitability of wealth. Furthermore, the "times" encompass the entire range of acts and events in life, with gainful employments mentioned only incidentally.

Though 'ŚH and 'ML are often equivalent in Qohelet, they are not precise synonyms, and they must be distinguished in v. 9a. *Ha'ośeh* is the more inclusive category, *'amel* a subset of it. "Toiling" — arduous labor — is a sort of "doing." One who does something — an *'oseh* — gets no profit if he toils at it — *overdoes* it, we might say. Toil, even when it yields a lot of wealth (as it is assumed to do in, for example, 2:21, cf. v. 9), achieves no more than a simple "doing," because human efforts hit up against the times, and these cannot be forced.

B. 3:10-15. The Implications of This Principle

3:11a   The first part of this verse does not (contrary to almost all interpreters) refer to God's original act of creation. "Everything" in v. 11 resumes "everything" in v. 1, and that, as the pairs in vv. 2-8 show, comprises the range of events and actions in human life rather than the major constituents of creation, described in Genesis 1. The pairs of events in 3:2-8 did not come into being in the act of creation. But God continues to "make" things at all times. In this way, he "made" the day of good fortune and the day of bad fortune (7:14). The qatal can also be translated as a present tense (Isaksson 1987:75-92); hence: "He made everything appropriate in its time."

Qohelet is focusing not on a moment in the past (the "making") but rather on the result — *what* things were made to be, the quality of events-types in the present (their appropriateness). Syntactically, *yapeh* is an adjective, not an adverb, and *yapeh be'itto* is an emphasized predicative complement. In other words, what is in focus is the *appropriateness* of "everything," not the making. We can reflect this by translating, "God made everything to be appropriate in its time." Qoh 7:29aβ has the same construction and uses *'asah* in the same way: *'asah ha'ělohim 'et ha'adam yašar,* "God made man to be straight."

Yapeh is not precisely an aesthetic evaluation — most of the events listed in the Catalogue are not beautiful — but a statement of rightness. Elsewhere in the Bible (with the exception of Qoh 5:17), *yapeh* does refer to visible beauty, but it comes to mean "fitting," "meet." Sir 14:16b, MS A[23] (probably influenced by Qoh 2:3bβ and 9:10) speaks of pleasures as things that are *yapeh la'ăśot,* "good to do." Jastrow's *Dictionary* (1.585) gives the following glosses for the RH usage of *yapeh:* "appropriate; strong; healthy; handsome, beautiful, fine (of build); auspicious; (adv.) well, right." The scope of this cluster of meanings suggests that Qohelet uses *yapeh* here in the RH sense, as a synonym of *ṭob,* "good." The Greeks called the universe the *kosmos,* "ornament," "order," because of the way everything fits together wonderfully. *Yapeh* here is close to κόσμιος, "well-ordered," as it is in 5:17.

In *Contradictions* (1987) I translated v. 11a as "he makes everything

---

23. The verse is lacking in the Greek and may be later.

happen appropriately in its time." While *'aśah* can mean "make happen," Qohelet does not seem to be saying here that God makes all things, including human actions, happen when they do. God does intervene in human lives, but not to that extent. The point of v. 11 is that God made a world in which all things, even events with a human agent, even death and disease, are good and serviceable in their proper time. Sir 39:33 (cf. v. 16), which is almost certainly dependent on Qoh 3:11 as well as on Pss 104:27 and 145:15 (see above), uses similar language in speaking of God's providence, not his acts of creation. Of course, this is not the only thing Qohelet believes. He also believes that God sometimes does some things (in particular, bringing death and executing judgment) in what do not seem to be the right times as far as man is concerned.

3:11b *'Amal:* MT's *gam 'et ha'olam natan b\u1e97libbam,* lit. "he also put the world in their heart," has lent itself to speculations about the "world" or "eternity" placed in the human mind. The word has been assigned a number of meanings: Gordis explains it as "world" (cf. Vul *mundum*), which he amplifies to "love of the world." He could as well expand it to "hatred of the world," since Qohelet both loves life (11:7) and hates it (2:17). An ancient explanation construes *ha'olam* as "eternity" (LXX αἰῶνα). This too can make sense only if considerably amplified, for example, ". . . [God] has also established in man an impulse leading him beyond that which is temporal toward the eternal" (Delitzsch). But that is irrelevant to this passage and foreign to the book. Qohelet shows no interest in an afterlife. At most he may be said to be skeptical toward it (3:21), but in practice he sees nothing but darkness beyond the grave (3:19; 9:10; 11:8). And even if *'olam* meant "eternity" (it more precisely means the farthest reaches of time), it certainly does not mean *desiderium aeternitatis,* as Delitzsch puts it. In fact, *'olam* does not mean the eternity of the afterlife; the rabbinic locution for that is *ha'olam habba',* "the world to come." Barr explains *'olam* as "perpetuity": "The reference to perpetuity would mean the consciousness of memory, the awareness of past events" (1962:117f.). But it is a big jump from "perpetuity" to "consciousness of memory." Jenni (1953:24-27), followed by Murphy, construes *ha'olam* as "duration," as opposed to *'et,* which is supposedly a defined moment or period of time. But "duration" is not one of the meanings of *'olam.* Isaksson (1987:176-89) explains *'olam* as "creation in its widest sense, in time and space, the created and ongoing history," to be translated "the eternal work," sc. of God (p. 183). Isaksson does not show that *'olam* means all this, but in any case, God didn't put all this, or even the desire for it, in man's heart.

Another approach is to vocalize *h'lm* as *hā'elem* and derive it from the root 'LM "concealed," "dark," hence "ignorance" (Barton) or "the unknown" (Crenshaw). *'Elem* is not attested in BH. It does exist in RH, but there it means "secret" rather than "ignorance."

The *'olam* in man's heart is a theologically fertile notion, but it is probably a mistake. MT's *h'lm* is most likely a metathesis for *h'ml (he'āmāl)*. This emendation was suggested by D. B. MacDonald (1899) and is followed by Ginsberg, ad loc. The best evidence for this reading is 8:17, which echoes 3:11 in wording and ideas. There Qohelet uses the verb *'amal* to designate man's hopeless endeavor to grasp *(limṣo')* that which God has brought to pass:

3:11b		8:17aβb
gam 'et <he'amal> natan b^elibbam	≈	*b^ešel 'ăšer ya'ămol ha'adam l^ebaqqeš*
mibb^eli 'ăšer lo' yimṣa' ha'adam	≈	*ki lo' yukal ha'adam limṣo'*
'et hamma'ăśeh 'ăšer 'aśah ha'ĕlohim	≈	*'et hamma'ăśeh 'ăšer na'ăśah taḥat haššemeš*
mero'š w^e'ad sop	≈	*w^egam 'im yo'mar* etc. (emphatic: "at all")

The *'amal* in 3:11 is the same as the *'inyan* ("business, activity, task") that, according to the preceding verse, God gave to man to busy himself with. This toil is *in the heart;* it is a mental labor, similar to the "heart's thoughts" mentioned alongside *'amal* in 2:22. To be sure, the phrase *'amal b^eleb* does not occur elsewhere, but Isa 53:11a *(me'amal napšo)* shows that the *nepeš* can have *'amal,* and Ps 73:16a *(wa'ăḥaššĕbah lada'at zo't, 'amal hi' b^e'eynay)* shows that an endeavor to understand something can be called *'amal.* Like Qohelet's labors, these too are mental and emotional, not physical.

The arduous task that God has placed in man's heart is defined by the rest of the verse. It is the attempt to understand "what God has brought to pass." The clause *'et <he'amal> natan b^elibbam* in 3:11bα resumes *ha'inyan 'ăšer natan 'ĕlohim libney ha'adam* in 3:10 and refers to what is called *'inyan ra' natan 'ĕlohim libney ha'adam la'ănot bo,* "an unfortunate business that God has given people to busy themselves with," in 1:13.

"Grasp" translates *maṣa',* usually glossed as "find," "discover." The two basic meanings of this word are "find" and "reach" (hence "acquire" and "seize"). See Ceresko 1982 and above, chapter 5, n. 1.

Hamma'ăśeh 'ăšer 'aśah ha'ĕlohim in v. 11b means "the totality of events that God has made" — or "made happen." It is this that man cannot "find out" or "grasp" *(yimṣa')*.

The phrase *mero'š wᵉ'ad sop* in v. 11bβ, lit. "from beginning to end," emphasizes negation of existence ("not any") rather than negation of universality ("not all"). The usual translation, "without man being able to find out the work that God has done from beginning to end" (or the like), has Qohelet complaining about the impossibility of knowing the entirety of God's work. Such a complaint would be trivial, because it would be senseless to hope for absolute knowledge of everything. Rather, Qohelet is saying that man can *in no way* understand *ma'ăśeh ha'ĕlohim.* To be sure, Qohelet does have things to say about divine activity, but he does not define that knowledge as "grasping" (lit. "finding") or "understanding" *(maṣa', yada')* what God brings to pass.

3:12-13 There is nothing better *(ṭob)* than to "do" pleasure *(ṭob)* in life. But doing this depends on God's will (v. 14). As in 2:24f., the advice to enjoy life comes in the context of God's control of all that happens.

"For man." Emending MT's *bm* "in them" to *b'dm* (*BHS* et al.) is conjectural but attractive. The emendation supplies a masculine singular antecedent for *ḥayyayw;* and compare *ba'adam* in 2:24.

3:14 "Forever" *(lᵉ'olam)* in *hu' yihyeh lᵉ'olam* does not indicate duration or perpetuity, as if Qohelet were asserting the eternality of everything God creates or makes happen.[24] That would be irrelevant here. Nor does it mean "unchanging" (contrary to Jenni 1953:22); *lᵉ'olam* never has that sense elsewhere. Rather, it is a sentence modifier placed as an afterthought. (Compare the positioning of *mero'š wᵉ'ad sop* at the end of the sentence in 3:11.) In other words, it is always the case that what happens is only what God has made happen. Hence (3:14aβ, repeating 1:15) man cannot add to or take away from what God does.

The usual translation of 3:14b is, "and God caused people to fear him" (lit. "God made that [people] fear him"). But this translation produces a short sentence unrelated to the preceding statement (v. 14a) and lacking motivation. Moreover, all Qohelet's statements about human wickedness, in particular 8:13b, show that Qohelet does not believe that God has caused mankind to fear him. After all, they do not. Rather, God *intends* for people to fear him (thus *še-*

---

24. Ben Sira may be interpreting Qohelet in this way in 42:23 (MS M, ≈ Gk): "All [of God's works, cf. 22] live and abide forever, and are preserved for the sake of every need." God's works, Ben Sira insists, are both permanent and purposive.

introduces a purpose clause), but he does not impose that fear. By enforcing human ignorance and helplessness, God *occasions* fear but does not directly cause or "make" it. The implicit direct object of *'aśah* is the immutability of divinely caused events, stated in v. 14b. *'Aśah* is used absolutely, with the direct object implicit in the immediate context, as in Prov 31:13; Ezr 10:4; 1 Chr 28:10; Ezek 20:44; 1 Sam 14:45; etc.; see also *GBH* §146*i.* "This" may be supplied.

"Whatever God makes happen" refers, as Rashbam says, to "all the times *(ha'ittim),* which are in God's hand." God has created a system of times that is opaque to man's wisdom (3:11) and constrained by God's control of events (3:14f.). Whoever has the wisdom to recognize this will fear God and share the humility epitomized in the confession of the psalmist: "My times *('ittotay)* are in your hand" (Ps 31:16).

Ben Sira paraphrases Qoh 3:14: "One cannot take away and one cannot add, and one should not investigate God's wonders" (18:6, Gk[25]). The first stich stays close to Qohelet's wording. The second draws a practical conclusion from Qoh 3:14b. Fearing God means accepting one's own limitations.

3:15a As Ibn Ezra observed, *mah šehayah* is equivalent to *ma'aśeh ha'ĕlohim:* that which happens and the events that God brings to pass are one and the same. Thus v. 15a uses the phraseology of 1:9a to restate 3:14. God's works steamroller over man's puny efforts, and nothing substantially new can interrupt the awesome course of events that God has ordained.

3:15b *Wᵉha'ĕlohim yᵉbaqqeš 'et nirdap:* for the early interpretations of this crux, see Salters 1976. The construction *'et* + bare noun is possible but awkward (GKC §117*e;* cf. 4:4; 7:7). The LXX, Syr, Tg, and Sir 5:3 apply the sentence to God's care for the persecuted (*nirdapim,* in Sira's paraphrase). Vul renders: "et Deus instaurat quod abiit" — "and God repeats what has passed away." Since *radap,* "pursue," is a near-synonym of *biqqeš* (see Ps 34:15, and compare Zeph 2:3 with Deut 16:20), the sentence means, approximately, "God seeks what has already been sought." This seems to be a variant of "nothing new under the sun." It is not clear what "seeking" or "pursuing" has to do with divine causation of events. Murphy suggests that the context is *time:* "*Nirdap* can be understood to designate what is rushed after, or even caught up with, such as time" (p. 30). But can this really be said of time? More viable is Crenshaw's surmise: "There is nothing new. Why? Because God ensures that events which have just transpired do not vanish into thin air. God brings them back once more, so that the past circles into the

25. Retroverting οὐκ ἔστιν ἐξιχνιάσαι to *'eyn laḥqor,* which has monitory force.

213

present" (p. 100). In any case, the gist of the sentence seems to be that God seeks to do things he has already done, hence "Whatever happens already has happened" (v. 15a).

◆ 3:16-22

(16) I further saw that under the sun, in the place where judgment should be, wickedness is there, and in the place where righteousness should be, wickedness is there. (17) I said in my heart, "God will judge the righteous and the wicked, for there is a time for every matter, and upon all that is done^a there [?]."

(18) I said in my heart with regard to mankind, "< — ^{b}> God, and to <show^c> that they are but beasts."< — ^{d}> (19) For what happens to humans and what happens to the beast is one and the same thing: as the one dies so dies the other, and both have the same life-breath, and man has no advantage over the beast, for all are absurd. (20) All go to the same place. All are from the dust, and all to the dust return. (21) And who knows whether the spirit of man goes upward^e while the spirit of the beast goes down^f to the ground?

(22) And I saw that there is nothing better than that a man take pleasure in his works, for that is his portion, for who can enable him to see what will happen afterwards?

^{a}*hanna'ăśāh* (MT *hamma'ăśeh*)
^{b}obscure; word missing? MT *lᵉbārām*
^{c}*wᵉlar'ôt* (MT *wᵉlir'ôt*)
^{d}omit *lāhem*
^{e}*hă'ôlāh* (MT *hā'ôlāh*)
^{f}*hăyōredet* (MT *hayyōredet*)

Injustice pervades the world. Qohelet affirms God's judgment but, reflecting that death eliminates distinctions, concludes that pleasure is the only recourse.

3:16 Lit. "in the place of judgment [*mišpaṭ*], . . . in the place of righteousness [*ṣedeq*]." These are the same, the place where righteous judgment *should,* but evidently does not, reside. "Judgment"/"righteousness" is a distributed word-pair equivalent to *mišpaṭ ṣedeq,* "righteous judgment." "The place of righteous judgment" is a place that can be called by these names even when this virtue is absent, and that is the court, the proper locus *par excellence* of righteous judgment. In English we can call a law court a "court of justice" in the same way, even if the particular one is corrupt.

214

3:17 Qohelet reports that when he observed violations of justice, he thought that God would judge the wicked. Inasmuch as everything has a right time, Qohelet reasoned, divine judgment too must have a time, and in it God will execute judgment. But this assurance is small comfort, because if the sentence is death, the universality of death makes that sentence meaningless as punishment, and if it is something else, death may intervene while the sentence is pending.

The observation of injustice — like others of Qohelet's melancholy observations — brings him to thoughts of death in vv. 19-21. Life is absurd, because all distinctions in life, even the difference between humans and animals, are obliterated by death.

According to the belief prevalent in Biblical times, death means loss of the life-breath *(ruah)* and descent to Sheol, a fate shared by all creatures. When God "takes back" *('osep)* the spirit (that is, the life-breath common to all creatures, not the "soul"), the creature dies (Ps 104:29; Job 34:14-15). This "taking back" of the life-spirit does not imply an afterlife, but merely the dissolution of the components of the living being.

Unusual in Qohelet is the notion — mentioned but not affirmed — that the spirit might go *up* rather than down to Sheol. The likely source of this non-Semitic idea is a belief common in popular Hellenistic religion that the human soul is made of a spark of ether and will return to the heavenly ethereal sphere upon death (see Hengel 1974:I, 124).

Qohelet refuses to draw comfort from mere speculation. Nevertheless, he has raised the concept of an afterlife as a higher state than eternal somnolence in the underworld. If the human soul did have an elevated fate — Qohelet implicitly concedes — then human life would not be pointless. But we cannot know whether this is the case, and we cannot rationalize a known injustice by appeal to an unknown remedy. Since man is ignorant of what lies ahead, nothing remains but to enjoy the present.

Šam "there" at the end of v. 17 is difficult. It is hardly an allusion, facetious or otherwise, to an afterlife (as Gordis holds) since an ironic reference would presume that there *is* an afterlife, and Qohelet does not have enough of a belief in judgment after death to say that there is a time for "everything" in the afterlife. It is the life "under the sun" that has a time for everything. Barton, Ginsberg, et al., emend to *śām* "set," but that places the verb awkwardly late in the clause. As it stands, "there" is the court of law (v. 16). There will be judgment for (*'al*) everything done *there, šam*. This idea would be better conveyed by *hanna'ăśah* rather than *hamma'ăśeh*, and perhaps we should read the former word here, a *mem-nun* graphic error.

Podechard's attractive conjecture, reading *mišpaṭ* (of which *šm* is a remnant) produces a meaningful, well-structured sentence, with *mišpaṭ* parallel to *ʿet,* a word-pair which appears in 8:6. In 12:14 as well, *mišpaṭ* is complemented by *ʿal* + the deed judged. The emendation is perhaps too extensive to be accepted in the absence of other evidence, but even without it the sentence affirms a time of judgment for all deeds. This sentence repeats the idea of 3:1, except that the focus here is limited to the time of judgment upon injustices.

Hammaʿăśeh (or *hannaʿăśah,* if we so emend in v. 17b) refers to human deeds, for these (and not events) are objects of judgment.

3:18 A crux. MT's *lᵉbārām* is apparently a by-form of BRR, which means "to sift, single out" in RH. A finite verb is missing. *Haʾĕlohim* as the subject of the infinitive after an inf. + dir. obj. construction is harsh. One reasonable conjecture is to read *lōʾ bārām* "(God) did not distinguish them" (Ehrlich).

In spite of some insoluble difficulties, we can get the gist of the verse. We should read *larʾôt* (an apocopated hiphil, understood thus by LXX) for MT's *lirʾôt.* In MT's *bᵉhemmah hemmah lahem, hemmah* could be a dittograph but can also be explained as a redundant copula used for paronomasia. *Lahem,* however, has no function, syntactic or literary. In the absence of a preceding verb it is not an ethical dative. There is no justification for glossing it as "per se, in themselves" (Gordis), and in any case that translation has no particular meaning. The letters *lhm* are probably a partial dittography of *hemmah* and should be omitted.

The point of the verse is that God made humans mortal to show them that they are but beasts, in order to distance them from divine powers. God's wish to prevent humans from gaining eternal life is the reason he banishes them from Eden in Gen 3:22f. Man should recognize this difference (5:1b) and regard God with humility and fear (3:14).

3:20 "All are from the dust. . . ." Or "both" (man and beast). The next verse implies that "going to the dust" includes spirit as well as body, since the possibility of the spirit going elsewhere is effectively denied. According to 12:7, however, the spirit returns to God. Thus too in Ps 104:29.

3:21 "Goes upward," "goes down." MT's *hāʿôlāh* and *hayyōredet* treat the *heh* as the article so that the verse can be construed, with some forcing, as in accord with the Jewish afterlife belief: "Who knows the spirit of man, which goes upward, and the spirit of the beast, which goes down to the ground?" But this is grammatically impossible and out of line with the context. The *heh* should be pointed as interrogative.

"And who knows. . . ." An unknowable possibility is of no use in solv-

216

ing present dilemmas. "Hence what he demands of himself is to live *solely* with what he knows, to accommodate himself to what is, and to bring in nothing that is not certain" (Camus, *Myth*, p. 39).

3:22 *'aḥărayw* has been understood in three ways: (1) "After him," with reference to what happens to an individual after his death (Delitzsch, Crenshaw). (2) "After him," with reference to what will happen on earth after one's death (Rashbam, Murphy). Qohelet earlier worried about what would happen to his property after his death (2:19). (Qohelet's concern may be, as Rashbam noted, that his son may be a fool and his property will not remain in his possession.) (3) "Afterwards," with reference to what will happen on earth within the individual's lifetime (Podechard [317-19], Gordis, Fox 1987). *'Aḥărayw* clearly has this sense in Qoh 9:3 and Jer 51:46. The suffixed *yw (-āw)* may be adverbial, as in *yaḥdaw* "together." The possibility of losing one's wealth sometime in the future makes present enjoyment all the more urgent (5:12-18; 6:1-3).

In the book as a whole, all three possibilities are relevant. Ignorance of the future, whether before or after death, whether on earth or elsewhere, is a reason to seize the present moment. But in the present context, following upon a verse that declares human ignorance of what follows death, the first alternative is probably in view. The rhetorical question in v. 22b rephrases the one in v. 21 and motivates the advice in 22a.

◆ 4:1-16

Qoh 4:1-16 is a thematic cluster of five sections commenting on desirable and undesirable patterns in human relations. The key-word is "two." The grouping is loose, but each section leads into the next in a way that shows that their composition was not haphazard.

A. 4:1-3. No fellowship for the oppressed
B. 4:4-6. Jealousy the fuel for toil
C. 4:7-8. The loner's obsessive labor
D. 4:9-12. The value of companionship
E. 4:13-16. Wisdom's failure to secure enduring fame

In 4:1 Qohelet "turns" to a new observation in five sections, each linked to the next. Section A is connected to B by the theme of fellowship and its lack. Section B is linked to C by the theme of toil, which is in turn spliced to D by the theme of the lone man, and that passage introduces the theme of the "companion" *(šeni),* which becomes important in E. This chaining is not by "Stichwort" or association but by thematic linkage. The sections are all speaking about the way that people can support one another in life's struggles or fail to do so. But in spite of these linkages, the handling of the theme is sufficiently varied that the sections are best examined separately.

A. 4:1-3. No Fellowship for the Oppressed

(1) When I turned and observed all the oppressions that occur under the sun, I saw the tears of the oppressed — and they have no comforter. Their oppressors ⟨*possess^a*⟩ *power — but they have no comforter. (2) So I declared the deceased — since they are already dead — more fortunate than the living — since they are still alive. (3) But better than either is the one who never existed, for he has never seen the evil things that occur under the sun.*

$^a b^e yad$ (MT *miyyad*)

Only occasionally does Qohelet observe wrongs committed by one person against another (3:16; 4:1-3; 8:9, 10; 9:15; 10:6f.), and in them he does not demand a change of behavior or rectification of the wrongs. The possibility that human character or social structure could be modified does not seem to cross his mind. Social injustice is just one of many warps and bends in his unchanging and unchangeable world.

Qohelet's focus is not the oppression itself (which is a given and not a discovery). While observing oppressions, Qohelet beholds *(w^{e}hinneh)* the weeping of the downtrodden and realizes that it goes without consolation. What troubles Qohelet in these tears is less the misery the tears express than the absence of a humane response to the suffering. This emphasis is shown by the repetition of the clause "and they have no comforter." Here then is the hope that Qohelet found frustrated: not that oppression disappear (such a possibility does not occur to him, even as a far-fetched hope), not that the persecuted cease their weeping (how could they?), but that others respond with sympathy to their anguish. Loyal companionship is truly good (4:9-12; 9:9), but the downtrodden are denied it. The inevitable absurdity of social oppression is thus unnecessarily exacerbated.

According to Ogden (1984a:449), Qohelet considers the pain the wise man feels when observing the human scene to be more intense than the pain suffered by the afflicted. It would be more precise to say that Qohelet is more sensitive to, and more troubled by, the wise observer's pain, which is, after all, his own. But he does not compare the two forms of suffering.

Qohelet does not view *himself* as a potential source of consolation. He feels sorry for the pain of the wretched and regrets that no one will offer them

218

solace, yet he seems more concerned with the disturbance to his own equanimity. He views the uncomforted oppression entirely from the perspective of an onlooker: how unfortunate is he who must behold such evils!

4:1 In *weʂabti ʾăni waʾerʾeh* (cf. 4:7; similarly 9:11) the verb ŠWB in effect is adverbial to the following verb. It does not mean "return" or "again," for prior to 4:1 Qohelet did not "see" oppressions, just as prior to 9:11 he did not "see" that "the race does not belong to the swift, etc." Here, as in 2 Chr 19:4; Isa 6:10, 13; Jer 18:4; etc., *šub* points to another in a series of actions or events and means "afterwards," "next," or the like. The verbs *panah* (Qoh 2:11, 12), *sabab* (2:20; 7:25), and *tur* (2:3) function similarly, except that *tur* describes the entire exploration, while the others mark new phases. I translate "turned" or "went about," to recall Qohelet's metaphorical geography, his "going about" and exploring all that occurs under the heavens (1:13).

Weʰinneh indicates perception or recognition (from the participant's perspective) and marks the preceding clause as virtually subordinate.

MT's *miyyad* "from the hand of" is difficult, since the oppressed cannot be said to get strength "from" the hand of their oppressors. *Koaḥ* never means oppression, or even the effects of the exercise of power. It is only power as *possessed* by someone. We should emend to *beyad* (*bet* and *mem* are very similar in some scripts). There is strength *in* the oppressors' hands, while their victims are weak.

4:2 The piel *šabbeaḥ* is declarative. Qohelet is not actually "praising" the dead (the usual translation) so much as favoring their condition, proclaiming it better than something else. On the inf. abs. used as the equivalent of a finite verb (also in 8:9; 9:11; and possibly 4:17 [*weqarob*]), see Schoors 1992:178-80. For syntactic parallels to the inf. abs. + subject, Schoors lists Lev 6:7; Num 15:35; Deut 15:2; Prov 17:12; Job 40:2 (dubious); Esth 2:3; and 9:1. In all these cases, however, as well as in the 25 cases noted by Huesman (1956:284-95), the infinitive can be explained otherwise: as consequential, as epexegetical, or as a gerund (cf. Prov 17:12). Qohelet's usage remains peculiar. (Even if the locution really reflects Phoenician influence, as Dahood [1952:49f.] claims, it is still peculiar in *Hebrew*.)

Parsing *še-* and *ʾăšer* as causal (Ginsberg) avoids producing pleonastic clauses ("the dead who have already died" and "the living who are still alive"). The two subordinate clauses give the grounds of the declaration, as does the second *ʾăšer*-clause in v. 3. The two subordinate clauses give the grounds of the declaration, as does the second *ʾăšer* in v. 3.

4:3 *Hamma'ăśeh hara' 'ăśer na'ăśah:* It is unclear whether this refers to oppressive actions, or to the fact that people suffer oppression yet have no one to comfort them (which might be called a *ma'ăśeh* "occurrence"), or to all the unfortunate events that occur in life. In any case, it is not the evil deeds alone that trouble Qohelet but rather something he sees *happening:* affliction going uncomforted.

Although Qohelet is burdened and grieved by the thought of death, in this same passage his despair drives him to prefer it to life and to pronounce it better not to have been born than to have lived and (inevitably) seen life's evils. This outburst, like 2:17 and 18, comes in a moment of despondency and is not determinative for Qohelet's philosophy.

B. 4:4-6. Jealousy the Fuel for Toil

(4) And I saw that all toil and all skilled work are [merely] one man's envy of another. This too is absurd and senseless.

(5) The fool locks his hands together and eats his flesh.

(6) Better is one handful earned calmly than two fistfuls of wealth with senseless thoughts.

4:4 *'Amal, 'ŚH: Ma'ăśeh* means "activity" and is partly synonymous with *'amal,* here meaning "toil." It is work, not wealth, that is driven by envy.

Kišron hamma'ăśeh means lit. "skill of work." Though *kišron* means both "skill" and "success" (5:10), the phrase here does not mean "success of work" (contrary to Ginsberg), since in context (4:5f.) it is the reasonableness of efforts rather than their outcome that is in question. Skilled work — a form of *hokmah* — is motivated by envy, which, as Prov 14:30 observes, is a "rotting of the bones." Driven by this unhealthy impulse, toil and ambition are inherently self-destructive and self-defeating.

4:5-6 Two proverbs, the first condemning indolence, the second toil.

"Locking" or "clasping" the hands together means to be idle (cf. Prov 6:10; 24:33). Eating one's flesh is a strikingly crass metaphor for self-destruction: the impoverished fool is forced to cannibalize himself. Imagine him sitting with hands clasped together while he gnaws on his knuckles. This is also an image of anxiety. Eating human flesh is a metaphor of destruction in Ps 27:2; Mic 3:3; and esp. Isa 49:26 ("I will feed your oppressors their own flesh . . ."). Lohfink construes *bᵉśaro* as the meat the fool possesses, making the verse a paradox. But the suffix of *baśar* always refers to the person or animal whose body the flesh is on.

4:6 Lit., "Better one handful of calm than two fistfuls of toil [*'amal*] and senseless thoughts [*re'ut ruaḥ*]." *'Amal* here means earnings rather than the activity of toiling, for "fistfuls" is something that can be possessed rather than an action. The conjunctive *waw* before *re'ut ruaḥ* signifies "together with," "accompanied by." For the phenomenon see GKC §254*a*, note 1 (b).

Although "locking of hands together" indicates mere idleness, *naḥat* is not mere inactivity, but rather an inner repose, without the buzz of frenetic busyness. In 9:17 *naḥat* is calm delivery of words. In 6:5 it must mean something besides simple absence of activity, because the stillbirth self-evidently has "more" inactivity than the living, and because it is not the non-activity that gives it an advantage over the living, but rather its lack of agitation. Isa 30:15 uses *naḥat* with reference to an inner state, composure. In Qoh 4:6, *naḥat* is probably a metonym for property gained through calm, moderate activity, just as *'amal* is a metonym for property gained through toil, its contrary.

Qoh 4:6 teaches that a small amount of property (or none at all) that is acquired without strain is better than twice as much gained through exertion and stress. Prov 15:16 expresses essentially the same idea, except that the preferred term in the comparison is a religious attitude rather than a psychological state: "Better a little in the fear of the Lord than great treasure with agitation in it [*me'oṣar rab ume'humah bo*]." *Re'ut ruaḥ* refers to much the same thing as *me'humah*.

By form and theme, both vv. 5 and 6aα are conventional proverbs. Whybray (1981:439-41) considers both verses (up to *re'ut ruaḥ*) to be quotations, while Gordis regards only v. 5 as a conventional proverb, which Qohelet answers by one of his own in v. 6. Either hypothesis may be right, or both verses may have been composed by the author. But whether they are quoted or not, we still have to determine Qohelet's stance toward them.

The second proverb does not invalidate the first; both are true: v. 5 condemns idleness, v. 6 censures toil. Both describe fools, the one frozen in inaction, the other grinding away and scrambling for money day and night. This is an actual instance of the "Zwar-Aber Tatsache" (see §1.51). To be sure, the lazy man harms himself (therefore Qohelet never recommends indolence), *and yet* the toiler, too, harms himself through his endeavors and the attendant aggravations. But the latter case, as Murphy notes, is worse. The ordinary, lazy fool harms himself, while the skillful (hence "wise") worker is motivated by envy, a source of social corrosion. Since v. 6 motivates v. 4, v. 5 is parenthetical, a transition to the comment on the more severe folly. The real topic of the unit is skill and industry, not laziness.

C. 4:7-8. The Loner's Obsessive Labor

(7) I turned and observed another absurdity under the sun: (8) There is a man all alone who has no companion, neither does he have a son or brother. Yet his toil is endless and, moreover, his eye is never sated by wealth. (So for whom am I toiling and depriving myself of pleasure?) This too is an absurdity and an unfortunate business.

4:8 Lit. "there is one and not a second" or "without a second." Both *'amel* and *'amal* here mean toil, for that rather than wealth is endless and entails deprivation.

In v. 8aβ *gam* is a coordinating conjunction introducing an additional datum (see Ellermeier 1967:234). In other words, there are two factors in this man's behavior: external — he never ceases working — and internal — he is never satisfied with what he has. And yet there is no one (at least no one he cares about) to enjoy what he earns and hoards. Such behavior is obviously absurd.

In the middle of v. 8, Qohelet shifts to the first person. Gordis supplies an italicized *"He never asks himself"* before the sentence, to make it an unmarked quotation of the hypothetical argument the lone man *should have* used. But the reader could not be expected to recognize an unmarked quotation of something the man never said, in fact, of something he never even *thought* of saying. Rather, the interjection in the middle of v. 8 shows that Qohelet is speaking out of his own experience. In 2:18-19 as well, Qohelet sees himself as the unfortunate toiler.

D. 4:9-12. The Value of Companionship

(9)   *Better two than one,*
      because they have a good reward in their toil.
(10)   *For if they fall, one can help the other get up,*
      but woe to the lone man who falls
      and has no companion to help him up.
(11)   *Also, if two lie down, they will keep warm,*
      but how can the lone man keep warm?
(12)   *And if someone attacks either of them,*
      the two can stand against him.
      And the three-fold rope will not quickly snap.

Qohelet recognizes benefits in friendship, albeit rather cheerless ones. Comrades can aid each other in difficulty, such as when one falls, is attacked, or is cold. Qohelet does not mention the emotional blessings of fellowship.

4:9 *'Amal* here means "toil" and refers not only to efforts directed at gaining wealth, but to life's activities in general.

4:10 "Companion": *šeni*, lit. "second." Since it is not ordinarily difficult to get up after a fall, we should understand the saying as alluding to any trouble or failure in life (cf. Mic 7:8; Ps 24:17; 145:14).

4:12 *Yitqᵉpô:* The subject of *yitqᵉpo* is awkward. It is not reflected in LXX (ἐπικραταιωθῇ "was overpowered") or Syr (*neˀšan* "became strong" — apparently with reference to the attacker). Ellermeier (1967:175) explains the sg. verb as indefinite and the suffix as objective ("if one attacks him"), with the "him" resumed by the following noun, "the one."

Ha'eḥad, lit. "the one," is either of the two companions, as in v. 10, not an indefinite "someone," which would not have the article. *Negdo* = "against him," namely the attacker. The antecedent of *negdo* is implicit in the indefinite subject of the verb.

"The three-fold rope will not quickly snap" is numerical heightening: if the companionship of two people is fortunate, how much the more so when there are three! This is an ancient proverb found in "Gilgamesh and Hubaba" (version A, 102-7; Shaffer, 1967, 1969).

102. Gilgamesh answered [Enkidu]:
103. Stop, Enkidu! The 'second' [= companion] will not die.
     The towed boat will not sink.
104. No one can sever the three-fold cord.
105. In the protection of the wall, no one will be swept away.
106. In the well-woven hut the fire will not be extinguished.
107. Help me, and I will help you — and who can trouble us?

Not only does the adage "No one can sever the three-fold cord" appear, but the context is similar — the protection a travelling companion affords one on a journey — and both teach the value of mutual aid against assault. The three-fold cord is, as l. 103 shows, the tackle of a ship or barge towed in the river. The three-fold cord does not fit into Qohelet's imagery as well as it does in the Sumerian poem's. This is an indication that the actual (though not, of course, immediate) source of the adage is Gilgamesh (Schaffer 1967:248f.). An Akkadian fragment of the epic with part of the adage (discussed by Schaffer 1969) helps bridge the gap between the Sumerian epic and the much later Qohelet. Menahem Haran (private communication) suggests that Qohelet is splitting up a graded numerical proverb (originally

223

"Two are better than one, and the three-ply cord will not quickly snap") and inserting his own comments in the middle. The graded numerical sequence in Gilgamesh supports this.

E. 4:13-16. Wisdom's Failure to Secure Enduring Fame

(13) Better a poor but wise young man than an old but foolish king who no longer knows how to be wary, (14) for he came forth from prison to rule, while in his rule too a poor man was born.

(15) I saw all the living — those who go about under the sun — with the next young man who would arise in his place. (16) There was no end to all the people, all those whom he led. Likewise, later people would not take pleasure in him. Now this too is absurd and senseless.

    a. What wisdom can accomplish (13-14)
        i. A "better than" saying praising wisdom (13)
        ii. An incident that supports the saying (14)
    b. The ephemerality of such accomplishments (15-16a)
        i. The outcome: the masses follow whoever arises next (15)
        ii. The exacerbation of the outcome (16a)
    c. Conclusion: This is absurd (16b)

The ambiguity in almost all the pronouns in this passage and in the subjects of the verbs hampers interpretation. There are syntactical ambiguities as well, especially in vv. 15-16. Also uncertain is how many youths enter into the story, whether it is one: the old king's immediate successor; or two: the wise youth and that youth's successor (called *hayyeled haššeni* in 15b); or three: the wise youth who came from prison ("youth[1]," 13a), a second youth, who was born in the reign of the latter ("youth[2]," 14b), and a third ("youth[3]," 15b), called *hayyeled haššeni,* namely whoever comes next in line. I will argue for the third alternative, which, I believe, has not been proposed elsewhere, including in my earlier study (1987:205-9).

The multiplicity of possibilities for resolving the ambiguities has given rise to a considerable variety of interpretations (summary and critique in Ellermeier 1967:217-28). Nevertheless, most commentators agree that the point of the story is that wisdom's practical value is limited and transient.

4:13 ". . . old *but* foolish" rather than "old *and* foolish." The king's age is not the cause of his folly, but a valuable attribute that is overcome by his folly. Age was universally thought to be associated with wisdom in the ancient world. This is the reverse of the young man's situation, in which a weakness (imprisonment) is overcome by wisdom. Since the king's folly is marked by a lack of circumspection, and since his successor was in prison, we may surmise that this youth had been incarcerated for presenting a danger to the old king.

4:14 The subject of "came forth" is youth[1], not the old king, for the king's past is irrelevant. This verse motivates the previous one by stating that the wisdom of youth[1] enabled him to attain the throne from a position of lowliness and apparent incapacity.

"A poor man was born [*nolad raš*]": Most commentators construe *raš* as adverbial to *nolad*, describing the circumstances of the birth of youth[1] ("was born poor"). This, however, makes no sense of *ki gam*, whether it is construed as concessive ("although") or causal ("for also"). Nothing would be added by saying that the poor youth who came out of prison was "born poor," and *bᵉmalkuto*, whether meaning "in his kingdom" or "in his reign," adds nothing to the fact that youth[1] was "born poor." (There is no need to say that he was born poor in the old king's *kingdom*. Otherwise his foreignness would be a factor. And it is impossible that he was born other than in the old king's *reign*, since he was younger.)

I suggest that *raš* is a noun meaning "a poor man"; this is youth[2]. The adverb *gam* "too" indicates that the sentence comments on another reign ("in his reign too") in addition to the old king's, namely, the reign of youth[1]. So far there is a series of an old king, succeeded by a former prisoner (youth[1]), who is succeeded by another formerly poor man (youth[2]). In fact, the "too" of *ki gam bᵉmalkuto* implies that youth[1] was also born poor.

Taking a new approach, D. Rudman (1997) vocalizes *lammelek* "to the king" instead of MT's *limlōk* "to rule" (inf.) and translates v. 14 as "For out of prison he shall come [*yāṣā'*] to the king, even though born poor in his kingdom" (p. 57). Rudman interprets this to mean that this youth became the king's companion or lieutenant *(haššeni),* and as counsellor he used his wisdom for the benefit of the kingdom. *Hayyeled haššeni* in v. 15 is thus the same person as the youth of vv. 13f. This youth enjoys the king's patronage but eventually falls out of public favor.

Rudman's interpretation is an overreading. For one thing, *yaṣa'* indicates motion from the standpoint of the place of origin, not the goal. (That would be *ba'*.) The phrase "go out to the king" says nothing about what happened when the youth arrived at the court. It does not in itself convey the idea that the youth became the king's protegé, and nothing else in the passage reinforces this notion.

The particle *ki gam* is discussed at 8:12.

4:15 *Hayyeled haššeni,* lit. "the second youth," is neither youth[1] nor youth[2], but their successor, youth[3]. *Hayyeled haššeni* does not mean "the lad, who was second," that is to say, the old king's successor (thus Gordis); *šeni* alone never has this sense. Nor is youth[2] the "second" with respect to rank, the king's deputy or "Stellvertreter" (Hertzberg), since if he arose from prison merely to that end, the old king's folly would be irrelevant. On the contrary, the choice of a wise viceroy would demonstrate wisdom on the king's part. *Haššeni* here means "next" (cf. Ex 2:13; Judg 20:24f.; thus Ellermeier, 1967, p. 232, who, however, thinks of only two young protagonists). Youth[3] is "second" to the previously mentioned one (youth[2]) but third in the sequence.

"The next youth" (youth[3]) is not a specific person and does not yet exist from Qohelet's standpoint. He is whoever comes next in line. The switch to yiqtol in *ya'ămod* in v. 15 also indicates the introduction of another person in the story, since it implies that the arising "in his place" occurs after the events of v. 14. (Qohelet never uses yiqtol for simple past tense.[26]) The change in tense also suggests that Qohelet's temporal perspective is contemporaneous with the reign of youth[2]. From that perspective, the ascendancy of the *next* young man is yet to come.

The sentence should be construed not as "I saw X" (X = "the living who go about under the sun with the next young man") but rather "I saw Y with Z" (Y = "the living who go about under the sun"; Z = "the next young man who would arise in his place"). Thus the MT, which places the major disjunctive on *haššameš*. The prepositional phrase *'im hayyeled haššeni* is an adjunct of the main verb, not the relative clause. In other words, the focus of Qohelet's seeing is not "the living" but rather the fact of their *being with* the next youth. The clause *ham^ehall^ekim taḥat haššameš* is adjectival, modifying *haḥayyim* (Ellermeier 1967:231f.) and equivalent to *ro'ey haššameš* (7:11; C. D. Ginsburg). Being "with" (*'im*) someone indicates alliance and support (e.g., Gen 28:20; 26:3; 1 Kgs 8:57; cf. 2 Kgs 6:16; 9:32 [using *'et* "with"]). The phrase "under the sun" emphasizes the universality of the phenomenon: *everyone's* loyalties attach themselves to whatever ruler comes along and are thus very erratic. The phrase also underscores the contrast between these people, who will be alive at the time to which the statement applies, and the previous rulers (youth[1] and youth[2]), who will by then be dead or supplanted.

---

26. B. Isaksson (1987:130-33) ascribes the following functions to the yiqtol in Qohelet: generalized cursive aspect (expressing a universal truth or ongoing event or action), actuality or facticity, the gnomic present, future (or future-in-past), and modal nuances.

Qohelet "sees" — that is, foresees — that all the living would be on the side of whoever comes to power next. Though Qohelet is looking to the future, he calls the supplanter (youth³) a *yeled,* "youngster," to imply that the people's loyalty is so unreliable that they will flock after anyone, *even* a mere stripling.

4:16 The phrase *lᵉkol 'ăšer hayah lipneyhem* does not mean "all who existed before them," for it is irrelevant how many people lived prior to the events of this anecdote. Rather it means, lit., "all those before whom he [youth³] was"; in other words, all the people he led (thus Tg, Ginsburg, Delitzsch, and Podechard). This clause refers to the same group as "all the living" (v. 15a). The subject of *hayah* "he was" is youth³.

"Would not take pleasure in him" *(lo' yiśmᵉḥu bo):* The antecedent of "him" is youth³. The verb *śamaḥ bᵉ-* is used of a king pleasing his subjects and being accepted by them (Judg 19:9). Not even youth³, though leader of limitless masses, would find favor with later people, because everyone is soon forgotten. The "next youth" (youth³) represents anyone who succeeds in the endless series of power-holders.

The antecedent of "this" in the *hebel*-judgment is a situation: one ruler passing on his power to the next with little rhyme or reason in the process.

The following paraphrase resolves the ambiguities:

(13) A poor youth [y¹] who is shrewd is better off even than an old king, if the latter is puerile and no longer has the sense to take precautions. (14) For it happened that one such youth [y¹] went forth from prison to rule. Yet in his reign too a poor man [y²] was born.

(15) I saw that all the living who go about on earth would join the following of whichever young man would take over next [y³]. (16) All the people — all whom such a young man [y³] would lead — would be beyond number. But, by the same token, subsequent generations wouldn't care a whit about him [y³]. This fact is absurd and senseless.

Many attempts have been made to identify the persons in this tale with Biblical characters, such as Nimrod and Abraham, Saul and David, Pharaoh and Joseph, Nebuchadnezzar and Daniel, or with later historical characters, such as Antiochus III and Ptolemy Philapeter, Antiochus Epiphanes and Alexander Balas, Ptolemy IV and Ptolemy V. But none of these personages fits the description, and some are too late to be mentioned in Qohelet. Nevertheless, the elliptical character of the narration does give the impression that the story was actual to the original audience (though perhaps dimly remembered, and perhaps legendary) and that he expects them to recognize the event and flesh it out. The audience must be able to grant the factuality of the episode in vv. 13-14 in order for the twist in vv. 15-16 to be effective. Further suggesting that the anecdote is supposed to be historical is the fact that one of the men came forth from prison. This datum does not further the message of the anecdote, which requires only that the protagonist comes to rule from a lowly station through wisdom. As Ogden observes (1980a:315), Qohelet is making a claim that requires "documentation," some rooting in the real world, to be rhetorically effective. Whether or not the event is historical, it is to be imagined as such.

Rudman (1997:72) traces the parallels between 4:13-16 and 9:13-15. The protagonist of the latter is a "poor wise man" (*'iš misken ḥakam)*; in the present passage he is a "poor but wise youth" *(yeled misken w^eḥakam)*. In both, the poor man is compared favorably to the king. Neither protagonist reaps the full rewards of his wisdom. Rudman also points out ways in which 4:13-16 fits in its nearer context: the concern for oppression of the poor in 4:1-3, the divisiveness of human strivings implied in 4:4, the importance of companionship, described in 4:8-12, as well as the recurrence of the "better than" formula in vv. 3, 6, 9, and 13 (1997:58f.). These connections do not, however, reinforce Rudman's idea that the first youth was the king's favorite and served as his counselor. There are further parallels with 6:8, q.v.

Qohelet's message emerges not from the details of the story but from its typical and recurrent features, above all the recognition that prized accomplishments, whether in wealth or power, even if obtained through wisdom, will be passed on to someone else (cf. 2:18-26). What Qohelet regards as valuable (and vulnerable) in rulership is the fame and favor it should bring. This popularity is the large-scale counterpart of the companionship that Qohelet prizes in 4:9-12.

The old king's loss of power was the expected and appropriate result of his folly. The subsequent transfers of power have no such rationale. The first transfer demonstrates the power of wisdom, the second its frailty. It is the instability of accomplishment, rather than the loss of power as such, that troubles Qohelet. As he will remind us, "favor does not belong to the knowledgeable" (9:11).

◆ **4:17–5:6**

> *(17) Tread carefully when you go to the House of God,*
> *for to obey is more acceptable*
> *than when fools offer sacrifice,*
> *since they do not know how to do wrong.*
> *(5:1) Do not be hasty with your mouth,*

> and let not your heart haste
> to utter a word to God,
> for God is in heaven
> and you are on earth.
> Therefore let your words be few.

(2) For a dream comes with much busyness,
and the fool's voice with much talk.

(3) When you make a vow to God
do not delay in paying it,
for no one takes pleasure in fools.
What you vow — pay!

(4) Better that you not vow
than that you vow and not pay.

(5) Do not let your mouth
bring punishment upon your flesh,
and do not say to <God*ᵃ*>
that it was a mistake,
lest God grow angry at your voice
and destroy the work of your hands.

(6) For much talk*ᵇ* is <like*ᶜ*> a lot of dreams and absurdities.
But fear God!

ᵃ*hāʾĕlōhîm* (MT *hammalʾāk*)
ᵇ*dᵉbārîm* (MT *ûdᵉbārîm*)
ᶜ*kᵉrōb* (MT *bᵉrōb*)

Admonitions to behave with proper trepidation toward God open (4:17) and close (5:6b) this unit. The central theme is vows. Qohelet warns of the folly of excessive and rash vows (5:1f.) and of the dangers in delaying payment (5:3). The remarks about sacrifices and speech are subordinate to this theme and allude to the circumstances of vows.

In form and content, this passage is conventional wisdom. Though Qohelet is known for his subversive and critical remarks, he *also* taught wisdom of a traditional cast. Qohelet never abandons moral and religious principles or repudiates the principle of divine justice.

The passage comprises a series of admonitions and motivations, addressed in the second person singular to an indefinite audience and structured, for the most part, in parallel stichs. As is usual in Wisdom Literature, the misdeed is condemned for its folly rather than its sinfulness. This focus is deliberate in v. 5; see the comment.

4:17 Although the difficulties of this verse have not been resolved, the essential message is clear: behave carefully in the temple, for obedience to God is better than the sacrifices fools bring. To be sure, obedience is better than *anyone's* sacrifice (1 Sam 15:22). Qohelet is warning against misbehavior in the cult, and is only incidentally associating such behavior with fools. A similarly superfluous addition of "fools" appears in Qoh 7:5.

The idiom *šᵉmor ragleyka* (qeré: *rglk,* sg.), lit. "guard your feet," means to behave with care (Tur-Sinai); hence: "tread carefully," "be careful what you do." Compare Ps 119:101 and especially Ps 26:12, where "my foot stands on level ground" is equivalent to "and I walk in my innocence" (v. 11); see further Job 23:11; 31:5; and Prov 4:27 ("remove your foot from evil"). The present verse counsels prudence in the temple generally and introduces the following section, which warns against precipitant vows. The basic idea of *šᵉmor ragleyka* is rephrased at the end of this unit by *'et ha'ĕlohim yᵉra',* "fear God."

Qarob apparently means "near to God's favor," "acceptable." The adjective/noun *qarob* is used of one who has an intimate relationship, whether divine (Ps 34:19; 85:10; 119:151) or human (Ps 148:14 [Israel]; Ezek 43:19 [Zadokites]; Lev 10:3 [priests]). Though it is not elsewhere used of actions, in 1 Kgs 8:59 words of prayer are said to be "near to the Lord," meaning acceptable to him.

The end of 4:17, *ki 'eynam yodᵉ'im la'ăśot ra',* can only mean, "since they do not know how to do wrong." This seems to imply that ignorance of doing evil is a bad quality and that *this* is what makes the fools' sacrifices inferior to obedience. All the proposals to explain the present text have been unpersuasive, and even so do not arrive at an appropriate meaning. The versions support MT.

Lohfink (1983) defends MT by parsing *yodᵉ'im* as stative and arguing that the ignorant are not fully conscious *('eynam yodᵉ'im),* as they themselves concede by making a *šᵉgagah*-offering (5:5). Without full awareness, they cannot have true fear of God, which alone allows for freedom, and they therefore lack the moral responsibility that makes it possible to truly do evil. But Lohfink's interpretation attributes to Qohelet an intricate psychological-ethical theory that has no anchoring in the text or the language, and it is self-contradictory. Wouldn't an evil act performed by a person who lacks full moral responsibility, a child for instance, be referred to as "doing *ra*'"? Also, if fools did possess the intellectual requisites for genuine moral responsibility (as is usually the case; that is why they are culpable), would that make their sacrifices better than obedience?

An emendation would be in order if that would solve the problem, but none proposed so far is persuasive. The emendation to *milla'ăśot* (haplography) supposedly yields the meaning "For they do not know (except) to do evil" (Barton; similarly McNeile, Podechard, *BHS,* and others). But there is no evidence that *min* has this function. Inserting *ki 'im* after *yodᵉ'im* (Renan) gives the same sense but is graphically too distant from MT to be justified without versional evidence. Ginsberg weighs emending *ra'* to *'od* "more." But the resulting clause, "for they do not know how to do anything else," does not motivate the advice of v. 17a, for it diminishes the moral responsibility of the fools. The words may be facetious: these fools are too stupid to do *anything,* even to do evil (cf. Gordis), but this too connects poorly with the preceding. Since the MT is clear and grammatically feasible, I translate the sentence literally without understanding its point.

Qohelet is in no way repudiating the cult. On the contrary, if he did not assume that offering sacrifice is essentially commendable, the comparison he draws would not enhance his praise of obedience. In 9:2, Qohelet lists those who offer sacrifice among other possessors of virtues.

5:1 As the phrase "to God" shows, the topic of this verse is circumspection in uttering vows rather than caution in speech generally, although Qohelet would undoubtedly advocate the latter as well (cf. 6:11; 10:14). To speak "before" God (thus, lit., in 5:1 and 5b [LXX]) is an Aramaism, equivalent to *'ămar* (or *'anpeq*) *'imra' qŏdam,* meaning "speak to." The vast disparity between God's lofty station and man's earth-bound lowliness is the reason to be sparing of speech, especially in vows. God's heavenly vantage point allows him to see all that goes on in the world (Ps 33:13; 102:20; 113:6; Job 28:24), while man's horizon is constricted and does not permit him to know what eventualities may keep him from paying his vows.

5:2 A parenthetical remark of proverbial character, motivating the advice in 5:1. The main point of this verse comes in the second line: it is foolish to talk too much.

The first line is generally understood as a warning that too much work during the day causes disturbing dreams at night. But Qohelet does not indicate that he is referring to nightmares. The proverb probably means that the dreams are accompanied by busyness (*'inyan*), rather than that busyness provokes dreams. Construing the phrase in the latter way would mean that in the parallel line, "much talk" was the source of "the fool's voice," whereas the causality is the other way around. The phrase *ba'bᵉ-* here means "come with," "come bringing," "accompanied by," a sense this locution has in Lev 16:3; Ps 66:13; etc. (BDB p. 98b; GKC §219n). Just as a dream holds much empty "activity," so does the voice of the fool convey only a lot of vapid verbiage. '*Inyan* therefore refers to the busy but meaningless stream of thoughts during dreams (thus Tyler), rather than to daytime tasks that might cause dreams. Ben Sira (34[31]:5) says that divination, omens, and dreams are *hebel*, "vain," "nonsense."

5:3-4 The impersonal locution, "No one takes pleasure in fools," may indicate a hesitancy (that recalls a Targumic characteristic) to speak of God's emotions directly.

5:3 "No one takes . . .": lit. "there is no . . ." reiterates 4:17 but phrases the admonition more narrowly. In both, as in 5:5b, God's favor or disfavor is the motivating consideration.

Qoh 5:3f. is a close reformulation of Deut 23:22-24, "(22) When you make a vow to the Lord your God, do not delay in paying it, for the Lord your God will seek it from you and it will be a sin in you. (23) But if you refrain from vowing, it shall be no sin in you. (24) Be careful (to fulfill) what comes forth from your lips, and do what you have vowed freely to the Lord your God, that which you spoke with your own mouth." Hasty vows are warned against in Prov 20:25 and Sir 18:22f., and payment of vows is demanded in Num 30:3 and Ps 50:14b.

5:5 *Laḥăṭî'*, an apocopated hiphil, means "bring harm upon," as in Isa 29:21 and Deut 24:4, but the word echoes *ḥeṭ'* "sin" in Deut 23:22f. Qohelet is concerned more with the harm the behavior may cause the doer than with its sinfulness.

MT reads "And do not say before the angel." The LXX and Syr (probably independently) have "God." There is no reason for those highly literalistic versions to have changed "angel" to "God." A change from "God" to "angel" was not necessary theologically, but it would have added a degree of caution. From the literary standpoint "God" is preferable, for it is the expression used in 5:1, and its repetition adds cohesiveness to the passage: Do not make rash vows to God *(lipney ha'ĕlohim)* (v. 1) so that you will not have to make excuses to God *(lipney ha'ĕlohim)* (v. 5). But since an angel simply carries out God's will or bears his message, the two readings are equivalent. Deut 23:22 envisions that God himself will "seek" payment of the vow, and this may be reflected in Qohelet's "do not say to God."

If you are delinquent in paying your vows, "your voice," as the object of God's anger, will turn out to be none other than the "voice of the fool," which is characterized by "much talk." *Ma'ăśeh-yadeyka* is earnings. The punishment will take the form of material loss, as is appropriate, since (in

232

terms of votive symbolism) a default on vows impinges on God's material dues.

For the history of interpretation of this verse, see Salters 1978.

5:6 A summary conclusion. The MT reads, lit., "(a) For in much dreams and vapors and many words. (b) But fear God." To make sense of v. 6a we must minimally remove the *waw* of *udᵉbarim,* making *dᵉbarim harbeh* the subject. But though the sentence thus emended is grammatical, it says the reverse of what is required, which is that there are many dreams and vapors "in" a lot of talk, and not the other way around. It would not disparage dreams and absurdities (senseless thoughts) to say that there is "much talk" in them, and at any rate, dreams and absurdities are not the topic in this unit. We should therefore also emend *brb* to *krb,* making the sentence comparative. The sentence then reads *kî kᵉrôb ḥălōmôt wahăbālîm dᵉbārîm harbēh,* lit. "for like much dreams and absurdities are many words."

Fearing God is the antithesis of the negligence implied by thoughtless vowing and vain excuses. The *ki*-clause in v. 6a reinforces the admonition of v. 5 in a general way. The *ki* in 6b introducing an imperative ("fear God") cannot be even loosely causal and must be in some way emphatic, or possibly adversative to the negatives in v. 5a. (*Ki* + impv. clauses can be motivations only when they are implicitly indicative, as in Deut 4:32; 1 Sam 12:24; and Jer 2:10.)

Hăbalim straddles its literal sense of "vapors" (which come from the mouth) and its figurative sense of pointless, senseless things — in other words, absurdities.

◆ **5:7-8**

(7) If you see oppression of the poor and robbery of justice and right in the state, do not be surprised at the matter, for every highly placed person has a higher one looking out for him, and there are higher ones over them. (8) And the advantage of a land in all regards is <in every worked field [?].ᵃ>

ᵃ*bᵉkōl śādeh ne'ĕbād* (MT *melek lᵉśādeh ne'ĕbād*)

5:7-8 is an epigram on the ubiquity of social oppression and greed. It is loosely connected to the following unit, especially 5:10a, by the theme of greed.

5:7 As the pointing of the *waw* and the conjunctive *mᵉhuppak* suggest, *mišpāṭ wāṣedeq* is a hendiadys equivalent to *mišpaṭ ṣedeq,* "righteous judgment" or "just due." This is something that people possess, in principle, and of which they can be "robbed" or deprived. Compare Deut 10:18: the orphan and widow possess a *mišpaṭ* ("the *mišpaṭ* of the orphan and widow") which God "does" or "carries out" (*'ośeh*).

A "province" (*mᵉdinah*) is an administrative unit, a province of an empire or, later, a city state. As Lohfink observes (1981:539), Qohelet speaks from the standpoint of a provincial subject of an empire. This would probably be the Ptolemaic empire ruled from Alexandria.

It is usually assumed that the cause of oppression described here is the bureaucratic hierarchy itself. But it is not a superior's *watching* his subordinates that would cause oppression and injustice. Instead, the verse observes the corrupting influence of "proteksia": people of rank watch *over,* look out for, their subordinates, making it impossible to protect against corruption. For *šamar* in the sense of "watch over" protectively, see 1 Sam 26:16 and Prov 6:22. The Egyptian Anii looks at bureaucratic layering as an insider and assumes it is positive: an official takes care of his subordinates and in turn "his prince is his protection" (B 20.4-7). Though there was always bureaucracy, it became most complex and burdensome in Ptolemaic times, when it was largely an instrument of tax gathering.

5:8 This verse is difficult, but it is possible to get at its gist. The verse speaks of an advantage (*yitron*) a land possesses. This suggests a comparison, the other term of which could be found in the preceding verse. ("Land" in v. 8 is a country — a polity rather than a physical land.) In 5:7 the disfavored land suffers under self-serving officials. In 10:16-17 too Qohelet contrasts an unlucky land, suffering from dissolute rulers, with a favored land, blessed with a responsible élite. But what "advantage" is intended here?

The text, particularly in 8b *(mlk lśdh nʿbd),* requires an emendation. One that yields a meaningful (if not entirely smooth) sentence is *bᵉkōl śādeh neʿĕbād,* "in every cultivated field." Consonantally, this is a fairly minor change, from *mlklśdh* to *bklśdh. Bakkol* in v. 8a can mean "in all respects"; cf. Gen 24:1 and 2 Sam 23:5. *Nʿbd* means "worked," that is, cultivated or tilled; this is the only meaning attested for *neʿĕbad,* e.g., Deut 21:4; Ezek 36:9, 34. Translating "for even a king is subject to the land" (Gordis; cf. Tg, Ibn Ezra) is impossible.

The point of the sentence thus read is that a country that has all of its fields cultivated has an advantage over others. Far better for a country to be thoroughly agrarian rather than to be burdened with a stratified and self-serving bureaucracy. In a similar spirit, Qohelet praises the possession of a *naḥălah,* a landed inheritance, in 7:11.

234

◆ **5:9–6:12**

This unit comprises five loosely related sections treating the themes of greed and satisfaction. Because of the length of the unit, the sections will be discussed separately.

A. 5:9-11. Preliminary observations on satisfaction
and dissatisfaction
B. 5:12-16. A bad scenario (a *ra'ah ḥolah*): a man hoards
his wealth and loses it
C. 5:17-19. A good scenario (a *ṭob*): a man gets to enjoy his wealth
D. 6:1-6. The bad scenario made worse (it is a *ra'ah* as well as
a *hebel woḥŏli ra'*): a man is not allowed to enjoy his wealth,
but another consumes it in his place
E. 6:7-9. Dissatisfaction
F. 6:10-12. Conclusion: human ignorance

A. 5:9-11. Satisfaction and Dissatisfaction

(9) He who loves silver will not be sated with silver, nor whoever loves wealthᵃ with income. This too is absurd.

(10) As goods increase, so do those who would consume them, and the only benefit (in it) for its owner is the sight of his eyes.

(11) Sweet is the sleep of the <slaveᵇ>, whether he has eaten little or much, whereas the rich man's surfeit does not allow him to sleep.

ᵃ*hāmôn* (MT *behāmôn*)
ᵇ*hā'ebed* (MT *hā'ōbēd*)

One reason people fail to derive satisfaction from their wealth is that others take it away. It is therefore imperative to enjoy what you have in front of you, even if it is just scraps.

5:9 *Mi* = "whoever" (Exod 24:14; 32:26; etc.). Read *hmwn* for *bhmwn* (dittography; *BHS* and most), because *'ahab* elsewhere governs a direct object without a preposition. *Lo' teḇu'ah* is elliptical for *lo' yiśba' teḇu'ah*, the force of the verb carrying over from the preceding sentence. "This too is absurd" refers to the situation or fact described in the verse as a whole: As Qohelet said earlier, "The eye is not sated with seeing" (1:8b); cf. 4:8.

Money should be a means, not an end in itself, for if one heads for riches the horizon ever recedes. Hence one should "get satisfaction from the goods [*tobah*]" (6:3) he already possesses.

5:10 *Ṭobah,* "good (things)," "property," can refer more specifically to food (Sir 30:18). Thus 5:10a can first of all be understood literally, then extended metaphorically to all property.

Mah is often used in rhetorical questions equivalent to negations. Sometimes the interrogative character seems to be lost and the word becomes synonymous with *'eyn* or *lo'* (e.g., Job 16:6; 31:1; 1 Kgs 12:16; compare Cant 8:4 with 5:8). Thus *mah* X *ki 'im* Y (like RH *'eyn* X *'ella'* Y) means "X is only Y." *Kišron,* as commonly recognized, here means "benefit," "prosper," corresponding to *yikšar* "succeed" in 11:6 (Ibn Ezra, Delitzsch, Ginsberg, Hertzberg, et al.).

The point of this verse is not that one who possesses something is soon left with only "the mere vision of his eyes" (Gordis). If he can see it, he probably still has it. Rather, "the sight of his eyes" *is* the benefit. *Rᵉ'ût* (qeré) *'eynayw* (like *mar'ey 'eynayim* in 11:9 and 6:9) is something desirable, not something worthless. (The Oriental reading, *rᵉ'ôt,* is the infinitive construct, with a slightly different meaning: *rᵉ'ût* is the abstract — seeing, vision. The infinitive indicates the action of seeing, which is somewhat more suitable here.) Wealth is in constant danger of disappearing because it attracts others who will try to take it for themselves. Therefore the only benefit *(kišron)* that wealth can offer is the immediate experience — the seeing — of pleasure.

5:11 Better the untroubled sleep of the slave than the rich man's insomnia, which is induced by worry over one's possessions.

Almost all MSS of the LXX have τοῦ δούλου, "the slave," construing the consonantal text as *hā'ebed,* "the slave." This is to be preferred to MT's *hā'ōbēd* "the worker." The contrast MT draws between the rich man and the worker is not meaningful, because the rich man too works hard. In fact it is his toil that keeps him awake. "Slave" is more meaningful because the contrast hinges on the possession of property to worry about. Moreover, in BH *ha'obed* is not used to designate the common laborer, the worker in contrast to other classes. (In Ezek 48:18f. *'obᵉdey ha'ir* are those who work within the city in contradistinction to those who work outside it. They are not a social class of workers as distinct from a leisure class.) The term that designates a physical laborer as opposed to one who earns his living through trade, properties, and the like, is *śakir.*

Haśśaba' is not the satiety or satisfaction felt by the rich man, but rather the surfeit of property he possesses (*śaba'* = "surfeit," "abundance" in Gen 41:29, 30, 31; Prov 3:10; etc.). Qohelet does not demean satisfaction. He considers it desirable (4:8; 6:3), whereas he regards satiety as unobtainable (6:7). The contrast between the rich man and the slave is not that the former brought on indigestion by overeating, since a slave too may have eaten much (v. 11aβ). The rich man has insomnia because he must worry about his wealth (Ibn Ezra, Rashbam, Podechard, Ginsberg; cf. 2:23 and Sir 31:1). As Rabban Gamaliel observes, "He who increases property increases worry" (Avot 2:7). After all, the more one earns the more he must fret that others will try to get hold of it (5:10). The slave, by contrast, can rest easy because he has no property to worry about losing.

B. 5:12-16. A Bad Scenario (a ra'ah holah)

(12) There is a sick misfortune that I have seen under the sun: Wealth is stored up by its owner to his harm, (13) and then that wealth is lost in an unfortunate business, and when he begets a son he owns nothing whatsoever. (14) Just as he came forth from his mother's womb, so shall he return naked — just as he came — and he will carry away nothing of his toil that he might take in his possession.

(15) This too is a sick misfortune: just as[a] he came so shall he go, so what profit is there that he should toil for the wind? (16) Moreover, all his days he eats in darkness and great irritation[b] and sickness[c] and wrath.

[a]*kil'ummat* (MT *kol 'ummat*)
[b]*w^{e}ka'as* (MT *w^{e}kā'as*)
[c]*wohŏlî* (MT *w^{e}holyô*)

Qohelet describes a complex scenario: A man toils and hoards his money, harming himself in the process by worry and self-deprivation, then suddenly loses it all. He has a son but nothing to give him. He is as poor when he leaves the world as when he entered it.

This scenario is worse than the similar ones described earlier. Vv. 12 and 16 pick up from the preceding section the theme of the rich man who toils in dismal discomfort ("to his harm" refers to the agitation and self-deprivation he undergoes; cf. 2:23). The man in the preceding section at least ate his full. When this one eats, he does so joylessly, sitting in the dark to skimp on lamp oil and suffering sickness and agitation. He grimly drives himself to amass wealth, then suddenly loses it in an unfortunate incident. This loss is further exacerbated by the fact that no one got any enjoyment out of the earnings, *not even* his heir. In 2:19, Qohelet brooded on the possibility that one's heir will be a fool. In 4:8 the absurdity of the toil is worsened by the worker lacking a relative to benefit from his labors. Here the toiler does have a son but, in an unhappy twist, has nothing to give him, whether during his, the toiler's, lifetime or after his death.

5:14 Vv. 14a and 15a probably speak of the father, the toiler, as vv. 14b and 15b clearly do. For the problem is not that some people (such as the son) die poor, but that some people (like the father) dissipate their lives on useless toil.

The Masoretic accents make *'arom* "naked" a modifier of the second clause, thus: "naked shall he return."

'Amal here probably means wealth, for that is what one would like to take with him but cannot. But possibly *ba'ămalo* means "by means of his toil."

"This too . . .": That is, the fact that he dies poor, after all that toil and deprivation.

5:15 *Ruaḥ* in *šeyya'ămol laruaḥ* designates something that is ephemeral, not something that is unattainable (the toiler did acquire wealth) or that lacks value (the defect was not in the wealth itself but in its loss). There can be no profit in an endeavor whose rewards evaporate.

5:16 LXX's καὶ πένθει, "and mourns," represents *w'bl*, for MT's *y'kl;* but mourning is not an appropriate term to describe the agitation of the miser. We should, however, follow LXX's καὶ αρρωστία and read *wḥly* for MT's *wḥlyw* (dittography). None of the versions reflects the suffix, which is awkward here. Even though *w'ḥolyo* can theoretically be an independent sentence ("and he has illness"), as Gordis argues, *waqaṣep* is left hanging. The LXX correctly takes *wk's* as one of three nouns coordinated with *ḥošek* and dependent on its *bet* (Euringer, Barton, Podechard). A single preposition can govern a series of coordinate nouns (see König 1897, §419l and *GBH* §132g). To eat "in" irritation and sickness and wrath, is the antithesis of eating and drinking "in pleasure" (*b'simḥah*) and "with a merry heart" (*b'leb ṭob,* lit. "in a good heart"), 9:7.

C. 5:17-19. A Good Scenario (a *ṭob*)

(17) Here is what I[a] have seen: It is a good thing that is beautiful to eat and drink and to experience enjoyment in all one's toil at which he labors under the sun during the few days of his life that God has given him, for that is his portion. (18) Furthermore, if God gives anyone wealth and property and enables him to partake of it and to take his portion and to get pleasure in his toil — that is a gift of God. (19) For then he will not much call to mind the days of his life, since God is keeping <him[b]> occupied with his heart's pleasure.

[a] *'ănî* (MT *'ānî*)
[b] *ma'ănēhû* (MT *ma'ăneh*)

Here is the fortunate situation: taking pleasure in one's possessions through-out life. This is the antithesis of the "sick misfortune" of 5:12-16. To be sure, man cannot determine whether he will be able to do this. God must grant the possibility of enjoyment. If he does, he allows man a great gift: oblivion. God keeps man occupied, distracts him with pleasures. Pleasure dulls the pain of consciousness, the same pain that wisdom exacerbates (1:18).

The Egyptian phrase for entertainment is "diverting the heart." Pictures of banqueting scenes, which show a man and wife eating, drinking, and lis-tening to music in the company of friends and relatives, are labeled "divert-ing the heart." The poet of the Egyptian "Harper's Song," despairing of the efficacy of mortuary rites to assure immortality, urges his listeners to enjoy themselves in the present, to divert their hearts from thoughts of mortality: "Hence rejoice in your heart! Forgetfulness profits you. Follow your heart as long as you live!" (*AEL* 1.196f.).

5:17 As Yaḥyah notes, this verse describes a "good thing," a benefit, to match the "evil thing," the misfortune, observed in v. 12. It is, in fact, "a good that is beautiful." *Yapeh* means "beautiful" or "appropriate"; see the comment on 3:11. A Stoic tenet, going back to Plato, identified goodness with beauty. Braun points out a striking parallel in the phrase ἀγαθόν ὅτι καλόν, a "good thing that is beautiful," found in Plato (Lysias 216d; cf. Aris-totle, Nichomachean Ethics 8.1, 1155b and Marcus Aurelius 2.1) (Palm 1885:17; Braun 1973:54f.). Schwienhorst-Schönberger (1996:305f.) too re-gards 5:17a as reflecting a popular Hellenistic concept.

The verse has no *'atnaḥ* or *zaqeph*. The main division is at the first *rᵉviaʿ*, on *'ānî* (with pausal pointing), and *ṭob 'ăšer yapeh* are subordinated by two *munaḥ*s to the disjunctive *tᵉlišah gᵉdolah* on *leʾĕkol-wᵉlištot*. This suggests the following phrasing: "Here is what I have seen: to-eat-and-drink is a good-thing, which is beautiful. . . ." In other words, Qohelet has not "seen a good-thing-which-is-beautiful." Rather, he has seen this: *that* eating and drinking is "a good thing, which is beautiful," etc. Gordis trans-lates *ṭob 'ăšer yapeh* as "it is meet and proper." But *'ăšer* is not a conjunc-tion, and Hos 12:9 (*'awon 'ăšer ḥeṭ'*), even if correct, does not support this. *'Ăšer yapeh* is a relative clause modifying *ṭob*. Thus *ṭob 'ăšer yapeh* is structurally equivalent (but semantically antonymic) to *raʿah ḥolah* a "sick misfortune" in 5:12.

5:18 This sentence is actually an anacoluthon, lit.: "Furthermore, every man to whom God has given wealth and property and enabled him to partake of it and to take his portion and to have pleasure in his toil — that is a gift of God."

In *le'ĕkol mimmennu,* "to partake of it" or "to consume some of it," the *m(in)* is partitive, a nuance ignored by most translations. By Qohelet's criteria, one need not consume *all* he owns in order to have something good. It is, to be sure, unfair if someone else gets part of the worker's wealth without himself expending effort (2:21-26), and this eliminates the "profit." Theoretically, this injustice need not spoil the pleasure the toiler received from his earnings, but it seems to have had that effect on Qohelet.

5:19 The verb *zakar* means "be aware of" or "call to mind" and can be used of awareness of present facts or future matters; e.g., Ps 8:5; Isa 47:7; and especially Lam 1:9: *lo' zak^erah 'aḥăritahh,* "she did not call to mind her future." The man blessed with pleasure, Qohelet says, will not often think of the days of his life, that is to say, brood about how few they are.

For MT's *ma'ăneh* read *ma'ănēhû,* following LXX περισπᾷ αὐτόν and Syr *m'n' lyh.* (It is also possible to regard the direct object as elided and implicit in 19a; on the phenomenon see *GBH* §146i). 'NH-hiphil corresponds to Syriac *'a'niy,* "busy one (with)." Thus Syr can translate precisely: *ma'ne' leh.* 'NH-qal means "be busy with" in 1:13 and 3:10, and in both cases it is said that God "gives" man an *'inyan* "task" to be busy with. "Giving *(natan)* an *'inyan*" is equivalent to the hiphil causative *ma'ăneh* (which may be a denominative from that noun and is probably an Aramaism). The *'inyan* there is "bad" (1:13), the one in this verse is good: God's keeping a man preoccupied, so that he does not brood on his mortality. 'NH is also used in this sense in 10:19, probably in the hiphil.

Gordis, believing that Qohelet would not consider joy a narcotic, derives *ma'ănehu* from 'NH-"answer" and assigns it the meaning of "provide." But he does not show that *'anah* (in any stem) has that sense. At any rate, the notion that pleasure might distract one from oppressive thoughts is already implied in the first part of the verse and is not foreign to Qohelet's attitudes.

Lohfink (1990), while providing arguments for the above interpretation, understands the verb *ma'ăneh* as additionally meaning "answers (him)," which supposedly indicates a form of divine revelation. The revelation by joy, Lohfink says, is superior to fear of God and renders it superfluous. "When we experience joy, at least in one small moment, we come in touch with that sense of things which normally God alone sees" (p. 634). This, I think, is an idiosyncratic understanding of "revelation," which usually includes propositional content or at least an immediate and extraordinary experience of the divine presence. Furthermore, even if *ma'ăneh* does

240

mean "answers," Qohelet does not say that God reveals *himself*. It is also peculiar to say that *śimḥah* — which is induced by eating and drinking — is superior to fear of God (ibid.). After all, *śimḥah* "does nothing" (2:1), and the heart of fools is in the house of *śimḥah* (7:4). Nor does "answer" (which is what *'anah* means in the qal, not the hiphil) imply revelation, except when the revelation is in response to something, in particular a query or a request.

D. 6:1-6. The Bad Scenario Made Worse

(1) There is an evil I have seen under the sun, and it weighs heavy on man: (2) God gives a man wealth and property and honor, so that he does not lack for his appetite anything he might desire, yet God does not allow him to consume any of it, but rather a stranger consumes it. This is an absurdity and an evil sickness. (3) Even if a man begets a hundred children and lives many years, however many the years he may live, if his appetite does not get satisfaction from (his) goods, and he doesn't even receive a proper burial — I say that the stillborn is better off than he. (4) For he comes into absurdity and goes into darkness, and in darkness his name is covered. (5) Even the one who neither saw nor knew the sun has more repose than he. (6) And even if a man should live a thousand years twice over, if he did not experience enjoyment. . . . Oh, everyone goes to the same place!

In 5:12-16 Qohelet related the "sick misfortune" of a man who derived no pleasure from his wealth while he toiled and hoarded his earnings, then lost it all anyway. In 6:1-6 Qohelet describes another "misfortune" or "evil" (*ra'ah*), similar to the earlier one except that now God turns the wealth over to a stranger. The second scenario doubles the injustice, for not only does the toiler fail to enjoy his wealth, but another, who did not toil, does so. See the comment on 2:26.

Qohelet places the blame squarely on God, with no moralizing terminology to rationalize the action. But the transfer of the wealth to a stranger — an obvious misfortune, observed in 4:7f. — is not the heart of the problem here. Even *before* the loss of wealth, and *even if* a man has sons for heirs, and *even if* he lives far beyond the human lifespan, his life is wasted if he himself has not known pleasure.

The injustices described in this passage and in 5:12-16 are worse than the one Qohelet protests in 2:18-26. There we heard of the toiler whose earnings God transferred to a more fortunate man. Here we learn that even an ostensibly fortunate man, upon whom God bestows wealth and prestige, may suffer the vagaries of the divine will, for God may take away that man's fortune before he dies, before he derives benefit from it. Such a man, and not only the unfortunate toiler, is worse off than a stillbirth, who was at least spared the misery of seeing life's evils (cf. 4:3).

6:1 "Weighs heavy on," lit. "is great upon," as in 8:6.

6:2 This verse is an anacoluthon, a sentence that changes syntactical direction in mid-course; see Ellermeier 1967:292-95. The effective predicate of the sentence is not "man" but the situation described in 2a.

"Appetite": In this unit, *nepeš* is translated by "appetite," since "soul" might be thought to imply a higher spiritual level. *Nepeš* is the seat of desire and was thought to be located in the throat or gullet.

Kabod here is the prestige attendant upon wealth (thus too in 2 Chr 1:11), rather than a deeper honor. This prestige will be consigned along with the wealth to the favored man. Compare how the recipient in 2:26 picks up "wisdom and knowledge" along with the toiler's material effects.

6:3 The clause *weᵉgam qᵉburah lo' hayᵉtah lo,* "and furthermore he doesn't even receive a proper burial," has perplexed the commentators, for it seems odd that Qohelet would place so much weight on the formality of burial, as if that could somehow compensate for a life of joyless toil. One exegetical expedient is to change the negative *lō'* into a conditional *lû',* "even if": "even if he have an elaborate funeral" (Gordis). But if this were a concessive clause it should have been placed with the other concessive clauses, before *weᵉnapšo lo' tiśbaʿ,* and the expected word order would be *weᵉlu' gam hayᵉtah lo qᵉburah.* Another expedient is to move the clause to v. 5a (Ginsberg, following Hitzig), but this is a major conjectural emendation that does not help much, since it makes that verse imply that a burial is a *bad* thing.

The MT is satisfactory in both the pointing and placement of the clause. Elsewhere too Qohelet places value on burial and the remembrance that it helps preserve. He is angered when the wicked receive honorable last rites while the righteous are neglected (8:10), and by the fact that everyone's name will perish in darkness (6:4). Concern for a proper interment was (and is) a deep-rooted attitude in Jewish society, not merely a philosophical position, and it is not surprising that Qohelet holds on to it. While he probably would not consider a stately burial sufficient to bestow meaning on a pleasureless life, he does take burial seriously and seems to feel that the lack thereof exacerbates life's tragedy.

Verses 2 and 3 comprise two convoluted series of conditionals and subordinate stipulations that lay out the criteria for a satisfactory life. Qohelet gives the impression that he is being pushed tortuously and reluctantly toward the harsh repudiation of life's intrinsic value at the end of v. 3.

(6:2) Conditions that make a gift of wealth absurd: IF God gives a man everything he might desire, AND IF God does not allow him to consume any of it (BUT a stranger consumes it), THEN this situation is absurd and evil.

(6:3) Things that might compensate for lack of pleasure but do not: EVEN IF a man begets a hundred children, AND EVEN IF he lives an unlimited number of years, IF he does not get satisfaction, OR IF he lacks a proper burial, THEN it is better for him not to have existed.

In other words, if a man does not get satisfaction, nothing makes life better than death. On the face of it, burial would seem to make life preferable, but this implication is probably not intended.

A Mesopotamian Wisdom book exclaims, "A gloomy life [lit. "a life without light"], what advantage does it have over death?"[27]

6:4 By itself, this sentence could describe either the stillbirth or the unfortunate man, an ambiguous fact that is itself ironic. All commentators apply it to the former, but there is some reason to read it as a description of the latter. Since the verse is a motivation of the preference for the stillbirth in v. 3, and since v. 4 does not say anything good about the stillbirth, v. 4 probably describes the miserable man. But a lengthy description of a stillbirth, such as vv. 4-5 is supposed to provide, would not be quite relevant here, because the stillbirth is mentioned only as a point of comparison. Also, the stillbirth does not have a name to be covered. Finally, the stillbirth does not "come into" *hebel,* which is the condition of life under the sun. The stillbirth cannot be even said to be ephemeral; he is less than that. A human comes into a life of absurdity and passes into darkness and oblivion. Only the little plus of pleasure makes him better off than the zero of the stillbirth.

MT's *yelek* is a generalizing present. 4QQoh[a] has *hlk (hōlēk),* agreeing with LXX's πορεύεται (in most MSS; the future in some minuscules and SyH is hexaplaric). This variant, with the participle, seems to be an attempt to fit the verb to context by a scribe who expected the yiqtol to indicate the future.

6:5 *Gam šemeš lo' ra'ah w^elo' yada':* The verbs are nominalized: "He who did not see or know." Compare *y^eladatka* "she bore you" = "she who bore you"//*'immeka* "your mother" in Cant 8:5. For the phenomenon see D. Grossberg 1979, 1980.

27. Trans. A. Gianto, forthcoming; text in D. Arnaud, *Emar* VI.4, 767.

Naḥat means "rest, repose"; see the comment on 4:6. (4QQohᵃ *nwḥt* = *nuḥat,* a variant form of the segolate.) This sentence is not a conclusion or a summation; it gives another reason why the stillbirth is better off: it, at least, has repose and quiet, in contrast to the toiler, who not only lives in a darkness analogous to the stillbirth's (6:4; 5:16a), but also knows incessant agitation (5:16b).

6:6 This sentence too goes off track. Qohelet starts out once again listing the conditions for a desirable life but suddenly gives up and just exclaims *(hălo')* in despair or frustration upon the universality of death's power. His outburst is not quite logical: if life is so bad, why complain that everyone dies? Jacob complains, "Few and evil have been the days of the years of my life" (Gen 47:9) — but if they are evil, what does it matter that they are few? Yet somehow it does matter, and however bad one's years have been, usually there endures hope for better times ahead, and even if they don't turn out better, they are better than nothing, for "sweet is the light" (11:7). Thus, in a sad and weary way, thinking of death steers Qohelet back to his fundamental affirmation of life.

E. 6:7-9. Dissatisfaction

(7) All a man's toil is for his mouth, but the appetite is never filled. (8) (For what advantage has the wise man over the fool? What good does it do the poor man to know how to get along with the living?) (9) Better the sight of the eyes than the wandering of the appetite. This too is absurd and senseless.

Thoughts on the importance of satisfying the appetite (6:2-6) give rise to comments on how voracious it is. It is impossible to satisfy a craving for wealth, so instead of striving for more, one should enjoy what he holds now. The wealth one sees before him (*mar'eh 'eynayim* = *rᵉ'ut 'eynayw;* 5:10) is better than something longed for but not presently possessed. Yet even immediate satisfactions are absurd (6:9). This section deals with a single issue — desire — but the movement of thought is choppy and the logic hard to follow, perhaps because it is citing proverbs without integrating them well. Sections A and E bracket the unit by their shared ideas and components:

- 6:7//5:9: a man toils to fill an insatiable appetite.
- 6:9//5:10b-11a: the possibility of getting some satisfaction from one's possessions.

244

6:7   A concessive sentence introduced by *w*ᵉ*gam;* see Ellermeier 1967:249-53. It is a fact that man ceaselessly strives to satisfy his appetite, even though, like the sea, it can never be filled up. "Mouth" and "appetite" (*nepeš;* originally perhaps "throat" or "gullet") do not, of course, refer to the hunger for food alone (5:11), but rather to a diffuse yearning for possessions of all sorts. This nagging desire is never assuaged by actual possessions.

6:8   V. 8 interrupts the connection between vv. 7 and 9 and is perhaps misplaced. It might, however, be taken as a parenthesis, a proverb (albeit a rather enigmatic one), about satisfaction through toil, which Qohelet is using to say: in this regard, the wise man, however much his skill and energy allow him to acquire, has no advantage over the incompetent and lazy fool.

Since the appetite is insatiable, the wise man, who has the skill to amass wealth, has no advantage over the fool, who, as a *k*ᵉ*sil,* must be incompetent in his occupation. In the context of 6:7 and 9, the statement of v. 8a does not deny an advantage to wisdom categorically, but only with respect to achieving satisfaction.

The second part of the verse, *mah le῾ani yodea῾ lahălok neged haḥayyim* is a crux. Ehrlich says that as it stands this phrase must mean "was hat der Arme zu verstehen?" ("what does the poor man have to understand?"). He calls this nonsense and emends to *mah hayyodea῾,* which is hardly an improvement, since he still finds the verse unclear. His first observation, however, was on the right track. In his comment on Judg 18:23, Ehrlich mentions Jon 1:6; m. Ker. 5:2; m. Middot 2:2; and Mekilta 7.135ff., as examples of the construction *mah l-* + undefined participle. The construction actually means "why should X do Y?" and expresses surprise and usually disapproval too. This is the syntax of Qoh 6:8b.

The point of the rhetorical question is: since the wise man has no advantage over the fool, there is no value in a poor man knowing how to get along with people or, perhaps, how to lead them in some capacity. After all, "the wisdom of the poor man is held in contempt, and his words are not heard" (9:16).

Lahălok neged haḥayyim: The closest parallel to the locution *lahălok neged* is Prov 14:7: *lek minneged l*ᵉ*ʾiš k*ᵉ*sil,* etc., "go around with [lit. "opposite"] a foolish man, and you will not know knowledgeable lips." In other words, if you consort with fools, you will hear only folly. "Go around with" is the notion required by Qoh 6:8 as well. *Minneged l-* bears the same sense as *neged,* in line with the series of near equivalences in prepositions based on location-nouns: *mittaḥat l-* = *taḥat; me῾al l-* = *῾al; miqqedem l-* = *qedem;* etc. Since *neged* is in turn nearly synonymous with *lipney* "before," we can compare the phrase *halak/hithallek lipney,* "go before," usually used of loyalty to God. It is also used of a leader vis-à-vis the people (1 Sam 12:2 — and also Qoh 4:16), and of a priest vis-à-vis the king (1 Sam 2:35). Thus the phrase can be applied to a variety of relationships. Comparison with Prov 14:7 suggests that *lahălok neged* is something one does with other people. Thus *hahayyim* probably means "the living" (Podechard, Barton) rather than "life" (Gordis).

In the light of these considerations, 6:8b recalls 4:16a, esp. *lᵉkol 'ăšer hayah lipneyhem* "all before whom he was," that is, whom he led. This in turn refers to the group called *hahhayim hammᵉhallekim tahat haššameš* in 4:15a. A further correspondence is that at least two youths in the anecdote were poor. In 6:8b, then, Qohelet casts doubt on the value to a poor man of knowing how to lead people, or even just how to get along with them, which is the form of wisdom possessed by the youths in 4:13-16.

6:9 The immediate experience of pleasure is better than the "wandering of the appetite" (lit. "the going of the soul"). For the soul to go after something means that one's mind concentrates on the object of desire, may even be obsessed with it, so much so that it is as if his soul had left his body and gone after what it covets. This idiom does not occur elsewhere, but the heart is said to "go" in a similar sense. When Elisha tells Gehazi that his heart "went" to the place where Naaman got off his chariot, he shows the notion that one's heart is in a place he is thinking about (2 Kgs 5:26). For one's heart to go after something means more specifically to desire it. Job declares that his heart did not "go after" his eyes, meaning that if he saw something desirable but illicit, he did not let himself covet it. Ezekiel (11:21; 20:16) uses the idiom in a similar way.

If one is walking through a lovely field and luxuriating in the beauties of the day, that is *mar'eh 'eynayim,* and that is good. If he starts to think of other things he craves — wealth, perhaps, or prestige, or success, or sex — he loses contact with the actual place and moment, and his soul departs, as it were, and goes off, uselessly, to another, nonexistent place, the object of his desire. Then the moment is depleted of meaning, and he has nothing.

It is difficult to identify the antecedent of "this" in the *hebel*-judgment. It might be "the wandering of the desire," though the absurdity of that is self-evident. A negative judgment beginning "this too is" is more meaningfully directed at the *preferred* term of a comparison, here — *mar'eh 'eynayim.* Granted that actual pleasure is better than yearning, nevertheless pleasure too is senseless. No reason is given here.

F. 6:10-12. Conclusion: Human Ignorance

(10) Whatever has happened was already called by name, and what it is, is known. <ᵃAnd one cannotᵃ> dispute with the one who is stronger than he is. (11) For (if) there are many words, they only increase absurdity, and what is the advantage for man? (12) For who knows what is good for man in life during the few days of his absurd life (which he passes like a shadow), for who can tell man what will happen afterwards under the sun?

ᵃwᵉʾadam lōʾ yûkal (MT ʾādām wᵉlōʾ yûkal)

Life is unchangeable and the future is hidden. Therefore it is futile to argue with God. The questions in vv. 11b, 12a, and 12b are equivalent to negations.

Section F seems isolated, but in fact it is a pivot between units. As in 3:22 and 7:14, Qohelet caps off a series of observations of absurdities by throwing up his hands, as it were, in a declaration of ignorance. At the end, he introduces the theme of 7:1-12: what is good.

6:10a resonates in 12b: *mah šehayah* and its complement *mah yihyeh; kᵉbar* and its complement *ʾaḥărayw; nodaʿ* and its negative *mi yodeaʿ; ʾadam* and *ʾadam*. These pairings bracket v. 11, whose topic is the futility of speech. It is absurd to waste words (as Job did) in arguing with God about what happens in the world, because man cannot really know or really change what has happened or will happen. Therefore man cannot say what is good to do — surely a self-directed irony, since Qohelet has done just that several times and is about to launch into a series of such statements in the next unit.

Mah šehayah and *mah yihyeh* are events past and future. 7:24 shows that *mah šehayah* is, more precisely, present perfect rather than mere past, for that verse speaks of the incomprehensibility of life generally, rather than only the hiddenness of past history. Again, *hayah* is better translated "happen" than "be," since Qohelet is not speaking of the simple existence of things. *Mah yihyeh* (v. 12b) does not refer to the future existence of beings or things, as if it were important to know that a certain person or a certain building, for example, will exist in the future. The knowledge that could bear on the decision about what is good for man (v. 12a) is knowledge of future *occurrence*.

Wᵉnodaʿ ʾăšer huʾ ʾadam: Gordis rightly observes that the clause *ʾăšer huʾ ʾadam* cannot mean "it is known what man is," but he is wrong in explaining it as "anticipation" (prolepsis), equivalent to *wᵉnodaʿ ʾăšer haʾadam lōʾ yukal*. As his own examples show, in prolepsis a noun or noun phrase that is the semantic subject of an object clause is treated as the direct object of the main verb; which is not the case here.

The minimal emendation that will make sense of this verse is to read a *waw* with *w^elo' yukal* rather than with *'adam*. This is the same construction as *lo' yukal 'iš l^edabber* (1:8a) and *lo' yukal ha'adam limṣo'* (8:17a). For a tighter correspondence, one could transpose *'adam* and *yukal* (Ginsberg). *'Adam* with a negative is sometimes better translated as indefinite — "no one" or "one . . . not." This usage pertains when *'adam* is not being implicitly distinguished from another kind of being. This construction is more frequent with *'iš*, but examples with *'adam* are Judg 18:7, 28; Isa 38:11; Prov 12:3; Lachish Ost. 4.5; and, quite clearly, Qoh 9:15.

The sentence *w^enoda' 'ăšer hu'* "and what it is, is known" is equivalent to *niqra' š^emo*, lit. "its name has been called." The "already" of v. 10aα applies to *noda'* as well. The knowledge in question is foreknowledge. The semantic subject of *noda'* (the implied knower) can only be God, who alone knows what happens before it occurs. (This is most clearly asserted in Sir 23:20.) God's exclusive foreknowledge makes it useless to dispute with him (Qoh 6:10b).

"Whatever has happened was already called by name" is a way of saying that it was already known, for that which can be named is known. In other words, there is nothing new under the sun.

6:11   The literal translation, "there are many words that increase absurdity," does not fit the context well, since it seems to exempt some words from the censure. Ginsberg explains *yeš* as emphatic. Elsewhere, however, the construction with *yeš* as predicate emphasizer occurs only in interrogative clauses or with the conditional particle, and the subject is always a pronoun (Gen 24:42, 49; 43:4; Deut 13:4b; and Judg 6:36; see Muraoka 1985:77-81). The present sentence is probably an unmarked conditional: *If* there are many words, they (merely) increase vapor, which is here a live metaphor for nonsense.

Mah yoter la'adam means that there is no advantage in many words, specifically when they are expended in disputation with God (6:10).

6:12   "Which he passes like a shadow" is a parenthetical remark about how life flees past. *'Ăšer* motivates the negation implicit in the rhetorical question of v. 12aα. *'Aśah* means "spend time," as in Ruth 2:19 and RH.

'Aḥărayw means "afterwards," "in the future" (see the note on 3:22), here with reference to future events in one's lifetime. Knowledge of what happens after death would not enable one to say what is good to do in life, unless the knowledge had to do with a judgment after death, a concept out-

side the purview of Wisdom prior to the Wisdom of Solomon. Moreover, in 7:14b, which reiterates 6:12b, the future in question is clearly in this life.

◆ **7:1-12 + 19**

(1)   A name is better than good oil,
  and the day of death than the day of one's birth.

(2)   It is better to go to a house of mourning
  than to go to a house of feasting,
  inasmuch as that is the end of every man,
  and the living should take it to heart.

(3)   Irritation is better than merriment,
  for the heart is improved by a scowl.

(4)   The heart of wise men is in the house of mourning,
  and the heart of fools is in the house of merrymaking.

(5)   It is better to hear the rebuke of a wise man
  than <to hear^a> the singing of fools,

(6)   for as the sound of thorns under the pot
  so is the merriment of the fool.
  And this too is absurd.

(7)   For a bribe makes the wise foolish,
  and a gift corrupts the heart.

(8)   Better the end of a matter than its beginning;
  better a patient spirit than a haughty spirit.

(9)   Do not let your spirit hastily become irritated,
  for irritation rests in the breast of fools.

(10) Do not say:
  "How has it happened that the former times were better than these?"
  for not <in wisdom^b> do you ask about this.

(11) Wisdom is good with an inheritance —
  an advantage for those who see the sun.

(12) For to be in the shelter of wisdom is to be in the shelter of silver.
  But the advantage of knowledge is that wisdom keeps its possessor alive.

(19) Wisdom helps the wise man
  more than the <wealth^c> of the magnates who are in a city.

^a*miššĕmōaʿ* (MT *mē'îš šōmēaʿ*)
^b*bᵉhokmāh* (MT *mēhokmāh*)
^c*mē'ōšer haššallîṭîm* (MT *mē'ăśārāh šallîṭîm*)

249

A. 7:1-6. Some good things
B. 7:7-10. The sensible and patient spirit
C. 7:11-12 + 19. The advantage of wisdom

The unit begins with a series of aphorisms on the theme of good things, including several "better than" proverbs. Qohelet has just declared that no one can say what is "good" for man to do (6:12); he now may be speaking with some self-mockery, but he is still serious about the advice itself and does not undermine its validity. Qohelet's skepticism does not prevent him from offering ordinary counsel and observations. Yet he does not place great stock in his own sagacity, and he deliberately undermines the *certainty* of his counsels by skeptical remarks (e.g., 7:6b) and by self-directed irony. These qualities moderate the assertive confidence of section A, as does the bracketing of the aphorisms of this section between reminders of human limitations, particularly with regard to knowledge of the future (6:12b//7:14b).

The unit is loose-knit and coheres largely because there is no clear subdivision. There is some associative and linguistic cohesion. The theme word is the recurrent *ṭob*. The proverbs of 7:1-6 are united by words belonging to two semantic fields: pleasure (*yiyṭab leb*, lit. "the heart is made good," *mišteh* "feasting," *śᵉḥoq* "laughter" or "merriment," *śimḥah* "pleasure," *šir* "song") and displeasure (*'ebel* "mourning," *ka'as* "irritation," *roa' panim*, lit. "badness of face," and *gᵉ'arah* "rebuke"). Vv. 2-6a proceed chiastically, with v. 2 elaborated by v. 4 and v. 3 by vv. 5-6a. Vv. 7-10 describe the proper disposition of the soul. Then follow six maxims on the superiority of wisdom (vv. 11-12 + 19), and this may be considered the theme of the unit as a whole.

N. Lohfink, largely followed by R. E. Murphy, sees in this unit (and throughout chapters 7–8) a critical dialogue with traditional wisdom. The weakness of this approach is its arbitrariness in separating out traditional wisdom from Qohelet's. And it sometimes involves projecting a notion of traditional wisdom from Qohelet's words which is not actually found in "traditional wisdom." See the comment on v. 10.

In the first part of the unit, Qohelet commends a somber awareness of death and derides merrymaking for its frivolity. Qohelet is not recommending sadness for its own sake. He (basically but not invariably) values life. But death is inescapable; hence "the living should take it to heart" (v. 2b). The wise man does so (v. 4), while fools play around (vv. 4b, 5b).

The aim of 7:1-4 is not to condemn feasting but to advocate an open-eyed awareness of mortality. Those who divert their mind from their mortality are fools. Qohelet is not wholehearted in this evaluation, for in 5:19 he commends *śimḥah* for providing distraction from the ache of finitude. This is certainly one of Qohelet's contradictions. It arises from frustration, of which he himself is quite aware and which he confesses in 7:23f. By displaying and venting his frustration, Qohelet is demonstrating by his own example a more fundamental truth: man (even the wisest) is hopelessly ignorant, and even when he can discover some truths (such as those expounded in the present unit), their validity is shaky and they clash with other things he knows. Therefore Qohelet proceeds in 7:13f., as in 6:13f., to a statement of human ignorance.

A. 7:1-6. Some Good Things

7:1 The first line glides off the tongue like oil: *ṭob šem miššemen ṭob.* "Name" with no further qualification often means reputation, which need not necessarily be for moral virtues; see Gen 6:4; 11:4 and Ezek 16:14. Even the reputation of the wicked is a "name" (Prov 10:7b). Like English "fame" and "reputation," *šem* is indifferent to moral value but can receive that connotation from context. In Prov 22:1a (of which Qoh 7:1a is a variant), the type of "name" in view is undoubtedly a *good* reputation: "A name is more desirable than great wealth, and a good regard than silver and gold." (The LXX here explicates "name" by adding "good.") A name can also be a memorial, parallel to *zeker* "memory" (Job 18:17; Prov 10:7; sim. Isa 14:22; 66:22). Since oils were used in preparing a corpse for burial, we can understand 7:1a in a double sense: a (good) reputation is better than a pleasant rub-down with fine oils; and a remembrance is better than a proper burial.

In any case, the importance of the saying lies in the second line (preference of the day of death) rather than in the first (praise of reputation), because the second line introduces the topic of the succeeding verses (2-4): death.

"Oil" (v. 1) is echoed by "house of feasting" (v. 2), and that in turn by "house of merrymaking" (v. 4), because oil for anointing was one of the luxuries offered at banquets. Similarly "day of death" (v. 1) is echoed by "house of mourning" (v. 2), and that by "house of mourning" in v. 4.

"One's birth": *hiwwāleᵈô,* lit. "his birth." The suffix must be indefinite or have its antecedent implied in the first line: the possessor of the name.

This verse is a proverb of ratio: just as a reputation is preferable to good oil, so is the day of death preferable to the day of birth. The reason for v. 1b is not given. Since reputation is mentioned in v. 1a, it may be that one's reputation is not secure until he dies and can no longer damage it (Ibn Ezra; cf.

Avot 2:4). Still, Qohelet does not believe that the dead are long remembered; see 2:16. Given Qohelet's recurring melancholy, he may well be praising death for releasing man from the awareness of injustice and the toils to which birth exposes him (4:3; 6:3).

7:2 + 4   *Beyt mišteh* (v. 2) = *beyt śimḥah* (v. 4). In v. 4, *śimḥah* means "merrymaking," "feasting"; on the usage see §7.3. In Esth 9:17, 18, 19, 22, *mišteh* and *śimḥah* are collocated in a way that suggests their synonymy. 4QQohᵃ in 7:2 substitutes the synonym *[ś]mḥh* for *mišteh*.

Qohelet believes that much wisdom makes one melancholy (1:18). Most of the sages would not agree, though LXX-Prov 14:10 does say that the mien of the wise man is generally grave: "As for the heart of a perceptive [αἰσθητική] man — his soul is sad. And when he rejoices, it is not mixed with pride." (This is based on a different Hebrew text, but the translator presumably considered this notion a reasonable one.) Such sadness is not, of course, a reason to avoid wisdom, but rather to accept solemnity.

7:3 + 5-6a   The value of reproof. Verse 3b presents a paradox: how can *roaʿ panim*, "badness of face" (which implies gloom; see Gen 40:7; Neh 2:2f.) make the heart "good" (which usually means cheerful; e.g., Prov 15:13)? Paradox invites resolution by the reinterpretation of its terms. The first part of the saying suggests that we revise our understanding by associating *roaʿ panim* with *kaʿas* ("irritation," "anger") and construe the sentence as teaching that another person's displeasure and scowl may improve one's own mind. Rebukes (often lauded in the book of Proverbs) are instructive and "improve the mind," while the sounds of merriment are hollow.

7:5   V. 5 reinforces the lesson: better to hear the wise man's rebuke than the sounds of foolish merriment. This is especially true of the fool's merriment, but it applies to others' as well, as the broader formulation in v. 3 shows. (Compare the way Qohelet adds "fools" in 4:17 without exempting other people's sacrifices from the comparison.) JPSV translates, "Vexation is better than revelry, for though the face be sad, the heart may be glad." But the fact that a sad face *may* hide a happy heart says nothing commendable about vexation.

In v. 5, MT has a lopsided comparison between an action ("to hear") and a person ("a man hearing"). Delitzsch's explanation, that the twofold act of hearing is distributed between two subjects (namely, the one who hears the rebuke, and the one who hears the song), is unsatisfactory, for that would require the first term of comparison to be a person *(ṭob šomeaʿ . . .).* We should emend consonantal *m'yš šm'* to *mšm' (miššᵉmōaʿ)*. The infinitive construction is typically used in the second half of "better than" comparisons; see Qoh 6:9; 7:2 (cf. 4:17); Gen 29:19; Exod 14:12; Ps 52:5; 118:8f.; Prov 16:19; 25:7.

Šir refers to the music that accompanies merrymaking; see Isa 24:9, where *šir* is the background for drinking; sim. Sir 35:5 and m. Sotah 8:11. Here it may be a synecdoche for all the sounds of revelry. As in v. 3, the antonymic pair (here *gᵉʿarah/šir*) opposes rebuke to merrymaking, not rebuke to praise. The wise man's anger is a reprimand and naturally conveys moral censure. *Śᵉḥoq*, lit. "laughter," which in v. 6 restates *šir*, lit. "song," likewise implies revelry, again as an effect-for-cause synecdoche (§7.5).

7:6a   This saying is highly alliterative; note the repetition of the k/q sounds, the sibilants, and the *î* vowel: *kî kᵉqol hassîrîm taḥat hassîr kēn śᵉḥōq hakkᵉsîl.*

7:6b   "This too is *hebel*" has four possible referents: (1) The fools' merriment, which is undoubtedly *hebel* in almost any sense of the word. But that is so obvious that it is hardly worth saying. (2) The "general theme of the passage" (Gordis), in other words the proposition that the wise man's rebuke is better than the fool's merriment (or praise, as Gordis understands *šir*). But nowhere is *hebel* used to invalidate a proposition, as if it meant "false" or (in Gordis's limp paraphrase) "to be taken with a grain of salt." (3) "The rebuke of a wise man" in v. 5a. Verse 6 is parenthetical, probably a proverb cited to strengthen the observation made in v. 5. The reason for calling the wise man's rebuke *hebel* might be seen in v. 7. Vv. 5-7 might form a "Zwar-Aber Tatsache": granted that the rebuke of the wise is better than the merry noise of the fool, yet even that rebuke is meaningless, because even a wise man's reason can be undermined by lust for wealth. (On the vulnerability of wisdom, see 9:18.) The idea that the purpose of a gift is to deflect rebuke appears in Sir 20:29: "Gifts and presents can blind the eyes of wise men and avert rebukes like a muzzle on the mouth." (4) *Hebel* is used of hollow and ineffective words in 5:6 and 6:11. It may be, however, that the motivation of the *hebel*-judgment is now missing; see the comment on v. 7.

B. 7:7-10. The Sensible and Patient Spirit

7:7   In spite of beginning with *ki*, this verse has little connection with the preceding. 4QQohᵃ has space for fifteen to twenty letters after 7:6 (Ulrich 1992:146). Although these letters are lost, the arrangement of the lines on the fragment indicates that something once stood before 7:7 — perhaps only a meaningless error, but perhaps a sentence, later deleted as a supposed addition. In fact, Delitzsch already conjectured that a couplet was lost before 7:7, perhaps a saying like Prov 16:8 ("Better a little in righteousness than great produce without justice"). A proverb of this length would fit well in the lacuna of the Qumran Qohelet, but that particular saying is not quite apropos.

Qoh 7:7 is a variant of a maxim found in Exod 23:8 and Deut 16:19. Sir 8:2b has similar warning about the corruptibility of princes *(rabbim, n^edibim)*. The "wise" (that is, the learned) served as judges; see Sir 38:33. *'Ošeq* is not here the act of oppression, but rather dishonest money, namely a bribe to judges. Compare Lev 5:23 and Ps 62:11, where *'ošeq* is a transferred usage, effect-for-cause. There is no need to emend to *'ošer* (Ginsberg) or *š^ehoq* (Ehrlich).

"Corrupts": *wiy'abbed,* lit. "destroys." 4QQoh^a has *wy'wh,* "perverts," "makes iniquitous," which appears to be a functional synonym used for the sake of greater specificity.

7:8 The first line recalls v. 1: the end of a matter is better than its beginning. Therefore, v. 8b says, one should wait patiently to see how things turn out. Only then will the nagging and incessant uncertainty about the future be resolved. "Patience" can serve as an antithesis of "haughtiness" because it is prideful to imagine that one can know the future.

7:9 The unit continues to speak about irritation *(ka'as),* but of a particular kind: anger at present misfortunes and injustices.

Verse 9b contains a striking image: anger rests in the fool's bosom. Delitzsch thinks of a demon making itself at home in the fool's bosom. More to the point is the image of a baby snuggling in its father's arms. The fool coddles his vexation, nurtures it, lets it grow, while all the while, of course, it is gnawing at his innards.

To resolve the apparent contradiction between this verse and v. 3, which praises irritation, Gordis opines the word has different meanings in the two verses: in v. 3 it means "serious of disposition," in v. 9 "uncontrolled bad temper." Other commentators similarly distinguish two meanings. The true distinction, however, lies not in the lexical meaning of the word but in its application. *Ka'as* refers to different kinds of anger or irritation: in v. 3 it is irritation at another's failing and is expressed as reproof; in v. 9 it is anger at one's own misfortunes. Neither verse makes a statement about anger in all circumstances, and the present verse does not condemn irritation flatly, but only hasty vexation.

7:10 For MT's *meḥokmah* "from wisdom" read *bᵉḥokmah* "in wisdom," with LXX (ἐν σοφίᾳ) and Syr *(bḥekmta').* "In wisdom" indicates the manner of the asking — "(not) wisely" — while MT's "from wisdom" would indicate the source or motive of the question, which is less relevant here. ἐν never corresponds to Hebrew *m(in)* elsewhere in LXX-Qoh. The LXX reading is not (contrary to Gordis) due to Greek idiom. LXX-Qoh has few compunctions about violating natural Greek usage, and in any case ἐκ σοφίας (= *mḥkmh*) would be good Greek.

According to Murphy (following Lohfink), v. 10 is an example of Qohelet's "dialogue" with traditional wisdom. Qohelet supposedly criticizes the "traditional wisdom" of vv. 8f., which promotes the ideal of the patient sage who cultivates the teachings of the past. "But," Murphy paraphrases, "it is not from *true* wisdom (v 10b) that one champions the past over the present." The idea in vv. 8-9 is, to be sure, a traditional one, but that does not mean that Qohelet rejects it. Rather than contradicting the preceding verses, v. 10 *supports* them. Murphy, along with many other commentators, misinterprets these verses. Wisdom did not view the past as a golden age. It did not even have a concept of historical movement that would allow the sages to favor one period over another.

Nor is it Qohelet's intent to repudiate a sentimental preference for the good old days. If it were, he would have *denied* the proposition that "the former times were better than these," not simply have cautioned against asking about this, thereby granting that they were indeed better. Yaḥyah (ad loc.) more aptly compares the question to Job's complaints. Some misfortunes occur "without cause":

> Therefore Qohelet said that one should not speak and utter words of complaint about one's troubles or inquire of God about their reason, "for not from wisdom do you ask about this." For you are obliged to put your hand on your mouth and to justify the judgment of Heaven, even if it is true that the former times were better, before the wealth was lost.

The issue is a change of fortunes in someone's life. The proper attitude toward a downturn in one's fortunes is exemplified in 7:14, which also speaks of the right response to the ups and downs of life: in good times, enjoy the good fortune, and when bad times come upon you, do not ask why things were better in the past. Keeping fortunes fluctuating inexplicably is God's way of keeping man uncertain and anxious and crumbling his self-confidence. This is one way God causes fear.

C. 7:11-12 + 19. The Advantage of Wisdom

7:11 Wisdom is especially good if one also has a material inheritance (after all, "the wisdom of the poor man is held in contempt, and his words are not heard"), but of the two, wisdom is the more advantageous. Verses 11 and 12 both say that wealth is good but wisdom is better. *Naḥălah* (in its non-metaphorical use) is almost always a landed inheritance. This is an especially desirable form of wealth because one supposedly obtains it without strain and toil.

7:12 V. 12 supports v. 11. The connection is somewhat imprecise, since *kesep* and a *naḥălah* are very different forms of wealth. This loose fit indicates that v. 12 was probably an existing proverb and not composed for this context.

"Shelter" is literally "shade," a metaphor for shelter and protection (Num 14:9; Isa 30:2, 3; Jer 48:45; etc.). Sym's ὅτι ὡς . . . ὁμοίως apparently represents *kṣl . . . kṣl;* LXX and SyH testify to the second *kaph*. The meaning of the proverb in that form ("The shade of wisdom is like the shade of sil-ver") is essentially the same as in the MT, but the latter formulation is stron-ger. The MT implies causality, meaning that wisdom brings with it the pro-tection of wealth (Prov 3:16; 8:18; 24:3f.). To be in the shade of wisdom is tantamount to being in the shade of wealth as well. The formulation with the *kaph*s says merely that wisdom's protection is "like" that of silver. Wisdom *(daʿat)* has an advantage over wealth, namely that it keeps its possessor alive, which is protection indeed. (The latter claim is implied in Prov 3:2, 16a, 18; 8:35a; and often). *(Daʿat* is resumed by its synonym *ḥokmah.)* Wealth, on the other hand, does not help its possessor escape death (cf. 8:8b, reading *ʿšr* for *ršʿ*); cf. Prov 11:4, 28. To keep alive (ḤYH piel) does not mean to bestow im-mortality but to give protection in danger and allow a full lifespan; see, e.g., Ps 33:19; Deut 6:24; Ezek 3:18; 13:19.

To say that wisdom "is" an advantage (a *yoter* or *yitron*) is equivalent to saying that it *has* an advantage (sc., for someone). Possession is implicit in the construction in 7:12b, as it is in 2:13 and 5:8. Wisdom is the subject of *yitron* in 10:10. Wisdom's advantage over an inheritance is spelled out in 7:12b — it keeps its possessors alive. That is why Qohelet refers to humans in this verse as "those who see the sun," which is to say, the living.

7:19 This saying is irrelevant in its current place, whether in its Masoretic form (". . . than ten magnates") or in the emendation adopted here (". . . than the wealth of the magnates"), and it interrupts the tight connection between

vv. 18 and 20. Galling (1969 edn.) justifies the placement of 7:19 as exempli-
fying the precept in v. 16, but v. 19 is too far removed to serve that function.
A transposition to after v. 12 is distant, but such dislocations are widespread
in Wisdom Literature, from Ptahhotep to Ben Sira.[28] The original location of
the verse is uncertain. Ginsberg places it after 7:12, where it continues the
teaching of wisdom's superiority to wealth.

For MT's *tā'ōz*, 4QQoh[a] reads *t'zr*, "helps," a reading found in several
Hebrew MSS and represented by LXX's βοηθήσει. The variants are a synonym interchange (on the synonymity of 'ZR and 'ZZ see Brin 1960). The
reading *t'zr* is probably a substitution of a more familiar expression for *'azaz
l-*, "show oneself strong on behalf of."

M'śrh šlytym: MT's reading, lit. "than ten magnates" (or "officials"), is
peculiar, for ten magnates are an unlikely source of help (or power) for a
wise man. Also, the indefinite form of the noun-phrase is inappropriate. If
there really were ten *šalliṭim*, we would expect a reference to "*the* ten magnates" (or "officials"). We should follow Perles (1895:42) in redividing the
words as *m'šr hšltym (mē'ōšer haššallîṭîm)*, "the wealth of the magnates."
These "magnates," *šalliṭim*, are rich and powerful men. They are not necessarily rulers or governors (Seow 1996:653), but they may have received their
wealth by holding positions in the officialdom whose corruption Qohelet observes in 5:7. By the emended reading, 7:19 is even more closely aligned thematically with 7:11-12. In 7:19, as in 7:11f., Qohelet is calling wisdom more
valuable than wealth.

◆ **7:13-18 + 20-24**

*(13) Observe what God has brought to pass! Who can straighten out
what he has warped?*

*(14) In a day of good fortune, enjoy the good, and in a day of misfor-
tune, observe: God has made the one to happen next to the other, so that man
is unable to grasp anything (that might happen) afterwards.*

(15) I have seen both in my absurd life:

28. This can easily be confirmed by perusing Žába's edition of Ptahhotep, in which
he collates the three main manuscripts and notes displacements in the margin. For Ben
Sira, the 1973 concordance of the Academy of the Hebrew Language lists displacements
in the Hebrew manuscripts on p. 69. There are further displacements in the Greek tradition of Sira, and numerous transpositions in the LXX of Proverbs vis-à-vis the MT. Transpositions occur in a great many ancient manuscripts, but are probably more tolerable in
Wisdom texts, where the precise sequence of sentences is usually less determinative of the
meaning.

> *there is a righteous man who perishes in his righteousness,*
> *and a wicked man who lives long in his wickedness.*
>
> *(16) Do not be very righteous or become excessively wise,*
> *lest you be dumbfounded.*
>
> *(17) Do not be very wicked or act the fool,*
> *lest you die before your time.*
>
> *(18) Better that you take hold of the one,*
> *and not let go of the other.*
> *For he who fears God fulfills them both. <(19) . . .ᵃ>*
>
> *(20) For there is no man on earth so righteous that he does only*
> *good and never sins.*

(21) Furthermore, you should pay no heed to all the things people say, so that you do not hear your slave reviling you. (22) For — as your heart well knows — many times you too have reviled others.

(23) All this I tested with wisdom. I said, "I shall become wise," but it was far from me. (24) Far off indeed is that which happens, and very deep. Who can find it?

ᵃ7:19 is placed after 7:12 and discussed there.

A. 7:13-14. Human ignorance and frailty before God
B. 7:15-18 + 20. The paradoxes of justice
C. 7:21-22. The ubiquity of wickedness
D. 7:23-24. The inevitability of ignorance

The theme of this unit, which is an extension of the preceding, is injustice and ignorance. The theological issues this unit probes are discussed in §3.4.

The connections between the sections are loose. Section A develops the theme of uncomplaining endurance of turns of fortune. Recognition of man's inability to understand and change things (B) can help one resign himself to adversities while waiting patiently for their outcome. Section C reminds the reader that he too is not free of sin. Section D expresses Qohelet's frustration at understanding injustices such as described in section A. In *Contradictions,* I joined 7:23f. to the next unit, but I now agree with Murphy (p. 69) that while vv. 23f. are transitional, they serve primarily to cap off the foregoing. In v. 23, "all this" looks backward and provides a conclusion and resting point, while in v. 25, "I turned, I and my heart" introduces a new phase of the exploration.

A. 7:13-14. Human Ignorance and Frailty Before God

7:13 *Ma'aśeh ha'ĕlohim* are events such as the misfortunes mentioned in v. 14 and the injustices described in v. 15. When inequitable, distorted things befall a man, he must accept them, because he cannot set them aright. V. 13b is a variant of 1:15a, but now God is held directly responsible for the distortion or "warping." Job uses the same word — *'iwwet* — in blaming God for perverting justice in his own case (27:1).

7:14 The gender distinction between *ṭob* and *ṭobah,* though not usually significant, here cues us to a shift in usage: when in *ṭobah,* a good situation, enjoy the *ṭob,* the good feeling. "Enjoy the good" *(hᵉyeh bᵉṭob)* is lit. "be in good"; cf. the similar expressions in Ps 25:13; Job 21:13.

'Aśah ha'ĕlohim, "God has made . . . to happen," refers to what befalls an individual, his fortunes, good or bad.

Yom here, like *'et* in *'et ra'ah* (9:12), means "time" (and not precisely "day"), in the sense of a complex of circumstances that occur together. By making different types of "times," God keeps man off balance. Man never knows what will happen next.

Yimṣa' 'aḥărayw, lit. "find after him," is sometimes explained as a calque on Aramaic *'ešᵉkah batreh,* an idiom meaning "find an occasion of complaint against"; see Whitley 1979:66. However, similar sentences in 3:22; 6:12; and 10:14 speak unambiguously of man's ignorance of the future.

B. 7:15-18 + 20. The Paradoxes of Justice

7:15 The *bet* ("in") of *bᵉṣidqo* and *bᵉra'ato* means "in the state of" and not "because of" (contrary to Hertzberg). The latter would imply that wickedness *causes* long life. The point is that someone may die young in spite of living in a state of righteousness and another live long in spite of being in a state of wickedness. Ginsberg renders "although," comparing Num 14:11; Lev 26:27; Ps 27:3; etc.; sim. Murphy. However, the adversative or concessive notion derives not from the preposition *b-* but from the tension between the subject and the condition it is in. It is because Qohelet had expected to see consistent justice that he was shocked when it is violated.

7:16-17a There are two main ways of interpreting the peculiar advice in these verses:

(1) Do not be *self-righteous* and do not make great pretensions to wis-

dom (for this view see particularly Whybray, 1978). But while *tiṯḥakkam* can mean "pretend to wisdom," *tĕhi ṣaddiq* does not mean "claim to be righteous." Also, this interpretation creates an awkward dissymmetry between a warning not to *pretend* to be something (righteous and wise) and a warning not to *be* something (wicked and foolish).

(2) Be neither *very* righteous and wise, nor *very* wicked and foolish. ("Very" may also apply to "foolish" in v. 17a.) One may wonder, however, why Qohelet would warn against a high degree of righteousness and wisdom. Even more puzzling is the implication that only a high degree of wickedness and folly is to be avoided. Is even a *little* vice acceptable?

In spite of the difficulties, the second interpretation is the better. One motive for the advice is that straining to be too righteous may be a form of hubris. Since, as v. 20 says, no one can be entirely righteous, living on too high a level of virtue gives the appearance of striving to go beyond human bounds. As examples of excessive "righteousness," Ibn Ezra and Yaḥyah mention praying all day and self-affliction, practices they consider un-Jewish. Rashi cites Saul's mercy to Agag.

Qohelet teaches us to accept in ourselves a mixture of good and bad, just as we should accept that same mixture in the events and circumstances we experience (v. 14). Only in this way can we show true fear of God. Pushing too hard in either direction displays a presumptuous confidence in one's own powers (cf. Hertzberg, p. 154).

Such a counsel of moderation has precedents. Ptahhotep says, "Follow your heart [= enjoy yourself] as long as you live. Do no more than is said. Do not reduce the time meant for following your heart. It is an offense to the Ka [soul, appetite] when its time is reduced" (ll. 186-88; cf. AEL 1.66). Kagemeni cautions: "Do not go beyond what is set down [sc., in this book]" (2.6; cf. *AEL* 1.60).

Qohelet's counsel of moderation should not be conflated with the Peripatetic ideal of μέσως ἔχειν or the "Golden Mean" (contrary to Delitzsch, Hertzberg, Gordis, and many). According to that principle, wisdom is not one of the extremes to be avoided. Wisdom is the mid-point between two extremes, which are too much and too little of any quality, while folly is defined as either extreme. For Qohelet, the continuum goes from extreme wisdom/righteousness to extreme folly/wickedness. He does not advise us to locate ourselves precisely in the mid-point. Judging from his advice elsewhere, it is desirable to be more wise and righteous than not, but not to push toward the maximum.

Another reason for the avoidance of an extreme of wisdom (such as Qohelet says he himself suffered from) is that it makes one aware of inequities such as those described in 7:15, and this awareness will leave one shocked (7:16b). As he said in 1:18, "in much wisdom there is much irritation, and whosoever increases knowledge increases pain." Being "too" righteous can cause a similar effect, making you "dumbfounded" or "devastated" *(tiššomem)* in frustration and chagrin at seeing the unworthy receiving the rewards that your righteousness merits.

Qohelet's advice is thus not only a humble expression of the acceptance of human limitations. It also holds a flash of indignation, perhaps with a bit of petulance, provoked by awareness of the injustices described in 7:15. If neither wise, righteous behavior nor wicked, foolish behavior definitely produces the deserved consequences, then one need not devote himself too intensely to either. After all, "no one can straighten out what God has warped" (7:13).

7:16 *Tithakkam:* the hitpael of ḤKM does not necessarily connote slyness or a pretense of wisdom. (In Exod 1:10, *nithakkᵉmah,* "let us deal cleverly," refers to *genuine* wisdom, for Pharaoh is speaking of his own plan.) *Hithakkem* does mean "to act wise" or "make a show of wisdom" in Sir 10:26, but it means "become (genuinely) wise" in Sir 6:32; 38:24, 25, and "to display (genuine) wisdom" in 35:4. In Qoh 7:16, the conjunction of *tithakkam* with "be righteous" and its contrast with "be wicked" and "act the fool" shows that it refers to wisdom and not just its pretense. The hitpael here indicates *becoming* wise rather than displaying wisdom, since the impression that one's wisdom makes on others is not at issue.

'Al tᵉhi ṣaddiq harbeh: This does not mean "do not claim to be a righteous man," as Whybray (1978:192-96) argues. A warning against pretense would be conveyed by a prohibition such as *'al to'mar ṣaddiq 'ani,* "Do not say, 'I am righteous'" (cf. Jer 1:7; Qoh 7:10). The syntactically and structurally parallel *'al tᵉhi sakal* (v. 17) clearly admonishes against actually being something, not only a pretense.

Tiššomem is a hitpael of ŠMM with assimilation of the *taw* (GKC §74c). ŠMM-hitpael means "be shocked, dumbfounded," e.g., Isa 59:16; 63:5; Ps 143:4; Dan 8:27; Sir 43:24; and that is its meaning here (thus LXX, Syr, Vul), rather than "be destroyed." Qohelet regards wisdom as a cause of emotional disturbance (1:18) rather than physical destruction.

7:17 By warning against acting *very* wickedly, Qohelet appears to be recommending a *little* wickedness. Some interpreters get around this by construing "wickedness" as something other than moral evil, such as transgression of the letter of the law (Delitzsch) or belonging to a party less rigorously attentive to divine precepts (Ehrlich). But one guilty of such behavior would not be called *raša'*, which is used only with reference to real wickedness. It is better to recognize that to condemn "much" is not to approve of a little. As Crenshaw points out, the curse on slaying one's neighbor in secret (Deut. 27:24) does not license doing so in public. "In the same way, Qohelet's warning against excessive wickedness does not endorse moderate evil. Rather, it accepts villainy as a harsh fact, one that Qohelet articulates in 7:20 and 7:29 ('no one is righteous'; 'everyone searches for ways to do wrong')" (p. 141). "Very" *(harbeh)* is simply a concession to human weakness, a recognition that man cannot be entirely blameless, even if he can avoid great wickedness (cf. v. 20; thus Whybray 1978:197).

". . . lest you die before your time": Qohelet holds to the principle that the wicked die early, though he knows the rule is sometimes violated.

7:18 "The one" and "the other" *(zeh . . . zeh)* must be the two counsels given in vv. 16f., since it is difficult to extract from the preceding context two things that one should "take hold of" and "not let go of."

Yeṣe' 'et kullam: Some take *yeṣe'* here to mean "leave," "escape" (e.g., Hertzberg, Zimmerli; thus LXX, Sym, Syr [in which we should read *npq* for *nqp*]). But "escape" does not work as a translation of *yeṣe'*, since its direct object *kullam,* if it means "both of them," must have its antecedent in the immediately preceding pronouns ("this . . . this"). These pronouns are not something one would wish to "escape" from, since they refer to counsels of *desirable* behaviors and not to the undesirable consequences threatened in 16b and 17b. *Yeṣe' 'et kullam* is best rendered "do his duty by both" on the basis of RH *yaṣa' y^edey ḥobah* "to do one's duty," which is sometimes shortened to *yaṣa'.* "Both" *(kullam)* here would be the two counsels in vv. 16f. (Tg, Rashi, Delitzsch, Gordis, etc.). It must be granted that there is a problem in retrojecting this usage to Qohelet's time. (In Sir 38:17, mentioned by Crenshaw, *ywṣ'* actually means "be fitting.")

7:19 See after 7:12.

7:20 To be human is to be flawed (cf. Ps 143:2; Prov 20:9; Job 4:17-19). Do not expect much righteousness from anyone, including yourself.

C. 7:21-22. The Ubiquity of Wickedness

7:21f. To the phrase "all the things people say," LXX (in B and S) supplies ἀσεβεῖς "the wicked" as subject; sim. Syr, and Tg. This is a gloss, possibly in the vorlage, restricting the scope of the warning to words spoken by evildoers, lest one think that it includes the rebukes of the wise.

These verses are an incidental pendant to v. 20, which says that sin is universal. The fact that one has himself sinned is not proposed as a reason to ignore the insults, as if Qohelet were trying to inspire a humble tolerance of others' flaws. Rather it explains the end of v. 21: you know that you are likely to hear nasty things said about yourself because you know that these are the sorts of things people say, because you too have done it. The aim of this advice is not to increase tolerance for others but to help the reader avoid discomfort to himself.

Yadaʿ libbeka, "as your heart well knows," lit. "your heart knows": You know privately; you have to admit to yourself, at least. The heart, having a certain independence from the "I" or ego (see §4.4), functions as a conscience, which can tell a person what he does not want to hear. Thoughts that reside in the heart are secret, known only to God (Ps 44:22; Prov 15:11; 24:12; etc.). Even if we pretend otherwise, our heart knows we are not free of the offenses we condemn in others.[29]

". . . so that you do not hear your slave reviling you": If your slave — *even* your slave — who is in your power and who has every reason to fear you, would insult you behind your back, how much more will others do so.

D. 7:23-24. The Inevitability of Ignorance

In the final section of this unit (7:23f.), Qohelet summarizes his investigation thus far by reformulating 1:13, when he determined "to investigate and to explore with wisdom all that occurs under the heavens." *Lidroš wᵉlatur* in 1:13 is functionally synonymous with *nissiti* in 7:23, *baḥokmah* appears in both verses, and *kol 'ăšer naʿăśah taḥat haššamayim* in 1:13 is equivalent to *mah šehayah* in 7:24. *Mah šeyahah* refers to the same thing as *zoh* in v. 23, namely, all that happens in life.

7:23 Qohelet says that he decided to become wise but failed. The admission is peculiar, because Qohelet has insisted all along that he succeeded quite well in becoming wise, and he never denies that his knowledge, whatever its limitations and vexations, was truly wisdom (and the epilogue agrees; see 12:9). Indeed, in this very verse he says that he availed himself of wisdom in his search.

---

29. This notion is an Egyptian one as well, very dramatically displayed in mortuary texts, where the deceased begs his heart to stay with him: "Say not against me 'He really did it' concerning what I have done. Bring no charges against me before the great god, the lord of the west" (Spell 30A; Allen 1974:40).

There must be a difference between the wisdom Qohelet aimed at but did not reach (implied by *'eḥkamah*) and the wisdom he *did* have. The problem is finding the defining marks in the context rather than coming up with a distinction *ad hoc* in order to eliminate the difficulty.

Delitzsch does the latter when he explains *'eḥkamah* as expressing no less than an intention "to possess [wisdom] fully and completely; *i.e.,* not merely to be able to record observations and communicate advices, but to adjust the contradictions of life, to expound the mysteries of time and eternity, and generally to solve the most weighty and important questions which perplex men" (p. 329). But is all this really packed into the verb *ḥakam?* And would the inability to obtain this exalted degree of knowledge be considered a failure to become wise? And surely Qohelet is not so arrogant as to demand a degree of wisdom no sage ever dared claim, wisdom of a breadth obviously reserved for God.

According to Gordis, *'eḥkamah* alludes to a special kind of wisdom, namely "*ḥokmah* par excellence," the "fundamental" or "speculative" wisdom, as distinct from the "lower" or "practical" wisdom (sim. Crenshaw). This distinction (which the Israelite sages would not have made) is of no help here, because the type of wisdom that Qohelet possessed includes not only "practical" but also "speculative" wisdom, the "organon" (see Gordis, p. 199) whereby he explored "all that occurs under the heavens" (1:13).

Another approach is to point *'ēḥkāmehā,* an Aramaism supposedly meaning "I will understand it" (Ginsberg, sim. Fox 1987). But an emendation (albeit just vocalic) to an otherwise unattested word is too tenuous a conjecture, and it is unnecessary.

More to the mark is Murphy's observation: "Obviously Qoheleth was a sage in the traditional sense; the entire book testifies to his deep roots in the wisdom tradition. But the tests he put it to made him realize that he was not truly wise or did not possess the wisdom he sought for" (p. 72). In other words, he possessed learning and employed his reason (both being forms of *ḥokmah*), but he could not attain the kind of wisdom he was aiming at. We can compare the analogous use of *yada'* in Qoh 8:17, where *wᵉgam 'im yo'mar heḥakam lada'at* shows that *yada'* can refer to a certain kind of understanding which is beyond the wise man's grasp, though he undeniably has *da'at* "knowledge" of some sort. In both cases the unattainable type of wisdom can be designated *ḥokmah* and *da'at* and be defined by specifying what was *not* attained, and this is far short of the god-like wisdom Delitzsch defines (above). The unattainable wisdom is, as the next verse indicates, an understanding of *mah šehayah.*

7:24 *Mah šehayah* signifies "that which happens," as in 1:9; 3:15; and 6:10. It is virtually synonymous with *hamma'ăśeh 'ăšer na'ăśah taḥat haššameš* ("the events that occur under the sun") and *ma'ăśeh ha'ĕlohim* ("what God makes happen"), which no one, *not even the wise man*, can grasp, according to 8:17. Grasping (lit. "finding") "what God brings to pass" means an understanding of the rationale of events, including anomalous and unjust occurrences. If Qohelet could understand, for example, why "there is a righteous man who perishes in his righteousness, and a wicked man who lives long in his wickedness" (7:15) — as purveyors of theodicy presume to do — that would be a successful conclusion to Qohelet's determination to "become wise," and *mah šehayah* would no longer be "far off." But he cannot.

Beyond frustration at his inability to reach this knowledge, Qohelet betrays a feeling of alienation from "that which happens." The events of life feel alien and distant to Qohelet. He is a stranger here, watching the world but not quite *of* it:

> A world that can be explained even with bad reasons is a familiar world. But, on the other hand, in a universe suddenly divested of illusions and lights, man feels himself an alien, a stranger. . . . This divorce between man and his life, the actor and his setting, is properly the feeling of absurdity. (Camus, *Myth*, p. 13)

◆ 7:25–8:1a

(25) I turned, I and my heart, to understand and to explore and to seek out wisdom and solutions, and to understand wickedness, stupidity, and folly, <and[a]> madness. (26) And I found woman more bitter than death, because she is nets, and her heart is snares, her hands bonds. He whom God likes will escape her, but he who is offensive will be caught by her. (27) See, this I have found, said the Qohelet,[b] (adding) one to one to find a solution: (28) A <woman[c]> I sought continually but did not find. One human being in a thousand I did find, but a woman in all these I did not find. (29) Only, see, this I did find: God made people straight, but they seek out great solutions.

(8:1a) Who is <so[d]> wise, and who knows the meaning of anything?

[a]*wᵉhôlēlôt* (MT *hôlēlôt*)
[b]*'āmar haqqōhelet* (MT *'āmᵉrāh qōhelet*)
[c]*'iššāh* (MT *'ăšer*)
[d]*kōh ḥākām* (MT *kᵉheḥākām*)

With regard to the starting point of this unit, see the introduction to the preceding one. As for its end, most commentators (including Delitzsch, Barton, Podechard, Gordis, and Zimmerli) set it at v. 29, others at 8:1 (Hertzberg, Galling, Lauha, Ellermeier [1967:138], et al.). Some divide this passage into two units, either at v. 25 (Zimmerli, Lauha) or at v. 26 (Gordis). I end the unit at 8:1a (sim. Lohfink, 1979), which is a summary statement echoing the statement of ignorance that concludes the preceding unit in vv. 23f. 8:1b introduces a topic (ingratiation) that belongs to the advice in 8:2-6 (behavior before the king) rather than to the matters treated in 7:25–8:1a.

This unit, with its ironic self-undermining calculations, flows out of the preceding insofar as it serves to demonstrate the remoteness of wisdom. Man cannot understand anything, not even — or especially — women.

Despite the valiant efforts of some exegetes, this passage remains irreparably misogynistic. The fact that Qohelet lists woman alongside other pleasurable things in 9:9 (and, for that matter, 2:8) does not buffer the acidity of the present passage.[30]

Lohfink (1979) rebuts various attempts to improve Qohelet's image, but his own effort is no more successful. According to Lohfink, in 7:26 Qohelet cites a traditional saying in order to debate traditional wisdom (in vv. 27f.). But Lohfink fails to show either that Qohelet is attributing the remark in v. 26 to someone else or that he in any way rejects that opinion. *Moṣe' 'ăni* can only introduce Qohelet's own conclusion, not an opinion he repudiates. Moreover, the sentiments of the supposedly refuted verses are far from the attitudes of traditional wisdom. (Only Ben Sira makes genuinely misogynistic remarks [25:24; 42:13f.], but even he reserves most of his spleen for the evil or loose woman [esp. in 9:3-9 and 25:13-26].) In Lohfink's reading, Qohelet is quoting a claim that woman is truly "stronger" *(mar)* than death (but who would claim that?), then replying that the people he observed were, after a while, not to be found (in other words, they had died), and all women had proved mortal (p. 283). But this interpretation has Qohelet contrasting the woman's mortality with the occasional immortality of men — a strange notion that would occur to no one. In any case, Qohelet's reply, thus understood, hardly contradicts or even softens 7:26.

D. Michel (1989:261; 225-38) follows Lohfink in assigning the misogynistic views to another voice. He says that in v. 26 the participle *moṣe'* with its connotation of continuing action, introduces an indirect quotation of a misogynistic "theory." Qohelet "finds" (that is, repeatedly comes upon) the

---

30. The fact that Ben Sira is fulsome in his praise of virtuous — and pretty — women (26:1-4, 13-18; 36:26-31[23-28]) would not be thought to disprove *his* misogyny.

opinion expressed in v. 26. He introduces his own opinion in v. 27, cites and rebuts another misogynistic theory *en passant* in v. 28, and delivers his response only in v. 29. What he himself found, the conclusion *(ḥešbon)* he reached *(maṣaʾ* = "reach," "grasp," "understand"; see §5.11), is that men distort their straight nature by seeking *ḥiššᵉbonot* — such as the repudiated opinions about women.

This explanation strains too hard. Too much depends on idiosyncratic interpretations of "I find." Insofar as the contrast between the participle (v. 26) and the perfect (in vv. 27-29, five times) is significant, it shows that v. 26, at least, expresses Qohelet's current and enduring view. "I find/found" always introduces a conclusion the speaker accepts or accepted at the time of finding. For an interpreter to insert "die Ansicht" ("the opinion") after "I find" (Michel 1989:225) is taking a liberty that could reverse the meaning of any verse. Nor is there any sign that v. 28b is a quoted proverb, or, if it is, that v. 29 rebuts it. Verse 29 does quip about seeking "solutions" (such as Qohelet came to when thinking about women), but it does not deny their truth, nor does it imply that Qohelet himself did not perform these calculations and come to these findings.

Though there are several uncertainties in this passage, there is no ambiguity about one thing: Qohelet is not defending the honor of women. Qohelet is crabby. He doesn't think too highly of men either, and there's no reason to expect him to have much good to say about women.

Nevertheless, Qohelet may not intend his dyspeptic remarks to be read with too much gravity. The arch and ironic tone in this passage, especially in the self-directed irony in v. 29, suggests that he does not intend to give all his remarks the weight of philosophical propositions. Grousing about the other sex — in both directions — is a commonplace of persiflage, wisecracks, folk song, and even serious literature throughout the world. It is because we care so much about members of the opposite sex that we are so easily bruised and frustrated — and bemused — by them, and also, if we think about it, by our own reactions to the game.

7:25 Lit. "I turned *(wᵉsabboti)* and my heart." Qohelet, in a way reminiscent of Egyptian usage, thinks of his heart as an entity distinct from his ego, the "I"; see §4.4.

The syntax of MT v. 25b is difficult. Treating *wᵉladaʿat rešaʿ kesel wᵉhassiklut holelot* as two sets of double accusatives and translating "to know that wickedness is foolishness; and folly, madness" (Barton; sim. Delitzsch, Gordis, et al.) produces a tautology and leaves the last clause detached from context. LXX points to a better reading. It translates this clause as καὶ τοῦ γνῶναι ἀσεβοῦς ἀφροσύνην καὶ σκληρίαν καὶ περιφοράν ("and to know the folly and stubbornness and madness [lit. 'revolutions, twistings'] of the wicked)," which can be retroverted to *wldʿt ršʿ ksl wsklwt whwllwt*. As Euringer observes, if LXX had *wsklwt hwllwt* it would have rendered it with a genitive construction, as it did for the first two nouns. In the retroverted Hebrew, all four nouns are direct objects of *ladaʿat,* though LXX construes the words otherwise. Syr reads ". . . and to know the wickedness of the fool and folly and transgression," which also assumes a *waw* on *hwllwt*. Minimally we should emend MT to *wᵉhôlēlôt*. In 1:17 and 2:12 as well, "folly" and "madness" are coordinated with a *waw*. The article on *whsklwt* can be preserved; compare the uneven use of the article in 2:8; for a discussion of the phenomenon see Schoors 1992:166-69.

Qohelet sets out to understand all sorts of human capabilities and dispositions. *Ḥešbon* "calculation" refers to both the process of reckoning and the solution reached. Its semantic range is well reflected by LXX's λογισμός in 7:27 and 9:12, though here it has ψῆφος "account," lit. "counting pebble." In this passage, *ḥešbon* first of all means "solution" (as of a problem in arithmetic), but it also has a metaphorical application. Machinist (1995) observes that *ḥešbon* is used in Qohelet at a higher level of abstraction than elsewhere. In Qohelet it means a "'considered assessment of life, that is, what is arrived at by a deliberate process of reasoning' (7:27-28; maybe 7:25; and 9:10) or, apparently, 'the reckoning process itself' (9:10; possibly 7:25)" (p. 170). Qohelet is thinking about thought and must shape the vocabulary to allow himelf to do so.

7:26 The "wickedness, stupidity, and folly, and madness" that Qohelet observed turn out to be . . . woman. There is both bathos and wit in these words: the result of his inquiries in the abstruse realms of intellect comes down to this: woman is dangerous. Qohelet's heart, which accompanies him (independently, as it were) on his investigation (7:25), leads him to an awareness of the woman's "heart." The unusual phrase *'ănî wᵉlibbi* in v. 25 (confirmed by LXX and Syr) both focuses attention on the word "heart" and imagines Qohelet's heart as an independent entity ready to meet — and be caught by — a woman's heart.

Mar means "bitter," not "strong," contrary to Dahood (1958:308f.; cf. Whitley 1979:68f.). In fact, Pardee (1978:257-66) throws doubt on the existence of a root MRR meaning "strong" in BH. He points out that death has the quality of bitterness elsewhere (see esp. 1 Sam 15:32 — certainly the *strength* of death has not departed from Agag), and the evil woman is associated with death in Prov 5:5.

The word *'ăšer* may be either a relative adjective or a causal conjunction. The latter is likely (thus Ginsberg, Lohfink [1979:278, n. 67]), because a reason for Qohelet's judgment is in order and because parsing the particle as causal explains the otherwise superfluous pronoun *hi'*. As a relative adjective, *'ăšer* would be non-restrictive: "woman, whose . . ." rather than "the woman whose . . ." — as if Qohelet were condemning only those women who fit the description (thus, e.g., Hertzberg, Kroeber, Crenshaw, Murphy). But 7:28 shows that Qohelet is sniping at all of womankind. Moreover, it would be a pointless assertion to state that those women who are nets, whose heart is a snare, and whose hands are bonds, are more bitter than death. A man who fit that description would likewise be more bitter than death. It is thus misleading to say that "[t]he theme of the woman who ensnares men is standard in ancient Near Eastern wisdom. It echoes the book of Proverbs' persistent warning against the 'foreign' woman" (Crenshaw, p. 146). Others did warn against the snares of *wicked* women (e.g., Prov 2:16-19), but they did the same for wicked *men* (e.g., 2:12-15, and very often in Proverbs). Qohelet does not limit his gibes to women of a certain type.

'Ăšer hi' meṣodim waḥăramim libbahh can be construed in two ways: (1) "because as for her — her heart is nets and snares" (treating *hi'* as the antecedent of the feminine singular possessive suffixes). Or (2) "because she is nets, and her heart is snares" (thus LXX). The singular-plural predication is not awkward in Hebrew, as it is in English. MT reads this way, making *hi' meṣodim* a prosodic unit.

Here, as in 2:26 (q.v.), the men called "he whom God likes" (*tob lipney ha'ĕlohim,* lit. "good before God") and "he who is offensive" (*hote',* usually "sinner") may be no more or less virtuous than others. Qohelet calls a man pleasing or offensive to God in accordance with his fate rather than his deeds. This verse may be jousting with Prov 18:22, "He who finds a woman finds something good, and receives favor from the Lord." "Good before God" (*tob lipney ha'ĕlohim*) in Qohelet is equivalent to "receives favor" *(wayyapeq raṣon)* in the proverb. Qohelet's comments on womankind resemble what is said in Proverbs about the adulterous "strange" woman (that is, a woman other than one's own wife); note especially Prov 22:14: "A deep pit is the mouth of strange women; he who is cursed by the Lord will fall therein"; similarly Prov 23:27. But Qohelet is speaking about all women, having failed to find even one who escapes the verdict.

7:27 MT's *'mrh qhlt* should be redivided to read *'mr hqhlt,* as in 12:8. "Qohelet" is here treated as a common noun and supplied with an article.

"This I have found" *(zeh maṣa'ti):* Michel (1989:229) correctly construes "this" as prospective. It refers to the same fact called "this" in 29a: that

God made men straight but they sought many solutions. Qohelet introduces his finding in v. 27 but gets sidetracked into an extended description of the search in v. 28. He then reintroduces his conclusion in v. 29.

"(Adding) one to one" shows that Qohelet is using an arithmetical image. Qohelet, who is much concerned with business matters like work, portions, and profits (see Kugel 1989), studies the opposite sex with an accountant's eye. But it doesn't add up. This verse reformulates the conclusion of v. 26 and pursues the arithmetical imagery. When considering women, Qohelet added one to one — a painstaking process — to arrive at a sum total, a *hešbon*. The feminine "one" (*'aḥat,* both times) suggests wryly that he surveyed the field of womanhood carefully and extensively, just like the other pleasures he finds absurd but (relatively) good (2:1-11).

7:28 The syntax of MT is difficult. If it were a relative clause, *'ăšer 'od biqšah napši wᵉlo' maṣa'ti* ("which my soul sought constantly, but I did not find"), it would be lacking an antecedent. *Hešbon* is not what Qohelet failed to find, because in the next sentence he says that he *did* find a *hešbon.* As a substantive (subject) clause, this sentence would lack a predicate. Therefore it is best to follow Perles (1895:33) and Ehrlich in emending *'šr* to *'šh,* "woman." Orthographically the *reš/heh* change is very slight (see the qeréketiv variants in 1 Kgs 22:49; for other possible examples see *LSF* §§216c, 123b). The emendation produces a simple and meaningful construction: "A woman I sought continually but did not find." This balances the end of the verse nicely: "but a woman in all these I did not find."

'Od = "continually," as in Gen 46:29; Ruth 1:14; Ps 84:5; cf. Qoh 12:9. The rest of the verse undergirds this conclusion by claiming a broad statistical base for the survey.

Qohelet found one *'adam* in a thousand (people), but among all these, he did not find even one *'iššah. 'Adam* means "person," "human being," not specifically male. It can be limited to males by contrast or pairing, as in *ha'adam wᵉ'išto,* "the man and his wife" (Gen 2:25); but "human being" is appropriate in the present context. In any case, *'adam* and *'iššah* cannot be simply a human (or man) and a woman, because Qohelet would obviously have found people (or men) and women among the thousand (people) he was appraising. Commentators suggest different ways to supply the ellipsis, for example, "a man who is reliable, useful to friends, and ethically upright" (Lauha), "a perfect person, an ideal person" (Ginsberg), "a woman, in the right and highest sense" (Hertzberg), "an honest, blameless woman" (Lauha), or "a woman as God created her, fulfilling her true woman's essence (Ellul 1990:201); sim. Delitzsch, Barton, Podechard, Gordis, et al.

Such an ellipsis does not appear elsewhere with *'adam* or *'iššah*. *'Iš* "man" does imply masculine virtue in 1 Sam 4:9b; 26:15; 1 Kgs 2:2; and Avot 2:5, but Qohelet would not be contrasting masculine virtue ("a real man") with feminine virtue ("a true woman") since he has a low regard for woman's nature. Since *'adam* is the term used for humans in contrast to an-imals (see 3:18, 19a [twice], 21), the unstated contrast is humans versus beasts. (Compare Prov 30:2, "I am more brutish than a man, nor is there human understanding [*binat 'adam*] in me.") Of a thousand people, Qohelet found one *real* human; the rest were dumb animals. And these rare people turned out to be all males, for, looking at the one-in-a-thousand, he found not so much as one woman.

Just how did Qohelet "find" the things mentioned in 7:23-29? Enough puzzles remain to suggest that Qohelet is playing on words, in this case by the rhetorical device of *antanaclasis*. Antanaclasis is the repetition of one word in different senses in a single passage. The polysemic MṢ' ("find/discover" or "reach/overtake/acquire," hence "grasp" [intellectu-ally], "understand") lends itself to antanaclasis. (Ceresko 1982 discusses antanaclasis of *maṣa'* in Qohelet, but does not address this passage.) V. P. Long (1997) argues that *maṣa'* means "understand," "figure out," or the like in vv. 27-29 (cf. the use of *maṣa'* in 8:17). Qohelet could *understand* one man in a thousand but not a single woman. Woman remained an enigma. Such a word play is possible, but the shifts in meaning of the verb in this passage are hard to follow, and *maṣa'* is best rendered consistently throughout.

Maṣa' 'iššah, lit. "find a woman," as Ehrlich observes, elsewhere means to "find a wife." This is clearly so in Prov 18:22 (quoted above). In Prov 19:14b too, *'iššah* (though indefinite and not in a bound construction) means "wife." (The only woman a man would receive "from the Lord" would be a wife.) Thus Qohelet could be saying that he searched diligently but failed to find himself a wife. (Qoh 9:9 does not show that he did so, but only that having one would be, all in all, a good thing.) This meaning works in the first and last clauses of v. 28, but Qohelet could not be said to have "found" a person *('adam)* in the same sense that he failed to "find" a wife. Still, perhaps this sense too is active as a double entendre. This passage, in spite of its sardonic tone, is meant to be wry and playful, so a series of double entendres is possible.

Prov 31:11 exclaims, "Who can find an excellent woman?" This is meant more as praise of her preciousness than a comment on her rarity, but it does imply the latter. Qohelet says they are too rare to be found.

"Only": The use of *l^ebad* to introduce a main clause is unparalleled in *BH.* It is probably a calque on Aramaic *l^eḥud,* often used at the beginning of

271

sentences. *L^{e}hud* translates sentence-initial *raq* in the Targumim to Gen 19:8; Exod 8:24, 25; Num 20:19; Deut 12:15; et al.

Yašar, "straight" or "straightforward," here refers not to the quality of moral integrity but to intellectual directness or simplicity, as is indicated by the contrast between being *yašar* and "seeking solutions."

Rabbim here means "great" rather than "many" (Ginsberg; cf. 10:6). It is not so much the quantity of the sought-for answers that exasperates Qohelet as their qualitative "greatness."

The upshot of all of Qohelet's *ḥešbon*-seeking is simply this: mankind seeks great *ḥišš^{e}bonot.* In mentioning the decline in human quality from essential straightness, Qohelet no longer has in mind the corruption ascribed to 99.9 percent of men and 100 percent of women in the preceding verse. He is, rather, speaking of a flaw common to humanity generally, namely the tendency to seek answers and make calculations. Qohelet is the prime example of this, for he sought a *ḥešbon* and got himself all tangled up in the computations. The entire book of Qohelet, in fact, tells of his search for great *ḥišš^{e}bonot.* Such cogitations, Qohelet says here, run contrary to the way man was created, though elsewhere we are told that God himself implanted the desire for them in man's heart (1:13; 3:11). Man may not be able to straighten what God has twisted, but it seems that he can twist what God has made straight.

8:1a Interrogative "who?" occurs seventeen times in the book, sixteen in rhetorical questions tantamount to "no one." Here, as in 2:16b, Qohelet recapitulates an earlier generalization (2:14b; 7:23f.) by a rhetorical question.

MT's *my khhkm* ("Who is like the wise man?") should be divided *my kh ḥkm* (Aq, Sym, and LXX, in which οἶδε is a misreading of an original ὧδε; see Euringer). The MT word-division in v. 1aα produces a sentence that evaluates the wise man positively: no one else is comparable to the wise man. But since v. 1aβ can only mean that no one knows the meaning of a matter, we require a negative evaluation in v. 1aα too, in other words, a statement that *even* the wise man has a limited capacity for understanding. To assert the incomparability of the wise man would require a sentence like *umi kamohu yodea' pešer dabar* in v. 1aβ. *Dabar* (unlike *haddabar*) need not refer to any specific word or thing but may mean "something, anything" (BDB 183b).

Since 8:1aβ ("who knows the meaning of anything?") restates 8:1aα ("who is <so> wise"), we may paraphrase v. 1a as: No one is so wise as to understand the meaning of anything. This statement is hyperbolic but understandable, since Qohelet has defined the kind of knowledge that no one can have in earlier verses. Together the rhetorical questions of v. 1a reiterate *mi yimṣa'ennu*, "Who can find it," of v. 24. The clause *mi koh ḥakam*, "who is so wise?," rephrases *'amarti 'eḥkamah*, "I said, 'I shall become wise,'" in 7:23. In 7:23 and 8:1aα (as in 2:18-20 + 21-23), Qohelet first makes a statement about himself and then recasts it as a sweeping principle.

◆ **8:1b-9**

    (1b) A man's wisdom illumines his face,
        while the impudence of his face <changes it.ᵃ>

    (2) Obey the king's orders, and with regard to the oath of God (3) be not hasty. Leave his presence; do not tarry in a bad situation, for he can do whatever he wishes. (4) For the king's word is authority, and who (dares) say to him, "What are you doing?"

    (5) He who keeps a command will experience nothing bad. And the wise man's heart knows time and procedure, (6) for every matter has a time and procedure. Truly man's misfortune weighs heavy upon him, (7) for he does not know what will happen, for who can tell him when *it will happen?*

    (8) No man has control over the life-spirit so as to retain the life-spirit, and there is no control in the day of death, and there is no release in war, and <wealthᵇ> will not give its possessor an escape.

    (9) All this I observed as I gave thought to all that happens under the sun when one man has authority over another — to his harm.

ᵃ*yᵉšannᵉ'ennû* (MT *yᵉšunne' 'ănî*)
ᵇ*ošer* (MT *reša'*)

A. 8:1b-4. The king's authority
B. 8:5-7. Time and procedure
C. 8:8-9. Other regards in which man lacks control

Beginning with admonitions on comportment in the presence of a king and obedience to his command, Qohelet moves to the theme of obeying commands, then to the issue of the right time (*'et umišpaṭ*, lit. "time and [right] procedure"). In v. 5 the topic shifts from obedience to the king to the right time to act, but the theme of control continues. Vv. 5b-7 digress from the topic of human control to underscore human ignorance of the right times.

Verse 8 returns to this topic in a more general fashion: what humans cannot control, emphasizing the limitations inherent in human powers. Although vv. 8-9 do not directly continue the thought of the foregoing verses, they belong to this unit, since the conclusion in v. 9, which speaks of "all this," must sum up all that has been said about authority. (ŠLṬ denotes both authority and control.)

The argument develops in 8:2-7 much the same as in 3:16-17. Qohelet observes injustices people commit, takes comfort in his belief that judgment will eventually be executed, then finds this comfort undermined — in 3:18-21 by the universality of death, in 8:7 by human ignorance of the time of judgment. These issues are discussed in §§3.32, 3.4.

Throughout this unit (and elsewhere), R. Murphy traces a "dialogue" or (better) a "dialectic" between Qohelet and "traditional wisdom." Since much of the present unit has easily identifiable antecedents in Wisdom Literature, this is a good place to consider the concept of dialectic and how it can be used in interpreting Qohelet. Murphy describes the dialectic in this unit thus:

> [Qohelet] is relativizing the role and prestige of the sage (v. 1) by following up with (wise!) admonitions that in fact are humiliating for the sage at court, even if they also save him from trouble. The wise advisor, for all his gifts, is confronted by royal power and is totally dependent upon the royal pleasure. It is all very well to praise the wisdom of the wise (v. 1), but one must attend to the risks they run at court (vv. 2-4). Hence Qoheleth's admonitions serve to qualify v. 1, even though they are themselves derived from traditional wisdom. He pits traditional wisdom against itself. (p. 83)

Now Qohelet undoubtedly is in dialectic with "traditional wisdom." But *where* is the dialectic, what are its phases, and where are its signs?

The practical problem facing the exegete is whether two phrases of a dialectic can be segregated in the text, with the (traditional) idea as hypothesis and Qohelet's as antithesis. Murphy (p. 82) sees the following pattern: vv. 2-4 modify v. 1; vv. 6-12a modify v. 5; vv. 14f. are in opposition to vv. 12b-13; 16f. are a conclusion about the impenetrability of the divine design.[31] There is, however, nothing in 1b-6a that is not entirely in line with traditional

31. Lohfink, who also reads the book as a dialectic, goes so far as to introduce v. 2 with "I (on the other hand say)." But v. 2 is unquestionably "traditional" advice. That would make Qohelet a "traditional" wise man in dialectic with something else. Such devices show that Qohelet has not given the reader the information necessary to separate out phases of a dialectic.

wisdom, as Murphy recognizes. The parallels in Proverbs and Aḥiqar (which may even be the sources of Qohelet's admonitions) are noted below.

If Qohelet "relativizes" v. 1 by vv. 2-4, he is doing nothing that any sage wouldn't do, since no one would say that a servitor of the king runs no risks at court or is immune to oppressive authority. A number of proverbs recognize such dangers; for example, "The anger of a king is like a lion's roar, while his favor is like dew on the grass" (19:12) and "A king's wrath is angels of death, but a wise man can assuage it" (16:14); cf. 24:21. The king's intentions are often enigmatic (Prov 25:3), and he must be feared (24:21). Aḥiqar (101-104, quoted below) would agree entirely with Qohelet's assessment of kingship. Traditional wisdom did not claim that the wise ran no risks when dealing with authority. It taught, as does Qohelet, that the wise man can reduce the risk by maneuvering carefully through the minefields of power.

In a sense, Proverbs relativizes itself no less than Qohelet does, because you can't squeeze the whole truth into a single sentence. Prov 16:14b relativizes 14a, as 19:12b does 12a (and 20:2) and 29:4b does 4a. Prov 26:5 relativizes 26:4 by bold contradiction, apparently indicating that the first proverb is not valid in all circumstances. Ben Sira does the same (10:3). There are many proverbs that remark on the king's dominion, whether for good (Prov 20:8) or ill (28:15), at once warning against that power and extolling it. They show that the wise man's skills do not guarantee him security even while advising their cultivation and use. In all matters we can find proverbs that "relativize" other proverbs, near or distant. Of course different sayings may have different sources, but many are in the same collections and were selected by a compiler who felt that they were all worthy guides to the truth. None of this is polemic or even dialectic, but simply an observation of various aspects of a situation.

Qohelet does have a more suspicious and even hostile attitude toward human authority than most of the sages (but not than Ben Sira! see Sir 9:13; 13:1-26), but he is not trying to replace their views with his own. He does not oppose or present antitheses to the doctrines of traditional wisdom. It is not even clear that he recognizes a difference. He is not "using traditional wisdom against itself." He is just using it.[32]

A. 8:1b-4. The King's Authority

8:1b-2 Wisdom makes the face bright and cheerful. Or, by a more cynical reading (probably more relevant in this context), it is prudent to put on a cheery

32. For general remarks about Wisdom dialectic, see §1.55.

face before the ruler. Brightness of face is indicative of contentment. When it is God's (e.g., Ps 4:7; 31:17; 44:4) it signals favor, as when it is the king's (Prov 16:15). In an underling, it indicates satisfaction and good spirits, which make a man less dangerous to his master: "The sign of a good heart is a shining face, while withdrawal [?] and brooding (are signs of) wicked plans" (Sir 13:26).[33]

MT's "and the impudence of his face is changed" is awkward, and *'ny* ("I") at the beginning of v. 2 is meaningless. It does not introduce a solution to a riddle supposedly asked in v. 1 (Gordis). Verse 1b is not a question requiring a solution. Nor is *'ăni* likely to be short for "I say," as if Qohelet were piping up and volunteering an answer to his own question. A bare "I" meaning "I say" would be unique in BH and only vaguely paralleled (once) in the Gemarah (b. Qid. 44a, Gordis's example). Another difficulty with MT's reading is that it implies that a man may have "insolence of face," which must be "changed" by his wisdom. But if he was wise, he would not be insolent to start with. The problems of vv. 1b-2a are solved by reading *yᵉšannᵉ'ennû*, "changes it" (sc. his face). Consonantally the emendation is from *yšn' 'ny* to *yšn'nw*. By this reading, the insolent man is a different one from the wise man of the first clause.

Significantly, the letters *'ny* are not represented in LXX, Syr, or Tg. In RH, verbs originally III-H can take an *'aleph* before the suffix. Ben Sira spells "change" with an *'aleph* in 9:18; 12:18 (*yšn' pnym* "he will change his face"); and 13:25. (The last verse is apparently a deliberate paraphrase of Qoh 8:1bf.: *lb 'nwš yšn' pnyw 'm ltwb w'm lr'*, "The heart of a man changes his face, whether for the better or for the worse.") In other words, the way one feels inside shows on the outside. "Change one's face" means to alter the facial expression, making it cheerful or (in this case) sullen. This is clearly the meaning the idiom has in Sir 12:18 and 13:25.[34]

A man's wisdom will not make him actually happy in the presence of a despot, but it does teach him to affect a cheerful demeanor so as to ingratiate himself with whoever is in power and disarm his suspicions. Impudence, on the other hand, betrays itself by a scowl, and this could very well cause trouble with the ruler.

8:2-3 *Wᵉ'al dibrat,* translated above as "with regard to," does not mean "and that, because of" (Gordis; similarly Barton, Hertzberg). The *waw* is in-

---

33. *'Qbt lb twb pnym 'wrym, wśyg yśyḥ* [read *wśyḥ*] *mḥšbt 'ml* (MS A).

34. The Greek of Sir 25:17 has "changes her face" where the Hebrew reads *wyqdyr p[ny]w ldwb*, "and darkens his face to that of a bear." In spite of the different pronoun, the Greek shows what "changing the face" meant to the translator by using that phrase to translate "darkens his face," which means to give one a surly (bearish) countenance.

trusive; it does not "emphasize the reason" (Gordis) but separates it from the foregoing. (GKC §254*a*, n. 1(b) does not apply here; none of the examples listed there have a *waw* before a causal or motive clause or phrase.) And while *'al tibbahel mippanayw telek* could mean "do not hasten to go from his presence" (in accordance with GKC §220*g*), such advice would not accord with the next sentence, "do not tarry [lit., stand] in a bad situation."

The verse division belongs after *tibbahel* (thus LXX and Syr; Ginsberg). By this division, 8:2b counsels circumspection in swearing oaths, and v. 3 advises leaving the king's presence when he is angry. MT, by ending the sentence after "oath of God," makes obedience to the king a moral issue based on an oath sworn by God rather than just a matter of prudence, as it clearly is in vv. 3f. The sentence as emended admonishes: do not be hasty to swear innocence when the ruler is angry at you; just leave his presence.

A striking parallel, which supports the interpretation favored here, is Aḥiqar 101-104:

> (101) See before you a difficult thing:
> Do not oppose [lit. "stand against the face of"] the king
> *([ʾl ʾ]npy m[lk] ʾl tqwm)*
> Quicker than lightning is his anger.
> As for you, take care for yourself.
> (102) May he not ignite it against your words
> and you depart before your time.
> (103) If the king's word is commanded you,
> it is a burning fire. Quickly do it.
> Let it not ignite against you and <burn> your hands.
> (104a) Also, let the king's words be the delight of your heart.[35]

Qohelet's *mippanayw telek 'al ta'ămod bᵉdabar ra'* looks like a reformulation of Aḥiqar's *ʾl ʾnpy mlk ʾl tqwm*.

If this advice were to have practical relevance to Qohelet's readers, the "king" could not actually be any of the imperial rulers of Judea after the exile, and the book is too early to allude to the Hasmoneans. Lohfink (1981:540f.) suggests that Qohelet has in mind the Alexandrian court as a fictive situation. But since Qohelet is not just describing royal behavior but is giving advice to subordinates on how to behave in the king's presence, it is more likely, as Murphy says, Qohelet has in mind local governors. Even if

---

35. This translation draws upon the comments and emendations of Lindenberger 1983:81-86.

these were not actually "kings," sayings using traditional language about royalty could be used in formulating such advice.

8:4 The king's authority is beyond questioning, just like God's, of whom this very phrase is used in Job 9:12b and Isa 45:9. In the latter, Deutero-Isaiah mocks the mortal who *rab 'et yoṣᵉro,* "who contends with his maker." It is as if a pot said to *its* maker, "What are you doing." This shows that the question "what are you doing" is a contention *(rib).*

B. 8:5-7. Time and Procedure

8:5 Verse 5a does not assert a universal truth to the effect that the obedient never suffer any misfortune. That would be too extreme even for the ortho-dox. Rather, the context in vv. 2-4 restricts v. 5a to obedience to the king's command. "He who keeps a command" *(šomer miṣwah)* in v. 5a is one who does what is counseled in v. 2, "obey the king's orders" *(pi melek šᵉmor).* The command one must obey is the king's, not (in this context) God's (Delitzsch, Gordis, Hertzberg, Ginsberg, et al.).

In both form and in content, v. 5 has the appearance of a proverb, and we may surmise that Qohelet quotes it in order to cap off his advice on how to behave in the king's presence, after which he pursues the theme introduced in the second line of the proverb.

Dabar ra' (here translated, with the negative, "nothing bad") echoes the *dabar ra'* (translated "bad situation") of v. 3, though there it refers to an action that angers the king, here to something the king may *do* when angry. One can avoid such circumstances by withdrawing from the king's pres-ence or by obeying his command — the heart of the wise man will know which is which, for "the wise man's heart knows time and (proper) proce-dure."

The phrase *'et umišpaṭ* can mean (1) "the appropriate time and manner of procedure" (Gordis) or (2) (as a hendiadys equivalent to *'et mišpaṭ*) "the right time." As a hendiadys, it can also mean (3) "the time of judgment" (Delitzsch, Ginsberg, Hertzberg). The LXX, which translates καιρὸν κρίσεως "a time of judgment," probably had *'et mišpaṭ* in its vorlage. (The LXX rep-resents the *waw* in v. 6.) The present passage does not discuss evils and injus-tices that call for rectification, so the first two interpretations, which give ba-sically the same meaning, are preferable.

Verse 5b asserts that the wise man knows (or *should* know) the "time and procedure" *('et umišpaṭ),* in other words, what to do when, which is the topic of 3:1-15, q.v. This does not mean that he will know *when* things will happen, a possibility that Qohelet never concedes and that he explicitly denies in 3:11b and 8:7. Rather the wise man knows the right, opportune time to do things. Hence this verse is not — *as a proposition* — contradicted by the assertion of ignorance of the future in v. 7. Within Qohelet's soul, however, there *is* a clash: between the confident sense that an intelligent man can have a pretty good idea about when and how to do things, and the feeling that even the wise are blind to the future and can do no more than respond to events as they come upon them.

8:6 The import of the first statement, "for every matter has a time and procedure," is clear. The second statement, "man's misfortune weighs heavy upon him," is unexpected here. What is the point of the juxtaposition?

Ra'at ha'adam might be translated "man's evil" and understood as the evil that man does, but the sore point in this passage is not the evil in man's actions so much as the misfortune he suffers: the human tragedy. The nature of this misfortune is explained in the preceding and following verses: Everything has an opportune time and a proper way of doing it, yet man cannot know the future, and so can only wait and watch for things to come to pass. Being ignorant, he lacks *šilṭon*, control over what befalls him.

The "man" upon whom the human tragedy weighs so heavily is, first and foremost, Qohelet himself. As he says, "for I was distressed by what happens under the sun" (2:17), using a very similar expression: *ra' 'alay,* lit. "evil upon me," which is synonymous with *ra'at (ha'adam) rabbah 'alayw,* lit. "for the evil (of man) is great upon him," in the present verse.

Verse 6b is introduced by *ki,* but the clause cannot be causal except in the vaguest way: the reason I'm saying all this is. . . .

In *Contradictions,* I explained vv. 5f. as referring to the evil done to man by human authorities and identified the *mišpaṭ* as the future judgment upon the evil ruler. But, though v. 9 may suggest otherwise, Qohelet has not yet described any wrongs committed by the ruler. He has, however, spoken of doing the right thing at the right time in the presence of the king, and this is a matter of *'et umišpaṭ.*

8:7 Knowledge of when something will be (7b) would allow knowledge of *what* will be (7a), because there is nothing new, and the real unknown is the timing. In insisting that the future is hidden, Qohelet is using, not challenging, traditional wisdom. Proverbs too insists that man cannot know the morrow (27:1; cf. Sir 11:19), and this is a commonplace of Egyptian Wisdom (see Fox 1985a). But Qohelet alone seems oppressed by the ignorance.

This unit conveys an impression of strain and struggle. This is not a struggle of Qohelet with traditional wisdom, but a struggle of Qohelet with himself, because the "traditional wisdom" is his as well. Qohelet is not setting forth traditional wisdom in vv. 5-6a in order to challenge it in vv. 6b-7, as Crenshaw maintains. The relation is more subtle. Qohelet elsewhere does contradict 8:5, if that statement is taken as an absolute, but not even the most conservative sages supposed that the wise man never suffers *any* misfortune. But the other sages had ways of resolving the dilemma of the unfair misfortunes they saw (§3.6), while Qohelet sees the dilemma as a deep contradiction. He broods on this dilemma in a number of verses. The problem cannot be resolved piecemeal. The issue is discussed in §§3.3, 3.4.

Qohelet does not dispute the unquestionably traditional and almost self-evident idea that the wise man knows the proper time and procedure (8:5b). Otherwise he would not, after all, be wise. On the contrary, Qohelet confirms it in a number of counsels and remarks that assume and praise the adaptability and dexterity of the wise (§5.3). *And yet* he is painfully (8:6b) aware that man, even the wisest, is blind to the future (v. 7). Logically, this is no more contradictory than 11:6, which does not trouble the commentators. Sowing in the morning and evening (11:6a) means knowing *'et umišpaṭ* (8:5b), and not knowing "which will prosper" (11:6b) is equivalent to not knowing "what will happen" (8:7a).

The sages would agree with both statements in this verse. Qohelet alone feels a tension. That must be because he expects more and is frustrated to get less. He assumes a strong definition of "knowledge," as if knowledge must be complete (within the relevant domain) and fully reliable. Anything less is too little.

C. 8:8-9. Other Regards in Which Man Lacks Control

8:8 "No man has control over the *ruaḥ* so as to retain the *ruaḥ*." Since *ruaḥ* means wind as well as spirit, the first sentence can be an analogy: "(Just as) no man controls the wind so as to cage *(liklo')* the wind, so too there is no control. . . ." But since *ruaḥ* also means soul or life-spirit, this sentence is immediately reread in the light of the next one as alluding to the escape of the life-spirit at death, when, as Qohelet says later, "the spirit returns to God, who gave it" (12:7).

This verse picks up the theme of control from v. 4 and reminds us that, however powerful the authority (*šilṭon*, v. 4) that one man may wield over others, no one has control (*šilṭon*) over his life-spirit (*ruaḥ*, as in 3:19) in the day of death, so as to keep hold of it. This incapacity has a positive side: a ruler's death frees his people from tyranny (Job 3:17-19), at least till the next one comes along.

"And there is no release *(mišlaḥat)* in war": Translating *mišlaḥat* as "delegation" (Rashbam: "a delegation of his soldiers to do battle with the angel of death"; cf. Ps 78:49) is far-fetched. *Mišlaḥat* here probably means "release," "furlough" (Barton), since this verse denies the possibility of different kinds of escape.

What is this "war"? Although we expect another reference to the inescapability of death, there is no evidence that dying itself was viewed as a battle, a "Todeskampf," "death struggle" (thus Ehrlich). Taken literally, the third sentence seems to be an adage to the effect that a soldier cannot be released once the battle is joined, Deut 20:5-7 to the contrary. In that passage, the reason for releasing certain men from battle — those who recently built a house, planted a vineyard, or betrothed a woman — is that they might die and others receive their new acquisitions. These eventualities constitute a curse in Deut 28:30. The law has a utopian cast, because it presumes that the mass of soldiers *want* to go to war and will leave only if dismissed for good reasons.[36] The law belongs to Deuteronomy's ideal of Holy War in the invasion of the Land (and might even be a reflex of a stereotypical curse), not to the ordinary business of running an army. If Qohelet, who is familiar with Deuteronomy (see the comment on 5:3f.), says there is no release from battle, he may be implying that a soldier cannot be protected from losing a precious new possession that he himself has not yet been allowed to enjoy. This is a type of tragedy Qohelet mentions in 6:2 and which recalls the patterns of futility curses, on which see the comment on 2:26. Read thus, this sentence gives an example of the inescapability of death and loss.

MT's "and wickedness will not give its possessor an escape" (from death) is a warning that no one would need, for though an evildoer might imagine that he could escape death *in spite of* his wickedness, no one would expect to escape *because* of it. Ginsberg's emendation of *rš'* to *'šr* "wealth" is attractive, especially since "possessor *(beʿalim)* of wealth" is a more natural idiom than "possessor of wickedness."

The truth of the statement that wealth will not allow its possessor to escape (death) is not self-evident. Escape from death does not mean immortality but rather avoidance of disaster in the here and now. One might suppose that he could bribe his way out of danger or hire guards, for example. Against this, Prov 11:4 warns, "Wealth [*hon*] will not avail in the day of wrath, but righteousness saves from death." Qoh 8:8b is the exact ob-

---

36. Judah Maccabee applied the law (at least according to the author of 1 Macc 3:56) in order to align his warfare with Joshua's, not because it was the common practice in his day.

verse of Prov 11:4b. The latter sentence is a coinage that Ezekiel rephrases as "Their silver and their gold will not be able to save them in the day of the Lord's wrath" (7:19aβ). Prov 11:28 says, "He who trusts in his wealth (*'ošro*) will fall, but the righteous will blossom like foliage." In other words, one *could* trust in wealth for deliverance, but he would be deluding himself.

8:9 *Kol ma'áśeh 'ăšer na'ăśah . . . :* These words refer to events, because the unit does not reflect on what people *do* when they have authority so much as what *happens* as a result.

"When one man has control over another — to his harm": It would have been enough to say "when one man has control over another." Qohelet reveals his suspicion of authority by appending *l^era' lo* "to his harm," recalling the way he introduces a parenthetical comment by adding a superfluous "fools" in 4:17 and 7:5. "To his harm" is ambiguous. Those who are subject to human authority are harmed, but Qohelet may also be claiming that the authorities themselves are injured by their power (Crenshaw).

◆ 8:10-15

(10a) And then I saw the wicked <brought to^a> the grave, and they proceeded from the holy place^b, while those who had acted honestly were neglected in the city.

(10b) This too is an absurdity: (11) the sentence for a wicked deed is not carried out quickly. That is why people's hearts are intent on doing evil. (12) For an offender may do evil <for years^c> but live long. And I also know that it will go well with the God-fearing, because they are afraid of him, (13) and that it will not go well with the wicked man, and, like a shadow, he will not live long, because he does not fear God.

(14) There is an absurdity that happens on the earth: there are righteous people who receive what is appropriate to the deeds of the wicked, and there are wicked people who receive what is appropriate to the deeds of the righteous. I said that this too is absurd.

(15) So I praised pleasure, because there is nothing good for man under the sun but to eat, drink, and experience pleasure, and this will accompany him in his toil throughout the days of his life, which God has given him under the sun.

^a*q^ebārîm mûbā'îm* (MT *q^ebûrîm wābā'û*)

^b*ûmimmāqôm* (MT *ûmimm^eqôm*)

^c*mē'āz* (MT *m^e'at*)

A. 8:10-14. Injustices

B. 8:15. Praise of pleasure

Contemplation of the unfair way that people are treated when they die (8:10a) provokes thoughts on an even more severe injustice: the way that God allocates their lifespans. In 8:10b-14, as in 2:18-26, Qohelet describes a single scenario in several ways, repeatedly calling it absurd. The absurdity considered here is that an offender (here, a sinner) may live a long life, while a righteous person may die young. Since the punishment that Qohelet has in mind here is a sentence of premature death, a delay in punishment is tantamount to failure to carry it out. The theological implications of this crucial passage are discussed in §§3.32, 3.4. *Hebel* throughout this unit is predicated of a fact or event rather than of an action. As often, when Qohelet descends too deeply into disheartening thoughts, he recovers by prescribing pleasure (8:15).

A. 8:10-14. Injustices

8:10a *Ub^eken* means "and then" or "next" in a series; cf. Esth 4:16 and Aramaic *bkyn*. MT's *qbrym wb'w wmmqwm* is garbled. (The MT of 10a has to be translated "I saw the wicked buried, and they came, and from a holy place they went about.") Ginsberg emends to *q^erēbîm* "approach," that is, they drew near to the priestly service, where they exercised their duties wickedly and "profaned the Holy Place" (reading *ûm^eqôm qādôš y^eḥallēlû*). These emendations are not large, but the context says nothing about priestly service and probably nothing about the temple. Instead, it reflects on the treatment of the wicked generally. LXX (εἰς τάφους εἰσαχθέντας) represents *qbrym mwb'ym*[37] *(BHS)*, which is definitely the better reading. The continuation, καὶ ἐκ τόπου ἁγίου ἐπορεύθησαν, agrees with MT's *wmmqwm qdwš yhlkw*. We should emend to *qeber mûbā'îm* "brought to (the) grave" (BHK, Gordis) or *q^ebārîm mûbā'îm*, lit. "brought to the graves." The latter seems awkward, but the plural has versional support and has a parallel in Job 21:32f., in which Job complains of the very injustice Qohelet describes: "But [the wicked man] is brought to the tomb [*w^ehu' liqbarot yubal*], and he keeps watch over

---

37. The retroversion of εἰσαχθέντας to *mwb'ym* is not certain, since εἰσάγω-passive twice represents BW'-qal (Num 27:17 [though there it is used in a free rendering of a fixed idiom] and 1 Kgs 7:14 [LXX 7:2]). Of the twenty-three times that BW'-hophal occurs in the Bible, it is represented by εἰσάγω-passive only three times. It is, however, represented by other compounds of ἄγω in the passive five times. In Aq, εἰσάγω (only active) always represents BW'-hiphil, so the passive is an expected rendering of the hophal.

a heap, and everyone draws after him, and before him people without number." The passive *yubal* recalls the proposed *muba'im*. The plural *q^ebarot* or *q^ebarim* can refer to the burial area, with multiple graves or burial niches. In sum, we should emend 10a to *ûb^ekēn rā'îtî r^ešā'îm q^ebārîm mûbā'îm*.

The "holy place" is either the temple (the τόπος ἅγιος of Matt 24:15) or the synagogue, not the cemetery, which was ritually unclean. The absence of the article favors the synagogue rather than the temple, *the* Holy Place *par excellence*. This is supported by the usage in synagogue inscriptions of the Talmudic period, which call the synagogue *'tr' qdyš* "the holy place." The verse presupposes a custom of honoring a dead person by beginning the funeral procession at the synagogue. The piel *y^ehalleku* means "go about" (focusing on the movement rather than the destination). "Go about" is suitable for the movement of a funeral procession, like *sab^ebu* "go about" in 12:5. A custom of eulogizing the dead (called *hesped*) in the synagogue is attested in the Talmud (b. Meg. 28b; b. Rosh Hashanah 25a; b. Moed Q. 21b). We should probably point *maqom* as absolute, as in Lev 6:9, 19, 20, etc.; see GKC §128w, n. 1 (MT may be understanding *qadoš* as an epithet of God).

Verse 10aβ, *w^eyištakk^ehu ba'ir 'ăšer ken 'aśu*, is usually thought to mean that honest people are forgotten soon after death. But that fate would not distinguish them from the wicked, since "in the days to come both [the fool and the wise man] are soon forgotten" (2:16), and furthermore the phrase "in the city" would be superfluous if *w^eyištakk^ehu* means that the memory of them is lost, for it is forgotten everywhere. Rather, the honest people are "forgotten" insofar as their corpses are *neglected* at the time of their death. This is not to say that the bodies of the dead are left within the city forever, but rather that immediately after their death, when they should be buried, they lie in neglect, while the wicked receive obsequies and are brought in procession from the city to the cemetery outside the walls. ŠKH "forget" can imply neglect in deed rather than a lapse of memory; for example, Ps 9:19 (neglecting a poor person, not caring for him); Ps 102:5 (neglecting to eat one's food); Isa 49:15 (a woman neglecting her baby); Deut 24:19 (leaving a sheaf lying in the field).

The variant *wyštbhw*, "were praised" (LXX, Aq, and some MSS), requires taking *ken* in *ken 'aśu* to mean "thus" ("and those who did thus were praised in the city"), but there is no antecedent action to which "thus" could refer.

8:10b   I take the *hebel*-judgment in 8:10b as introducing a new passage (thus Wildeboer, Ginsberg). To be sure, the exact clause *gam zeh hebel* does not elsewhere introduce a scenario, but Qohelet does label a phenomenon *hebel* prior to describing it in 8:14 (and cf. 4:7). In 5:15, *w^egam zoh ra'ah holah* introduces the description of a misfortune. This clause is structurally the same as *gam zeh hebel* in 8:10b, except for the additional *waw,* which should perhaps be read in this verse as well (haplography; thus Ginsberg). If *gam zeh hebel* were retrospective, in accordance with the Masoretic verse-division and most commentators, *'ăšer* in v. 11 would begin a new section and lack a discernible function. Causality would be inappropriate, since v. 11 does not motivate v. 10, and *'ăšer* as a causal conjunction is never prospective. But whether the clause is applied to v. 10a or to vv. 11-13, the meaning of *hebel* is the same, because both the preceding and the following passages describe an unjust, absurd situation. If "this too is an absurdity" looks forward, the "too" shows that the preceding likewise is an absurdity.

8:11 *'Ăšer* here is best translated "namely," "the fact that," or represented by a colon. Syntactically, it is noun-equivalent (Ginsberg) in apposition to a preceding substantive (in this case, *hebel*); similarly in 8:14a (second *'ăšer*) and 9:1aβ.

Na'ăśāh should be pointed *na'ăśeh* (masculine). The MT regularly points *'ŚH-*niphal as the perfect, *na'ăśāh,* even where the participle *(na'ăśeh)* seems appropriate. This pointing is supported by the plural perfect *na'ăśû* in 1:14. In 8:11, however, a participle is required, since the negator is *'eyn.*

"Hearts are intent on doing evil"; lit. "the heart of people is full in them to do evil." Most commentators understand this to mean "dare" (Ginsberg, Delitzsch, Gordis, Hertzberg, et al.); others explain it as "be inclined," "desire" (Podechard). The parallel commonly adduced for the former, *'ăšer mĕla'o libbo la'ăśot,* "whose heart has filled him to do . . ." (Esth 7:5), is itself ambiguous, and the expression "(his) heart filled him" may imply something quite different from "(their) heart is full." The notion of the heart being "full" of something is an extension of having something "in" one's heart (see the two phrasings in 9:3bα), and the latter idiom implies desire or intention (Isa 63:4; Jer 20:9; Ps 84:6; Prov 2:10a [note the parallel "be pleasant to your soul" in 10b]); it can also imply knowledge; e.g., Isa 51:7. In Qoh 9:3, the notion of desire and inclination is clearly more relevant than daring, for there the phrase is not followed by an infinitive that might indicate what they dare to do.

Just how the punishment is delayed is shown by v. 12a: the sinner is allowed to live long. A timely judgment, then, would be an early death. Qohelet is not denying the working of divine retribution in all cases. He is observing that there are cases where God postpones the punishment past the point where it would be an effective warning.

Ma'ărik lo = ma'ărik lo yamim, lit. "lengthens days for him" (cf. 8:13).
The subject of *ma'ărik* may be the man (as in 7:15 and 8:13) or God (as in 1
Kgs 3:14).

8:12f.   Here the "offender" *is* a sinner, as usually in the Bible, for if he were
not immoral, his long life would not affront Qohelet's sense of justice.

MT's *me'at,* lit. "does evil one hundred of," is impossible. LXX's ἀπὸ
τότε (SyH *mn hydyn*) reflects *me'az,* "from of old," "for years" (ἀπὸ τότε =
me'az in Exod 4:10 [Aq]; Ps 76:8; 93:2 [LXX, Sym]; Prov 8:22 [Aq, Theod];
and Isa 16:13 [Theod]). LXX's reading hardly arises from misunderstanding
m't as *mē'ēt* "from" (contrary to Euringer and Gordis), which would have
been translated ἀπὸ καιροῦ (as it is in five of its six occurrences in the HB),
and which would make no sense here. *Me'az* is precisely what is required by
the context, to emphasize that the punishment is delayed.

The assumption that *ki gam* (v. 12b), like *gam ki,* means "although"
(Gordis, and widely followed) is not well established. Even if it were, that
would not help Gordis's case, since Qohelet would be saying: "(I observe
that) an offender may do evil <for years> but live long, *although* I also know
that it will go well with the God-fearing, etc." There is indeed a concessive
relationship between the sentences (*X although Y* means that Y could be expected to negate X but does not), but it is not inherent in the phrase *ki gam.*
The particle *gam* can introduce a concessive or adversative clause, but this is
a function of the semantic relationship between it and the preceding clause,
not of the particle itself. (See Ellermeier 1967:247-53, esp. 252.) The problem lies in the use of *ki,* which often seems depleted of any explanatory or
causal function and may be labeled emphatic for lack of a more specific explanation. Nowhere else is the force of *ki gam* clearly concessive. In 7:22, *ki
gam* comprises two independent particles, "for" + "also" (as is the case elsewhere in the Bible). In 4:14, 16; 8:16; and 9:12 its force is unclear, but it is
not concessive. It seems that *ki + gam* in Qohelet usually introduces and calls
attention to a concomitant fact, much like *w'gam.* Thus *ki gam zeh hebel* in
4:16b is equivalent to *w'gam zeh hebel* in 7:6.

There is no sign that 8:12b-13 are the words or opinion of another person or party. See §1.53. Rather, v. 12 says: "It is a fact that . . . and I also
know that. . . ." Although Qohelet "knows" the principle of retribution and
nowhere denies it, he *also* knows there are cases that violate the rule. It is because Qohelet holds to the axioms of Wisdom that he is shocked by their violation and finds the aberrations absurd.

In v. 13, *kaṣṣel* is parenthetical to the preceding negative clause: *lo'
ya'ărik yamim.* Man does not endure just as the shadow does not endure.

8:14 Qohelet restates vv. 10b-13. Given this context, v. 14 is best understood as a complaint about undeserved brevity or length of life rather than
about all sorts of undeserved contingencies.

Ma'ăśeh haṣṣaddiqim and *ma'ăśeh har^eša'im* are probably the deeds of
people, their behavior seen as a whole. It is also possible that the phrases refer to what *happens to* the righteous and the wicked (thus Ehrlich, Crenshaw;
cf. Isa 32:17 and Hab 3:17).

B. 8:15. Praise of Pleasure

8:15 *'Amal* here seems to mean toil in a broad sense — the burdens of
life — for pleasure should accompany a person in life generally, not precisely when he is doing his work; see §6.14.

Praise of pleasure is not an obvious response to the injustice Qohelet has
just described. Elsewhere, when Qohelet broods about the impossibility of
holding on to the fruits of toil, it is logical to advise their immediate enjoyment.
But the fact of undeserved lifespans is not directly relevant to the enjoyment of
life. The ideas are connected by an unstated link: the effect of diversion. Here,
as in 5:17f., Qohelet is recommending pleasure as a distraction from the painful awareness of realities such as he has just described. Man cannot change
these things; he can only alleviate the distress they cause him as observer.

◆ 8:16–9:10

*(16) When I set my heart to gain wisdom and to observe the business
that occurs on the earth (<my^a> eyes seeing sleep neither by day nor by
night), (17) I saw that man cannot grasp anything that God makes happen,
that is to say, the events that occur under the sun, for even if a man seeks arduously, he will not grasp (them). And even if the wise man intends to understand, he is not able to grasp (them).*

*(9:1) Now I considered all this carefully, and <my heart saw^b> all this,
that the righteous and the wise and their deeds are in the hand of God. Also,
man has no knowledge of love or hate. Everything one sees is (2) <absurd^c>,
inasmuch as all have the same fate: the righteous and the wicked, the good
<and the bad^d>, and the pure and the impure, and he who gives sacrifice and
he who does not give sacrifice; the good man just as the offender, the one
who swears oaths just as the one who fears to swear. (3) This is <the worst^e>
of all that happens under the sun, that all have the same fate. What's more,
people's heart is full of evil, and inanity is in their hearts while they live. And
afterwards: to the dead!*

*(4) Now whosoever is still joined to all the living has something he can
be sure of (for a live dog is better off than a dead lion), (5) for the living know*

*that they will die, while the dead know nothing and no longer have any rec-
ompense, for their memory is forgotten. (6) Even their love, their hatred, and
their jealousy have already perished, and they never more have a portion in
all that happens under the sun.*

*(7) Go, eat your bread in pleasure and drink your wine with a merry
heart, for God has already favored what you are doing. (8) Let your garments be white at all times, and let oil not be lacking for your head. (9) Enjoy
life with a woman you love during all your absurd days that God gives you
under the sun, all your absurd days, for this is your portion in life and in your
toil at which you labor under the sun. (10) All that you are able to do, do <in
accordance withᶠ> your strength, for there is no activity or calculation or
knowledge or wisdom in Sheol, where you are headed.*

ᵃ*beʿêynay ʾêynennî* (MT *beʿêynāyw ʾêynennû*)
ᵇ*welibbî rāʾāh* (MT *welābûr*)
ᶜ*hābel* (MT *hakkōl,* joined to v. 2)
ᵈadd *welāraʿ*
ᵉ*zeh hārāʿ* (MT *zeh rāʿ*)
ᶠ*kᵉkōḥăkā* (MT *bᵉkōḥăkā*)

A. 8:16-17. The failure of the search for understanding
B. 9:1-3. The universality of death
C. 9:4-6. Life's superiority to death
D. 9:7-10. The enjoyment of life

The unit strings various topics in a single train of thought. The observation of
8:16f. is rephrased and explained in 9:1: The fact that people cannot understand what happens in life means that they cannot even understand the ways
of God's favor. And everything they see is absurd (9:1-2), inasmuch as all
people, whatever their merits, suffer the same fate. 9:2 *(ka'ăšer . . .)* is the
pivot, linked syntactically to v. 1 while introducing a new topic — death, the
ultimate absurdity.

Vv. 7-10 constitute the climax of this unit, because the advice to enjoy
the pleasures of life always comes in response to a depressing thought about
its unfairness.

A. 8:16-17. The Failure of the Search for Understanding

8:16f. Man cannot understand what happens in life. Wisdom, which alone
might be expected to provide this understanding, can only lead to frustration.

These verses echo 1:13-18, where Qohelet defined his task and summed up the results. The meaning and implications of this important passage are discussed in §5.11. §6.23 examines the phraseology of 8:16f., in particular the ways it designates what the wise man is searching for.

Lada'at ḥokmah in 8:16 means "to attain (or possess) wisdom," as in 1:17, q.v. In 1:18, Qohelet said that wisdom leads to misery. In 8:17 he says it leads nowhere, for it cannot achieve its goal of understanding life. Qoh 8:16f. (a single complex sentence) restates 7:23f., which says that it is impossible to grasp *(mi yimṣa'ennu)* "that which happens," in other words, "what God makes happen."

In 8:16a, the "business" *(ha'inyan)* that is done on earth is the same as *kol hamma'ăśim šenna'ăśu taḥat haššameš* in 1:14a. (The "business" in 8:16a is not, however, the search for wisdom, though that is called *'inyan ra'* in 1:13b.) Qohelet is observing wisdom (8:16aα) in the course of examining life (16aβγ). The *'inyan* and *ma'ăśim* in 8:16f. are events (§6.23).

In 8:16b, MT has "he does not see sleep with his eyes." There is no antecedent for the third person, and emendation to the first person is called for. This assumes only a minor *waw-yod* confusion.

8:17a   This is a proleptic construction with a precise parallel in Jon 3:10, where *ki* introduces epexegesis of the direct object of *wayyar'*: "God saw what they had done, namely that they had repented of their evil ways." See Ellermeier 1967:295-300.

Since *kol . . . ha'ělohim* is the proleptic direct object of *lo yukal limṣo'*, the *kol* is negatived, and a negatived *kol* may mean "not any" as well as "not all." "Not any" is to be preferred here rather than "not all," which would impute to Qohelet the ludicrous complaint that he was unable to understand the *totality* of the events that God makes happen (similarly in 3:11). We should translate, "cannot grasp them." This, however, must be understood as hyperbole, since Qohelet nowhere insists on absolute and utter ignorance, and he himself "grasps" or "finds" *(maṣa')* many things. Qohelet is asserting that no one can understand the rationale of events in life as a whole. This statement is still hyperbolic, but it is more meaningful than complaining about the inability to know *everything*.

8:17b   *B'ešel ăšer* is an Aramaism, from *b'dil d-*. In a nearly identical form, *b'ešel še-*, the idiom appears in 4QMMT B 12, C 32 and in a letter of Bar Kokhba (DJD 2.165f.), where it means "so that" (Qimron 1986:89). In this verse, the phrase introduces a causal clause (as the Aramaic equivalent can do) rather than a final or result clause.

W^egam 'im yo'mar hehakam lada'at: This clause is usually understood to refer to the wise man's *claim* to have this knowledge. This understanding is reflected in most translations, for example, Zimmerli's: "Und auch wenn der Weise behauptet es zu erkennen, er kann es nicht herausfinden." ("And even if the wise man claims to know, he can not find it out.") Barton, on the basis of inadequate parallels, translates: "Even if the wise man thinks he is about to know. . . ." Delitzsch correctly interprets this phrase in accordance with *'amarti 'ehkamah* in 7:23, where *'amar* (lit. "say") undoubtedly means "intend" rather than "claim." *'Amar* often indicates intention (BDB 56a). Note also that *w^egam 'im yo'mar hehakam lada'at* generalizes Qohelet's description of his own activity in 8:16, *ka'ăšer natatti 'et libbi lada'at hokmah. Yo'mar* ("says") corresponds to *natatti 'et libbi,* "I set my heart," lit. "gave my heart," which means "determined," *not* "claimed." The point of the verse is: *Even* a wise man — the one best equipped to gain knowledge — who undertakes to attain this knowledge must fail in the quest.

B. 9:1-3. The Universality of Death

9:1-2 The opening *ki* is a loose causal particle that explains why the above is said rather than why it is true. (On the "evidential" function of *ki* see Claasen 1983:37-44.) It is often impossible to render this relation in English without overloading the sentence ("I am led to say all this by the fact that . . .").

The LXX has καὶ καρδία μου σὺν πᾶν εἶδεν τοῦτο (followed by SyH). The translation is mechanical (with an Aquilan σύν for *'et*), but the Greek cannot be directly retroverted, because that would produce an impossible word order in Hebrew *(wlby 't kl r'h zh).* Thus there is an inner-Greek transposition in the LXX. Nevertheless, the Greek does represent *wlby r'h,* which is preferable to MT's syntactically impossible *wlbwr 't* ("and to examine . . ."). The only consonantal changes assumed in emending to *wlby r'h* are a *waw/yod* interchange and a loss of *'h* through near-haplography with *'t.*

'Ăbādêhem "their deeds" (not *'abdêyhem,* "their slaves"!) is an Aramaism equivalent to Hebrew *ma'ăśeyhem.* LXX correctly renders ἐργασίαι. Though Ginsberg does not adduce this case on behalf of his hypothesis that the Hebrew of Qohelet is a translation from Aramaic, this is a case where his theory works well. It is difficult to understand why an author composing in Hebrew would use a common Hebrew word, *ma'ăśeh,* numerous times, then suddenly use an Aramaism (apparently unattested in Hebrew of any period) that expresses no more than the Hebrew equivalent does. It seems more likely that a translator would understand *'bd'* (pl. *'bdy'*) correctly

most of the time but misread it in one occurrence. He may have been misled by the conjunction of *'bdyhwn* (which can be read either "their deeds" or "their slaves") with two nouns that refer to classes of people. The Masoretes, however, did recognize the correct sense of the word and indicated it in vocalization.

"In the hand of God" means "under God's control." Of course, *everyone* is under God's control, but the righteous and the wise might be thought to determine their own fate, because (Wisdom teaches) they shape their own blessings, unlike the wicked, who suffer disasters they cannot control and which are (to them) a surprise. As Job says of the wicked, "their good fortune *(ṭubam)* is not in their hand" (21:16a).

That the deeds *('ăbādêyhem)* of the wise and righteous are "in God's hand" need not mean that he allows humans no slack, that he predetermines every little thing that they do. Rather, it means that he *can* control the outcome. Even an absolute monarch allows his subjects some room for maneuver, and to some extent they determine what happens to them. But they are not free, and if the monarch is not consistent in his rewards and punishments, they can never know quite where they stand.

"Also, man has no knowledge of love or hate" in 9:1aβ reformulates 8:16-17, which says that no one can understand *ma'ăśeh ha'ĕlohim,* "God's doing," which is to say, all that he brings to pass. To understand "God's doing" means to understand the workings of his favor and displeasure. Hence "love" and "hate" in 9:1 are not human emotions in the abstract, as if to say that human psychology is incomprehensible. That would not be relevant to the immediate context or the book as a whole. "Love" and "hate" here are God's favor and disfavor toward individuals. It is the *divine* psychology that is obscure. You cannot know whom or what God loves and hates until you see the effects of his attitude. And this applies *even* to the wise and the righteous. Qohelet spoke about the wise earlier: the man who labors in wisdom but loses his earnings to one God favors (2:21-26).

MT ends v. 1 with *hkl lpnyhm,* lit. "all is before them," and starts v. 2 with *kl k'šr lkl,* "All as to all," neither of which says much. We should read *hkl lpnyhm hbl (hakkōl lipnêyhem hābel)* (Barton, McNeile). *Hakkol lipneyhem,* lit. "all that is before them," means "all that they see," or, since the third plural is indefinite: "everything one sees." Compare *lipney* in *ṭob lipney ha'ĕlohim* (2:26), where "before" indicates mental perspective, not futurity. The verse division should fall before *ka'ăšer* in v. 2a, and *hkl* should be emended to *hbl.* LXX (SyH), Sym, Vul, and Syr read *hbl* at the juncture of vv. 1 and 2. (Syr has *hbl' kl = hbl hkl,* probably a conflate reading.)

The text as emended — "Everything one sees is absurd" — is an amplification of "man has no knowledge of (God's) love or hate." God's inexplicable allocation of fates makes his attitudes inscrutable and, to human eyes, arbitrary.

9:2-3a In 8:11-14, Qohelet described an injustice that befalls some people — they are assigned lifetimes shorter or longer than they deserve. Now he remarks on an injustice that befalls all: death. Equal fates for unequal persons is an absurdity from which not even the fortunate are exempt. Qohelet alone in the Bible complains about the universality of death.

In the otherwise paired series, *laṭṭob* stands alone. We should add *wᵉlāraʿ* with LXX (καὶ τῷ κακῷ). (LXX-Qoh is too mechanical to have added a word for the sake of literary balance.) This is confirmed by SyH, as well as Syr and Vul.

9:3b Observing the universality of death provokes man to inane, irrational behavior. In 8:11f., it was the observation of inequitable lifespans that had this effect.

Zeh raʿ bᵉkol ʾăšer naʿăśah: Vul, Ibn Ezra, Ginsburg, and others understand this phrase as a superlative (*"the* worst thing"), and some interpret it as a virtual superlative without emending (Gordis: "the root of the evil"; Lauha, in comment: "das Grundübel"). A superlative does seem required here, for the universality of death is not a misfortune or evil *in* all events; it is rather *the* worst of all that happens, for it is a fundamental and irreparable inequity. Since the anarthrous noun + *bᵉ*- does not (contrary to Ginsburg) constitute a superlative, we should read *zh hrʿ* (haplography; thus Ehrlich).

C. 9:4-6. Life's Superiority to Death

9:4 What advantage do the living have over the dead? Only their awareness of death. *Biṭṭaḥon* is not a feeling of hope or inner security (knowing that one will die brings neither), but rather something that one can rely on and be confident of (cf. Isa 36:4). It is in this regard that a living dog is better off than a dead lion, because the living possess one trustworthy scrap of knowledge while the dead lack even this. The tone is ironic, perhaps sardonic, but Qohelet is not undermining the statement.

The *lamed* of *lᵉkeleb* is not emphatic (contra Gordis), because an emphatic particle would precede the predicate. It is a *lamed* of benefit (or "interest"), and the *huʾ* is impersonal (and strange, before an impersonal verbal adjective). Thus: "because it is better for a live dog than (for) a dead lion" or, more idiomatically: "a live dog is better off than a dead lion." The first part of the sentence is a variant of the common expression, *ṭob l^e-X* (with X indicating the beneficiary); e.g., 2:3; 6:12; 8:12. The *lamed* is elided after the preposition in *min ha'aryeh*.

9:5 The dead know nothing and have no more recompense. What is the recompense they *did* have while alive? *Śakar* essentially means "wage" or "reward." A *śakar* is never an outright gift, but is always a benefit or payment given in compensation for something of value, usually work or merit (Gen 15:1; Ps 127:3). Qohelet applies the word, somewhat strangely, to benefits that are not really recompense. The benefits two men gain from their companionship are "a good *śakar* in their toil," yet the examples listed are instances of mutual aid, not remuneration or rewards for labor or merit. When he says that the dead have no more *śakar,* the implication is that there *are* cases of recompense in life. Some of them will be enumerated in 9:7-9: eating one's bread, etc. These are equivalent to the *ḥeleq* one may get from his toil, meaning life's toil generally (see esp. 9:9, where *'amal* is parallel to *ḥayyim* "life"). These "compensations" or "portions" evaporate with death. *If* remembrance persisted, *that* might be reckoned an adequate compensation for righteousness, but it does not (2:16). In this regard, Qohelet unequivocally departs from traditional wisdom, for example Prov 10:7: "The memory of the righteous is for a blessing, while the name of the wicked will rot." Qohelet (like the cynics quoted in Wis 2:4) sees no distinctions.

In 9:5, Qohelet asserts that (contrary to 4:3) "[c]onsciousness on any terms is preferable to nonexistence, and knowledge, however limited and melancholy in content, is better than ignorance" (Gordis).

> "Actually," says the stranger, "I was sure of myself, sure about everything, far surer than he; sure of my present life and of the death that was coming. That, no doubt, was all I had; but at least that certainty was something I could get my teeth into — just as it had got its teeth into me." (Camus, *The Stranger,* p. 151)

9:6 Man's "portion" includes his feelings, among them his love, hatred, and envy. One who has these has a "portion in all that happens under the sun." They are man's portion because he holds them as his rightful possession. These emotions, so important to their possessors, are not necessarily persistent or pleasant. Nevertheless, they belong to the totality of life's experiences, and are therefore (according to this verse, at least) better than the darkness that awaits us.

D. 9:7-10. The Enjoyment of Life

It is good to enjoy life and take hold of its possibilities, simply because that is what we have in the present, while the void of death stretches on forever. Ben Sira, in dependency on this passage, offers similar advice in 14:11-15, especially: "Remember that there is no pleasure to be had in Sheol, and death will not tarry, and the limit of Sheol has not been told you" (v. 12).[38] The strikingly similar advice in the Egyptian "Harper Song" is quoted in §1.43.

9:7 As always when praising pleasure, Qohelet observes that it is God's gift. Now he goes farther: not only does God allow you enjoyment, he *wants* you to have it — if you are one of the fortunate.

$K^e bar\ ra\d{s}ah$ "has already favored" functions in context as a future perfect, with the "already" situated vis-à-vis the moment of enjoyment rather than the present (the narrative present of speaking and hearing), and we could translate, though awkwardly, "will have favored." For other examples see *GBH* §112i. In other words, the sentence does not imply that God has at some time in the past chosen you as one who will enjoy life, but if and when you do so, that will be *post facto* a sign of divine approbation of your pleasures. We may compare the way that the Puritans regarded material good fortune as a token of belonging to God's elect.

9:9 "A woman you love": Some commentators assure us that despite the lack of an article, *'iššah* must mean a specific woman, namely one's wife. But a bare noun followed by a relative clause is indefinite, and "a woman" is the correct translation. Ginsburg and Barton did understand "a woman" to allow for concubines and felt it smacked of "voluptuousness." Still, it is hard to see what Qohelet could have in mind besides marriage. "Enjoy life" — lit. "see life" — means more than an occasional dalliance, and a concubine was an unusual luxury and unlikely to be a man's sole companion ("*a* woman you love," not "women"). The point is that a man should marry a woman he loves, not, say, one who only brings a hefty dowry or family connections.

'Amal means "toil" in a very broad sense, not "wealth," for enjoying life with one's wife is not a portion a man has in his wealth, but is one that may accompany him throughout life's activities. Here too *'amal* is a near-synonym of *ḥayyim*.

---

38. This also recalls Qoh 3:21. Both authors are aware of a concept of afterlife, whether in heaven (Qohelet) or after resurrection (Ben Sira), but both are skeptical about it and set it aside as a viable response to life's difficulties.

The repetition *kol y^emey ḥayyey hebleka . . . kol y^emey hebl^eka* sounds a note of quiet melancholy and resigned finality reminiscent of the ending of Robert Frost's "Stopping by Woods on a Snowy Evening": "But I have promises to keep, / and miles to go before I sleep. / And miles to go before I sleep."

9:10 *Ma'ăśeh* here means "action" rather than "events." The reason for being active in life (v. 10a) is the absence of any *activity* afterwards (v. 10b).

Timṣa' yad^eka: The hand "finding" or "reaching" signifies metaphorically the concept of *ability* or of *affording* something (most clearly in Lev 12:8; 25:28; and Isa 10:10). Nowhere does it mean "happen to do (something)" without also implying the ability to do it. Qohelet is advising us to expend effort only in accordance with our abilities, to do what we can manage to do. The disjunctive accent belongs after *la'ăśot*.

For MT's *b^ekoḥăka,* "with your strength" (i.e., with your full strength), read *k^ekoḥăka,* "according to your strength," with LXX (and SyH) ἡ δύναμίς σου. (In 86 percent of its occurrences in Qohelet, ὡς corresponds to Heb *k^e-* [or *k^eše-*]. The one other occurrence of ὡς = MT *b^e* in Qohelet [9:10a], probably reflects *kaph* in the vorlage.) Qohelet does not recommend all-out expenditure of effort (as would be implied by *b^ekoḥăka*), but only moderate exertions in accordance with one's abilities.

Ibn Ezra, apparently with attention to the preceding context, applies 9:10a only to pleasurable acts rather than to other sorts such as work. But since the next sentence (v. 10b) motivates this one by reference to the entire range of human activities, the broadening of scope probably starts in v. 10a.

◆ 9:11-12

> *(11) I turned and saw that under the sun*
> *the race does not belong to the swift,*
> *nor the war to the mighty,*
> *nor bread to the wise,*
> *nor wealth to the intelligent,*
> *nor favor to the knowledgeable,*
> *for a time of mishap befalls them all.*

(12) Moreover, man does not know his time. Like fish caught in an evil net and birds caught in a trap, so are humans ensnared by a time of misfortune, when it falls upon them suddenly.

Talents and merits do not secure their deserved and expected results, because everyone is subject to the vagaries of chance and fortune.

9:11 *Ḥăkamim, nᵉbonim,* and *yodᵉ'im* are synonyms; compare the series in Dan 1:4.

"The race does not belong to the swift," lit. "the race is not to the swift" *(lo' laqqallim hammeroṣ),* does not mean that the swift always lose the race, but that they do not *possess* it. They do not control it, do not *necessarily* win it. It is not the loss of a race by the swiftest runner that troubles Qohelet, nor the poverty of a wise man as such, but rather the evidence such inequities provide of the ineffectuality of human skills and powers.

The wise *should* have bread, if not wealth (Prov 3:16; 8:18, 21; 22:4; 24:4), and the knowledgeable *should* have favor (Prov 3:4, 22; 4:9; 13:15). This is not a matter of moral deserts, but of fairness: skills and efforts should get their due rewards, as when the mighty man wins the battle and the swift wins the race.

The cause of this ineffectuality is *'et wapega',* lit. "time and accident" or "mishap." The phrase governs a singular verb and is a hendiadys equivalent to "a time of mishap." A time, as well as a misfortune, may "meet" *(yiqreh)* or befall someone (cf. 9:12b), because it is not a moment in the temporal continuum but a set of circumstances (a war, say, or a disease) that people find themselves in. See the introduction to 3:1-15.

Pega', like English "accident," can have connotations either neutral ("happening," "chance") or negative ("mishap," "disaster"). In its only other occurrence (1 Kgs 5:18), *pega'* is modified by *ra',* "evil," and it is unclear whether *ra'* is a necessary modifier or an addition for emphasis. In RH, according to Jastrow, *Dictionary,* it always connotes misfortune. The verb *paga'* can mean "encounter with hostility," "harm" (e.g., Josh 2:16; Judg 8:21), or simply "meet" (e.g., Gen 32:2; 1 Sam 10:5). But even if *'et wapega'* is semantically neutral, the occurrences Qohelet has in mind in this verse are unfortunate and deprive people of their due. Hence *'et wapega'* is equivalent to *'inyan ra'* "a bad business" in 5:13. It is synonymous with *'et ra'ah* "a time of misfortune" in v. 12, except that the latter verse refers to a particular misfortune while this one refers to any mishap.

Ginsberg says that *'et wapega'* is specifically the time of death. But the fact that everyone dies would not explain why the swift do not necessarily win the race, and so on. Verse 12 describes *another* evil, namely the arbitrary and inequitable character of death, which sets the seal on the misfortunes of life.

Murphy (p. 95) notes two passages with affinities to Qoh 9:2f. In Mal 1:2 (cf. Rom 9:13), God says, "Jacob I have loved, but Esau I have hated." This is a declaration of free divine choice, and it defines the poles of love and hate as God's two basic modes of relating to man. In the Babylonian "Dialogue of Pessimism," the slave seconds his master's statement that he will not do a benefit to his country: "Go up on the ancient ruin heaps and walk around, look at the skulls of the lowly and great. Which was the doer of evil, and which was the doer of good deeds?" (*BTM* 2.817). Death, as Qohelet emphasizes, wipes out distinctions.

9:12 Qohelet turns from discussion of mundane misfortunes to the time of the misfortune *par excellence:* death. *'Itto* here refers to the time of one's death, like *'itteka* in 7:17.

'Et ra'ah is a genitival phrase, "time of misfortune" like the synonymous *yom ra'ah* in 7:14. This time "falls" upon people, trapping them like a net. Again, *'et* is conceived of as a reality independent of the time-line and is in some sense external to individual lives. "Misfortune" can in itself refer to any calamitous circumstance or interval that may occur on earth; compare 7:14; 11:2. In this verse, misfortune is the particular calamity that causes one's death. In the Hebrew Bible, the quality of suddenness is usually associated with disaster (Daube 1964:5 and *passim*).

◆ **9:13–10:3**

(13) This too I have seen < — ᵃ> under the sun, and I regard it as significant:

(14) There was a small city with few people in it. And a great king came and encompassed it and built great siege works against it. (15) And he found in it a man who was poor but wise, and it was he who saved the city by his wisdom. Yet no one remembered that poor man.

(16) I said, "Better wisdom than might," yet the wisdom of the poor man is held in contempt, and his words are not heard.

(17) The words of the wise spoken gently are heard
more than the shout of a ruler among fools.

(18) Better wisdom than weapons,
yet one offender can destroy much of value.

(10:1) A fly <diesᵇ> and spoils a <chaliceᶜ> of perfumer's ointment.
Weightier than wisdomᵈ is a bit of folly.

(2) The wise man's heart is at his right,
and the fool's heart is at his left.

(3) And even when the fool walks in the road his heart is absent,
and it says to everyone, "He is a fool!"

[a]omitting *ḥokmah*

[b]*z^ebûb yāmût* (MT *z^ebûbêy māwet*)

[c]*g^ebîa'* (MT *yabbîa'*)

[d]omitting *mikkābōd*

A. 9:13-16. An anecdote about wisdom
B. 9:17–10:1. Wisdom's excellence and vulnerability
C. 10:2-3. How the fool harms himself

Qoh 9:13–10:1 is constructed like 8:11-14:

- An injustice: 8:11-12a//9:13-16
- The principle this violates: 8:12b-13//9:17-18a
- Reassertion of the injustice: 8:14//9:18b–10:1

While wisdom's preciousness makes its vulnerability to folly all the more absurd, folly hurts the fool above all. The topics of rulers and speech, wise and foolish, recur throughout 9:13–10:20, but there is no overall design or movement of thought, and the topical clusterings seem merely associative.

A. 9:13-16. An Anecdote about Wisdom
The anecdote demonstrates both wisdom's excellence and its vulnerability.

9:13 *Gam zoh ra'iti ḥokmah:* As MT stands, *ḥokmah* must be a predicative complement, which is to say, it defines the state in which the first accusative is perceived to be (e.g., Gen 7:1: "I have seen you to be a righteous man"), hence: "I have seen this too as wisdom" or "as an example of wisdom." However, the event Qohelet is about to describe is *not* an example of wisdom; rather, it is an incident in which wisdom was wronged. Moreover, in the verse as it stands the *gam* ("too") seems to introduce an additional instance of wisdom, but there is no such instance in the previous passage for this one to be additional to. Omitting *ḥokmah* would be more in line with Qohelet's style elsewhere; compare 3:16; 4:7; 5:12; and 9:11, none of which uses a predicative complement. But because *ḥokmah* is superfluous, its presence does not affect the meaning of the passage.

9:14 *M^eṣodim* means "snares," cf. 7:26; 9:12, and elsewhere. Either "snares" is also a term for siege-works or we should read *m^eṣûrîm*. The versions perforce translate "siege-works" and are not evidence either way, nor are two late manuscripts with this reading.

298

9:15 Most commentators take *umaṣa'* as impersonal (Gordis, Barton, Hertzberg, et al.). But even if the third masculine singular *maṣa'* means "one found," *someone* did the finding. The transitive qal *maṣa'* is not the same as the niphal "there was found," meaning "there existed." Ehrlich and Delitzsch correctly identify the subject as the foreign king mentioned in the immediately preceding sentence.

The king "found" — came across — a citizen in the way that the Josephite spies happened upon a man of Bethel, who, however, betrayed his city rather than saving it (Judg 1:22-26). The word *maṣa'* is used similarly of the watchmen "finding," or "coming upon," the Shulamite in Cant 5:7. Delitzsch says that *maṣa'* may mean "met with" as in "met with his match" without implying a physical meeting, but he gives no examples of this usage. *Maṣa'* may indicate that the king *captured* the wise man. (Iwry [1966] identifies this sense of the word *maṣa',* though not for the present passage.) If the king found the poor man literally "in" the city, then he had already penetrated the defenses. Perhaps, however, he found him not within the city walls but in its environs. In either case, the citizen proved able by persuasion or guile to get the king to spare the city. The wise woman of Tekoa did just that in 2 Sam 20:15-22.

Did the poor man succeed in saving the city? According to one interpretation, he *would have* done so but no one paid attention *(wᵉ'adam lo' zakar)* to his counsel (thus Hertzberg, Zimmerli, Ginsberg). The reasoning is that if no one *remembered* that man, there would be no story for Qohelet to tell. There are two answers to this objection: First, "no one" can mean no one besides the narrator, who, after all, may have invented the incident. Second, even though the event was remembered, the name of the story's hero was forgotten, and no one "remembers" him in that sense. Moreover, *lo' zakar* is not the verb that would be used to indicate that the potential deliverer was ignored. Even when *zakar* means "to pay attention to," "be aware of," and not just to recall forgotten facts (e.g., Qoh 5:19; 11:8; 12:1), the verb still implies an awareness of facts already known. *Zakar* would not be used in the sense of paying attention to new information, new advice, or the like. For that reason *zakar* is not among the many verbs used in Proverbs to indicate the son's hearkening to his father's advice.

The verb in *umillaṭ hu'* is indicative: the wise man *did* save the city. It would be entirely unpersuasive for Qohelet to claim that this man could have saved the city but was ignored and not allowed to try. The reader would wonder how Qohelet could know that the wise man *could* have done this.

In *millaṭ hu'* the subject is displaced from its usual position (a background clause would be *wᵉhu' millaṭ*) and thereby emphasized: it was he (a poor man, of all people!) who saved the city.

Qohelet is treating the event as historical and using it as evidence for a proposition, and not just as an analogy or parable. It is uncertain whether an actual event underlies the anecdote.

9:16 V. 16 is commonly thought to prove that the wise man of v. 15 *could have* saved the city but was ignored. The point of the verse is, however, quite different. "Better wisdom than might" is the conclusion Qohelet learns from the fact that the poor man *did* save the city. (If he had not, then "Better wisdom than might" would not be true.) Then, in v. 16b, Qohelet complains that despite the fact (demonstrated by the anecdote) that wisdom is powerful enough to save a city, people tend to forget a wise man if he is poor. Verse 16b does not restate what happened in the case described in vv. 13-15 any more than v. 17 or v. 18b does. Rather it exposes a further affront to wisdom which, as the story shows and v. 16a declares, deserves better treatment.

B. 9:17–10:1. Wisdom's Excellence and Vulnerability

9:17 The disjunctive should be moved forward to *bᵉnaḥat*. The constituent phrase is *dᵉbar(im) bᵉnaḥat*, describing the manner in which the words are spoken, in contrast with the ruler's shouting. The *mošel* "ruler" would be a local governor of some sort, one to whom Qohelet's readers might have access (Lohfink 1981:542). The same is true of *hammošel* in 10:4. *Mošel bakkᵉsilim* is not an immediate constituent of the sentence, a single phrase describing a kind of ruler, a "ruler among fools" (thus Delitzsch, Barton, Gordis, etc., comparing 2 Sam 23:3 and Prov 30:30). Rather, "among fools" is adverbial to *nišmaʿim* "are heard"; hence: ". . . more than the shout of a ruler (is heard) among fools." Ben Sira shares the proverb's optimism: "The opinion of the intelligent man is consulted in the assembly, and they pay attention to his words" (21:17).

In 9:16b Qohelet quoted the discouraging thought that came to him when he mulled over the way the wise man was neglected after having saved his city. Verse 17 modifies that thought by stating the rule: the words of the wise, *even when* spoken quietly, though vulnerable and often disdained, are nevertheless more effective than the words of a ruler are among fools, even when those words are shouted. This *is* a dialectic, but one that takes place within Qohelet's thoughts, not between him and other persons.

9:18 Qohelet restates his complaint of v. 16b, that in spite of wisdom's power, its benefit can easily be nullified. As in 2:26, *hote'* does not mean "sinner," because it is not immorality but incompetence or obtuseness that undoes the efficacy of wisdom.

10:1 reinforces 9:18 by a proverb. There are several difficulties in this verse, and the solutions are all conjectural. But the image of a fly spoiling the ointment sets up the ratio for fools and wisdom, so that the gist of the verse is clear: a little folly can undo much wisdom.

MT's $z^e bubey$ *mawet* does not mean "dead flies" (NRSV, JPSV, etc.). It must be rendered "deadly flies" (cf. *moqšey mawet* [2 Sam 22:6] and $k^e ley$ *mawet* [Ps 7:14]) or "doomed flies" (cf. *ben mawet* [2 Sam 12:5] and *'iš mawet* [1 Kgs 2:26]). But flies are not deadly, and in any case their deadliness would not spoil the ointment. Nor would their being doomed (thus still alive) hurt anything. We should redivide *zbwby mwt* as *zbwb ymwt* (Perles 1895:43). This slight emendation commends itself also because the idea of the proverb requires setting a minimal quantity of the bad substance (one dead fly, a bit of folly) over against a large quantity of the valuable substance (much ointment, much wisdom), and MT's plurality of flies does not strengthen the contrast. Moreover, the emendation provides a singular subject for *yab'iš*. *Yamut yab'iš* is an asyndeton showing quick succession: no sooner does a fly die than it decays and spoils the ointment.

MT's *yabbia'* is not meaningful, for though a dead fly might ruin the ointment, it will not make it bubble or ferment, as *yabbia'* is sometimes thought to mean (e.g., BDB). In fact, the only established meaning of *hibbia'* is "pour out," hence "express," which makes no sense here. Reading $g^e bîa'$ "chalice" *(BHS)* produces a meaningful sentence. In some forms of the square script (e.g., Qumran, as in 1Q Isaᵃ) the left diagonal of the *yod* extends down far enough that the letter resembles a *gimel*. LXX σκευασίαν, "preparation" (supported by SyH *twqn'*), is more likely to be a rendering of *gby'* than of *yby'*, assuming that the translator took "chalice" as a metonym for its contents.[39] "Chalice" is hyperbolic: even a little dead fly can ruin a whole pot of perfume.

10:1b is a crux. The versions differ radically from MT and from one another and offer no help. It is ad hoc to construe *mikkabod* as "in abundance" (thus, e.g., Gordis). One expedient is to take *yaqar* with 10a as a modifier of *šemen roqeaḥ* (contrary to MT, which sets the *'atnaḥ* on *roqeaḥ*) and to emend *mkbwd* to *tkbd*. (For *taw/mem* interchange see *LSF* §129b and *TAOT* 98f.) Thus read, the line explains the analogy in v. 1a (John Hobbins, private communication; thus Fox 1987). But the order of the comparison seems awk-

---

39. The only other appearance of σκευασία in the Greek versions is in Ezek 24:10, where Sym uses it to translate *merqaḥah*, "spice pot" or "spice." Syr's *m'n* "vessel" does not actually support the emendation, because it is derived from the LXX, confusing the rare σκευασία with σκεῦος (Syr would render *gabia'* by *'sqp'* or *'gn'*).

ward. (The prepositional phrase with "than" can precede when the subject is provided in the preceding context, as in 2 Sam 1:23.)

MT has two items of comparison, "than wisdom" and "than honor." These look like conflated doublets. I suggest reading *yāqār miḥokmāh* [or *mikkābôd*] *siklût me'āṭ*, "weightier than a little wisdom [or "honor"] is a bit of folly." *Yaqar* is an Aramaism meaning "heavy," "onerous"; see its use in Aḥiqar 111 and 130.

Wisdom's superiority to power is, of course, a tenet of traditional wisdom, stated clearly in Prov 21:22. It is also close to self-evident, since wisdom includes intelligence and expertise. Qohelet shares this axiom, as shown by his anecdote and reinforced by 10:2f. The vulnerabilities he observes do not void this truth, but they do show that people fail to appreciate the wise man or give proper attention to his wisdom, and others' folly may impair or nullify its value.

C. 10:2-3. How the Fool Harms Himself

Having taken account of the damage that fools can wreak on wisdom, Qohelet hastens to stress that they even more surely hurt themselves.

10:2-3 Even when the fool is merely walking along the road, his folly is evident to everyone, perhaps because he goes astray (10:15). The unusual syntax of v. 3a (lit. "also in the way when the fool walks") places emphasis on "the way" rather than on "walking." One does not need much intelligence when treading along a well-beaten path, such as the highway to a city, whereas in other places, such as the market, the activity may require some application of thought. Yet *even* when he's just walking along the road, the fool's heart betrays him. As Prov 12:23b puts it, "The heart of fools cries out, 'Folly!'"

The parallel with Prov 12:23b suggests that the subject of "says" in Qoh 10:3b is the fool's heart, which is, so to speak, absent, not "with" him. (Contrast the way that Qohelet, being wise, goes about *with* his heart [7:25].) The lack of a conjunction before *sakal hu'* favors taking that phrase as the heart's ridicule of its owner: "He is a fool!" Thus it is that the heart of the fool is "at his left": it is working against him, as are his lips (10:12). On the concept of the heart as a distinct entity, see §4.4.

In the Egyptian conception, when one's heart "leaves" him he is deprived of resources. A girl in an Egyptian love song scolds her heart for deserting her and making her foolish (see Fox 1985b:53, 59). The notion of the fool's heart betraying its owner's stupidity also recalls the Book of the Dead, in which the heart is perceived as a potential accuser of the deceased. In Spell

302

28, the deceased declares: "I have my heart and control it. It shall not tell what I have done. . . . Obey me, my heart, (for) I am thy lord while thou art in my body" (trans. Allen 1974:38).

Evidence that Qohelet is not just sniping at traditional wisdom is that he ends the unit by affirming wisdom's superiority. Hertzberg and Murphy read 9:16-18 as a "yes but statement" *(Zwar-Aber Tatsache),* or a case of "relativization," with v. 18b limiting the power of wisdom. That is true, but it is only part of the picture, because Qohelet does not stop there. In 10:2f. he returns to the positive view. This may be called "relativization," but if so it is in the other direction to what is commonly supposed to happen. Qohelet does not simply relativize traditional wisdom by pessimistic and skeptical observations *or* the other way around. He swings back and forth without settling on one side to the exclusion of the other.

◆ 10:4-7

(4) *If the ruler grows angry at you, do not leave your place, for the ability to soothe anger can set aside great offenses.*

(5) *There is an evil I have seen under the sun, an error that proceeds from a magnate: (6) a fool is appointed to great heights while rich men sit in lowly places. (7) I saw slaves on horses and princes walking on the ground like slaves.*

The rest of chapter 10 is a loosely grouped collection of miscellaneous maxims.

10:4 As Ibn Ezra observes, this verse reverts to the topic of 9:17: a soft-spoken wise man in contrast to a shouting ruler. However, its closest affiliation is to 8:1b-4, which teaches how to behave in the presence of authority.

Marpe' designates the *power* of healing or soothing as well as the act of healing or soothing. For the potential sense of *marpe'* see Mal 3:20, where it refers to the power to heal; Prov 14:30, where *leb marpe'* is a heart that has the ability to heal others; and Prov 15:4, where *marpe'* is a quality (the power to soothe) inhering in the tongue, just as deceit can be "in" it (4b). In its meaning, *marpe'* seems to be associated with both RPH ("soft") and RP' ("heal"), though etymologically it derives from the latter. *Marpe'* is healing (RP') in the sense of soothing (RPH), which is, for the most part, all that ancient medicines could do anyway. *Marpe'* is a near-synonym of *nahat* (9:17).

The MT correctly points *ynyh* as *yannîah,* which conventionally means "set (down, aside)," as distinct from *yānîah,* "give rest," "assuage" (LXX). The latter meaning should not be simply assigned to the former form without revocalization, as, e.g., Barton and Gordis do. When the non-geminated form *hēnîaḥ* etc. means "to give rest" in the sense of "assuage," it takes as direct object the anger (e.g., Ezek 5:13; 16:42), the uneasy spirit (Zech 6:8), or the person (Prov 29:17, meaning "reassure"), not the cause of the anger.

The assumption bridging 4a and 4b is that when the wise man stays in his place he will make use of his *marpe'*, "soothing ability," to pacify his superior. Prov 16:14 makes a similar observation, "The king's wrath is angels of death, but a wise man can assuage it." Even closer is Sir 20:28b, "The man who pleases the great atones for wrongdoing."

The difference between Qoh 8:2 and 10:4 may reflect a distinction between a *melek* "king" (8:2) and a *mošel* "ruler" (10:4), the latter probably being a local or provincial authority; see Lohfink 1981:541f. Still, for practical purposes the author could not have expected the readers to have face-to-face dealings with an actual monarch.

10:5-7 In Qohelet's eyes it is "evil" when people are placed in inappropriate positions, such as when fools are given high appointments or slaves elevated to privilege. Such things offend Qohelet's sense of propriety. This "evil" is introduced by "there is," as often when anomalies are described. Such anomalies, we should note, were observed by "traditional wisdom" too; see Prov 19:10 and 30:21-23.

10:6 "Folly" *(hassekel)* = "fool" (abstract-for-concrete, as noted by Ibn Ezra). Qohelet, like the author of Prov 30:21-23, is indignant at warps in the social order. According to the Proverbs passage, a slave coming to rule makes the earth tremble (Prov 30:22a; cf. 23b); see at 10:16. In the eyes of both Qohelet and this sage, there is something ridiculous and unaesthetic in dislocations of the proper order. This is also the attitude of the Egyptian "prophetic laments" of Neferti and Ipuwer (see §2.3), for whom rapid shifts in social status indicate social chaos. For Proverbs, such human failings are extraneous burdens placed upon the orderly world, and they will be shaken off as if by an earthquake. For Qohelet, they are symptomatic of a deep disorder in life, one that is systemic and chronic and not confined to certain phases of history.

◆ **10:8-11**

(8) He who digs a pit may fall into it, and he who breaks through a wall may be bitten by a snake. (9) He who moves stones may be hurt by them, and he who splits logs may be endangered by them.

(10) If the iron is dull and he has not sharpened the blade, then he must exert more force. But the skilled man[a] has the advantage of wisdom. (11) If a snake bites for lack of a spell, what profit is there for the snake charmer?

[a]*hakkaššîr* (MT *hakšēr* Q, *hkšyr* K)

10:8-9 These proverbs build on a topos found in Psalms (7:16; 9:16f.; 35:7f.; 57:7), Proverbs (26:27), and Ben Sira (27:25-27): a person's deeds rebound upon him. Falling into a pit one dug for someone else is usually a figure for the peripety that the wise found so satisfying. The topos is glossed with an explicit interpretation in Ps 7:16f.:

> He digs a hole and excavates it —
> and falls in the pit he dug.
> His wickedness returns upon his own head,
> and upon his own skull his lawlessness comes down.

Such a reversal may surprise the guilty, but the wise can predict it, for they know that a higher principle overrides human expectations. The causal link need not be understood theologically, but it may be so interpreted, as in Ps 9:16f., where the nations' sinking in the pit and net they prepared for Israel is glossed as God's judgment, "The Lord is known; he has executed judgment: by the deeds of his own hands the evildoer is ensnared . . ." (v. 17).

The topos is given a twist in Qoh 10:8-9. Digging a pit is one of four actions of the sort that would be performed in the course of one's everyday chores. These injuries may be simply unexpected misfortunes, and not necessarily retribution. The message is summed up in v. 14: "Man does not know what will happen." A man labors day in and day out to earn a living and ends up causing his own loss. He digs a pit or a cistern, or takes down a tottering wall, or moves stones, or splits firewood, and he is injured in carrying out these ordinary tasks. Such reversals could well be called *hebel*. Because these accidents do not happen every time one does something, I translate "may fall" rather than "will fall" etc.

10:10 In "and he has not sharpened," the antecedent of "he" is "he who splits logs" in v. 9. *Panim* means "surface(s)," hence "blade" (Ezek 21:21). The meaning of *qilqal* can be surmised from context and from the adjective *qalal* "burnished/polished (bronze)" (Ezek 1:7; Dan 10:6). The pilpel suggests a rapid, back-and-forth motion (it means "shake" in Ezek 21:26), hence "sharpen." In *waḥăyalim yᵉgabber,* the noun is probably not the subject, for the non-coordination of number with a conjoined predicate would be unusually rough. Possibly *hăyalim* is adverbial: "then he overcomes [pointing *yigbar*] by force." Most likely *ḥăyalim* is the direct object of *yᵉgabber* and the clause means: "then he must exert more force" (Yaḥyah). If one neglects to sharpen his axe, he must chop harder. This might explain the danger mentioned in v. 9, because a dull axe wielded with force is more likely to slip.

The word-order *lo'* — direct object — verb is peculiar. It puts an emphasis on *panim* that is hard to explain. The MT joins *lo'-panim* as a prosodic unit, perhaps understanding it as an adverbial, "not-earlier." Some Oriental MSS read *lw pnym,* perhaps to be understood "and he damaged [the RH sense of *qilqel*] its surface."

Verse 10b is obscure. The best expedient is to point *hakkaššir* (= Aramaic *kaššira'*), "the skilled man." *Yitron hakkaššir ḥokmah,* lit. "the advantage of the skilled man is wisdom," means that wisdom (here, technical expertise) gives the skilled man an advantage over him who substitutes force for preparedness and good sense. One must use his skill and good sense in a timely fashion, before it becomes necessary to apply force — just as the "possessor of a tongue" in the next verse must use his magical competence in a timely fashion.

10:11 "Snake charmer" is literally "possessor of a tongue." If a snake bites before the spell mesmerizes it, it is too late for the snake charmer's skill to benefit him, and he has no advantage over the unskilled. Generalized, the point is that no one, *not even* the skilled man, can undo damage after the fact. This proverb too recognizes at once the efficacy and vulnerability of wisdom.

Technical skills, including magic, are within the compass of the Biblical concept of wisdom. Magicians are *ḥăkamim;* e.g., Gen 41:8; Ex 7:11; Isa 44:25; Dan 2:27, 13; Isa 3:3 (where *nᵉbon laḥaš,* "one knowledgeable in spells," stands alongside *ḥăkam ḥărašim,* "one skilled in spells"). The snake charmer is called *mᵉḥukkam,* "skilled" or "learned," in Ps 58:6.

◆ **10:12-15**

(12) The words of a wise man's mouth are gracious, while the fool's lips devour him. (13) The fool starts out speaking folly and ends up speaking evil inanity. (14) And it is the fool who speaks at length. Man does not know what will happen, for who can tell him what will happen afterwards?

(15) The ⟨fool's toil exhausts him[a]⟩, because he doesn't even know how to get to town.

[a]*hakkᵉsîl mᵉyaggᵉʿennû* (MT *hakkᵉsîlîm tᵉyaggᵉʿennû*)

These verses concern wise and foolish speech (associated with the preceding by the phrase *baʿal hallašon* in v. 11).

A wise man's talk benefits him, the fool's harms him — yet it is the latter who talks the most.

10:12 Lit. "the wise man's words are favor," in other words, gracious, and as such they bring him good regard (see Sir 6:5, e.g.) — but not always (Qoh 9:11). This verse states more generally the theme of 8:1b; 9:17; and 10:4. "The fool's lips devour him," taken literally, suggests self-cannibalism. Compare "The fool locks his hands together and eats his flesh" (Qoh 4:5).

10:13 The fool starts out speaking nonsense and ends up talking vicious inanity. *'Aḥărit* also can be understood as "after effect"; cf. Prov 5:4; 23:32.

10:14 A different word is used for "fool" — *sakal* here, *kᵉsil* in v. 12. This suggests that the author draws on existing materials, perhaps an adage in v. 12.

No one can tell man "what will be *meʾaḥărayw.*" Since death is not mentioned in this unit, *meʾaḥărayw* probably means "afterwards," including the future in this life; thus in 6:12, which this verse closely resembles (with the clauses reversed). It is ignorance of the future in this life, rather than ignorance of what happens after death, that makes a lot of talk so much babble. See also the comment at 3:22.

10:15 *'Ml hksylym tygʿnw:* The text is undoubtedly corrupt. The non-coordination of number ("fools" — "him"), though possible, is very awkward, and the non-coordination of gender is almost certainly an error. (The fact that some nouns are epicene does not, contrary to Delitzsch, mean that *this* noun is.) One suggested emendation is *'ml hksyl mty yygʿnw,* "The toil of the fool — when will it weary him?" (Ehrlich, Hertzberg). But this reading implies that the fool is *not* wearied by his toil, whereas the rest of the verse declares his feebleness, not his stamina. Albrecht (1896:113), noting that this verse is the only example in which an abstract form (*ʿāmāl*) and its gender are not coordinated, emends to *yᵉyaggᵉʿennû* "wearies him." This emendation, however, still leaves a non-coordination of number in the suffix ("fools") . . .

307

"him") and does not account for the *taw*. I suggest emending to *'ml hksyl myg˓nw*. LXX (S, A) has the singular (τοῦ ἄφρονος . . . αὐτόν). The error could arise from associating the *mem* of *myg˓nw* with the preceding word. The second *yod* of MT *hksylym* would have been added after the *mem* was incorrectly joined to *hksyl*. The *taw* is probably a dittograph of the *mem* of *myg˓nw* (for examples of *t-/m* interchange, showing that they were at times similar enough to lead to near-dittographies, see *LSF* §229b and *TAOT* 98f.; see esp. 1 Kgs 6:8).

10:15 is an isolated and not quite relevant afterthought. It continues the thought of 10:3 and may originally have been located there. Combined, vv. 3 and 15 say: even when he's just walking along the road, the fool reveals to everyone that he is stupid (v. 3), for he wearies himself by getting lost on the way to town (v. 15), the best-known place in the region.

The phrase "doesn't even know how to get to town" may have meaning both literally and idiomatically. As an idiom it may signify incompetence. Compare the Egyptian phrase, "does not reach the city," which means to fail in attaining a goal. In "The Eloquent Peasant" (B1.326f.), this idiom stands in antithesis to "reach land," an Egyptian cliché for success. The fool's toil wearies him because he is unable to accomplish what he sets out to do.

◆ 10:16-20

(16) Woe to you, O land whose king is a lackey and whose princes feast in the morning! (17) How fortunate you are, O land whose king is a nobleman and whose princes feast at the proper time, in a manly fashion and not in drunkenness!

(18) *(Through sloth[a] a roof sags,*
and through slackness of hands a house leaks.)
(19) *For merriment they prepare food*
and wine, which cheers the living.
And money keeps them all occupied!
(20) *Even in your thoughts do not insult the king,*
and insult not a rich man even in your bed chamber,
for the birds of the heavens will carry the sound,
and a winged creature report the matter.

[a] *˓aṣlût* (MT *˓ăṣaltayim*)

Remarks on virtues and vices of the ruling class. Does Qohelet have his own land in mind when condemning lazy aristocrats?

10:16 Hitzig (pp. 122-24; sim. Lohfink 1981) identifies the youth as Ptolemy V Epiphanes, who ascended the throne in 205 BCE at age 5. But *na'ar* probably means "servant" or "slave" rather than "youth," since it stands in antithesis with *ben ḥorim,* a member of the well-to-do classes. If so, *na'ar* refers to this person's origins rather than to his current position and calls to mind the youth of 4:13, though that one was wise. Qohelet betrays class bias even when mocking the behavior of some members of the upper classes. He feels it is as indecorous for a servant to ascend to power as for noblemen to lounge about drinking in the morning. Such a bias, we should note, does not reveal the author's own social class, since the servitors of the rich can be snobs no less than their masters, while members of the ruling classes can be sharply critical of their peers.

Qohelet shares the attitude of the author of Prov 30:22, who believes that the very earth shakes "under a slave [*'ebed*] coming to rule [*yimlok*], and a fool [*nabal*] being sated with bread." Prov 19:10 agrees: "Luxury is not fitting for a fool. How much the less so for a slave [*'ebed*] to rule among princes." These complaints belong to a widespread "world turned upside down" topos, on which see Van Leeuwen 1986. When Qohelet complains that the dissolute ruling class "feasts [lit. "eats"] in the morning" he means not just that they have breakfast, but that they eat and drink *all day,* or, in the words of Prov 30:22, "are sated with bread."

10:18 A proverb serving as a parenthetical reinforcement of vv. 16f. It is slightly out of line with the context and was probably not written for this place.

'Aṣaltayim: Most commentators (including Delitzsch, Hertzberg, and Gordis) explain the dual form as intensive. But there is no evidence for this function of the dual, and, moreover, a *non*-intensive form of "laziness" is required here. An admonition against indolence should warn that laziness — any laziness, and not only a double portion thereof — brings a house to ruin. We should emend to *'aṣlût,* omitting the final *-ym* as a dittograph (Zimmerli). The two hemistichs combine to make a single point: indolence causes the roof of a house to sag and leak. Flat roofs in Palestine were covered with lime, which would crack and allow seepage if not maintained (Murphy).

10:19 This verse describes the banquets that the wealthy, both the worthy and the dissipated, prepare for themselves daily. The subjects of the verbs are found in vv. 16f. — the princes and nobility. *'Aśah leḥem* is an Aramaism, equivalent to *'ăbad lĕḥem,* "prepare food, a feast" (Dan 5:1) (Ginsberg). *Śeḥoq* means "merriment," "amusement," as in 2:2. The remark on wine is an old saw, appearing in Ps 104:15a ("And wine which cheers the heart of man") and Judg 9:13 (". . . my wine, which cheers gods and man"). These verses show that y*ᵉ*śammaḥ ḥayyim is a relative clause modifying wine (as Ibn Ezra notes), and also that ḥayyim means "living people" not "life."

The usual meaning of ya*ʿăneh*, in the qal at least, as this verb is usually parsed, is "answer." In this verse, ya*ʿăneh* is commonly explained to mean "answer for," whence (by a jump) "provide," on the basis of Hos 2:23f. (thus, e.g., Gordis). But in the Hosea passage, *ʿanah* cannot mean "provide" in the first three sentences, for God does not "provide" the heavens, nor do the heavens "provide" the earth. Hosea apparently envisions a cosmic conversation of the sort mentioned in Ps 19:2-3 and Anat (III:10-28), a notion inapplicable, even metaphorically, to our verse. In any case, to point out that money provides food and drink would be trivial and to say that it responds affirmatively to everyone would be irrelevant if not meaningless. *Yaʿăneh* here is best parsed as a hiphil meaning "to occupy, keep busy," as in 5:19, q.v. In both verses the "busyness" intended is the enjoyment of pleasures.

This verse is not in itself cynical or even critical of the wealthy. Neither Qohelet nor the other sages objected to the preparation of food and wine for merry-making. As Ben Sira says, "Joy of heart and happiness of soul: (this is) wine drunk at the proper time and temperately" (31:27, Greek). They censured only the failure to confine these pleasures to the appropriate time and measure ("Wine drunk to excess is bitterness of soul," Sira says [31:29a]). The criticism of the rich and royal is voiced in Qoh 10:16 and 18, and there it is only certain members of the class who are censured. Verse 19 is an incidental remark on the good fortune of the wealthy: they have the means to keep themselves preoccupied, a state Qohelet considers a divine blessing (5:19). There is a grievance behind this remark: While such pleasures are legitimate, it is unfair that the dissolute rich have the resources to supply themselves with diversions.

10:20 *Madda*ʿ = "mind," "thought." *Madda*ʿ means "mind" (rather than "knowledge") in 1QS 7.3 (if a man "gets angry in his *madda*ʿ") and 7.5 (if a man commits deceit "in his *madda*ʿ"; similarly 6.9). In Aramaic it sometimes means "thoughts" or "mind" (rather than "knowledge," its usual sense), e.g., Tg-Ps 34:1. Other suggested translations of *madda*ʿ are "intimates," "bed," and "bedroom." Some emend, unnecessarily, to *maṣṣaʿăka* (thus Ehrlich and Perles 1895:71f.). But "mind" is a meaningful hyperbole, as if to say: Don't even *think* about it!

This remark is an afterthought, a wry quip evoked by the reproach against the lazy king and nobility in v. 16. Qohelet realizes that he himself has just insulted the king and the rich man.

◆ **11:1-6**

(1) Send forth your bread upon the waters, for in the course of time you will find it. (2) Give a portion to seven people, even eight, for you do not know what misfortune will occur on earth.

(3) If the clouds fill up, they will empty out rain on the earth. If a tree should fall, whether in the south or in the north, wherever the tree may fall, there will it be. (4) He who watches the wind will not sow, and he who looks at the clouds will not reap.

(5) Just as you cannot understand what the life-breath does <in the limbs[a]> (of the fetus) in the womb of a pregnant woman, so you cannot understand the work of God, who makes everything happen. (6) In the morning sow your seed, and in the evening let not your hand go slack, for you do not know which will prosper, this or that, or whether both will be equally good.

[a] *ba'ăṣāmîm* (MT *ka'ăṣāmîm*)

In a world of uncertainties, prepare for all eventualities, because you cannot know which will come to pass (vv. 1b, 2b, 4, 5, 6), and in any case you cannot change the course of events (vv. 3, 4). What will be will be, so do not waste time puzzling over the future (cf. 6:12b; 10:14; etc.). Instead, adapt yourself as well as you can to various contingencies. Instead of straining for wisdom, just go ahead and do what you must. This is similar to the message of 3:1-15; see the introduction to that passage.

11:1f. There are four main ways of interpreting these maxims:

(1) Send your merchandise over the seas, but divide it among several boats (= enterprises) for safety's sake (Delitzsch, Gordis, Zimmerli, et al.).

"Bread" does stand for merchandise in mercantile commerce in Prov 31:14. Nevertheless, this interpretation is problematic because when someone makes an investment, he hopes to gain *more* than the principal (Ginsberg).

(2) At a further level of abstraction: take chances, even long shots, and in the future you may benefit from them (v. 1), but protect yourself against unexpected misfortunes by spreading the risk around (v. 2) (Podechard).

This interpretation depends on the meaning of "sending bread upon the waters." The parallels mentioned below suggest that the "bread" metaphor has another meaning, but the thrust of this reading may be valid.

(3) An unreflective, improvident deed (v. 1a) may, contrary to expectations, succeed (v. 1b), while a prudent and cautious deed (v. 2a) may, contrary to expectations, fail (v. 2b). The consequences of a man's actions are not in his control and are unpredictable (Hertzberg, Galling, Ellermeier [1967:253-61]).

This interpretation turns the advice into a statement, whereas in this passage Qohelet is drawing rules for human activity based on the fact of human ignorance, as we see clearly in vv. 4 and 6. The imperatives in 11:1-2 also are most naturally read as actual advice. Moreover, v. 2b is not the opposite of 2a but the principle motivating it.

(4) Do deeds of charity, giving alms and assistance to various people in need. You may not know how compensation will come, and you should not act in expectation of reward, but it will eventually come (Qoh. Rab., Tg, Rashi, Ibn Ezra, Barton, et al.).

Interpretation 4 is supported by the parallels discussed below, but the element of surprise (from interpretation 2) should be given greater emphasis. In other words: wager on charitable and gracious deeds, even if this seems like a long shot, because the unexpected may happen and your deeds pay off. As Rashbam puts it: "Do a favor for a man from whom you never expect to benefit, because in the far future he will do a favor for you."

To this advice we may compare the strikingly similar counsel in the Instruction of Onchsheshonqy, an Egyptian wisdom book from about the same period as Qohelet: "Do a good deed and throw it in the water; when it dries up you will find it" (19.10; *AEL* 3.174; similarly *AW* 255). This maxim looks like a partially demetaphorized version of Qohelet's. One should do a good deed and forget about it. Then in hard times it will pay off, in an unexpected way. Ben Sira similarly advises: "Lose your money for the sake of a brother or friend" (29:10). As the context shows, this means that if you give charity without expecting repayment or make an unsecured loan, you may anticipate some future reward from God (vv. 11-13) (see also Sir 3:31 and Ps 112:9).

An ancient topos in Wisdom Literature is the value of helping others so that they will reciprocate in time of need. Ptahhotep advises:

(339) Satisfy your acquaintances with what has accrued to you,
(340) as is possible for the one whom god favors.
(341) As for him who neglects to satisfy his acquaintances,
(342) it will be said, "This is a selfish soul!"[40]

---

40. The *Ka*, the aspect of human nature with appetites and desires.

(343) One does not know what will happen, such that he might understand the morrow.[41]

(344) A (true) soul is an honest soul, in which one can find repose [?].

(346) If misfortunes[42] occur,

(347) it is (one's) acquaintances who say, "Welcome!"

(348) One does not receive relief from one's town.[43]

(349) When there is misfortune, one receives (aid) [from] one's acquaintances.

Ptahhotep teaches that it is prudent to give of your wealth to others because you do not know what the future will bring. In a time of trouble, you will receive help only from people you have treated kindly.

Anii has much the same advice to offer in 21.4-10, from which the following is a selection:

Eat no bread, while another stands nearby
and you neglect to stretch out your hand to him. . . .
Should your own property come (to harm),
another will do you a benefit. . . .
One year's stream of water disappears
and it is (in) another [channel] this year. . . .
A single plan does not happen <to> man.
It is mixed in life.[44]

At the same time that Qohelet recommends generosity, he is also reiterating his lesson of life's uncertainties.

Šallaḥ: ŠLḤ-piel usually means "to release," occasionally "to send." It nowhere means "to throw" (an object). (ŠLḤ-piel is once used of shooting an arrow [1 Sam 20:20; the direct object is implicit], but an arrow may be said to be "released.") Thus Qoh 11:1a suggests the image of a person placing or dropping his bread on the water and letting it float away, rather than throwing

41. Line 345 is a variant (MSS L1, L2): "There is no one who knows (the outcome of) his plans, so that he might plan for the morrow."

42. *Ḥsswt,* which usually means "praised things" or the like, is clearly a euphemism for misfortune; see Volten 1955:362f.

43. In other words, you cannot take your neighbors' help for granted, so you must prepare the ground for receiving aid in time of trouble. Manuscript L2 introduces a more obvious concept by replacing "town" by "enemies."

44. The last couplet (21.9f.) teaches that life does not proceed in a single fashion, all good or all bad, but is a mixture of the two. Compare Qoh 7:14.

it into the water. The image of letting something go rather than throwing it accords better with the preposition *'al p*^{e}*ney*, lit. "on the surface of" (rather than *bammayim* or *'el tok hammayim*). "Sending" or just "letting go" *(šallaḥ)* is a gentler, less goal-directed action than "casting." We may think of a hard, rounded "pita" which can float briefly, instead of a Western breadloaf that would sink immediately.

"Find it" *(timṣa'ennu):* "Finding" can mean to come across something accidentally and does not necessarily entail a search.

Mah yihyeh ra'ah "what will happen bad" = *mah ra'ah tihyeh*, lit. "what bad thing will happen" (Ginsberg); cf. Esth 6:3.

11:3 South-north is a merism signifying "everywhere." The rain and the falling tree are events totally beyond human control. The Masoretic accents place the secondary pause at *gešem*, hence "If the clouds fill up with rain."

The verb *y*^{e}*hû'* is peculiar. Phonetically, it could be Mishnaic-type plural. However, the expected spelling would be *yhw* and the sentence requires a singular verb. A possible emendation is *hw'* "it" (GKC §75s), but the future seems more natural. Consonantal *yhw'* looks like a mechanical transcription of the Aramaic third masculine singular form, *yehĕwē'*. This too seems to point to an Aramaic origin.

11:4 A farmer who constantly frets about the weather will never get around to doing his tasks. If he delays sowing until the western wind blows, the harbinger of rain, he may wait until it is too late. If he is always peering at the clouds, postponing the harvest until he is certain of dry weather (out of fear that rain immediately upon harvesting might spoil the grain), he may delay till the grain rots on the stalk and harvest is useless. There is, to be sure, a time to plant and a time to harvest, but man cannot calculate them too precisely.

Generalized, the maxim teaches that the attempt to plan too meticulously for the future can paralyze initiative. Generalized further, it teaches the uselessness of brooding and speculating about *ma'ăśeh ha'ĕlohim*, as is made explicit in v. 5b.

11:5 MT's *k*^{e}*ṣmym* "like the limbs" (of the fetus) brings in the comparison too soon. This produces a disjointed analogy between the "way" of the life-breath on the one hand and the limits of understanding on the other ("Just as you cannot understand the way of the life-breath like the limbs [of the fetus] . . ."). What is required is an analogy between not understanding the mystery of gestation and not understanding the work of God. We should read *b*^{e}*ṣmym*, with many MSS and possibly Tg. *Derek X b-* does not mean "the way that X takes into" (contrary to Fox 1987), but "the behavior of X *in* something." *Derek* "way" is a habitual behavior, something one regularly does (e.g, Gen 19:31; 31:35; Prov 6:6). ("The way of a man in a maid," one of four marvelous "ways" in Prov 30:19 may be a euphemism for the process of impregnation.) The unknown is what the spirit does to animate the fetus within the womb. *'Ăṣamim* (masc.) seems to mean limbs or organs rather than "bones," which is *'ăṣamot* in the plural *(HALAT)*. Still, the masculine/feminine distinction is not certain (*'ăṣamim* definitely means "bones" in Am 6:10), and in light of Ezek 37:5-11, in which the bones are brought to life by the infusion of the "spirit" (*ruaḥ,* as here), it is possible that *'ăṣamim* in the present verse means "bones."

"Pregnant woman" is lit. "the full (one)," a noun; cf. *m^ele'ah* "pregnant" in the Temple Scroll 50.10; m. Yeb. 17:1; b. Bek. 20b, etc.

The "work of God" *(ma'ăśeh ha'ĕlohim)* is not creation, which is not relevant here, but God's ongoing governance of the world, manifest in his causation of processes, such as a misfortune, the clouds emptying, a tree falling, a particular planting succeeding, and the life-spirit animating the fetus.

11:6 *La'ereb* = "in the evening" (see 1 Chr 23:30; Ps 30:6; Brockelmann 1956:§207b), not "until evening," or "toward evening," because two distinct times are spoken of ("the one" and "the other"). Nevertheless, as a merism the phrase includes the entire workday. This is not to say that Qohelet is advocating work without rest. His message is that one should perform his work whenever the opportunity or need arises, rather than trying to ascertain the best moment — though, to be sure, there is such a thing (3:1-8) — "for you do not know" which effort will succeed (3:11). In structure and message, 11:6 recapitulates 11:1f. and thereby rounds out the unit with its central teaching: compensate for ignorance by preparing for multiple eventualities.

"Morning and evening" might also call to mind early and late in life. One must exploit the possibilities that arise throughout life. This thought is thus a pivot to the subsequent advice to enjoy oneself while young.

Yikšar = "be successful," "useful," translated by χρησιμεύειν "to be useful" in Sir 13:4.

◆ **11:7–12:8**

    A. 11:7-10. The light: carpe diem
       a. Enjoy all of life (7-8),
       b. especially the time of youth (9-10)
    B. 12:1-7. The darkness: *memento mori*
       a. And remember your creator when young (1a)

      b. before the miseries of old age (1b)
      c. before your death and funeral (2-5)
      d. before your burial (6-7).
   C. 12:8. All is absurd

11:7–12:8 is a single unit, organized as a series of imperatives advising enjoyment of life when one is young. Qoh 12:8 is a linchpin between the body of the work and the epilogue and could be attached to either unit.

Because of the length and complexity of this unit, section A will be discussed apart from sections B and C. The advice of section A extends into 12:1a, which thus links the two sections structurally. Then 12:1b begins a series of temporal clauses that describe aging and death, all of which serve to bring out the urgency of the advice of section A. *Hebel*-judgments in 11:8 and 10 demarcate the two segments of section A, and the phrase *ʿad ʾăšer lo'* subdivides B.

Although the theme of the unit is *carpe diem,* far greater attention is given to the negative — the somber limits on this opportunity — than to the positive enjoyment itself.

H. Witzenrath (1979:5-27) shows how this unit receives textural cohesiveness from repetition of certain lexemes (*harbeh*, ŚMḤ, ZKR, *hebel, yaldut, yamim, qol,* ŠWB) and by the clustering of words in certain semantic fields (light, ages of life, time, house, voice, plants, valuables, vessels, wells).

A. 11:7-10. The Light: Carpe Diem

   (7) Sweet is the light,
        and it is good for the eyes to see the sun.
   (8) Now even if a man live many years,
        he should take pleasure in them all,
        and remember that the days of darkness are many.
        All that comes is absurdity.

   (9) Rejoice, young man, in your youth,
        and let your heart give you cheer in the days of your prime.
        And follow your heart
        and the sights of your eyes.
        And know that for all these things
        God will bring you to judgment.
   (10) And remove irritation from your heart,
        and banish unpleasantness from your flesh,
        for youth and juvenescence are fleeting.

11:7 Just to be alive is sweet, even if much of life is bitter. Qohelet does not say "it is good to see the sun," but rather "it is good for the eyes to see the sun," which is a statement of a subjective value. Whatever a wise man may discover about the absurdity and bitterness of life, the fact remains that people desire to live. Therefore they should cherish every minute of life, because the darkness stretches on forever.

Ellermeier (1967:303-6) explains 11:7-8 not as advice but as a statement of the fact that people consider life good. He takes v. 8abα as the reason for this observation: even someone who lives a long life never considers the years excessive but loves them all. I agree that 11:7 is indicative, but it is also the basis for advice, which v. 8 provides in the jussive *(yiśmaḥ, yizkor)*. The *ki* in v. 8a is evidentiary, motivating the sequence of thought ("I say this because"). The sheer experience of life is desirable, so we should savor it to the extent allowed us.

11:8 Death is absurd. So is life, but it, at least, is sweet. See the discussion in §2.5 (g). In 11:8 Qohelet says that people should think of death so as to appreciate life all the more. In 5:19 he praised pleasure for diverting the mind from its brevity. These paradoxical attitudes are inherent in the *carpe diem*. The Antef Song, for example, first describes the gloom of death, then advocates pleasure as diversion (see on 5:19). We are reminded of death in order to persuade us to lay hold of the pleasures that will divert our thoughts from death. People often contemplate most what they most wish to avoid.

11:9a The "ways of your heart" are the ways in which your heart goes; we might translate: "Go where your heart goes." Underlying this idiom is the notion that one who desires something moves in imagination toward the desired situation. (Hence desire is *hălok nepeš,* lit. "the wandering of the soul"; 6:9; see the discussion there.) In this sense, the heart or soul goes ahead of a person, who may then decide whether to follow or not.

The phrase *ubᵉmarʾey ʿeyneyka,* lit. "and in the sights of your eyes," is elliptical for "and (go) in (the ways of) the sights of your eyes," with the elided components derived from the previous clause. In 6:9, "the sight of the eyes" means satisfaction as opposed to vain yearning. It is the same here, for "the sight of your eyes" denotes not desire but the destination of the "going." In other words, go after your heart and what your eyes see. For *marᵉʿey* "sights" the LXX, Syr, Vul, and MSS read the singular, but the plural is meaningful. It indicates the multiplicity of pleasures to be pursued rather than the abstract "vision."

11:9b   Commentators often delete this sentence as a gloss (thus Zimmerli, Galling, Ginsberg, and many). The sentence is indeed somewhat intrusive in the series of imperatives, and of all proposed glosses in the book this is the most likely. But the arguments are not compelling. The belief in man's accountability for his deeds is not foreign to Qohelet; see 3:17 and 8:6a (and note that the latter is rarely considered a gloss). Moreover, Qohelet undoubtedly disapproves of excessive indulgence: consider his contempt for the dissolute nobility in 10:17-19.

"Days of your prime": *b^eḥurot* is youth extending into adulthood. Basically, a *baḥur* is a young man of the age of military service (e.g., 1 Kgs 12:21; 2 Chr 25:5).

The advice to follow the ways of one's heart caused discomfort to early readers. LXX (sim. Syr) moralizes by translating *šaḥărut* as ἄνοια, "ignorance," and by adding ἄμωμος, "innocent(ly)," after "your heart" in v. 9a (in SyH with an obelus; B and MS 68 omit, erroneously, καρδίας σου). In the same vein, several Greek witnesses simply add a negative (μή) to the next clause, reading, "and (go) not in the sight of your eyes" (B, S*, and several minuscules). A similar tendency is manifest in Ben Sira's cautionary reversal of Qohelet's advice: "Do not follow your heart and your eyes, to go in evil delights" (5:2, MS A).[45]

11:10   V. 10 is the complement, not the converse, of v. 9. Though that verse advises pleasure and this one counsels the removal of displeasures, psychological and physical, they are not saying the same thing in different words. It is possible to steep oneself in pleasures while feeling malaise and irritation. That was Qohelet's own experience in chapter 2, and in 5:11 he speaks of a rich man robbed of repose. Qohelet here goes beyond his usual advice and teaches that in addition to embracing pleasures, one must pull the thorns out of body and soul. One gets the impression that by now, and perhaps as early as 9:7, Qohelet has pretty much succeeded in doing so for himself.

"Unpleasantness from your flesh" (*ra'ah mibb^eśareka*, lit. "[remove] evil from your flesh"): Ginsberg says that this means sadness, the opposite of *leb tob*, "a good [i.e. merry] heart." But since "flesh" commonly means the body, the expression refers more directly to physical discomfort, like the rich man's insomnia (5:11).

---

45. The Greek lacks the additional moralizing element, reading, "Do not follow your soul and your strength, going in the desires of your heart." Sir 5:2 is probably a response to Qohelet, since v. 3 certainly is. V. 3 uses the peculiar phrase *m^ebaqqeš nirdapim*, which is derived from *y^ebaqqeš 'et nirdap* in Qoh 3:15.

The unique *šaḥărut*, which must signify the time of youth, has been explained as dawn of life (deriving it from *šaḥar* "dawn") and as the time of black hair (deriving it from *šaḥor* "black," sc. of hair). The latter derivation is the better, because a Hebrew term for old age is *śeybah* "gray head," and "black hair" is a natural epithet for youth. Also, as a metaphor, the "dawn" of life would probably signify infancy and not include young adulthood.

Hebel here denotes ephemerality, for that is the only quality of youth that makes pleasure-seeking pressing. At the same time, it connotes illusoriness and thus absurdity, because the very brevity that makes it precious also makes it deceptive; and what deceives the mind is absurd. See §2.5 (f).

The ostensibly hedonistic exhortation in vv. 9-10a raised concerns that it might provoke heresy (Qoh. Rab. 1:4; see chap. 1, n. 3). Such concerns may have earlier inspired a prudential gloss at the end of the verse, but the author himself could have been similarly motivated.

B. 12:1-7. The Darkness: *Memento Mori*

aa	(1)	And remember your creator
aβ		in the days of your youth —
ba		before the days of unpleasantness arrive,
bβ		and the years of which you will say:
bγ		"I take no pleasure in them."
aa	(2)	Before the sun and the light grow dark,
aβ		and the moon and the stars,
b		and the clouds return after the rain —
aa	(3)	in the day when the keepers of the house tremble,
aβ		and the powerful men writhe,
ba		and the grinders are idle, (their numbers) having dwindled,
bβ		and the (ladies) looking through the windows darken,
aa	(4)	and the doors in the street are closed,
aβ		as the sound of the mill fades low;
ba		and the bird begins to sing,
bβ		and all the songstresses are bowed low,
aa	(5)	and they also fear what is on high,[a] and terrors are along the way.
aβ		But the almond tree blossoms, and the locust becomes laden,
aγ		and the caperberry <buds[b]> —
ba		for the man is going to his eternal home,

bβ		and the mourners walk about in the streets.
aa	(6)	Before the silver cord <snaps[c]>,
aβ		and the golden bowl is smashed,
ba		and the jug breaks at the spring,
bβ		and the wheel is smashed[d] in the pit,
a	(7)	and the dust returns to the earth as it was before,
b		and the spirit returns to God, who gave it.

[a]*miggōbāhh* (MT *miggāboahh*)

[b]*w^etiprah* (MT *w^etāpēr*)

[c]*yinnātēq* (MT *yērātēq* Q; *yrhq* K)

[d]*w^etāruṣ* (MT *w^etērōṣ*)

The opening poem describes the unending cycles in the world of nature. The closing poem describes the undoing and cessation of the individual life, which is the world to that person. The sun arises after setting (1:5), but man's light is extinguished forever (12:2a). The injunction to "remember your creator" in 12:1 may recall the failure of memory of the past in 1:11. In chapter 1, the natural elements go round and round. In chapter 12, the mourners do "go around" (v. 5bβ), but the movement of the whole is one-directional, heading to the "eternal home." *This* world does not "remain forever the same" (1:4).[46]

The exegetical comments will address the surface meaning — the *p^ešaṭ* — of the sentences, leaving considerations of metaphorical applications and broader literary issues to the excursus to follow. I should note in advance, however, that the interpretation I favor explains many of the enigmatic sentences as descriptive of communal mourning, as will emerge from the exegesis.

Section A spoke of taking pleasure in the light of life. Now section B describes the limit point of this possibility: the advent of eternal darkness. Qoh 12:1a is introductory to 12:1-7. The body of the poem, 12:1b-7, divides into three parts, unequal in length but unmistakably marked by the conjunction *'ad 'ǎšer lo'* "before": (a) 12:1b, (b) 12:2-5, and (c) 12:6f.

Though the above translation could not represent it, all of 12:1-7 is one long sentence consisting of an imperative (*z^ekor*, v. 1a) and three complex temporal ("before") clauses describing the time-limit to the "remembering." Qoh 12:2-5 itself incorporates a long temporal clause (vv. 3-5b), which elaborates the description of "the day when" the luminaries go dark (v. 2). The

---

46. The way that 1:3-8 and 12:1-8 bracket the book by reversal was pointed out to me by my student Rick Painter.

long sentence at first seems to reach a conclusion with v. 5, but v. 6 resumes the series of "before" clauses and must itself be dependent on the imperative in v. 1a.

The key to understanding the movement of the passage is recognizing that 12:3-5 is a complex temporal clause depicting the events that occur simultaneously with those of v. 5b, which can only be on the day of the funeral.

The phrase *'ad 'ăšer lo'* does not mark a caesura so much as give renewed momentum to the scenic development. Without this impetus, such an intricate series of dependent clauses would peter out in vagueness. With it, the restless movement toward the climactic return of the dust to the earth adumbrates man's relentless advance to the grave. With the metaphors explicated, the temporal structure of the entire unit can be diagrammed as follows:

A. Enjoy life while young (11:7-9) and
B. Remember your creator (12:1a)

before	before	before
old age (1b)	death (2), which is "the day when" mourning takes place (3-5)	death and disintegration (6-7)
⟶	⟶	

The three columns are progressive, but the third takes a step back and represents death as well as the subsequent process. 12:5αβγ ("But the almond tree blossoms, etc.") adduces three annual events in nature whose occurrence is external to the time-frame of the scene.

12:1a Alongside *bwr'yk (bôr'eykā)*, the reading common in printed Bibles, an inner-Masoretic variant is *bwr'k (bôr'ᵉkā);* see Baer (1886:68f.) and Euringer (1890:124-26). The *yod* of *bwr'yk*, however, is not an error but a fuller representation of the segol. Both variants are singular nouns and are alternative realizations of III-H verbs with consonantal suffixes.[47]

47. Examples of infixed *y* with singular nouns: *mḥnyk*, Deut 23:15; *mštyhm*, Isa 5:12; *mqnyk*, Isa 30:23; *nwtyhm*, Isa 42:5. These examples appear on disjunctive accents. The other examples in GKC §93*ss* may be plurals. Cf. 1QIsa^a 43:1: *bwr'yk* "your creator" (the *yod* was added interlinearly).

Commentators have often felt the reference to the creator to be inappropriate here, because remembering God does not seem to motivate the enjoyment of life and is not something one does only before old age. 12:1a cannot be removed as a gloss (contrary to McNeile, Barton, et al.), because v. 1b cannot be joined directly to 11:10b as a temporal clause, and if we mark a new sentence at 12:1b, as Barton does, the entirety of vv. 3-7 lacks a main clause. Various emendations have been suggested,[48] but they are unnecessary because, as M. Gilbert (1981:100) observes, in this context to think on one's creator is to think of death, for the life-spirit returns to its giver (12:7). Gilbert believes that the sentence also implies an admonition not to sin, but that does not seem relevant to context. The only counsels that would be meaningful in 12:1a are advice to enjoy life (found in five forms in 11:9-10) and advice to keep death in mind (as in 11:8bα). The latter is what is intended by the injunction to remember one's creator.

12:1b The "days of unpleasantness" (lit. "badness") are the years of old age, contrasting with the time of youth. They are not (contrary to Ogden 1984b:34) the eternity of death. Once in Sheol, one would not be able to say "I take no pleasure in them," which, at any rate, would be a feeble way to complain about the eternity in the underworld. Old age is described here from the perspective of the adverse reaction of the old-man-to-be, the universal addressee. The funeral is described later from the perspective of the disturbed onlookers.

12:2 "The light and the moon and the stars": Gordis says that this is a hendiadys meaning "the light of the moon and the stars," but he gives no examples of three nouns combining in this way. Qohelet uses "light" to create a double pairing: sun and light//moon and stars. The parallelism could not be perfect because there is no other daytime luminary to pair with the sun. Light as such is independent of the sun and the other luminaries. After all, light can come from other sources, and according to Gen 1, it was created before the sun, moon, and stars. Light itself will go dark at death.

The return of the clouds after the rain is an obscure image. It is suggestive of darkness and gloom. Compare the mention of clouds in eschatology (Ezek 30:3; 32:7).

12:3 *Bayyom še-* links the events of v. 2 to those of vv. 3-5. The long temporal clause that it introduces must modify "the sun and the light grows dark,

---

48. E.g., *bôrʾăkā* or *bôryᵉkā* "health" (RH) (Ginsberg); *bôrᵉkā* "your pit" = grave (Levy); *bᵉʾērᵉkā* "your well" = wife.

etc." and not "remember your creator" (1a), for the remembering must take place prior to, not during, the events of vv. 3-5. All of vv. 3-5 refers to the same time. Whether *yom* means "day" or a less definite "time," the events are depicted as concurrent. That "day," as v. 5b shows, is the time of death. Although the events are described as if concurrent, the processes they signify may not be so in actuality. It is a question of how much time one brackets as a "day."

"The keepers of the house" are servants, not watchmen, though watching over the estate may belong to their duties. The term "keeper" is applied to various kinds of servants, not only to guards (2 Sam 20:3 refers to ten concubines David left "to keep the house"). Taylor suggests that *'anšey hehayil*, the "powerful men," are men of influence and position, in contrast to the servants or keepers of the house (1874).

Hayil often means wealth (e.g., Isa 30:6; 60:5; Jer 17:3; Job 5:5). *'Anšey/b^eney hayil* sometimes are skillful, worthy men (e.g., Gen 47:6; Ex 18:21; 2 Kgs 2:16). In some places *'iš/ben/gibbor hayil* seems to indicate social status, as in Ruth 2:1, where Boaz's military prowess is irrelevant. In 1 Chr 9:13, *gibborey heyl-* seems to mean "those in charge of," a designation of status. In Ps 76:6, LXX (75:6) translates *'anšey hayil* as οἱ ἄνδρες τοῦ πλούτου. Although this translation is not appropriate in that context, it does show an early understanding of the phrase as referring to wealth or social status.

Yazu'u: The only other occurrence of ZW'-qal in BH is Esth 5:9, where it means to tremble in fear of someone. The root clearly has that sense in Aramaic, in Dan 5:19 and 6:27.

W^ehit'aww^etu: In context this term seems to indicate a gesture of mourning. The verb means "twist," "writhe," and is not a common term for bowing down. Prostration in grief is expressed by other verbs: *napal ('al panayw/'arṣah)* "fall" (on his face/to the ground) (Josh 7:6; Ezek 9:8; 11:13), *hištahăwah* "prostrate oneself" (Job 1:20), and ŠḤḤ-qal "bow down" (Ps 35:14; 38:7 [together with *na'ăweyti*]; 44:26; 107:39; Isa 5:15). (On *napal 'arṣah* and *na'ăweyti* see Gruber 1980:463-79.) The derivatives of 'WT never mean simply "to bow/make bow" but indicate twisting or distortion, always — except in the present verse — connoting moral deviance. While moral connotations are not appropriate here, the term does seem to indicate more than merely bowing down. The men are twisted and distorted out of their normal form. The by-form 'WH has nearly the same semantic range as 'WT. Like Qoh 12:2f., Ps 38:7 joins the motifs of writhing ('WH-niphal), bowing low, and gloominess: *na'ăweyti šahoti 'ad m^e'od, kol hayyom qoder hillakti,* "I writhe and am bowed exceedingly low; every day I go about in gloom."

The three actions in Ps 38:7 evince violent grief (in the psalm, this is due to feelings of guilt). In Isa 21:3, writhing (ʿWH-niphal) and consternation (BHL-niphal) are reactions to a frightening vision.

Since an estate or village is being described, the "grinders" (*haṭṭo-ḥănot*, fem. pl.) are first of all the maidservants, the counterparts of the men who look after the house. The ladies who look through the windows are the well-to-do women, women of leisure, the counterparts of the "powerful (rich) men." If Taylor is right that *ʾanšey ḥayil* refers to influential, well-to-do men, the four types of people mentioned form an ABAʹBʹ pattern and encompass the range of social classes in the village.

Baṭᵉlu . . . ki miʿeṭu: BṬL (a hapax in BH; common in RH) means "be idle," "cease" from work. The question is in what way the decrease in the number of grinding women would make their work come to a halt.

Ibn Ezra takes the verb as elliptical for *miʿăṭu haṭṭᵉhinah* (better: *miʿăṭu ṭaḥon;* inf. abs.), "they do little grinding." Jenni (1968:52) explains *miʿeṭu* as elliptical for "(ihre Zahl) verringern" ("diminish [their number]") — though it seems like an unnecessary fiction to assume an ellipsis, as he does, when the fuller phrase *(miʿăṭu misparam?)* does not occur. More helpful is his observation that since the root MʿṬ in the qal describes the process *in actu,* the piel intransitive can be resultative: "weil ihrer wenig geworden sind" ("because there have become few of them"; ibid.).

In v. 3bα, the *ki* is not necessarily causal. Even by the figurative interpretation ("grinders" = teeth), *ki miʿeṭu* does not provide a good reason for the cessation of the grinding, for even when only a few teeth are left, they still have to "grind." *Ki* here might have demonstrative force, which can develop into an intensifier (Muraoka 1985:158-64). (For example, Job 22:12b, "and see the highest stars, they are so high"; sim. Gen 18:20.) We could translate, "and the grinding-maids are idle — (their numbers) have so dwindled!" Nevertheless, a causal function is possible here insofar as diminution in the number of grinding maids might bring the work at least to a partial halt, if several people were needed to work together to operate the mill.

"The ladies . . .": lit., "the lookers [fem. pl.] grow dark": *ḥašᵉku* means "grow dark" in the sense of becoming gloomy. ḤŠK alone is not elsewhere used in this sense, but the phrase *ḥašᵉku ʿeyneynu* (lit. "our eyes grew dark") in Lam 5:17 means to become despondent — blind with grief, so to speak. The metaphorical transfer from "dark" to "gloomy" is a natural one. This transfer is lexicalized in the synonymous QDR, which indicates the gloom of mourning; e.g., Jer 8:21; 14:2; Job 5:11; and Ps 38:7. In the last verse, emotional darkness (QDR) appears in conjunction with bowing (ŠḤḤ) and writh-

324

ing ('WH). Within the literal level of the events described, then, the sentence means that the women of the locale are in grief. If this image is also a figure for the eyes, it may also imply the loss of eyesight with age. But the choice of ḤŠK instead of KHH, the latter being usual for loss of eyesight, shows that this is not merely a physiological process, but also an emotional one, namely the loss of joy.

12:4a During the funeral, doors are closed and the mill grows silent (thus Anat 1970:379), probably because the owner of the estate has died.

The pual of *weᵉsuggᵉru* indicates not merely that the doors are now in the state of being closed, but that they are the object of an active closing. In other words, in our mind's eye we should picture not shut doors but doors *being* shut during the time-frame of the scene.

"Doors," *dᵉlatayim,* in the dual, are double-doors that swing together to close. City gates have double-doors (Deut 3:5; Jer 49:31; Josh 6:26), but so do some houses (Josh 2:19; Job 31:32) and great buildings (2 Kgs 18:16).

12:4b *Weᵉyaqum lᵉqol haṣṣippor* is obscure. The usual translation, "He rises to the voice of the bird," is awkward because the presumed subject, the old man, has not been mentioned previously, and also because it is not a great affliction to be awakened by the birds, especially when the usual time of rising was near dawn. At any rate, the discomfort a bird might cause at dawn would be *awakening* a sleeper rather than making him *rise up* (from bed), and QWM means "rise up," not "awaken," which is expressed by QWṢ and 'WR.[49] Furthermore, a sudden jump from the figurative plane of an elaborate allegory to a literal statement (without the subject of the sentence being specified) then back again would be abrasive and hard to follow.

Anat (1970:379) reads *weᵉyiqmal qôl* (suggested earlier by Zapletal), "the voice of the birds withers"; this he interprets to mean that even the birds join in the public lamentations. QML, however, is used only of plants (Isa 19:6; 33:9).

Taylor (1874:19f.) translates, "and the bird rises to voice," in the sense of "starts to sing" (cf. *qum lammišpaṭ,* Ps 76:10; see also Ps 132:8; etc.). He understands this to refer to birds of ill omen. In particular, the owl is thought to make mournful sounds, as in Mic 1:8: "I will make lamentation like jackals, mourning like ostriches"; see also Job 30:28-31. A reference to the hooting of desert birds would indeed intensify the dreariness of the scene. This suggestion is problematic only insofar as the generic term *ṣippor* "bird"

---

49. In Prov 6:9b, *taqum* [*miššᵉnateka*] means "rise up" (for work); it is the antonym of *tiškab,* "lie down" (9a).

would not call to mind specifically an owl or another bird of ill-omen. Still, Taylor's translation fits the MT and requires no emendations. (The non-coordination of gender between the verb and the non-adjacent subject [*ṣippor* is fem.] is not a major drawback (see GKC §245*o*), especially if the bird represents a man. The singing bird is aligned with the songstresses in the parallel line, who are probably the female mourners bowing in lament. Perhaps the bird's song is a cheerful one, contrasting with the dirge (v. 5a draws a similar contrast with v. 5b). Possibly it reinforces the dirge. Just possibly, the "bird" is a metaphor for singer. If so, it could be used generically of chanters of laments, or it could refer to a male mourner, perhaps the leader of the "daughters of song." (2 Chr 35:25 refers to both male and female singers — *šarim* and *šarot* — of laments.)

Wᵉyiššaḥu kol bᵉnot haššir: Taylor (1874:25-27) understands this sentence to mean that women who sing for merriment and entertainment become silent. But the verb means "bow low," not "cease." In accordance with a well-known use of *ben/bat* as a noun of relation (BDB 121b, §8), *bᵉnot haššir* can indeed mean "songstresses." We can compare Ugaritic *bnt hll snnt*, "the daughters of praise (songs), swallows" (Aqhat ii 27). These are the Kotharot, female singers.[50] The combination of "daughters of praise (songs)" and "swallows" resembles the proximity of "bird" and "daughters of song" in v. 4b.

Bᵉnot haššir, the songstresses, are mourning women, probably professionals, who intone their laments. (In Am 8:3, the songs of the palace have a mournful sound.) In 2 Chr 35:25, the singers *(šarim)* and the songstresses *(šarot)* utter laments *(qinot).* According to Matt 9:23, lamentations were accompanied by flutes. The songstresses in Qoh 12:4 are bent down in the traditional posture of lamentation. Bowing low, sitting on the ground, and prostrating oneself are expressions of mourning (see Gruber 1980:460-79). Note in particular: "I went about as in mourning for a mother, I was bowed down *(šaḥoti)* in gloom" (Ps 35:14; see further Ps 38:7; 107:39; Isa 2:9; 5:15). Mourning women are represented in this posture in numerous Egyptian paintings.

12:5aα *Gam miggaboahh yira'u:* Most commentators suppose this to mean that old people are afraid of heights, either because they develop acrophobia (is that so?) or because they are adverse to walking up hills (though then the

50. Dahood 1952:215. This does not mean that the Kotharot *are* swallows; this is their epithet. Gibson (1978:106), however, translates "the swallow-like daughters of the crescent moon."

object of their "fear" should be "heights" [m*romim], "hills," or "ascents" [ma'ălot], not "a tall thing" [gaboahh]). Moreover, there is no previous mention of old people to provide a subject for "fear." These interpretations also must assume a sudden switch from a description of an old man to a description of old people, and from figurative to literal statement. Also, m*romim, not gaboahh, designates heights in the abstract. Gaboahh is an adjective applied to tall or lofty entities and could serve as a noun meaning something tall or high, but not heights or high places. Taylor construes the clause "When also they fear from on high, and terrors are on the path" as a merism equivalent to "terrors are on all sides" (1874:28). But "high" and "path" are not opposites.

I favor a solution along the lines suggested by Yaḥyah (sim. Anat 1970:379), who construes gaboahh as the "High One," that is, God. Compare Job 22:12, "Is God not (in) the height of heaven [gobahh šamayim]?" By this reading, it is the fear of God (real fear, not just reverent piety) that encompasses the mourners as they accompany the dead. This nicely echoes 12:1a, as interpreted above. One problem is that bare gaboahh "high," without an article, is not a recognizable epithet for God. The essence of Yaḥyah's interpretation can, however, be maintained by vocalizing miggōbahh, "(they fear) from on high." The mi(n) "from" indicates the source of the fears: heaven, an allusion to God.

The subject of yira'u is the songstresses or the members of the procession they lead. As they bow down, they dread the power lurking over their heads. This clause and the next describe the fear and dismay (at once ritual and genuine) of the mourners.

W*ḥatḥattim badderek, "and terrors are along the way": The exact sense of the hapax ḥatḥattim is unclear. It presumably is related to ḤTT-niphal, which means "be broken," hence "fear." The sentence probably refers to the emotions of those walking in the cortège (cf. Anat 1970:379). Scenes of dismay mark the processional. Vivid depictions of a formalized outpouring of emotions, compounded of misery and fear, are frequent in Egyptian funerary scenes in tomb murals. Needless to say, funerary practices in Egypt were very different than in Israel. But the outward demonstrations of grief in Egypt were similar to what we know from Mesopotamia and were probably common throughout the ancient Near East.

12:5aβγb A new topic begins in v. 5aβ and a verse division would have been appropriate here.

The almond, "locust," and caperberry have most often been read as deliberately obscured sexual allusions. This is always easy to do, but there is no reason whatsoever to associate these plants with sexuality or its decline. They are best understood literally, as descriptions of nature that stand in *contrast* to man. Nature, but not man, is reborn in the spring (Hertzberg; Loretz 1964:191f.). This same bleak contrast is drawn in Job 14:7-10: "A tree has hope: if it is cut off, it will be renewed. . . . But man dies and is helpless. A human expires and disappears."

"But the almond tree blossoms, etc." *W^eyānē's* is correctly pointed by MT as NṢṢ-hiphil, in spite of the superfluous *'aleph*. Deriving the word from N'Ṣ and pointing as *yinnā'ēṣ* "is despised" (e.g., Podechard) makes little sense and requires wild guesses as to why an almond tree should be detested.

W^eyistabbel hehagab: Since this occurs between and parallel to two sentences describing the blossoming of trees, the *hagab* also is probably a kind of plant. "Be laden" would describe the growth of buds or fruit. *Ḥagab* elsewhere is a kind of locust (the insect), but here it might be the name of a tree. In English "locust" is also used of several related kinds of trees, including *Robinia pseudo-acacia* and the carob, whose pods resemble the locust (grasshopper). The latter grows in Palestine and could be the *hagab* here. (In RH the carob is called *harub*.) The carob's pods appear in autumn but do not ripen until summer. That process could be well described as the tree "becoming laden" with the heavy fruit. *Histabbel* can mean "be laden" in the sense of "be fecund," like the SBL-pual in Ps 144:14. But we know little of the flora terminology in BH, and *hagab* could be any tree or bush. This is more likely than that the locust is an unparalleled, and rather weird, figure for the rump (b. Shab. 152a and Rashi), the male genitals (mentioned by Ibn Ezra), the ankles (Tg), or the back of the pelvic cavity (Delitzsch).

Ginsberg (p. 137; followed by Fox 1987) emends *hāgāb* to *hāṣāb* (which is known from RH). The *haṣab,* sc., "sea onion," "squill," gives the appearance of dying in May, when it contracts into its bulb. With the increase of moisture in August, the bulb becomes laden (thus, *w^eyistabbel*) and quickly bursts into life again. But since we do not know that *hagab* is the wrong word, it is facile to emend it to one we know slightly better, especially since *ṣadé-gimel* interchanges are not well attested and hard to explain.

For *w^etāpēr* "will annul" read *w^etiprah* (*h-h* haplography) "blossoms" (Perles 1895:30). PRḤ is parallel to NṢṢ in Cant 7:13. The LXX correctly translates *ha'ăbiyyonah* as ἡ κάππαρις "the caperberry," which is the meaning of the word in RH.

Ki holek ha'adam 'el beyt 'olamo (v. 5bα): This happens at the same time as "the mourners walk about in the streets" and thus describes the processional to the grave. *Halak* is used of going from life to the underworld or to the grave in Qoh 3:20; 9:10; Ps 39:14; 1 Chr 17:11; etc. The *ki* at the beginning of v. 5b may be understood as giving the reason for the entire complex of occurrences of vv. 3-5a, not only for the events of v. 5a. "House of eternity" *(beyt 'olam)* is a euphemism for the tomb in Nabatean, Syriac, and Palmyrene inscriptions (Healey 1995:190).

12:6 The poem shifts its focus from the funeral to a series of mysterious figures. But the mystery is in their surface meaning — the identity of the physical objects — not in their figurative sense. The following verse shows that they signify death, or possibly death and burial. At the same time, the physical images of falling and breaking intensify the atmosphere of disintegration and neglect in the village or estate. Whatever these objects are, they suffer sudden and irreparable destruction. The fragments of the vessels and wheel are enduring witnesses to their former wholeness. The wheel lies in a *bor,* which also means grave. All this is evocative of death and burial, with the bones lying dry and disjointed in the grave.

There are several ways to identify the objects that serve as symbols. There may be (1) a cord, one vessel (the *gullah* may also be a *kad* or a component of it), and a wheel (a *galgal*); (2) a cord, two vessels (a *gullah* and a *kad*), and a wheel *(galgal);* or (3) either of the above, but understanding *galgal* too as a vessel. Interpretation #2 is the most likely and the most faithful to the usual senses of these words. The uses of *gullah* and *kad* elsewhere suggest they are distinct, the former an ornamental bowl, the latter a simple clay jug, while *galgal* consistently means wheel.

The multiple images for a single referent may serve to emphasize that death is universal and inescapable, whatever kind of "vessel" a person may be. (Compare the way that Joseph interprets the repetition of a single pattern in Pharaoh's dreams as signifying certainty in Gen 41:32.) Ginsberg decodes the three symbols variously: the golden bowl is the nobleman, the clay jug is the common man, and the wheel (jar?) (a *galgal*) is the poor man. But there is no gradation apparent in the last two items.

12:6aα The cord snaps. In *yrḥq* [qeré: *yērātēq*] *ḥebel hakkesep* the ketiv is *yrḥq = yirḥaq* "be far," followed by LXX ἀνατραπῇ "is removed." But *yirḥaq* would not be used of the cord's playing out. The vessel might "go far" but this would not be said of the cord. Syr has *ntpsq* "be snapped"; sim. Tg. As for the qeré, RTQ is rare; the verb occurs elsewhere only in Nah 3:10 (in the pual), where it means "bind," which does not make sense here. Gordis posits a privative niphal, a nonexistent category. We should emend the qeré to *yinnātēq,* which is used of a cord's snapping in Qoh 4:12 (thus McNeile, Barton,

Podechard, et al.). On *nun/resh* interchanges see *LSF* §211 and *TAOT* 100f. Some *nun/resh* interchanges may be phonetic in origin (as in Nebuchadnezzar/ Nebuchadrezzar), but graphic confusion may explain others.

12:6aβ A golden bowl [*gullat hazzahab*] is smashed [pointing *wᵉtērōṣ*]: A *gullah* is a round bowl that holds liquids. It can hold lamp oil, as in Zech 4:2f., or wine and honey, as in Keret i 71-72, 164-66: "Pour wine in a *gl* of silver, in a *gl* of gold (pour) honey." In Josh 15:19 (= Judg 1:15), *gullah* is a geological feature, apparently a basin-shaped concavity with water springs. In 1 Kgs 7:41, it is a feature of the temple columns Jachin and Boaz, probably part of the capital. A *gullah* would not be used for drawing water from a well, but it could be suspended on a cord as an oil lamp. *Gullah* sounds like *gulgolet* "skull," and this may also be a play on words, as if to say, "the skull is smashed," as when a stone that falls on Abimelech's head *wattariṣ 'et gulgolto* "and smashed his skull"; Judg 9:53.

The MT pointing, *wᵉtāruṣ,* parses the word as a qal from RWṢ "run." Perhaps the Masoretes imagined the bowl "running" to the ground as the well-wheel spins freely and the rope plays out. But "run" would not describe a fall. Pointing *tērōṣ,* a niphal from RṢṢ, "smash," gives better sense.

12:6bα The jug falls and breaks at the spring. The *kad* is a simple clay vessel for drawing water. It must have been a common occurrence for a heavy, wet jug to slip out of the water-drawer's hands and shatter on the rocks at the spring of water. *Mabbua'* is a water source (Isa 35:7; 49:10), not the fabricated stone housing of the well. Water would typically well up through rocks, upon which the jug could smash.

The smashing of a clay vessel represents the destruction of life in Jer 18:6; Isa 30:14; and Ps 2:9. Man is compared to a vessel in Isa 45:9 and 64:7 and is called a "precious vessel" *(kᵉli ḥemdah)* in a dirge in b. Meg. 6a.

12:6bβ "The wheel [*galgal*] is smashed in the pit [*bor*]": Objections have been raised to the appropriateness of a wheel in the series of vessels. More-over, a pulley would not be dislodged by the snapping of the cord wound around it.

For these reasons, Dahood (1952:216f.; followed by Fox 1987) glosses *galgal* as "pot" or the like, deriving this sense from the meaning of the root GLL "round." Dahood refers to a vase on which *galgal* is inscribed in Punic characters, and to Akkadian *gulgullu,* which in addition to meaning "skull" is also a water pitcher or cooking pot.

Since a wheel has a place among the array of water-drawing implements, and since these are enigmatic to start with, we cannot say that it is *not* a wheel that is breaking. As I now read the passage, this item is distinct from the cord, the bowl, and the jug. The wheel used for drawing water from a *bor* was called *galgal* in RH (e.g., m. Mid 5; t. Erub 8:14). Well-wheels are attested in Tannaitic literature, which refers to one in the temple court (m. Mid 5:4; m. Erub 10; t. Erub 8:14).

A wooden wheel would not shatter in the well or cistern if there were still water left. We can picture an old cistern, dry and neglected, with its wheel apparatus having fallen into disrepair and lying broken on the bottom. The image of a broken object falling into a cistern — *bor* — is especially appropriate because the grave is also called *bor* (Prov 28:17[?]; Isa 14:15; 38:18; etc.).

Wᵉnārōṣ is a niphal qatal-form from RṢṢ. Here it is probably a *waw*-conversive; compare *yiqtol//wᵉqatal* in v. 1 and various other *waw*-conversives in this unit.

The snapping of the cord is the instant when a person's connection to life is ruptured.

12:7 "And the dust returns to the earth as it was before" straddles the figurative and the literal. This image looks two ways, to the preceding image, for clay vessels are made from *'apar,* "dust" (actually, "dirt"), and to the following process, for man is composed likewise. Human death is seen as one of a series of entropic processes, and the corpse is one of several fragmented, useless, forgotten implements.

The *ruaḥ,* the life-spirit, returns to God, who gave it. At death, whether of man or beast, the elements of life — body and breath — separate, and God takes back his gift of life. Ps 104:29, in describing the death of all creatures, says: "You gather in their spirit and they expire, and they return to their dust"; see also Job 34:14f.: "If [God] pays attention to him, He gathers back his spirit and breath. Then all flesh dies at once, and man returns to the dust."

In the Hebrew conception, the person *is* the body, no less than the animal's body *is* the animal, and he *has* a life-spirit or breath *(ruaḥ* or *nᵉšamah).* This concept is evident in Ezek 37:8-10 and Gen 2:7. The creature God forms is a man even before he gets the life-breath (there called *nišmat ḥayyim*), at which time he becomes a *nepeš ḥayyah,* a living being (Gen 2:7). When the spirit is removed, the person, and not only the body, is said to go to the earth, or to Sheol, or to darkness (Ps 104:29; Qoh 6:4; 9:10; and often). Thus Qoh 12:7 does not imply continued existence of the sort that would overcome death and compensate for the miseries of life.

In 3:20f., Qohelet said that no one knows whether man's spirit goes upward at death. In 3:21 Qohelet was countering someone else's idea: the ascent of the soul to eternal life. In 12:7, Qohelet states that man's spirit goes back to God, and this must be upwards, but he means only that God takes back the life-spirit and deprives the individual of it. This does not affirm an afterlife. The verse says that at death a person's body returns to the dirt and his life-spirit is withdrawn; in other words, he is deprived of breath, without which he is a helpless, somnolent semi-being in Sheol. Having discounted the possibility of an enduring soul as unknowable and thus irrelevant, Qohelet leaves it aside. When, at the climax of his harsh description of death in chapter 12, he speaks of the departure of the life-breath, he conceives of it in the ancient way as God's repossession of the life force.

Since 12:7 does not imply an afterlife, it is actually *more* pessimistic than 3:21. The earlier verse at least grants that the spirit's ascent to God would redeem humanity from absurdity, whereas the present verse assumes that the spirit does ascend and yet sees no escape from death's obliterating power.

C. "All Is Absurd"

(8)   *Utterly absurd, said the Qohelet,*
      All is absurd.

12:8 In the most memorable inclusio in the Bible, the book of Qohelet returns to its opening declaration. This verse and 1:2 bracket the book, and the external (authorial) perspective reappears. But the reader does not stop suddenly at 12:7. Qoh 12:8 is both the climax of this poem and an encapsulation of the book.

Qoh 12:1-8 reverses the direction of 1:2-8. There the declaration of universal absurdity is demonstrated by examples of futility in nature. In 12:1-8 a description of the futility of human life — futile in the sense that it ends up back where it started ($k^e\check{s}ehayah$; v. 7) — culminates in and justifies the declaration that all is absurd. In both cases, circularity is felt to show futility and thus absurdity.

EXCURSUS II

How Worlds End: Aging and Death in Qohelet 12

1. Approaching an Enigma

This is a powerful poem, even if we don't quite know what it means. Actually, we do know what it means: enjoy life before you grow old and die. What we don't know is *how* it means it. The poem retains its power even over those who do not understand it completely — and no one does. It is important to take stock of just what the poem does communicate, and how it does so, even as it withholds the meaning of many details.

Qoh 12:1-7 is section B of a longer unit (11:7–12:8), but it has a large degree of independence from section A and makes its own demands on interpretation. I will begin by considering the perspectives from which it can be read. *How* a poem means belongs to *what* it means. Qohelet is not simply plying us with information; if that were his goal, he would not make it so hard for us to get at it. He makes us go through a challenging and uncertain process of reading, and that process will presumably have effects beyond the conveyance of information. There is nothing in the encoded facts (by any interpretation) that is not already known to all, so *how* we know them is important.

There are three ways of reading Qoh 12:1-7: the literal, the symbolic, and the allegorical. These ways of reading are not mutually exclusive. On the contrary, the figurative and the symbolic require a literal base line from which both types of extended meaning can proceed.

2. Facing the Surface

Rather than thinking of imagery as an expendable outer garb, we should compare it to the visible surface of a painting. The imagery *is* the painting. The symbolism, emotive overtones, religious or political message, and so on, exist only as projections and constructions of the surface imagery, not as substitutes for it. To understand even a manifestly allegorical painting — or poem — we must first look carefully at the surface the author shows us.

The literal meaning is the one given by a reading that attends to the things, actions, and events that the images depict. It is the meaning most adequately captured by paraphrase. Literal meaning may be conveyed in part by metaphor, but in a literal reading, the metaphors aid in illuminating the explicit meaning and are strictly subordinated to it.[51] A literal reading does not assume the presence of a governing metaphor or look for meanings conveyed by the imagery independently of the surface content.

Or we may think of this as a "cinematographic" reading. A movie showing the literal meaning of Jotham's allegory (Judg 9:7-15), for example, would show trees discussing who will rule over them. Looking at Qoh 12:1-7 that way, we ask: if we were watching a movie with these events depicted, what would we be seeing?

One literal reading, proposed by M. Gilbert (1981), takes the poem as a description of the realities of aging: shaking, bending, blindness, obscurity, and isolation. Different people are described: guards trembling, old women going blind, etc. Against this it must be noted that the scene does not show different people growing old. And doors in the street would not actually be closed as one grows old, nor would milling cease as the aged died off (Gilbert construes *mi'etu* as impersonal), for others would take their place. Moreover, the phrasing of these verses implies that all this happens more or less at once, whereas everyone in a town would not grow old simultaneously.

Some literal readings, without denying a further metaphorical meaning, attend to the surface meaning of the scene as a whole rather than decoding its elements atomistically.

Along these lines, C. D. Ginsburg sees the scene as a cohesive description of a gathering storm, which in turn serves as a figure for the approach of death.

Similarly, M. Leahy (1952) sees in the scene a depiction of fearful reactions to a thunderstorm. These represent the emotions in a household when someone dies. The problem is that the rain has stopped (v. 2b), and anyway a rainstorm is not *that* frightening. Moreover, the sun, moon, and stars would not be darkened all at once by a downpour.

O. Loretz (1964) reads the scene as a description of winter followed by spring. The winter is a metaphor for aging; the coming of spring (v. 5b) reminds us that man cannot revive. But winter, especially in Israel, would not make men twist and tremble unless they were extraordinary cowards, nor

51. For example, the lamentation in Ezek 28 calls the prince of Tyre a beautiful "seal" (read *ḥotam*) in the garden of Eden (v. 12). This is a trope for beauty and embellishes the portrayal of the first man in Eden. It remains within the parameters of the literal meaning, which is the depiction of the Edenic man's resplendence. Similarly, within a literal reading of Jotham's allegory, "shade" (Judg 9:15) is a metaphor for "protection" as well as a reference to actual blockage of sunlight.

would it cause the maids to halt their grinding, because preparation of bread is an endless chore.

J. F. A. Sawyer (1976) traces an extended description of a ruined estate, which represents the failure of human efforts. He assumes many accretions to the basic picture. Similarly H. Witzenrath (1979:46-50) uses a structuralist analysis to argue that the scene shows the deterioration of a house as a symbol of human ephemerality (12:3-4a). She says that the images of these sentences (like the others in 12:2, 4-5aα, 6) describe the movement from a positive state (strength/activity/brightness/openness) to a negative one (weakness/inactivity/darkness/closure). But the images in Qoh 12:3-4a do not suggest decay and dilapidation so much as pain and cessation of normal activity. To be precise, the scene does not depict the experience of dying and death but rather the observers' *response* to a death.

The most convincing of the various literal interpretations proposed is that of C. Taylor, *The Dirge of Coheleth* (1874). Taylor argues vigorously that 12:2-5 is a "dirge describing the state of a household or community on an occasion of death and mourning" (pp. iii-iv). Although Taylor calls the poem a dirge, he seems to mean that it is a dirge-like description of a funeral day. M. Anat (1970) goes further and maintains that the poem is a reworking of an actual dirge, which he attempts to reconstruct by stripping away whatever does not fit his metrical scheme. In spite of some arbitrary methods and far-fetched interpretations, Anat does show that some of the statements in this passage pertain to mourning. But the poem itself is not a dirge, for the purpose of a dirge is to bewail the loss of the deceased and to extol his virtues, and these are not the concerns of Qoh 12:1-8.

The strength of Taylor's approach lies in his attempt to grasp what is happening on the literal plane rather than jumping quickly, as most commentators do, to figurative meanings. He is, however, wrong in his insistent exclusion of all meaning other than the literal in vv. 3-5, for the literal meaning may well hold symbolic or figurative significances, which may, conversely, reinforce the literal picture. The funerary interpretation can account for the passage as a whole better than the figurative approach can, but many gaps remain, and not all details accommodate themselves to the funeral-scene interpretation.

It is possible that some of the lines are taken from actual dirges. Except for 2 Sam 1:17-27 and 3:33f., all we know of dirges of Biblical times is at one remove.[52] The prophets almost certainly draw on existing *qinot* either to create mocking laments (e.g., Isa 14:4-20; Ezek 26:17f.; 27:3b-10; 28:12-

---

52. Laments are quoted in rabbinic sources, e.g., m. Sem. 1:9; b. B. Bat. 91 a-b; b. Meg. 6a; 28b; b. Ber. 6b; b. Mo'ed Q. 25b.

19), or to dramatize an impending national disaster by bewailing it or by quoting the future lamentations of those destined to suffer the calamity (e.g., Mic 2:4). Lam 1, 2, and 4 are laments for a communal disaster, though not necessarily spoken by the community. Lam 3 and 5 and several psalms are communal entreaties with embedded expressions of lamentation (e.g., Pss 44; 60; 74; 79; 80; 85). References to communal mourning include Amos 5:16; 2 Sam 1:12; 1 Macc 1:27; 9:41.

On behalf of the interpretation of 12:2-5 as depicting the events surrounding a death and funeral, we may observe that although Qohelet urges enjoyment of life during one's youth, he does not elsewhere show much anxiety about physical decrepitude. There is no reason to expect him to conclude his teachings with an extended threnody on the ailments of aging. He is, on the other hand, deeply disturbed by death, and it is no surprise to see his gaze returning to that subject as he brings his teachings to a close.

The gross syntax of the passage, described in the introduction to 12:1-7, supports the idea that 12:2-5 depicts the time of death and mourning rather than the process of aging. Qoh 12:3-5a is an extended temporal clause describing the events that occur *at the same time as* "the man is going to his eternal home, and the mourners walk about in the streets" (v. 5b). Though a man's going to his "eternal home" might be construed as an allusion to aging and a gradual approach to death, the mourners' procession (v. 5bβ) can only signify the funeral, and thus v. 5bα too must refer to the cortège. Also, the darkening of the luminaries (v. 2) occurs "in the day when" (that is, in the time when) the events of the long temporal clause (vv. 3-5) take place, rather than long before them. The blossoming described in v. 5aβ-αγ, however, is stated as a fact in the universal (atemporal) present, not as an event on the day of the death or burial.

Before the funeral, the luminaries go dark. Even in a literal interpretation this must be read metaphorically. The light that is snuffed out in 12:2 is the light that is sweet in 11:7, namely the light of life. The day the lights go out is "the day when" all that is described in 12:3-7 happens, and that is the time of death and the funeral.

The significance of the rain's and the clouds' return is unclear. "Return after" may mean "follow" (e.g., Ruth 1:15, *šubi 'aḥărey yᵉbimtek* "return after your sister-in-law," where *'aḥărey* is spatial) (John Hobbins, private communication). In that case, the rain has not necessarily ended when the clouds come in. Usually clouds disappear after the rain, especially after the rainy season. When the clouds return right away, the day remains gloomy.

If the darkening in 12:2a alludes to death, as the contrast with "seeing the sun" in 11:7 suggests, then the clouds' return may be a further description

336

of life's light going out rather than a metaphor for the sadness of aging. The rain here is usually understood as a sign of gloom, but elsewhere rain is a cause and sign of vitality and fertility. It is the clouds' coming *after* the rain that betokens death.

If we came into a village and saw these things happening, we would conclude we were witnessing a funeral procession. During the funeral, doors are closed and the mill grows silent. The mill maids cease their work, because they have grown few in number, perhaps because they have gone to join the mourning. The passing cortège brings normal activities to a halt.

While Qohelet's description of the gloom that a funeral casts on a village or estate may be overstated, some evidence does suggest that a funeral procession could and in principle should bring activities temporarily to a halt. Josephus says that "all who pass by when a corpse is being buried must accompany the funeral and join in the lamentations" (*Contra Apionem,* 2.205). The Talmudim, in b. Moʿed Q. 27b and j. Bik. 65c (cf. Shulḥan Arukh, Y. D. 361.4), define a duty to rise and accompany a cortège for at least a symbolic four paces. Closer to Qohelet's time, Ben Sira's monitions in 7:34 and 38:16-17 show that participation in funerals was an important communal obligation.

Qohelet leads us through a village, painting the scene item by item but leaving many puzzles. What village is this? We may wonder if this is in some sense the place, the situation, we will reach when we grow old or when we die. We see sturdy men writhing. What nameless dread terrifies them so? The "grinders" (fem. pl.), whatever else they represent, are first of all grinding-maids. When they suspend their work, one of the background sounds of everyday life stops. Milling was a never-ending task, and its sound would drone on unabated. Its cessation would leave a perturbing absence. The darkening (gloom? disappearance?) of the ladies at the windows darkens the mood of the village. In the past their half-hidden presence, scarcely noticed, signaled human contact. They observed, noted, and registered the bustle of everyday life. Now their faces darken and somber. What grieves them? Doors are shut — against what? — and the sounds of daily life cease, perhaps because the master of the estate has departed forever. Suddenly we realize that the background hum of human activity was reassuring, a constant reminder that we belong to the land of the living. Now it is gone. All we hear now is the chirping (hooting?) of the bird and the keening of the mourners. They alone are going about their business. The mourning women bend low. People fear what is above their heads, an anxiety whose unnamed source may be God. All about them too, as they walk along the way, lurk unnamed terrors. There will be rebirth, the annual budding, growing, and blooming of nature. But this is without cheer, because it mocks the finality of *our* end. For man there is only snapping, falling, and shattering. The vessel lies shattered beyond repair.

Still leaving aside the symbolic significations (though these soon begin to intrude themselves into a literal reading) we may ask about the connotations of the imagery. The imagery of the poem, whatever its further meanings, creates an atmosphere of loss, pain, contortion, and constriction. This atmosphere is almost independent of the way we decode the images, if at all. The poem draws us into a world of decay, fear, and silence. Then it makes us look through this atmosphere to see our own aging and death, whose pain is only made worse by contrast with the rejuvenation of nature.

The scene is unsettling in an almost surrealistic way. The luminaries and light itself are extinguished. Clouds hang overhead. All is murky. Then we encounter a succession of images of distortion and despair: trembling, writhing, stoppage of activity, darkening, shutting, silence, bowing, fear, and the plangent song of grief.

What do all these people see that terrifies and afflicts them so? For whom are they mourning so intensely? The answer is inevitable: they see your death and mourn for *you*, you to whom Qohelet addressed his advice and warnings, the "you" of v. 1. Qohelet wants you to look upon your death and funeral from the outside. It is *your* fate that appalls the village. Your death is eclipsing their world, and you are present at the terrible scene. The bell tolls for you, and for everyone.

3. Seeing Through Symbols

Even in the literal reading, some features of the scene — again visualizing it as in a movie — obtrude and disturb the construction of the funeral scene. This is no ordinary funeral. By diverting our attention from the mundane, the obtrusive, hyperbolic features provoke a reading on another level, a symbolic one.[53]

The distinction between symbolism and allegory is not sharp-etched or widely agreed upon. The most helpful definition of symbolism, for present purposes at least, is Samuel Taylor Coleridge's, who says that, in contrast to allegory,

a symbol is characterized by a translucence of the Special in the Individual or of the General in the Especial or of the Universal in the General. Above

53. The following discussion of symbolism draws especially on G. Kurz 1982:65-83.

all by the translucence of the Eternal through and in the Temporal. It always partakes of the Reality which it renders intelligible; and while it enunciates the whole, abides itself as a living part in that Unity, of which it is the representative. (1832:40)

Coleridge is defining a particular type of symbolism, sometimes called "inherent symbolism,"[54] in which conception and embodiment are simultaneous and interpenetrating. Such symbols are characterized by an "immediate presentation of something not immediate," thus evoking an ineffable, "total organic response" (Mischel 1952:72). Since the symbol carries with it an indefinite penumbra of connotations, paraphrase cannot exhaust its meaning, nor can a symbolic image be directly translated into an entity in another domain, as an allegorical figure can (e.g., grinders = teeth; thornbush = Abimelech). Rather, in a symbol we observe a reality concentrated and instantiated. For example, Adam both *is* a man and represents humanity. Dust symbolizes the body and *is* its substance. Esther both *is* a Jew in the diaspora and symbolically embodies the experience of diaspora Jewry; Abel's murder is an instance of brotherly conflict and also represents all human strife. By this understanding of symbolism, how can we read Qoh 12:1-7 symbolically?

Through the prism of symbolism the reader sees more than an ordinary death and burial. The poem depicts a community at mourning, but also something beyond that. After all, rarely does an individual's death cause communal grief so extreme and so pervasive. The sun, moon, and stars do not truly go dark when someone dies, and light itself, the primal light of creation, does not disappear. Nor does the return of actual clouds and rain (usually a welcome phenomenon) cause consternation.

Behind the surface, looming in the background, is a disaster of cosmic magnitude. The universal darkness and silence — which blanket everything from the stars to the mills, from the powerful men to the menials, from the rich women to the maids — evokes the prophetic vision of the national and universal desolation awaiting Israel and all humanity at the end of this age. Normal sounds are stifled and the land is enveloped in darkness and terror.[55]

54. Following Levin 1956:15. "Symbolism" includes more kinds of signification than Coleridge's definition allows. Symbols may also be related to their referents by convention, prescription, or extrinsic association. Allegory, for its part, is a symbolic mode; see further Fletcher 1964:14. In this discussion I am using "symbol" to refer to what Levin calls "inherent" or "natural" symbols.

55. The patristic commentator Gregory Thaumaturgus, in his *Metaphrasis,* apparently interprets Qoh 12:1-6 as describing "that great and terrible day of God" (quoted in Plumptre 1881:90f.).

> I will eliminate from them
> the voice of gladness and the voice of happiness,
> the voice of the groom and the voice of the bride,
> the sound of the millstones and the light of the candle.
> And all this land will become a desolate waste. (Jer 25:10-11a)

> And when you are extinguished,[56] I will cover the heavens,
> and I will make their stars go dark.
> I will cover the sun with a cloud,
> and the moon will not shine its light.
> All the luminaries in the heavens
> I will blacken above you;
> and I will set darkness upon your land,
> says the Lord God. (Ezek 32:7-8)

The day of the Lord is dark and overhung with clouds. It is "a day of clouds" (Ezek 30:3), which represent misery and fright. It is

> a day of darkness and gloom,
> a day of cloud and mist. . . .
> Before it peoples writhe,
> and all faces gather blackness [pa'rur]. . . .
> The sun and the moon go dark,
> and the stars withdraw their radiance.
>
> (Joel 2:2a, 6, 10b; compare Zeph 1:15)

On the cruel and violent day of retribution, the Lord will come

> to make the earth a desolation;
> and he will destroy the sinners from upon it.
> For the stars of the heavens and their constellations
> will not shine their light:
> The sun will go dark when it arises,
> and the moon will not radiate its light. (Isa 13:9b-10)

Threat of darkness is a frequent prophetic topos, as in Isa 5:30; 8:22; Amos 5:18-20; and Zeph 1:15. The extinguishing of light symbolizes the undoing

---

56. Pointing *bikbōtᵉkā* (qal for piel) with LXX. Ehrlich emends to *bmwtk* "in your death," which is graphically feasible but lackluster.

of creation, the return to primeval darkness. The prophetic eschatology does not regard the day of the Lord as the end of the universe,[57] but it does use hyperbolic, end-of-the-world imagery to suggest the extremity of the day's horror.

Here the literal and the symbolic readings crisscross. The "literal" sense of Qoh 12:2 (the luminaries go dark) fits into the symbolic reading of the passage (as eschatological disaster), while the "literal" interpretation of the passage (as depicting an actual death and funeral) requires that we read the darkening of the lights figuratively, as a metaphor for an individual death.

The prophets' eschatological symbolism draws upon imagery and possibly phraseology familiar from mourning practices, while applying the images and phrases to a personified city, land, or world, for example: "The field is robbed, the land mourns" (Joel 1:10); "Shall the earth not quake for this, and all its inhabitants mourn?" (Amos 8:8); "The earth mourns and is withered; miserable, withered, is the land" (Isa 24:4); "Her doors moan and mourn. Wiped out, she sits on the ground" (Isa 3:26); "For this the earth mourns, the heavens grow dark above" (Jer 4:28); and many more like these.

In Qoh 12:3bα, the cessation of the daily chore of milling, restated in 4aβ, epitomizes the disruption of ordinary activities. What has happened to the maids? In terms of the surface-scene, their numbers around the mill may simply have dwindled as they stopped their chores in order to join the mourning. But the event calls to mind the inactivity that follows depopulation; compare, for example, Isa 13:12: "I will make man scarcer than fine gold, people than gold of Ophir." Depopulation will silence the millstones (Jer 25:10, quoted above; cf. Rev 18:22f.).

The reaction of the denizens of Qohelet's village transcends a community's formalized expressions of grief. Everyone, and not only the immediate family, seems to be deeply smitten with grief, and not only grief but terror, which funerals would not normally evoke. Everyone, from the wealthy to the most humble servants, has his normal condition interrupted — like the population facing the cataclysm Isaiah predicts, when social distinctions become nugatory: "Laymen shall be like priest, servant like his master, maidservant like her mistress, buyer like seller, lender like borrower, creditor like debtor" (24:2).

The behavior of the population of Qohelet's village recalls the horrified quaking and writhing common in eschatological depictions. The men in Qoh 12:3 tremble and twist just as people will do on the day of the Lord, when

57. See the definition and discussion of "eschatology" in Lindblom 1952. Eschatology refers to visions of a new age in which the relations of history or the world are altered and conditions in general are radically changed (p. 81).

> . . . all hands will grow slack,
> and every human heart melt,
> and they will be terrified.
> Pangs and pains will seize them,
> they will writhe like a woman in labor.
> They will look at each other in dismay,
> their faces flames of fire. (Isa 13:7f.)

Such torment recalls the prophet as he contemplates the approaching cataclysm:

> Therefore my loins are full of trembling.
> I am seized with pangs,
> like the pangs of a woman in labor.
> I am too twisted [*na'ăweyti*] to hear,
> too terrified to see. (Isa 21:3)

The shaking and writhing of males was considered especially shocking (Jer 30:6). The terror or grief — or both — of the men in Qohelet's village suggests they have seen a disaster of high magnitude.

The light that is extinguished in 12:2 is the light that is called sweet in 11:7, namely the light of life, and the darkening of the light is the onset of the eternal darkness mentioned in 11:8. In one sense this is the extinction of an individual life; in another, the extinction of a universe. Every individual is a microcosm and every death the end of a world. For the person who dies, the stars blink out, the sun goes dark (only the living "see the sun"), rigor mortis sets in, and all sound ceases.

Both Qohelet and the prophets draw upon images of mourning and universal cataclysm. In the prophets, these depict the disaster to a nation or the world. Qohelet uses them to represent the demise of the individual. Symbolism usually views the general through the particular, the great through the small (Daniel representing the Jewish people in exile; a woman's mourning representing Jerusalem's; Jerusalem's mourning representing Israel's misery). Qohelet perceives the particular through the general. He sees the small writ large.[58] He audaciously musters images of universal disaster to evoke

58. John Donne excelled in metaphors of this sort, such as when he calls his beloved "my America, my new-found land" or proclaims that "She is all States, and all Princes, I" ("The Sun Rising"). For Donne and his contemporaries, such images gave voice to the concept of man as microcosm. "I am a little world made cunningly of elements," Donne wrote in *Holy Sonnets,* V. Qohelet, I think, shares this view.

the unimaginable experience of one's own death. He makes the reader see his death from the standpoint of an outside observer.

The hyperbole in Qohelet's dirge recalls Talmudic statements that apply apocalyptic imagery to the death of great sages, such as: the columns of Caesarea ran with tears; roof gutters ran with blood; stars were visible in the daytime; all cedars were uprooted; hail stones fell from heaven; the palms were laden with thorns (from B. Mo'ed Qaṭan 25b; see Feldman 1977:131f.).

In comparison with prophetic eschatology, Qohelet's imagery is restrained. Still, Qohelet does choose to evoke a vast catastrophe to suggest a vision of individual death, that most ordinary of tragedies. The angst he thereby reveals is not restricted to this poem. Throughout the book, Qohelet betrays a virtual obsession with death, not because it is the end of life but because it annuls life's achievements.

There may be no explanation for this unusual obsession with death besides the author's personality. Not every literary phenomenon can be mapped onto social or historical realities. Qohelet's obsession with death intersects another of his peculiarities: he reveals no awareness of himself as part of a nation or a community. His values are solitary, all his judgments gauged by benefit or harm to the individual. This individualism culminates in his view of death. Every death is an unmitigated loss, for its shock cannot be buffered by communal continuity.

4. Deciphering Allegory

A. *How Allegory Works*

Allegory works by substitutions. Whereas the symbolic meaning of an image extends the literal, its figurative meaning displaces it through a series of substitutions: the thornbush for Abimelech (Judg 9:14f.), the vineyard for Israel (Isa 5:1-6), (Orwell's) pigs for Bolsheviks, and so on. As such, the contours of figurative meaning are more sharply defined than the symbolic. The signifier (farm animals, etc.) and the signified (political parties, etc.) are kept in two distinct domains. A figurative reading calls for a decoding or a translation between these two domains. A reading of Qoh 12:1-7 as an allegory of aging translates the "grinders" into teeth, the women at the windows into eyes, and so on.

An effective allegory, however, is not depleted by such decoding. The imagery is not (though it has usually been so treated) a disguise cloaking the "true" meaning of the poem. The interpreter's task is not to strip away the disguise and triumphantly expose what lies hidden behind it. We have also to ask about the author's purpose in applying the disguise to start with. The rhetorical gain in allegory inheres in the process of reading itself. This process, whatever answers it arrives at, requires the reader to give careful attention to the individual images while simultaneously calling to mind the realities signified.

Any interpretation of 12:1-7 must reckon with the fact that Qohelet is being deliberately enigmatic — which is no surprise, since enigmas were one of the vehicles of wisdom (Prov 1:6; Sir 39:1-3). This means that ambiguities and uncertainties are inevitable — and intended.

B. An Allegory of Aging?

The allegorical interpretation of this poem, first attested in the Midrash (Qoh. Rab.) and the Talmud (b. Shab. 131b-132a), is still dominant. In this reading, each object mentioned in the poem is transposed into an organ of the body and its deterioration.

Here are some of the decodings that have been proposed in the commentaries, ancient and modern:

- *The sun grows dark:* The light of the face or the forehead dims. Or the eyes cannot see the sun. Or the enjoyment of life fades.
- *The light:* The eyes or nose lose their keenness.
- *The moon:* The cheeks or the soul grows dim.
- *The stars:* The eyeballs or the cheeks grow dim.
- *The clouds return after the rain:* The eyes darken (grow blurry) after weeping.
- *The keepers of the house tremble:* The knees, or ribs, or legs, or arms, or hands, tremble.
- *The powerful men writhe:* The arms, or loins, or spinal column weaken or bend.
- *The "grinders" cease:* The teeth fall out.
- *Those (fem.) looking through the windows darken:* The eyes grow weak or blind.
- *The doors in the street are closed:* The feet or bodily apertures or ears or lips suffer or close. The anus and bladder suffer retention.
- *The sound of the mill fades low:* The appetite or mouth or digestion or voice diminishes.

- *He arises to the voice of the bird* (the usual translation): The old man is easily awakened. Or his voice rises in pitch.
- *The daughters of song bow low:* The voice rasps or loses pitch or becomes weak. Or deafness sets in.
- *They fear a high thing* (or: *from on high*): Non-allegorical: old people fear heights.
- *Frights are along the way:* Literal: the aged become timid.
- *The almond tree blossoms:* The hair goes white.
- *The grasshopper becomes laden* (or: *becomes a burden*): The back of the pelvic cavity becomes sore. Or breathing becomes labored. Or the joints grow stiff. Or the old man is bent over. Or the ankles swell up. Or the buttocks droop. Or sex becomes onerous. Or the penis fails to become erect. Or a (literal) grasshopper feels heavy to the weakened oldster.
- *The caperberry is annulled (?):* Desire is dulled. Or aphrodisiacs fail.

A few of these decodings do seem to suit the images, but most are arbitrary and some do not fit at all. For example, the eyes would grow dim during not after weeping. It is largely out of exegetical habit that we see the watchmen, for example, as the legs (or the arms), and the doors in the street as the lips (or the orifices, or the ears), and the stars as the pupils of the eyes (or the cheeks, or the five senses). Little argumentation accompanies these decodings. Almost invariably, a commentator will propose an identification and leave it at that.

The procrustean character of this interpretation may make it appear more effective than it really is. It is easy enough to connect almost any image with some ailment in the manifold physical and psychological processes of aging and death. And when this approach runs into difficulties, the interpreter is free to construe the image as literal or as a metaphor outside the allegorical frame. Difficulties in accommodating the text to the interpretation can also be dismissed by invoking the author's "Oriental richness of imagination and carelessness in exact use of metaphor" (Barton, p. 187). Yet even with all this hermeneutic flexibility, the allegorical interpretations leave much unexplained.[59] Though some of the images of the poem are undoubtedly figurative (this cannot be denied for vv. 2 and 6, at least), the poem as a whole is not an allegory, and it is certainly not *only* that.

59. C. Taylor (1874:51-63) summarizes various forms of the "anatomical" interpretation and shows that it requires a convoluted and self-justifying exegesis. His arguments are basically valid, but his all-or-nothing assumption, as if there must be consistent anatomical figuration or no figuration at all, is unwarranted.

A few of the images in Qoh 12:2-7 do lend themselves to translation into the infirmities of aging, though only two do so with much clarity. The women looking through the windows can easily represent eyes, because they are said to "look," and because "grow dark" is elsewhere predicated of eyes (Ps 69:24; Lam 5:17) but not directly of people. The grinding-maids seem to represent the teeth, because milling is physically similar to chewing, and because the maids are said to "grow few," which happens more often with teeth than with maids. The other decodings are rather arbitrary, except for v. 6, where the idea is clear even if the symbols themselves are not.

The aging-allegory has not only question marks but stumbling blocks. If the "grinders" are the teeth, the mill in v. 4aβ should be something else. We might think first of the mouth, but the mouth does not grow silent in old age, and if the mill in 4aβ were the mouth, the "double-doors" in 4aα would be the lips. But in what sense is the silencing of the mouth the *circumstance* of the lips' closing? And if the doors are figurative, what "street" are they on? Is that street different from the literal street in the next verse? The attempt to decode the other images in vv. 2, 4b, and 5 leads to similar blind alleys. The images that do work as figures are stranded and do not add up to an allegory on aging.

It is *a priori* possible that this poem includes several figures for aging interspersed with literal statements. A Sumerian epigram does just that:

> My grain roasting fails,
> Now my youthful vigor, strength and personal god
>   have left my loins like an exhausted ass.
> My black mountain has produced white gypsum.
> My mother has brought in a man from the forest;
>   he gave me captivity.
> My mongoose which used to eat strong smelling things
>   does not stretch its neck towards beer and butter.
> My urine used to flow in a strong torrent,
>   but now you flee from my wind.
> My child whom I used to feed with butter and milk,
>   I can no more support it.
> And I have had to sell my little slave girl;
>   an evil demon makes me sick. (Alster 1974:93)

This text, however, has two interpretive controls that Qohelet's poem lacks: a first-person possessive directing attention away from the literal plane (e.g., "my" black mountains) toward something the speaker actually possesses (white hair), and a coherence in the domain of the signified — the difficulties of aging. Nevertheless, the Sumerian example does neutralize one objection made against the allegorical interpretation of Qoh 12:1-7, that the figures are not coordinated with one another.[60] There is no reason to expect them to be.

C. An Allegory of Death?

In my view, the theme of aging does not continue beyond 12:1. With the extinguishing of the luminaries in v. 2, the perspective shifts to dying and does not move backwards thereafter. I suggest a different allegorical reading, one more consonant with the syntax and structure of the passage, though still including much that is speculative. This one sees in the imagery events occurring at the time of death, when the lights go out. Not all images are allegorical, but those that are, are ciphers for death.

This interpretation does not clash with the literal and symbolic readings suggested above but reinforces them. As literal depiction, the scene in 12:2-7 represents the day of a funeral. As symbolism, the constellation of imagery is suggestive of a world-end, which in turn signifies individual death. As allegory, the details of the depiction, or at least many of them, can be translated into aspects of death and dying. Thus whether we just picture what is happening, or stand back to take in the background as well, or peer closely to resolve the blurry details, we see the same thing: death.

- *The luminaries grow dark:* the darkness of death.
- *The clouds return after the rain:* the darkness of death, which obscures the sun of life (?).
- *The keepers of the house tremble:* mortal illness and the spasm of the limbs.
- *The powerful men writhe:* death throes.
- *The grinding-maids are idle:* At the end of old age, few teeth are left in the mouth.[61]
- *The (ladies) looking through the windows grow dark:* The eyes go dark at death.

---

60. Taylor, for example, asserts that it is "scarcely possible to harmonize the various details on any rational plan. But assuredly, unless a consistent whole can be made out, there is but slight reason for granting the details of the interpretation" (1874:53).

61. In this case, the *ki* may have an asseverative function; cf. *GBH* §164b.

- *The doors in the street are closed:* The apertures of sensory input (perhaps specifically the ears), previously open to the external world, cease functioning. Or: the mouth and/or eyes of the corpse are closed by attendants. (Both organs are "double-doors.")[62]
- *The sound of the mill fades low:* Man's voice is eternally silenced. Or, possibly, the gasps and rasps of the dying, which may recall the grinding sounds of a mill, fall silent.
- *The bird arises to voice:* The "bird" — perhaps a man who keens the lament — begins a threnody. Or perhaps it is an actual bird whose song resonates in the keening of the wailing women.
- *The daughters of song bow low:* Non-allegorically, the wailing women bow down.

The remaining images are to be taken literally, as discussed above.

If the poem draws on actual dirges, it may well have borrowed cryptic tropes from them. Some Biblical dirges are called *mᵉšalim* or speak of the dead figuratively. Isa 14, called a *mašal* in v. 4 (correctly glossed in the LXX as θρῆνον "lament"), speaks allegorically and cryptically of Babylon as a god, Helel son of Dawn. Ezekiel's dirge *(qinah)* over Tyre imagines the prince as the first man and as a precious seal (Ezek 28:12-19). Num 21:27-30 is a dirge over Moab spoken by *hammošᵉlim,* "the mashal makers." Some *mᵉšalim,* at least, require exegesis (Prov 1:6). Some of the dirges recorded in the Talmud use ciphers, some of these quite mysterious. For example: "Our brothers are merchants whose goods are examined at the customs house" (b. Mo'ed Q. 28b); "I have many coins but no money changer to accept them" (b. San. 68a); "Borrow a Milesian robe for a free man who left no provision" (b. Mo'ed Q. 28b).[63]

The accurate decoding of allegorical figures and the information conveyed by them, whether pertaining to aging or death, is of secondary importance in Qoh 12:1-7. First of all, the reader must *start* with the knowledge of what the presumed figures communicate or they can convey nothing at all. The reader can know that the strong men's quaking represents the legs' shaking (if this is indeed so) only if he knows that legs grow shaky with age — or tremble in disease. If the "daughters of song" indeed

---

62. In Greece, the deceased's eyes and mouth were closed by the next-of-kin as part of the ritual preparation of the corpse (Garland 1985:23). This was probably a very widespread practice, if only for aesthetic reasons.

63. Talmudic laments are collected, translated, and analyzed by Feldman, 1977:109-37.

represent mourning women, the reader can know this only if he is already familiar with funerary practices. It cannot be the poem's goal merely to inform us of such things. How great would our gain be if we knew for certain that Qohelet intended the powerful men to signify legs or the almond blossoms white hair? Not even the young need a sage to tell them that aging weakens the legs and grays the hair, or that people die and all their bodily functions cease.

The poem's purpose is not to convey information, but to instil an attitude toward aging and (more important) death. A reader, especially a young one like the youth ostensibly addressed in this unit, can have little notion of the fear, loneliness, and nostalgia for a past irretrievably lost, which are the lot of many, perhaps all, the aged, Qohelet among them. As we stare into the darkened glass of Qohelet's enigmas we strain to see what lies beyond. We see and sense a troubling scene, even if we cannot make out the details. Indeed, however we decode the symbols, we will come to the same insights and the same uneasiness. We finally descry ourselves. We see our own death, and Qohelet will not let us turn away.

◆ 12:9-14

(9) Furthermore, Qohelet was wise, and he also taught the people knowledge, and having listened and investigated, he composed many sayings. (10) Qohelet sought to find pleasing words and wrote^a the most honest words of truth.

(11) The words of the sages are like goads, and the [words of] masters of collections are like implanted nails set by a shepherd.

(12) Furthermore, my son, of these things be wary: Making many books is endless, and studying^b too much wearies the flesh.

(13a) (Here is) the conclusion of the matter. Everything has been heard.

(13b) Fear God and keep his commandments. For this is (the substance) of every man. (14) For God will bring every deed into judgment, (even) every secret deed, whether good or evil.

^{a}*w^{e}kātôb* (MT *w^{e}kātûb*)
^{b}*lahăgôt* (MT *lahag*)

The book's motto, "Utterly absurd, said the Qohelet, All is absurd" (12:8), has a janus quality, as it both concludes the poem on death and introduces the epilogue.

    A. 12:9-12. The epilogue
       a. Qohelet the wise man (12:9-10)
       b. The words of the wise (12:11)
       c. The study of wisdom (12:12)
    B. 12:13-14. Postscript: man's main duty

The epilogue looks back on Qohelet and reports that he was a sage and a writer of *meʿšalim* who sought for and wrote pleasing and true words. Then it comments on the words of all the sages: they prod their readers to better things. Turning next to the instructional mode (a quick sign of which is the address to "my son"), the epilogist warns about excesses in intellectual endeavors. Finally a postscript — probably a later addition, but not alien to the spirit of the foregoing — reminds us that the main thing is to devote oneself to piety and righteous deeds, for God's judgment is sure. The perspective of the book's ending becomes progressively broader, moving from Qohelet's life-work to God's universal judgment.

A. 12:9-12. The Epilogue

12:9 The phrase *yoter še-* has (as shown by Lohfink 1996:131-39) no good parallels in BH or RH. There are basically two ways of reading it: as an additive conjunction ("Not only X but also Y") or a sentence adverb ("Furthermore, X . . ."). Lohfink believes the issue cannot currently be resolved. In my view, only the second is possible. Its meaning cannot be derived from RH *yoter misše-* meaning "beyond the fact that," as is commonly done (Podechard, Barton, Gordis, and most), because the *m(in)* before the first member is indispensable to mark the lesser term of the comparison and is used consistently in this construction in RH. *Yoter* is a noun in Qoh 6:8, 11; and 7:11, where it means "the positive balance," "remainder"; this notion can be applied here. The clause introduced by *še-* is predicated of the noun. Hence *weyoter šehayah qohelet ḥakam,* translated mechanically, means: "and something remaining is (the fact) that Qohelet was a sage." This can be rendered "furthermore" or "moreover" (cf. Hertzberg, Ginsberg). The disjunctive *zaqeph gadol* on *weyoter* reflects this interpretation. (LXX περισσόν is probably to be taken adverbially, "exceedingly was Qohelet. . . .")

    The additional or remaining information (the *"yoter"*) is not the fact that Qohelet was wise — that was asserted clearly enough in 1:16 — but the fact that he was a sage *and* a diligent teacher of the public. Hence the "furthermore" is adverbial to the entire sentence.

    'Od means either "constantly" (Ibn Ezra, Galling, Hertzberg; cf. Qoh

7:28; Gen 46:29; Ruth 1:14; Ps 84:5; etc.) or "additionally," "also." If the latter is its sense here, it may mean: in addition to the wisdom quoted thus far (Ginsberg), or, in addition to being a wise man. In either case, the sentence implies that Qohelet's teaching was extensive and that the "many sayings" he constantly examined and composed went beyond those quoted in this book.

Gordis maintains that this verse draws a distinction between a professional wisdom-teacher for the rich (a *ḥakam*) and a teacher of knowledge to the common people, both of which Qohelet was. But the authors of Wisdom Literature would not have distinguished teachers of the upper class from teachers of the general populace. The Wisdom writers never saw their instruction as directed to certain social classes (though they do reveal an unconscious class orientation). The knowledge and virtues of wisdom are accessible to all (Prov 8). Personified Wisdom calls from the city walls and at the thoroughfares (Prov 1:20f.; 8:1-3) and summons all men (8:4). Nor does *ḥakam* ever designate a professional educator of the well-to-do as opposed to a teacher of the general populace. Indeed, Seow draws a causal connection: "*Because* Qohelet was a sage, he constantly taught people knowledge" (1997b:129; emphasis added).

Although I do not think that *yoter še-* is contrastive and to be translated "Not only was Koheleth a sage himself, but he also taught the people knowledge . . ." (Gordis) or the like, I do think that the sentence mentions two areas of activity. These correspond to the distinction between just being wise, which can be confined to the private sphere, and the *additional* role of teaching and writing. Not every wise man is a teacher of the public or an author of proverbs, though, of course, authors of proverbs and other wisdom could be called *ḥăkamim* (Prov 22:17; 24:23; and Qoh 12:11). The latter is an additional role, for a *ḥakam* may be, as Ben Sira puts it, merely "wise for himself":

He who is wise for himself [*ḥakam leⁿapšo*] will be sated with delights, and all who see him will call him blessed.
But he who is wise for the people [*ḥăkam ʿam*] will inherit honor, and his name will remain everlastingly in life.
(Sir 37:24, 26 [contiguous in Hebrew, MS D])

Ben Sira calls both types *ḥakamim*. The latter type is a *ḥăkam ʿam*, which could be translated "a teacher of the people" and which is the nominal equivalent of the clause *ʿod limmad daʿat ʾet haʿam*.

Weⁱizzen weⁱḥiqqer tiqqen meⁱšalim harbeh: Ginsburg says that the asyndeton in the series of verbs shows that the first two are adverbial modifiers of the third. Syr, 10 MSS K-R, and, more significantly, Aquila have a conjunction before *tiqqen*. *W^etiqqen* may have been an actual Hebrew variant, but it is not preferable to MT (otherwise in Fox 1987). In the MT, the first two verbs are circumstantial to the third, and this makes sense, because listening and examining would precede and be the background of *composing m^ešalim*. Moreover, listening would precede investigating.

'Izzen probably does not mean "weigh" (Delitzsch, Hertzberg, Podechard, and most); that would be *šaqal*. It is also unlikely that a prefixed noun-form would be the source for a denominative, which would require the extraction of 'ZN as the root of *mo'znayim*, though the *'aleph* is quiescent (the root is etymologically *WZN [as in Arabic]). *'Izzen* might be a direct verbal derivation from *WZN, though that root is not attested in NW Semitic except in *mo'znayim* and cognates. 'ZN-piel is probably a denominative from *'ozen*, "ear," equivalent to 'ZN-hiphil. *'Izzen* was understood as "listen" by Syr, Aq, and Tg, as well as Rashbam and Ginsberg.

A sage listens to others' wisdom (see Prov 1:5-6; Sir 3:29; 6:33-35) so that he can compose proverbs of his own. As Ben Sira remarks, "When a man of understanding hears a wise word, he praises it and adds to it" (21:15).

M. Fishbane (1985:30-32) compares the description of Qohelet's activities to Assyrian and Babylonian colophons. But while both mention writing and (sometimes) composing, they do not show the "striking similarity" Fishbane sees (ibid., p. 30). Colophons are always reflexive, referring to the act of copying the tablet (its source, the name of the scribe, date of completion, the owner of the tablet, etc.) (see Leichty 1964). Typically the scribe refers in the first person to his activity in writing, composing, or collating the text. The epilogue to Qohelet speaks in praise of teaching, not scribal work. The activity of the sages praised here is not the inscription, editing, or preservation of documents, but the formulation of their own wise teachings.

12:10 *W^ekātûb:* MT's consonants and pointing are supported by LXX's γεγραμμένον, but the passive participle is very awkward here. Aq, Sym, Syr, and Vul use a finite verb ("and wrote"), but they may have had the same consonants as MT and could be interpreting an infinitive absolute as a finite verb. An infinitive absolute would be in agreement with Qohelet's usage (4:2 and 8:9) and should probably be read here. In a Hebrew fragment of Tobit (13:1) (4QTob^e), *wktwb thlh btšbwḥt* is translated (in recension G^I) as "and (Tobit) wrote a prayer for rejoicing (ἔγραψεν προσευχὴν εἰς ἀγαλλίασιν) (= 4Q200, frg. 6, l. 4; see C. A. Moore 1996:277). The structure (though not word order) is similar: infinite absolute *kātôb* + direct object (of words) written + adverb (of manner).

Yošer dibrey 'ĕmet: An Aramaizing equivalent of this phrase appears in Prov 22:21, *qošṭ 'imrey 'ĕmet. Qošṭ,* which corresponds to *yošer,* is the bound form (of *qošeṭ;* see Ps 60:6), suggesting that in Qoh 12:10 *yošer* is a bound form. In that case, *yošer dibrey 'ĕmet* is a superlative: "the most honest words of truth." Compare *qomat 'ărazayw* "his tallest cedars" (*//mibḥar b^eróšayw* "his choicest cypresses"; Isa 37:24) and *ḥakmot śaroteyha* "her wisest princesses" (Judg 5:29).

12:11 "The words of the sages": In Proverbs (outside the headers), mention of the speech of the wise refers either to the content and manner of their speech in daily life (12:18; 14:3; 15:2, 7), or to the message of their teachings (13:14; 16:23), rather than to specific proverbial utterances. Here the words of the wise are the teachings of learned men. Since their teachings are meant to be inclusive of the words Qohelet wrote, the former too are to be understood as written teachings.

With rare exceptions, a *ḥakam* in the Bible is any person possessing special expertise or the virtue of wisdom, not to a member of a professional class or one who subscribes to a particular school of thought. Whybray (1974, *passim*) has argued this at length and his view is now widely accepted.

In a few verses from the latest stages of Biblical Wisdom, *ḥăkamim* refers to a specific group, the sages or the learned, who are experts in Wisdom Literature and other written lore. This is the meaning of *ḥăkamim* in Prov 22:17 (reading *dibrey ḥăkamim* "words of the wise"), 24:23a, *gam 'elleh laḥăkamim* "these too are by the wise," and 1:6b, *dibrey ḥăkamim w^eḥidotam* "the words of the wise and their enigmas." *Ḥăkamim* seems to designate the scripturally learned in Sira 3:29; 8:8; and 44:4b. In the latter verse, Sira speaks of men who are *ḥkmy śyḥ bsprtm* "wise of speech in their writings." The scholar [*soper*] of God's law is *ḥakam* (Sir 38:24; 39:1-14). "How can one grow wise who guides the plow?" (38:25) does not mean that the plowman cannot fear God, act judiciously, and the like, but that he cannot become learned in scripture. This is the meaning of *ḥakam* in Qoh 12:11. It is not used in exactly that way in the body of the book, but this does not show that the author did not know that meaning, since the *ḥokmah* that Qohelet amasses (1:16), is certainly to be understood as erudition, not life-skills.

Ba'ăley 'ăsuppot: 'ăsuppot probably refers to collections of sapiential sayings; thus LXX συναγμάτων "collections." *Ba'ăley-* has been taken to mean "members of"; thus Delitzsch, Barton, Gordis, and Hertzberg, who compare *baʿal* "participant" (in a covenant or vow) in Gen 14:13 and Neh 6:18. But the meaning of *baʿal* in those verses is not quite the same, because participants in a covenant may be said to be *beʿalim* in the sense that they "possess" it. The basic sense of *baʿal* is "possessor," "master," and that is appropriate in the present verse as well. *Baʿăley ʾăsuppôt* are the "masters of (proverb) collections," parallel to *ḥăkamim.* The force of *dibrey* "words of" carries over from v. 11aα (thus C. D. Ginsburg, who notes the very same ellipsis in 10:12 and 13). RH uses *beʿalim* of men *expert* in different types of literature: *baʿăley miqraʾ* = experts in Scripture; *baʿăley ʾaggadah* = experts in Aggadah, and so on (see, e.g., the listings in Gen. Rab. 41.1, Lev. Rab. 36.2, and the Alpha Beta d'Ben Sira §24). These *beʿalim* are not the authors of the texts in question but rather learned specialists in them. By this parallel we should translate *baʿăley ʾăsuppôt* as "experts in collections." But these experts are themselves the wise, and their words in writing are Wisdom Literature.

This sentence assumes that Qohelet belongs to this category. He was a *baʿal ʾăsuppah.* His words, then, constitute an *ʾăsuppah.* This does not necessarily mean that they were collected from different sources or authors, but rather that in terms of its form it is a collection of sayings — *debarim, mešalim,* and *ʾămarot.* All could have been "collected," brought together, by the author. A *mašal* can be quite lengthy, e.g., Num 24:3-9; Hab 2:6-12; Ezek 17:1-10; and apparently the entirety of Ps 49:6-21 and 78:5-72. Thus not only could Qohelet's proverbs and short units be considered *mešalim,* but the longer units too, such as 1:3-11, 3:1-15, and 11:7–12:8, could each be called a *mašal* in Biblical usage.

Dārebōnôt (sic) are the nails on the end of ox goads, parallel to *maśmerot* "nails" in v. 11aβ. (Sira 44:4b apparently uses *mśmrwt* in reference to proverbs, parallel to *sprt* "writings"; see Di Lella ad loc.) Commentators have invariably considered the tenor of the comparison between goads and words of sages to be the fact that both spur people to better behavior. The similarity between *baʿăley ʾăsuppôt* (however that may be construed) and implanted nails is thought to be that the latter are difficult to move or remove. If that were so, however, the parallel comparisons would refer to completely different qualities: an extrinsic quality in v. 11a (they induce better behavior in others) and an intrinsic one in v. 11b (they are in themselves unchanging and stable). I suggest that the "nails" share a referential function with the "goads," which are called "implanted" either by virtue of being stuck in the flesh or by virtue of being fixed in the end of the staff. In either case the *tertium comparationis* of the words of the sages and goads/nails is not that they are immovable but that they both sting. A goad prods one on to thought and better behavior, but it also hurts. As Ibn Ezra recognized, goads "afflict and open the mind *(mᵉyassᵉrim umĕpaqqᵉhim hannepeš).*" The words of the sages, in other words, can be uncomfortable, even dangerous.

Nittᵉnu meroʿeh ʾehad, lit. "given from a/one shepherd": All commentators have assumed that what is given by the shepherd is "the words of the wise." The shepherd is almost always thought to be God. But in the Bible, God is called "shepherd" in his capacity as keeper and protector, which is not relevant here, and the epithet "shepherd" is never used by itself to refer to God (see Galling). Nor are the words of the wise ever said to be given by God. Wisdom as a personified entity and as a personal intellectual and moral power is given by God, and perhaps the essential, abstract message of Wisdom is also a divine gift. But the specific teachings of the sages do not come from him directly. Similar reasons militate against identifying the shepherd as Solomon (contrary to Delitzsch and McNeile). Qohelet is not identified with Solomon in the epilogue, nor could it be said that Solomon "gave" the words of the sages.

Another difficulty in the identification of the shepherd as God (or Solomon) is the modifier *ʾehad.* If the point were that there is only one divine shepherd who gives the words of the wise, rather than several, the "one" would be very emphatic. The weight of the verse would rest there rather than in the similes of v. 11a, and the verse would become an avowal of monotheism divorced from context.

Whatever "shepherd" may represent metaphorically, the sentence must first make sense literally. The fact that the images of "shepherd" and "goads" belong to one domain shows that the vehicle of the simile is continuing and the clause *nittᵉnu meroʿeh ʾehad* is something that could be done by an actual shepherd. In the usual interpretation, an irrelevant comparison is sandwiched between subject and verb. A more natural reading of the sentence locates the subject of *nittᵉnu* not in the distant "words of the sages," but the immediately preceding nouns, the goads and nails that a shepherd "gives" or "puts" in the sense that he prods his herd with them. Within the simile, it is not the words but the goads that are "given," and they are "given" — set or stuck — not by God or Solomon but by a *shepherd,* any shepherd. NTN means "to stick" (an awl) in Deut 15:17. *ʾEhad* can function as an indefinite article.[64]

Within the vehicle of the simile, "shepherd" is an actual shepherd, just

---

64. As in 1 Sam 24:15; 26:20; 1 Kgs 19:4, 5; Ezek 8:8; 17:7 (see *GBH* §137u, GKC §125b, BDB *ʾehad*); similarly Aramaic *hădah/hăda'*: Ezr 4:8; Dan 2:31; 6:18. In all these cases enumeration is not the point, since there is no need to mark unity in opposition to plurality. The modifier could be removed with little effect on the sentence.

as goads are real goads.[65] When applied to the tenor, "shepherd" does have a metaphoric function, which is created and controlled by the ratio implied in the simile: words are to the sage as goads are to the shepherd. Goads and shepherds are not independently figures for words and sages. Rather, the *relation* between the two elements of the image, shepherd and goads, is an analogy to the relation between the sage and his words. Words and goads are tools to guide people on the right path, but their effect is not always pleasant. Any reader of Qohelet knows this.

12:12 *W^eyoter mehemmah b^eni hizzaher: Yoter* presents the same problem as in 12:9. In my view, it does not mean "And besides these . . . ," as if the listener were to beware of words other than those of the wise, for the exclusion "than these" would require *miyyoter.* Moreover, by this translation the sentence would be warning against words and collections other than those of the wise. What could those be, since the authors of all of Jewish literature were wise, that is, learned? (It is only modern scholarship that enrolls "the wise" in a "school" of their own.) The warning against books other than those of the wise would at least require a clearer identification of the words or books of the non-wise. Otherwise how could we know what to avoid? Simply to say "other than these" would not identify the proscribed category, when "these" is not well-defined.

We must set the pause at *w^eyoter* (against MT, which takes *yoter mehemmah* as a prosodic unit) and translate *w^eyoter* (literally) as "and an additional thing (is)," hence "there's something else to be said," or "furthermore," or the like. It is not problematic (contrary to Lohfink 1996:138) that *nizhar* does not govern a *min* elsewhere in the Bible. It often does so in RH when it means "be wary of" (e.g., Qoh. Rab. 4.9; Lev. Rab. 16.1; Num. Rab. 10.4). (When *nizhar* means "be careful" [to obey or to do something], it governs *b-* or *šello*.) The antecedent of *mehemmah* "of these" must be the subject of the preceding sentence, the words of the sages/proverb collections. Lohfink (p. 139) says that, on the face of it, "these" could refer either to the object of the warning ("*of* these be wary") or to the *source* of the warning ("*from* these take this warning"). *Nizhar min* is not used in the latter sense in RH. The latter, moreover, would imply that the admonition in v. 12b came

---

65. The words "literal" and "metaphorical" intersect in discussion of the functioning of metaphor. In "he was a lion in battle," it is the "literal" feline creature that is a "metaphor for" human bravery. We commonly apply "literal" in this context to the metaphor prior to transposition to another domain, but we also apply the term to the tenor of the metaphor, its sense *after* transposition. Both uses are correct, for a metaphor takes us from one "literal" domain (e.g., animals) to another (humans).

from the words of the sages, but I do not think that one could find such a warning in Jewish literature.

The caution about the words of the sages is reinforced by the next sentence (12b), which reveals a certain hesitancy about the effects of much writing and study. Those are the very activities attributed to Qohelet in v. 9.

'Ăśot s^eparim harbeh 'eyn qeṣ: This clause, like the next one (v. 12bβ), is structurally an affirmative sentence of classification with two nominal members; the predication places the subject-clause in the category of *'eyn qeṣ*. Literally: "making many books is a thing-of-no-end"; in other words, endless. *'Eyn qeṣ* is a noun phrase, literally, "a nothingness of end" or "an absence of end," hence "a thing of no end." The negative particle *'ayin* is a noun, and the nominal use of the bound form *'eyn* (+ noun) is clear in prepositional phrases such as *b^e'eyn musar,* "because of lack of instruction" (Prov 5:23); *me'eyn mayim,* "because of lack of water" (*//baṣṣama';* Isa 50:2); *l^e'eyn 'onim,* "to the one-of-no-strength" (*//layya'ep;* Isa 40:29); and often. Note also the strict parallelism in Prov 26:20 between *'eyn* and *'epes* "nothing," whose nominal character is clear.

Contrary to my comment in *Contradictions,* I do not now follow Tur-Sinai in construing *qeṣ* as "purpose, profit" and *'eyn-qeṣ* as "profitless." This usage is inadequately attested elsewhere. However, the traditional translation, "without end," comes down to the same thing. The sentence is not just an observation on the unremitting enterprise of authorship; it is an evaluation of the activity. Making many books is endless in the sense of leading nowhere, like the interminable movements of natural phenomena in 1:3-8, which Qohelet considers profitless. In Qoh 12:12b, the epilogist shares Qohelet's assumptions about the preconditions of profit and their lack.

In 12:12bα, *harbeh* "many" is not superfluous. It is not that writing books itself is endless, hence pointless. It is the *excessive* production of books whose value the epilogist doubts. Qoh 12:12bα is thus an application of one of Qohelet's own lessons: Do what you will, but don't *overdo* it (9:10).

A different understanding of the phrase is suggested by the translation in R. B. Y. Scott's commentary: "book learning is an endless occupation"; but Scott offers no further comment. P. de Boer (1977) argues that *'ăśot s^eparim* means "working at books" (p. 88) and notes that the Targum first translates the phrase as *lm'bd spry ḥwkmt'* "to make books of wisdom" then paraphrases *wlm'sq bptgmy 'wryt'* "to busy oneself in words of Torah." Tg, however, may be extending the application of the idea paraphrastically rather than explicating it. N. Bronzik (1980) interprets the phrase to mean "book-learning" and compares *'aśah torah* in RH, meaning "to study Torah." Mid. Ps. 119:42 shows that this was one ancient interpretation of Qoh 12:12bβ:

"What is the meaning of 'It [the Torah] belongs to me forever' [Ps 119:98]? It means that I did not busy myself with other books besides it, as Solomon says, *'ăśot separim harbeh 'eyn qeṣ*." In the Midrash the line must be rendered, "there is no end in studying many books." By this interpretation, the phrase is in synonymous parallelism with the end of the verse, "and studying too much wearies the flesh." The problem with this intriguing interpretation is that even though *'aśah torah* means "to study Torah," there is no evidence that *'aśah separim* ever meant "to study books." In Aramaic, *'ăbad sipra'* (see below) means "write a document," and this supports the interpretation of *'ăśot separim* as "writing books."

M. Fishbane (1985) translates *'ăśot* as "compose" or "compile," comparing Akkadian *uppušu* (D-stem of *epēšu*, the equivalent of Hebrew *'aśah*), used in scribal colophons. But whether *ăśot separim* means to compile or to write books (or, most likely, both), the epilogist does not ascribe the original composition of Qohelet's sayings to someone other than Qohelet. The equivalent Aramaic phrase, *'bd spr'*, occurs in a fifth century B.C.E. papyrus (*spr' znh zy 'nh 'bdt;* Kraeling 1953:9, 22), where *'bd* means "write," not "collect." ʽŚH is used of scribal activity in Jer 8:8, but we cannot know just what these scribes were doing — composing, compiling, or copying.

Lahag is a crux, usually explained by reference to Arabic *lahija*, "apply oneself assiduously." But that root is not otherwise productive in Hebrew. Qoh. Rab. on this verse rephrases *lhg* as *lahăgot:* "They [the words of the wise] were given (to us) to study *(lahăgot);* they were not given for weariness of flesh." This seems to grasp the gist of the verse. We should, however, emend to *lhgt* (Perles 1895:29), a haplography with the similar *heh* of *hrbh;* see *LSF* §205. *Hagah* means "meditate, study" (see especially Josh 1:8 and Ps 1:2). It also (and originally) means "utter, speak" and is used of teaching wisdom in Ps 37:30a: "The mouth of the righteous utters *(yehgeh)* wisdom." The "uttering" probably refers to studying (by reading aloud, perhaps in a singsong) rather than to teaching. By this interpretation, the verse warns against excess in the two aspects of the sage's activity attributed to Qohelet: studying others' sayings *(lahăg<ot>* = *'izzen* and *hiqqer)* and writing one's own wisdom *('ăśot separim* = *tiqqen* and *katob).* The clause "and studying too much wearies the flesh" means that excessive study is tantamount to, or produces, this discomfort. (For this type of predication compare 2:23.)

B. 12:13-14. Postscript: Man's Main Duty

12:13a *Sop dabar hakkol nišmaʽ,* "(Here is) the conclusion of the matter. Everything has been heard": The Masoretes make the *samekh* of *sop dabar* a *samekh rabbati,* a "large *samekh.*"[66] The *rabbati* letters call attention to something special, such as a beginning of a new section. Here the function is to mark the start of the book's conclusion. It is significant that the Masoretes marked v. 13a rather than v. 9 by the large letter. Regardless of the authorship of vv. 13-14 (Hertzberg, Lauha, Zimmerli, et al. identify them as later than vv. 9-12), they constitute a "postscript" (as Seow [1997b:138] aptly calls the passage, with reference, however, only to vv. 13b-14).

The epilogue has thus far appraised Qohelet and his intellectual setting: the production and study of wisdom, probably meaning book-learning generally. The postscript has a different perspective: man's religious duty prior to, and apart from, wisdom. This is supplementary, not contradictory, to Qohelet's (and Wisdom's) perspective, even though it may well be a later addition (thus too Seow 1997b:139). But it is not of a piece with the rest of the epilogue. A new voice enters, one which probably belongs to a later scribe.[67]

An examination of *sop dabar hakkol nišmaʿ* (v. 13a) shows how the postscript stands apart. It marks the end of the epilogue proper (12:9-12) but stands outside it.

Qohelet's *sop dabar* has a precise Aramaic equivalent in *sopaʾ di-millᵉtaʾ,* in Dan 7:28a. The full phrase in Daniel is *ʿad kah sopaʾ di-millᵉtaʾ,* lit. "up to here is the conclusion of the matter." This phrase concludes Daniel's report of an angelic interpretation of a symbolic vision. The commentary of Hartman and Di Lella (1978:207) explains Dan 7:28a as a conflation of two expressions, *ʿad kah millᵉtaʾ* "thus far the matter" and *kah sopaʾ di-millᵉtaʾ* "here is the conclusion of the matter," but neither expression is attested independently. More likely, the clause is a fusion of *ʿad kah* and *sopaʾ di-millᵉtaʾ,* each of which is a meaningful phrase and attested elsewhere. The latter is found in Qoh 12:13a, the former has precise Hebrew equivalents: *ʿad hennah* and *ʿad kaʾn.* Jeremiah's words end with *ʿad hennah dibrey yirmᵉyahu* "until here the words of Jeremiah" (Jer 51:64), after which follows the historical appendix from 2 Kgs 24:18–25:30. The RH equivalent *ʿad kaʾn* is often used to close quotations (e.g., Sifra *Behar Sinai* §5; b. Bek. 20a).

Daniel's fusion of two synonymous phrases resembles the present verse, in which *sop dabar* is reinforced by *hakkol nišmaʿ.* In Daniel the phrase marks the end of a long quotation of the angel's explanation, draws a

---

66. Not writen in the Leningrad codex proper, but listed in its Masorah Finalis and noted in *Diqduqey Haṭṭĕamim* (ed. Baer-Strack, §61).

67. In *Contradictions* (pp. 310-23; 328f.), I read these verses as integral to the epilogue and construed v. 13a as prospective.

line under it, as it were. If we apply this to Qohelet, the "matter" *(dabar)* is not what is about to be said in vv. 13b-14 but what has been said so far.

These considerations support the perception of Seow (1997b:138f.) that v. 13a marks the end of the book proper. Seow calls v. 13a a colophon, comparing the colophons at the end of Egyptian Wisdom books. (The usage is in fact common to many genres.) Vv. 13b-14, Seow says, are a "postscript" by a later editor. To be precise, a colophon is the addition of a scribe to a text he has copied, assuring the reader of the accuracy of the inscription and adding data relating to the copy itself, such as its date (see Leichty 1964 on Assyro-Babylonian colophons).[68] However, Qoh 12:13a can (somewhat loosely) be called a colophon along the lines of Jer 51:64 and Ps 72:19 ("Amen and Amen. The prayers of Jesse son of David are finished"), which apparently mark what was originally the end of a scroll.

Verse 13a is *not* said by the author of the epilogue, just as Dan 7:28a is not said by the preceding speaker, the angel. Likewise, Jer 51:64 is certainly the words of the scribe who added the historical appendix, not Jeremiah himself. Qoh 12:13a, then, is a colophon, and vv. 13b-14 an extension of it. The scribe (whom we need not dub an "editor") has, fairly enough, sealed the book with v. 13a before adding an admonition of his own.

The blunt "everything has been heard" suggests a certain impatience with excessive study and rumination, just like v. 12. In context, the "everything" that has been heard is the words of the wise (the *hemmah* of v. 12), Qohelet's among them. The author puts wisdom in perspective: wisdom (meaning booklearning, not good sense or sagacity) is all very fine, but don't overdo it.

The next sentence begins with "fear God," which is also blunt but grammatical. Ben Sira rephrases Qoh 12:13a by the sentence '*wd k'lh l' nwsp, wqṣ dbr hw' hkl* (43:27), a difficult line that is probably to be translated, "More (things) such as these we shall not add, and the end of the matter is: He [God] is everything." It must be granted that Sira seems to read *sop dabar* as prospective. Sira's sentence, however, does support the suggested reading in part, because *k'lh*, like *hakkol* in Qohelet, is retrospective, and the verse as a whole concludes a passage. The structure of Sir 43:27b and the first-plural verbs in 27f. suggest that Ben Sira is construing Qohelet's *hakkol nišma'* as an independent sentence in apposition to *sop dabar*, as I have done here.

---

68. A typical Egyptian colophon says "Finished successfully [lit. "It has come well, in peace], (made) by the (soul of the) scribe PN son of PN [sometimes with titles and self-praise], on (such-and-such a date)."

"The conclusion of the matter" means that the book of Qohelet, together with its epilogue, is finished. The author of Qoh 12:13a considered 12:9-12 as belonging to the *dabar,* the "matter" or "word" that is the book of Qohelet. In v. 13b, he contributes something beyond that book.

As Excursus III will argue, the speaker of the epilogue (and 1:1 and 7:27) presents himself as a teacher transmitting the words of Qohelet, a literary persona, whom he comments on in 12:9-12. The speaker of the postscript, however, has a different relation to the preceding: He is not looking in retrospect on the most recent speaker, the epilogist. If we imagine the epilogist writing vv. 9-12 and continuing into v. 13, he would have had no reason to say "end quote," so to speak, marking v. 12 as the end of the book proper, for he would not yet have finished speaking. Hence it is probable that a later scribe added vv. 13f. in order to bring the discussion to an end, respectfully but definitively.

A difference in ideological nuance too, discussed below, supports this ascription of the postscript to a different author, though not conclusively. It is not that the postscript contradicts the rest of the book, but it does take a different tack and adds a new dimension.

12:13b The postscript reminds us that what really counts is fear of God and obedience to his commands. Basic knowledge of this principle is accessible to everyone — *kol ha'adam* — from the start, even without "much study." Prov 1:7 and 9:10 teach the same.

The theme of fear of God belongs to traditional (pre-Sira) Wisdom, but keeping his commandments diverges from it insofar as it speaks of a revelation of the divine will. The postscript goes beyond earlier Wisdom Literature and, like Ben Sira, explicitly subordinates wisdom to the Law. That does not make vv. 13-14 "alien to everything Qohelet has said thus far" (Crenshaw, p. 192). Vv. 13b-14 do stand outside of Wisdom epistemology, but Wisdom Literature, including the book of Qohelet, does not repudiate divine revelation of commandments; that is simply not its province. Wisdom Literature, including Qohelet, seeks to show the way to a righteous and successful life through the exercise of human intellect. There is much that the Law does not regulate, and that vast area is largely Wisdom's realm. With rare exceptions, most notably with regard to adultery, the behavior Wisdom deals with is not in categories covered by law. The same is true of Pirqey Avot, which is, of course, thoroughly aware of God's law and committed to its fulfillment. While Avot counsels study of Torah and obedience to it, it does not itself reiterate the law or tell people to do what the law already commands.

Ki zeh kol ha'adam, lit. "for this is every man" or "this is the entirety of man." The Aramaic translation hypothesis explains this difficult phrase as reflecting, approximately: *ky dyn* [i.e., *dāyēn*] *kl 'nš,* "For he [sc., God] judges every man." *Dyn* "judge" was supposedly misread as *deyn* = "this" (Zimmermann 1973:163; followed by Ginsberg). An Aramaic writer, however, would probably have supplied *hu'* as a copula, which would have eliminated the ambiguity that supposedly faced the Hebrew translator.

Kol ha'adam means "every man" throughout the Bible (see, e.g., Qoh 3:13; 5:18; 7:2), not "all of man." In this verse, the phrase is elliptical, but it is not clear how the ellipsis is to be filled out. AV, Gordis, Murphy, and many supply "duty": "For this is the entire duty of man." But the notion of "duty" is not really provided by context and supplying it seems rather *ad hoc*.

The predicate in such nominal predications can have a variety of functions. It can designate the material from which something is made, the thing contained, the measure, the thing numbered (for *mispar*), the abstract quality, and a concrete particularity (*GBH* §154e). These can be boiled down to the notion of content — the substance that constitutes, or fills up, the entity in the predicate. For example, *'ăṣabbeyhem kesep wᵉzahab* (Ps 115:4) means "their idols are made of silver and gold"; *mᵉlo' kol ha'areṣ kᵉbodo* (Isa 6:3) means that God's glory fills up the earth, is its very substance and material; *'ăni šalom* (Ps 120:7) means that I am peace and nothing but peace, I have no hostile thoughts; *'ăni tᵉpillah* (Ps 109:4) means that "I am all prayer" (in the way we might say, "I am all ears"); *'ammᵉka nᵉdabot* (Ps 110:3) (lit. "your people are voluntariness" [abstract]) means that the entire nation is composed of volunteers; *kullo mahᵃmadim* (Cant 5:16aβ) means that "he is entirely delights," with nothing bland or base mixed in. This explanation fits most of the examples *GBH* (§154e) gives.[69] The effect of this construction seems to be an intensification of the equation: Not only am I prayerful, I am prayer itself; or, we might say, I am the very soul of prayer, and similarly for the other examples. By this measure, *zeh kol ha'adam* in Qoh 12:13 means that *this* — the fear of God and obedience to his commandments — is the substance, the "material" of every person. There should be no alloy.

"Every man" implies a distinction between the statements and admonitions in 12:9-12, which have to do with the sages and their pupils, and *this,* the demand stated in 12:13bβ, which applies to everyone. *Zeh* is thus emphatic, italicized so to speak. Verse 14 provides a logical motivation for v.

---

69. "The seven good ears are seven years" (Gen 41:26), which *GBH* classes as "explanation," is different. It is an equation formula typical of glossing.

13bβ: this rule applies to everyone, whatever his learning and wisdom, because God will bring every single deed into judgment.

12:14 "For God will bring every deed into judgment, (even) every secret deed, whether good or evil": This recalls 3:17, "God will judge the righteous and the wicked," which also emphasizes the globality of the judgment. In *'al kol ne'lam,* the preposition *'al* is governed by the verbal notion implicit in *mišpaṭ.* As in 11:9, *'al* indicates the deeds with respect to which one is judged. Compare Jer 1:16, "And I will pronounce my judgments (on) them [*'otam*] upon [*'al*] all their evil," in which the deed being judged is introduced by *'al.* The final warning is that God will judge every deed, even hidden ones.

On the theology of the postscript see §9.6.

EXCURSUS III

The Voices in the Book of Qohelet

After being introduced in 1:1 and epitomized in 1:2, Qohelet speaks. In 12:8, Qohelet's message is again epitomized, with a third-person quoting-verb. An external speaker, the epilogist, steps forward in 12:9-12. In 12:13f., a postscript, probably by a later hand, sums up with an exhortation to fear God and obey him, since his judgment is certain. This excursus examines the interrelations and functions of these three voices.

1. The Epilogist

The epilogist speaks in a pronouncedly didactic tone. He marks off the points to be learned: "Furthermore, . . . Furthermore." He commends the wise Qohelet, generalizes about the words of sages, and cautions the listener against excess in writing and study. He addresses the ostensive audience of his remarks as *b'ni,* "my son," in the customary Wisdom fashion, thus implying the discourse-setting almost universal in didactic Wisdom Literature: a father giving instruction to his son. The epilogist thus represents himself as a sage, a teacher of Wisdom, as he describes the work of an earlier wise man, Qohelet. Who, then, is the epilogist, and what did he do?

363

A. *A Later Editor?*

Traditional commentators assumed that because the epilogue is part of the book of Qohelet, it was composed by him. Modern commentators have assumed that because the epilogue speaks *about* Qohelet it was added secondarily, by a later editor. The latter proposition involves two separable assumptions: that the epilogue is secondary, and that it was written by an editor.

Apart from the question of the identity of the epilogist, we should consider whether there are indications of editorial activity in the formation of this book, for the concept of "editor" is often applied rather facilely in Bible studies.

(1) One hypothesis is that an editor created the book of Qohelet by compiling it from short, originally independent written teachings. This is very unlikely. Surely an editor did not find fifty-five short essays on little scraps of papyrus[70] and copy them one after the other. Qohelet would not have composed units such as 2:24-26 or 5:7-8 or 11:6–12:7 as independent bits of wisdom and expected them to be copied and transmitted as such. Few of the units, even by a grosser division, have much meaning in isolation.

(2) Nor is compilation from oral transmission likely. It is also hard to imagine that Qohelet spoke his teachings on various occasions and that they were memorized and transmitted separately until an editor collected and put them in writing. Some of Qohelet's sayings may have been spoken and transmitted separately, but most of the units do not stand alone, nor are his teachings and reflections the sort of thing that tradents would be likely to memorize. In any case, the epilogist says that Qohelet *wrote* his wisdom (12:10).

(3) One might surmise that Qohelet inscribed only some of his teachings and spoke others, and a later scholar, perhaps a disciple, wrote down what he recalled of the former and drew together the latter. If so, that scholar would be as much an author as an editor, and the Qohelet we know would be a *created* character, a construct based on recollections of an actual person.

(4) Another possibility is that Qohelet wrote down all of 1:3–12:7 (or possibly 1:2–12:8), and that the epilogist added only 12:9-12 (or 12:9-14) and some framing material in 1:1f. and 12:8. But that activity could hardly be called editing, since it would not have intervened in the book proper. Furthermore, the vocative *bᵉni* is appropriate not to an editor but to someone who, at least by convention, is addressing his son.

---

70. Ellermeier divides the book into fifty-five units, whose assembly he ascribes to the major editor of Qohelet, who also added "words of Qohelet" in 1:1 as well as 1:2-3 and 12:8-12. The rest of 1:1 and 12:13f. is assigned to a second editor (1967:93-103, 131-41).

B. The Author?

The last-mentioned alternative, that a later scribe added an epilogue and perhaps the opening verses (1:1-2), is a possibility but not quite what is suggested by the way the epilogue regards Qohelet. The epilogist speaks as "teller of the tale," who is telling about Qohelet by quoting his teachings. In my view, the words of Qohelet (1:3–12:7), the title (1:1), the motto (1:2; 12:8), and the epilogue proper (12:9-12) are all the creation of the same person, the author of the book, who is not to be identified with Qohelet, his persona. In other words, it is not that the epilogue is by Qohelet, but that Qohelet is "by" the epilogist.

The speaker we hear referring to Qohelet in the third person in 1:1-2; 7:27; and 12:8, who comes to the fore in the epilogue, and whose "I" we hear just once in the suffix of b^eni in 12:12 — this speaker is the frame-narrator whose words encompass Qohelet's. This speaker looks back and, using the traditional stance of wisdom teacher, tells his son about the sage Qohelet, transmits to him some of his teachings, then appreciatively but cautiously evaluates the work of Qohelet and other sages. The body of the book is formally a long quotation of Qohelet's words. The frame-narrator presents himself not as the author of Qohelet's teachings or as their editor but as their transmitter. He keeps himself well in the background, but he does not disappear.

The authorial voice (saying "Qohelet said") also appears in 7:27, in the middle of a sentence, though there is no necessity for a quoting-phrase at that point. Qohelet elsewhere, and often, uses the first-person to quote his own words and thoughts. Unless we posit an additional third-person voice, it is the epilogist (the frame-narrator) who is quoting Qohelet here too. And since he is actively joining two halves of a sentence, he has composed the verse. It is unlikely that 7:27 alone was created thus. If another person besides Qohelet gathered and edited Qohelet's sayings, this activity went so deep as to make the editor, for all practical purposes, the *author* of the book.

C. Taylor (pp. 79-85) argued that the epilogue is by the author, but on quite different grounds, namely the supposition that "Qohelet" is a "representation of Philosophy as a personified assembly." The *author's* point is supposedly that "Philosophy" self-destructs by arriving at contradictory conclusions from the same facts and premises, after which the epilogue sets forth the positive conclusion. But, contrary to Taylor, the epilogue in no way dismisses or repudiates Qohelet. Also, as one of Taylor's early reviewers noted (ibid., pp. 82f.), the religious exhortation of the epilogue is too short to constitute a refutation of the "philosophic" doctrines that make up most of the book.

E. Christianson's *Narrative Strategies in Ecclesiastes* builds on the recognition that the book of Qohelet tells a *story* and as such can be analyzed by tools of narrative-criticism. Christianson proceeds to explore the deliberate artistry of both the sequential story-line of the book and the complex interplay of voice. Qohelet is a "dynamic character who is actively communicating with effective narrative strategies" (chap. 1). Christianson demonstrates the value of reading with attention to the narratival qualities of the book as well as to the ideas it expounds.

A recent study by C. L. Seow (1997b) supports the idea that the epilogue (12:9-13a) was an integral part of the original book. The epilogue serves as an apology for the rest of the book and gives it a stamp of legitimacy. Seow identifies 12:13b-14 as a postscript (see the commentary, above). He maintains that both sections of the ending are in harmony with the rest of the book.

The most determined application of the theory of the frame-narrator is by T. A. Perry (1993). Perry identifies the external voice as that of a pious sage (the "Presenter," P), who transmits the wisdom of the skeptical Kohelet (K), which he appreciates but disagrees with; see the summary above, p. xi. Perry's "P" includes my "frame-narrator" but is much more active throughout the book, entering into dialogue with Qohelet at numerous points. But Perry's division of voices is tendentious. There is simply no sign that "P" speaks in the book other than in the few verses I note. The author chooses to allow the persona's voice to dominate until the end.

2. The Hierarchy of Perspectives

The book of Qohelet, then, is built of nested levels of perspective, each one with its own time-frame and each encompassed in the next:

(1) The frame-narrator, who tells about
(2) Qohelet-the-reporter, the narrating "I," who speaks from the vantage point of old age and looks back on
(3) Qohelet-the-observer, the experiencing "I," who undertook the investigation that the book reports.

Levels 1 and 2 are different persons (different, that is, within the text; the distinction may, however, be fictive). Levels 2 and 3 are different perspectives of the same person. The time-frame of level 1 is the present tense of the speaker in the epilogue; it is the temporal context in relation to which the phrase "Qohelet said" is past tense. The time-frame of the frame-narrator is supposed to be some time after Qohelet lived. The time-frame of level 2 is the one in which Qohelet speaks, when he reflects on his experiments and experiences and reports them. This is the present to which the past tense of certain verbs of observation, cognition, and speaking ("I saw," "I realized," "I said," and the like) is relative. The time-frame of level 3 is the context in which the exploring, experiencing, and cognition took place. The postscript is an attachment and outside the hierarchy.

3. Parallels

There are several parallels in ancient Wisdom Literature to the use of an anonymous third-person, retrospective narrative framing the monologue of the teacher. We find this technique in Kagemeni, Ptahhotep, Neferti, Ipuwer, Anii, Onchsheshonqy, Suruppak, and Aḥiqar, as well as in Deuteronomy and Tobit.

- *Kagemeni:* The beginning of the Instruction for Kagemeni is missing. In the body of the book, the old vizier, Kagemeni's father, declaims to his children words of advice and *then* writes them in a book. The epilogue speaks about the vizier in retrospect and tells how Kagemeni benefited from his father's counsels and became vizier himself. The narrative frame thus looks back on both the teacher and his son as figures in the past and praises the teachings.
- *Ptahhotep:* The framework is not prominent in Ptahhotep, but the book opens with an introduction speaking *about* Ptahhotep and describing the circumstances in which he delivered his teaching to his son, then quoting his request to Pharaoh to allow him to appoint his son as his successor.
- *The Prophecy of Neferti,* written in the reign of Amenemhet I (12th dynasty), begins with a frame-narrative set in the reign of Snefru (4th dynasty). The frame-narrative looks back on the ancient sage Neferti and introduces his words in an attitude of esteem. From the point of view of the speaker of the frame-narrative, Neferti and his words lie well in the past. The work is fictional, a prophecy *ex eventu* of the "future" triumph of Amenemhet I, and Neferti is a persona for the anonymous author.

367

- *Ipuwer:* The introduction of the prophecy of Ipuwer is lost, but it probably defined the setting indicated by the ending of the work, which refers to Ipuwer in retrospect: "What Ipuwer said when he answered the Majesty of the All-Lord" (15.5). The introduction must have told how Ipuwer (like Neferti) was called to address the king. The body of the work quotes Ipuwer's words of lament over the breakdown of the social order, though his "I" occurs only occasionally (6.5, 8; 12.6). The speech of Ipuwer, which comprises the main part of the book, is thus bracketed by the perspective of an anonymous narrator who looks back on the sage, quotes him, and speaks about him.
- *Anii:* After the scribe Anii instructs his son, the son speaks up and enters into debate with him. This epilogue, as Seow notes (1997b:113) includes praise of the father's wisdom and (the son's) awareness that the teachings are difficult to grasp. There is a significant difference, however, in that the praise and the caution are the son's, and his hesitancy is viewed as a protest against his father's attempts to teach him and is met with a vehement rebuttal by the father (see Fox 1997b). Qohelet's epilogist is not concerned with the difficulty of the teachings, and his warnings pertain to all wisdom, not just Qohelet's.
- *Onchsheshonqy:* The instruction opens with a narrative explaining how the (otherwise unknown) vizier Onchsheshonqy came to write his instruction on potsherds while in prison, having been falsely implicated in an assassination plot against Pharaoh. Onchsheshonqy's words — the body of the book — are a long quotation (see the extended quoting-phrases in 4.17-21; 5.14, 19). After the introduction, his advice to his son is delivered. The introductory story is almost certainly fictional. The book as a whole has an anonymous frame-narrator telling the story of that sage: what he did and what he said.
- *Suruppak* (Sumerian fragment; Alster 1974:35, lines 1-8 [a reconstruction]): The gist is that in ancient days, the wise Suruppak gave instruction to his son Ziusudra. The book ends (lines 278-82) by praising the goddess Nisaba for the wisdom of Suruppak. Though as far as the author was concerned, Suruppak was a historical personage, he was an antediluvian and thus legendary. Some of the contents of the instruction may have existed prior to the time the introduction was added, but that is conjecture, and in any case, the *book* of Suruppak was not authored by the sage himself.
- *Aḥiqar:* The introductory narrative tells a complex story about the betrayal of the childless vizier Aḥiqar by his nephew Nadin, whom he adopted and instructed in wisdom. In the Aramaic text, the transition

368

between the story and the proverbs is lost, as is the end of the text, which probably returned to the frame-narrative. In other versions, the proverbs are Aḥiqar's instruction to Nadin, and they are followed by the story of the betrayal and Nadin's undoing.

- *Deuteronomy:* On Deuteronomy's affinities with Wisdom Literature see Weinfeld 1972:244-319. In its present state, but excluding the additions in 4:41-43; 32:48-52; and 34:1-12, Deuteronomy is an extended first-person monologue of Moses set within a sparse third-person framework, which is indicated by a number of quoting-phrases. Deut 1:1-5 is an extended quoting-introduction; 28:69 is a retrospective summary. Brief quoting-phrases are more numerous, e.g., 5:1; 27:1, 9, 11; 29:1. Deut 31:14-25, whose relation to D is problematic, is a short narrative about Moses. Thus in Deuteronomy too there is a voice telling *about* the main speaker, looking back on him from an indefinite distance, while itself remaining well in the background. Polzin (1980) has carefully examined the interplay between the narrator's voice and Moses'.

- *Tobit:* Immediately after the title and brief identification of Tobit, which is not part of the frame-narrative, Tobit introduces himself by a personal retrospect similar to Qohelet's. Both sages reflect upon their earlier experiences from the vantage-point of old age. Tobit says: "I, Tobit, walked all the days of my life in ways of truth. . . ." Then follows a monologue of typical Wisdom counsels and observations. The book taken as a whole, however, is a third-person narrative. In 3:7ff. the author begins to speak *about* Tobit, with Tobit quoted at length throughout the book. Tobit 14:15 is an authorial retrospect taking us down to a time after the destruction of Nineveh, when Tobit's son dies. (Even if chapters 13 and 14 are later additions, as Zimmermann argues [1958:24], the essential narrative structure of the book is as described here, though in that case the distance of the frame-narrative's retrospect would be foreshortened.) Although the emphasis here is quite different from that of Qohelet, with the frame-narrator's voice much more prominent in Tobit, the essential narrative design is the same: a frame-narrator who looks back on Tobit who looks back on himself. What is of special interest is that the first-person speaker (Tobit) can appear right after the title without a frame-narrator's introduction, even in a work where the voice of the latter does not hesitate to make itself heard throughout the work.

Seow (1997b:136) draws a further parallel. At the end of Kagemeni the father says, "All that is written in this book, heed it as I have said it. Do not go beyond what has been set down" (*AEL* 1.60). The perspective of this sentence, however, is quite different. It is the teacher's admonition that his words be followed precisely, not an epilogist's caution about a body of literature *including* the teaching just concluded.

Analogies from distant cultures can suggest the possible rhetorical functions of literary devices. One such analogy is the Foreword of *Gulliver's Travels,* in which the fictional editor, Richard Sympson, coolly assesses the accounts he supposedly received from Gulliver. In this way Swift bestows a certain verisimilitude on the "author" though no one would *really* imagine that Gulliver's experiences were historical: "I have carefully perused [these papers] three times: the style is very plain and simple; and the only fault I find is, that the author, after the manner of travelers, is a little too circumstantial. . . . There is an air of truth apparent throughout the whole" (from the Foreword).

An even closer analogy is the Preface to Daniel Defoe's *Moll Flanders,* in which the author begins "The world is so taken up of late with novels and romances that it will be hard for a private history to be taken for genuine where the names and other circumstances of the person are concealed. . . ." The "editor" testifies (fictitiously!) that, in spite of the pseudonym, the memoir is authentic, though conceding that "the original of this story is put into new words." He then proceeds to assure the reader of the morality and propriety of the story to follow, although it reports debauchery and vice, because immodesties have been veiled and all misdeeds are finally punished. The "editor" thus professes a moralism that is stricter and more solemn than Moll's but that is not in conflict with it. *Moll Flanders,* like Qohelet, is a vision of stark realism conveyed through the voice of a fictional character. Moreover, Qohelet, like Moll Flanders, is an expression of "classical realism" — defined by Kenneth Rexroth as "an archetype of carefully selected 'abstracted' characteristics."[71] Material facts are supplied not to increase the character's individuality, but are chosen "as facets of their typicality."[72]

Most of these narrative frames, especially the shorter notices, could have been written by the authors of the instructions or by a later scribe, or perhaps the sage's son, but they all testify to an ancient convention of framing the sage's words from a retrospective viewpoint. It seems likely that adherence to this convention in Qohelet belongs to the original creative stage of the work.

71. From the Afterword to the New American Library edition, New York, 1964, 305f.

72. Ibid.

Since there is an implied author mediating Qohelet's words, we cannot simply identify Qohelet with the author. Qohelet is a character created in the work who may be a close expression of the author's attitudes, but whose words cannot be assumed to be inseparable from the ideas of his creator.

4. Qohelet Through the Epilogist's Eyes

The epilogue conveys a certain attitude toward the teachings of Qohelet and the other sages.

(1) The epilogue bolsters the verisimilitude of Qohelet, simply by talking about him as having lived and speaking about him in the matter-of-fact, reliable voice of a sage. This is not, of course, historical evidence, but is a common novelistic device, recognizable in texts as disparate as Gulliver and Suruppak. However, the epilogist of Qohelet succeeded in convincing many readers that he was intimately familiar with Qohelet.[73]

(2) The epilogue projects an attitude of respect toward Qohelet. The epilogist's rhetorical stance as wisdom teacher helps to establish his own reliability and to guide the reader in the attitude he is to take toward Qohelet's words. The epilogist, speaking in a voice that is reassuringly conventional, testifies that Qohelet was indeed a sage with praiseworthy goals who spoke honest words of truth. The epilogue praises Qohelet's diligence in studying Wisdom and teaching it to the people. He was, we are told, a public figure, dedicated to the people, an author of quantity as well as quality. He listened to and examined the wisdom of the past (for a sage is a link in the chain of tradition) and created many sayings of his own. He sought fine words (for the sages placed great emphasis on elegant speech) and wrote the truth. This testimony is especially important in the case of a bold and unorthodox thinker whose thought may appear bizarre and even dangerous. The reader is assured that Qohelet's teachings remain within the limits of tolerability.

Whether he is best described as an author or as an editor, the author of the epilogue basically supports Qohelet's teachings. Otherwise he could have refrained from writing, editing, or transmitting the book.

(3) While evincing respect and appreciation for Qohelet, the epilogist sets a certain distance between himself and the words of Qohelet — and of

---

73. For example: "1:2 thus shows the same familiarity ("dieselbe Vertrautheit") with the man Qohelet as has been emphasized for 12:9-11. We see here the same hand at work. It is the first epilogist, who knew Qohelet personally — perhaps as pupil, perhaps as disciple" (Ellermeier 1967:100).

other sages as well. The epilogist is somewhat chary of all the sages. Their words are like goads, so they can sting. This must be stressed: the epilogue's circumspection is directed not toward Qohelet's words in particular, but toward wisdom as such, of which Qohelet's teaching is a part.

(4) This same distance serves a protective buffer between the book as a whole and the views expressed by its persona. The caution the epilogue expresses is a public, protective stance, intended to ease acceptance of Qohelet's pungent words. He does not simply warn the reader away from Qohelet's pessimism and unorthodoxy. The distance the epilogist sets between himself and Qohelet is basically protective rather than polemical. The author may be attempting to soften resistance to the book by presenting it as a report of what Qohelet said.[74]

5. Qohelet as Persona

In his comment on 12:9, Delitzsch makes the acute observation that "In the book [viz., 1:2–12:8] Koheleth-Solomon speaks, whose mask the author puts on. Here, letting the mask fall off, he speaks *of* Koheleth." (In Latin, "persona" originally was the mask through which an actor spoke; it now means a character through whom an author speaks.)

Qoheleth is, and is meant to be recognized as, a persona based on a historical character, Solomon. If there was an actual sage in the background, he is lost behind the fictional character. After all, there *was* no king called Qohelet, so the face we are shown must be a literary construct.

Though he regards Qohelet with a certain wariness, the epilogist does not undermine the persona's ethos or subvert his teachings. In fact, we can easily imagine Qohelet himself urging circumspection about the teachings of the sages, for he demonstrates wisdom's pains and perils in his own flesh.

T. Longman (1998), who has done much to delineate the genre of fictional autobiography (see §10.2), shifts the core of the book's meaning from the persona to the epilogist (including all of 12:9-14), whom Longman identifies as the author. This author uses Qohelet, the fictional persona, as a teaching device for demonstrating the dangers of speculative, skeptical wisdom. The book's conclusion directs the reader away from such wisdom to a theology consonant with the rest of the Old Testament (pp. 38f.) In my view, the epilogue does not undermine the persona, but only takes a cautious and

---

74. Romberg (1962:77ff.) discusses the comparable case where an author detaches himself from his creation by concealing himself behind an editorial fiction.

cautionary stance toward him. The book's ending does not invalidate Qohelet's complaints or observations. These are never said or shown to be wrong. Rather, the epilogue and postscript say: Granted that the world is full of absurdities and injustices and frustrations, and granted that human wisdom wears blinders, still, what counts is fear of God and obedience to his commands. The book's ending does not contradict Qohelet, but only changes the emphasis. It should be noted that this is the canonical meaning of the book as a whole even if the epilogue is by a later writer.

Qohelet is not an unreliable persona; he does not self-destruct. To be sure, Qohelet is well aware of the uncertain basis of his knowledge, but this awareness is part of *his* message and does not undermine his reliability. There is little doubt that the author means us to take Qohelet's words seriously — his pessimistic, querulous reflections as well as his affirmations of ethical-religious values. Qohelet represents the best that human intellect can do, and his inadequacies are common to all. Nor is there an ideological conflict between Qohelet's teachings and the epilogue. Both express the author's views, but with different tones and emphases.

The author employs the figure of Qohelet in a sort of thought experiment: Let us posit a man, Solomonic in wisdom, who employed his wisdom to amass Solomonic-scale wealth, then used it to purchase a great array of pleasures. (At first, it sounds wonderful.) What would happen if such a man used his wisdom to examine his pleasures and accomplishments, to evaluate wisdom itself, and to assess all of life? The author allows Qohelet to play out the experiment honestly (as the author obviously has done in his own heart), but then steps back and reminds us that such activities must be approached with circumspection and moderation.

The persona of Qohelet is formed not for the proclamation of fixed and timeless truths. That could be better achieved by impersonal statement, such as we have in most of Wisdom Literature, even in texts with an identified author. Qohelet gives expression to one man's observations and evaluations. His subjectivity is on display. The book is, as I argued earlier, about *meaning,* and this, the author realizes, exists relationally, inhering in perception.

6. The Postscript

The postscript seals the book with a proper and orthodox conclusion. The postscript, which makes fear of God and obedience to his commands the highest values (these are a single value, as the singular "this" in v. 13b indicates). The postscript undoubtedly succeeded in promoting the book's acceptance for public use, on the grounds that it "ends with words of Torah" (b. Shab. 30b). Since it is the last word in the book, the familiar piety of the conclusion could outweigh the uncomfortable observations of the preceding twelve chapters. Jerome (in his commentary to Qoh 12:13) says:

> The Hebrews say that, among other writings of Solomon which are obsolete and forgotten, this book ought to be obliterated, because it asserts that all the creatures of God are vain, and regards the whole as nothing, and prefers eating and drinking and transient pleasures before all things. [But] from this one paragraph [12:13f.] it deserves the dignity that it should be placed among the number of the divine volumes, in which it condenses the whole of its discussion, summing up the whole enumeration, as it were, and says that the end of its discourse is very easily heard, having nothing difficult in it, namely, that we should fear God and keep his commandments. (trans. Ginsburg, p. 15)

Fear of God is important in Proverbs (esp. in 1:7 and 9:10), but concern with obedience to God's commands is not a factor in Wisdom Literature prior to Ben Sira. For that reason many commentators have understood this belief as irreconcilable with those of the body of the book. Zimmerli says:

> If, then, the epilogist nevertheless describes this fear of God as the adherence to the commandments and as the divine judgment of good and evil, then he is interpreting Qohelet according to the alien criterion of orthodox legal piety, which believes that in the revealed command of God, wisdom too — which also brings the right outcome for life — is revealed. (pp. 250f.)[75]

In fact, however, the idea expressed in vv. 13-14 is not contrary to Qohelet's thought. Qohelet (like Proverbs), simply does not deal with this aspect of religion. He does not *contradict* "legal piety," he just does not advocate it. When the postscript does the latter, it is not rebutting or repudiating Qohelet's wisdom, any more than wisdom generally, but only placing human wisdom lower on the ranking of values.

The postscript relegates all the words of the sages — Qohelet's among

---

75. "Wenn der Epilogist dann allerdings diese Furcht Gottes als Halten der Gebote und Glauben und das göttliche Gericht über Gute und Böse beschreibt, dann interpretiert er Kohelet nach einem diesem fremden Massstab der rechtgläubigen Gesetzesfrömmigkeit, die glaubt, dass im geoffenbarten Gebot Gottes die Weisheit, die auch den rechten Lebenserfolg bringt, geoffenbart sei" (pp. 250f.).

them, but not more so than the others' — to a place of secondary importance by summing up the essence of wisdom as fearing God and keeping his commandments. Teachings such as Qohelet's and the other sages', though fine in themselves, are not identical with piety and obedience. Fear of God and obedience override wisdom in case of conflict, or, rather, this principle constitutes the essence of wisdom.

Placing a boundary to wisdom — or all wisdom other than the essential and highest rule — allows the wise some freedom of movement. It allows everything to be heard and considered as long as everything is finally subordinated to the fundamental principle. By circumscribing wisdom's scope, the epilogist suggests that Qohelet's probing and complaining are not truly dangerous, for his conclusions cannot undermine what ultimately counts, the fundamentals of action and belief.

7. Wisdom and Canon in the Book's Ending

The book's ending sets Qohelet's words in a broader literary and religious context. The epilogue includes Qohelet's teachings among the "words of sages." What does this classification show about the epilogist's concept of the organization of literature and Qohelet's place in the emerging canon?

G. Sheppard (1980:120-29) has probed the way the epilogue and particularly the postscript understand wisdom and canon. He points to some well-recognized correspondences between 12:13f. and the body of the book: the admonition to fear God and keep his commandments and the affirmation of God's judgment upon all actions at the appointed time, as well as some lexical items (pp. 124f.). These correspondences show that the postscript answers the dilemma of delayed justice raised by Qohelet by "thematizing," that is to say, extracting a particular aspect of Qohelet's teachings. Sheppard considers the ideology of the thematization as the same as Sira's (p. 126). "In other words, Qoheleth has been thematized by the epilogue in order to include it fully within a canon conscious definition of sacred wisdom, one that is remarkably close to that of Sirach and Baruch" (p. 127). With regard to the epilogue proper, the reference to "these" in 12:12 may show an awareness of a circumscribed canonical group of sacred Wisdom books, perhaps just those ascribed to Solomon, to which Qohelet belongs but to which one may not add (pp. 127f.).

Sheppard is right that the postscript and Ben Sira share some key concepts, in particular, the fear of God and his judgment *(mišpaṭ),* but they by no means express the same ideology. Unlike Sir 1:26, the postscript does not say that obedience to God's commandments *produces* wisdom, nor does it bring

375

wisdom under the aegis of Torah or identify the two, which is Sira's great contribution in chapter 24. On the contrary, the postscript implies a *distinction* between the words of the sages on the one hand and pious obedience on the other.

Neither part of Qohelet's ending reveals any "canon-consciousness," though 12:11 does recognize a genre of writings associated with the *ḥăkamim.* "These" in v. 12a are the words of the wise whatever they may be. If the epilogist wanted to warn us not to add to the body of Solomonic writings, he would have called them "the words of Solomon" or the like, not "the words of the sages." Also, *yoter mehemmah . . . hizzaher,* as noted above, does not mean "beware of more than these"; that would require *miyyoter.* We are not to be wary of *other,* additional, words of the wise but of the very ones mentioned in the preceding verse, the ones that are praised.

G. Wilson (1984) ascribes a different sort of canonical function to the postscript. He construes "the words of the sages" in 12:11 as a reference specifically to the book of Proverbs. He argues that correspondences between the prologue to Proverbs and the postscript to Qohelet associate the two books and imply a hermeneutical principle: that fearing Yahweh and keeping his commandments constitute "the proper context within which to understand and evaluate the wisdom endeavor" (p. 192).

Wilson says that a canonical editor of Qohelet sought to make explicit the connection, implicit in Prov 1–9, between "fearing God" and "keeping his commandments" (p. 189). But this is not implicit in Proverbs, which never equates the *miṣwot* of the sage with those of God.

More fundamentally, it should not be assumed that wisdom was in itself classed as sacred and worthy of canonization. Nothing in the Bible bestows that status on human wisdom or Wisdom Literature. Even in Ben Sira's concept of wisdom, according to which wisdom was in essence given to mankind at creation and has Torah at its pinnacle, human wisdom is not *ipso facto* sacred. In rabbinic usage, Torah is divine wisdom, and any Biblical mention of *ḥokmah* can be so understood for exegetical purposes, but the rabbis did not regard the Wisdom books as sacred just by virtue of being wisdom. In questioning whether the book of Qohelet was sacred scripture, they did not adduce the fact that it is wisdom. On the contrary, if it had been human wisdom — *merely* Solomon's wisdom, as one opinion has it — then it would be profane and would *not* "defile the hands" (t. Yad. 2:14).[76]

---

76. The view that Qohelet was merely Solomon's wisdom is ascribed to R. Shimon b. Menasia (170-200 C.E.). The argument for sacred status was that Solomon did not write whenever he pleased, hence his writing was under divine control, and when he did write, his words were "spoken" in the Holy Spirit, that is, divinely inspired.

The epilogue, which speaks with the voice of a pious and cautious sage, places Qohelet well within the scope of legitimate Wisdom activity. The epilogist reports that Qohelet was a sage doing what sages generally do: weighing and composing proverbs, writing true and elegant words of wisdom, and teaching the people knowledge. The postscript implicitly agrees, by complementing rather than contradicting the preceding speakers. And this view is not a whitewashing. Qohelet is less orthodox and optimistic than most sages, but he belongs to the same tradition.

That is not to say that Qohelet's views are quite comfortable. On the contrary, he was one of the wise, and, the epilogist tells us, the words of the wise can prick like ox goads or nails (Qoh 12:11), or (as Rabbi Eliezer b. Hyrcanus was later to put it), "they burn like fiery coals, bite like jackals, sting like scorpions" (Avot 2:15). And indeed, Qohelet's words sometimes do that, but that is not the end of the matter.

Bibliography

Throughout the book, commentaries (marked below by an asterisk) are referenced by name of author only, other works by author + publication date.

Page numbers in English translations ("ET") of these works are noted for the reader's convenience, but unless otherwise indicated, all translations (sometimes made with a certain freedom for the sake of clarity) are my own. Quotations from Camus are taken from the English editions listed below.

AḤIQAR
1983   Text, translation, commentary: Lindenberger.

ALBRECHT, Karl
1896   "Das Geschlecht der hebräischen Hauptwörter." *ZAW* 16:41-121.

ALBREKSON, Bertil
1981   "Difficilior lectio probabilior." *OTS* 21:5-17.

ALBRIGHT, William F.
1955   "Some Canaanite-Phoenician sources of Hebrew wisdom." *VTSup* 3:1-15.

ALLEN, Thomas G.
1974   *The Book of the Dead.* Chicago.

ALLGEIER, A.
1925   *Das Buch des Predigers oder Koheleth.* HSAT 6.2. Bonn.

ALSTER, B.
1974   *Studies in Sumerian Proverbs.* Copenhagen.

ALSTON, William P.
1967   "Pleasure." In *Encyclopedia of Philosophy,* VI, 341-47. New York.

AMENEMHET
            Pap. Millingen, Pap. Sallier I, II, et al. Text: Helck, 1969; Volten, 1945. "The Instruction of King Amenemhet I for His Son Sesostris I," *AEL* 1.135-39.

AMENEMOPET
            Pap. BM 10474 et al. Text: Lange, 1925. "The Instruction of Amenemope," *AEL* 2.146-63.

ANAT, M. A.
1970   "The lament on the death of man in the scroll of Qoheleth" [Hebrew]. *Beth Mikra* 15:375-80.

ANDERSEN, Francis I.
1974   *The Sentence in Biblical Hebrew.* Janua Linguarum 231. The Hague.

ANDERSON, Gary
1991   *A Time to Mourn, A Time to Dance.* University Park, Penn.

ANII
            Pap. Boulaq IV et al. Text: J. F. Quack, *Die Lehren des Ani* (OBO 141), Göttingen, 1994. ET "The Instruction of Ani," *AEL* 2.135-46.

ASTOUR, Michael C.
1968   "Two Ugaritic serpent charms." *JNES* 27:13-36.

BACKHAUS, F. J.
1993   "Qoheleth und Sirach." *BN* 69:32-55.

BAER, Seligmann
1886   *Quinque Volumina.* Lipsiae.

BAILEY, Lloyd R., Sr.
1979   *Biblical Perspectives on Death.* Philadelphia.

BARR, James
1961   *The Semantics of Biblical Language.* London.
1962   *Biblical Words for Time.* SBT 33. London.
1985   "Hebrew orthography and the Book of Job." *JSS* 30:1-33.

BARTHELEMY, Dominique
1963   *Les Devanciers d'Aquila. VTSup* 10.

380

BARTON, George A.
*1908   *The Book of Ecclesiastes.* ICC (Repr. 1959.) Edinburgh.

BARUCQ, André
1968   *Ecclésiaste.* Paris.

BAUMGÄRTEL, Fr.
1969   "Die Ochsenstachel und die Nägel in Koh 12, 11." *ZAW* 81:98.

BAUMGARTNER, Walter
1933   *Israelitische und altorientalische Weisheit.* Tübingen.

BENDAVID, Abba
1967   *Biblical Hebrew and Mishnaic Hebrew* [Hebrew], vol. 2. Jerusalem.

BERTRAM, Georg
1952   "Hebräischer und griechischer Qohelet." *ZAW* 64:26-49.

BIANCHI, Francesco
1993   "The Language of Qohelet: A Bibliographical Survey." *ZAW* 105:210-23.

BICKERMAN, Elias
1967   *Four Strange Books of the Bible.* New York.

BIRNBAUM, Solomon A.
1971   *The Hebrew Scripts.* Leiden.

BLANK, Sheldon H.
1962   "Ecclesiastes." In *Interpreter's Dictionary of the Bible,* II, 7-13. New York.
1970   Prolegomenon to Ginsburg's *Cohelet* (1861). New York.

BLENKINSOPP, Joseph
1995   "Ecclesiastes 3.1-15: Another Interpretation." *JSOT* 66:55-64.

BOER, P. A. H. de
1977   "A note on Ecclesiastes 12:12a." In *A Tribute to Arthur Vööbus,* ed. by
        R. H. Fischer, pp. 85-88. Chicago.

BOMAN, Thorleif
1960   *Hebrew Thought Compared with Greek.* Philadelphia.

BÖSTROM, Lennart
1990   *The God of the Sages.* Stockholm.

BRAUN, Rainer
1973   *Kohelet und die frühhellenistische Popularphilosophie.* BZAW 130. Berlin.

BRETON, Santiago
1973   "Qoheleth studies." *Biblical Theology Bulletin* 3:22-50.

BRICHTO, Herbert C.
1963   *The Problem of "Curse" in the Hebrew Bible.* SBLMS 13. Philadelphia.

BRIN, Gershon
1960   "The roots 'ZR and 'ZZ in the Bible." *Lešonenu* 24:8-14.
1975   *Studies in the Book of Ezekiel* [Hebrew]. Tel Aviv.

BROCKELMANN, Carl
1956   *Hebräische Syntax.* Neukirchen.

BRONZIK, Nahum
1980   "'aśot sᵉparim harbeh 'eyn qeṣ. (Qoh 12:12)." *Beth Mikra* 25:213-18.

BROWN, Francis, S. R. DRIVER, and Charles A. BRIGGS
1907   *A Hebrew and English Lexicon of the Old Testament.* (Repr. 1966.) Oxford (= BDB).

BROWN, William P.
1996   *Character in Crisis.* Grand Rapids, Mich.

BRUNER, Jerome
1986   *Actual Minds, Possible Worlds.* Cambridge, Mass.

BRUNNER, Hellmut
1957   *Altägyptische Erziehung.* Wiesbaden.
1963   "Der freie Wille Gottes in der ägyptischen Weisheit." *SPOA,* pp. 103-17.
1979   "Zitate aus Lebenslehren." In *Studien zu altägyptischen Lebenslehren,* ed. by E. Hornung and O. Keel, pp. 105-71. OBO 28. Freiburg.
1988   *Altägyptische Weisheit.* Zurich (= AW).

BRUNS, J. Edgar
1965   "The imagery of Eccles 12,6a." *JBL* 84:428-30.

BUDDE, Karl
1922   *Der Prediger.* In *Die Fünf Megillot.* KHAT XVII. Tübingen.

BUZY, Denis
1932   "Le Portrait de la vieillesse (Ecclésiaste, XII,1-7)." *RB* 41:329-40.
1934   "La Notion du bonheur dans l'Ecclésiaste." *RB* 43:494-511.

CAMUS, Albert
1948   *The Plague.* (ET Stuart Gilbert.) New York. (Original publication in French: 1947.)

Bibliography

1953   *The Rebel.* (ET Anthony Bower.) London. (Original publication in French: 1951.)

1955   *The Myth of Sisyphus.* (ET Justin O'Brien.) London. (Original publication in French: 1948).

1956   *The Stranger.* (ET Stuart Gilbert.) New York. (Original publication in French: 1942.)

CASTELLINO, G.
1968   "Qohelet and his wisdom." *CBQ* 30:15-28.

CERESKO, Anthony R.
1982   "The function of antanaclasis. . . ." *CBQ* 44:551-69.

CHRISTIANSON, Eric S.
1996   "Narrative Strategies in the Book of Ecclesiastes." Ph.D. dissertation, the University of Sheffield.

1997   "Qoheleth and the Existential Legacy of the Holocaust." *The Heythrop Journal* 38:35-50.

forthcoming   *Narrative Strategies in Ecclesiastes.* JSOTSup. Sheffield.

CLAASEN, W. T.
1983   "Speaker-oriented functions of *ki* in Biblical Hebrew." *JNSL* 11:29-46.

COLERIDGE, Samuel Taylor
1832   *The Statesman's Manual.* Burlington.

COPPENS, J.
1979   "La structure de l'Ecclésiaste." In *La Sagesse de l'Ancien Testament,* ed. by M. Gilbert, pp. 288-92. Gembloux, Belgium.

COSSER, William
1953-54   "The meaning of 'Life' in Prov., Job and Ecc." *Glasgow University Oriental Society Transactions* 15:48-53.

CRENSHAW, James L.
1969   "Method in determining wisdom influence upon 'historical' literature." *JBL* 88:129-42. (Repr. Crenshaw, *Studies,* 481-94.)

1970   "Popular questioning of the justice of God in ancient Israel." *ZAW* 82:380-95. (Repr. Crenshaw, *Studies,* 289-304.)

1974   "The Eternal Gospel (Ecc. 3:11)." In *Essays in Old Testament Ethics* (FS J. P. Hyatt), ed. by J. L. Crenshaw & John T. Willis, pp. 25-55. New York.

1975   "The problem of theodicy in Sirach: on human bondage." *JBL* 94:47-64 (= Crenshaw, 1983b:119-40).

1976   *Studies in Ancient Israelite Wisdom.* New York (= *Studies*).

1978   "The shadow of death in Qoheleth." In *Israelite Wisdom* (FS Samuel Terrien), pp. 205-16. Missoula, Mont.

1981a   *Old Testament Wisdom.* Atlanta.

1981b   "Wisdom and authority: sapiential rhetoric and its warrants." *VTSup* 32:10-29.
1983a   "Qoheleth in current research." *HAR* 7:41-56.
1983b   *Theodicy in the Old Testament* (edited with an introduction by J. L. Crenshaw). London.
1986a   "The expression *mi yoe'a* in the Hebrew Bible." *VT* 36:274-88.
1986b   "Youth and old age in Qoheleth." *HAR* 10:1-13.
*1987   *Ecclesiastes*. OTL. Philadelphia.
1992   "Prohibitions in Proverbs and Qoheleth." In *Priests, Proverbs and Scribes,* ed. by E. Ulrich, pp. 115-24. JSOTSup 149. Sheffield.

CRUICKSHANK, John
1959   *Albert Camus*. London.

CRÜSEMANN, Frank
1979   "Die unveränderbare Welt." In *Der Gott der kleinen Leute,* ed. by W. Schottroff and W. Stegemann, 1.80-104.

DAHOOD, Mitchell J.
1952   "Canaanite-Phoenician influence in Qoheleth." *Bib* 33:30-52, 191-221.
1958   "Qoheleth and recent discoveries (Qumran)." *Bib* 39:302-18.
1960   "Immortality in Prv 12,28." *Bib* 41:176-81.
1962   "Qohelet and Northwest Semitic Philology." *Bib* 43:349-65.
1965   "Canaanite words in Qoheleth 10,20." *Bib* 46:210-12.
1966   "The Phoenician background of Qoheleth." *Bib* 47:264-82.
1968   "The Phoenician contribution to Biblical wisdom literature." In *The Role of the Phoenicians in the Interaction of Mediterranean Civilizations,* ed. by W. A. Ward, pp. 123-48. Beirut.

DAUBE, David
1964   *The Sudden in the Scriptures*. Leiden.

DAVIDSON, Donald
1980   *Essays in Actions and Events*. Oxford.

DELITZSCH, Franz
*1875   *Koheleth*. Leipzig. (ET James Martin; Grand Rapids, Mich., 1989.)

DELITZSCH, Friedrich
1920   *Die Lese- und Schreibfehler im AT.* Berlin/Leipzig (= *LSF*).

DELL, Katharine J.
1994   "Ecclesiastes as Wisdom: Consulting Early Interpreters." *VT* 44:301-29.

DHORME, E.
1923   "L'Ecclésiaste ou Job?" *RB* 32:5-27.

DIESEL, A. A., R. G. Lehmann, E. Otto, and A. Wagner, eds.
1996   *"Jedes Ding hat seine Zeit . . ."* (FS D. Michel). BZAW 241. Berlin.

DI LELLA, Alexander
1966   *The Hebrew Text of Sirach.* The Hague.
*1987   *The Wisdom of Ben Sira.* AB 39. New York.

DRIVER, G. R.
1954   "Problems and solutions." *VT* 4:225-45.

DUESBERG, Hilaire, and I. FRANSEN
1938   *Les Scribes inspirés.* Paris.

DUNCKER, Karl
1940   "On pleasure, emotion, and striving." *Philosophy and Phenomenological Research.* 1:391-429.

EHLICH, Konrad
1996   *"Hebel* — Metaphern der Nichtigkeit." In *"Jedes Ding hat seine Zeit . . . ,"* ed. by A. A. Diesel et al. BZAW 241, pp. 49-64. Berlin.

EHRLICH, Arnold B.
*1908-14 *Randglossen zur hebräischen Bibel.* Leipzig. (Repr. Hildesheim, 1968.) (Qohelet is in vol. 7.)

EICHRODT, Walther
1934   "Vorsehungsglaube und Theodizee im Alten Testament" (FS Otto Procksch), ed. by A. Alt et al., pp. 45-70. Leipzig. (ET in Crenshaw, 1983b:17-41.)

ELIADE, Mircea
1954   *The Myth of the Eternal Return.* New York.

ELLERMEIER, Friedrich
1963a   "Das Verbum ḤWŠ in Koh 2,25." *ZAW* 75:197-217.
1963b   "Die Entmachung der Weisheit im Denken Qohelets." *ZThK* 60:1-20.
1967   *Qohelet.* I, 1. Herzberg.

ELLUL, Jacques
1990   *Reason for Being: A Meditation on Ecclesiastes* (trans. J. M. Hanks). Grand Rapids, Mich.

ELOQUENT PEASANT
Pap. Berlin 3023, 3025, 10499, Pap. BM 10274. "The Eloquent Peasant," *AEL* 1.169-84.

ENCYCLOPEDIA OF PHILOSOPHY. 7 vols. New York, 1967.

EPPENSTEIN, Simon
1888   *Aus dem Kohelet-Kommentar des Tanchum Jerushalmi.* Berlin.

EURINGER, Sebastian
*1890   *Der Masorahtext des Koheleth kritisch untersucht.* Leipzig.

FAHLGREN, K. H.
1932   *Ṣᵉdāqâ, nahestehende und entgegengesetzte Begriffe im Alten Testament.* Uppsala.

FELDMAN, Emanuel
1977   *Biblical and Post-Biblical Defilement and Mourning: Law as Theology.* New York.

FICHTNER, Johannes
1933   *Die altorientalische Weisheit in ihrer israelitisch-jüdischen Ausprägung.* BZAW 62. Giessen.

FISHBANE, Michael
1985   *Biblical Interpretation in Ancient Israel.* Oxford.

FLETCHER, Angus
1964   *Allegory.* Ithaca, N.Y.

FOHRER, Georg
1964   "Die Weisheit im Alten Testament." In *Theologisches Wörterbuch zum Neuen Testament,* 7.476-96.

FORMAN, Charles C.
1958   "The pessimism of Ecclesiastes." *JSS* 3:336-43.
1960   "Koheleth's use of Genesis." *JSS* 5:256-63.

FOSTER, Benjamin
1993   *Before the Muses.* 2 vols. Bethesda, Md. (= BTM).

FOX, Michael V.
1977a   "Frame-narrative and composition in the Book of Qohelet." *HUCA* 48:83-106.
1977b   "A Study of Antef." *Orientalia* 46:393-423.
1980   "The identification of quotations in Biblical literature." *ZAW* 92:416-31.
1985a   "LXX Proverbs 3:28 and Ancient Egyptian Wisdom." *HAR* 8:63-69.
1985b   *The Song of Songs and the Ancient Egyptian Love Songs.* Madison, Wis.
1986   "The meaning of *hebel* for Qohelet." *JBL* 105:409-27.
1987   *Qohelet and his Contradictions.* JSOTSup 71. Sheffield. (Repr. 1989.)

1993a	"Wisdom in Qohelet." In *In Search of Wisdom. Essays in Memory of John Gammie,* ed. by L. Perdue, B. B. Scott, W. J. Wiseman, pp. 115-32. Philadelphia.

1993a   "Wisdom in Qohelet." In *In Search of Wisdom. Essays in Memory of John Gammie,* ed. by L. Perdue, B. B. Scott, W. J. Wiseman, pp. 115-32. Philadelphia.
1993b   "Words for Wisdom." *ZAH* 6:149-69.
1995   "World order and Ma'at: A Crooked Parallel." *JANES* 23:37-48.
1996   "The social location of the book of Proverbs." In *Texts, Temples, and Traditions: A Tribute to Menahem Haran,* ed. by M. V. Fox et al., pp. 227-39. Winona Lake, Ind.
1997a   "The ideas of wisdom in Proverbs 1–9." *JBL* 116:613-33.
1997b   "Who can learn? A Debate in Ancient Pedagogy." In *Wisdom, You are my Sister* (FS R. E. Murphy), ed. by M. L. Barré (CBQMS 29), pp. 62-77. Washington.
1997c   "Words for folly." *ZAH* 10:1-12.
forthcoming   *Proverbs.* AB. Garden City, NY.

FRANKL, Viktor
1962   *Man's Search for Meaning.* New York.
1963   *The Doctor and the Soul.* New York.
1969   *The Will to Meaning.* New York.

FREDERICKS, Daniel C.
1988   *Qohelet's Language: Re-evaluating its Nature and Date.* Lewiston, N.Y.
1993   *Coping with Transience.* Sheffield.

FREEDMAN, David N.
1969   "Orthographic peculiarities in the Book of Job." *EI* 9:36-44.

FRENDO, Anthony
1981   "The 'broken construct chain' in Qoh 10,10b." *Bib* 62:544-45.

GALLING, Kurt
1932   "Kohelet-Studien." *ZAW* 50:276-99.
1934   "Stand und Aufgabe der Kohelet-Forschung." *ThR* n.F. 6:355-73.
1950   "The scepter of wisdom. A note on the gold sheath of Zendjirli and Ecclesiastes 12,11." *BASOR* 119:15-18.
1952   *Die Krise der Aufklärung in Israel.* Mainz.
1961   "Das Rätsel der Zeit im Urteil Kohelets (Koh 3,1-15)." *ZThK* 58:1-15.
*1969   *Prediger Salomo.* HAT I, 18 (1st ed. 1940). Tübingen.

GAMMIE, John G.
1985   "Stoicism and anti-Stoicism in Qoheleth." *HAR* 9:169-87.

GARDINER, Alan H.
1909   *The Admonitions of an Egyptian Sage.* Leipzig. (Repr. Hildesheim, 1969.)

GARLAND, Robert
1985   *The Greek Way of Death.* Ithaca, N.Y.

GEMSER, Berend
*1937   *Sprüche Salomos.* HAT I, 16. Tübingen.
1968   "The spiritual structure of Biblical aphoristic wisdom." In *Adhuc Loquitor,*
          pp. 138-49. (Repr. Crenshaw, *Studies,* 208-19.) Leiden (= *Homiletica in*
          Bib 21 [1962]:3-10).

GESE, Hartmut
1958   *Lehre und Wirklichkeit in der alten Weisheit.* Tübingen.
1963   "Die Krisis der Weisheit bei Kohelet." *SPOA,* pp. 139-51. (ET in
          Crenshaw, 1983b:141ff.)

GIANTO, Agustus
1998   "Human Destiny in Emar and Qohelet." In *Qohelet in the Context of Wis-*
          dom (Colloquium Biblicum Lovaniense XLVI). *BETL* 136:473-49.

GIBSON, J. C. L.
1971-1982 *Textbook of Syrian Semitic Inscriptions.* Vols. I-III. Oxford (= *TSSI*).
1978   *Canaanite Myths and Legends.* 2nd ed. Edinburgh.

GILBERT, Maurice
1981   "La description de la vieillesse en Qohelet XII 1-7 est-elle allégorique?"
          VTSup 32:96-109.

GINSBERG, H. L.
1955a   "The original language of Ben Sira 12:10-14." *JBL* 74:93-95.
1955b   "The structure and contents of the Book of Koheleth." *VTSup* 3:138-49.
1956   "Koheleth 12:4 in light of Ugaritic." *Syria* 33:99-101.
*1961   *Kohelet* [Hebrew]. Jerusalem.
1963   "The quintessence of Koheleth." In *Biblical and Other Studies,* ed. by
          A. Altmann, pp. 47-59. Cambridge.

GINSBURG, Christian D.
*1861   *Coheleth.* New York. (Repr. 1970.)

GLADSON, Jerry A.
1978   "Retributive Paradoxes in Proverbs 10–29." Ph.D. dissertation, Vanderbilt
          University, Nashville.

GLANVILLE, Stephen R. K.
1955   *The Instructions of 'Onchsheshongy. Catalogue of Demotic Papyri in the*
          British Museum, vol. 2. London.

GLASSER, E.
1970   *Le Procès du bonheur par Qohelet.* Paris.

GOOD, Edwin M.
1965   *Irony in the Old Testament.* London.

1978	"The unfilled sea: style and meaning in Ecclesiastes 1:2-11." In *Israelite Wisdom* (FS S. Terrien), pp. 59-73. Missoula.

GORDIS, Robert

1937	"Eccles. 1:17 — its text and interpretation." *JBL* 56:323-30.
1939/40	"Quotations in wisdom literature." *JQR* 30:123-47.
1943	"The asseverative kaph in Ugaritic and Hebrew." *JAOS* 63:176-178.
1943/44	"The social background of wisdom literature." *HUCA* 18:77-118 (= Idem, *Poets, Prophets, and Sages,* Bloomington, 1971, pp. 160-97).
1946/47	"The original language of Qohelet." *JQR* 37:67-84.
1949	"Quotations as a literary usage in Biblical, oriental and rabbinic literature." *HUCA* 22:157-219 (= *Poets, Prophets, and Sages,* pp. 104-59).
1949/50	"The translation-theory of Qohelet re-examined." *JQR* 40:103-16.
1952	"Koheleth — Hebrew or Aramaic?" *JBL* 71:93-109.
1955	"Was Kohelet a Phoenician?" *JBL* 74:103-14.
1960	"Qohelet and Qumran — a study of style." *Bib* 41:395-410.
1965	*The Book of God and Man.* Chicago.
*1968	*Koheleth — the Man and His World* (2nd ed.; orig. 1955). New York.

GORDON, Cyrus H.

1955	"North Israelite influence on post-exilic Hebrew." *IEJ* 5:85-88.
1965	*Ugaritic Textbook* (Analecta Orientalia). Rome.

GOSHEN-GOTTSTEIN, Moshe

1957	"The history of the Bible-text and comparative semitics." *VT* 7:195-201.

GRAETZ, Heinrich

1871	*Kohelet.* Leipzig.
1872	"Die Integrität der Kapitel 27 und 28 im Hiob." *Monatschrift für die Geschichte und Wissenschaft des Judenthums* 21:241-50.

GREENBERG, Moshe

1960	"NSH in Exodus 20:20 and the purpose of the Sinaitic theophany." *JBL* 79:273-76.

GROSSBERG, Daniel

1979	"Nominalization in Biblical Hebrew." *HS* 20:29-33.
1980	"Noun/verb parallelism: syntactic or asyntactic." *JBL* 99:481-88.

GRUBER, Mayer I.

1980	*Aspects of Nonverbal Communication in the Ancient Near East.* Studia Pohl 12/I-II. Rome.

HARAN, Menahem

1996	*Ha'ăsuphah Hamiqra'it* ["The Biblical Collection"]. Jerusalem.

HARDJEDEF

	"The Instruction of Prince Hardjedef," *AEL* 1.58-59.

HARTMAN, Louis F., and Alexander A. DI LELLA
1978 *The Book of Daniel.* AB 23. New York.

HEALEY, John F.
1995 "Death in West Semitic texts: Ugarit and Nabataea." In *The Archaeology of Death in the Ancient Near East* (Oxbow Monograph 51), ed. by Stuart Campbell and Anthony Green, pp. 188-91. Oxford.

HELCK, Wolfgang
1969 *Der Text der "Lehre Amenemhets I. für seinen Sohn."* Wiesbaden.
1970 *Die Prophezeiung des Nfr.tj.* Wiesbaden.

HENGEL, Martin
1974 *Judaism and Hellenism.* (ET J. Bowden.) Philadelphia.

HERMISSON, Hans Jürgen
1968 *Studien zur israelitischen Spruchweisheit.* WMANT 28. Neukirchen.

HERTZBERG, Hans Wilhelm
*1963 *Der Prediger.* KAT n.F. XVII, 4. Gütersloh.

HILLERS, Delbert
1964 *Treaty-Curses and the OT Prophets.* BO 16. Rome.

HIRSCHBERG, H. H.
1961 "Some additional Arabic etymologies in Old Testament lexicography." *VT* 11:372-85.

HITZIG, F., and W. NOWACK
1883 *Der Prediger Salomos erklärt.* 2nd ed. KEHAT 7. Leipzig.

HO, Ahuva
1991 Sedeq *and* Sᵉdaqah *in the Hebrew Bible.* New York.

HÖFFKEN, Peter
1985 "Das Ego des Weisen." *ThZ* 4:121-35.

HOLLADAY, William
1958 *The Root šubh in the Old Testament.* Leiden.
1962 "Style, irony, and authenticity in Jeremiah." *JBL* 81:44-54.

HOLM-NIELSEN, Svend
1974 "On the interpretation of Qoheleth in early Christianity." *VT* 24:168-77.

HORTON, Ernest
1972 "Koheleth's concept of opposites." *Numen* 19:1-21.

HUESMAN, John
1956   "Finite uses of the infinitive absolute." *Bib* 37:271-95.

HURVITZ, Avi
1990   (Review of D. Fredericks's *Qoheleth's Language*). *HS* 144-53.

HYVÄRINEN, Kyösti
1977   *Die Übersetzung von Aquila.* Coniectanea Biblica, OT Ser. Lund.

IPUWER
            Papyrus Leyden 344 recto. "The Admonitions of Ipuwer," *AEL* 1.149-63.

IRWIN, William A.
1944   "Eccles. 4:13-16." *JNES* 3:255-57.

ISAKSSON, BO
1987   *Studies in the Language of Qohelet.* Studia Semitica Upsaliensia, 10. Stockholm.

IWRY, Samuel
1966   "*whnmṣ'* — a striking variant reading in 1QIsaᵃ." *Textus* 5:34-43.

JAMES, Kenneth W.
1984   "Ecclesiastes: precursor of existentialists." *The Bible Today* 22:85-90.

JAMES, William
1902   *The Varieties of Religious Experience.* New York.

JAPHET, Sara, and Robert SALTERS
1976   "A note on the exegesis of Ecclesiastes 3:15b." *ZAW* 88:19-22.
1977   "Text and exegesis in Koh 10:19." *ZAW* 89:423-26.
1978   "Notes on the history of the interpretation of Koh 5:5." *ZAW* 90:95-101.
1985   *The Commentary of R. Samuel ben Meir Rashbam on Qoheleth.* Jerusalem.[1]

JARICK, John
1993   *A Comprehensive Bilingual Concordance of the Hebrew and Greek Text of Ecclesiastes.* SBLSCS. Atlanta.

JASTROW, Marcus
1950   *A Dictionary of the Targumim, the Talmud Babli and Yerushalmi, and the Midrashic Literature.* New York.

1. With regard to the authorship of the commentary in Hamburg Codex Heb. 32 (catalogue no. 37; first published by Jellinek), Japhet (pp. 19-33) argues persuasively that it indeed is the work of Rabbi Samuel ben Meir. I will refer to the author of this commentary as "Rashbam," though the identification is still disputed.

JENNI, Ernst
1952   "Das Wort *'ôlâm* im Alten Testament." *ZAW* 64:197-248.
1953   "Das Wort *'ôlâm* im Alten Testament." *ZAW* 65:1-35.
1968   *Das hebräische Pi'el.* Zurich.

JOHNSTON, Robert K.
1976   "'Confessions of a workaholic': A reappraisal of Qoheleth." *CBQ* 38:14-28.

JONG, Stephan de
1994   "Qohelet and the Ambitious Spirit of the Ptolemaic Period." *JSOT* 61:85-96.

JOÜON, Paul
1930   "Notes philologiques sur le texte hébreu d'Ecclésiaste." *Bib* 11:419-25.
1991   *A Grammar of Biblical Hebrew.* Translated and revised by T. Muraoka. 2 vols. Rome.

KAGEMENI
            Papyrus Prisse 1-2. "The Instruction Addressed to Kagemni," *AEL* 1.59-61.

KAISER, Otto
1995a   "Beiträge zur Kohelet-Forschung." *ThR* 60:1-31.
1995b   "Die Botschaft des Buches Kohelet." *ETL* 71:48-70.
1995c   "Qohelet." In *Wisdom in Ancient Israel* (FS J. A. Emerton), ed. by John Day et al., pp. 83-93. Cambridge.

KAMENETZKY, Abraham S.
1904   "Die P'šita zu Koheleth." *ZAW* 24:181-239.
1914   "Der Rätselname Koheleth." *ZAW* 34:225-28.
1921   "Die ursprünglich beabsichtigte Aussprache der Pseudonyms QHLT." *OLZ* 24:11-15.

KAWIN, Bruce F.
1972   *Telling It Again and Again.* Ithaca, N.Y.

KEDAR-KOPFSTEIN, Benjamin
1977   "Semantic aspects of the pattern *qôtēl.*" *HAR* 1: 155-76.

KENNEDY, James
1928   *An Aid to the Textual Amendment of the Old Testament.* Edinburgh (= *TAOT*).

KHAKHEPERRE-SONB
            "The Complaints of Khakheperre-Sonb," *AEL* 1.145-49.

KLEINERT, Paul
1883   "Sind im Buche Koheleth ausserhebräische Einflüsse anzuerkennen?"
            Theologische Studien und Kritiken 56:761-82.

KLOPFENSTEIN, Martin A.
1972   "Die Skepsis des Qohelet." *ThZ* 28:97-109.

KNOPF, Carl S.
1930   "The optimism of Koheleth." *JBL* 49:195-99.

KOCH, Klaus
1972   "Gibt es ein Vergeltungsdogma im Alten Testament?" In *Um das Prinzip
            der Vergeltung in Religion und Recht des Alten Testaments,* ed. by
            K. Koch, pp. 130-80. Darmstadt (= *ZTK* 52 [1955]: 1-42). (ET in
            Crenshaw 1983b, 57-87.)

KÖNIG, Eduard
1897   *Lehrgebäude der hebräischen Sprache,* II, 2. Leipzig.

KOPF, L.
1959   "Arabische Etymologien und Parallelen zum Bibelwörterbuch." *VT* 9:247-87.

KRAELING, G. E.
1953   *The Brooklyn Museum Aramaic Papyri.* New Haven.

KROEBER, Rudi
1963   *Der Prediger.* Berlin.

KROPAK, Arno
1909   *Die Syntax des Autors der Chronik.* BZAW 16. Giessen.

KRÜGER, Thomas
1996   "Dekonstruktion und Rekonstruktion prophetischer Eschatology im Qo-
            helet-Buch." In *"Jedes Ding hat seine Zeit . . . ,"* ed. by A. A. Diesel et al.
            BZAW 241, pp. 107-30. Berlin.

KUGEL, James
1989   "Qohelet and money." *CBQ* 51:32-49.

KUHN, Gottfried
1926   *Erklärung des Buches Koheleth.* BZAW 43. Giessen.

KURZ, Gerhard
1982   *Metapher, Allegorie, Symbol.* Göttingen.

KUTSCHER, Eduard Yechezkel
1974   *The Language and Linguistic Background of the Isaiah Scroll (1QIsaᵃ)* (Studies on the Texts of the Desert of Judah, VI). Leiden.

LAMBERT, W. G.
1960   *Babylonian Wisdom Literature.* Oxford.

LANDSBERGER, Benno
1936   "Die babylonische Theodizee." *Zeitschrift für Assyriologie* 43:32-76.

LANE, D. J.
1979   "Peshiṭta Institute Communication XV: 'Lilies that fester....'" *VT* 29:481-89.

LANG, Bernhard
1972   *Die weisheitliche Lehrrede.* Stuttgart.

LANGE, H. O.
1925   *Das Weisheitsbuch des Amenemope.* Copenhagen.

LAUHA, Aarre
1960   "Die Krise des religiösen Glaubens bei Kohelet." *VTSup* 3:183-91.
*1978   *Kohelet.* BKAT 19. Neukirchen-Vluyn.

LAVOIE, Jean-Jacques
1996   "Temps et finitude humaine: étude de Qohélet IX 11-12." *VT* 46:439-47.

LAZERE, Donald
1973   *The Unique Creation of Albert Camus.* New Haven and London.

LEAHY, Michael
1952   "The meaning of Ecclesiastes (12:2-5)." *Irish Theol. Quart.* 19:297-300.

LEICHTY, Erle
1964   "The Colophon." In *Studies Presented to A. Leo Oppenheim,* pp. 147-53. Chicago.

LEIMAN, Sid Z.
1976   *The Canonization of Hebrew Scripture: The Talmudic and Midrashic Evidence* (Trans. Conn. Acad. of Arts and Sciences, 47). Hamden, Conn.

LEVIN, Harry
1956   *Symbolism and Fiction.* Charlottesville, Va.

LEVY, Ludwig
1912   *Das Buch Qoheleth. Ein Beitrag zur Geschichte des Sadduzäismus kritisch untersucht.* Leipzig.

LICHTHEIM, Miriam
1945   "The Song of the Harpers." *JNES* 4:178-212.
1973-80   *Ancient Egyptian Literature.* Berkeley, Calif. vol. 1: 1973; vol. 2: 1976; vol. 3: 1980 (= *AEL*).
1983   *Late Egyptian Wisdom Literature in the International Context.* OBO 52. Göttingen.

LIEBERMAN, Saul
1962   *Hellenism in Jewish Palestine.* New York.

LIEDKE, Gerhard
1971   *Gestalt und Bezeichnung alttestamentlicher Rechtssätze.* WMANT 39. Neukirchen.

LINDBLOM, Johannes
1952   "Gibt es eine Eschatologie bei den alttestamentlichen Propheten?" *Studia Theologica* 6:79-114.

LINDENBERGER, James M.
1983   *The Aramaic Proverbs of Ahiqar.* Johns Hopkins Near Eastern Studies. Baltimore.

LOADER, J. A.
1969   "Qohelet 3:2-8 — a 'sonnet' in the Old Testament." *ZAW* 81:240-42.
1979   *Polar Structures in the Book of Qohelet.* BZAW 152. Berlin.

LOHFINK, Norbert
1979   "War Kohelet ein Frauenfeind?" *BETL* 51:259-87.
*1980   *Kohelet* (Neue Echter Bibel, 2nd ed.). Stuttgart.
1981   "*Melek, šallîṭ* und *môšēl* bei Kohelet und die Abfassungszeit des Buchs." *Bib* 62:535-43.
1983   "Warum ist der Tor unfähig, Böse zu handeln?" *ZDMG* Sup. 5:113-20.
1989   "Koh 1,2, 'Alles ist Windhauch' — universale oder anthropologische Aussage?" In *Der Weg zum Menschen. FS A. Deissler,* ed. by R. Mosis and L. Ruppert, pp. 201-16. Freiburg.
1990   "Qoheleth 5:17-19 — revelation by joy." *CBQ* 52:625-35.
1994   "Grenzen und Einbindung des Kohelet-Schlussgedichts." In *Altes Testament Forschung und Wirkung* (FS H. Graf Reventlow). Frankfurt a.M.
1995a   "Les Epilogues du livre de Qohélet et les débuts du canon." In *"Ouvrir les Ecritures"* (FS P. Beauchamp), ed. by P. Bovati and R. Meynet. Paris.
1995b   "Freu dich, Jüngling — doch nicht, weil du jung bist: zum Formproblem im Schlussgedicht Kohelets (Koh 11,9–12,8)." *Biblical Interpretation* 3: 158-89.
1996   "Zu eigen Satzeröffnungen im Epilog des Koheletbuches." In *"Jedes Ding hat seine Zeit . . . ,"* ed. by A. A. Diesel et al. BZAW 241, pp. 131-48. Berlin.

LONG, V. Philips
1997   "One man among a thousand, but not a woman among them all." *VTSup* 48, Congress volume, ed. by K. D. Schunk and M. Augustin.

LONGMAN, Tremper, III
1991   *Fictional Akkadian Autobiography.* Winona Lake, Ind.
1998   *The Book of Ecclesiastes.* NICOT. Grand Rapids, Mich.

LORETZ, Oswald
1963   "Zur Darbietungsform der 'Ich-Erzählung' im Buche Qohelet." *CBQ* 25:46-59.
1964   *Qohelet und der alte Orient.* Freiburg.
1965   "Gleiches Los trifft alle! Die Antwort des Buches Qohelet." *Bibel und Kirche* 20:6-8.
1980   "Altorientalische und kanaanäische Topoi im Buche Kohelet." *UF* 12:267-86.

LÖW, I.
1924-34   *Die Flora der Juden.* Hildesheim. (Repr. 1967.)

LYONS, John
1977   *Semantics.* 2 vols. Cambridge.

LYS, Daniel
1977   *L'Ecclésiaste ou que vaut la vie?* Paris.
1979   "L'Etre et le Temps. Communication de Qohèlèth." In *La Sagesse de l'Ancien Testament,* ed. by M. Gilbert, pp. 249-58. Gembloux, Belgium.

MacDONALD, Duncan Black
1899   "Eccl. iii 11." *JBL* 18:212f.
1936   *The Hebrew Philosophical Genius.* Princeton.

MACHINIST, Peter
1995   "Fate, *miqreh,* and reason: some reflections on Qohelet and Biblical thought." In *Solving Riddles and Untying Knots,* ed. by Z. Zevit et al., pp. 159-75. Winona Lake, Ind.

MacINTOSH, A. A.
1969   "A consideration of Hebrew GʻR." *VT* 19:471-79.

MARGOLIOUTH, D. S.
1911   "The prologue of Ecclesiastes." *The Expositor* 8:463-70.

McKANE, William
1965   *Prophets and Wise Men.* London.
1970   *Proverbs: a New Approach.* London.

McNEILE, Alan H.
1904   *An Introduction to Ecclesiastes.* Cambridge.

MERIKARE
Pap. Leningrad 116A, Pap. Moscow 4658, P. Carlsberg 6. Text: Volten, 1945. "The Instruction Addressed to King Merikare," *AEL* 1.97-109.

MICHEL, Diethelm
1988   *Qohelet.* EdF 258. Darmstadt.
1989   *Untersuchungen zur Eigenart des Buches Qohelet.* BZAW 183. Berlin.

MILLER, Athanasius
1934   "Aufbau und Grundproblem des Predigers." *Miscellanea Biblica* 2:104-22.

MILLER, Patrick D., Jr.
1982   *Sin and Judgment in the Prophets.* SBLMS 27. Chico, Calif.

MISCHEL, Theodore
1952   "The meanings of 'symbol' in literature." *Arizona Quarterly* 8:69-79.

MITCHELL, Hinckley G.
1913   "'Work' in Ecclesiastes." *JBL* 32:123-38.

MONTGOMERY, James A.
1924   "Notes on Ecclesiastes." *JBL* 43:241-44.

MOORE, Carey A.
1996   *Tobit.* AB 40A. New York.

MORAN, William
1975   "Amarna Glosses." *RA* 69.

MORENZ, Siegfried, with Dieter MÜLLER
1960   *Untersuchungen zur Rolle des Schicksals in der ägyptischen Religion.* Abh. Sächsischen Ak. Wiss. zu Leipzig, Phil.-hist. Kl., 52,1. Berlin.

MOWINCKEL, Sigmund
1960   "Psalms and wisdom." *VTSup* 3:205-24.

MUILENBURG, James
1954   "A Qoheleth scroll from Qumran." *BASOR* 135:20-28.

MULDER, J. S. M.
1982   "Qoheleth's division and also its main point." In *Von Kanaan bis Kerala,* ed. by W. C. Delsman et al. Neukirchen.

MÜLLER, Hans-Peter
1968   "Wie sprach Qohälät von Gott?" *VT* 18:507-21.
1986   "Theonome Skepsis und Lebensfreude — zu Koh 1,12–3,15." *BZ* 30:1-19.
1996   "Kohelet und Amminadab." In *"Jedes Ding hat seine Zeit . . . ,"* ed. by A. A. Diesel et al. BZAW 241, pp. 149-68. Berlin.

MURAOKA, Takamitsu
1985   *Emphatic Words and Structures in Biblical Hebrew.* Jerusalem.

MURPHY, Roland E.
1955   "The *Pensées* of Coheleth." *CBQ* 17:304-14.
1962   "A consideration of the classification 'wisdom psalms'." *VTSup* 9:156-67. (Repr. Crenshaw, *Studies,* 456-67.)
1967   "Assumptions and problems in Old Testament wisdom research." *CBQ* 29:407-18.
1969   "Form criticism and wisdom literature." *CBQ* 31:475-83.
1979   "Qohelet's 'quarrel' with the Fathers." In *From Faith to Faith* (FS Donald G. Miller), ed. by D. Y. Hadidian, pp. 235-45. Pittsburgh.
1981   *Wisdom Literature.* In *Forms of OT Literature,* 13. Grand Rapids, Mich.
1982   "Qohelet interpreted: the bearing of the past on the present." *VT* 32:331-37.
1985   "Wisdom and creation." *JBL* 104:3-11.
1991   "On translating Ecclesiastes." *CBQ* 53:571-79.
*1992   *Ecclesiastes.* WBC 23A. Waco, Tex.

NAGEL, Thomas
1971   "The absurd." *Journal of Philosophy* 68:716-27.

NEFERTI
        Papyrus Leningrad 1116B. Text: Helck, 1970. "The Prophecies of Neferti," *AEL* 1.139-45.

NEHER, André
1951   *Notes sur Qohelet.* Paris.

NEL, Philip Johannes
1982   *The Structure and Ethos of the Wisdom Admonitions in Proverbs.* BZAW 158. Berlin.

NÖTSCHER, F.
1954   *Kohelet.* Würzburg.
1959   "Schicksal und Freiheit." *Bib* 40:446-62.

OGDEN, Graham S.
1977   "The 'Better'-Proverb (Tôb-Spruch), rhetorical criticism, and Qoheleth." *JBL* 96:489-505.
1979   "Qoheleth's use of the 'Nothing is Better'-Form." *JBL* 98:339-50.

1980a	"Historical allusion in Qoheleth IV 13-16?" *VT* 30:309-15.
1980b	"Qoheleth IX 17–X 20." *VT* 30:27-37.
1983	"Qoheleth XI 1-6." *VT* 33:222-30.
1984a	"The mathematics of wisdom: Qoheleth IV 1-12." *VT* 34:446-53.
1984b	"Qoheleth XI 7–XII 8: Qoheleth's summons to enjoyment and reflection." *VT* 34:27-37.
1986	"The interpretation of *dor* in Ecclesiastes 1.4." *JSOT* 34:91-92.
1987	*Qoheleth.* Readings. Sheffield.

ONCHSHESHONQY
    Pap. BM 10508. Glanville, 1955; Lichtheim, 1983. "The Instruction of Ankhsheshonq," *AEL* 3.159-84.

PALM, August
1885   *Qohelet und die Nach-Aristotelische Philosophie.* Mannheim.

PARDEE, Dennis
1978   "The semitic root *mrr* and the etymology of Ugaritic *mr(r)//brk.*" *UF* 10:249-88.

PEDERSEN, Johannes
1926   *Israel. Its Life and Culture,* vols. 1-2 combined. Copenhagen.

PENNACCHINI, Bruno
1977   "Qohelet ovvero il libro degli assurdi." *Euntes Docete* 30:491-510.

PERLES, Felix
1895   *Analekten zur Textkritik des Alten Testaments.* München.
1922   *Analekten zur Textkritik des Alten Testaments,* n.F. Leipzig.

PERRY, T. A.
1993   *Dialogues with Kohelet.* University Park, Penn.

PFEIFFER, Egon
1965   "Die Gottesfurcht im Buche Kohelet." In *Gottes Wort und Gottes Land* (FS H.-W. Hertzberg), pp. 133-58. Göttingen.

PHEBHOR ("The Demotic Wisdom Book")
    Pap. Insinger etc. *AEL* 3.184-217.

PIOTTI, Franco
1977   "Osservazioni su alcuni usi linguistici dell'Ecclesiaste." *BeO* 19:49-56, 129-40.
1978   "Osservazioni su alcuni problemi esegetici nel libro dell'Ecclesiaste." *BeO* 20:169-81.

PLÖGER, Otto
1965   "Wahre die richtige Mitte; solch Mass ist in allem das Beste!" In *Gottes Wort und Gottes Land* (FS H.-W. Hertzberg), pp. 159-73. Göttingen.

PLUMPTRE, E. H.
1881   *Ecclesiastes.* Cambridge.

PODECHARD, E.
1912   *L'Ecclésiaste.* Paris.

POLZIN, Robert
1980   *Moses and the Deuteronomist.* New York.

PRIEST, John F.
1963   "Where is Wisdom to be placed?" *JBR* 31:275-82.

PTAHHOTEP
Pap. Prisse. Text, transl.: Žába, 1956. ET *AEL* 1.61-80.

QIMRON, Elisha
1986   *The Hebrew of the Dead Sea Scrolls.* HSS 29. Atlanta.

RAD, Gerhard von
1953   "Josephgeschichte und ältere Chokma." *VTSup* 1:120-27.
1966   "Das Werk Jahwes." In *Studia Biblia et Semitica* (FS Th. Vriezen), 290-99. Wageningen.
1970   *Weisheit in Israel.* Neukirchen-Vluyn. (ET James D. Martin: *Wisdom in Israel.* London, 1972.)

RANKIN, Oliver S.
1936   *Israel's Wisdom Literature.* Edinburgh.
1956   *The Book of Ecclesiastes. Interpreter's Bible,* V. Nashville.

RANSTON, Harry
1923   "Koheleth and the early Greeks." *JTS* 24:160-69.
1925   *Ecclesiastes and the Early Greek Wisdom Literature.* London.
1930   *The Old Testament Wisdom Books and Their Teaching.* London.

RASHBAM (R. Samuel ben Meir). See Japhet and Salters.

REIF, Stefan C.
1981   (Review of C. F. Whitley's *Koheleth*). *VT* 31:120-26.

REINES, C. W.
1954a   "Koheleth on wisdom and wealth." *JJS* 5:80-84.
1954b   "Koheleth VIII,10." *JJS* 5:86-87.

RENAN, E.

1882   *L'Ecclésiaste traduit de l'hébreu avec une étude sur l'âge et le caractère du livre.* Paris.

RIESENER, Ingrid

1996   "Fraufeindschaft im Alten Testament? Zum Verständnis von Qoh 7,25-29." In *"Jedes Ding hat seine Zeit . . . ,"* ed. by A. A. Diesel et al. BZAW 241, pp. 193-207. Berlin.

ROFÉ, Alexander

1978   " 'The Angel' in Qoh 5:5 in the light of a wisdom dialogue formula" [Hebrew]. *EI* 14:105-9.

ROMBERG, Bertil

1962   *Studies in the Narrative Technique of the First-Person Novel.* Lund.

ROUSSEAU, François

1981   "Structure de Qohelet I 4-11 et Plan du Livre." *VT* 31:200-217.

ROWLEY, H. H.

1963   *From Moses to Qumran.* New York.

RUDMAN, Dominic

1997   "A contextual reading of Ecclesiastes 4:13-16." *JBL* 116:57-73.

RYLAARSDAM, J. Coert

1946   *Revelation in Jewish Wisdom Literature.* Chicago.

SABOURIN, Leopold

1974   *The Psalms.* New York.

SALTERS, Robert B.

1975   "Qohelet and the Canon." *ExpT* 86:339-42.
1976   "A Notes on the Exegesis of Ecclesiastes 3:15b." *ZAW* 88:419-22.
1977   "Text and exegesis in Koh 10,19." *ZAW* 89:423-26.
1978   "Notes on the history of the interpretation of Koh 5,5." *ZAW* 90:95-101.
1979   "Notes on the interpretation of Qoh 6,2." *ZAW* 91:282-89.

SALZBERG, M.

1873   "Septuagintalübersetzung zum Buche Kohelet." *MGWJ* 22:168-74.

SAWYER, John F. A.

1976   "The ruined house in Ecclesiastes 12: A reconstruction of the original parable." *JBL* 94:519-31.

SCHIFFER, S.

1884   *Das Buch Kohelet, nach der Auffassung der Weisen des Talmud und Midrasch und der jüdischen Erklärer des Mittelalters I.* Frankfurt a.M.

SCHMID, Hans Heinrich

1966   *Wesen und Geschichte der Weisheit.* BZAW 101. Berlin.

1968   *Gerechtigkeit als Weltordnung.* Beiträge zur historischen Theologie, 40. Tübingen.

SCHOORS, Antoon

1981   "The particle *ki.*" *OTS* 21:240-76.

1982a   "Kethibh-Qeré in Ecclesiastes." *Studia Paulo Naster Oblata. OLA* 13:215-22.

1982b   "La structure littéraire de Qohéleth." *OLP* 13:91-116.

1985a   "Koheleth: a perspective of life after death?" *ETL* 61:295-303.

1985b   "The Peshitta of Kohelet and its relation to the Septuagint." *OLA* 18:347-57.

1992   *The Preacher Sought to Find Pleasing Words,* Part I: Grammar (*OLA* 41).

1998   *Qohelet in the Context of Wisdom.* BETL 136. Leuven.

SCHWIENHORST-SCHÖNBERGER, Ludger

1996   *"Nicht im Menschen gründet das Glück."* Herders Biblische Studien 2. Freiburg.

1997   "Kohelet: Stand und Perspektiven der Forschung." In *Das Buch Kohelet. Studien zur Struktur, Geschichte, Rezeption und Theologie,* ed. by idem, pp. 5-38. Berlin.

SCOTT, R. B. Y.

*1965   *Proverbs, Ecclesiastes.* AB 18. New York.

SEGAL, Moshe T.

*1958   *The Complete Book of Ben Sira* [Hebrew]. Jerusalem.

SEOW, Choon-Leong

1995   "Qohelet's Autobiography." In *Fortunate the Eyes that See: Essays in Honor of David Noel Freedman,* ed. by A. B. Beck et al., pp. 275-87. Grand Rapids, Mich.

1996   "Linguistic Evidence and the Dating of Qohelet." *JBL* 115:643-66.

1997a   *Ecclesiastes.* AB 18c. Garden City, N.Y.

1997b   "The epilogue of Qohelet revisited." In *Wisdom, You are my Sister* (FS R. E. Murphy), ed. by M. L. Barré (CBQMS 29), pp. 125-41. Washington.

SERRANO, J. J.

1954   "I saw the wicked buried (Ecc 8,10)." *CBQ* 16:168-70.

SHAFFER, Aaron

1967   "The Mesopotamian background of Qohelet 4:9-12" [Hebrew]. *EI* 8:246-50.

1969   "New information on the origin of the 'three-fold cord'" [Hebrew]. *EI* 9:159-60.

SHEPPARD, Gerald T.

1977   "The epilogue to Qoheleth as theological commentary." *CBQ* 39:182-89.

1980   *Wisdom as a Hermeneutical Construct.* BZAW 151. Berlin.

SIEGFRIED, K.

*1898   *Prediger und Hoheslied.* HAT II, 3/2. Göttingen.

SIMPSON, William K., ed.

1972   *The Literature of Ancient Egypt.* New Haven & London.

SIRA (Ben Sira)

1973   *The Book of Ben Sira: Text, Concordance and an Analysis of the Vocabulary.* Academy of the Hebrew Language. Jerusalem.[2]

SKEHAN, Patrick W.

1938   *The Literary Relationship between the Book of Wisdom and the Protocanonical Wisdom Books of the Old Testament.* Washington.

1967   "Wisdom's house." *CBQ* 29:468-86.

SNAITH, Norman H.

1963   "Time in the Old Testament." In *Promise and Fulfillment, Essays Presented to S. H. Hooke.* Edinburgh.

SNEED, Mark

1997   "Qohelet as 'Deconstructionist'." *OT Essays* 10:303-11.

STAERK, W.

1942-43   "Zur Exegese von Koh 10,20 und 11,1." *ZAW* 59:216-18.

STAPLES, W. E.

1943   "The 'vanity' of Ecclesiastes." *JNES* 2:95-104.

1945   "'Profit' in Ecclesiastes." *JNES* 4:87-96.

1965   "The meaning of *ḥepeṣ* in Ecclesiastes." *JNES* 24:110-12.

TANCHUM JERUSHALMI. See Eppenstein.

TAYLOR, C.

1874   *The Dirge of Coheleth.* London.

2. Word-counts and textual references in the present book are based on this volume.

TORREY, Charles C.
1948-49 "The question of the original language of Qohelet." *JQR* 39:151-60.
1952 "The problem of Ecclesiastes IV,13-16." *VT* 2:175-77.

TUR-SINAI, Naphtali H.
1962ff. *Pᵉšuṭo šel Miqra'* [Qohelet in vol. 4b]. Jerusalem.

TYLER, Thomas
*1899 *Ecclesiastes*. London.

ULRICH, Eugene
1992 "Ezra and Qoheleth Manuscripts from Qumran (4QEzra, 4QQoh^{A,B})." In *Priests, Prophets, and Scribes*. JSOTSup 149, ed. by E. Ulrich et al., pp. 139-57. Sheffield.

VAN LEEUWEN, Raymond
1986 "Proverbs 30:21-23 and the Biblical world upside down." *JBL* 105:599-610.
1992 "Wealth and poverty: system and contradiction in Proverbs." *HS* 33:25-36.

VAWTER, Bruce
1972 "Intimations of immortality in the Old Testament." *JBL* 91:158-71.

VERGOTE, Jozef
1963 "La notion de Dieu dans les livres de sagesse égyptiens." *SPOA*, pp. 159-90.

VOLTEN, Aksel
1937 *Studien zum Weisheitsbuch des Anii*. Copenhagen.
1945 *Zwei altägyptische politische Schriften*. AnÄg IV. Copenhagen.
1955 "Zwei ägyptische Wörter." *Ägyptologische Studien*, ed. by O. Firchow, pp. 362-65. Berlin.

WAARD, Jan de
1979 "The translator and textual criticism (with particular reference to Eccl 2,25)." *Bib* 60:509-29.
1982 "The structure of Qoheleth." In *Proc. Eighth World Congress of Jewish Studies*, pp. 57-63. Jerusalem.

WALDMAN, Nahum M.
1979 "The *dabar raḥoq* of Eccl 8:3." *JBL* 98:407-8.

WALTKE, Bruce, and Michael Patrick O'CONNOR
1990 *An Introduction to Biblical Hebrew Syntax*. Winona Lake, Ind. (= *IBHS*).

WEINFELD, Moshe
1972 *Deuteronomy and the Deuteronomic School*. Oxford.
1995 *Justice and Righteousness in Israel and the Nations* [Hebrew]. Jerusalem.

WESTERMANN, Claus
1977   *Der Aufbau des Buches Hiob.* Calwer Theologische Monographien, A.6. Stuttgart.

WHITLEY, Charles F.
1979   *Koheleth, His Language and Thought.* BZAW 148. Berlin.

WHYBRAY, R. N.
1965   *Wisdom in Proverbs.* London.
1974   *The Intellectual Tradition in the Old Testament.* BZAW 135. Berlin.
1978   "Qoheleth the immoralist? (Qoh 7:16-17)." In *Israelite Wisdom* (FS S. Terrien), pp. 191-204. Missoula, Mont.
1981   "The identification and use of quotations in Ecclesiastes." *VTSup* 32:435-51.
1982   "Qoheleth, Preacher of Joy." *JSOT* 23:87-98.
1989   *Ecclesiastes.* NCB. Grand Rapids, Mich.

WILCH, John R.
1969   *Time and Event.* Leiden.

WILDEBOER, Gerrit
*1898   *Der Prediger* (in K. Budde et al., *Die Fünf Megillot*). Freiburg.

WILLIAMS, James G.
1971   "What does it profit a man?: The wisdom of Koheleth." *Judaism* 20:179-93. (Repr. Crenshaw, *Studies,* 375-89.)
1981   *Those Who Ponder Proverbs.* Sheffield.
1987   "Proverbs and Ecclesiastes." In *The Literary Guide to the Bible,* ed. by R. Alter and F. Kermode, pp. 263-82. Cambridge, Mass.

WILSON, Gerald R.
1984   "'The words of the wise': the intent and significance of Qoheleth 12:9-14." *JBL* 103:175-92.
1987   (Review of J. A. Loader's *Ecclesiastes*). *HS* 28.

WITTGENSTEIN, Ludwig
1958   *Philosophical Investigations.* ET G. Anscombe. Oxford.

WITZENRATH, Hagia
1979   *Süss ist das Licht.* St. Ottilien.

WÖLFEL, Eberhard
1958   *Luther und die Skepsis.* Munich.

WOLFF, Hans W.
1937   *Das Zitat im Prophetenspruch.* Beiheft zu Evangelische Theologie, 4. München.

WRIGHT, Addison G.
1968   "The riddle of the sphinx: the structure of the Book of Qoheleth." *CBQ* 30:313-34.
1980   "The riddle of the sphinx revisited: numerical patterns in the Book of Qoheleth." *CBQ* 42:38-51.
1983   "Additional numerical patterns in Qohelet." *CBQ* 45:32-43.

YAḤYAH = Yosef ben David ibn Yaḥyah
*1539   *Peruš Ḥameš Hamm^egillot* [Hebrew]. Bologna.

YOUNG, Ian
1993   *Diversity in Pre-Exilic Hebrew.* FAT 5. Tübingen.

ŽABA, Zbynek
1956   *Les Maximes de Ptahhotep.* Prague.

ZAPLETAL, Vincenz
*1911   *Das Buch Kohelet kritisch und metrisch untersucht.* Freiburg.

ZER-KAVOD, Mordecai
*1973   *Qohelet* [Hebrew]. Jerusalem.

ZIMMERLI, Walther
1933   "Zur Struktur der alttestamentlichen Weisheit." *ZAW* 51:177-204. (ET in Crenshaw, *Studies,* 175-207.)
*1962   *Das Buch des Predigers Salomo.* ATD XVI, 1. Göttingen.
1963   "Ort und Grenze der Weisheit im Rahmen der alttestamentlichen Theologie." *SPOA,* pp. 121-38. (ET in Crenshaw, *Studies,* 314-26.)
1974   "Das Buch Kohelet — Traktat oder Sentenzensammlung?" *VT* 24:221-30.

ZIMMERMANN, Frank
1945/46 "The Aramaic provenance of Qohelet." *JQR* 36:17-45.
1949/50 "The question of Hebrew in Qohelet." *JQR* 40:79-102.
1958   *The Book of Tobit.* New York.
1973   *The Inner World of Qohelet.* New York.

ZIRKEL, G.
1792   *Untersuchungen über den Prediger mit philosophischen und kritischen Bemerkungen.* Würzburg.

ZUCK, Roy B., ed.
1994   *Reflecting with Solomon.* Grand Rapids, Mich.

Subject Index

Author Index

411

AUTHOR INDEX

Scripture Index

Note: This index follows the order of the Hebrew Bible.

Index of Hellenistic
and Rabbinic Texts

Index of Ancient Texts

Index of Hebrew Words